Microsoft® Excel® 2010 Formulas & Functions Inside Out

Egbert Jeschke
Helmut Reinke
Sara Unverhau
Eckehard Pfeifer
Bodo Fienitz
Jens Bock

Published with the authorization of Microsoft Corporation by:
O'Reilly Media, Inc.
1005 Gravenstein Highway North
Sebastopol, California 95472

ISBN: 978-0-7356-5802-8

1 2 3 4 5 6 7 8 9 QG 6 5 4 3 2 1

Printed and bound in the United States of America.

Microsoft Press books are available through booksellers and distributors worldwide. If you need support related to this book, email Microsoft Press Book Support at *mspinput@microsoft.com*. Please tell us what you think of this book at *http://www.microsoft.com/learning/booksurvey*.

Acquisitions and Developmental Editor: Kenyon Brown
Production Editor: Teresa Elsey
Editorial Production: Online Training Solutions, Inc.
Technical Reviewer: Judith Mills
Indexer: Angela Howard
Cover Design: Twist Creative • Seattle
Cover Composition: Karen Montgomery

Contents at a Glance

Table of Contents

Introduction

In the beginning there was the idea....The proposal to write about every single Microsoft Excel function with interesting and comprehensible examples came from Helmut Reinke—and everyone on the team agreed. "Yes, this is what Excel users need—a comprehensive reference book with all of the functions." That was eight years ago, and the enthusiasm hasn't diminished.

At the beginning of this year, the idea to translate our reference book into English arose. And what could we say? There they were again: the same enthusiasm as in 2007, and along with it the tremendous task of translation. But we have persevered, and now we are really proud and happy to present to you the first edition of our function book in English. Since we wrote the German edition, a couple of small Excel revolutions took place: A few years ago, Excel 2007 was launched with many new properties and possibilities. For a year and a half now, we also have had Excel 2010 at our disposal, which includes even more new possibilities. We will address them partially in this book.

We hope that you, dear reader, will welcome this concept, and that this reference work will give you many ideas and support you when needed.

Who This Book Is For

Functions are the most powerful tools in Excel. Our goal is to give readers an understanding of every single function with the aid of plausible examples so that everyone can be capable of realizing the inexhaustible possibilities.

So this book is aimed at everyone who is interested in working with Excel—whether you are a beginner or a power user and whether you are using Excel privately or for business. We want to make readers with little experience familiar with the functions so that they will find meaningful scenarios for using them. But we also want to address the reader who is more familiar with Excel, and so we provide several scenarios to help that reader move to the next level of knowledge.

Do you want to calculate the probability of winning the lottery? Do you have to provide a meaningful report of your company's annual sales? No problem. Let's get started.

Assumptions About You

We make a basic assumption that you are generally experienced in working with Microsoft Office and know a few Excel basics. We do not spend time explaining the user interface of Excel and the buttons on the ribbon.

If you are an experienced Excel user, you can just skim over Chapter 1, "Solving Problems with Functions," and Chapter 2, "Using Functions and PowerPivot." If you are not so experienced, we hope to give you an idea of the general possibilities offered by Excel. We hope that the many pages you have in front of you will be helpful to you. Use them to your advantage, and if you like the book, please don't keep your opinion to yourself. Write to us and let us know what you like about it, and especially what we should improve.

We promise that we will be here for you if you have questions or are running into problems. You can write to us at: *info@mindbusiness.de*.

How This Book Is Organized

All the functions have been tested in Microsoft Office Excel 2000 through Excel 2010. With the exception of characteristics specific to Excel 2007 and Excel 2010, most descriptions can even be used with Excel 97. Where necessary, we added comments regarding the particularities of the different versions.

The book is divided into four sections.

Introducing Formulas and Functions in Excel

The first section contains Chapters 1 through 4. They describe working with Excel, provide a general introduction to using Excel 2010, and give you a first look at formulas and functions. For beginners and experts alike, we have outlined the use of formulas and table functions with all the important notes, instructions, tips, and tricks.

Because we consider the Excel 2010 PowerPivot add-in quite extraordinary, we have introduced it briefly in this section. It has relatively little to do with spreadsheet functions, but we still wanted to acquaint you with it.

Creating Your Own Solutions in Excel

Chapter 5, "Functions in Special Operations," and Chapter 6, "Custom Functions," show that you can do a lot more with most functions than just use them in a worksheet. You can create and program your own functions.

Chapter 5 provides examples for using special functions in names and conditional formatting, as well as for validity and data checks. We hope you will find many ideas and clues for your own Excel solutions here.

Chapter 6 introduces you to programming in Excel. You can create any custom functions in Excel and then use them just like the built-in functions.

Functions

Chapters 7 through 17 provide the descriptions of the main Excel functions:

- Chapter 7, "Date and Time Functions"

- Chapter 8, "Text and Data Functions"

- Chapter 9, "Logical Functions"

- Chapter 10, "Lookup and Reference Functions"

- Chapter 11, "Information Functions"

- Chapter 12, "Statistical Functions"

- Chapter 13, "Database Functions"

- Chapter 14, "Cube Functions" (new in Excel 2007)

- Chapter 15, "Financial Functions"

- Chapter 16, "Mathematical and Trigonometry Functions"

- Chapter 17, "Engineering Functions"

Appendices

This book includes three appendices: Appendix A and Appendix B list the functions alphabetically and categorically (respectively), and Appendix C explains what is new in Excel 2007 and Excel 2010.

And now we wish you lots of success for your work with Microsoft Excel!

Features and Conventions Used in This Book

This book uses special text and design conventions to make it easier for you to find the information you need.

Text Conventions

Convention	Meaning
Abbreviated commands for navigating the ribbon	For your convenience, this book uses abbreviated commands. For example, "Click Home, Insert, Insert Cells" means that you should click the Home tab on the ribbon, then click the Insert button, and finally click the Insert Cells command.
Boldface type	**Boldface** indicates text that you type.
Initial Capital Letters	The first letters of the names of tabs, dialog boxes, dialog box elements, and commands are capitalized. Example: the Save As dialog box.
Italicized type	*Italicized* type indicates new terms.
Plus sign (+) in text	Keyboard shortcuts are indicated by a plus sign (+) separating key names. For example, Ctrl+Alt+Delete means that you press the Ctrl, Alt, and Delete keys at the same time.

Design Conventions

INSIDE OUT   An example of an "Inside Out" heading

These are the book's signature tips. In these tips, you get the straight scoop on what's going on with the software—inside information about why a feature works the way it does. You'll also find handy workarounds to deal with software problems.

Sidebar

Sidebars provide helpful hints, timesaving tricks, or alternative procedures related to the task being discussed.

See Also Cross-references point you to locations in the book that offer additional information about the topic being discussed.

CAUTION !

Cautions identify potential problems that you should look out for when you're completing a task or that you must address before you can complete a task.

Note

Notes offer additional information related to the task being discussed.

Certain parts of the text are specially marked to draw your attention to important comments. We have used the following categories:

Category	Meaning
Note	Additional information about this topic that's worth knowing
Important	Makes you aware of facts you must know and keep in mind
Tip	Tips and tricks regarding the current context

Your Companion eBook

The eBook edition of this book allows you to:

- Search the full text

- Print

- Copy and paste

To download your eBook, please see the instruction page at the back of this book.

Using the Sample Files

You'll find the sample files that are used in this book at:

http://go.microsoft.com/FWLink/?Linkid=229604

Important

The Microsoft Excel 2010 software is not available from this website. You should purchase and install that software before using this book.

Tip

Microsoft offers special updates and file converters for opening an Excel 2007 and Excel 2010 workbook in a previous Excel versions (97–2003). If the converters are not installed with the Office update, you might be prompted to install them when opening an Excel 2007 or Excel 2010 workbook.

After you install the updates and the converter, you can open Excel 2007 and Excel 2010 workbooks. You can edit and save the workbooks. However, the new features and formats of Excel 2007 and Excel 2010 are not displayed in previous Excel versions. You will find detailed information at the following Microsoft website: *http://office.microsoft. com/en-us/excel/HA100775611031.aspx*

You should also read the information that is provided for the sample files in each chapter.

The following table lists the names of the sample files that are used in the book. Because some users who are working with older Excel versions (Excel 2000 through Excel 2003) might not be able to open the new file formats of Excel 2007 and Excel 2010 (.xlsx, .xlsm, and so on), the sample files are provided in both formats: .xls (Excel 97 through Excel 2003) and .xlsx (Excel 2007 and Excel 2010).

Important

When you open a sample file in Excel and then close Excel, you can save the file in the same format or in a different format. By default, Excel offers the standard format again. However, if you choose the standard format (*.xlsx), Excel will display a message box that contains the information that you are going to save your work as a macro-free workbook. You should click No and save your work in a macro-enabled file type (*.xlsm).

Chapter Folder	Workbook/Worksheet Name	Location and/or Description
Chapter01	Excel_Example.xlsx	Chapter01 folder
	Excel_Pivot_Data.xlsx	Chapter01 folder
Chapter02	InformationFunctions.xls or InformationFunctions.xlsx	Chapter02 folder
	Date_Time.xls or Date_Time.xlsx	Chapter02 folder
	Text_Data.xls or Text_Data.xlsx	Chapter02 folder
	DifferentialCalculation.xls or DifferentialCalculation.xlsx	Chapter02 folder

Chapter Folder	Workbook/Worksheet Name	Location and/or Description
	Lookup.xls or Lookup.xlsx	Chapter02 folder
	Practice_Statistics.xls or Practice_Statistics.xlsx	Chapter02 folder
	DBFunction empty.xls or DBFunction empty.xlsx	Chapter02 folder
	Practice_Database.xls or Practice_Database.xlsx	Chapter02 folder
	Financial mathematics.xls or Financial mathematics.xlsx	Chapter02 folder
	Math.xls or Math.xlsx	Chapter02 folder
Chapter03	Arithmetic Operators	Chapter03.xls or Chapter03.xlsx
	Priority	Chapter03.xls or Chapter03.xlsx
	Comparison Operators	Chapter03.xls or Chapter03.xlsx
	Text Operator	Chapter03.xls or Chapter03.xlsx
	Relative Reference	Chapter03.xls or Chapter03.xlsx
	Absolute Reference	Chapter03.xls or Chapter03.xlsx
	Mixed Reference	Chapter03.xls or Chapter03.xlsx
	Array Formula	Chapter03.xls or Chapter03.xlsx
Chapter05	Fct_Names	Chapter05_Names.xls or Chapter05_Names.xlsx
	Comparison	Chapter05_CF.xls or Chapter05_CF.xlsx
	Training	Chapter05_Names.xls or Chapter05_Names.xlsx
	Weekend	Chapter05_CF.xls or Chapter05_CF.xlsx
	Holidays	Chapter05_CF.xls or Chapter05_CF.xlsx
	Accident1, Accident2	Chapter05_CF.xls or Chapter05_CF.xlsx
	Print Layout	Chapter05_CF.xls or Chapter05_CF.xlsx
	Top3	Chapter05_CF.xls or Chapter05_CF.xlsx
	Empty	Chapter05_CF.xls or Chapter05_CF.xlsx
	Credit	Chapter05_CF.xls or Chapter05_CF.xlsx
	Groups	Chapter05_CF.xls or Chapter05_CF.xlsx
	Subtotals	Chapter05_CF.xls or Chapter05_CF.xlsx
	Depending list, Paygrouplist	Chapter05_DV.xls or Chapter05_DV.xlsx
	Duplicates	Chapter05_DV.xls or Chapter05_DV.xlsx
	Completed	Chapter05_DV.xls or Chapter05_DV.xlsx

Chapter Folder	Workbook/Worksheet Name	Location and/or Description
Chapter06	Circle	Geometry.xls or Geometry.xlsm
	Fundamentals	Geometry.xls or Geometry.xlsm
	Quadrilateral	Geometry.xls or Geometry.xlsm
	Sector of a circle	Geometry.xls or Geometry.xlsm
Chapter07	WORKDAY	Date_Time.xls or Date_Time.xlsx
	WORKDAY.INTL	Date_Time.xlsx
	Practice	Date_Time.xls or Date_Time.xlsx
	YEARFRAC	Date_Time.xls or Date_Time.xlsx
	DATEDIF	Date_Time.xls or Date_Time.xlsx
	DATE	Date_Time.xls or Date_Time.xlsx
	DATEVALUE	Date_Time.xls or Date_Time.xlsx
	EDATE	Date_Time.xls or Date_Time.xlsx
	TODAY	Date_Time.xls or Date_Time.xlsx
	YEAR	Date_Time.xls or Date_Time.xlsx
	NOW	Date_Time.xls or Date_Time.xlsx
	WEEKNUM	Date_Time.xls or Date_Time.xlsx
	MINUTE	Date_Time.xls or Date_Time.xlsx
	MONTH	Date_Time.xls or Date_Time.xlsx
	EOMONTH	Date_Time.xls or Date_Time.xlsx
	NETWORKDAYS	Date_Time.xls or Date_Time.xlsx
	NETWORKDAYS.INTL	Date_Time.xlsx
	SECOND	Date_Time.xls or Date_Time.xlsx
	HOUR	Date_Time.xls or Date_Time.xlsx
	DAY	Date_Time.xls or Date_Time.xlsx
	DAYS360	Date_Time.xls or Date_Time.xlsx
	WEEKDAY	Date_Time.xls or Date_Time.xlsx
	TIME	Date_Time.xls or Date_Time.xlsx
	TIMEVALUE	Date_Time.xls or Date_Time.xlsx
Chapter08	ASC	Text_Data.xls or Text_Data.xlsx
	BAHTTEXT	Text_Data.xls or Text_Data.xlsx
	CODE	Text_Data.xls or Text_Data.xlsx
	DOLLAR	Text_Data.xls or Text_Data.xlsx
	REPLACE	Text_Data.xls or Text_Data.xlsx
	FIXED	Text_Data.xls or Text_Data.xlsx
	FIND	Text_Data.xls or Text_Data.xlsx

Chapter Folder	Workbook/Worksheet Name	Location and/or Description
	TRIM	Text_Data.xls or Text_Data.xlsx
	UPPER	Text_Data.xls or Text_Data.xlsx
	PROPER	Text_Data.xls or Text_Data.xlsx
	EXACT	Text_Data.xls or Text_Data.xlsx
	LOWER	Text_Data.xls or Text_Data.xlsx
	LEN	Text_Data.xls or Text_Data.xlsx
	LEFT	Text_Data.xls or Text_Data.xlsx
	RIGHT	Text_Data.xls or Text_Data.xlsx
	CLEAN	Text_Data.xls or Text_Data.xlsx
	SEARCH	Text_Data.xls or Text_Data.xlsx
	T	Text_Data.xls or Text_Data.xlsx
	MID	Text_Data.xls or Text_Data.xlsx
	TEXT	Text_Data.xls or Text_Data.xlsx
	CONCATENATE	Text_Data.xls or Text_Data.xlsx
	SUBSTITUTE	Text_Data.xls or Text_Data.xlsx
	VALUE	Text_Data.xls or Text_Data.xlsx
	REPT	Text_Data.xls or Text_Data.xlsx
	CHAR	Text_Data.xls or Text_Data.xlsx
Chapter09	Samples	Logical_values.xls or Logical_values.xlsx
	Properties and Interpretation	Logical_values.xls or Logical_values.xlsx
	IF	Logical_values.xls or Logical_values.xlsx
Chapter10	Address.xls or Address.xlsx	Chapter10 folder
	Offset.xls or Offset.xlsx	Chapter10 folder
	References.xls or References.xlsx	Chapter10 folder
	Misc	References.xls or References.xlsx
	Index	References.xls or References.xlsx
	MTRANS	References.xls or References.xlsx
	exampleRTD.xls, exampleRTD.xlsx, or exampleRTD.xlsm, exampleRTD.dll	Chapter10 folder
	Column-Row	References.xls or References.xlsx
	LOOKUP	Lookups.xls or Lookups.xlsx
	test.doc or test.docx	Chapter10 folder
	VLOOKUP	Lookups.xls or Lookups.xlsx
	MATCH	Lookups.xls or Lookups.xlsx
	HLOOKUP	Lookups.xls or Lookups.xlsx

Chapter Folder	Workbook/Worksheet Name	Location and/or Description
Chapter11	Misc	Informations.xls or Informations.xlsm
	Error	Informations.xls or Informations.xlsm
	Info	Informations.xls or Informations.xlsm
	IS-functions	Informations.xls or Informations.xlsm
	ISEVEN	Informations.xls or Informations.xlsm
	ISODD	Informations.xls or Informations.xlsm
	NA	Informations.xls or Informations.xlsm
	Cell	Informations.xls or Informations.xlsm
Chapter12	INTERCEPT	Regression.xls or Regression.xlsx
	RSQ	Regression.xls or Regression.xlsx
	BETAINV or BETA.INV	Probability.xls or Probability.xlsx
	BETADIST or BETA.DIST	Probability.xls or Probability.xlsx
	BINOM.INV	Probability.xlsx
	BINOMDIST or BINOM.DIST	Probability.xls or Probability.xlsx
	CHIINV or CHI.INV	Probability.xls or Probability.xlsx
	CHISQ.INV or CHISQ.INV.RT	Probability.xlsx
	CHITEST or CHI.TEST or CHISQ.TEST	Probability.xls or Probability.xlsx
	CHIDIST or CHISQ.DIST or CHISQ.DIST.RT	Probability.xls or Probability.xlsx
	CRITBINOM	Probability.xls or Probability.xlsx
	EXPONDIST or EXPON.DIST	Probability.xls or Probability.xlsx
	FINV or F.INV or F.INV.RT	Probability.xls or Probability.xlsx
	FISHER	Probability.xls or Probability.xlsx
	FISHERINV or FISHER.INV	Probability.xls or Probability.xlsx
	FTEST or F.TEST	Probability.xls or Probability.xlsx
	FDIST or F.DIST or F.DIST.RT	Probability.xls or Probability.xlsx
	GAMMAINV or GAMMA.INV	Probability.xls or Probability.xlsx
	GAMMALN	Probability.xls or Probability.xlsx
	GAMMALN.PRECISE	Probability.xls or Probability.xlsx
	GAMMADIST or GAMMA.DIST	Probability.xls or Probability.xlsx
	GEOMEAN	Average.xls or Average.xlsx
	TRIMMEAN	Average.xls or Average.xlsx
	ZTEST or Z.TEST	Probability.xls or Probability.xlsx
	HARMEAN	Average.xls or Average.xlsx

Chapter Folder	Workbook/Worksheet Name	Location and/or Description
	Web access	WEBACCESS.xls or WEBACCESS.xlsx
	COUNT	Count.xls or Count.xlsx
	COUNTA	Count.xls or Count.xlsx
	COUNTBLANK	Count.xls or Count.xlsx
	FREQUENCY	Count.xls or Count.xlsx
	HYPGEOMDIST or HYPGEOM.DIST	Probability.xls or Probability.xlsx
	LARGE	Count.xls or Count.xlsx
	SMALL	Count.xls or Count.xlsx
	CONFIDENCE or CONFIDENCE.NORM	Probability.xls or Probability.xlsx
	CONFIDENCE.T	Probability.xls or Probability.xlsx
	CORREL	Probability.xls or Probability.xlsx
	COVAR	Regression.xls or Regression.xlsx
	COVARIANCE.P	Regression.xls or Regression.xlsx
	COVARIANCE.S	Regression.xls or Regression.xlsx
	KURT	Symmetry.xls or Symmetry.xlsx
	LOGINV or LOGNORM.INV	Probability.xls or Probability.xlsx
	LOGNORMDIST or LOGNORM.DIST	Probability.xls or Probability.xlsx
	MAX&MIN	Count.xls or Count.xlsx
	MAXA&MINA	Count.xls or Count.xlsx
	MEDIAN	Average.xls or Average.xlsx
	AVEDEV	Variance.xls or Variance.xlsx
	AVERAGE	Average.xls or Average.xlsx
	AVERAGEA	Average.xls or Average.xlsx
	AVERAGEIF	Average.xls or Average.xlsx
	AVERAGEIFS	Average.xlsx
	MODE or MODE.SNGL	Average.xls or Average.xlsx
	MODE.MULT	Average.xlsx
	NEGBINOMDIST or NEGBINOM.DIST	Probability.xls or Probability.xlsx
	NORMINV or NORM.INV	Probability.xls or Probability.xlsx
	NORMSINV or NORM.S.INV	Probability.xls or Probability.xlsx
	NORMDIST, NORMSDIST or NORM.DIST or NORM.S.DIST	Probability.xls or Probability.xlsx

Chapter Folder	Workbook/Worksheet Name	Location and/or Description
	PEARSON	Regression.xls or Regression.xlsx
	POISSON or POISSON.DIST	Probability.xls or Probability.xlsx
	PERCENTILE	Average.xls or Average.xlsx
	PERCENTILE.INC or PERCENTILE.EXC	Average.xlsx
	PERCENTRANK	Average.xls or Average.xlsx
	PERCENTRANK.INC or PERCENTRANK.EXC	Average.xlsx
	QUARTILE	Average.xls or Average.xlsx
	QUARTILE.INC or QUARTILE.EXC	Average.xlsx
	RANK	Count.xls or Count.xlsx
	RANK.EQ	Count.xlsx
	RANK.AVG	Count.xlsx
	LINEST	Regression.xls or Regression.xlsx
	LOGEST	Regression.xls or Regression.xlsx
	FORECAST	Regression.xls or Regression.xlsx
	SKEW	Symmetry.xls or Symmetry.xlsx
	STDEV or STDEV.S	Variance.xls or Variance.xlsx
	STDEVA	Variance.xlsx
	STDEVP or STDEV.P	Variance.xls or Variance.xlsx
	STDEVPA	Variance.xlsx
	STANDARDIZE	Probability.xls or Probability.xlsx
	SLOPE	Regression.xls or Regression.xlsx
	STEYX	Probability.xls or Probability.xlsx
	DEVSQ	Regression.xls or Regression.xlsx
	TINV or T.INV or T.INV.2T	Probability.xls or Probability.xlsx
	TREND	Regression.xls or Regression.xlsx
	TTEST or T.TEST	Probability.xls or Probability.xlsx
	TDIST or T.DIST or T.DIST.2T	Probability.xls or Probability.xlsx
	T.DIST.RT	Probability.xlsx
	VAR or VAR.S	Variance.xls or Variance.xlsx
	VARA	Variance.xls or Variance.xlsx
	VARP or VAR.P	Variance.xls or Variance.xlsx
	VARPA	Variance.xls or Variance.xlsx
	GROWTH	Regression.xls or Regression.xlsx

Chapter Folder	Workbook/Worksheet Name	Location and/or Description
	PERMUT	Probability.xls or Probability.xlsx
	PROB	Probability.xls or Probability.xlsx
	WEIBULL or WEIBULL.DIST	Probability.xls or Probability.xlsx
	COUNTIF	Count.xls or Count.xlsx
	COUNTIFS	Count.xlsx
Chapter13	Raw data	DBFUNCTION_empty.xls or DBFUNCTION_empty.xlsx
	DCOUNT	DBFUNCTION2.xls or DBFUNCTION2.xlsx
	DCOUNTA	DBFUNCTION2.xls or DBFUNCTION2.xlsx
	DGET	DBFUNCTION2.xls or DBFUNCTION2.xlsx
	DMAX or DMIN	DBFUNCTION2.xls or DBFUNCTION2.xlsx
	DAVERAGE	DBFUNCTION2.xls or DBFUNCTION2.xlsx
	DPPRODUCT	DBFUNCTION2.xls or DBFUNCTION2.xlsx
	DSTDEV	DBFUNCTION2.xls or DBFUNCTION2.xlsx
	DSTDEVP	DBFUNCTION2.xls or DBFUNCTION2.xlsx
	DSUM	DBFUNCTION2.xls or DBFUNCTION2.xlsx
	DVAR	DBFUNCTION2.xls or DBFUNCTION2.xlsx
	DVARP	DBFUNCTION2.xls or DBFUNCTION2.xlsx
	GETPIVOTDATA	DBFUNCTION2.xls or DBFUNCTION2.xlsx
Chapter14	Cube Test.cub	Use the offline cube file to test the cube functions without Microsoft Analysis Services
	offline cubeTest.xlsx	This workbook contains the example applications for the cube functions
	offLine.odc	Use the office data connection file to access data through workbook connections
	offLine.oqy	Use the office data connection file to access data through Microsoft Query

Chapter Folder	Workbook/Worksheet Name	Location and/or Description
Chapter15	AMORDEGRC	Depreciation Calculation.xls or Depreciation Calculation.xlsx
	AMORLINC	Depreciation Calculation.xls or Depreciation Calculation.xlsx
	ACCRINT	Simple Interest Calculation.xls or Simple Interest Calculation.xlsx
	ACCRINTM	Simple Interest Calculation.xls or Simple Interest Calculation.xlsx
	Bill of Exchange	Simple Interest Calculation.xls or Simple Interest Calculation.xlsx
	PV	Compound Interest Calculation.xls or Compound Interest Calculation.xlsx; Repayment Calculation.xls or Repayment Calculation.xlsx; Annuity Calculation.xls or Annuity Calculation.xlsx
	SYD	Depreciation Calculation.xls or Depreciation Calculation.xlsx
	Treasury Bonds	Simple Interest Calculation.xls or Simple Interest Calculation.xlsx
	DURATION	Price Calculation.xls or Price Calculation.xlsx
	EFFECT	Compound Interest Calculation.xls or Compound Interest Calculation.xlsx
	DDB	Depreciation Calculation.xls or Depreciation Calculation.xlsx
	DB	Depreciation Calculation.xls or Depreciation Calculation.xlsx
	IRR	Investment Calculation.xls or Investment Calculation.xlsx
	ISPMT	Simple Interest Calculation.xls or Simple Interest Calculation.xlsx
	PRICE	Price Calculation.xls or Price Calculation.xlsx
	SLN	Depreciation Calculation.xls or Depreciation Calculation.xlsx
	MDURATION	Price Calculation.xls or Price Calculation.xlsx
	NPV	Investment Calculation.xls or Investment Calculation.xlsx

Chapter Folder	Workbook/Worksheet Name	Location and/or Description
	DOLLARFR	Other.xls or Other.xlsx
	DOLLARDE	Other.xls or Other.xlsx
	MIRR	Investment Calculation.xls or Investment Calculation.xlsx
	YIELD	Price Calculation.xls or Price Calculation.xlsx
	YIELDMAT	Simple Interest Calculation.xls or Simple Interest Calculation.xlsx
	PMT	Annuity Calculation.xls or Annuity Calculation.xlsx
	TBILL	Simple Interest Calculation.xls or Simple Interest Calculation.xlsx
	ODDFPRICE	Price Calculation.xls or Price Calculation.xlsx
	ODDFYIELD	Price Calculation.xls or Price Calculation.xlsx
	ODDLPRICE	Simple Interest Calculation.xls or Simple Interest Calculation.xlsx
	ODDLYIELD	Simple Interest Calculation.xls or Simple Interest Calculation.xlsx
	VDB	Found in Depreciation Calculation.xls or Depreciation Calculation.xlsx
	XIRR	Investment Calculation.xls or Investment Calculation.xlsx
	XNPV	Investment Calculation.xls or Investment Calculation.xlsx
	RATE	Compound Interest Calculation.xls or Compound Interest Calculation.xlsx; Annuity Calculation.xls or Annuity Calculation.xlsx
	PRICE and YIELD	Price Calculation.xls or Price Calculation.xlsx
	FV	Compound Interest Calculation.xls or Compound Interest Calculation.xlsx; Annuity Calculation.xls or Annuity Calculation.xlsx; Repayment Calculation.xls or Repayment Calculation.xlsx
	FVSCHEDULE	Compound Interest Calculation.xls or Compound Interest Calculation.xlsx

Chapter Folder	Workbook/Worksheet Name	Location and/or Description
	NPER	Compound Interest Calculation.xls or Compound Interest Calculation.xlsx; Annuity Calculation.xls or Annuity Calculation.xlsx; or Repayment Calculation.xls or Repayment Calculation.xlsx
Chapter16	AGGREGATE.xlsx	Chapter16 folder
	ARRAY_FUNCTION	Chapter16.xls or Chapter16.xlsx
	ARRAY_FUNCTION2	Chapter16.xls or Chapter16.xlsx
	ATAN2	Chapter16.xls or Chapter16.xlsx
	COMBIN	Chapter16.xls or Chapter16.xlsx
	Data&Chart and Example	ACosH.xls or ACosH.xlsx
	Data&Chart	ASinH.xls or ASinH.xlsx
	Data&Chart	ATanH.xls or ATanH.xlsx
	Data&Chart and Example	CosH.xls or CosH.xlsx
	Data&Chart and Distribution	SinH.xls or SinH.xlsx
	Data&Chart and Water waves	TanH.xls or TanH.xlsx
	EXP	Chapter16.xls or Chapter16.xlsx
	EXP_LOG_LN	Chapter16.xls or Chapter16.xlsx
	FACT	Chapter16.xls or Chapter16.xlsx
	FLOOR	Chapter16.xls or Chapter16.xlsx
	GCD_LCM	Chapter16.xls or Chapter16.xlsx
	LOG_LN	Chapter16.xls or Chapter16.xlsx
	MOD	Chapter16.xls or Chapter16.xlsx
	POWER	Chapter16.xls or Chapter16.xlsx
	PRODUCT	Chapter16.xls or Chapter16.xlsx
	PRODUCT_SUM	Chapter16.xls or Chapter16.xlsx
	RAND	Chapter16.xls or Chapter16.xlsx
	ROMAN	Chapter16.xls or Chapter16.xlsx
	ROUND	Chapter16.xls or Chapter16.xlsx
	ROUNDUP	Chapter16.xls or Chapter16.xlsx
	Seriessum	Seriessum.xls or Seriessum.xlsx
	SIGN	Chapter16.xls or Chapter16.xlsx
	SIN_COS	Chapter16.xls or Chapter16.xlsx
	SQRT	Chapter16.xls or Chapter16.xlsx

Chapter Folder	Workbook/Worksheet Name	Location and/or Description
	SUBTOTAL	Chapter16.xls or Chapter16.xlsx
	SUBTOTAL2	Chapter16.xls or Chapter16.xlsx
	SUMIF	Chapter16.xls or Chapter16.xlsx
	SUMIFS	Chapter16.xls or Chapter16.xlsx
	SUMIFS2	Chapter16.xls or Chapter16.xlsx
	SUMPRODUCT	Chapter16.xls or Chapter16.xlsx
	SUMXY	Chapter16.xls or Chapter16.xlsx
	trigon	Chapter16.xls or Chapter16.xlsx
Chapter 17	Binary	Numbers.xls or Numbers.xlsx
	Decimal	Numbers.xls or Numbers.xlsx
	Hexadecimal	Numbers.xls or Numbers.xlsx
	Octal	Numbers.xls or Numbers.xlsx
	Sheet1	Convert.xls or Convert.xlsx
	Complex	Complex.xls or Complex.xlsm
	BESSEL I and Chart	Bessel_I.xls or Bessel_I.xlsx
	BESSEL J and Chart	Bessel_J.xls or Bessel_J.xlsx
	Bessel K and Chart	Bessel_K.xls or Bessel_K.xlsx
	Bessel Y and Chart	Bessel_Y.xls or Bessel_Y.xlsx
	Data and Chart	Gauss.xls or Gauss.xlsx
	Sheet1	Delta.xls or Delta.xlsx
	Longjump	GESTEP.xls or GESTEP.xlsx

Acknowledgments

In this introduction we would like to thank our editors Kenyon Brown and Thomas Braun-Wiesholler at O'Reilly Media and Kathy Krause at Online Training Solutions, Inc. (OTSI) for their inspiration, patience, and effort. The first edition of this book we published eight years ago in German for Microsoft Excel users in Germany, Austria, and Switzerland. Now we are proud to present you with our book translated into English. It was a great experience to transfer all of the chapters and sample files to readers in the United States and all over the world. Sometimes it was easy because we could remove the German-specific and European-specific topics. Other times it was challenging to find the U.S. analogy for some topics and samples. None of us is a native speaker, but with the great teamwork of the O'Reilly translators and editors, we learned a lot.

We have tried to bring you substantiated descriptions, practical examples, and solutions in all chapters, and to present the wide range of material without errors. Whether we have succeeded in fulfilling our own requirements is up to you to decide. We are realists and know that a book like this can always be improved in spite of all our efforts. We are therefore looking forward to receiving your critiques, suggestions, and notes.

Support and Feedback

The following sections provide information on errata, book support, feedback, and contact information.

Errata & Support

We've made every effort to ensure the accuracy of this book and its companion content. Any errors that have been reported since this book was published are listed on our Microsoft Press site at oreilly.com:

http://go.microsoft.com/FWLink/?Linkid=229605

If you find an error that is not already listed, you can report it to us through the same page.

If you need additional support, email Microsoft Press Book Support at *msinput@microsoft.com*.

Please note that product support for Microsoft software is not offered through the addresses above.

We Want to Hear from You

At Microsoft Press, your satisfaction is our top priority and your feedback our most valuable asset. Please tell us what you think of this book at

http://www.microsoft.com/learning/booksurvey

The survey is short, and we read every one of your comments and ideas. Thanks in advance for your input!

Stay in Touch

Let's keep the conversation going! We're on Twitter: *http://twitter.com/MicrosoftPress*

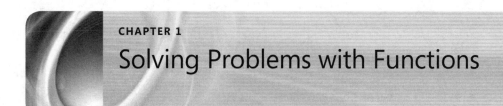

Solving Problems with Functions

T his chapter introduces Microsoft Excel and its functions. There are more practical examples with detailed function descriptions in Chapters 7 to 17 of this book.

First you will become familiar with Excel 2010, because there have been some notable changes since Excel 2007. Even if you are already using Excel 2010, you should be able to find some interesting points and suggestions.

Introducing the New Functions in Excel 2010

Microsoft Excel 2010 includes several new functions, many of which are introduced in the following Profit Margin example. Calculating a profit margin is important for price calculations and for planning operating results. By calculating the profit margin, you can build a decision-oriented cost accounting system.

Scenario and Goals

The Contoso, Ltd. company wants to evaluate and analyze its profit margins, focusing on overall percentages and variances. After you complete this example, you should be able to perform the following actions in Excel:

- Automatically fill in a month series and create your own fill styles

- Enter formulas

- Work with tables and style sheets

- Format cells

- Add and format graphics and charts

- Create a PivotTable and PivotChart

> **Sample Files**
>
> Use the Profit margin, Namerows, and Table profit margin worksheets in the Excel_
> Example.xls or Excel_Example.xlsx sample file. The sample files are found in the
> Chapter01 folder. For more information about the sample files, see the section titled
> "Using the Sample Files" on page xxiii.

The New Way to Work with Data, Formulas, and Functions

In this section, you will learn how to effectively work with Excel 2010 and explore the new possibilities.

Creating the Month Data Series

To quickly create a list of all months of the year, perform the following steps:

1. Select File/New and click Create to open an empty Excel workbook.

2. Enter the following text in columns A2 through E2 (see Figure 1-1):

   ▫ **Month** (A2)

   ▫ **Purchase** (B2)

   ▫ **Sales** (C2)

   ▫ **Profit margin** (D2)

	A	B	C	D
1				
2	Month	Purchase	Sales	Profit margin

Figure 1-1 Naming the table columns.

3. To enter the names of the months, you will use the fill feature. Start by entering **January** in cell A3.

4. Select cell A3 and point to the small square in the lower-right corner of the selected cell, the fill handle (see Figure 1-2). The mouse pointer changes to a black crosshair pointer.

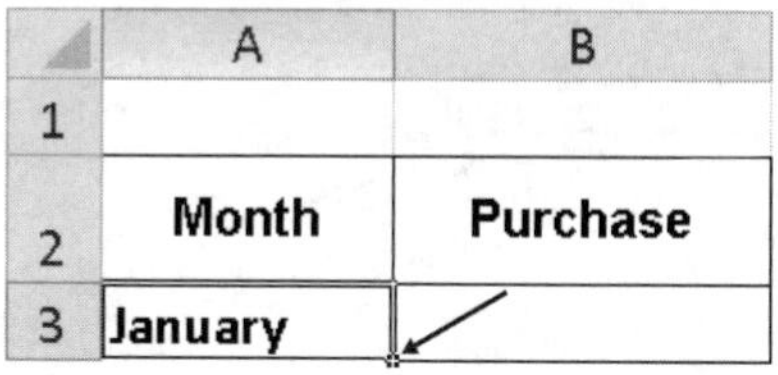

	A	B
1		
2	**Month**	**Purchase**
3	January	

Figure 1-2 The fill handle for extending the data series.

5. Drag the crosshairs into cell A14. While you drag the crosshairs down, you will see the names of the months in the preview (see Figure 1-3).

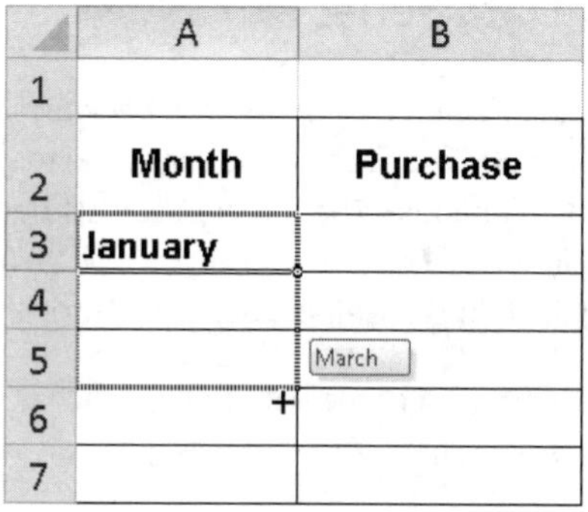

	A	B
1		
2	**Month**	**Purchase**
3	January	
4		
5		March
6	+	
7		

Figure 1-3 The months are added by using the fill handle.

6. Release the mouse button in cell A14 to display all months from January through December (see Figure 1-4).

	A
1	
2	Month
3	January
4	February
5	March
6	April
7	May
8	June
9	July
10	August
11	September
12	October
13	November
14	December

Figure 1-4 The names of the months are automatically filled in.

Creating an Individual Data Series

This feature can be used to fill rows or columns; it works for weekdays, months, and dates. To fill a number series, fill in the first two numbers in the sequence manually, select the two completed cells, and then drag the fill handle. The function can also be useful if you want to create your own data or AutoFill series. For example, if you don't want to enter a list of sales managers over and over again, you can define your own AutoFill list:

1. Click the last sheet tab at the bottom of the workbook, which is the one with the new sheet symbol, to open a new sheet. Alternatively, you can press the Ctrl+F11 key combination.

2. Enter **Sales manager** in a free cell.

3. Enter the names of the sales managers in the cells below the Sales manager title (see Figure 1-5).

	A
1	Sales manager
2	Jay Hamlin
3	Lori Penor
4	Ben Andrews
5	Michael Patten
6	Roxanne Kenison
7	Chris Sells

Figure 1-5 Creating a custom data series.

4. Select the range containing the names.

5. Click the File tab and select Options (see Figure 1-6).

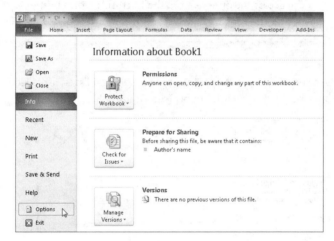

Figure 1-6 Selecting Excel options.

6. In the Excel Options dialog box, select the Advanced category and click Edit Custom Lists in the General section (see Figure 1-7).

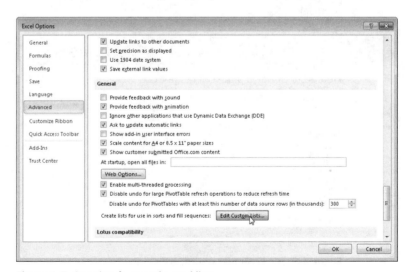

Figure 1-7 Opening frequently used lists.

> **Tip**
> In Excel 2003, the Excel options are located in the Custom menu. In Excel 2007, you can access the options from the Microsoft Office button, and in Excel 2010 they are on the File tab. Click Excel Options or Options, respectively.

7. Make sure that the cell reference for the selected list is displayed in the Import List From Cells field, and click Import (see Figure 1-8).

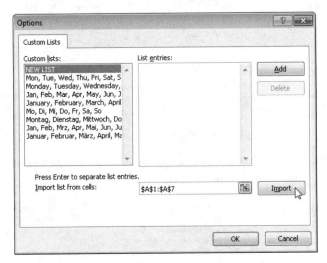

Figure 1-8 Specifying the cell range to be imported.

The elements in the selected list are added to the List Entries field (see Figure 1-9).

Figure 1-9 The list entries are added.

8. Click OK twice.

Now you have to enter only the name of one sales manager in a cell and drag the fill handle in the desired direction to generate the list of the sales managers on any spreadsheet. The series is created automatically.

This strategy gives you almost unlimited possibilities for creating a data series.

Entering Test Data Fast

Now let's return to the scenario described earlier in the chapter, in the section titled "Scenario and Goals." To complete the table with sales and purchase values, you need a set of sample data so that you can create and check the example. A convenient way to do this is to generate a set of random data by using the RANDBETWEEN() function.

1. Select cell B3 in the Excel sheet that contains the table you created previously.

2. Enter the following function: **=RANDBETWEEN(1000,500000)**. The values 1000 and 500000 indicate the minimum and maximum values and are divided by the comma (see Figure 1-10).

	A	B
1		
2	Month	Purchase
3	January	=RANDBETWEEN(1000,500000)
4	February	
5	March	

Figure 1-10 Working with formulas.

3. Press the Enter key. A random number from 1,000 through 500,000 appears in the cell (see Figure 1-11).

	A	B
1		
2	Month	Purchase
3	January	178314

Figure 1-11 The RANDBETWEEN function calculates a random value.

4. Select the cell and double-click the fill handle. The Purchase column is automatically filled through December (see Figure 1-12).

	A	B	C
1			
2	Month	Purchase	Sales
3	January	178314	
4	February	100419	
5	March	181190	
6	April	60947	
7	May	66849	
8	June	57386	
9	July	2957	
10	August	4410	
11	September	183933	
12	October	102958	
13	November	172501	
14	December	83044	

Figure 1-12 Values are added within seconds.

5. Edit the table however you want.

Converting Formula Results into Fixed Values

To ensure that the random values in the Purchase and Sales columns don't change, create a permanent copy of the entries by performing the following steps:

1. Select the cells in the Purchase column from January through December.

2. Point to the right edge of the selected column. The pointer changes into an arrow.

3. Click the right mouse button and drag the selection to the right and back. The movement is illustrated by a dashed line (see Figure 1-13).

	A	B	C
1			
2	Month	Purchase	Sales
3	January	178,314.00	
4	February	100,419.00	
5	March	181,190.00	
6	April	60,947.00	
7	May	66,849.00	
8	June	5 C3:C14	
9	July	2,957.00	
10	August	4,410.00	
11	September	183,933.00	
12	October	102,958.00	
13	November	172,501.00	
14	December	83,044.00	

Figure 1-13 The selected values are moved to the right and back.

Tip   Use the Paste Values icon

If you are working with Excel 2010, there is an easier way to copy the values. Copy the values in the Purchase column, and then paste them by opening the Paste menu and clicking the Paste Values icon (see Figure 1-14).

Figure 1-14 The Paste Values icon.

4. When the selection is back in the original position, release the mouse button and select Copy Here As Values Only in the shortcut menu (see Figure 1-15).

	A	B
1		
2	**Month**	**Purchase**
3	January	178,314.00
4	February	100,419.00
5	March	181,190.00
6	April	60,947.00
7	May	66,849.00
8	June B3:B14	57,386.00
9	July	2,957.00
10	August	4,410.00
11	September	183,933.00
12	October	102,958.00
13	November	172,501.00
14	December	83,044.00
15		
16		
17		
18		

Move Here
Copy Here
Copy Here as Values Only
Copy Here as Formats Only
Link Here
Create Hyperlink Here
Shift Down and Copy
Shift Right and Copy
Shift Down and Move
Shift Right and Move
Cancel

Figure 1-15 Converting numbers into fixed values.

The random values in the column are now fixed values and not formula-generated.

5. Repeat these steps and those in the section titled "Entering Test Data Fast" for the values in the Sales column, after you generate a fixed set of random values there, too.

Formatting Numeric Values

To format the numeric values in the Purchase and Sales columns as currency values, perform the following steps:

1. Select the cells B3 to C14.

2. Click the Accounting Number Format button in the Number group on the Home Tab (see Figure 1-16).

Figure 1-16 Formatting numbers as dollar values.

The selected values are automatically displayed as decimal numbers with two decimal places, in the currency format (see Figure 1-17).

	A	B	C
1			
2	**Month**	**Purchase**	**Sales**
3	**January**	$ 178,314.00	$ 219,572.00
4	**February**	$ 100,419.00	$ 205,043.00
5	**March**	$ 181,190.00	$ 385,835.00
6	**April**	$ 60,947.00	$ 201,285.00
7	**May**	$ 66,849.00	$ 213,776.00
8	**June**	$ 57,386.00	$ 397,653.00
9	**July**	$ 2,957.00	$ 283,100.00
10	**August**	$ 4,410.00	$ 334,551.00
11	**September**	$ 183,933.00	$ 247,343.00
12	**October**	$ 102,958.00	$ 362,121.00
13	**November**	$ 172,501.00	$ 340,069.00
14	**December**	$ 83,044.00	$ 379,739.00

Figure 1-17 The numbers are displayed as dollar amounts.

Calculating Profit Margin

To calculate the profit margin, do the following:

1. Click in cell D3 and subtract the Purchase amount from the Sales amount. To do this, enter an equal sign (=) in cell D3, click in cell C3, enter a minus sign (–) and then click in cell B3 (see Figure 1-18).

SUM	▾	✕ ✓ ƒ✕	=C3-B3	
	A	B	C	D
1				
2	Month	Purchase	Sales	Profit margin
3	January	$ 178,314.00	$ 219,572.00	=C3-B3

Figure 1-18 Subtracting values.

2. Press the Enter key.

3. Double-click the fill handle to calculate the profit margin through December (see Figure 1-19).

	A	B	C	D
1				
2	Month	Purchase	Sales	Profit margin
3	January	$ 178,314.00	$ 219,572.00	$ 41,258.00
4	February	$ 100,419.00	$ 205,043.00	$ 104,624.00
5	March	$ 181,190.00	$ 385,835.00	$ 204,645.00
6	April	$ 60,947.00	$ 201,285.00	$ 140,338.00
7	May	$ 66,849.00	$ 213,776.00	$ 146,927.00
8	June	$ 57,386.00	$ 397,653.00	$ 340,267.00
9	July	$ 2,957.00	$ 283,100.00	$ 280,143.00
10	August	$ 4,410.00	$ 334,551.00	$ 330,141.00
11	September	$ 183,933.00	$ 247,343.00	$ 63,410.00
12	October	$ 102,958.00	$ 362,121.00	$ 259,163.00
13	November	$ 172,501.00	$ 340,069.00	$ 167,568.00
14	December	$ 83,044.00	$ 379,739.00	$ 296,695.00

Figure 1-19 The profit margin is calculated for all months.

Formatting Data as a Table

In Excel 2007 and Excel 2010, a selection of preset table formats can be readily accessed from the ribbon.

1. Select the cells containing the entire table (A2:D14).

2. On the Home tab, click the Format As Table button in the Style group and select one of the table layouts shown in Figure 1-20.

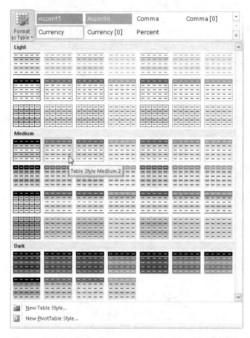

Figure 1-20 Table formats in Excel 2007 and Excel 2010.

3. The Create Table dialog box shows the range to be formatted (see Figure 1-21). Click OK.

Figure 1-21 Confirming the table range to be formatted.

The table is formatted in the selected layout (see Figure 1-22).

	A	B	C	D
1				
2	Month ▾	Purchase ▾	Sales ▾	Profit margin ▾
3	January	$ 178,314.00	$ 219,572.00	$ 41,258.00
4	February	$ 100,419.00	$ 205,043.00	$ 104,624.00
5	March	$ 181,190.00	$ 385,835.00	$ 204,645.00
6	April	$ 60,947.00	$ 201,285.00	$ 140,338.00
7	May	$ 66,849.00	$ 213,776.00	$ 146,927.00
8	June	$ 57,386.00	$ 397,653.00	$ 340,267.00
9	July	$ 2,957.00	$ 283,100.00	$ 280,143.00
10	August	$ 4,410.00	$ 334,551.00	$ 330,141.00
11	September	$ 183,933.00	$ 247,343.00	$ 63,410.00
12	October	$ 102,958.00	$ 362,121.00	$ 259,163.00
13	November	$ 172,501.00	$ 340,069.00	$ 167,568.00
14	December	$ 83,044.00	$ 379,739.00	$ 296,695.00

Figure 1-22 Formatting tables in only a few steps.

After you have formatted the data as a table, you can use the filter options that have been placed in the table header.

INSIDE OUT   Format data as a table for added functionality

Formatting data as a table provides a convenient way to arrange the information neatly and concisely and also provides access to additional table features.

Calculating Profit Margin as a Percentage

This section explains how to calculate the profit margin as a percentage for the full year. To do this, perform the following steps:

1. Select cell D15, which is below the profit margin for December.

2. On the Home tab, in the Editing group, click the AutoSum button (see Figure 1-23).

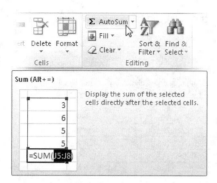

Figure 1-23 Calculating the sum with one mouse click.

The sum is automatically calculated and displayed in the Profit Margin column (see Figure 1-24).

	A	B	C	D
1				
2	**Month** ▾	**Purchase** ▾	**Sales** ▾	**Profit margin** ▾
3	January	$ 178,314.00	$ 219,572.00	$ 41,258.00
4	February	$ 100,419.00	$ 205,043.00	$ 104,624.00
5	March	$ 181,190.00	$ 385,835.00	$ 204,645.00
6	April	$ 60,947.00	$ 201,285.00	$ 140,338.00
7	May	$ 66,849.00	$ 213,776.00	$ 146,927.00
8	June	$ 57,386.00	$ 397,653.00	$ 340,267.00
9	July	$ 2,957.00	$ 283,100.00	$ 280,143.00
10	August	$ 4,410.00	$ 334,551.00	$ 330,141.00
11	September	$ 183,933.00	$ 247,343.00	$ 63,410.00
12	October	$ 102,958.00	$ 362,121.00	$ 259,163.00
13	November	$ 172,501.00	$ 340,069.00	$ 167,568.00
14	December	$ 83,044.00	$ 379,739.00	$ 296,695.00
15				$ 2,375,179.00 ▾
16				Σ ▾

Figure 1-24 Simplified calculation options with table formatting.

Tip   Choose calculations options

Did you notice the arrow to the right of the sum field? Click the arrow to open a menu, select one of the different options, and view the result (see Figure 1-25).

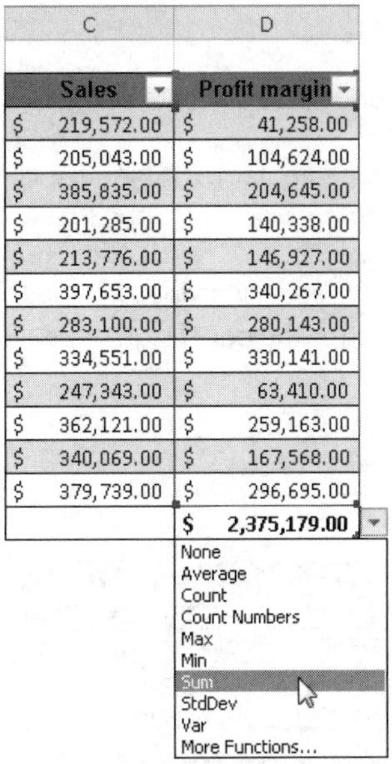

	C	D
	Sales ▾	**Profit margin** ▾
	$ 219,572.00	$ 41,258.00
	$ 205,043.00	$ 104,624.00
	$ 385,835.00	$ 204,645.00
	$ 201,285.00	$ 140,338.00
	$ 213,776.00	$ 146,927.00
	$ 397,653.00	$ 340,267.00
	$ 283,100.00	$ 280,143.00
	$ 334,551.00	$ 330,141.00
	$ 247,343.00	$ 63,410.00
	$ 362,121.00	$ 259,163.00
	$ 340,069.00	$ 167,568.00
	$ 379,739.00	$ 296,695.00
		$ 2,375,179.00 ▾

None
Average
Count
Count Numbers
Max
Min
Sum
StdDev
Var
More Functions…

Figure 1-25 The calculation options for table ranges.

3. Create the profit margin percentage in the column next to the Profit Margin column. When you enter the text in column E, the table formatting is automatically extended to the additional column (see Figure 1-26).

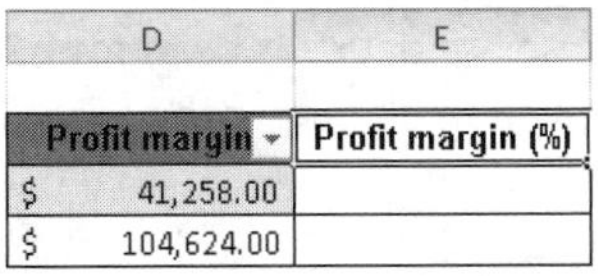

D	E
Profit margin ▾	**Profit margin (%)**
$ 41,258.00	
$ 104,624.00	

Figure 1-26 Adding columns to the table.

4. Press the Enter key. The column is added to the table automatically and inherits the table layout (see Figure 1-27).

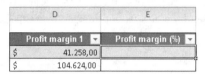

Figure 1-27 New columns are automatically adjusted to the table layout.

5. To calculate the profit margin as a percentage for January, click cell E3 (Profit Margin (%) column, January row).

6. The formula is "the profit margin of January divided by the total profit margin." To enter this in the cell, click cell D3 after the equal sign, type a forward slash, and then click cell D15 (see Figure 1-28).

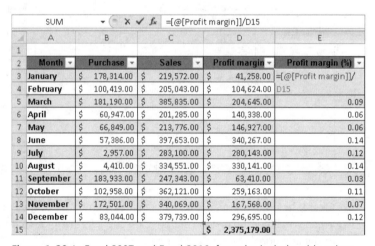

Figure 1-28 In Excel 2007 and Excel 2010, formulas include table values.

7. Press the Enter key to confirm. Because the data has been formatted as a table, the formula entered is automatically applied to all cells in the Profit Margin (%) column (see Figure 1-29).

D	E
Profit margin ▼	**Profit margin (%)** ▼
$ 41,258.00	0.02
$ 104,624.00	0.04
$ 204,645.00	0.09
$ 140,338.00	0.06
$ 146,927.00	0.06
$ 340,267.00	0.14
$ 280,143.00	0.12
$ 330,141.00	0.14
$ 63,410.00	0.03
$ 259,163.00	0.11
$ 167,568.00	0.07
$ 296,695.00	0.12
$ **2,375,179.00**	

Figure 1-29 The formula is applied to all cells in the column.

8. Select the numeric values in the Profit Margin (%) column, and click the Percent Style button in the Number group on the Home Tab (see Figure 1-30).

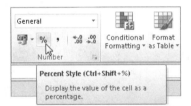

Figure 1-30 Numbers are displayed as percentages.

The values are now displayed as percentages (see Figure 1-31).

E
Profit margin (%) ▼
2%
4%
9%
6%
6%
14%
12%
14%
3%
11%
7%
12%

Figure 1-31 The profit margins as percentages.

Applying Conditional Formatting

To make data easier to interpret, use the conditional formatting feature to automatically format the data. With conditional formats, values are selected if they meet certain criteria, and the cell range is formatted accordingly. Conditional formats visually highlight the distribution and variation of data.

With regard to our example, the condition could be "Format in green all cells in the Profit Margin column that contain a value of at least $200,000." To enter this format, perform the following steps:

1. Select the cell range in the Profit Margin column.

2. Click the Conditional Formatting button in the Style group on the Home tab, and then click New Rule (see Figure 1-32).

Figure 1-32 Creating a new rule.

3. In the New Formatting Rule dialog box, under Select A Rule Type, select Format Only Cells That Contain.

4. Specify the settings in the Edit The Rule Description pane. Select Cell Value and Greater Than Or Equal To in the list boxes.

5. Enter the value **200000** in the third field (see Figure 1-33).

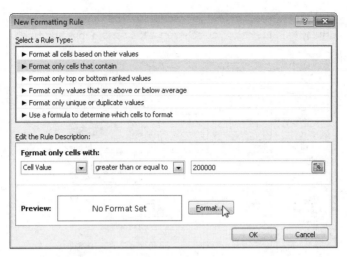

Figure 1-33 Defining the formatting rule.

6. Click the Format button.

7. Click the Fill tab of the Format Cells dialog box, and select a background color (see Figure 1-34).

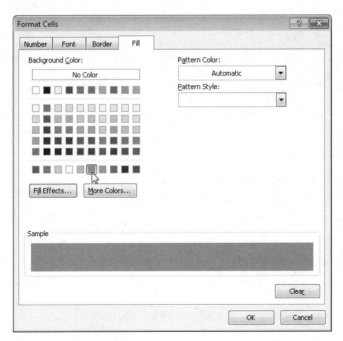

Figure 1-34 The condition is displayed in color.

8. Click OK twice to confirm your selection. The values in the Profit margin column are displayed in the color you selected if the condition is met (see Figure 1-35).

	A	B	C	D
1				
2	**Month**	**Purchase**	**Sales**	**Profit margin**
3	January	$ 178,314.00	$ 219,572.00	$ 41,258.00
4	February	$ 100,419.00	$ 205,043.00	$ 104,624.00
5	March	$ 181,190.00	$ 385,835.00	$ 204,645.00
6	April	$ 60,947.00	$ 201,285.00	$ 140,338.00
7	May	$ 66,849.00	$ 213,776.00	$ 146,927.00
8	June	$ 57,386.00	$ 397,653.00	$ 340,267.00
9	July	$ 2,957.00	$ 283,100.00	$ 280,143.00
10	August	$ 4,410.00	$ 334,551.00	$ 330,141.00
11	September	$ 183,933.00	$ 247,343.00	$ 63,410.00
12	October	$ 102,958.00	$ 362,121.00	$ 259,163.00
13	November	$ 172,501.00	$ 340,069.00	$ 167,568.00
14	December	$ 83,044.00	$ 379,739.00	$ 296,695.00

Figure 1-35 Values meeting the condition have a green background.

You can use conditional formatting to automatically display the values in your table in different colors to give them significant visual impact.

You can also use other color fill options or an icon set to format cells. Conditions can apply to text, numeric, date, or time values, as well as to values that fall below or above the average.

Data bars are also a quick way to visually highlight values in tables (see Figure 1-36).

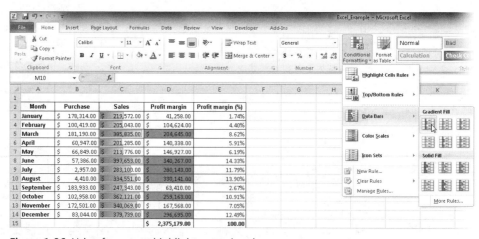

Figure 1-36 Using formats to highlight numeric values.

There are many different options to choose from.

Tip   Apply conditional formats to highlight data

In Excel 2007 and Excel 2010, conditional formats have improved significantly (see Figure 1-37). Now you can add not only colors but also arrows, traffic lights, and other icons. This functionality is also referred to as KPI (Key Performance Indicators).

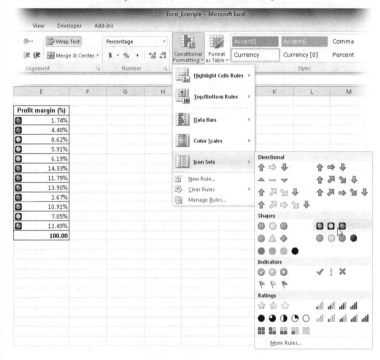

Figure 1-37 New elements for conditional formats in Excel 2007 and Excel 2010.

Creating Meaningful Charts

Sometimes it is useful to display data in a chart instead of in a table. In Excel 2007 and Excel 2010, the options for creating bar charts, pie charts, and other charts have been enhanced.

Creating a Column Chart

To convert our example table into a simple but informative column chart, perform the following steps:

1. Select the table cells starting from Month to the profit margin December (see Figure 1-38).

A2		▾	fx	Month	
	A	B	C	D	
1					
2	**Month**	**Purchase**	**Sales**	**Profit margin**	
3	January	$ 178,314.00	$ 219,572.00	$ 41,258.00	
4	February	$ 100,419.00	$ 205,043.00	$ 104,624.00	
5	March	$ 181,190.00	$ 385,835.00	$ 204,645.00	
6	April	$ 60,947.00	$ 201,285.00	$ 140,338.00	
7	May	$ 66,849.00	$ 213,776.00	$ 146,927.00	
8	June	$ 57,386.00	$ 397,653.00	$ 340,267.00	
9	July	$ 2,957.00	$ 283,100.00	$ 280,143.00	
10	August	$ 4,410.00	$ 334,551.00	$ 330,141.00	
11	September	$ 183,933.00	$ 247,343.00	$ 63,410.00	
12	October	$ 102,958.00	$ 362,121.00	$ 259,163.00	
13	November	$ 172,501.00	$ 340,069.00	$ 167,568.00	
14	December	$ 83,044.00	$ 379,739.00	$ 296,695.00	

Figure 1-38 Selecting a value to create a chart.

2. On the Insert tab in the Chart group, click the Column button and select the first chart under 2D Column (see Figure 1-39).

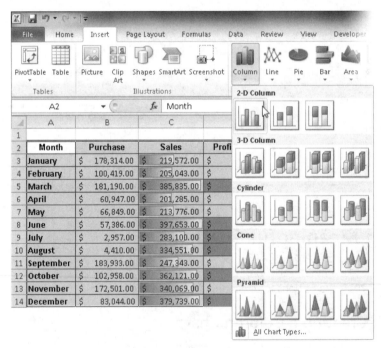

Figure 1-39 Selecting the chart format.

The chart is immediately displayed on your Excel sheet (see Figure 1-40).

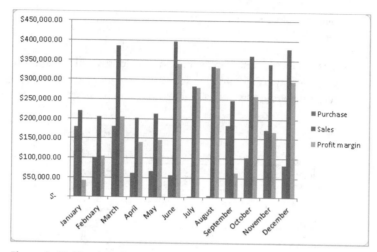

Figure 1-40 The data displayed as a chart.

In the same way you created a column chart, you can create a 2D, 3D, or line chart (see Figure 1-41). To do this, select a chart format by clicking the Line button to open the menu.

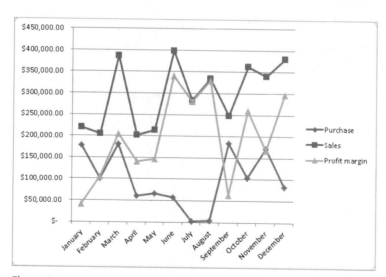

Figure 1-41 Another view of the chart.

Creating a Pie Chart

To display the values in the Profit Margin column by month, you can use a pie chart. Do the following:

1. Select the cells containing values in the Months and Profit Margin columns. To select only these two columns, first select the Months column. Then press the Ctrl key and select the Profit Margin column. Both columns are selected (see Figure 1-42).

	A	B	C	D
1				
2	**Month**	**Purchase**	**Sales**	**Profit margin**
3	January	$ 178,314.00	$ 219,572.00	$ 41,258.00
4	February	$ 100,419.00	$ 205,043.00	$ 104,624.00
5	March	$ 181,190.00	$ 385,835.00	$ 204,645.00
6	April	$ 60,947.00	$ 201,285.00	$ 140,338.00
7	May	$ 66,849.00	$ 213,776.00	$ 146,927.00
8	June	$ 57,386.00	$ 397,653.00	$ 340,267.00
9	July	$ 2,957.00	$ 283,100.00	$ 280,143.00
10	August	$ 4,410.00	$ 334,551.00	$ 330,141.00
11	September	$ 183,933.00	$ 247,343.00	$ 63,410.00
12	October	$ 102,958.00	$ 362,121.00	$ 259,163.00
13	November	$ 172,501.00	$ 340,069.00	$ 167,568.00
14	December	$ 83,044.00	$ 379,739.00	$ 296,695.00

Figure 1-42 Selecting only certain columns of the list.

2. Click the Pie button to open the menu, and select the first chart type under 3D Pie (see Figure 1-43).

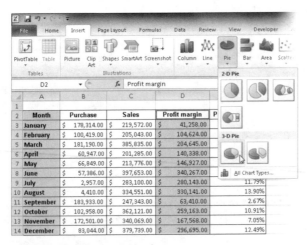

Figure 1-43 Selecting a pie chart.

The pie chart is displayed immediately (see Figure 1-44).

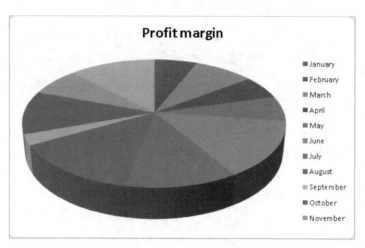

Figure 1-44 The pie chart shows the profit margin.

Formatting a Chart

Excel 2010 provides many formatting options you can use to emphasize values in pie charts.

Do the following:

1. Click the frame of the chart.

    The Chart Tools contextual tab opens. On this tab, you can choose between the available formatting options (see Figure 1-45).

Figure 1-45 The Chart Tools tab in Excel 2010 for editing charts.

2. With these tools, you can select any of the format options. For example, click Layout 6 in the Chart Layouts section (see Figure 1-46).

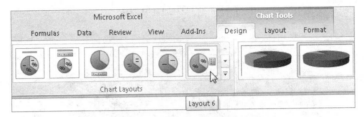

Figure 1-46 Changing the chart layout.

Layout 6 displays your pie chart with percentages, or values (see Figure 1-47).

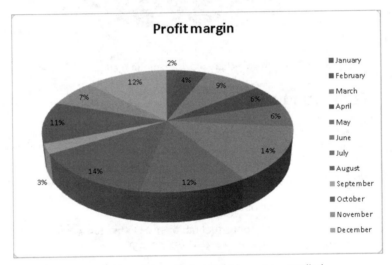

Figure 1-47 The settings of the selected chart layout are applied.

3. With the chart formats, you can also adjust the chart colors. Just click one of the available formats (see Figure 1-48).

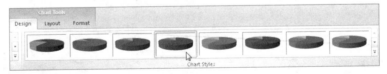

Figure 1-48 Using chart formats to adjust the color.

The color of the chart changes according to your selection (see Figure 1-49).

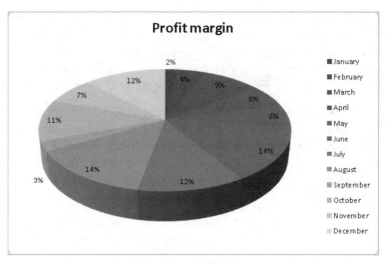

Figure 1-49 The selected chart colors are applied.

4. In Excel 2010—as in Excel 2007 and Excel 2003—more chart format options are available in the shortcut menu of the selected chart. Right-click the chart to open the menu, and then select Format Data Labels or Format Data Series to change the format of your chart (see Figure 1-50).

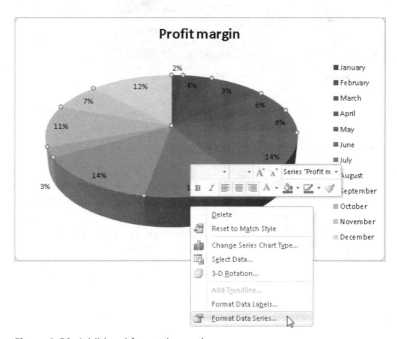

Figure 1-50 Additional formatting options.

In Excel 2010, working with charts is a lot easier. The options for editing and formatting are more extensive, and fully formatted charts can be created with just a few clicks.

INSIDE OUT   Use sparklines to graphically represent values

Check out the new sparklines in Excel 2010. These "word graphics" illustrate values by using miniature line, bar, or profit-and-loss charts. Sparklines illustrate numeric values so that the values can be interpreted more easily (see Figure 1-51).

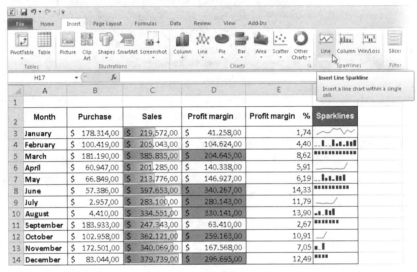

Figure 1-51 Values illustrated by the new sparklines.

Working with PivotTables

PivotTables help you arrange and consolidate data into well-defined tables. With a Pivot-Table, you can easily generate cross-tabulations and analyze information by rotating and moving column and row selections and by filtering. The original data remains unchanged, and the PivotTable is quickly generated even with large amounts of data. In Excel 2007 and Excel 2010, PivotTable data can also easily be displayed as a PivotChart.

> **Tip**
> A PivotTable is useful for quickly obtaining summary information from long lists or large amounts of data.

Creating a PivotTable

> **Sample Files**
> Use the Basic data worksheet in the Excel_Pivot_Data.xls or Excel_Pivot_Data.xlsx sample file. The sample files are found in the Chapter01 folder. For more information about the sample files, see the section titled "Using the Sample Files" on page xxiii.

To create a PivotTable, perform the following steps:

1. Open the Excel_Pivot_Data.xlsx file from the sample files.

2. In the table, select the cell range for which you want to create the PivotTable. In this case, select cell A1 (Customer Name) through cell J100 (Total Price), or select the entire table by pressing Ctrl+A from anywhere within the table.

3. On the Insert tab, in the Table group, click the arrow on the PivotTable button and select PivotTable (see Figure 1-52).

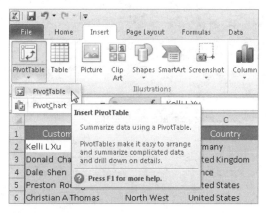

Figure 1-52 Creating a PivotTable.

> ### Tip   Find Pivot functions on the Insert tab
>
> In Excel 2003, the Pivot functions were located on the File menu. In Excel 2007 and Excel 2010, you can open the Pivot functions by clicking a button on the Insert tab. The functions open in a separate tool window as soon as you start creating a PivotTable.

Because you have already selected the data, the PivotTable range is displayed in the Select Table Or Range box in the PivotTable dialog box.

4. Select an option under Choose Where You Want The PivotTable Report To Be Placed. Selecting the New Worksheet option is recommended (see Figure 1-53).

5. Click OK. The PivotTable framework is displayed.

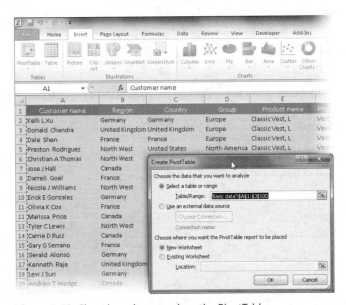

Figure 1-53 Choosing where to place the PivotTable.

An empty PivotTable report is added, in this case in a new worksheet, and the PivotTable field list is displayed. In this list, you can select fields, create a layout, and change the Pivot-Table report.

You can also use the PivotTable tools on the PivotTable Tool contextual tab, which you can access from the ribbon (see Figure 1-54).

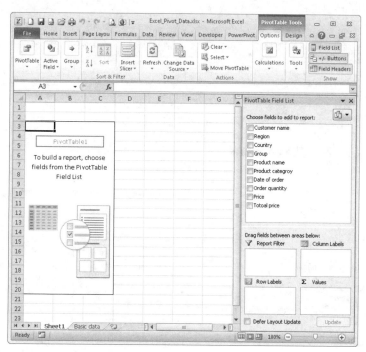

Figure 1-54 The PivotTable layout.

Using a PivotTable

The following example illustrates the functionality of a PivotTable. Assume that you want to find out in which country the most orders for gloves are placed. For this you need the PivotTable fields Country, Product Category, and Order Quantity.

Follow these steps:

1. Select the Country, Product Category, and Order Quantity check boxes in the PivotTable field list.

   After you have enabled the fields, the associated data are automatically positioned in the default range of the layout, but you can move the fields to any position (see Figure 1-55).

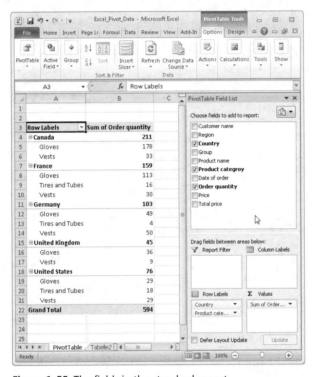

Figure 1-55 The fields in the standard report.

2. Because you want to view the order quantity for gloves per country, you should move the Product Category column into the Report Filter area. This will allow you to filter by country. Drag the Product Category field into the Report Filter area within the PivotTable field list (see Figure 1-56).

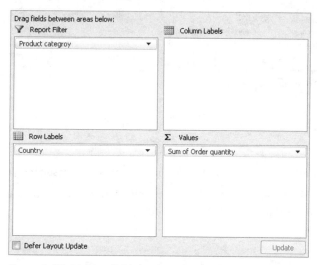

Figure 1-56 Moving fields by dragging.

As soon as you release the mouse button, the data is arranged in the PivotTable (see Figure 1-57).

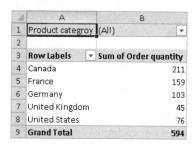

Figure 1-57 The newly arranged fields.

3. In the (All) list, select Gloves and click OK (see Figure 1-58).

Figure 1-58 Select Gloves from the list so that only the result for gloves will be displayed.

Only the order quantities for gloves in the individual countries are displayed (see Figure 1-59). Canada is the frontrunner!

Figure 1-59 Getting meaningful results with only a few clicks.

> **Note**
>
> Don't worry if a report is not what you were expecting. With Excel, you can try various options to see how the data looks in different formats by rearranging the data, moving data, or even starting again.

Using PivotCharts: Graphical Pivot

The new user interface also makes it easier to create PivotCharts. All filter enhancements for PivotTables are also available for PivotCharts. There are special PivotChart tools and short-cut menus you can use to create a PivotChart to analyze the data within a chart.

You can change the layout and the format of charts or the chart elements in the same way you make changes for Pivot Tables. Unlike in previous Excel versions, in Excel 2007 and Excel 2010, the chart format is maintained if you change the PivotChart.

Creating a PivotChart

Creating a chart for a PivotTable takes only seconds. Use the previous PivotTable example to practice. Do the following:

1. Click in the PivotTable, and select the PivotTable Tools contextual tab above the default tab (see Figure 1-60).

Figure 1-60 Working with PivotTable tools.

2. In the Tools group, click the PivotChart button (see Figure 1-61). The Insert Chart dialog box opens. The first layout under Column is selected (see Figure 1-62).

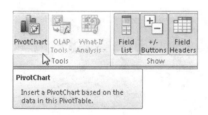

Figure 1-61 Creating a chart from PivotTable data.

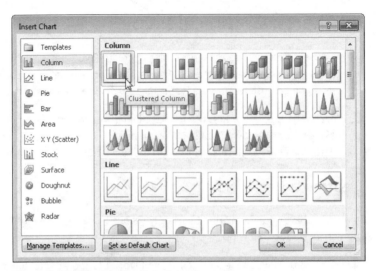

Figure 1-62 Selecting the chart format.

3. Keep this setting and click OK. The chart and a PivotChart filter range are displayed (see Figure 1-63).

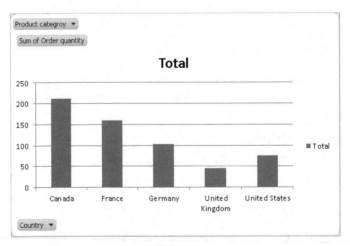

Figure 1-63 The PivotChart is created.

4. As soon as you change the filter, the chart also changes. In the Country list, select Germany and click OK (see Figure 1-64).

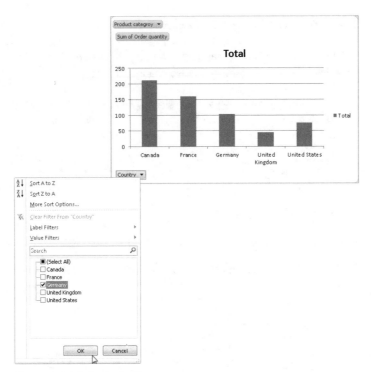

Figure 1-64 Selecting a filter.

The chart changes automatically, and the corresponding values are displayed (see Figure 1-65).

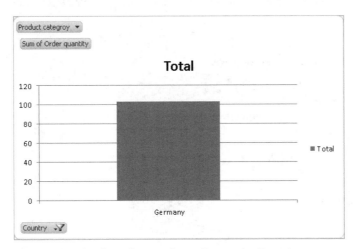

Figure 1-65 The chart changes depending on the Pivot data.

Changing the Original Data

PivotTables and PivotCharts change dynamically: If a value changes in the original data, the PivotTable and the associated chart also change. Try it out:

1. In the original data, increase the order quantity for gloves in Germany in any row (see Figure 1-66).

	A	B	C	D	E	F	G	H
37	Alexandra E Washington	Canada	Canada	North America	Half-Finger Gloves, L Gloves		11.05.11	6
38	Cassidy Washington	United Kingdom	United Kingdom	Europe	Half-Finger Gloves, L Gloves		04.05.11	1
39	Elijah Alexander	Canada	Canada	North America	Half-Finger Gloves, L Gloves		29.04.11	2
40	Bruce G Suri	Germany	Germany	Europe	Half-Finger Gloves, L Gloves		28.03.11	2568

Figure 1-66 Changing the original data.

2. Go back to the PivotTable and open the PivotTable Tools contextual tab.

3. On the Analyze tab, in the Data group, click the Refresh button (see Figure 1-67).

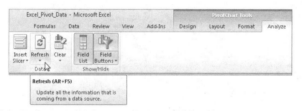

Figure 1-67 Applying changes to the original data by clicking Refresh.

The PivotTable as well as the PivotChart are automatically updated (see Figure 1-68).

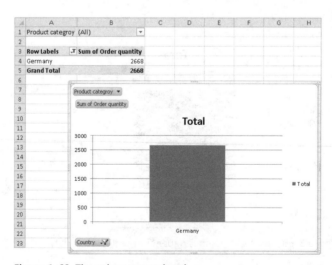

Figure 1-68 The values are updated.

Note

You can change additional settings for PivotCharts: Select a chart element and open the shortcut menu (see Figure 1-69).

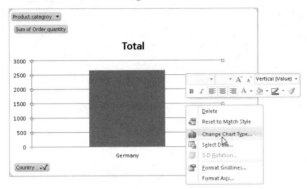

Figure 1-69 The shortcut menu allows quick access to the settings.

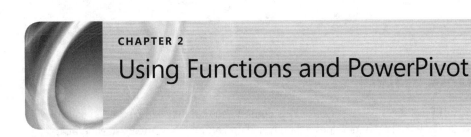

Using Functions and PowerPivot

This chapter describes many important functions in Microsoft Excel, including functions that can be used to manipulate date and time values. You can use these functions in conjunction with the system time of your computer, but you need to ensure that your system time is correct.

Using Date and Time Functions

When Excel recognizes a date value, the corresponding cell is automatically formatted as a date. For example, the value 10-7 is interpreted as October 7th of the current year, and the cell is formatted accordingly. Any subsequent entries made in this cell will be displayed as date values. So, for example, entering the number 123456 will display 1/3/2238. (See the section titled "The Excel Date System" later in this chapter for more information about these numbers.)

INSIDE OUT Entering date values

When dates are entered, Excel recognizes a slash (/) or a minus sign (–) as a separator. For example, Excel recognizes 8/13/08 or 4-26-11 as dates. These two characters are located on the keypad and are easy to enter.

The Excel Date System

Microsoft Excel saves dates as continuous numbers so that they can be used in calcula-tions. By default, Excel determines a date based on continuous numbers starting at 1, which is January 1st, 1900, and ending with the number 2,958,465, which is December 31st, 9999. This means that Excel can calculate date values only between these two dates.

CAUTION!

Microsoft Excel for Mac uses a different date system. The calendar starts at 01/01/1904. For compatibility reasons, the Windows version of Excel provides an option for working with the date system starting at 1904. Select this option only if you have to change worksheets between Windows and Mac computers. But be careful: This setting applies to the active worksheet, and the dates already entered will be changed!

To display the continuous number for a date or time value, restore the General format of the cell. In versions of Excel before Excel 2003, you can select the Delete option on the Edit menu and click Formats to restore the General format. In Excel 2007 or Excel 2010, you only need to click the number format on the Home tab (see Figure 2-1).

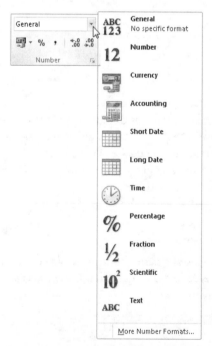

Figure 2-1 Number format selection on the Home tab of Excel 2007 and Excel 2010.

Here is how dates and times together are displayed as continuous numbers: The number before the period is the date. For example, the number 39448 indicates the number of days since 01/01/1900. The result is January 1st, 2008. The numbers after the period indicate the time. If you divide this value by the number of hours in a day, you get the decimal fraction for an hour: 1/24 = 0.04166667. The number 0.5 indicates that half a day has passed and it is noon. The number 0.25 indicates 6:00 A.M., and 0.75 indicates 6:00 P.M.

Date and Time Number Formats

You can view the date and time by using the formats listed in Table 2-1. The example worksheets for Chapter 7, "Date and Time Functions," include many more examples of formats.

Table 2-1 Number Formats for Dates and Times

Format	Description/Result
Number	=SUM(number1,number2...)
Text	=CONCATENATE(Text1,Text2,...)
T	Day without leading zero
TT	Day with leading zero for one-digit numbers
TTT	Abbreviated name of the day (Mo, Tu, We, Th, Fr, Sa, Su)
TTTT	Name of the day (Monday, Tuesday, and so on)
M	Month without leading zero
MM	Month with leading zero for one-digit numbers
MMM	Abbreviated name of the month (Jan, Feb, Mar, and so on)
MMMM	Name of the month (January, February, March, and so on)
J or JJ	Two-digit year
JJJ or JJJJ	Four-digit year
h	Hour without leading zero
hh	Hour with leading zero
m	Minute without leading zero
mm	Minute with leading zero
[h] or [hh]	Hours for more than 24 hours
[m] or [mm]	Minutes for more than 60 minutes
[s] or [ss]	Seconds for more than 60 seconds
hh:mm AM	Twelve-hour format (A.M.): *Ante meridian* (Latin for "before noon," the hours between midnight and noon)
hh:mm PM	Twelve-hour format (P.M.): *Post meridian* (Latin for "after noon," the hours between noon and midnight)

Leap Years

When programming date calculations, you have to consider leap years. In the Gregorian calendar, every fourth year is a leap year in which the month of February has 29 days. If the year can be divided by 100 without a remainder, the year isn't a leap year, with one exception: If the year is divisible by 400 without a remainder, the year is a leap year anyway. If this last rule is disregarded, there will be further mistakes instead of a 29th of February.

Analysis Functions

Though most of these date and time functions are available with the standard Excel 2003 installation (and earlier), some need to be enabled. You can enable them by selecting Tools/ Add-Ins and making a selection in the Add-Ins dialog box (see Figure 2-2).

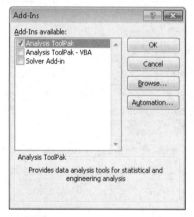

Figure 2-2 In Excel 2003 and earlier, certain analysis functions have to be enabled in the Add-Ins dialog box.

In Excel 2007 and Excel 2010, you can use all functions without having to enable the add-in.

Date and Time Functions in Practice

The following practice examples show typical calculations that use the date and time functions of Excel.

> ### Sample Files
> Use the Praxis worksheet in the Date_Time.xls or Date_Time.xlsx sample file. The sample files are found in the Chapter02 folder. For more information about the sample files, see the section titled "Using the Sample Files" on page xxiii.

Calculating the Start and End of Daylight Saving Time

Assume that Daylight Saving Time starts on the last Sunday in March and ends on the last Sunday in October. The start of Daylight Saving Time in the current year is calculated with the following formula:

`=DATE(YEAR(TODAY()),31,3)-WEEKDAY(DATE(YEAR(TODAY()),31,3),2)`

`DATE(YEAR(TODAY()),31,3)` returns March 31st of the current year. `WEEKDAY(DATE(YEAR(TODAY()),31,3,)` returns the weekday number of the last day of March in the current year. Because of the argument 2 at the end of the formula, Excel starts with number 1 for Monday. So by subtracting this value from the last day of the month and adding one day, you get the date of the last Sunday of March.

The following formula returns the end of Daylight Saving Time for the current year (the last Sunday of October):

`=DATE(YEAR(TODAY()),11,)-WEEKDAY(DATE(YEAR(TODAY()),11,))+1`

Identifying What Day of the Year Today Is

You can use a nested date function to find out the continuous number of today's date:

`=TODAY()-DATE(YEAR(TODAY())-1,12,31)`

This formula subtracts December 31st of last year from today's date. The result is the difference between both dates in days—in this case, the number of the day for today in the current year.

Calculating with Time

Enter the current time by pressing Ctrl+Shift+: (colon). The time is displayed in the hh:mm number format. For example, the cell might display 2:25 P.M., and the formula bar would also show 2:25 P.M. If you select the General number format, the value (in this example, 0.60069444) is displayed. If you are calculating times, you should remember that the time is always a value from 0 through 1.

Usually you don't have to take care of the conversion, because Excel automatically converts dates and times. To calculate the difference between two date and time entries, you can subtract the start date/time from the end date/time. This way, you can create a table with working hours to calculate the hours for each working day, as in the example that follows in the next section.

Chapter 2

Calculating Working Hours

Assume that you want to create a worksheet with shift work hours. Some employees work from 10:00 P.M. to 6:00 A.M. How do you calculate the correct working hours?

If the employees work from 10:00 P.M. to 6:00 A.M., and you calculate the difference, the result is ######. Even if you change the column width, the problem is not solved. If, however, you change the format of this number to General, the value is displayed. It is interesting that Excel can calculate the time when you set the number format to General, but not when it is set to a time format. As you can see, the Excel time format does not work with negative numbers.

You have two options for solving this problem: Change the general setting to the 1904 date system (see Figure 2-3), or use a formula.

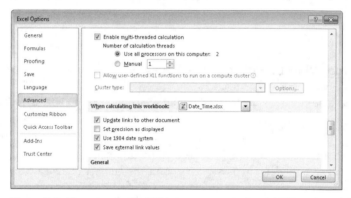

Figure 2-3 Changing to the 1904 date system in Excel 2007 and Excel 2010.

CAUTION

Use the Tools/Options menu command (Excel 2003 or earlier) to select the 1904 date system check box on the Calculation tab. With this option enabled, Excel can perform calculations with negative times. However, this has disadvantages: This setting applies only to the active worksheet. If other worksheets refer to these time values, you must change those worksheets accordingly. All entered date values change by four years, and you must change all existing dates. Therefore, this option isn't a reliable solution.

Calculating Beyond the Date Limit

To calculate a time interval that crosses over to another day, you can enter the times and include the date. If work begins at 8/4/2008 10:00 P.M. and ends at 8/5/2008 06:20 A.M., you can easily calculate the difference. This is done with the formula =End-Beginning.

However, you should display the number format of the result cell in the hh:mm format (see Figure 2-4).

	F	G	H
H12		fx =G12-F12	
7	**Calculate working hours (date/time)**		
8			
9	*Beginning*	*End*	*Hours*
10	8/5/2012 6:00 AM	8/5/2012 2:30 PM	8:30
11	8/5/2012 2:00 PM	8/5/2012 10:15 PM	8:15
12	8/5/2012 10:00 PM	8/6/2012 6:20 AM	8:20

Figure 2-4 When you include the date with the time, calculating the difference causes no problem.

Another approach is to check which time value is higher if the times are available for the beginning and end. With the logical IF(test;value_if_true,value_if_false) function, you get the result with the formula

```
=IF(Beginning>End,1-(Beginning-End),End-Beginning)
```

This formula can be used to calculate the difference up to 24 hours. Figure 2-5 shows an example.

	B	C	D	E
D12			fx =IF(B12>C12,1-(B12-C12),C12-B12)	
7	**Calculate working hours (time only)**			
8				
9	*Beginning*	*End*	*Hours*	
10	6:00 AM	2:30 PM	8:30	
11	2:00 PM	10:15 PM	8:15	
12	10:00 PM	6:20 AM	8:20	

Figure 2-5 A possible day overrun has to be considered when only times are specified.

If the time intervals are less than 24 hours, and the start time is greater than the end time, you could take the absolute difference between the two times and then subtract this from 1.

```
=If(Beginning>End,1-(Beginning-End), End - Beginning)
```

Another option is to insert a comparison of Beginning>End. The result is one of the two logical values TRUE or FALSE. If Excel finds a logical value in a calculation, the value is converted into 1 or 0. Because an entire day corresponds to the value 1, you can add 1 to a time (when the beginning is larger than the end) and get the result in the next day. Use this formula:

```
=(Beginning>End)+End-Beginning
```

Chapter 2

Adding Time Intervals

When adding times, you need to be aware of several factors. In Excel, the addition of two times will not exceed 24 hours; the result of 15 hours plus 12 hours is 3 hours. You can resolve this problem by using the correct number format:

1. Select the result cell and click the Format/Cells menu option (Excel 2003 and earlier), or click the arrow in the lower-right corner of the Number group on the Home tab (Excel 2007 and Excel 2010), as shown in Figure 2-6.

2. Click the Number tab of the Format Cells dialog box, and select Custom in the Category list field.

3. Select the number format [h]:mm. Pay attention to the brackets. If you cannot find the exact format, just modify a similar entry.

   The result is displayed in the 24:00 format.

Figure 2-6 In Excel 2007 and Excel 2010, click the arrow at the bottom of the Number group on the Home tab to open the Format Cells dialog box.

Calculating the Salary for Working Hours

Because Excel treats hours as fractions of a day, you have to be careful when calculating values based on the number of working hours. For example, if an employee works 6.25 hours and is paid $21 per hour, and you simply multiply these values, the result is only $5.61. The employee would not be happy with this amount.

To calculate the correct result, you have to multiply the number of hours by 24. The correct calculation would be =("6:25"*24)*21 resulting in $134.75 (see Figure 2-7).

	D21	▼		f_x	=(D19*24)*D20	
	B		C		D	
17	Calulate salary for working hours					
19	Hours		6:25		6:25	
20	Hourly rate	$	21.00	$	21.00	
21	Salary	$	5.61	$	134.75	

Figure 2-7 Multiplying the hours by the hourly salary returns the wrong result in C37.

Rounding Time Values

Because the exact minute or second is not always needed, you can round time values. Remember that Excel uses the value 1 for a day. An hour is a fraction of a day, or 1/24, and a minute is 1/1440. If you set these values as the arguments of the MROUND() table function, the time is rounded accordingly.

Suppose, for example, that cell B42 contains the time 08:52:36 in the number format hh:mm:ss. The formula =MROUND(B42,1/24) results in 09:00:00, and the formula =MROUND(B42,1/1440) in 08:53:00.

Identifying the Quarter

Supposed you want to identify which quarter of the year a given date falls in. For this example, the first quarter includes January through March, the second April through June, and so on.

Divide the number of the month by 3, and round the result to the next integer in the formula =ROUNDUP(MONTH(date value)/3,0) as shown in Figure 2-8.

	C27	▼	f_x	=ROUNDUP(MONTH(B27)/3,0)	
	B	C	D	E	
24	Determine quarter in calendar year				
25					
26	Date	Quarter	Alternative		
27	1/14/2013	1	1		
28	5/16/2013	2	2		
29	7/1/2013	3	3		
30	9/2/2013	3	3		
31	11/12/2013	4	4		

Figure 2-8 Identifying the quarter of the year.

Converting Normal Hours into Decimal Hours (Industrial Hours)

You may want to convert a time into decimal hours and minutes. If the hours and minutes are integers, use the following formula to calculate the decimal hours:

```
Time = Hour(date value) + Minute(date value)/60
```

If the time is shown as a fraction, multiply this value by 24. Here are some examples:

- 06:30 is 6.5 decimal hours.

- 07:15 is 7.25 decimal hours.

- 09:45 is 9.75 decimal hours.

> ## Sample Files
>
> Use the Praxis worksheet in the Date_Time.xls or Date_Time.xlsx sample file. The sample files are found in the Chapter02 folder. For more information about the sample files, see the section titled "Using the Sample Files" on page xxiii.

Using Text and Data Functions

With the text and data functions of Excel, you can view your data in a variety of formats as well as convert data or perform calculations in combination with other functions. You will find further solutions in the following practical examples.

> ## Sample Files
>
> Use the worksheet found in the the Text_Data.xls or Text_Data.xlsx sample file. The sample files are found in the Chapter02 folder. For more information about the sample files, see the section titled "Using the Sample Files" on page xxiii.

Separating Text Strings Such as ZIP Code and Location

Assume that you have an address list in which one column contains a location consisting of the state and a five-digit ZIP Code. You do not need the state but want to pick up just the five-digit ZIP Code. Therefore, you need to query for the last five characters of the complete address.

Assuming that cell A38 contains the address, the formula reads:

```
=RIGHT(A38,5)
```

In this case, the RIGHT() text function returns the five characters at the right end of the string (see Figure 2-9).

	B38	▾	f_x	=RIGHT(A38,5)	

	A	B
37	**ZIP Code state**	**ZIP Code**
38	New York 10001	10001
39	Arizona 85003	85003
40	Iowa 50206	50206
41	Michigan 48198	48198
42	Louisiana 71323	71323
43	Georgia 31909	31909
44	West Virginia 24970	24970

Figure 2-9 The five-digit ZIP Code is extracted with the RIGHT() table function.

Separating First and Last Names

Assume that a list of names contains both the first and last name. Separating the first names from the last names is more difficult than extracting the five-digit ZIP Code, because the names are not of standard length.

Assuming that cell A21 contains the first and last name separated by a space, enter the following formula in B21 to extract the first name (Figure 2-10):

```
=LEFT(A21,FIND(" ",A21)-1)
```

	B21	▾	f_x	=LEFT(A21,FIND(" ",A21)-1)	

	A	B	C
20	**First name Last name**	**First name**	**Last name**
21	Ed Banti	Ed	Banti
22	Darcy Jayne	Darcy	Jayne
23	Evan Dodds	Evan	Dodds
24	Kelly Rollin	Kelly	Rollin
25	David Jones	David	Jones
26	Soha Kamal	Soha	Kamal

Figure 2-10 The first name is extracted by specifying the separator.

Because first names are different in length, you have to use the FIND() function to find the first space. This function returns the position of the space in the text as a number. This number is decreased by 1 and used in the LEFT() function as an argument for the number of characters to return the first name.

To extract the last name, enter the following formula in cell C21:

```
=RIGHT(A21,LEN(A21)-FIND(" ",A21))
```

The RIGHT() function extracts the last name. To calculate the number of characters to extract from the right, you use the length of the entire name and subtract from this the number of characters in the string up to the first space, using the FIND() function again to find the position of the space. But this is not sufficient. It would be a coincidence if the space was at the same position as the number of characters read from the right.

Therefore, you use the LEN() function. This function identifies the total number of characters in the text. If you subtract the position number of the space from the total number of characters, as in LEN(A21)-FIND(""",A21), you get the length of the last name.

Switching the First and Last Names

If in one column the last name is placed in front of the first name, you may want to reverse the order. Assume that cell A5 contains the name *Jayne, Darcy*. As long as the order of the last names and first names is the same and the separator is a comma and a space, you can use the following formula to switch the names:

```
=RIGHT(A5,LEN(A5)-FIND(",",A5)-1)&"  "& LEFT(A5,FIND(",",A5)-1)
```

The result is *Darcy Jayne* (see Figure 2-11).

The first name is extracted by using the function

```
=RIGHT(A5,LEN(A5)-FIND(",",A5)-1
```

Note that the FIND function finds the position of the comma, and a further character must be subtracted to allow for the space after the comma. The last name at the beginning of the text string uses the function

```
=LEFT(A5,FIND(",",A5)-1)
```

Then the two names are concatenated together, with a space as a separator, using

```
& " " &
```

	B5	▾	*fx*	=RIGHT(A5,LEN(A5)-FIND(",",A5)-1)&" "&LEFT(A5,FIND(",",A5)-1)		
	A		B		C	D
1	**Change first and last name**					
2						
3	**Last name, first name**		**First name Last name**			
4	Banti, Ed		Ed Banti			
5	Jayne, Darcy		Darcy Jayne			
6	Dodds, Evan		Evan Dodds			
7	Rollin, Kelly		Kelly Rollin			
8	Jones, David		David Jones			
9	Kamal, Soha		Soha Kamal			
10	Rubin, Idan		Idan Rubin			

Figure 2-11 Nested but effective—switching names by using a formula.

Resolving the IBAN

The IBAN (International Bank Account Number) is required for international money transactions. Because this number consists of parts with a fixed length, you can pick out individual components of the IBAN. The IBAN can be up to 34 characters long. A German IBAN consists of 22 characters in the following order (see Figure 2-12):

1. Country code DE (two characters).

2. Check digits (two characters).

3. Routing number (eight characters).

4. Account number (ten characters). If the account number is shorter, leading zeros are added.

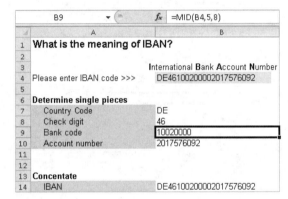

Figure 2-12 Separating out the IBAN parts by using the MID() function.

To separate out the parts of the IBAN in cell B4, use the following formula:

- Country code: =LEFT(B4,2)

- Check digits: =MID(B4,3,2)

- Routing number: =MID(B4,5,8)

- Account number: =MID(B4,13,10) or =RIGHT(B4,10)

You have already used the LEFT() and RIGHT() functions in the previous examples. To extract strings from the middle of a text string, use the MID(text,start_num,char_num) function.

Chapter 2

Calculating the Frequency of a Character in a String

For journalistic tasks and text analysis, it might be necessary to determine how often a certain character or string appears in a block of text. With the following trick, you can do this in Excel: If cell B3 contains the string and cell A7 contains the text to be analyzed, use the following formula:

```
=(LEN(A7)-LEN(SUBSTITUTE(A7,$B$3,"")))/LEN($B$3)
```

The LEN(A7) function calculates the number of characters in cell A7. The SUBSTITUTE() function in the second part of the formula replaces any occurrence of the characters in the test string with nothing ("") and calculates the new length. If you subtract this length from the original length of the string and divide by the length of the test string, you will calculate the number of occurrences (see Figure 2-13).

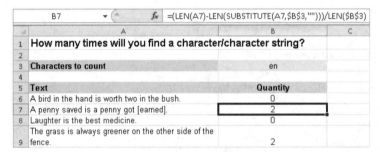

	B7		f_x	=(LEN(A7)-LEN(SUBSTITUTE(A7,$B$3,"")))/LEN($B$3)	
	A		B	C
1	**How many times will you find a character/character string?**			
2				
3	Characters to count		en	
4				
5	Text		Quantity	
6	A bird in the hand is worth two in the bush.		0	
7	A penny saved is a penny got [earned].		2	
8	Laughter is the best medicine.		0	
9	The grass is always greener on the other side of the fence.		2	

Figure 2-13 The trick for counting the frequency of characters.

Removing All Spaces

In some cases, you may want to remove blank characters from a text string. To do this, you can use the SUBSTITUTE() function (see Figure 2-14). If you want to remove all spaces from the text in cell A15, for example, you can use the following formula:

```
=SUBSTITUTE(A15," ","")
```

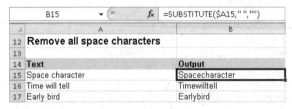

	B15		f_x	=SUBSTITUTE($A15," ","")
	A		B	
12	**Remove all space characters**			
13				
14	Text		Output	
15	Space character		Spacecharacter	
16	Time will tell		Timewilltell	
17	Early bird		Earlybird	

Figure 2-14 The SUBSTITUTE() function replaces strings.

Here is the function with its syntax:

```
SUBSTITUTE(text,old_text,new_text,[instance_num])
```

This function replaces the old text with the new text in a string. In this example, the space (" ") is replaced with an empty string (""). New York becomes NewYork. You can also use the SUBSTITUTE() function to replace certain characters in a text string.

> **Tip**
> To remove excessive spaces before and after text, use the TRIM() function.

Correcting the Position of Signs

When you are importing data, sometimes the minus sign for negative numbers appears after the value. Because Excel doesn't accept this expression as a number, it cannot be used in calculations. In fact, the position of the minus sign leads to the number being interpreted as a text value.

To convert the value in cell A4 into a number, use the following formula (see Figure 2-15):

```
=IF(RIGHT(A,1)="-",LEFT(A4,LEN(A4)-1)*(-1),A4)
```

	B4	f_x =IF(RIGHT(A4,1)="-",LEFT(A4,LEN(A4)-1)*(-1),A4)		
	A	B	C	D
1	Correct the placement of the negative sign			
2				
3	Import	Value		
4	2500.00-	-2,500.00		
5		545.60		
6	1.99-	-1.99		
7	14500.00-	-14,500.00		

Figure 2-15 Converting a number by changing the placement of the negative sign.

The IF() function is used to verify the content of parts of a cell. The RIGHT() function checks whether a minus sign is present. The LEFT() function separates the number part and converts it into the negative value of the number by multiplying it by –1.

Displaying the File and Worksheet Name

The following formula displays the name of the current file. Enter the following formula in cell A21:

```
=CELL("filename")
```

This function returns the file name of the current worksheet; the full file path and sheet name are displayed. If the current worksheet has not yet been saved, the function returns an empty string.

Within the string, the file name is enclosed in brackets, which can be useful in extracting the name from the string. The following formula extracts the file name from the result:

```
=MID(A21,FIND("[",A21,1)+1,FIND("]",A21,1)-FIND("[",A21,1)-1)
```

The MID() function calculates the number of characters from the start position. The FIND("[",A21,1)+1 expression determines the start position after the left bracket. The FIND("]",A21,1)-FIND("[",A21,1)-1 expression calculates the number of characters between the left and the right brackets.

You can also use this function to display the name of the worksheet. To do this, use the following formula:

```
=MID(A21,FIND("]",A21,1)+1,LEN(A21))
```

Concatenating the Content of Cells

Figure 2-16 shows a typical address list. To concatenate the data in the list, use the following formula:

```
=A4 & " " & C4 & " " & B4 & " lives in " & D4 & " " & E4 & "."
```

	B12		▼	_fx_	=A4&" "&C4&" "&B4&" lives in "&D4&" "&E4&"."		
	A	B		C	D	E	
1	**Concatenate names and data**						
2							
3	**Title**	**Last name**		**First name**	**State**	**ZIP Code**	
4	Mr.	Banti		Ed	New York	10001	
5	Ms.	Rollin		Kelly	Arizona	85003	
6	Mr.	Rubin		Idan	Louisiana	71323	
7	Mr.	Capek		Karel	Georgia	31909	
8							
9							
10	**All segments in one phrase**						
11	Alternative I						
12	(&-Operator)	Mr. Ed Banti lives in New York 10001.					
13		Ms. Kelly Rollin lives in Arizona 85003.					
14		Mr. Idan Rubin lives in Louisiana 71323.					
15		Mr. Karel Capek lives in Georgia 31909.					

Figure 2-16 The & concatenation operator combines text and values in more complex expressions.

You can concatenate text and references with the & concatenation operator. You can also use the CONCATENATE() text function, which returns the same result.

```
=CONCATENATE(A4," ",C4," ",B4," lives in ",D4," ",E4,".")
```

Breaking Lines in Concatenated Text

For some text concatenations, you might want to insert a line break in a place other than at the right margin, such as after a certain number of characters or after a certain word. You can press Alt+Enter to insert the break at any position. As soon as you press the Enter key, the line break is visible in the cell.

You can also link two strings with a newline character (see Figure 2-17). The newline character has a character code of 10 and can be added with the CHAR() function:

```
=CONCATENATE(A4," ",C4," ",B4,CHAR(10),"lives in ",D4," ";E4;".")
```

		B26	▼	*fx*	=A4&" "&C4&" "&B4&"	
	A	B		C	D	E
1	Concatenate names and data					
2						
3	**Title**	**Last name**		**First name**	**State**	**ZIP Code**
4	Mr.	Banti		Ed	New York	10001
5	Ms.	Rollin		Kelly	Arizona	85003
6	Mr.	Rubin		Idan	Louisiana	71323
7	Mr.	Capek		Karel	Georgia	31909
8						
24	**All segments in one phrase with line break**					
25	Alternative I					
26	(&-Operator Alt+Enter)	Mr. Ed Banti lives in New York 10001.				
27		Ms. Kelly Rollin lives in Arizona 85003.				
28		Mr. Idan Rubin lives in Louisiana 71323.				
29		Mr. Karel Capek lives in Georgia 31909.				

Figure 2-17 Text concatenations can contain line breaks and other special characters.

INSIDE OUT   View line breaks in cells

For a line break to become apparent, the cell must have the wrap option enabled. On the cell's shortcut menu, select Format Cells, and then on the Alignment tab, select the Wrap Text check box.

Visualizing Data

You probably use Excel charts to present numbers. However, you can use in-cell graphics instead of charts to display data. To do this, you can use the REPT() function, as shown in Figure 2-18.

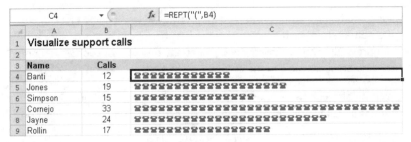

Figure 2-18 Creating graphics with the REPT() function.

In this example, the calls answered by the support personnel are captured in a list. The formula

```
=REPT("(",B4)
```

converts the number 12 in B4 into twelve phone icons. You will need to select the Wingdings font for the formula cell to display the opening parenthesis as a phone icon.

> **Sample Files**
>
> Use the Support Calls worksheet in the Text_Data.xls or Text_Data.xlsx sample file. The sample files are found in the Chapter02 folder. For more information about the sample files, see the section titled "Using the Sample Files" on page xxiii.

Using Logical Functions

The logical functions are some of the most versatile tools in Excel. They can be used to automate calculations, customize displays, and provide decision options. The example in this section introduces a basic decision statement. In this example, a company has a procedure for generating commodity prices. Figure 2-19 shows the calculation on a worksheet.

	B	C	D
2	**Differential calculation (margin)**		
3			Profit
4	List price		$ 4,500.00
5	-Delivery discount	20%	$ 900.00
6	=Intented purchase price		$ 3,600.00
7	-Delivery discount	3%	$ 108.00
8	=Cash purchase price		$ 3,492.00
9	+Delivery costs (net)		$ 54.00
10	=Delivery price (cost price)		$ 3,546.00
11	+General expenses	26%	$ 936.82
12	=Primary costs		$ 4,482.82
13	+Profit	21%	$ 956.85
14	=Cash purchase price		$ 5,439.66
15	+Customer discount	2%	$ 116.98
16	+Agent's commission	5%	$ 292.46
17	=Intended purchase price		$ 5,849.10
18	+Customer discount	10%	$ 649.90
19	=Sales listprice (net)		$ 6,499.00
20			
21	Profit ratio		OK

Figure 2-19 A typical differential calculation.

A retailer buys commodities from a supplier and gets a discount. The retailer also gets a cash discount. The delivery costs are added to the cash purchase price, and after other costs (such as rent and salaries) are considered, the primary cost amounts to $4,482.82.

The retail price for the customer has to include a discount, and the sales representative has to be paid. The difference between the cash sales price and the original costs is the profit. The profit is calculated as a percent of the original cost.

Each stage of the calculation is performed in Excel. The profit is calculated from

```
=D14-D12
```

and the percentage as

```
=D13/D12
```

Calculating Profitability

But how does Excel know if the required profit is OK? Let's assume that the retailer is content with 20 percent. He enters the following formula in cell C21 (in the figure this is shown linked with the next cell):

```
=IF(C13>=20%,"OK","Too low")
```

The IF() function checks the percentage and performs a calculation depending upon the result. The function checks whether the value in cell C13 is greater than or equal to 20 percent. If the value is greater than or equal to 20 percent, the text "OK" is displayed. If it is not, the alternative text "Too low" is displayed.

This example checks only one condition, but it can be extended to more complex conditions with additional logical functions, such as the AND() function and further IF() statements. For instance, perhaps the retailer doesn't want to reduce his profit but needs to consider the competition as well as the price ceiling. He might want to visually emphasize the cell containing the percentage profit. In Excel 2007 and Excel 2010, he can open the dialog box shown in Figure 2-20. The New Rule option can be reached from the Home tab by clicking Conditional Formatting in the Style group.

If you are using an earlier version of Excel, select Format/Conditional Formatting.

The formula

`=AND(($C$13>=20%),($D$19<6500))`

verifies whether two conditions are met:

- The value in cell C13 is greater than or equal to 20 percent.

- The entered sales price is less than $6,500.

If both conditions are met, the cell turns green.

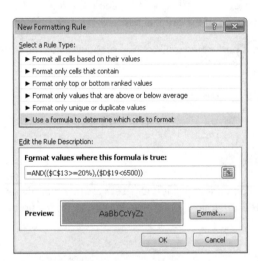

Figure 2-20 Conditional formatting and logical functions.

> **Sample Files**
>
> Use the Differential calculation worksheet in the DifferentialCalculation.xls or Differential calculation.xlsx sample file. The sample files are found in the Chapter02 folder. For more information about the sample files, see the section are titled "Using the Sample Files" on page xxiii.

See Also Chapter 9, "Logical Functions," considers logical functions in more detail.

Using Search and Reference Functions

Lookup &
Reference ▾

The table structure of Excel worksheets allows the user to systematically search worksheets for information.

Searching Through a Cross Table

Assume that you have tabulated price information for an item (in this example, shirts in different colors and sizes). After selecting a color and size, you want to look up the price and use this price in further calculations (see Figure 2-21). To do this, you use a typical cross tabulation.

	B	C	D	E	F	G	H
2	**Shirt**						
3							
4		XS	S	M	L	XL	XXL
5	blue	$ 24.99	$ 25.49	$ 25.99	$ 26.49	$ 26.99	$ 27.49
6	yellow	$ 27.99	$ 28.49	$ 28.99	$ 29.49	$ 29.99	$ 30.49
7	white	$ 29.99	$ 30.49	$ 30.99	$ 31.49	$ 31.99	$ 32.49
8							
9	Color	yellow					
10	Size	M		Column:		3	
11							
12	Price:	$ 28.99					

Figure 2-21 Prices based on size and color.

Chapter 2

Excel offers a range of lookup functions that can be used for this kind of task. There are three main functions: LOOKUP(), VLOOKUP(), and HLOOKUP(), as well as the MATCH() and INDEX() functions, which provide similar facilities. All of these functions find information in a rectangular area according to some criteria and return the information or the position of the information from the table. The following examples demonstrate how some of these functions can be used.

See Also You will find detailed descriptions of the other functions in Chapter 10, "Lookup and Reference Functions."

The VLOOKUP() function takes a value and tries to match it to values in the first column of a table. When a match is found, the function will return any of the information associated with the item matched in the table. There are two ways that it can perform the search:

- Look for an exact match of the item in the first column of the table.

- Look for a value, either the exact value or the value nearest to but lower than the value being searched for. In this case, the lookup table must be sorted on the first column.

The MATCH() function searches an array of values and returns the position of the first match in that array, either the column or the row. Matches can be exact, or the lowest or highest value.

Figure 2-21 shows the prices for shirts in different colors over a range of sizes. You are searching for information not only in a certain row but also in a certain column. Just proceed one step at a time. First, find the column containing the required size. The third column contains size M. If you want Excel to recognize this, press F10 to enter 3 in an auxiliary cell. The formula =MATCH(C10,C4:H4,1) finds the value in cell C10 (size M) in the heading of cells C4 through H4 and returns the column number. Chapter 10 explains these functions in detail.

The second step is achieved by using the VLOOKUP() function. Enter the following formula in cell C12:

```
=VLOOKUP(C9,B5:H7,F10+1,FALSE)
```

This formula searches for the content of cell C9 (yellow) in the first column of cells B5 through H7. If a value is found, the formula returns the value in the fourth column. The job is done!

There are several things that you can do to make this more elegant. Instead of using two formulas, you can embed the MATCH() function into the VLOOKUP() function to get the result from a single formula. Conditional formatting would provide a nice feature to emphasize the selected cell.

> ## Sample Files
> Use the Shirts worksheet in the Lookup.xls or Lookup.xlsx sample file. The sample files
> are found in the Chapter02 folder. For more information about the sample files, see the
> section titled "Using the Sample Files" on page xxiii.

Another popular function in this category is the OFFSET() function. This function focuses
on a specific range and allows you to dynamically adjust this by defining row and column
offsets.

Take a look at the following example (see Figure 2-22), in which daytime temperatures are
tabulated over a five-day period. Assume that you want to display the daytime temperatures for a selected day.

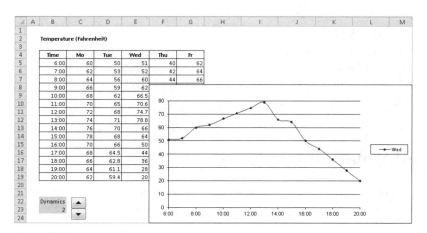

Figure 2-22 Dynamic charts.

The solution is to dynamically link the column used by the temperature chart to an input
value on the worksheet. Start by creating a line graph to display the temperatures throughout the day for Monday.

There are some tricks you can use. First, you can name not only ranges but also formulas.
In Excel 2007 and Excel 2010, on the Formulas tab, select Defined Names/Define Names,
and in previous versions select Insert/Names/Define to name formulas. Use these to define
dynamic ranges for the legend and the data series for the chart. Define the name chartDay as:

```
=OFFSET(charts!$C$4,0,charts!$B$23)
```

The reference in cell C4 on the Charts worksheet is moved zero rows down and the number
of columns to the right as indicated in cell B23 (see Figure 2-22).

Do the same for the chart data. Use the name chartData and link it with the formula

`=OFFSET(charts!$C$5:$C$19,0,charts!$B$23)`

This formula applies to the entire column instead of to only one row. The reference is moved in the same way. After the chart is created, click the drawn line. Something similar to the following is displayed in the input box:

`=SERIES(charts!$C$4;charts!$B$5:$B$19;charts!$C$5:$C$19;1)`

Change this entry by replacing the absolute cell references with your dynamic references:

`=SERIES(Lookup.xlsx!chartDay;charts!$B$5:$B$19;Lookup.xlsx!chartData;1)`

You have to use the name of the workbook, and the names have to be separated by an exclamation mark. For a perfect solution, you should also add a spinner control to select the value in cell B23.

> ### Sample Files
>
> **Use the Chart worksheet in the Lookup.xls or Lookup.xlsx sample file. The sample files are found in the Chapter02 folder. For more information about the sample files, see the section titled "Using the Sample Files" on page xxiii.**

Using Information Functions

Similar to the logical functions, the information functions serve to supplement and support other functions and formulas.

At the center of the information functions are the so-called *IS functions* (see Table 2-2), which provide information about expression types or the cell content. This information can be viewed or, more usefully, used for other calculations. The names of these functions are self-explanatory, and the returned values are always logical values. The logical value confirms whether the value of the cell specified in the argument is of the required type. Usually the argument for the functions is a cell reference, but sometimes—for example, for the ISREF() function—a specific value is provided for testing.

Table 2-2 **Overview of the IS Functions**

Function	Definition
ISBLANK()	The cell is empty.
ISTEXT(), ISNONTEXT()	The value of the cell is text or is not text.
ISNUMBER()	The value of the cell is a number.
ISLOGICAL()	The value of the cell is a logical value.
ISERR(), ISERROR()	The cell contains an error.
ISNA()	The cell contains an #NA! error.
ISEVEN(), ISODD()	The value of the cell is an even or odd number.

When you work with named ranges and use these ranges as references, you get a #REF! error if you accidentally delete the name. For example, assume that cells B2 through D5 have the name Sales, and that cell F7 contains

```
=SUM(sales)
```

This works as long as the name Sales exists. However, the formula

```
=IF(ISREF(sales),SUM(sales),"Name Sales was removed.")
```

is somewhat safer. The ISREF(sales) function returns FALSE if the name Sales is removed. Instead of calculating the sum for the unknown range and generating an error, Excel displays a message stating the cause of the error. If the range name exists, the total is calculated.

Errors can often occur when you are using the VLOOKUP() function, particularly when you are searching for an item that is not in the list. In Figure 2-23, the formula

```
=VLOOKUP(B13,D13:E15,2,FALSE)
```

generates an #N/A error (N/A=not available) indicating that the Blouse item is not in the list. The formula

```
=IF(ISERROR(VLOOKUP(B13;D13:E15;2;FALSE)),"not found", VLOOKUP(B13;D13:E15;2;FALSE))
```

is longer, but it first verifies whether VLOOKUP() was successful. If it was not, the message "not found" appears; if the function was successful, the price is displayed.

Figure 2-23 Searching for information in lists.

Often simple calculations can lead to errors; consider, for example, the use of a function such as 1/*x* (*x* cannot be zero) or LOG(*x*) (*x* has to be positive). If you want to create a chart from a series of numbers, you can manipulate the data to ensure that incorrect values "disappear" from the source range of the chart.

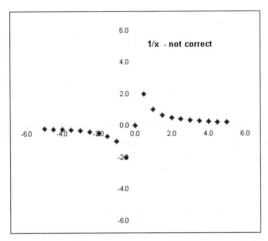

Figure 2-24 This presentation of 1/*x* is incorrect because the error values are shown as zero.

To avoid the incorrect presentation in Figure 2-24, enter

```
=IF(ISERROR(1/B13),NA(),1/B13)
```

This way you intercept the #DIV/0! error and replace it with the NA() function that indicates that the value doesn't exist. Do the same for other error values.

> **Note**
> You also can delete your formula from the cell containing the error and select the chart option that allows you to not draw empty cells.

See Also You can find more examples of the IS functions as well as other information functions in Chapter 11, "Information Functions."

Using Statistical Functions

Statistics is the science of using methods to handle quantitative information (data). However, most people associate the word *statistics* with extensive tables and graphics illustrating (or sometimes concealing) diverse facts, for example, about demographic groups, economic activities, diseases, or environmental impacts.

But that is only part of the field of statistics, sometimes called *descriptive statistics*. Statistics are used to illustrate extensive data as well as to summarize large quantities of information with a few simple measures, such as average and variance.

Data is collected for many purposes. Often the data consists of random samples from a larger (real or hypothetical) population, and this is used to form generalized statements for the entire population, taking into account random variations in the sample values.

Analytical statistics is based on probability models and principles derived from probability theory. Assume that you manage a company and want to find out if it would be more beneficial to invest in extensive advertising or to reduce costs. You want to investigate the revenue based on a chosen strategy. You also want to know the months with the lowest and highest revenues, and you are interested in the correlation between costs and sales.

Here's another example that almost everyone has come across at some point: How high is the probability of winning the lottery and retiring to the Caribbean?

All of these questions are statistical questions, and Excel can help you find the answers.

Overview

For better understanding, this book divides the statistical functions into six areas. The areas and their corresponding functions are introduced in the following sections.

The Path to a Happy Medium

Excel provides several functions for calculating different mean values. Mean values provide a quick review of the available data and are a first step in the analysis. These values help you find the middle value in a list of values.

The *mean average* or *arithmetic mean* is one of the most common measures of comparison. Because of its simple calculation and its popularity, the mean average appeals even to nonstatisticians. There are, however, several other average measures that can be utilized, as shown in Table 2-3.

Table 2-3 **Functions of the Mean Value Type**

AVERAGE()	HARMEAN()	PERCENTRANK.EXC()
AVERAGEA()	MEDIAN()	PERCENTRANK.INC()
AVERAGEIF()	MODE.MULT()	QUARTILE.EXC()
AVERAGEIFS()	MODE.SNGL()	QUARTILE.INC()
GEOMEAN()	PERCENTILE.EXC()	
TRIMMEAN()	PERCENTILE.INC()	

Correlation and Regression

Correlation allows you to consider the relationship between two variables. For example, a manufacturing company may want to evaluate whether further quality tests are justified. Or a company may look at the relationship between sales and advertising. Several correlation and regression measures and tests are available in Excel (see Table 2-4).

Table 2-4 **Functions of the Regression Type**

CORREL()	GROWTH()	RSQ()
COVARIANCE.P()	INTERCEPT()	SLOPE()
COVARIANCE.S()	LINEST()	TREND()
DEVSQ()	LOGEST()	
FORECAST()	PEARSON()	

Symmetry

Two symmetry statistics are available (see Table 2-5):

- The SKEW() function characterizes the degree of asymmetry around the mean. If the data is symmetrically distributed, the mean value, modal value, and median coincide.

- The *kurtosis* of a data group measures the shape and spread of the distribution compared to a normal distribution.

Table 2-5 **Functions of the Symmetry Type**

KURT()	SKEW()

Excel and Spreads

The more the individual data values deviate from the mean, the less representative the mean is of the distribution. The mean value alone is not sufficient to characterize a frequency distribution; you also need to consider to what extent the values deviate from the mean value. For this, you calculate the *spread*. The functions in Table 2-6 show all types of variance.

Table 2-6 **Functions of the Variance Type**

AVEDEV()	STDEVPA()	VAR.P()
STDEVA()	STDEV.S()	VARPA()
STDEV.P()	VARA()	VAR.S()

Trends and Forecasts

Probability calculations are an essential part of statistics. Because you often don't work with complete populations but only with smaller samples, you have to understand the probability of the derived conclusions. Probability calculations are used to predict study results based on certain assumptions.

Analytical statistics often compare results to determine whether the statistical values of empirically captured data are different. An example is the assessment of the efficacy of pharmaceuticals. The relative frequency of events observed in random experiments is analyzed and used to determine the probability of events. Table 2-7 shows the probability functions available in Excel.

Table 2-7 **Functions of the Probability Type**

CONFIDENCE.T()	LOGNORM.DIST()	PROB()
EXPON.DIST()	LOGNORM.INV()	T.DIST()
F.INV()	NEGBINOM.DIST()	T.DIST.2T()
F.INV.RT()	NORM.INV()	T.DIST.RT()
FISHER()	NORM.S.DIST()	WEIBULL.DIST()
F.TEST()	NORM.S.INV()	
GAMMA.INV()	PERMUT()	

One Plus One

The analysis of statistical data involves a lot of counting. For example, if you analyze a survey, you need to know how many questionnaires were returned. Next, you may count how often single results appear—that is, individual characteristics with the same value. Usually this is called *univariate data analysis*. To count combinations of characteristics—for example, the sales in a particular district—you need to consider a *bivariate distribution*. If more variables are added, it becomes a multidimensional or *multivariate distribution*.

Several tools are available for grouping, consolidating, and analyzing data. Table 2-8 shows the Excel analysis functions.

Table 2-8 **Functions of the Counting Type**

COUNT()	FREQUENCY()	MINA()
COUNTA()	LARGE()	RANK.AVG()
COUNTBLANK()	MAX()	RANK.EQ()
COUNTIF()	MAXA()	SMALL()
COUNTIFS()	MIN()	

The range of statistical functions and analyses is extensive, and Excel provides a comprehensive set of tools for analyzing most types of data. Some tools also generate charts in addition to tables.

See Also Chapter 12, "Statistical Functions," describes the statistic functions in more detail, and has some general statistical overviews as well as a section with practical examples.

New in Excel 2010

Excel 2010 provides some new statistical functions For example, the TINV() function has been replaced with the T.INV() and T.INV.RE() functions to increase the accuracy of the results. Also, the left and right T distributions are now shown separately. To ensure the backward compatibility of T.INV() and T.INV.RE(), the TINV() function is still available.

Statistical Functions in Practice

The following practice examples show typical calculations that use the statistic functions in Excel.

Sample Files

Use the List worksheet in the Practice_Statistics.xls or Practice_Statistics.xlsx sample file. The sample files are found in the Chapter02 folder. For more information about the sample files, see the section titled "Using the Sample Files" on page xxiii.

A training center conducted a survey of participants in seminars on Excel, Microsoft Power-Point, and Microsoft Outlook on each day of July 2008, and the information shown in Figure 2-25 was collected. A total of 184 questionnaires were handed out.

	A	B	C	D
1	**Date**	**Coaching**	**female/male**	**Rating**
2	7/1/2008	Excel	male	2
3	7/1/2008	Excel	female	1
4	7/1/2008	Excel		
5	7/1/2008	Excel	female	3
6	7/1/2008	Excel	male	2
7	7/1/2008	Excel	male	1
8	7/1/2008	Excel	female	1
9	7/1/2008	Excel		
10	7/2/2008	PowerPoint	male	2
11	7/2/2008	PowerPoint	male	2
12	7/2/2008	PowerPoint	male	1
13	7/2/2008	PowerPoint	male	1
14	7/2/2008	PowerPoint	female	1
15	7/2/2008	PowerPoint	female	4
16	7/2/2008	PowerPoint	female	3
17	7/2/2008	PowerPoint		
18	7/3/2008	Outlook	female	3

Figure 2-25 The survey results are consolidated in a table.

Finding the Number of Answers

Assume that, although you handed out 184 questionnaires, you want to know the number of answers you received, because not everyone participated in the survey. You do this by using the COUNTA() function to count the number of questionnaires returned, and you use the AVERAGE() function to evaluate the mean rating of responses (see Figure 2-26).

	G2		f_x	=COUNTA(C2:C185)			
	A	B	C	D	E	F	G
1	**Date**	**Coaching**	**female/male**	**Rating**			
2	7/1/2008	Excel	male	2		How many participants answered?	149
3	7/1/2008	Excel	female	1			

Figure 2-26 The formula =COUNTA(C2,C185) returns 149 participants.

Average Rating

How do the participants rate the training center's seminars? Good, medium, bad? To get a fast result, you calculate the average value by using the AVERAGE() function. All ratings are added together, and the total is divided by the number of ratings (see Figure 2-27).

	G3		f_x	=AVERAGE(D2:D185)			
	A	B	C	D	E	F	G
1	**Date**	**Coaching**	**female/male**	**Rating**			
2	7/1/2008	Excel	male	2		How many participants answered?	149
3	7/1/2008	Excel	female	1		What is the average of the ratings?	2.26
4	7/1/2008	Excel					

Figure 2-27 Calculating the average rating for all seminars.

The formula =AVERAGE(C2:C185) returns an average rating of 2.26.

Who Gives Better Ratings—Men or Women?

The training center wants to know whether men or women rated the seminars more favorably. The AVERAGEIF() function returns this result.

> **Note**
>
> The AVERAGEIF() function is available in Excel 2007 and Excel 2010.

AVERAGEIF() calculates the average value for all entries that meet specified criteria—in this case, men or women (see Figure 2-28).

	G4	▼	*fx*	=AVERAGEIF(C2:C185,"male",D2:D185)		
	A	B	C	D	E	F	G
1	Date	Coaching	female/male	Rating			
2	7/1/2008	Excel	male	2		How many participants answered?	149
3	7/1/2008	Excel	female	1		What is the average of the ratings?	2.26
4	7/1/2008	Excel				Average rating by male?	2.50
5	7/1/2008	Excel	female	3		Average rating by female?	2.06

Figure 2-28 Calculating the average rating for the seminars by men and women.

The formula =AVERAGEIF(C2:C185,"male",D2:D185) returns the average rating of 2.50 for men. With an average rating of 2.50, men rate the seminars significantly better.

In addition, the training center also wants to know how women rate the Excel seminars. The AVERAGEIFS() function returns the result.

> **Note**
>
> The AVERAGEIFS() function is available in Excel 2007 and Excel 2010.

AVERAGEIFS() calculates the average value for all cells in a certain range that meet several specified criteria—in this case, women and Excel (see Figure 2-29).

	G6	▼	*fx*	=AVERAGEIFS(D2:D185,C2:C185,"female",B2:B185,"Excel")		
	A	B	C	D	E	F	G
1	Date	Coaching	female/male	Rating			
2	7/1/2008	Excel	male	2		How many participants answered?	149
3	7/1/2008	Excel	female	1		What is the average of the ratings?	2.26
4	7/1/2008	Excel				Average rating by male?	2.50
5	7/1/2008	Excel	female	3		Average rating by female?	2.06
6	7/1/2008	Excel	male	2		**Average rating of Excel coachings by female?**	**1.38**

Figure 2-29 Calculating the average rating of Excel seminars by women.

The formula =AVERAGEIFS(D2:D185,C2:C185,"female",B2:B185,"Excel") returns the average rating of 1.38 for the Excel seminars by women.

Using Database Functions

The database functions are particularly useful because they analyze data from tables with headings (field names) and data rows (data records). The block of information in rows and columns constitutes a database.

Using the database functions is made easier if the following rules are observed:

- Make sure lists have column headings.

- Make sure lists don't contain empty rows or columns.

- Make sure lists don't contain linked cells.

In Excel 2003 and earlier, the usage of Excel as a database was stretched to its limits pretty quickly because a table was limited to 65,536 rows. In Excel 2007 this limit was extended: Now each table for data lists can have 1,048,576 rows. The same applies to columns: In Excel 2003, a table could have 256 columns, and in Excel 2007, up to 16,384 columns are allowed.

Dynamic Database Names

Dynamic names are an effective way to simplify working with data in Excel databases. If you specify a dynamic name, you can open a data template to view and capture data and then browse the data records, find data, or enter data.

When using dynamic names, it is important to remember to include an empty row below and an empty column next to the last entry. This avoids problems if you add new columns or rows at a later time.

> ### Sample Files
>
> Use the Raw data worksheet in the DBFunction_empty.xls or DBFunction_empty.xlsx sample file. The sample files are found in the Chapter02 folder. For more information about the sample files, see the section titled "Using the Sample Files" on page xxiii.
>
> To simplify subsequent evaluations, this database was given a dynamic name. Independent from the size of the list, this name is always the same, and you can use the name in database functions.

Chapter 2

See Also The OFFSET() function used in the following example is explained in more detail in Chapter 13, "Database Functions."

To assign a dynamic name to the Excel list, perform the following steps in Excel 2007 or Excel 2010:

1. Click in cell A1 or the first cell of your database, and then click the Define Names button (see Figure 2-30) in the Defined Names group on the Formulas tab.

Figure 2-30 Defining names in Excel 2007 or Excel 2010.

2. Enter the name **Start** in the New Name dialog box, and click OK (see Figure 2-31).

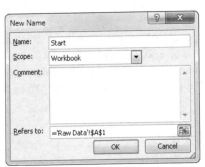

Figure 2-31 Specifying the starting point of the database.

The starting point of the database is now set. Next you have to generate the dynamic name of the database with the OFFSET() function. First you have to find out how many entries exist in column A and row 1.

3. Click the header of column A to select the entire column, and enter the name **Row** in the name box (see Figure 2-32). Press the Enter key to confirm.

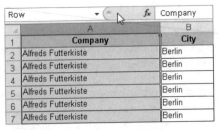

Figure 2-32 Assigning a name to column A.

> **Note**
>
> The name *Row* for column A makes sense because you want to calculate the entries in column A (in other words, the rows).

4. To test the settings, calculate the number of rows in column A by using the COUNTA() function. Click any empty cell in the worksheet and enter the following formula:

   `=COUNTA(row)`

   Because column A has the name Row, you have to click only column A to select the argument for the function. Because the number of rows was calculated with the COUNTA() function, the content of all cells, including text and logical values, is taken into account.

5. Press the Enter key to confirm.

   If you are working with the Excel table in the DBFunction empty.xlsx file from the sample files, the result is 7,008. Next you will calculate the number of entries in row 1. To do this you use the same procedure you used to calculate the number of entries in column A.

6. Click the row header to select the entire row, and enter the name **Column** in the name box (see Figure 2-33).

	A	B	C	D	E
1	Company	City	Date	Country	Name of article
2	Alfreds Futterkiste	Berlin	3/12/08	Deutschland	Chai
3	Alfreds Futterkiste	Berlin	1/11/08	Deutschland	Chang
4	Alfreds Futterkiste	Berlin	8/1/08	Deutschland	Aniseed Syrup

Figure 2-33 Assigning a name to row 1.

7. To test the settings, calculate the number of entries in row 1 by using the COUNTA() function. Click any empty cell in the worksheet and enter the following formula:

   `=COUNTA(column)`

If you are working with the Excel table in the DBFunction empty.xlsx file from the sample files, the result is 6.

> **CAUTION**
>
> Remember to delete the functions you used to calculate the entries in the row and column.

By naming the column and row and by calculating the entries within the column and row, you have already created the basis for the dynamic name of the matrix (database). If you add or delete columns or rows, the value within your formula cells will increase or decrease, respectively.

Now you can actually assign a dynamic name to the database in the following range: The database range starts at cell A1, to which you gave the name *Start*. This position is extended down by the number of rows calculated with the =COUNTA(row) function; in this case, 7,008 entries. At the same time, the position is extended six columns to the right, beginning at the Start cell, based on the result of the calculation

```
=COUNTA(column)
```

You then need to subtract one position in each dimension of the database range. The following function assigns the dynamic name and defines the database range:

```
=Start:OFFSET(start,COUNTA(row)-1,COUNTA(column)-1)
```

Perform the following steps:

1. On the Formulas tab, click the Define Name button in the Defined Names group.

2. In the New Name dialog box, enter the name **Database**.

3. Enter in the Refers To field the formula shown just before these steps, as shown in Figure 2-34. If you aren't using the worksheet in the Chapter02 sample files folder, adjust the entry accordingly.

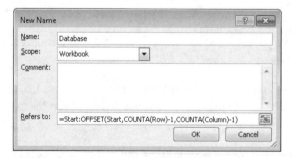

Figure 2-34 Specifying the database range.

4. Click the OK button.

To check the name, press the F5 key and enter the name **Database** in the Reference field in the Go To dialog box (see Figure 2-35) that appears. Click OK.

Figure 2-35 Searching for and showing specific database areas.

If the dynamic name was assigned properly and the database range is correct, the entire database range between cell A1 and cell F7008 should be selected (see Figure 2-36, but note that only a portion of the range is shown).

	A	B	C	D	E	F
1	**Company**	**City**	**Date**	**Country**	**Name of article**	**Turnover**
6970	Wolski Zajazd	Warszawa	08/10/07	Polen	Chartreuse verte	$ 1,827.00
6971	Wolski Zajazd	Warszawa	07/10/07	Polen	Boston Crab Meat	$ 1,499.00
6972	Wolski Zajazd	Warszawa	28/03/08	Polen	Jack's New England Clam	$ 1,388.00
6973	Wolski Zajazd	Warszawa	20/07/08	Polen	Singaporean Hokkien Fried Mee	$ 1,239.00
6974	Wolski Zajazd	Warszawa	12/08/08	Polen	Ipoh Coffee	$ 1,007.00
6975	Wolski Zajazd	Warszawa	03/08/08	Polen	Gula Malacca	$ 1,235.00
6976	Wolski Zajazd	Warszawa	08/09/07	Polen	Røgede sild	$ 1,585.00
6977	Wolski Zajazd	Warszawa	15/06/08	Polen	Spegesild	$ 1,546.00
6978	Wolski Zajazd	Warszawa	25/03/08	Polen	Zaanse koeken	$ 1,495.00
6979	Wolski Zajazd	Warszawa	26/08/07	Polen	Chocolade	$ 1,949.00

Figure 2-36 The entire database is selected, but only a portion is shown here.

Excel 2003, Excel 2007, and Excel 2010 offer an alternative way to assign your own dynamic names: You can define the list range to be evaluated as a list (Excel 2003) or a table (Excel 2007 or Excel 2010). Perform the following steps in Excel 2003:

1. Place the insertion point in the list.

2. Select the Date/List/Create list menu option.

3. If necessary, correct the suggested list range reference and specify whether the list has a header.

4. Click OK to confirm.

In Excel 2007 and Excel 2010, the list is called a table. To create the table range in Excel 2007 or Excel 2010, perform the following steps:

1. Place the insertion point in the list.

2. On the Insert tab in the Tables group, click the Table button.

3. If necessary, correct the suggested table range reference and specify whether the list has headings.

4. Click OK to confirm.

In both cases, you get a qualified list range. Excel extends all references in this list range as soon as the range is extended.

Database Functions in Practice

The following practice examples show typical calculations that use the database functions of Excel.

> **Sample Files**
>
> Use the Practice worksheet in the Practice_Database.xls or Practice_Database.xlsx sample file. The sample files are found in the Chapter02 folder. For more information about the sample files, see the section titled "Using the Sample Files" on page xxiii.

A training center has created a database to capture information about seminars conducted by the trainer. This data needs to be evaluated. The database has the dynamic name CourseInfo. The following database fields are available (see Figure 2-37):

- Date
- Training
- Coach
- Male/Female
- Company
- Rating
- Revenue

I17

Date	Training	Coach	Male/ Female	Company	Rating	Revenue
7/1/2008	Excel	Chris Preston	M	A	1	$ 1,059.00
7/1/2008	Word	David Jaffe	M	B	2	$ 1,121.00
7/1/2008	PowerPoint	Matt Berg	M	C	3	$ 1,073.00
7/1/2008	Visio	Chris Meyer	M	D	1	$ 1,193.00
7/1/2008	Outlook	Daren Waite	M	E	2	$ 1,124.00
7/1/2008	Publisher	Linda Tim	F	F	3	$ 1,063.00
7/1/2008	OneNote	Holly Dickson	F	G	1	$ 1,127.00
7/1/2008	Access	Richard Turner	M	H	2	$ 980.00
7/2/2008	Excel	Chris Preston	M	A	1	$ 842.00
7/2/2008	Word	David Jaffe	M	B	2	$ 1,121.00
7/2/2008	PowerPoint	Matt Berg	M	C	3	$ 908.00
7/2/2008	Visio	Chris Meyer	M	D	1	$ 994.00
7/2/2008	Outlook	Daren Waite	M	E	2	$ 1,181.00
7/2/2008	Publisher	Linda Tim	F	F	3	$ 893.00

Figure 2-37 The results in the database.

The training center wants to know how many Excel seminars were conducted since it started to collect information. The DCOUNTA() function returns the result.

How Many Excel Seminars Took Place?

The DCOUNTA() function counts the number of cells in a column, list, or database that are not empty and that meet the specified conditions (see Figure 2-38).

J2 =DCOUNTA(Kursinfos,B1,L1:L2)

Date	Training	Coach	Male/ Female	Company	Rating	Revenue			
7/1/2008	Excel	Chris Preston	M	A	1	$ 1,059.00		How many seminars took place?	23

Figure 2-38 Calculating the number of Excel seminars in the database.

Define the criteria range for the filter. The criteria range consists of the column heading and the filter criterion in the cell below. To do this, copy the range B1:B2 into cells L1:L2. The formula =DCOUNTA(CourseInfo,B1,L1:L2) returns 23 Excel seminars.

You can find the number of other seminars by changing the filter in L2, for example, to Microsoft Word.

Calculating Revenue

Next, the training center wants to know how much revenue the Excel seminars generated. You can use the DSUM() function to find this answer. This function adds the numbers in a column in a database that meet the specified conditions (Figure 2-39).

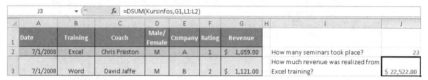

Figure 2-39 Calculating the revenue generated by Excel seminars.

The formula =DSUM(CourseInfo,G1,L1:L2) returns a revenue of $ 22,522 generated from Excel seminars.

Finding the Average Rating of the Seminars

The training center is also interested in the average rating for the trainers and the seminars. You find this by using the DAVERAGE() function. This function provides the average of the ratings that meet the specified conditions (see Figure 2-40).

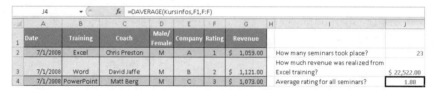

Figure 2-40 Calculating the average values from the database values in the Rating column.

In this case, you don't need the criteria range L1:L2, because no filter is required. The formula =DAVERAGE (CourseInfo,F1,F:F) returns an average rating of 1.88.

Using Cube Functions

Cube functions were introduced in Excel 2007. Data cubes are complex, multidimensional sets of data derived from raw information stored in a standard database. Cube functions are a little daunting on a technical level (they require at least Microsoft SQL Server 2005 and Microsoft SQL Server Analysis Services) and also because they include many new terms that may not be familiar.

This book tries to explain complex tasks based on a simple example. The example uses two store groups named North and South, which sold sweets (chocolate and cookies) from 2008 to 2010. Each store group consists of two stores. The sales are saved in a database and can be summarized and evaluated by using common methods. You can use views prepared in Microsoft Access or another database, use Excel data connections, or use Microsoft Query to create the query.

OLAP (online analytical processing) cubes, also known simply as *cubes*, offer the advantage that the data is already aggregated on the server and linked with the cube to make the information more readily available. This allows an analysis of complex sets of data.

The sales list could look like the one in Figure 2-41. Because the list repeats information for groups, stores, years, and products, it needs to be summarized.

GroupName	StoreName	Year	Product	Sales
South	SouthWest	2008	Chocolate	1300
South	SouthWest	2008	Cookies	1100
North	NorthEast	2009	Chocolate	1040
North	NorthEast	2009	Cookies	1560
North	NorthWest	2009	Chocolate	824
North	NorthWest	2009	Cookies	1751
South	SouthEast	2009	Chocolate	1260
South	SouthEast	2009	Cookies	1155
South	SouthWest	2009	Chocolate	1352
South	SouthWest	2009	Cookies	1144
North	NorthEast	2010	Chocolate	1081
North	NorthEast	2010	Cookies	1622
North	NorthWest	2010	Chocolate	848
North	NorthWest	2010	Cookies	1803
South	SouthEast	2010	Chocolate	1323
South	SouthEast	2010	Cookies	1212
South	SouthWest	2010	Chocolate	1406
South	SouthWest	2010	Cookies	1189
South	SouthWest	2011	Chocolate	1300
South	SouthWest	2011	Cookies	1100
North	NorthEast	2011	Chocolate	1040
North	NorthEast	2011	Cookies	1560
North	NorthWest	2011	Chocolate	788
North	NorthWest	2011	Cookies	2300
South	SouthEast	2011	Chocolate	1250

Figure 2-41 The sales of the company stores.

You can prepare the summary with programming tools, such as those in Microsoft Visual Studio 2005, Visual Studio 2008, and Visual Studio 2010. To do this you have to examine the data structure and preprocess the data (see Figure 2-42).

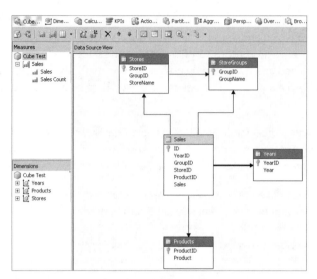

Figure 2-42 Preparing the cube for Analysis Services

Years, products, and stores become dimensions (cube axes), and the sales become measures. You can extend the measures as required (for example, for gross sales, average values, and other statistical values). The Key Performance Indicators (KPIs) allow you to use additional measures with different properties.

If the cube exists on the server (unlike a table in a database, it is not changed until it is regenerated) and you have access to the server, you have two options for creating the PivotTable:

- Select Insert/PivotTable/Use External Data Source and then select a workbook connection.

- Select Data/From Other Sources with these options:

  ○ From Analysis Services

  ○ From Microsoft Query

If you use the second option, you will be asked to insert the PivotTable afterwards. Microsoft Query also allows you to attach to offline cubes. Chapter 14, "Cube Functions," explains this in more detail.

The field list of the PivotTable in Figure 2-43 reflects the dimensions and configuration of the cube.

Figure 2-43 From the cube to the PivotTable.

It is up to you to display the data you are interested in. You can select report filters and column and row headings and values (see Figure 2-44).

	A	B	C	D
1	Years	All Years ▼		
2				
3	**Sales**	**Column Labels** ▼		
4	**Row Labels** ▼	Chocolate	Cookies	Grand Total
5	⊟ **North**	**7421**	**13796**	**21217**
6	NorthEast	4161	6242	10403
7	NorthWest	3260	7554	10814
8	⊟ **South**	**10391**	**8000**	**18391**
9	SouthEast	5033	3467	8500
10	SouthWest	5358	4533	9891
11	**Grand Total**	**17812**	**21796**	**39608**

Figure 2-44 Creating the overview.

The cube functions can be used in two different ways:

- The OLAP tools include the Convert To Formulas option (see Figure 2-45). This command converts the entire PivotTable (with the exception of the report filter). Afterwards you can still format the table as desired, but the table cannot be rearranged further.

Figure 2-45 Applying cube functions automatically.

- You can manually enter formulas into the worksheet to query information from the cube.

Cube functions are not tied to the PivotTable, because a cube connection in the workbook is sufficient. The following formula returns the gross sales for cookies sold in 2008 in the NorthEast store:

```
=CUBEVALUE("offLine","[Measures].[GrossSales]","[Stores].[Store].[All].[NorthEast]","
[Years].[Year].[All].[2008]","[Products].[Product].[All].[Cookies]")
```

The following formula returns the year with the highest sales for this store:

```
=CUBERANKEDMEMBER("offLine",CUBESET("offLine","([Stores].[Store].[All].[NorthEast],
[Years].Children)","all sales",2,"[Measures].[Sales]"),1)
```

Using Financial Math Functions

If you want to use the financial math functions of Excel, you will need to be familiar with their use. Excel can provide the calculations but not the interpretation. The Excel functions and the corresponding offline help aren't a substitute for a relevant textbook.

There is a mistaken belief that the financial math functions of Excel are specially tailored to business and financial mathematics in the United States and have only partial relevance for other countries. Maybe this is the reason that the majority of financial math books steer clear of Excel. If Excel is integrated, it is typically used only as a pure spreadsheet program, and the functions are rarely used. This book is one of the few that explains all the financial math functions of Excel in detail and includes examples.

Financial mathematics spans several areas, including statistics and differential and integral calculus, but there are areas such as the evaluation of equity warrants and other derivative financial products that cannot be handled by Excel.

A *simple interest calculation* is characterized by the fact that the interest is not added to the capital at the due date. This kind of calculation is mostly used for short periods. A simple interest calculation is basically a simple percentage calculation. Financial mathematics offers many different interest terms.

In all cases, the interest is the price for borrowed (*borrowing rate*) or loaned (*credit interest*) capital. The interest rate relates to a certain *period* (often a year). Initially there are two different interest calculations: *annuity* and *anticipative interest yield*. Additional interest terms are *nominal interest*, *real interest*, and *market interest*. There are also terms that directly relate to interest: *cash discount*, *bonus*, *rebate*, *markup*, and *markdown*.

Annuity refers to a normal savings account or a common mortgage loan. The interest is calculated and paid at the end of the interest period for the initial capital. The anticipative interest yield is usually used to honor a bill, for federal funding, and for building loan contracts.

The interest is paid for the capital due at the end of the period and calculated based on the interest rate.

If a customer deposits money in his savings account in the middle of the year, calculating the interest at the end of the year is not difficult. If the money is in the account for four months and the interest rate is 3 percent, only a third of the interest per annum is paid. But this simple percentage calculation should take into account the correct days when determining the proportion of the year, and for this you can use the DAYS360() function. If a bill with a maturity of one month is presented and the bank sets an interest per annum of 6 percent, the bank keeps (without fees) 0.5 percent (a twelfth of the interest per annum) of the bill amount and pays the difference. To count the days, you could use the DAY360() function again. However, for this task Excel provides the PRICEDISC() function.

The table in Figure 2-46 outlines the step-by-step calculations. The number of days in the period is calculated in F2, and this is applied to the annual interest rate to determine the rate for the period. Applying this rate to the principal results in a value of $9,950. Excel provides the function PRICEDISC() to perform this calculation. This example makes it clear that functions simplify calculations but that the use of these functions requires some knowledge of their functionality.

⊿	A	B	C	D	E	F
1						
2		Day of filing	10/1/2010		Days	30
3		Day of maturity	11/1/2010		Interest rate	0.50%
4		Note total	$ 10,000.00		Deduction	$ 50.00
5		Bank rate	6%		Payment	$ 9,950.00
6						
7		DISAGIO	$ 9,950.00			

Figure 2-46 Bill calculation as percentage calculation.

The example reveals something else: At what (annual) interest rate do you have to invest $9,950.00 to be paid $10,000.00 after one month, including interest? The answer is 50/9950*12=6.03 percent. This is also a simple percentage calculation. For this calculation, Excel offers the YIELDDISC() function. There is another function you can use: INTRATE(). You have to pass the data on the left in Figure 2-46 to this function to get the result.

Sample Files

Use the Practice worksheet in the Practice_Database.xls or Practice_Database.xlsx sample file. The sample files are found in the Chapter02 folder. For more information about the sample files, see the section titled "Using the Sample Files" on page xxiii.

In this example (for annuity), the interest to be paid is added to the initial capital and thus becomes part of the capital. This results in *compound interest*. This use of formulas requires the interest rate to remain the same over the entire period. This is not always realistic, but it is common in some investment models. If you invest $10,000 for 10 years, the bank might offer an interest rate of 4.8 percent. A detailed overview of this account is shown in Figure 2-47.

	D	E	F	G	H
1					
2		Year	Opening balance	Interest	Closing balance
3		1	$ 10,000.00	$ 480.00	$ 10,480.00
4		2	$ 10,480.00	$ 503.04	$ 10,983.04
5		3	$ 10,983.04	$ 527.19	$ 11,510.23
6		4	$ 11,510.23	$ 552.49	$ 12,062.72
7		5	$ 12,062.72	$ 579.01	$ 12,641.73
8		6	$ 12,641.73	$ 606.80	$ 13,248.53
9		7	$ 13,248.53	$ 635.93	$ 13,884.46
10		8	$ 13,884.46	$ 666.45	$ 14,550.91
11		9	$ 14,550.91	$ 698.44	$ 15,249.35
12		10	$ 15,249.35	$ 731.97	$ 15,981.32

Figure 2-47 Progress of an account with an opening balance of $10,000.

To calculate the result of $15,981.32, you don't need any functions; you only have to add the interest to the capital at the end of the year.

Excel contains a function group that includes the FV() function. The name of this function is an acronym for *future value*, which is also called *accumulated value*. This function in the formula

```
=FV(4.8%,10,,-10000)
```

where $10,000 is invested for 10 years at an interest rate of 4.8 percent, returns $15,981.33. Why the difference? The deviation occurs because each amount entered as a deposit, withdrawal, or interest credit has to be rounded to two decimal figures (there are no smaller monetary units). This fact cannot be incorporated by the function in a math formula, because the math formula calculates to a high degree of accuracy. So you have to use the ROUND() function to round the amount at each stage. Limiting the cells to only two decimal figures is not sufficient and can lead to errors.

The calculation of compound interest serves as the basis for the examples in the remainder of this section.

An Annuity Calculation Example

An annuity is the periodic payment of the same amount. All functions available in Excel assume that the payment date for the annuity is the same as the interest date. The only differences are for annuities in advance and annuities in arrears, which are paid at the end of the period.

This example can be extended with the depositor adding another $2,000 to the account each year. The calculation of the account is shown in Figure 2-48.

	D	E	F	G	H	I
14						
15		Year	Opening balance	Interest	Closing balance	Incoming payment
16		1	$ 10,000.00	$ 480.00	$ 10,480.00	$ 2,000.00
17		2	$ 12,480.00	$ 599.04	$ 13,079.04	$ 2,000.00
18		3	$ 15,079.04	$ 723.79	$ 15,802.83	$ 2,000.00
19		4	$ 17,802.83	$ 854.54	$ 18,657.37	$ 2,000.00
20		5	$ 20,657.37	$ 991.55	$ 21,648.92	$ 2,000.00
21		6	$ 23,648.92	$ 1,135.15	$ 24,784.07	$ 2,000.00
22		7	$ 26,784.07	$ 1,285.64	$ 28,069.71	$ 2,000.00
23		8	$ 30,069.71	$ 1,443.35	$ 31,513.06	$ 2,000.00
24		9	$ 33,513.06	$ 1,608.63	$ 35,121.69	$ 2,000.00
25		10	$ 37,121.69	$ 1,781.84	$ 38,903.53	

Figure 2-48 Investment plus savings.

Here the FV() function is also useful:

`=FV(4.8%,10,-2000,-10000)-2000   = 38903.52`

$2,000 is invested each year for 10 years at an interest rate of 4.8 percent and added to the opening balance of $10,000. Because there is no deposit made on the last day, you have to subtract the last $2,000 from the payments calculated with FV(). In this calculation there is also a small rounding error.

Chapter 2

Calculating Repayment

Financial mathematics uses three basic forms for the repayment of a loan—repayment through a single payment at the end (often in connection with life insurance), repayment through installments in consistent amounts (common for the purchase of merchandise), and repayment through annuity payments for which the repayment amount plus interest stays the same (the type of credit commonly used to finance real estate).

The last type is basically an annuity calculation, but the roles of the creditor and debtor are switched. The Excel function to calculate repayments covers only the first and the third types.

The formula used previously can also be used to calculate annuity repayments. In most cases, the annual interest rate has to be divided by 12 to calculate the monthly interest. The monthly interest is then used in the formula.

For example, assume that a bank offers the following financing for real estate: a $100,000 loan, at 5.6 percent per annum (p.a.) nominal interest (a five-year fixed rate), and 1 percent p.a. repayment. The bank also provides the following information:

- Monthly payment: $550.00

- Initial annual percentage rate: 5.75 percent

The monthly payment ensues from a twelfth of the interest rate of 5.6 percent plus a repayment of 1 percent: 6.6 percent/12 of the loan amount. The total is $550.00. With the following formula, you can calculate the effective rate:

=EFFECT(5.6%,12)

Figure 2-49 shows the repayment plan for the first year, which you can create without any special financial functions.

	A	B	C	D	E	F	G
9							
10	Year			Remainder of debt	Interest	Amortization	Remainder of debt
11				Beginning			End
12		1	Jan	100000.00	466.67	83.33	99916.67
13		1	Feb	99916.67	466.28	83.72	99832.95
14		1	Mar	99832.95	465.89	84.11	99748.84
15		1	Apr	99748.84	465.49	84.51	99664.33
16		1	May	99664.33	465.10	84.90	99579.43
17		1	Jun	99579.43	464.70	85.30	99494.13
18		1	Jul	99494.13	464.31	85.69	99408.44
19		1	Aug	99408.44	463.91	86.09	99322.35
20		1	Sep	99322.35	463.50	86.50	99235.85
21		1	Oct	99235.85	463.10	86.90	99148.95
22		1	Nov	99148.95	462.70	87.30	99061.65
23		1	Dec	99061.65	462.29	87.71	98973.94

Figure 2-49 A repayment plan for an annuity loan.

This repayment plan shows that more than the agreed-upon one percent is repaid at the end of the year. This is caused by monthly payments during the year (the twelfth part). The effective rate has to be higher than the nominal interest because the agreed-upon amount had to be repaid faster. The Excel functions allow you to calculate single items, such as the interest of the fifth month, the principal balance at the end of the 16th month, or the annual percentage rate that usually cannot be calculated in a simple equation.

The order of the current quotation of prices isn't based on divided durations but on parts of the year.

Calculating Exchange Rates

Calculations of the exchange rate and the overall return on an investment are a sophisticated area of financial mathematics. Many of the integrated functions are focused on these areas. The *exchange rate* is always defined as relative cash value of future payments after the accrued interest is subtracted, if necessary. The overall return is the figure (as an interest rate) for an actual value.

Investment Appraisal Example

Investments are often calculated with static or dynamic investment analyses. These might include cost/revenue comparisons as well as the payoff period and are based on cost and payment calculations. Dynamic methods consider the compound interest and evaluate deposits and withdrawals. These methods are not commonly used in commerce because of the models and the static collection of data. Excel provides several functions for dynamic investment calculations (capital value method and internal interest rate method). These methods are ideal for investment analyses.

For calculating the income returns, take the values shown in Figure 2-50 and enter them in a worksheet.

C6			f_x	=IRR(C3:C5)
	A	B	C	D
1				
2		End of year	Payments	
3		0	$ -495.20	
4		1	$ -	
5		2	$ 500.00	
6		IRR	0.48%	
7				
8		RATE	0.48%	

Figure 2-50 A simple example for a internal capital return.

Here the IRR() function provides the fastest result, but you could also use the RATE() function or GOAL.SEEK.

Amortization Calculation Example

Remember that payments are not only defined by the amount but also by the payment date. The payments could be illustrated in a timeline. It makes a difference whether a debtor pays his debt today or in a year. The longer it takes to pay the debt back, the higher the amount due. The interest is added to the debt, and the debt is capitalized.

This principle can be defined the other way around: Late money is worth less. This has nothing to do with inflation. From a financial point of view, it is irrelevant whether $11,000 is repaid in a year or $10,000 is repaid today (based on an annual interest rate of 10 percent).

Therefore, amortization calculations are not really part of financial mathematics. Traditionally, amortization calculations are discussed in textbooks. Excel provides the corresponding functions in a separate group.

Using Math and Trigonometry Functions

The math and trigonometry functions include the SUM() function. This function is probably the most commonly used function in Excel. To enhance the SUM() function, Excel offers the SUMIF() function. Assume that you have a list containing customer sales. To filter the sales for one customer and calculate the sum, use the SUMIF() function as shown in the following example.

The customers are listed in A2:A20, and the sales are listed in B2:B20 (see Figure 2-51). Cell D6 contains the customer whose sales you want to query. The formula in E6 for the sum of the sales is:

```
=SUMIF(A2:A20,D6,B2:B20)
```

E6		▼	𝑓ₓ	=SUMIF(A2:A20,D6,B2:B20)	

◢	A	B	C	D	E
1	**Customer**	**Invoice total**			
2	Smith	$ 26,711.00			
3	Young	$ 27,519.00			
4	Gallagher	$ 20,790.00			
5	Yokim	$ 14,770.00		**Customer**	**Total revenue**
6	Gonzales	$ 15,281.00		Smith	$ 43,196.00
7	Earls	$ 21,915.00			
8	Truher	$ 8,015.00			
9	Losa	$ 21,865.00			
10	Young	$ 33,453.00			
11	Gallagher	$ 29,747.00			
12	Barcley	$ 21,496.00			
13	Smith	$ 3,524.00			
14	Earls	$ 8,413.00			
15	Losa	$ 25,304.00			
16	Gonzales	$ 10,020.00			
17	Young	$ 18,623.00			
18	Earls	$ 18,784.00			
19	Smith	$ 12,961.00			
20	Gallagher	$ 4,210.00			

Figure 2-51 Filtering values with the SUMIF() function.

If you enter the name of the customer in D6, you can calculate the sum of the sales.

Generating Random Test Data

Another function of the math and trigonometry function is the RANDBETWEEN() function, which makes life with Excel easier. With this function you can quickly fill tables with test and demonstration data.

> **Note**
>
> For Excel 2003 and earlier, you might have to activate this add-in function (see the section titled "Analysis Functions" earlier in this chapter). In Excel 2007 and Excel 2010, the function is available by default.

Enter the RANDBETWEEN() function in any cell, and then enter the minimum and maximum value for the number range. If the values range from 500 through 1000, use the formula =RANDBETWEEN(500,1000). Now you can copy the formula in the other value cells to display a different value from 500 through 1000 in those cells (see Figure 2-52).

Chapter 2

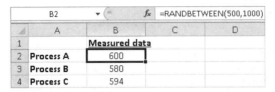

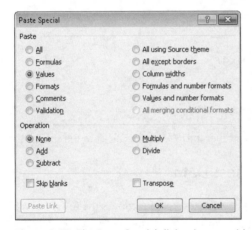

Figure 2-52 Filling a table with random values.

If you open the file or press the F9 key, all values are recalculated. To convert the random values in the cells to fixed values, copy the range containing the random values and select the Insert Values command in the shortcut menu to insert the range. Select the Values option in the Paste Special dialog box (see Figure 2-53), and click OK.

Figure 2-53 The Paste Special dialog box provides several useful options.

Sample Files

Use the Maths and Random worksheet in the Math.xls or Math.xlsx sample file. The sample files are found in the Chapter02 folder. For more information about the sample files, see the section titled "Using the Sample Files" on page xxiii.

These are just two examples of the functions in the math and trigonometry section. You will find further examples in Chapters 7 to 17 of this book.

PowerPivot

The best is saved for last. Microsoft offers a powerful analysis tool: the free PowerPivot for Excel 2010 add-in. This add-in is based on the latest technology, allowing processing of large data groups (up to several million rows), optimized integration of data, and the ability to publish analyses on the Internet with Microsoft SharePoint 2010. The following list details PowerPivot's advantages:

- PowerPivot combines native Excel 2010 functions with an in-memory engine to allow users to evaluate large data groups interactively and to use the results for calculations. This is possible with the new memory management system, which uses column-oriented compression. Everything is done in the memory of your computer to accelerate data operations.

- PowerPivot optimizes the integration of data from different sources, including enterprise databases, spreadsheets, reports, CSV files, and data feeds.

- PowerPivot also overrides the row limits for Excel 2007 and Excel 2010 worksheets.

- You can access PivotTables, data averages, and other familiar analysis features of Excel to create reports.

- You can publish your analyses in SharePoint 2010 to share them with other users in your organization. Other users working with Excel Services reports can use the same functions, such as data averages and fast queries.

- Applications and reports in SharePoint 2010 are automatically updated with simultaneous version tracking.

Further information, tutorials, and the download of the PowerPivot add-in can be found at *http://www.powerpivot.com*.

Using PowerPivot in Excel 2010

In Excel 2010, with the PowerPivot add-in installed, click the PowerPivot button on the PowerPivot tab to switch from Excel to the PowerPivot window. At first the window is empty and the ribbon contains many unavailable buttons. You have to embed the data to be analyzed. Click the From Database button (see Figure 2-54) and select From SQL Server.

Figure 2-54 The Get External Data group on the Home tab of the PowerPivot window.

> ## Note
>
> The Microsoft example database used is ContosoRetailDW, which at the time of this writing is available for download at
>
> *http://www.microsoft.com/download/en/details.aspx?displaylang=en&id=18279*
>
> The ContosoBIdemoBAK.exe download file contains two files to extract: ContosoRetailDW.bak and an Excel list. ContosoRetailDW.bak is a Microsoft SQL Server backup that you will need to restore in SQL Server.

Enter the server name in the Table Import Wizard, specify the credentials, and select the database name (see Figure 2-55).

Figure 2-55 The first step in getting the database connection in the Table Import Wizard.

In the next step, keep the preselected option to make a selection from the table and view list (see Figure 2-56).

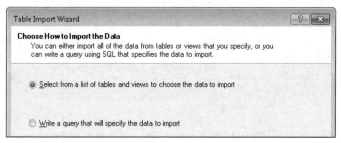

Figure 2-56 The second step in the Table Import Wizard.

Select the FactSales table. This table contains 3.4 million rows of transaction data. Click the Select Related Tables button (see Figure 2-57). Six related root data tables are included. Click the Finish button.

Figure 2-57 Selecting tables and views from the SQL Server database.

If you select large tables, it can take a few minutes to load the data. The wizard shows the loading progress (see Figure 2-58).

Figure 2-58 The data is loaded.

After the data is loaded, the tables are displayed in the PowerPivot window. The window (see Figure 2-59) looks like an Excel worksheet but has different functionality. Save the workbook. It has a size of 87 MB.

If you want to be able to publish the data in SharePoint, ask your administrator to increase the maximum size for uploaded data (which is 50 MB by default).

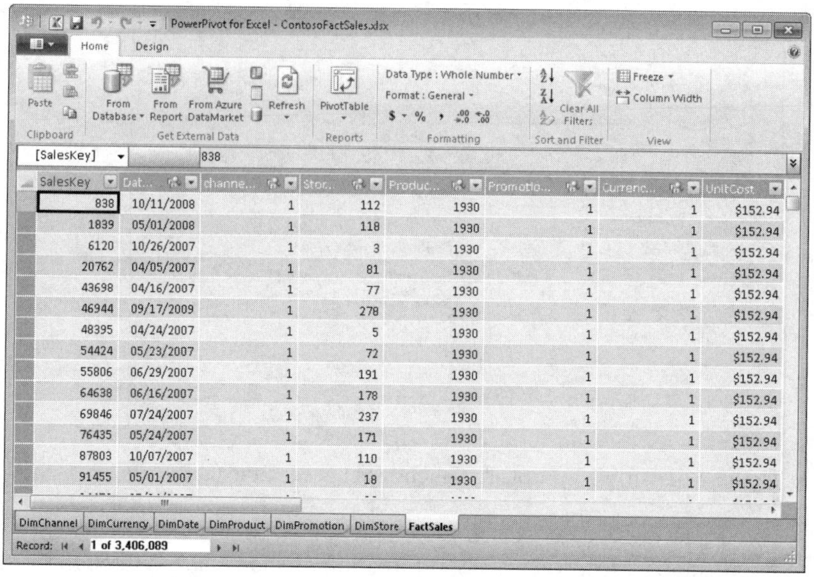

Figure 2-59 The PowerPivot window contains the loaded tables.

If the source database has a database relationships chart—that is, a definition of all relationships—the chart will be automatically used by PowerPivot. Right-click a column in the
lookup table to view the associated table. You can check and add table relationships on the
Design tab (see Figure 2-60).

Figure 2-60 The Design tab in PowerPivot.

If you click Manage Relationships on the Design tab, you get an overview of the defined
relationships (see Figure 2-61). You can edit the relationships and create any new relationships necessary to embed tables from other sources.

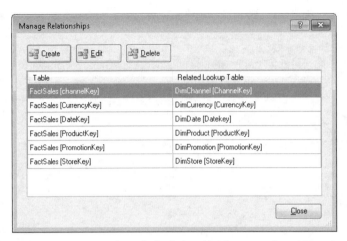

Figure 2-61 An overview of all relationships between the tables.

If you view the DimStore table, you might notice that the region, country, and location information for the stores is missing. This information is linked through the GeographyKey field in the DimGeography table. To add the DimGeography table from the same source, perform the following steps:

1. Click the From Database button and select From SQL Server (see Figure 2-54, shown earlier).

2. Enter the server name and the credentials in the Table Import Wizard. Select the ContosoRetailDW database.

3. In the next step, keep the option to make a selection from the table and view list (see Figure 2-56, shown earlier).

4. In the last step of the Wizard, select the check box for the DimGeography table and click the Finish button.

5. Select the DimStore table and click the Create Relationship button on the Design tab.

6. In the Edit Relationship dialog box, select the GeographyKey column for the DimStore table. Select DimGeography as the linked search table and GeographyKey as the linked search column. Click OK to exit.

The list you need for data analyses is complete. You don't need to add more tables to create a Pivot evaluation. Perform the following steps:

1. On the Home tab in the PowerPivot window, click the PivotTable arrow (see Figure 2-62). As you can see, templates for PivotTables and PivotCharts are available.

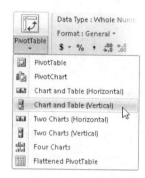

Figure 2-62 Templates for Pivot evaluations.

2. In the menu, select Chart And Table (Vertical). You will be switched to the Excel window with both empty Pivot objects on the worksheet.

3. Select the chart area and drag the ChannelName field from the DimChannel table into the Slicers Vertical area.

4. Right-click the new data average element and, in the shortcut menu, select the Field Settings command. Enter **Sales Channel** in the Custom Name box. Click OK to exit.

5. Drag the ContinentName and RegionCountryName fields from the DimGeography table into the Slicers Horizontal area. In the field settings for the elements, change the custom names to **Continent** and **Country/Region**.

6. Drag the CalendarYear field from the DimDate table into the Row Labels area. The custom name in the field settings should be Year.

7. Drag the TotalCost and SalesAmount fields from the FactSales table into the Values area.

8. Select the Measure command in the shortcut menus for both elements. In the measure settings for the elements, change the custom names to **Costs** and **Revenue**.

Figure 2-63 shows the settings you have made so far.

Figure 2-63 The design of the PivotChart in the PowerPivot report.

If necessary, format the chart (for example, set the number format for the axes). The second set of steps revolves around the PivotTable. To complete the PivotTable, perform the following steps:

1. Select the area for the PivotTable below the chart. You might notice that the slicers for the chart are already set. Keep these settings.

2. Drag the CalendarYear field from the DimDate table into the Column Labels area. The custom name in the field settings should be **Year**.

3. Drag the Manufacturer field from the DimProduct table into the Row Labels area. The custom name in the field settings should be **Manufacturer**.

4. Drag the TotalCost and SalesAmount fields from the FactSales table into the Values area. Again, change the custom names to **Costs** and **Revenue**.

Change the formats in the PivotTable (see Figure 2-64)—for example, change the number format or column width. The result should look similar to Figure 2-65. Name the sheet containing the PowerPivot report, and save your work.

Figure 2-64 The design of the PivotTable in the PowerPivot report.

A new worksheet with the associated PivotTable was created for the chart. Don't delete this worksheet, and remember that each time you change the PivotTable this change is also applied to the chart.

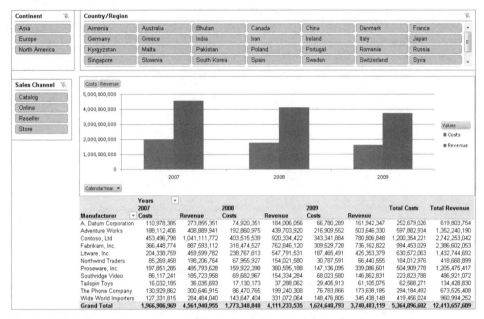

Figure 2-65 A PowerPivot report consisting of a chart and a table using the same slicers.

For PowerPivot reports, you need only to know how to create and design PivotTables and PivotCharts. In other words, your Excel know-how is sufficient to work with PowerPivot.

From Numbers to Formulas

Calculations in Microsoft Excel are achieved through formulas. Formulas are entered differently than other data, although you probably won't notice the difference.

The procedure for working with Excel worksheets and working on paper is basically the same, except that when you work on paper you have to write down the initial values and then manually work through each step of the calculation. In Excel, the initial values are called *input values,* and you specify the algorithms in a formula to produce a result based on the input values.

A spreadsheet has the advantage of letting you use the calculation scheme you have created over and over again. All you have to do is enter new input values, and the formulas containing the algorithms calculate the result. If you create a table of values, you can perform any number of calculations based on the same rules.

Remember that Excel cannot work directly with algebraic formulas, because the components must refer to real values. Excel also cannot calculate and draw graphs directly from a formula. The values must be calculated in a table.

Entering Formulas

If an entry in Excel starts with the equal sign (=), the subsequent string is treated as a calculation formula. You can start a formula with the plus or minus sign, but Excel will always add the equal sign at the beginning of the formula.

A formula consists of operands and operators. The *operands* are the values for the calculation, and the *operators* are the rules (see Figure 3-1).

Figure 3-1 Operands and operators are the basic elements of a formula.

Operators

The operators that can be used in Excel formulas span the entire range of commonly used symbols. These operators are listed in this section, with the most frequently used described first.

Arithmetic Operators

Arithmetic operators are used for basic calculations and return numeric values. Table 3-1 lists the arithmetic operators used in Excel formulas.

Table 3-1 Arithmetic Operators in Excel Formulas

Operator	Operation	Example Formula	Result
+	Addition	=15+13	28
−	Subtraction	=104–74	30
/	Division	=42/3	14
*	Multiplication	=5*8	40
^	Exponentiation	=2^8	256
%	Division by one hundred (percent)[1]	=140%	1.4

[1]Like algebraic signs, the percent sign is also an operator.

> ### Sample Files
> Use the Arithmetic Operators worksheet in the Chapter03.xls or Chapter03.xlsx sample file. The sample files are found in the Chapter03 folder. For more information about the sample files, see the section titled "Using the Sample Files" on page xxiii.

You create formulas in Excel worksheets by using these operators and entering the formulas directly into a cell. After you enter a formula, the result is displayed in the cell and the formula is shown as the cell content in the formula bar.

INSIDE OUT   Avoid using constants in formulas

The direct input of numeric values in formulas is also known as *entering constants*. However, constants are rarely used in formulas. You should avoid constants and replace them with references to input cells that contain the values for the constants. This way you can always update the constant by entering a new value in the cell, and it should be clear what values have been used in the calculation. The formulas listed in Table 3-1 use constants only to illustrate the functionality of the operators.

Specifying the Priority of Operations by Using Parentheses

To change the priority of calculation operations, put the expressions you want to calculate first in parentheses. Enter both formulas shown in Table 3-2 in different cells and compare the results to test the functionality of parentheses.

Table 3-2 **Result with Parentheses**

Formula	Result
=3+8*4	35
=(3+8)*4	44

Note

In a formula, the number of opening parentheses must match the number of closing parentheses. Otherwise, Excel reports an error and highlights the incorrect part of the formula or offers to correct the formula.

Sample Files

Use the Priority worksheet in the Chapter03.xls or Chapter03.xlsx sample file. The sample files are found in the Chapter03 folder. For more information about the sample files, see the section "Using the Sample Files" on page xxiii.

Chapter 3

Excel provides input assistance to ensure that you don't lose track of the parentheses and to verify that the number of opening parentheses matches the number of closing parentheses:

- If you enter a closing parenthesis, the opening parenthesis is highlighted for a few seconds in the formula bar or in the cell.

- If you edit an existing formula and point to one of the parentheses, the matching parentheses are highlighted for a few seconds (depending on your settings).

Priority of Arithmetic Operators

If an expression contains several operators, the priority for calculation is determined by the priority of the operators. You can change the standard priority by using parentheses within a formula. Table 3-3 shows the priority for the operators within an Excel formula.

Table 3-3 **Operator Priority**

Priority	Operator	Description
1	–	Negation of a value (for example, –34)
2	%	Division of a value by 100 (percent)
3	^	Exponentiation of a value
4	* and /	Multiplication and division
5	+ and –	Addition and subtraction

You might remember the old arithmetic rule, PEMDAS, which can help you when you are in doubt.

> **Note**
> If a formula contains operators with the same priority, Excel calculates the formula from left to right.

Comparison Operators

Use the comparison operators to compare values, text, or cells. These expressions are often used in logical functions; a common example is IF(). The result is always a logical value (Boolean value). Table 3-4 lists all of the Boolean operators and illustrates them with sample formulas.

Table 3-4 **Boolean Comparison Operators**

Operator	Operation (Comparison)	Sample Formula	Result
=	Equal to	=5=8	FALSE
<	Less than	=5<8	TRUE
>	Greater than	=5>8	FALSE
<=	Less than or equal to	=5<=8	TRUE
>=	Greater than or equal to	=5>=8	FALSE
<>	Not equal to	=5<>8	TRUE

Sample Files

Use the Comparison Operators worksheet in the Chapter03.xls or Chapter03.xlsx sample file. The sample files are found in the Chapter03 folder. For more information about the sample files, see the section "Using the Sample Files" on page xxiii.

Chapter 3

The & Text Operator

In some cases, you might want to combine the results from several formulas or cells in a single cell. For this task you use the & (ampersand) operator. If you connect two values of any type with the ampersand, the result always has the Text data type. In other words, Excel converts number values automatically into text. This way you can use the text operator to include two number values as text in one cell. However, you cannot use the resulting string directly for other calculations.

Note

If you use text instead of a cell reference in a formula, you must put this text in quotation marks. You don't have to put numbers in quotation marks. Quotation marks are also not necessary if you use references to cells, which can contain any data type.

To connect the content in cells A1 and A2 by using the text operator, use the following formula:

=A1&A2

The text operator connects the contents of the two cells without a space in between them. To include a space between the values, you must use quotation marks. If you want a space between the values in cell A1 and cell A2, use the following formula:

`=A1&" "&A2`

Sample Files

Use the Text Operator worksheet in the Chapter03.xls or Chapter03.xlsx sample file. The sample files are found in the Chapter03 folder. For more information about the sample files, see the section "Using the Sample Files" on page xxiii. Figure 3-2 shows the content of this worksheet.

	A	B	C	D	E
1	**Text Operator**				
2				Calculation	Formula
3	Nether	land		Netherland	=A3&B3
4	white	feather		featherwhite	=B4&A4
5					
6	Excel	2011		Excel 2011	=A6&" "&B6
7	Excel	Functions		Excel-Functions	=A7&"-"&B7
8	50000	townsfolk		50000 townsfolk	=A8&" "&B8
9					
10	47	11		4711	=A10&B10
11	6	49		6 from 49 (lottery)	=A11&" from "&B11&" (lottery)"
12	1	25000		1:25000	=A12&":"&B12
13					
14	John	Smith		John Smith	=A14&" "&B14
15	Sara	Conner		Conner, Sara	=B15&", "&A15
16					

Figure 3-2 Text operator examples you find in the sample file.

Reference Operators

With *reference operators*, you can pass cells or cell ranges to a formula or function for calculation. The following operators are available:

- **Range separator : (colon)** Creates a reference to all cells between two references, including the reference cells themselves; for example—B3:B20

- **Connection operator , (comma)** Allows the connection of several cells or references in an expression—for example, SUM(B3:B20,D3:D20)

- **Intersection operator (space)** Creates a reference to cells that occur in both ranges that are referenced; in other words, the cells are the intersection of both ranges—for example, B7:D7 C6:C8

The Range Operator

A *range* is an area of a worksheet consisting of cells next to and/or below each other. If two cell references are connected with a colon, these references together with the cells in between form a range. Ranges can have different sizes and shapes. In functions, a range is an argument independent of its size.

Possible Range References   Range references are easily specified. Figure 3-3 shows all of the possible variations.

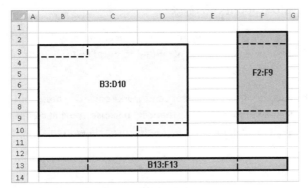

Figure 3-3 Possible range shapes and syntaxes to use in formulas.

The ranges shown demonstrate the following rules for range reference syntax:

- For a range spanning several columns and rows, the cell in the upper-left corner is connected with the cell in the lower-right corner, as in B3:D10.

- For a range spanning one row, the left cell is linked with the right cell, as in B13:F13.

- For a range spanning one column, the upper cell is linked with the lower cell, as in F2:F9.

References to Entire Columns or Rows

If you want to reference columns or rows from the first to the last cell, use the references listed in Table 3-5. You can create references for other columns and rows based on the references in this table.

Table 3-5 Syntax for References to Entire Columns or Rows

Reference to	Syntax
Entire column E	E:E
Entire row 7	7:7
All rows from row 2 to row 5	2:5
Entire worksheet	A:XFD or 1:1048576

·INSIDE OUT More about references

The references for the entire worksheet in Table 3-5 are valid only in Excel 2007 and Excel 2010, because these versions have extended row and column limits. You can find more information in Appendix C.

References can be used in other worksheets and workbooks. Be careful not to reference a cell in a formula that already references that cell, because you will create a circular reference. See the section "What is a Circular Reference?" later in this chapter for further information.

The Connection Operator

You can pass nonadjacent cells to a function for calculation by using a connection, or union, operator. The connection operator is the comma (,). If you use the connection operator to pass several cells to a function, each cell reference that is separated from another by a comma is treated as a separate argument.

If you wanted to add the three ranges shown earlier in Figure 3-3, you would have to specify each cell group in the SUM() function. The function would have three arguments separated by commas:

```
=SUM(B3:D10,F2:F9,B13:F13)
```

The Intersection Operator

The intersection operator is rarely used but should be included on this list. With the intersection operator (the space), you define a reference to the cells shared by several different references. In other words, an intersection in Excel describes the values in the area where two or more ranges overlap.

The intersection shown in Figure 3-4 is where the ranges B2:E11 and C8:G14 overlap. In a formula or function, this intersection would look like this: B2:E11 C8:G14.

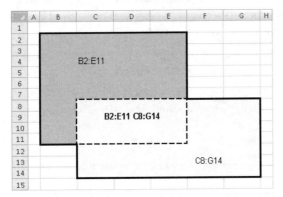

Figure 3-4 Simple example of an intersection.

The result of the intersection is called an *explicit intersection*. The values in the cells in the explicit intersection are added up with the following formula:

`=SUM(B2:E11 C8:G14)`

Intersections are mostly used in the context of range names and are rarely used as pure cell references.

References in Formulas

As mentioned at the beginning of this chapter, the use of constants in formulas defeats the purpose of a spreadsheet. When you use constants, you have to change the formula each time a value changes.

The content of a cell is handled through a cell reference. A reference tells Excel which cell contains the values used in a formula (see Figure 3-5).

D3	▾ (ⁿ	*f*ₓ	=B3*C3	
▲ A	B	C	D	E
1				
2	Day rate	Days	Total	
3	$ 66.00	5	$ 330.00	
4				

Figure 3-5 Using cell references to multiply the day rate by days.

When you enter references, make sure that the formula doesn't contain spaces.

> **Note**
>
> Formulas are not case sensitive. Excel converts all references from lowercase to upper-case if the syntax of the formula is correct. If Excel does not convert the reference, check your entry for syntax and typing errors.

You will find it easier to enter cell references by selecting the cell or cell range you want to use rather than typing it. To enter a formula, perform the following steps:

1. Type the equal sign.

2. Enter any function name, parenthesis, or character with which a formula can begin.

3. Select the cell or cell range you want to include in the formula as the cell reference. The selection is marked by a dashed line, and the cell reference appears in the formula.

4. Enter the operator or another part of the formula.

5. Select other required cells or ranges.

6. Repeat steps 2 through 5 until the formula is complete.

7. Press the Enter key to complete the formula.

Cell references allow you to use all the advantages offered by a spreadsheet. You can create any number of calculation schemes and change a scheme to get different results.

This means that you have to create a calculation scheme only once and can use it for simi-lar calculations over and over again. In the table in Figure 3-6, you can change the values in columns B and C to immediately get the result in column D.

	A	B	C	D	E
			D3	f_x =B3*C3	
1					
2		Day rate	Days	Total	
3		$ 66.00	5	$ 330.00	
4		$ 55.00	2	$ 110.00	
5		$ 45.00	3	$ 135.00	
6		$ 75.00	4	$ 300.00	
7		$ 60.00	5	$ 300.00	
8		$ 50.00	6	$ 300.00	
9		$ 70.00	7	$ 490.00	
10					

Figure 3-6 The formula containing cell references can be copied in the cells below it.

Another advantage of using cell references in a formula is that you can copy the formula by dragging the fill handle down. In this way you create all of the required calculations within seconds, which would not be possible if you were using constants.

> **Sample Files**
>
> Use the Relative Reference worksheet in the Chapter03.xls or Chapter03.xlsx sample file. The sample files are found in the Chapter03 folder. For more information about the sample files, see the section "Using the Sample Files" on page xxiii.

Relative References

If you copy the formula shown earlier in Figure 3-6 by dragging the fill handle down, you get the correct result for each line. This is because Excel adjusts the references in the formula by using the current row number. However, this works only because the row number in the formula is relative.

Consider a relative reference to be the relation between two cells. The relation—not the literal syntax of the reference—is copied.

The formula in cell D3 in the table shown in Figure 3-6 would read like this: "Take the value in the cell two columns to the left in the same row (=B3) and multiply (=B3*) this value by the value in the cell one column to the left in the same row (=B3*C3)."

> **CAUTION**
>
> The following applies when you are copying a formula containing a relative cell reference:
>
> - If you are copying horizontally, the column references change according to the location.
> - If you are copying vertically, the row references change according to the location.

Absolute References

An absolute reference is the counterpart to a relative reference. An *absolute reference* is a cell reference that doesn't change when it is copied or filled. You use absolute references to anchor a reference in a formula to a particular cell. Assume that you want to calculate the sales tax for several net prices, and the sales tax rate is entered in a particular cell. You need to be able to copy the formula you created (see Figure 3-7).

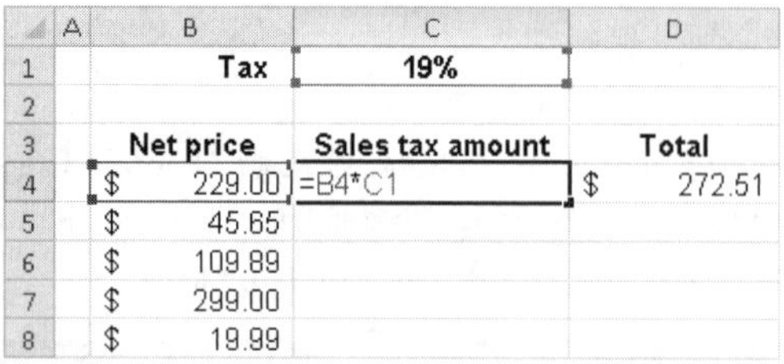

	A	B	C	D
1		Tax	19%	
2				
3		Net price	Sales tax amount	Total
4		$ 229.00	=B4*C1	$ 272.51
5		$ 45.65		
6		$ 109.89		
7		$ 299.00		
8		$ 19.99		

Figure 3-7 Initial situation with the formula in cell C4.

The formula entered in cell C4 calculates the sales tax for the net price in cell B4. The formula is:

```
=B4*C1
```

If you copy this formula to the cells below it, you get the wrong results because the relative cell references change. Cell C6 even displays the error message `#VALUE!`. Because cell C3 contains the text "sales tax amount", the `#VALUE!` error is generated.

When you analyze the formula in cell C4, you will see that the reference to the sales tax should not be changed. To ensure that the sales tax doesn't change, enter a dollar sign ($) before the column (C) and the row (1) references. Now this cell reference won't change when copied or filled and is called an absolute reference in Excel.

The formula in cell C4 in the table shown in Figure 3-7 should read:

```
=B4*$C$1
```

If you fill the range with this formula starting at cell C4 and copy the formula in the cells below it, the entire table shows the correct results (see Figure 3-8).

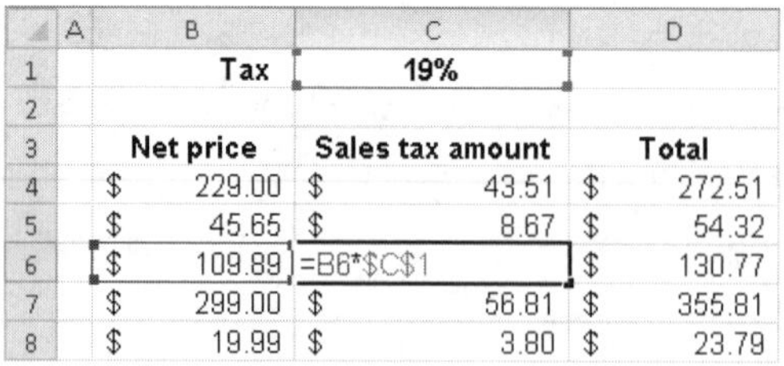

	A	B	C	D
1		Tax	19%	
2				
3		Net price	Sales tax amount	Total
4		$ 229.00	$ 43.51	$ 272.51
5		$ 45.65	$ 8.67	$ 54.32
6		$ 109.89	=B6*$C$1	$ 130.77
7		$ 299.00	$ 56.81	$ 355.81
8		$ 19.99	$ 3.80	$ 23.79

Figure 3-8 Correct results are a result of the absolute cell reference to cell $C$1.

> ## Sample Files
> Use the Absolute Reference worksheet in the Chapter03.xls or Chapter03.xlsx sample file. The sample files are found in the Chapter03 folder. For more information about the sample files, see the section "Using the Sample Files" on page xxiii.

Mixed References

Actually, you didn't need an absolute reference to copy the formula in the example shown in earlier Figure 3-8. Because you copied the formula in the same column, the column reference didn't have to be absolute. This knowledge leads us to a discussion of mixed references which are, as the name implies, a mix of relative and absolute references.

Assume that you want to create a multiplication table. The calculation method to use is simple to figure out. Look at the formula for cell F6 in the formula bar of the table shown in Figure 3-9: =A6*F2. In B3, the formula would be: =A3*B2. As you probably can guess, the formula doesn't have to be rewritten for each cell.

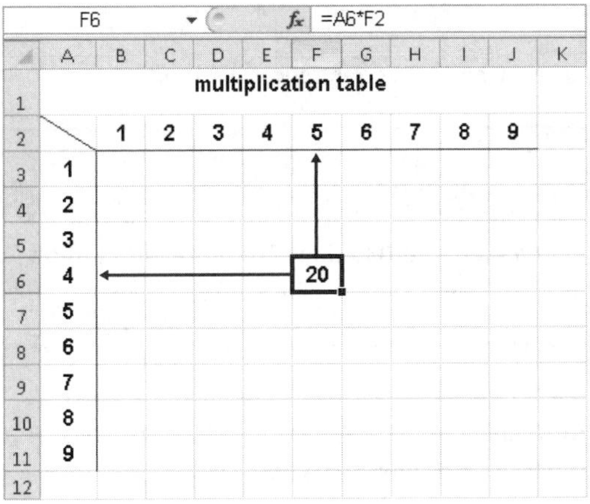

Figure 3-9 A multiplication table as an example for using mixed references.

If you could lock the column or row reference, you could copy the formula created in cell B3 in the table shown in Figure 3-9 to the cells below and to the right of it. The solution:

- You have to lock the column reference for the values in column A to copy the formula horizontally and to always use the values in column A. The row reference for the values in column A has to remain relative so that it can be adjusted when copied vertically. The result is the cell reference $A3.

Chapter 3

- For the reference to the values in row 2, it is the other way around. The column reference has to remain relative, and the row reference has to be locked with the $ sign. This way, the reference to the row is not changed when the formula is copied vertically, but the column references are adjusted when it is copied horizontally. This leads to the following formula for cell B3:

  ```
  =$A3*B$2
  ```

Try this in your table. You will always get the correct results (see Figure 3-10).

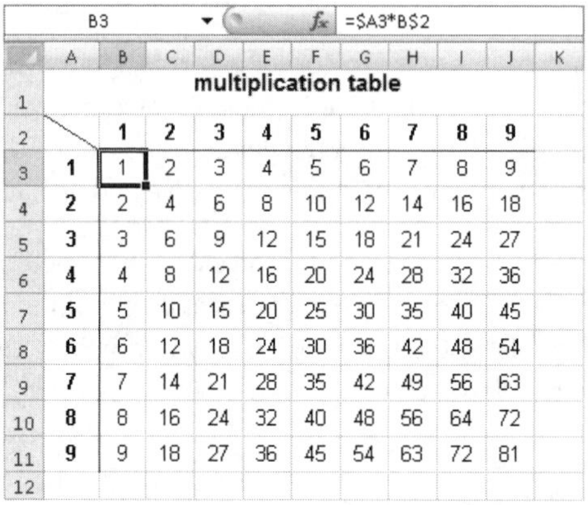

	A	B	C	D	E	F	G	H	I	J	K
1	multiplication table										
2		1	2	3	4	5	6	7	8	9	
3	1	1	2	3	4	5	6	7	8	9	
4	2	2	4	6	8	10	12	14	16	18	
5	3	3	6	9	12	15	18	21	24	27	
6	4	4	8	12	16	20	24	28	32	36	
7	5	5	10	15	20	25	30	35	40	45	
8	6	6	12	18	24	30	36	42	48	54	
9	7	7	14	21	28	35	42	49	56	63	
10	8	8	16	24	32	40	48	56	64	72	
11	9	9	18	27	36	45	54	63	72	81	
12											

Figure 3-10 The results are correct when mixed references are used.

> ## Sample Files
> **Use the Mixed Reference worksheet in the Chapter03.xls or Chapter03.xlsx sample file. The sample files are found in the Chapter03 folder. For more information about the sample files, see the section "Using the Sample Files" on page xxiii.**

The basic principle is this: For a mixed reference, the part after the dollar sign is locked and cannot be changed when copied. Remember these two rules:

- To always apply the values in a certain column, lock the column reference with the dollar sign.
- To always apply the values in a certain row, lock the row reference with the dollar sign.

You can press the F4 key to change the reference type. Click into the cell reference in a formula and press F4 several times. Each time you press F4, the syntax changes (relative to absolute to mixed to relative, and so on).

Finally, you should be aware of a new feature in Excel 2007 and Excel 2010: In list ranges marked as Table, you'll find a new syntax for relative references, as in the following example:

```
=[@Price]*[@Quantity]
```

The example multiplies the values in the columns with the Price and Quantity headings for each line. If you enter a formula in row 1, Excel fills the adjacent empty cells below it with the new formula.

What Is a Circular Reference?

Circular references are mostly generated by input errors. A *circular reference* is a reference to a cell containing the formula, in other words, a reference to itself. Excel cannot resolve formulas with a circular reference. Instead you receive the message shown in Figure 3-11.

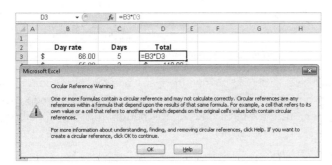

Figure 3-11 Wrong input in cell D3 and error message.

If you click OK in the error message, the circular reference toolbar appears in the table window of Excel 2003 (see Figure 3-12).

Figure 3-12 The circular reference toolbar in Excel 2003.

You can use the circular reference toolbar to iterate through the cells within the circular reference. Use the Trace Dependents and Trace Precedents buttons to see what caused the problem.

If you click OK in the circular reference warning in Excel 2010, a help window shows instructions on how to handle circular references (see Figure 3-13).

Figure 3-13 Excel 2010 help for circular references.

In Excel 2007 and Excel 2010, you can find the search and remove options for circular references on the ribbon, on the Formula tab. In the Formula Auditing group, click the Error Checking button and then the Circular References button. Then click the displayed references (see Figure 3-14). However, here (and in the status bar), only the circular reference entered last is displayed.

> **CAUTION**
>
> If you close the warning and the help windows and don't correct the circular reference, no other warning is displayed when you enter another formula with a circular reference in a cell. However, the status bar shows circular references. So you'll want to correct circular references immediately, because you might forget later.

Figure 3-14 Finding circular references in Excel 2007 and Excel 2010.

INSIDE OUT   More about circular references

Excel cannot calculate all open workbooks automatically if one workbook contains a circular reference. You have to remove the circular reference, or you can calculate each cell included in the circular reference by using the results of the previous iteration. If you don't change the default settings for iterations, Excel ends the calculation after 100 iteration steps or when the values in the circular reference change by less than 0.001 between two iterations (depending on which happens first).

Array Formulas

To understand array formulas, take a look at the functionality of a standard single-value formula. A single-value formula generates a result from several operands. For example, the formula =A4*B4 generates the product of both cells (see Figure 3-15). Compare this with the array formula {=E4:E8*F4:F8}. This formula generates five results—in this case, the product of the cells to the left and right of the multiplication sign.

	A	B	C	D	E	F	G
1	**Array Formula**						
2		Single value formula				Array formula	
3	Day rate	Days	Total		Day rate	Days	Total
4	$ 55.00	5	$ 275.00		$ 55.00	5	$ 275.00
5	$ 50.00	5	$ 250.00		$ 50.00	5	$ 250.00
6	$ 45.00	4	$ 180.00		$ 45.00	4	$ 180.00
7	$ 60.00	3	$ 180.00		$ 60.00	3	$ 180.00
8	$ 63.00	7	$ 441.00		$ 63.00	7	$ 441.00
9							

Figure 3-15 Comparing a single value formula and an array formula.

Sample Files

Use the Array Formula worksheet in the Chapter03.xls or Chapter03.xlsx sample file. The sample files are found in the Chapter03 folder. For more information about the sample files, see the section "Using the Sample Files" on page xxiii.

A single-value formula is created with relative references that change if the column is filled line by line. In contrast, the array formula doesn't change. The formula is the same line by line; however, the results per line are different as in the case of the single-value formulas.

An array formula can save time when you are entering the same formula repeatedly, because it can return several results. However, array formulas use more memory than the corresponding single value formulas.

> **Note**
>
> An array formula is enclosed in braces that are automatically added by Excel. Braces cannot be entered manually. To enter a formula as an array formula, you have to complete the formula by pressing Ctrl+Shift+Enter.

If you edit formulas, you have to consider several important differences between array formulas and single-value formulas. A change made to an array formula affects the entire range. This means that you cannot change only one part or one cell. The following operations are not possible:

- Changing the content of only one cell

- Deleting or moving cells included in the array

- Pasting cells, rows, or columns in an existing array

If you try one of these operations, you will receive an error message.

> **Tip   Determine where an array formula starts and ends**
>
> If you are not sure where an array formula starts or ends, perform the following steps:
>
> 1. Select a cell in the array.
> 2. Press the F5 key to open the Go To dialog box.
> 3. Click the Special button in the Go To dialog box.
> 4. In the Go To Special dialog box, select the Current Array option and click OK. The array containing the cell is selected.

Tips and Tricks

In this section, you see some tips and tricks you can use when working with formulas. Depending on how often you use Excel, you might find some of the following procedures more useful than others.

Turning the Formula View On and Off

To get an overview of a sheet with many formulas and connections, you can view the underlying formulas instead of the results. This is often useful if the sheet was created by someone else:

1. Open the worksheet.

2. Press Ctrl+` (the key to the left of the number 1 on the keyboard).

Excel switches from displaying the results to displaying the underlying formulas. Because the formulas need more space, Excel adjusts the column width automatically.

> **Note**
>
> The Ctrl+` key combination doesn't change the data in your table. This command only affects the view; you can reset by pressing Ctrl+` again.
>
> You can also switch to the formula view by clicking the Show Formulas button on the Formula tab in the Formula Auditing group. You can also make this change in the Excel Options dialog box. Figure 3-16 shows the Show Formulas In Cells Instead Of Their Calculated Results check box in the Advanced section of the Excel 2010 Options dialog box.
>
>
>
> **Figure 3-16** The worksheet options in Excel 2007 and Excel 2010.
>
> In all Excel versions, these settings apply only to the active worksheet.

Entering Formulas in Several Cells

If you know that a formula has to be entered into several cells, you can enter the formula in three simple steps:

1. Click the cell in which you want to enter the formula and extend the selection to the range that will contain the copied formula. A multiple selection is also possible.

2. Enter the formula in the active cell.

3. Press Ctrl+Enter after you enter the formula.

The selected range is filled with the formula.

Entering Formulas in Several Worksheets

In workbooks with similar sheets, you can enter formulas (or other content) in several worksheets at the same time. You just have to select (group) the desired sheets:

1. Hold down the Ctrl key and select the sheet tabs of the sheets you want to group. Group mode is indicated in the title bar of the window.

> **Tip**
> To select successive sheets, click the first sheet, hold down the Shift key, and click the last sheet. To select noncontiguous sheets, hold down the Ctrl key and click the sheets you want.

2. Enter the formula (or formulas) in the active sheet.

3. To ungroup, select a sheet or use the Ungroup command to ungroup all the sheets, right-click a selected sheet tab to display a shortcut menu.

The formula (or formulas) are written in all selected sheets. You can also combine the method shown previously for entering formulas in several rows with the method for entering formulas in several sheets.

Selecting Formula Cells

Excel highlights all cells containing formulas if you perform the following steps:

1. Press the F5 key or Ctrl+G.

2. Click the Special button.

3. In the Go To Special dialog box, select the Formulas option. You can then identify the formulas that will be selected.

4. Click the OK button.

If you have to work through all selected formula cells, press the Tab key to switch between the selected cells. You can also edit a formula in the formula bar. Press Shift+Tab to move in the opposite direction.

To unselect but still work through all formulas, assign a color to the selected cells (you can remove the color later).

Determining Which Cells Are Referenced in a Formula

To see which cells a formula refers to, press the F2 key. This opens the cell for editing and shows the cell references in different colors (see Figure 3-17).

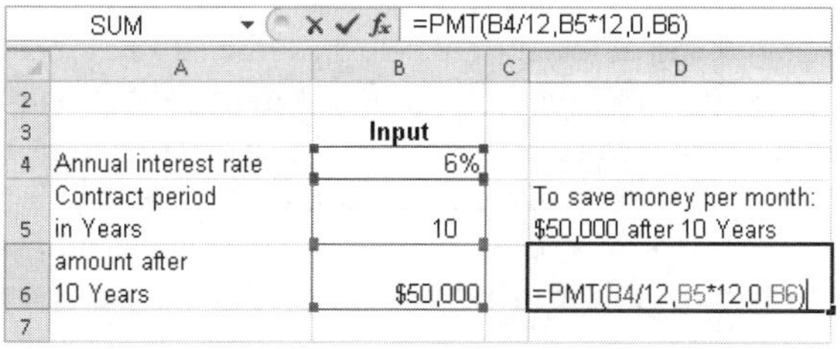

Figure 3-17 If you press the F2 key to open the cell for editing, all references in the formula and on the sheet are shown in different colors.

Copying and Moving Formulas

In large tables, entering each formula requires a lot of effort. If you know how to copy formulas you can reduce the amount of work required to enter formulas. The same applies to corrections. If you know how to move formulas and values, you can quickly rearrange your table.

You must always select the range you want to copy or move. As with all Windows applications, you have two options for making a selection:

● You can use the keyboard or a command.

● You can use the mouse.

Using the Keyboard to Make a Selection

The most comfortable way to make a selection is by using the mouse. However, sometimes it makes sense to make a selection by pressing a key combination. Table 3-6 lists several key combinations you can press to make a selection.

Table 3-6 Making a Selection by Using the Keyboard

Selection	Key Combination
Current row	Shift+Spacebar
Current column	Ctrl+Spacebar
Current data block	Ctrl+Shift+*
From the current cell in any direction	Shift+arrow key
From the current cell to the end of the data block	Shift+Ctrl+End
From the current cell to the beginning of the data block	Shift+Ctrl+Home
Entire sheet	Ctrl+Shift+Spacebar or Ctrl+A

To extend the selection beginning at the current cell, press the F8 key. Excel switches into "extension mode," as indicated by EXT (in Excel 2003) or Extend Selection (in Excel 2010) in the status bar. In this mode, you can use the arrow keys to extend the selection in any direction. To disable extension mode, press F8 again or press the Esc key.

Using the Mouse to Make a Selection

To select a cell range, drag over the range you want to select. Table 3-7 lists useful approaches for making a selection with the mouse.

Table 3-7 Making a Selection by Using the Mouse

Selection	Action
A single cell	Click in the cell.
A column	Click the column heading.
Several columns	Drag over the column headings.
A row	Click the row heading.
Several rows	Drag over the row headings.
A connected cell range	Drag diagonally from the first to the last cell.
Unconnected cells or noncontiguous cell ranges	Hold down the Ctrl key and click additional cells or cell ranges, columns, or rows.
All cells in the worksheet	Click the button in the upper-left corner of the worksheet window.

You have to select the entire table to make a global change (for example, to change the font).

> **Note**
> To move down or right in a selected cell range, press the Tab key. To move up or left, press Shift+Tab.

Moving Formula Cells

To move a formula cell, you actually delete the formula in the original cell and paste it into another cell. There are two approaches to do this:

- In Excel 2003, select the Cut and Paste options on the Edit menu or click the corresponding buttons on the toolbar. In Excel 2007 and Excel 2010, click the buttons in the Clipboard group on the Home tab.

- Move a formula by using the mouse.

Using the Clipboard to Move a Formula Cell

To move a formula cell to another location within a table, perform the following steps:

1. Select the cell or cells you want to move.

2. Click the Cut button in the Clipboard group on the Home tab or press Ctrl+X.

3. Select the target cell. If you move a cell range, the target cell is the upper-left cell of the new range.

4. Click the Paste button in the Clipboard group on the Home tab or press Ctrl+V.

After you have moved the cell, check whether the formula or the result has changed. The result is displayed in the table and should match the previous result. To review the formula, click the cell you moved and check the formula bar. The cell content as well as the formula stay the same if a cell is moved.

Using the Mouse to Move a Formula Cell

If you don't want to use the Clipboard, you can move a formula cell by using the mouse. With the mouse, you can move cells easily to another location within the table. Do the following:

1. Select the cell or cells you want to move.

2. Move the mouse pointer to the border of the selection. The pointer changes to a white arrow with a black double arrow (see Figure 3-18).

3. Drag the cell or cells to the new location.

Price	Quantity	Total
$ 22.55	4	$ 90.20
$ 33.50	3	$ 100.50
$ 17.56	5	$ 87.80

Figure 3-18 The mouse pointer changes to a double arrow.

While being dragged, the moved range is highlighted in gray. Next to the highlighted range, a tooltip shows the cell reference or the cell range to which the highlighted range will be moved when you release the mouse button.

If you move the cells into a range already containing data or formulas, Excel asks if you want to overwrite the content of the target range. This ensures that no data will be lost if cells are moved accidentally.

Copying Formula Cells

If you copy data, the data remains in the initial location and a copy of the data is pasted at another location. When copying formulas, it is important to know whether the formula references are relative, absolute, or mixed (see the section "References in Formulas" earlier in this chapter).

The following approaches are available for copying formulas:

- Selecting the Copy and Paste options in the Clipboard group on the Home tab

- Copying the formula cell by using the mouse

- Dragging the fill handle of the formula cell

The results of the first two approaches are the same.

Using the Clipboard to Copy

To copy by using the a key combination or the buttons on the Home tab, perform the next set of steps:

1. Select the cell or cells you want to copy.

2. Click the Copy button in the Clipboard group on the Home tab, or press Ctrl+C.

3. Select the target cell or cells. If you copy a cell range, the target cell is the upper-left cell of the range.

4. Click the Paste button in the Clipboard group on the Home tab, or press Ctrl+V.

> **Note**
>
> To paste the copied cells again, repeat step 4. This also applies to pasting by using the Cut command in the Clipboard group on the Home tab.
>
> If you press Enter to finish the move or copy operation, Excel deletes the content of the Clipboard, and the data cannot be moved or copied again from the Clipboard.

Using the Mouse to Copy

To copy cells by using the mouse, you basically do the same as you would to move cells with the mouse. Perform the following steps:

1. Select the cell or cells you want to copy.

2. Move the mouse pointer to the border of the selection. The pointer changes to a white arrow with a black double arrow.

3. Press the Ctrl key. The double arrow is replaced by a plus sign (see Figure 3-19).

4. Holding down the Ctrl key, drag the cell or cells to the new location. Release the mouse button and then the Ctrl key.

Price	Quantity	Total
$ 22.55	4	$ 90.20
$ 33.50	3	$ 100.50
$ 17.56	5	$ 87.80

Figure 3-19 The mouse pointer changes to an arrow with a plus sign.

Make sure you release the mouse button first and then the Ctrl key. If you release the Ctrl key first, the copy command is canceled and the cell content is moved.

Chapter 3

Click the copied cells and review the cell content in the formula bar to check whether the content has changed. For a better understanding, see the next section.

In Figure 3-20, the formula in cell D4 was copied to several different locations. Remembering the section "Relative References" earlier in this chapter, ask yourself the following questions: What calculation is related to the original cell (cell D4 in Figure 3-20)? Which cells, starting at cell D4, should be multiplied? What does the calculation look like after the cells are copied?

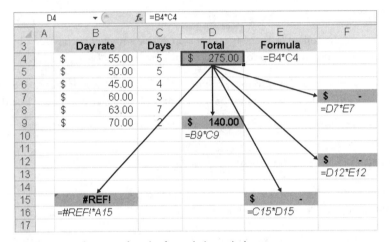

Figure 3-20 Changes after the formula is copied.

The calculation in cell D4 could read like this: "Multiply the two adjacent cells on the left." This calculation was copied exactly to all other cells:

- In cells E15, F7, and F12, the result is 0 because the two adjacent cells on the left are empty.

- In cell B15, the first cell reference generates the error message #REF!, which is returned by the formula as the final value. The referenced cell B4 cannot be transformed when you copy the formula two columns to the left.

- Only the result in cell D9 makes sense, because the two adjacent cells contain values that can be multiplied.

In other words: The cell references changed in relation to their locations, but the initial calculation—embedded in the formula—remains the same at all locations.

As you already know, a cell reference with these properties is called a relative reference. If you want the copied formulas to anchor on particular cells, you have to use absolute or mixed cell references.

Using the Fill Function to Copy

The Fill function in Excel offers several possibilities for copying formulas quickly and accurately.

The Fill Menu Command in Excel 2003   The Edit/Fill menu command achieves good results. Do the following:

1. Click the cell containing the formula you want to copy, and extend the selection in any direction (down, up, right, or left).

2. In Excel 2003, select the Edit/Fill menu option and select a fill direction. In the case shown in Figure 3-21, you would have to select Down.

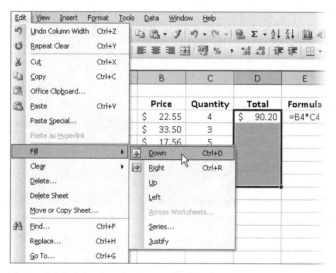

Figure 3-21 Selecting the Down fill direction.

In Excel 2007 and Excel 2010, only a few clicks are necessary to select the fill direction: Select the direction on the Fill list in the Edit group on the Home tab (see Figure 3-22).

Tip
For the two most commonly used fill directions, you can press the following key combinations: Ctrl+D for down and Ctrl+R for right.

Figure 3-22 The Fill list in the Edit group on the Home tab of Excel 2007 and Excel 2010.

Using the Mouse to Fill Cells

Using the mouse is probably the easiest and most commonly used approach for filling cells. In the lower-right corner of the active cell or of a selected range is the *fill handle*. If you point to the fill handle, the mouse pointer changes into a black plus sign. Drag the fill handle over the range into which you want to copy the formula.

If you drag over the cell (or cells) containing the formula, the cell is highlighted in gray. If you release the mouse button at this point, the content of the gray cell is deleted. If this happens, click the Undo button on the toolbar or in the Quick Access Toolbar (Excel 2007 and Excel 2010), or press Ctrl+Z.

Filling with a Double-Click

The smartest way to fill cells is to double-click. However, this approach has the following restrictions:

- Cells can be filled only from the top down.

- The fill range follows the data in the column to the left and fills down as far as data is displayed. (Note, however, that if columns are hidden, the fill range will follow the data in the column that is visible to the left of the fill range.)

- Any existing data or formulas in the fill range may be overwritten without warning.

To fill adjacent cells with a double-click, perform the following steps:

1. Select the cell that contains the formula you want to copy.

2. Point to the fill handle until the mouse pointer changes into a plus sign.

3. Double-click to fill the range with the formula.

Converting Formula Results into Fixed Values

There are many occasions when you may want to fix your data. For example, you might need to archive a snapshot of the results and want to avoid recalculation, or you might want to avoid having data linked back to other workbooks.

To convert results to fixed values, you use the right mouse button:

1.   Select the cells containing formulas or connections.

2.   Right-click the border of the selected cells and drag the selection one column to the right and then back again.

3.   On the shortcut menu, select Copy Here As Values Only.

Or use the Copy and Paste functions:

1.   Select the cells containing formulas or connections.

2.   Select the Edit/Copy option or press Ctrl+C.

3.   Select the Edit/Paste Special option (Excel 2003) or Paste/Paste Special in the Clipboard group on the Home tab (Excel 2007 and Excel 2010).

4.   Select the Values option in the Paste Special dialog box and click OK. Alternatively, you can select Values (Excel 2003) or Paste Values (Excel 2007 and Excel 2010) on the Paste list on the toolbar. Excel 2010 provides more options for pasting values (see Figure 3-23).

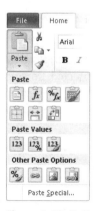

Figure 3-23 Options for pasting values in Excel 2010.

Chapter 3

> **Tip**
> Take a closer look at the Paste Special dialog box, and try the other options. One of these options is explained in the next section. You have many possibilities for making your work easier—use them!

Converting Existing Values

Assume that you have a table of readings in meters that you want to convert to feet. Follow these steps:

1. Enter the conversion factor **3.2808399** into any cell, and press the Enter key.

2. Select the cell containing the conversion factor.

3. Press Ctrl+C.

4. Select the range containing the readings in meters.

5. Select the Edit/Paste Special option (Excel 2003) or Paste Special on the Paste list (Excel 2007 and Excel 2010).

6. Select the Divide option, and click OK.

Protecting Formulas

To prevent your formulas from being changed by other users, you can protect certain cell ranges or formula cells.

There are two points to remember when protecting cells. First, all cells are locked by default. Second, the lock is activated only when the sheet is protected. Common practice is to leave all cells protected and unlock only those in which you want users to enter information.

To do this, perform the following steps:

1. Select the cell range in which you will allow users to enter information.

2. Right-click the selected range, and select the Format Cells option.

3. Click the Protection tab, and clear the Locked check box. Click OK.

4. On the Tools menu, select Protection/Protect Sheet (Excel 2003), or click the Protect Sheet icon on the Review tab (Excel 2007 and Excel 2010).

5.   Create a password if you want to add a further layer of protection.

6.   Click OK to activate the sheet protection.

Now other users cannot enter information into any cells other than those that have been unlocked.

If you want to protect only a limited number of cells, start by selecting the entire sheet and unlocking the cells by using the Format Cells option. Then repeat the preceding steps to lock a selection of cells. Finally, protect the sheet.

Hiding Formulas

You can go one step further and ensure that the formulas in your formula cells are not displayed in the formula bar. To do this, perform the following steps:

1.   Select the cell range containing the formulas you want to protect.

2.   Right-click the selected range, and select the Format Cells option.

3.   Select the Hide check box on the Protection tab, and click OK.

4.   On the Tools menu, select Protection/Protect Sheet (Excel 2003), or click the Protect Sheet icon on the Review tab (Excel 2007 and Excel 2010).

5.   Create a password if you want to add further protection.

6.   Click OK to activate the sheet protection.

Regardless of whether the cell is locked, the formula is not displayed in the formula bar when the sheet is protected.

Specifying the Formula Calculation Type

You can specify when Excel should perform a calculation. You can find the options for this in Tools/Options on the Calculation tab (Excel 2003). In Excel 2007 and Excel 2010, use the buttons in the Calculation group on the Formulas tab (see Figure 3-24).

Figure 3-24 The three icons in the Calculation group on the Formulas tab of Excel 2007 and Excel 2010.

Chapter 3

The following options are available:

- **Automatic** Calculates all dependent formulas if a value, a formula, or a name changes. This is the default setting.

- **Automatic Except For Data Tables** Calculates all dependent formulas except data tables. To calculate data tables, click the Calculate Now button on the Formulas tab or press the F9 key.

- **Manual** Only calculates open workbooks if you press the F9 key or click the Calculate Now button on the Formulas tab. If you select Manual, Excel automatically activates the option to recalculate the workbook before saving.

All settings are available on the File tab, by choosing Options and clicking the Formulas tab. Figure 3-25 shows the calculation options in Excel 2007 and Excel 2010, which reduced the selection available from previous versions.

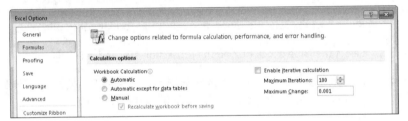

Figure 3-25 The calculation options in Excel 2007 and Excel 2010.

Analyzing Formulas

When you edit a formula, Edit mode shows all of the cells and cell ranges referenced in the formula, as well as their borders, in specific colors. This way you can easily create cell references.

To switch into Edit mode, double-click the formula cell or select the formula cell and press the F2 key.

Formula Auditing

You can use formula auditing to show the relationships between cells. To check which cells are used by a formula, enable formula auditing.

Until Excel 2007, this command was on the Tools menu and was called Formula Auditing. The descriptions in this book are for Excel 2002, Excel 2003, Excel 2007, and Excel 2010.

Formula auditing reduces the task to a few mouse clicks and shows the result (see Figure 3-26). Select the relevant formula cell and then the Tools/Formula Auditing/Trace Precedents option.

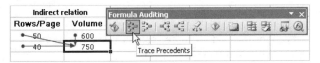

Figure 3-26 The Trace Precedents option shows the formula cell references.

Tracer arrows show the flow of values and formula results in a worksheet. This allows you to find and view precedents (cells referenced in a formula) and dependents (cells with references to other cells).

The Formula Auditing toolbar in Excel 2003 (shown in Figure 3-26) was replaced with the Formula Auditing group on the Formulas tab in Excel 2007 and Excel 2010 (see Figure 3-27).

Figure 3-27 The formula auditing functions in Excel 2007 and Excel 2010 are within easy reach.

INSIDE OUT   Displaying tracer arrows

To display the tracer arrows for formula audits, make sure that the following options are selected on the View tab in Tools/Options (Excel 2003): Enable the Show All or Show Placeholders option in the Objects group. If the Hide All option is selected, the tracer arrows are not displayed.

The same applies in Excel 2007 and Excel 2010 if you select the Nothing (Hide Objects) option instead of the All option on the Excel Options page on the Advanced tab, under the Display options for this workbook.

Chapter 3

Tracing the Data and Formula Flow

Assume that you want to find out which cells or cell results are included in the formula in a certain cell. The formula audit allows you to trace the flow of formulas and data. To do this, perform the following steps:

1. Select the start cell for the audit. This cell can include a formula, or a formula might refer to the cell or contain an error message.

2. In Excel 2003, select Formula Auditing from the Tools menu. In Excel 2007 and Excel 2010, select the Formulas tab to access the Formula Auditing options (shown earlier in Figure 3-27). The following options are available:

   ○ **Trace Precedents** The first time you select this option, you see traces to all cells directly referenced in the formula. Select the option again to trace the next precedents level.

   ○ **Trace Dependents** Select this option to display the traces to the cells that depend on the value or result in this cell. Select this option again to trace the next dependents level.

   ○ **Trace Error** If the selected cell contains an error message, you can trace the cell causing the error. The traces to cells with errors are displayed in red. If the selected cell cannot be used with this command, the program shows a corresponding message.

   ○ **Remove All Arrows (Excel 2007 and Excel 2010)** This command removes all previous traces.

If the tracer arrow points to a formula, the line is blue and the cell ranges used in the formula have blue borders (see Figure 3-28).

	A	B	C
10	**Investment profit calculation**		
11	Profit: $	185,000.00	
12	Person	Capital	Quota of profits
13	A	$ 124,000.00	$ 58,304.74
14	B	$ 85,700.00	$ 40,296.10
15	C	$ 183,750.00	$ 86,399.16
16	Total	$ 393,450.00	$ 185,000.00
17			

Figure 3-28 Traces to the precedents on two levels.

The tracer line to an error is red. If a trace includes several errors, the formula audit stops, and you can chose the next action.

Excel 2003, Excel 2007, and Excel 2010 all mark each error in the worksheet with a green triangle in the upper-left corner (if you didn't disable this option). If you select a cell with an error, the Caution symbol appears. The tooltip for this symbol shows the error message.

If a trace points to an external reference (for example, a table in the same workbook), the line is black.

The Formula Auditing Toolbar in Excel 2003

If you prefer to work with a toolbar instead of commands, select the Formula Auditing option on the Tools menu and click Show Formula Auditing Toolbar (see Figure 3-29).

Figure 3-29 The Formula Auditing toolbar.

The buttons on the Formula Auditing toolbar and their tooltips, from left to right, are listed in Table 3-8.

Table 3-8 **The Buttons on the Formula Auditing Toolbar**

Button	Action
Trace Error	Excel starts the error audit to show all errors and their causes (see Figure 3-30 in the next section).
Trace Precedents	The traces from the selected cell to the precedents are marked. To trace additional precedent levels, click the button again.
Remove Arrows To Precedents	The tracer arrows to the precedent level are removed. If several precedent levels were traced, you have to click this button for each level.
Trace Dependents	The tracer arrows point to all formulas with references to the selected cell. Click again to show tracer arrows at the next level.
Remove Arrows To Dependents	The tracer arrows to the dependent level are removed. If several dependent levels were traced, you have to click this button for each level.
Remove All Arrows	All tracer arrows in the active sheet are removed.

Button	Action
Trace Error	Click this button to point tracer arrows to an error source.
New Comment	This button corresponds to the Paste/Comment menu option.
Circle Invalid Data	Cells or data that don't meet the specified criteria are marked with a red oval.
Clear Validation Circles	Click this button to delete the validation circles. You can find more information about validation in Excel help.
Show Watch Window	You can watch the content of selected cells while searching for errors (see Figure 3-31 in the next section).
Evaluate Formula	Use this function to resolve formulas step by step. With this analysis process, you can quickly find errors.

> **Note**
>
> Note the following differences in Excel 2007 and Excel 2010:
>
> - The Circle Invalid Data and Clear Validation Circles options are available on the Data tab.
>
> - The New Comment option is available on the Review tab.

Troubleshooting: Example 1

In this example, the calculation results on a worksheet are not the expected results. You want to find out whether the data or the formulas contain errors. Select the error-checking option to start the validation. The dialog box for the first error found appears (see Figure 3-30). Select the next step.

Alternatively, select a cell that has a green triangle in its upper-left corner, and click the Caution symbol. Select the next step in the menu that appears.

Figure 3-30 The Error-Checking mode validates all formulas and data that contain errors.

Troubleshooting: Example 2

Here's another example: Several calculation steps based on each other don't return the expected result. You want to watch all intermediate steps. To do this, perform the following steps:

1. Click the Formula Auditing/Watch Window option. The Watch Window dialog box appears (see Figure 3-31).

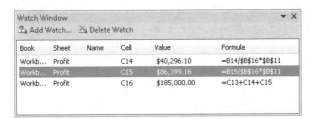

Figure 3-31 Observing the content of selected cells in the watch window.

2. Click the Add Watch button and select the first cell with an intermediate calculation. Click Add.

3. Do the same for all other cells with intermediate calculations.

4. Change the initial values. The Watch window shows the intermediate calculations.

If you don't need this window, close it. If you open the window later, the window displays the watched cells again.

The evaluation of formulas is useful in checking for errors, because Excel allows you to resolve the formula step by step.

Select a formula cell and then select Formula Validation/Formula Evaluation. In the dialog box that appears, click the Step In or Step Out button to resolve the formula (see Figure 3-32). This way you can also find out whether your formula includes errors in reasoning not found by Excel.

Figure 3-32 Formula evaluation shows how Excel resolves a formula.

> ## Note
>
> To control the behavior of the error-checking and formula auditing features, enable or disable the settings on the Error Checking tab (by using the Tools/Option menu option in Excel 2003), or select the Formula category in the Excel Options dialog box (click the Office button in Excel 2007 or the File tab in Excel 2010).
>
>

CHAPTER 4

Formulas and Functions

C hapter 3, "From Numbers to Formulas," explained the basics of editing formulas. However, you will quickly reach a point where the formulas for calculations get more complicated. An example is the summation in Figure 4-1. Do you really want to type such a long formula?

⊿	A	B	C	D	E
1					
2		**Store 1**	**Store 2**	**Store 3**	
3	January	$ 20,066.00	$ 10,792.00	$ 17,934.00	
4	February	$ 20,421.00	$ 10,445.00	$ 16,989.00	
5	March	$ 18,849.00	$ 11,130.00	$ 16,767.00	
6	April	$ 18,682.00	$ 10,865.00	$ 15,318.00	
7	May	$ 19,427.00	$ 10,181.00	$ 15,777.00	
8	June	$ 20,155.00	$ 10,032.00	$ 17,754.00	
9	July	$ 18,939.00	$ 10,290.00	$ 15,871.00	
10	August	$ 19,080.00	$ 10,162.00	$ 17,445.00	
11	September	$ 18,490.00	$ 11,111.00	$ 15,593.00	
12	October	$ 18,218.00	$ 11,130.00	$ 15,193.00	
13	November	$ 19,955.00	$ 10,912.00	$ 15,658.00	
14	December	$ 20,416.00	$ 11,663.00	$ 15,404.00	
15	**Total**	=B3+B4+B5+B6+B7+B8+B9+B10+B11+B12+B13+B14			

Figure 4-1 Who wants to enter such a long formula to add something up?

What if you need to add up not 12 but 100 or more numbers? At this point, you should learn about functions. In this specific case, the Microsoft Excel SUM() function simplifies the formula (see Figure 4-2). Chapter 16, "Mathematical and Trigonometry Functions," includes a detailed description of this function.

	A	B	C	D
1				
2		**Store 1**	**Store 2**	**Store 3**
3	January	$ 20,066.00	$ 10,792.00	$ 17,934.00
4	February	$ 20,421.00	$ 10,445.00	$ 16,989.00
5	March	$ 18,849.00	$ 11,130.00	$ 16,767.00
6	April	$ 18,682.00	$ 10,865.00	$ 15,318.00
7	May	$ 19,427.00	$ 10,181.00	$ 15,777.00
8	June	$ 20,155.00	$ 10,032.00	$ 17,754.00
9	July	$ 18,939.00	$ 10,290.00	$ 15,871.00
10	August	$ 19,080.00	$ 10,162.00	$ 17,445.00
11	September	$ 18,490.00	$ 11,111.00	$ 15,593.00
12	October	$ 18,218.00	$ 11,130.00	$ 15,193.00
13	November	$ 19,955.00	$ 10,912.00	$ 15,658.00
14	December	$ 20,416.00	$ 11,663.00	$ 15,404.00
15	**Total**	=SUM(B3:B14)		
16		SUM(**number1**, [number2], ...)		

Figure 4-2 Summation with an Excel function.

What Is a Worksheet Function?

Imagine a function as a complete computing program that can perform certain calculations. Each function has a unique name, which usually starts with a short description of the arithmetic problem solved by the function. Functions perform complex mathematical, statistical, technical, or logical calculations; search for certain information; and manipulate text.

Functions are mostly used in formulas, although you can use them in names and macros. (Names are covered in Chapter 5, "Functions in Special Operations," and macros are covered in Chapter 6, "Custom Functions.") Functions can be nested or used multiple times within formulas.

In Microsoft Office Excel 2003, a formula can include up to seven levels of nested functions. In Excel 2007 and Excel 2010, up to 64 levels are supported. The user—not the function—must ensure that the arithmetic correctness of the formula is maintained.

Functions not only make it easier to create formulas, they are also faster. You should always try to use a function instead of writing your own formulas. Functions can:

- Quickly perform calculations

- Use less space within a formula

- Reduce the risk of typing errors

To perform a calculation, functions require information (data), which is referred to as *arguments* or *parameters* in Excel. In Excel, the Help facility for functions provides comprehensive information on the number and type of required arguments, as well as guidance on the optional parameters.

The Syntax of a Function

The *syntax* of a function is the input rule and sets out the exact format required for the function. If you don't follow the syntax exactly, you get an error message from Excel.

The syntax of a function always follows these rules (see Figure 4-3):

- A function always starts with the function name. If the function is at the start of a formula, enter an equal sign first.

- The name is followed by a opening parenthesis. The opening parenthesis tells Excel where the arguments start. Spaces are illegal before and after a parenthesis.

- Arguments are entered after the opening parenthesis. The arguments have to match the data type required by the function. Some functions have optional arguments, which are not required to run the function. You will find more information in Excel Help.

- Arguments can be constants or formulas matching or calculating the required data type:

    - Arguments are separated by commas (,).

    - If an argument requires the Text data type, the text has to be in quotation marks. If an argument is a calculation, this calculation can also contain functions.

    - If you enter a function for an argument of a function, this function is said to be *nested*. In Excel 2003, a formula can include up to seven levels of nested functions. This was extended to 64 in Excel 2007.

- After you have entered all of the arguments, insert a closing parenthesis to complete the function.

Remember always to use parentheses in pairs. This means that for each opening parenthesis you have to enter a closing parenthesis.

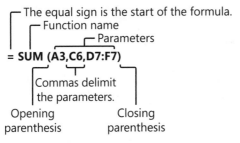

Figure 4-3 The general syntax for the SUM() function.

Arguments as Arithmetic Data in a Function

The data passed to a function for processing is referred to as *arguments*. In this book, in Excel Help, or in other reference books, the description of a function outlines the details of the required arguments, the optional arguments, and the data type:

- You can use any expression (a constant, a formula, and so on) as an argument as long as the expression (or its result) matches the required data type.

- In the Function Wizard (explained in more detail in the section titled "Using the Function Wizard" later in this chapter), the required arguments are bold. Optional arguments appear in normal type.

- Multiple arguments are separated by commas (,).

- Avoid spaces within functions, because they can cause errors. This is a general rule when writing formulas.

To pass arguments, you have to consider the required data type. Table 4-1 shows the data types used in Excel.

Table 4-1 **Data Types Used in Excel**

Data Type	Sample Function	Possible Input
Number	=SUM(number1,number2,...)	A number (constant); a cell reference; a formula with a number as its result
Text	=CONCATENATE(Text1,Text2,...)	Text in quotation marks; a cell reference
Cell reference	=ROW(reference)	A cell reference
Date/Time Value	=MONTH(number)	A number; a date in quotation marks; a cell reference
Logical	=AND(logical value1,logical value2,...)	Comparison output; TRUE; FALSE; a cell reference

You should also make sure that the data is passed efficiently. The faster the data is passed, the faster the function works. This is demonstrated in the following example.

Options for Passing Arguments

Consider the SUM() function in Figure 4-4. What options are available for passing arguments to this function?

Figure 4-4 These values are passed to the SUM() function.

Option 1: Values as Constants

You can pass the four values as constants, as shown in this example:

```
=SUM(27.5,20.0,12.5,30.0)
```

Even though the function calculates the correct result, it misses the point of a spreadsheet. If you change a value in the table, you also have to modify the function accordingly.

Option 2: Values as Cell References

You can pass each value as a cell reference, as in this example:

```
=SUM(B2,B3,B4,B5)
```

This function also returns the correct result. The input is correct but inconvenient, because the syntax could be shorter.

Option 3: Values as Addition Expressions

You can pass the four values as an addition formula, as in:

```
=SUM(B2+B3+B4+B5)
```

The function calculates the correct result again, because the sum of the four cells is a numeric value. However, this doesn't make any sense. If the addition is already performed in the parentheses, why do you still need the SUM() function? If constantly repeated, such meaningless arguments impact the calculation speed. (However, this example does show that an arithmetic expression can be passed as an argument.)

Option 4: Values as Range References

You can pass the four adjacent values as a range reference; for example:

```
=SUM(B2:B5)
```

This function returns the correct result. Because the values are passed in the shortest format, the function can work with only one argument (the range). This format provides the most concise and efficient approach.

Including Calculations in a Function

If a function requires several numeric values that result from a series of calculations, it is possible to include the calculations directly in the formula itself.

This arithmetic problem is explained in the example in Figure 4-5. The initial row calculations could be performed independently, and then the SUM() function used to combine the results. It is, however, possible to include the calculations directly in the SUM() function.

	A	B	C	D	E
1					
2		40	+	9	?
3		100	-	51	?
4		7	*	7	?
5		245	/	5	?
6				Sum	?
7					

Figure 4-5 The results of the four calculations must be added.

In this case, the formula looks like this:

```
=SUM(B2+D2,B3-D3,B4*D4,B5/D5)
```

For the SUM() function, the four arguments to be calculated can be entered in any order. In sum calculations, the order of the arguments doesn't matter. Remember: A function is always solved from the inside out.

But of course, the summation with the =SUM(E2:E5) formula would be faster and clearer if partial results were available in column E.

Entering Functions

Functions can be entered manually, but to do this you need to know the name of the function and the syntax for the arguments.

In Excel 2002, Excel 2003, Excel 2007, and Excel 2010, if you enter the name of the function, syntax-specific help is displayed to help you complete the parameters. Programmers who work with Microsoft Visual Basic for Applications are already familiar with this type of help, which displays a ScreenTip as soon as you enter the function name and the opening paren-thesis (see Figure 4-6). Each argument in turn is shown in bold as you enter the individual parameters.

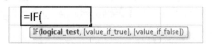

Figure 4-6 The ScreenTip for the IF() function.

If you are familiar with a function, you can probably enter the function faster without assis-tance. The section titled "Viewing Arguments," later in this chapter, explains how the syntax information is displayed in the versions of Excel prior to Excel 2002.

In Excel 2007 and Excel 2010 the support for entering formulas was further improved. If you start typing a formula, a list with suggestions appears (see Figure 4-7).

Figure 4-7 Excel 2007 and Excel 2010 suggest functions starting with "I" and display a description.

Chapter 4

INSIDE OUT Display ScreenTips

To display the ScreenTips, select the Show Function ScreenTips check box on the Gen-eral tab of the Excel Options dialog box in Excel 2003 or, in Excel 2007 or Excel 2010, in the Advanced/Display category in the Excel Options dialog box. The function list shown in Figure 4-7 appears if the Formula AutoComplete check box in the Formulas category (in the Working With Formulas area) in the Excel Options dialog box (Excel 2007 or Excel 2010) is selected. This option is enabled by default.

The names of functions are not case sensitive. Excel converts all letters in function names to uppercase.

Using the Function Wizard

The Function Wizard helps you select a function and enter the appropriate parameters. The Function Wizard button disappeared from the standard toolbar in Excel 2002 and was replaced by more options in the AutoSum menu, but the functionality is still available in Excel 2003, Excel 2007, and Excel 2010.

To start the Function Wizard, use one of the following methods:

- On the Insert menu, select Function (Excel 2003) or click the Insert Function button on the Formulas tab (Excel 2007 and Excel 2010).

- Click the Insert Function button in the edit box (see Figure 4-8).

- Select More Functions in the AutoSum list on the standard toolbar (Excel 2003) or on the Home tab (Excel 2007 and Excel 2010).

Figure 4-8 The Function Wizard can be started from the edit box.

The Function Wizard helps you enter functions and offers explanations of the arguments. During the entry process, you can terminate the creation of a function at any time by clicking the Cancel button in the Function Wizard or by pressing the Esc key.

Hands-On Practice

Assume that you want to calculate the monthly repayments for a loan of $100,000 over a period of ten years and at an interest rate of 7 percent. Of course you can use a function for this calculation (see Figure 4-9).

	A	B	C
1			
2		Loan	$ 100,000.00
3		Interest	7.0%
4		Credit period (years)	10
5			
6		Monthly payment	?
7			

Figure 4-9 Performing the interest calculation.

Follow these steps:

1. Select cell C6 to insert the function.

2. Click the Insert Function button in the edit box or select the Insert/Function menu command. The Function Wizard's Insert Function dialog box opens.

3. Click the function type you want in the Or Select A Category box. In this instance, click Financial (see Figure 4-10). When you select the category, the large number of available functions is filtered to the appropriate subset of options.

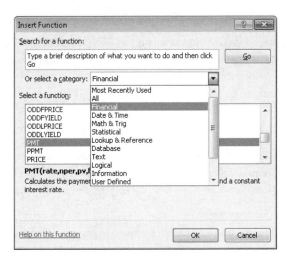

Figure 4-10 The Insert Function dialog box of the Function Wizard.

4. Select the PMT function in the Select A Function box. The general syntax for the function and a short description are displayed at the bottom of the dialog box. Click OK.

5. The next dialog box provides a text box for each function argument. The required arguments appear in bold, and the optional arguments appear in normal type (see Figure 4-11).

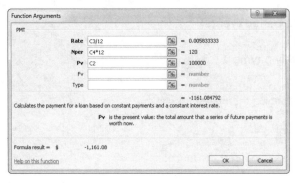

Figure 4-11 Dialog box to enter arguments.

6. Complete the text boxes according to Figure 4-11.

7. To add the function to the table, click OK. The formula is =PMT(C3/12,C4*12,C2). The result is a monthly installment of $1,161.08 displayed as a negative number.

8. To display the result as a positive number, set the present value, Pv, as **–C2**.

The interest is the annual percentage rate and has been divided by 12 to provide the monthly interest rate. In the *Nper* argument, you have to multiply the duration of 10 years by 12 to obtain the total number of monthly installments (120).

INSIDE OUT   Efficiently enter data in the Function Arguments dialog box

When you enter the function arguments in the Function Wizard text boxes, make sure that you use the required data type. Always use cell references rather than constants. To complete a cell reference in a text box, click in the cell on the spreadsheet or select a cell range.

If you click in a text box, an explanation for the current argument is displayed at the bottom of the dialog box.

To enter already-existing names for cells or cell ranges, enter the name or press F3 to insert the names from the Add Names dialog box.

Searching for Functions

A question frequently asked by Excel users is, "How can I find out if Excel provides a function for my problem?" This book was written to address this problem, but the Function Wizard can also offer some help.

Open the Function Wizard and enter your question in the Search For A Function box (see Figure 4-12).

Figure 4-12 The Function Wizard provides a search function.

A selection of suggested functions will be offered. Some of the suggestions will not be useful, but this facility provides a good starting point and searches for functions across all categories (see Figure 4-13).

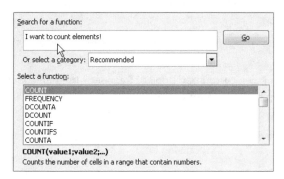

Figure 4-13 The result list in Excel 2003 includes functions for counting.

Entering Cell References

When you are entering function parameters in the Function Arguments dialog box, to the right of each text box is a small button with a red arrow (see Figure 4-14).

Figure 4-14 Text boxes for arguments include buttons for selecting references.

If you click this button, the rest of the dialog box is hidden, leaving just the text box and allowing more of the underlying spreadsheet to be viewed and selected. This feature allows you to complete cell references simply by selecting cells on the sheet.

All general selection rules apply: If you select a range, the range operator (:) is inserted, and for single cells (use the Ctrl key and click to select two or more single cells), the combination operator (,) is used. This method is not only easier than entering information manually but also helps to avoid errors.

To return to the full Function Wizard view, click the button at the right end of the text box again.

Getting Excel Help for Functions

The Function Wizard also allows quick access to the Excel Help facility. Excel Help explains each function with all arguments and provides detailed examples. The Help facility has improved considerably since Excel 2002, and although this section focuses on the Excel 2007 Help facility, help for functions in older versions of Excel can easily be accessed.

The Function Wizard displays tips for the selected function when you click the Help On This Function link in the lower-left corner of the dialog box, which opens the corresponding help topic (see Figure 4-15).

> **Tip**
> It is useful to create your own customized book of frequently used functions by printing off some of the help topics. To print a topic, click the Print button at the top of the help window.

Figure 4-15 The help text for the SUM() function in Excel 2007.

Specifying Nested Functions

When defining a function, you often need to specify a function as one of the arguments of the function. This is known as *nesting* functions.

For example, assume that you want to calculate the sine of an angle. The angle is specified in degrees (see Figure 4-16). Because the sine function in Excel expects a radian measure, you have to use the RADIANS function. This is a nested function because you use both functions.

⁄	A	B	C	D
1				
2		Angle	150 °	
3				
4		Sine	?	
5				

Figure 4-16 For the sine function, the degrees have to be converted into radians.

To enter a nested function, perform the following steps:

1. Select the cell in which you want to enter the formula (in this example, C4). Select the Insert Function command.

2. In the Or Select A Category list, click Math & Trig.

3. In the Select A Function list, click SIN, and then click OK.

4. To enter a function instead of an argument into a text box, click the arrow in the Name Box at the left end of the formula bar. For this example, select the RADIANS function (see Figure 4-17) to insert it into the SIN function argument text box.

> **Note**
>
> **If the list doesn't contain the function you need, select More Functions. The list shows only recently used functions, and you might not be able to select the RADIANS function directly.**

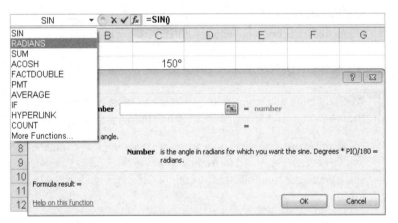

Figure 4-17 Enter the function as an argument.

5. The Function Wizard now shows the RADIANS function. You can view the status of the formula in the edit box (see Figure 4-18).

Figure 4-18 The nested functions in the edit box.

6.   Enter the cell reference **C2** as the argument for the RADIANS function. Click OK to exit.

The finished formula is

=SIN(RADIANS(C2))

For a 150° angle, the formula calculates the sine as 0.5.

> ## Important
>
> **Click OK in the second nested function to complete the formula entry. If you use nested functions and need to return to either function, click the name of the function in the formula bar, and then click the Insert Function button. The dialog box displays the arguments of the selected function for editing.**

Editing Formulas

You can manually edit a function in the formula bar. After you make a change, press the Enter key. To directly edit the function in the cell, double-click in the cell or press the F2 key.

You can also use the Function Wizard to edit formulas with functions. To do this, click in the cell containing the function and then click the Insert Function button in the formula bar or select the Insert/Function menu option. Change the arguments as required. Click OK to close the dialog box.

See Also Read the tips in Chapter 3, "From Numbers to Formulas," for information about entering, testing, and modifying formulas.

Tips and Tricks

To complete this chapter, you need a few more tips and tricks for entering functions.

Viewing Arguments

If you forgot to enter the arguments for a function, you can view them in the edit box. For example, to use the VLOOKUP() function, enter the equal sign, VLOOKUP, and an opening parenthesis. Press the Ctrl+Shift+A key combination to enter the arguments for the function in the formula bar.

To use the Function Wizard instead, press the Ctrl+A key combination. The Function Wizard starts up for the defined function.

> **Note**
>
> In Excel 2002, Excel 2003, Excel 2007, and Excel 2010, the arguments for a function are shown in a ScreenTip (see Figure 4-6 earlier in this chapter). For this to work, you have to select the Show Function ScreenTips check box in the Excel Options dialog box.

Using a Complex Formula in Several Workbooks

If you are constantly using complex functions, you can save the formulas by using the AutoCorrect option. The AutoCorrect feature is mostly used to correct common typing errors. You probably know this feature from Microsoft Word. Use the AutoCorrect feature to replace a string with a formula.

For example, assume that you often use the same table structure, and you want to calculate the sum for the 500 cells below the current cell without having to consider the reference. The following formula calculates the sum of the 500 cells below the active cell:

```
=SUM(INDIRECT(ADDRESS(ROW()+1,COLUMN(),4,TRUE),TRUE):INDIRECT(ADDRESS(ROW()+501,
COLUMN(),4,TRUE),TRUE))
```

To make this formula globally available, perform the following steps:

1. In Excel 2003, select the Tools/AutoCorrect menu option. In Excel 2007 or Excel 2010, select the Proofing category in the Excel Options dialog box and click AutoCorrect Options. Enter a string in the Replace box on the AutoCorrect tab.

INSIDE OUT   Use a unique string for AutoCorrect entries

Make sure you enter a unique string, because the AutoCorrect list is used by all Microsoft Office programs. You could enter a string containing a seldom used special character, as in _sum500.

2. Enter the formula shown just before these steps in the With box. Remember that you have to enter an equal sign in front of the string (see Figure 4-19).

3. Click Add and then OK.

Figure 4-19 Using AutoCorrect to streamline the entry of a formula.

Now you can just use the string _sum500 to reproduce the formula.

Chapter 4

Partial Calculations in Formulas

To analyze complex formulas or to search for errors, you can calculate parts of the formula, such as function arguments, in the form of references or nested function calls. The reference or the function call is replaced by a value. Perform the following steps:

1. Select the cell containing the formula, and press the F2 key or double-click the cell.

2. Select the part of the formula you want to calculate.

3. Press the F9 key. Excel replaces the selected part of the formula with the result.

This way you can solve a formula step by step and analyze the individual parts of the function.

Note

Be sure to cancel the formula changes when you are done by pressing the Esc key, because you don't want to change the formula permanently.

Functions in Special Operations

This chapter explains the use of worksheet functions and in particular how to integrate them with other features of Microsoft Excel to provide a very powerful tool with endless possibilities.

You will find out what role the functions can play together with:

- Names

- Conditional formatting

- Validation

> **Note**
>
> In this chapter, an effort is made to provide descriptions for the Excel versions up to Microsoft Office Excel 2003, as well as for Excel 2007 and Excel 2010, when the user interface changed dramatically. The first examples contain both commands and approaches that should provide enough information for you to assume the correct approach for the remaining examples.

Functions in Names

Using Excel functions in names can extend a simple naming facility and offer possibilities for specifying arguments in these functions. In Chapter 2, "Using Functions and PowerPivot," you learned about the different syntaxes for references. In addition to basic relative, mixed, and absolute cell references, the use of names for functions provides further possibilities.

A name can be used for a:

- Reference

- Constant

- Formula

Querying Current Information

You can use an information function (see Chapter 10, "Lookup and Reference Functions") to query the path, file name, and sheet name of the currently saved workbook. The workbook must be saved, otherwise an empty string ("") will be returned. The formula is:

```
=CELL("filename")
```

but the function returns all the information in a single string; for example:

```
C:\Excel-Functions\Chapter05\[Chapter05_Names.xls]Fct_Names
```

The text functions in Chapter 8, "Text and Data Functions," provide an approach to isolate the individual sections of information; this is often called *parsing*. This approach can be useful if you want to insert this information directly into the sheet rather than use the text modules &[Path], &[File], and &[Tab], which are available in the worksheet header or footer sections.

Querying the Path of the Current Workbook

The path of the workbook is at the beginning of the string and ends at the left bracket "[". To isolate the string to the left of this point, the following syntax is used:

```
=LEFT(CELL("filename"),FIND("[",CELL("filename"))-1)
```

The FIND() function calculates the position number of the left square bracket, and LEFT() determines the string up to the position of this bracket. The following steps describe how these functions are used:

1. In Excel 2007 and Excel 2010 on the Formulas tab, click the Define Name icon (see Figure 5-1). In Excel 2003, select the Insert/Names/Define menu option.

2. Enter the text **Path** in the Name text box (Excel 2007 and Excel 2010) or New Name text box (Excel 2003).

3. Enter the formula shown earlier in this section in the Refers To field, and click OK (Excel 2007 and Excel 2010) or Add (Excel 2003).

Figure 5-1 The Defined Names group on the Formulas tab in Excel 2007 and Excel 2010.

Figure 5-2 shows the New Name dialog box in Excel 2007 and Excel 2010, which is different from the old Define Name dialog box.

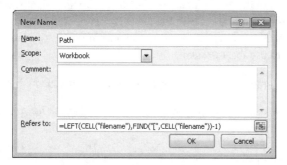

Figure 5-2 Entering a calculation for the name *Path*.

Querying the File Name of the Current Workbook

Extracting file names requires a little more effort. You need to query the string between the square brackets:

```
=MID(CELL("filename"),FIND("[",CELL("filename"))+1,FIND("]",CELL("filen
ame"))-(FIND("[",CELL("filename"))+1))
```

Identify the file name with the MID() function, using the FIND() function to locate the [character to determine the *start_char* parameter, and combine this with the FIND() function that locates the] character to determine the *num_chars* parameter. Here's how you use this formula:

1. Select the Define Names command and enter **File name** in the Name box.

2. Enter the formula just shown in the Refers To field, and click OK (or Add, in Excel 2003).

Chapter 5

Querying the Current Sheet Name

Isolate the current sheet name with the RIGHT() function or the MID() function. If you use the CELL() information function, make sure that the sheet name displays the tab label on each sheet by defining the optional second argument, which must contain a reference to any worksheet cell. Use the INDIRECT() function for this worksheet cell reference so that Excel doesn't attach the sheet name to references (for example, Table1!A1). Here we use the MID() function because it is shorter than using the alternative RIGHT() function:

```
=MID(CELL("filename",INDIRECT("A1")),FIND("]",CELL("filename",
INDIRECT("A1")))+1,255)
```

Identify the sheet name with the MID() function. The *Start_num* argument is set by determining the position of the right bracket with the FIND() function. Use the number 255 for the *num_chars* argument. This covers names up to the maximum allowed length. The following steps show how to use this formula:

1. Select the Define Names command. Enter **Sheet name** in the Name box.

2. Enter the formula just shown in the Refers To field, and click OK (or Add, for Excel 2003).

Excel 2007 introduced a new tool: the Name Manager (see Figure 5-3). This provides a much improved facility for defining, editing, and managing the names used in a workbook.

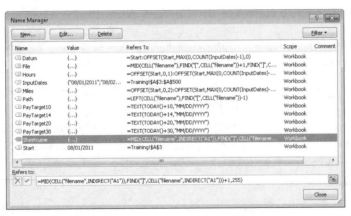

Figure 5-3 The Name Manager in Excel 2007 and Excel 2010 provides significantly better options for working with names.

Payment Targets as "Text Modules"

Assume that your company uses different payment targets for billing. These targets range from immediate payment to due dates in 10, 14, 20, or 30 days. To specify a payment target, you should enter a term that provides the date in a text format:

1. Select the Define Names option. Enter **PaymentTarget10** in the Name box. Then enter the formula

   `=TEXT(TODAY()+10,"MM/DD/YYYY")`

   in the Refers To field and click OK.

2. Repeat these steps to create the second name, **PaymentTarget14**. Enter the formula

   `=TEXT(TODAY()+14,"MM/DD/YYYY")`

   in the Refers to field and click OK.

3. Create the names **PaymentTarget20** and **PaymentTarget30** with the formulas

   `=TEXT(TODAY()+20,"MM/DD/YYYY")`

   and

   `=TEXT(TODAY()+30,"MM/DD/YYYY")`

You can now use the formula =″Please pay the invoice amount by ″ & PaymentTarget20″ to set the payment target in an invoice form by specifying the name—PaymentTarget10, PaymentTarget14, and so on—in the formula.

> ## Sample Files
>
> Use the Fct_Names worksheet in the Chapter05_Names.xls or Chapter05_Names.xlsx sample file. The sample files are found in the Chapter05 folde. For more information about the sample files, see the section titled "Using the Sample Files" on page xxiii.

Dynamic Range Names

The following example demonstrates how powerful names can be: Assume that you have a list to which entries are added on a daily or weekly basis. When you evaluate the list, you want the calculation to expand automatically to cover the additional entries. How can you achieve this?

Chapter 5

> **Note**
> Another example of using dynamic range names can be found in Chapter 2, in the section "Using Database Functions."

Assume that each day you enter fitness training data into a table. Column A contains the date, column B the time taken, and column C the distance covered (see Figure 5-4).

	A	B	C	D	E	F	G	H	I	J
1					List of training runs in 2011					
2	Date	Hours	Miles		No of training runs	18				
3	08/01/2011	1.8	9.0		Total hours	23.4				
4	08/02/2011	1.4	7.0		Total miles	117.0				
5	08/03/2011	1.2	6.0							
6	08/04/2011	1.8	9.0							
7	08/05/2011	0.5	2.5							
8	08/06/2011	1.4	7.0		Current ranges					
9	08/07/2011	1.0	5.0		Date	A3:A20				
10	08/08/2011	0.7	3.5		Hours	B3:B20				
11	08/09/2011	1.2	6.0		Miles	C3:C20				
12	08/10/2011	1.4	7.0							
13	08/11/2011	1.1	5.5		Used names on this sheet					
14	08/12/2011	1.4	7.0		Start	=Training!$A$3				
15	08/13/2011	0.7	3.5		Entry	=Training!$A$3:$A$500				
16	08/14/2011	1.8	9.0		InputDates	=Start:OFFSET(Start,MAX(0,COUNT(Entry)-1),0)				
17	08/15/2011	1.4	7.0		Hours	=OFFSET(Start,0,1):OFFSET(Start,MAX(0,COUNT(Entry)-1),1)				
18	08/16/2011	1.8	9.0		Miles	=OFFSET(Start,0,2):OFFSET(Start,MAX(0,COUNT(Entry)-1),2)				
19	08/17/2011	1.4	7.0							
20	08/18/2011	1.4	7.0							
21										

Figure 5-4 The names point to the extended range if new values are entered

The maximum number of rows in the worksheet will be 367 (including the title row and 366 leap year days) if each calendar year has its own worksheet. Create a name that will reference the maximum used range.

The solution lies in how the names are assigned:

1. Give the date range A3:A500 the name **Entry**.

2. Specify the name **Start** for cell A3.

3. Specify the name **InputDates**. Enter the following formula in Refers To:
   ```
   =start:OFFSET(start,MAX(0,COUNT(Entry)-1),0)
   ```

4. For the name **Hours**, use the reference
   ```
   =OFFSET(start,0,1):OFFSET(start,MAX(0,COUNT(Entry)-1),1)
   ```

5. For the name **Miles**, use the reference
   ```
   =OFFSET(start,0,2):OFFSET(start,MAX(0,COUNT(Entry)-1),2)
   ```

To identify the dynamic range, you can use the following function to return a reference that is offset from a specified reference:

$OFFSET(reference, rows, columns, height, width)$

In this case, the range starts in the row defined by the name Start, with the appropriate column selected by the Offset parameter. The MAX function identifies the number of numeric entries in the Entry range and is used in the OFFSET function to extend the range out to this point.

It is important to remember that the names *Hours* and *Miles* are based on the entries made in the Date column and thus this example relies on a date being entered for each line of information.

Note

The functions associated with names are not displayed in the Name box and in the Go To dialog box. To check these names, click in the Name box and enter the name, or press F5 to open the Go To dialog box, enter the name Hours or Miles in the Reference field, and click OK.

Add new entries to the data to the test the ranges. Press the F5 key to open the Go To dialog box and locate the reference again. You will notice that the name now points to the extended range, and the calculated values for sessions, time, and distance are based on the extended range.

Sample Files

Use the Training worksheet in the Chapter05_Names.xls or Chapter05_Names.xlsx sample file. The sample files are found in the Chapter05 folder. For more information about the sample files, see the section titled "Using the Sample Files" on page xxiii.

Please note that you can also use dynamic range names as a source for charts.

Functions for Conditional Formatting

Excel 2003 offered a range of conditional formatting options with up to three rules. This feature has been greatly improved in Excel 2007 and Excel 2010, and now offers an unlimited number of rules. Also, in addition to standard formatting, you now have a range of color scales, data bars, and icons to choose from. There is also a Rules Manager, offering a much improved way to define and manage the rules (see Figure 5-5).

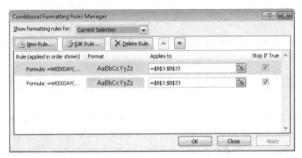

Figure 5-5 The Rules Manager for conditional formatting in Excel 2007 and Excel 2010.

In addition to simple data range selections, conditional formatting can also be applied to formulas.

In Excel 2003, select Formula Is in the left side of the Conditional Formatting dialog box (see Figure 5-6) and enter the formula in the field to the right. The formulas must return the value TRUE or FALSE. If the formula returns TRUE, the formatting is applied according to your settings.

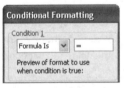

Figure 5-6 In Excel 2003, select Formula Is instead of Cell Value Is.

In Excel 2007 and Excel 2010, on the Home tab, click the Conditional Formatting button and select New Rule. Then select the Use A Formula To Determine Which Cells To Format rule type.

With the ability to use a formula to set conditional formatting, the range of functions available in Excel, and the unlimited number of rules in Excel 2007 and Excel 2010, the possibilities are endless. The following examples explore just a few of the capabilities.

> **Note**
>
> The Chapter05_CF.xlsx workbook in Excel 2007 and Excel 2010 file format, and the additional New in Excel 2007 and Excel 2010 sheet, show the new possibilities based on the temperature example in the section later in this chapter, "Emphasizing the Top Three Elements."

Highlighting Weekends in Color

Assume that you want to highlight Saturdays and Sundays as weekends in a column containing dates. Use the WEEKDAY() function in Excel to return the weekday for a date value (see Chapter 7, "Date and Time Functions," for more information) where a value of 1 corresponds to Sunday, and 7 corresponds to Saturday. This can be used to set a light green background for weekends by using the conditional formatting options.

Assume that the range B3:B33 contains the dates for one month. Select this date range, and then follow these steps:

For Excel 2007 and Excel 2010:

1. Select the date list and then select Conditional Formatting, New Rule, and Use A Formula To Determine Which Cells To Format.

2. Enter the following formula in the input field:

   `=WEEKDAY(B3)=1`

3. Click the Format button and, in the Format dialog box, select the Fill tab. Select light green as the color.

4. Confirm the format and the condition by clicking OK.

5. Repeat these steps to add another rule, but this time use the formula

   `=WEEKDAY(B3)=7`

   to highlight Saturdays.

For Excel 2003:

1. Select the date list and, on the Format menu, select Conditional Formatting.

2. In Condition 1, change the option Cell Value Is to Formula Is and enter the following formula in the input field:

    `=WEEKDAY(B3)=1`

3. Click the Format button and, on the template, select light green as the color.

4. Click Add to add a further condition, and repeat the previous steps, entering

    `=WEEKDAY(B3)=7`

    in the input field of Condition 2.

Using a combination of conditional formats and Excel functions is a useful way to visually highlight information. Figure 5-7 shows the completed dialog box and the result for the date list.

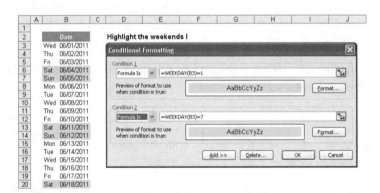

Figure 5-7 Using the WEEKDAY() function for conditional formatting in Excel 2003.

Another possibility is to combine the two conditions with an OR function if the same formatting is to be used in both instances. With the logical function OR() (see Chapter 9, "Logical Functions"), you need only one condition:

`=OR(WEEKDAY(B3)=1,WEEKDAY(B3)=7)`

This is particularly useful in Excel 2003, in which the number of conditions is limited.

Alternatively, the TEXT() function could be used to determine the day rather than WEEKDAY():

```
=OR(TEXT(B3,"ddd")="Sun",TEXT(B3,"ddd")="Sat")
```

In this formula, the "ddd" formatting command returns the first three letters of the weekday.

> **Sample Files**
>
> Use the Weekend worksheet in the Chapter05_CF.xls or Chapter05_CF.xlsx sample file. The sample files are found in the Chapter05 folder. For more information about the sample files, see the section titled "Using the Sample Files" on page xxiii.

Highlighting Weekends and Holidays

Color-highlighting weekends in calendar overviews is useful, but what about other days, such as national and cultural holidays? It also might be useful to automatically highlight days such as payment dates, deliveries, maintenance, and monthly or quarterly reports.

These dates can be added to a list to be considered for highlighting. In our example, besides processing weekends, two more requirements have to be met: holidays and other free days. This means that four conditions have to be checked:

- Saturdays

- Sundays

- Holidays

- Other free days

Start by setting up the Free Days list. Enter the information into the spreadsheet and name the list.

1. Select the range G27:G31 and click in the Name Box.

2. Enter the name **FreeDays**.

3. Press the Enter key.

Figure 5-8 on the next page shows the result. The highlighted range now has the name *FreeDays*.

Chapter 5

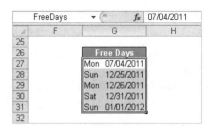

Figure 5-8 The list with the free days has the name *FreeDays*.

Using the MATCH() Function

To check whether a date is included in the Holidays range, you need to use the MATCH() function. This function has the following syntax:

```
=MATCH(Lookup_value, Lookup_array, Match_type)
```

The lookup_value is each cell of the date list. The lookup_array is the FreeDays range. Match_type specifies how Excel is to match the matrix values with the lookup_value. This example uses the type 0 for an exact match. Data in the lookup_array does not need to be sorted.

The MATCH() function returns a number for the position of the value found in the lookup_array. If the date is not contained on the FreeDays list, the error value #N/A is returned.

Finally, the ISNUMBER() function is used to determine whether a match has been found. If the MATCH function returns a numeric value, the date is included on the FreeDays list.

```
=ISNUMBER(MATCH(B3,FreeDays,0))
```

Add this condition to the conditional formatting already set to highlight weekend days. Assign the free days a red background color and a bold white font color in contrast

1. Select the date range and invoke conditional formatting.

2. Don't change the rules currently set for weekends. Click New Rule (or Add, in Excel 2003).

3. Select Formula Is again, and enter the formula
   ```
   =ISNUMBER(MATCH(B3,FreeDays,0))
   ```

4. Click the Format button, and set the background and font colors.

5. Click OK.

   The result is shown in Figure 5-9.

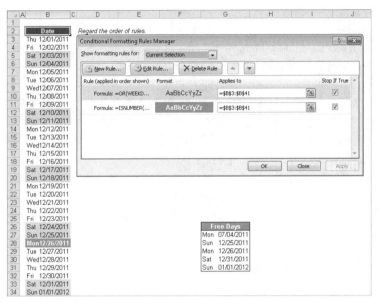

Figure 5-9 In addition to the weekends, the free days are highlighted.

Note that the order of the conditional formatting conditions is important. The formatting will be applied sequentially, so if the Free Days condition is checked first, the holiday format will be applied rather than the weekend format for a holiday that falls on a weekend. Reverse the conditions to give preference to the weekend formatting. In Excel 2007 and Excel 2010, with the Conditional Formatting Rules Manager, you can move rules up and down in order. In Excel 2003, each condition will need to be reset.

Sample Files

The Chapter05_CF.xls and Chapter05_CF.xlsx files contain this example, including the comparison between the different order of the conditions on the Holidays worksheet. The sample files are found in the Chapter05 folder. For more information about the sample files, see the section titled "Using the Sample Files" on page xxiii.

The example of the calendar overviews demonstrates some of the facilities available for highlighting information.

Chapter 5

> **Note**
>
> When you are editing the formula in the condition formula box, using the arrow keys may change the cell referencing instead of moving the mouse pointer along the edit box. To avoid this, activate the input field for the formula and press the F2 key to switch from Point mode to Edit mode. Now the arrow keys should work as expected.

Highlighting Identical Values

Sometimes it may be useful to highlight cells with identical content. Several functions are available to compare the content of cells, and conditional formatting can be used to highlight the results.

When Everything Is the Same

To format the cells in the range B3:B7 as light blue if all of the cells contain the same content (see Figure 5-10), perform the following steps:

1. Select the range B3:B7, select Conditional Formatting, and then select Use Formula.

2. For the condition, enter the formula

    `=COUNTIF($B$3:$B$7,$B$3)=COUNTA($B$3:$B$7)`

3. Click the Format button and select the light blue color format.

    The cells are formatted only if all of the cells contain the same content.

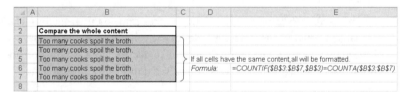

Figure 5-10 All of the cells need to have the same content for the format to be applied.

When Only One Matches

Let's take a look at a different scenario: All cells in the range B10:B14 have to be formatted if the range B11:B14 includes a cell that matches cell B10. Perform the following steps:

1. Select the range B11:B14, and then select Conditional Formatting and Use Formula.

2. Enter the following formula for the condition:

   `=COUNTIF($B$10:$B$14,$B$10)>1`

3. Click the Format button and select the format you want.

4. Confirm the format and the condition by clicking OK.

All cells are formatted if the range B11:B14 contains a cell with the same content as cell B10 (see Figure 5-11).

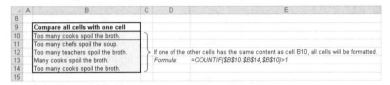

Figure 5-11 Only one cell has to match B10.

When Two or More Are the Same

The following example also compares the cells in a range. It formats those cells in the selected range that have identical contents. Perform the following steps:

1. Select the range B17:B21, and then select Conditional Formatting and Use Formula.

2. Enter the following formula for the condition:

   `=COUNTIF($B$17:$B$21,B17)>1`

3. Click the Format button and select the format you want.

4. Confirm the format and the condition by clicking OK.

Cells are only formatted if they match the content in cell B17. The COUNTIF function counts the number of matches and if it is greater than 1, formatting is applied (see Figure 5-12).

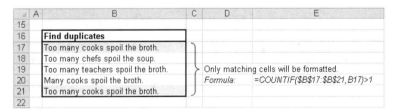

Figure 5-12 The duplicates are highlighted.

Sample Files

Use the Comparison worksheet in the Chapter05_CF.xls or Chapter05_CF.xlsx sample file. The sample files are found in the Chapter05 folder. For more information about the sample files, see the section titled "Using the Sample Files" on page xxiii.

Finding the Differences Between Tables on Different Worksheets

Sometimes you might have two versions of a table, and you want to compare them to see if there are any differences. Conditional formatting can help.

Assume that you have two versions of a worksheet containing accident statistics—Accident1 and Accident2. On the Accident2 worksheet, you want to highlight the cells that have different content from the matching cell or cells on Accident1.

This task should be simple, because you need to compare only the cell content. But there is a problem you need to consider. Try these steps:

1. Select the data area on the Accident1 worksheet.

2. Select Conditional Formatting and Use Formula.

3. Enter the formula

    `=A1<>Accident2!A1`

4. Select the desired format (via the Format button) and click OK to confirm the format.

You get an error message. Conditional formatting cannot handle external references to other worksheets or workbooks. The solution is to use a table function to calculate these references.

Note

Select a range big enough for comparison with conditional formatting to also highlight new or deleted records.

To use an external sheet reference for conditional formatting, do the following:

1. Select the Accident2 worksheet and select the data range.

2. Select the Conditional Formatting command and then Formula.

3. Enter the following formula as the condition:

    `=B4<>INDIRECT(ADDRESS(ROW(B4),COLUMN(B4), , ,"Accident1"))`

4. Click the Format button and select the format you want.

5. Confirm the format by clicking OK.

Now the cells in which Accident2 differs from Accident1 are visible (see Figure 5-13). The functionality of the INDIRECT(), CELL(), and COLUMN() functions is explained in Chapter 11, "Information Functions."

Note that the reference to the worksheet is entered as a string, which means that the formula is not automatically updated if the name of the worksheet changes. In this case, remember to modify the formula for conditional formatting.

	A	B	C	D	E	F	G	H
1	History of reported accidents from road traffic							
2								
3	Country	2005	2006	2007	2008	2009	2010	
4	A	847,919	802,800	485,202	188,577	152,628	232,426	
5	B	710,654	664,802	587,084	780,685	618,273	188,409	
6	CH	396,347	535,543	159,472	354,137	632,883	379,262	
7	D	558,784	695,357	633,524	559,837	548,559	631,978	
8	ES	352,400	652,646	216,647	749,896	358,148	834,914	
9	F	192,579	201,340	560,000	260,539	683,464	375,280	
10	GB	851,526	382,802	431,882	380,567	640,104	580,925	
11	I	387,490	239,883	226,285	524,396	424,771	109,108	
12	N	135,889	189,133	318,886	146,005	747,328	471,613	
13	NL	329,809	386,825	865,007	340,281	453,471	428,973	
14	PL	117,222	160,589	198,056	879,868	710,976	265,116	
15	RU	123,608	843,000	214,100	259,151	213,288	325,060	
16	S	552,060	274,995	425,132	841,377	676,841	309,595	
17	USA	610,516	279,053	829,739	743,316	567,779	763,007	
18								
19	This sheet shows the differences from the Accident1 worksheet by using conditional formatting							

Figure 5-13 The differences between the tables are highlighted with conditional formatting.

This solution also works with tables in different workbooks, but both workbooks must be open. You can use the following formula to apply conditional formatting to reference an external workbook:

`=B4<>INDIRECT(ADDRESS(ROW(B4),COLUMN(B4),TRUE,TRUE,"[Accident.xlsx]Accident 1"))`

Note that the workbook extension in Excel 2003 is .xls.

Sample Files

Use the Accident1 and Accident2 worksheets in the Chapter05_CF.xls or Chapter05_CF.xlsx sample file. The sample files are found in the Chapter05 folder. For more information about the sample files, see the section titled "Using the Sample Files" on page xxiii.

List Print Layout

If you print a list, it might be better to highlight every other row with a color rather than use borders (see Figure 5-14). But for large lists, it would be very tedious to format every other line manually, and a single sorting process would undo your work. Conditional formatting can help:

1. Select the list range without the titles.

2. Select Format/Conditional Formatting and then Formula Is (Excel 2003), or click the Conditional Formatting button on the Home tab, select New Rule, and then select Use Formula (Excel 2007 and Excel 2010).

3. For Condition 1 (Excel 2003) or Rules Description (Excel 2007 and Excel 2010), enter the formula

    `=MOD(ROW(),2)=1`

    to highlight the rows with uneven numbers.

4. Click the Format button and select the format you want.

5. Confirm the format by clicking OK.

	A	B	C
1	**Function**	**Description**	**Category**
2	AMORDEGRC	Returns the depreciation for each accounting period by using a depreciation coefficient	Financial functions
3	AMORLINC	Returns the depreciation for each accounting period	Financial functions
4	ACCRINT	Returns the accrued interest for a security that pays periodic interest	Financial functions
5	ACCRINTM	Returns the accrued interest for a security that pays interest at maturity	Financial functions
6	RECEIVED	Returns the amount received at maturity for a fully invested security	Financial functions
7	PV	Returns the present value of an investment	Financial functions
8	SYD	Returns the sum-of-years' digits depreciation of an asset for a specified period	Financial functions
9	DISC	Returns the discount rate for a security	Financial functions
10	DURATION	Returns the annual duration of a security with periodic interest payments	Financial functions
11	EFFECT	Returns the effective annual interest rate	Financial functions
12	DDB	Returns the depreciation of an asset for a specified period by using the double-declining ba	Financial functions
13	DB	Returns the depreciation of an asset for a specified period by using the fixed-declining bala	Financial functions
14	IRR	Returns the internal rate of return for a series of cash flows	Financial functions
15	ISPMT	Calculates the interest paid during a specific period of an investment	Financial functions
16	PPMT	Returns the payment on the principal for an investment for a given period	Financial functions
17	CUMPRINC	Returns the cumulative principal paid on a loan between two periods	Financial functions

Figure 5-14 The rows with uneven numbers are highlighted in gray.

The functionality of the MOD() function is described in Chapter 16, "Mathematical and Trigonometry Functions."

Even if the list is dynamic, the current formatting will always be applied to the same range. The formatting can be extended dynamically by combining two tests with the AND() function, as follows:

```
=AND(MOD(ROW(),2)=1,$A2<>"")
```

With this formula, conditional formatting also tests the first column of the list. If this column contains a value and the line number meets the condition, a reference line is displayed. To use this formula, select a larger range before you enter the condition. The formatting takes place only if this range is filled with data.

> **Sample Files**
>
> Use the Print Layout worksheet in the Chapter05_CF.xls or Chapter05_CF.xlsx sample file. The sample files are found in the Chapter05 folder. For more information about the sample files, see the section titled "Using the Sample Files" on page xxiii.

Emphasizing the Top Three Elements

Emphasizing the top elements should not be a problem with conditional formatting. Assume that you measured the temperatures of different places for a month. You now want to emphasize the three warmest and the three coldest temperatures (see Figure 5-15).

	A	B	C	D	E
1	Temperature measurement in September				
2					
3		**Berlin**	**London**	**New_York**	**Sydney**
4	09/01/2011	**49°F**	67°F	62°F	70°F
5	09/02/2011	64°F	59°F	52°F	65°F
6	09/03/2011	67°F	62°F	59°F	59°F
7	09/04/2011	68°F	**50°F**	62°F	**51°F**
8	09/05/2011	55°F	59°F	59°F	52°F
9	09/06/2011	67°F	64°F	**51°F**	63°F
10	09/07/2011	64°F	54°F	66°F	62°F
11	09/08/2011	**52°F**	67°F	52°F	54°F
12	09/09/2011	58°F	54°F	63°F	65°F
13	09/10/2011	63°F	66°F	53°F	66°F
14	09/11/2011	60°F	53°F	**51°F**	56°F
15	09/12/2011	66°F	70°F	63°F	52°F
16	09/13/2011	66°F	56°F	62°F	56°F
17	09/14/2011	67°F	52°F	57°F	52°F
18	09/15/2011	64°F	**51°F**	**48°F**	**51°F**

Figure 5-15 The warmest days are shown in red, and the coldest days are shown in blue.

Chapter 5

To perform this task, do the following:

1. Select the columns containing the temperatures, including titles (in this example, the range B3:E33). Press Ctrl+Shift+F3 to open the Create Names dialog box.

2. Select the Top Row check box to create the names from the top row, and click OK to confirm.

3. The data columns now have range names (the strings in the titles). These are required for the formulas for conditional formatting.

4. Select the range with the temperatures (in this example, the range B4:E33) and select Conditional Formatting. In the Conditional Formatting dialog box, select Formula as the first condition and enter the following formula:

   `=OR(B4=MAX(INDIRECT(B$3)),B4=LARGE(INDIRECT(B$3),2),B4=LARGE(INDIRECT(B$3),3))`

5. Click the Format button and select a format on the Font tab (for example, bold and red). Click OK to confirm.

6. In Excel 2003, click the Add button, and in Excel 2007 and Excel 2010, click New Rule. Enter the following formula for the second condition or rule:

   `=OR(B4=MIN(INDIRECT(B$3)),B4=SMALL(INDIRECT(B$3),2), B4=SMALL(INDIRECT(B$3),3))`

7. Click the Format button and choose a format on the Font tab (for example, bold and dark blue). Click OK to confirm.

The INDIRECT() function creates the range names from the titles, which allows you to create conditional formats for all of the columns in one step. Chapter 12, "Statistic Functions," describes the static MIN(), MAX(), SMALL(), and LARGE() functions in more detail.

Tip

In Excel 2007 and Excel 2010, you can use AutoFilter to filter for formats such as font or background color.

Sample Files

Use the Top3 worksheet in the Chapter05_CF.xls or Chapter05_CF.xlsx sample file. The sample files are found in the Chapter05 folder. For more information about the sample files, see the section titled "Using the Sample Files" on page xxiii.

Highlighting Cells Containing Spaces

Importing data from a text file can cause problems if the information contains blank characters, particularly if the cell content ends with a space, because this is not immediately obvious. Although you can search for spaces with the Find And Replace dialog box, it might not be possible to replace all spaces, because those in the center of a text string may be perfectly valid. The TRIM() function can be used to remove leading and trailing blanks, but a case-by-case review may be more useful. Conditional formatting can be used to highlight cells that contain blanks.

You can use conditional formatting for this purpose by applying the formulas shown in these examples:

- **=LEFT(C5,1)=CHAR(32)** Identifies a leading space. C5 is the upper-left corner of the selected area.

- **=RIGHT(D5,1)=CHAR(32)** Identifies a space at the end. D5 is the upper-left corner of the selected area.

- **=OR(LEFT(E5,1)=CHAR(32),RIGHT(E5,1)=CHAR(32))** Identifies a space either at the beginning or the end. E5 is the upper-left corner of the selected area.

- **=FIND(CHAR(32),F5)>0** Identifies any space. F5 is the upper-left corner of the selected area.

> ### Sample Files
> Use the Empty worksheet in the Chapter05_CF.xls or Chapter05_CF.xlsx sample file. The sample files are found in the Chapter05 folder. For more information about the sample files, see the section titled "Using the Sample Files" on page xxiii.

Navigating in Tables with Reference Lines

Often you might need to choose a value from a table at the intersection of a certain row and a certain column. In this example, we want to make sure that the installment amount and the number of partial payments can quickly be found (see Figure 5-16). On a piece of paper, you can use a ruler and pencil; on the screen, conditional formatting can help.

The PMT() table function calculates the installment amount in cell C9 with the following formula:

```
=PMT($C$5/12,C$8,-$B9)
```

Chapter 5

The combination of absolute (interest) and relative references (payment periods and cash value) allows you to copy the formula for the range C9:J28. Chapter 15, "Financial Functions," describes the math functions for finances, especially PMT(), in more detail.

	A	B	C	D	E	F	G	H	I	J
1										
2		**Credit Calculator**								
3		Amount	$15,000							
4		Duration (months)	36		Monthly rate		$ 451.25			
5		Interest rate	5.25%		Effective buy price		$ 16,244.97			
6										
7						Duration (months)				
8		Amount	4	8	12	18	24	36	48	60
9		$ 1,000.00	$ 252.74	$ 127.47	$ 85.72	$ 57.89	$ 43.98	$ 30.08	$ 23.14	$ 18.99
10		$ 2,000.00	$ 505.48	$ 254.95	$ 171.44	$ 115.79	$ 87.97	$ 60.17	$ 46.29	$ 37.97
11		$ 3,000.00	$ 758.22	$ 382.42	$ 257.17	$ 173.68	$ 131.95	$ 90.25	$ 69.43	$ 56.96
12		$ 4,000.00	$ 1,010.96	$ 509.89	$ 342.89	$ 231.57	$ 175.93	$ 120.33	$ 92.57	$ 75.94
13		$ 5,000.00	$ 1,263.70	$ 637.37	$ 428.61	$ 289.47	$ 219.92	$ 150.42	$ 115.71	$ 94.93
14		$ 6,000.00	$ 1,516.44	$ 764.84	$ 514.33	$ 347.36	$ 263.90	$ 180.50	$ 138.86	$ 113.92
15		$ 7,000.00	$ 1,769.18	$ 892.31	$ 600.05	$ 405.25	$ 307.88	$ 210.58	$ 162.00	$ 132.90
16		$ 8,000.00	$ 2,021.92	$ 1,019.79	$ 685.78	$ 463.15	$ 351.87	$ 240.67	$ 185.14	$ 151.89
17		$ 9,000.00	$ 2,274.66	$ 1,147.26	$ 771.50	$ 521.04	$ 395.85	$ 270.75	$ 208.28	$ 170.87
18		$ 10,000.00	$ 2,527.40	$ 1,274.73	$ 857.22	$ 578.93	$ 439.83	$ 300.83	$ 231.43	$ 189.86
19		$ 11,000.00	$ 2,780.14	$ 1,402.21	$ 942.94	$ 636.82	$ 483.82	$ 330.92	$ 254.57	$ 208.85
20		$ 12,000.00	$ 3,032.88	$ 1,529.68	$ 1,028.67	$ 694.72	$ 527.80	$ 361.00	$ 277.71	$ 227.83
21		$ 13,000.00	$ 3,285.62	$ 1,657.16	$ 1,114.39	$ 752.61	$ 571.78	$ 391.08	$ 300.86	$ 246.82
22		$ 14,000.00	$ 3,538.36	$ 1,784.63	$ 1,200.11	$ 810.50	$ 615.77	$ 421.17	$ 324.00	$ 265.80
23		$ 15,000.00	$ 3,791.11	$ 1,912.10	$ 1,285.83	$ 868.40	$ 659.75	$ 451.25	$ 347.14	$ 284.79
24		$ 16,000.00	$ 4,043.85	$ 2,039.58	$ 1,371.55	$ 926.29	$ 703.73	$ 481.33	$ 370.28	$ 303.78
25		$ 17,000.00	$ 4,296.59	$ 2,167.05	$ 1,457.28	$ 984.18	$ 747.72	$ 511.42	$ 393.43	$ 322.76
26		$ 18,000.00	$ 4,549.33	$ 2,294.52	$ 1,543.00	$ 1,042.08	$ 791.70	$ 541.50	$ 416.57	$ 341.75
27		$ 19,000.00	$ 4,802.07	$ 2,422.00	$ 1,628.72	$ 1,099.97	$ 835.69	$ 571.58	$ 439.71	$ 360.73
28		$ 20,000.00	$ 5,054.81	$ 2,549.47	$ 1,714.44	$ 1,157.86	$ 879.67	$ 601.67	$ 462.85	$ 379.72

Figure 5-16 The colored leader lines highlight the selection in the installment matrix.

Using data validation, you can easily handle the input of the amount in cell C3 and the input of the duration in cell C4. For the input of the amount, use the named range Amount (this name stands for the range B9:B28), and for the input of the duration, use the named range Months (this name stands for the range C8:J8). The section titled "Functions for Validation" on page 187 contains more examples of data validation.

Highlighting the Amount or Duration

To highlight the amount in column B:

1. Select the range B9:B28 and open the Conditional Formatting dialog box.

2. In the dialog box, select Formula.

3. Enter the formula

   =B9=$C$3

4. Select the format you want and click OK to close the two dialog boxes.

Next, select the duration values in row 8:

1. Select the range C8:J8.

2. Select Conditional Formatting. In the dialog box, select Formula.

3. Enter the formula

   `=C8=$C$4`

4. Select the format you want, and click OK to close the two dialog boxes.

Highlighting the Result Cell and the Leader Line

Displaying the leader line is a bit more difficult. Several conditions have to be checked, because all of the cells in the row and all of the cells in the column should be formatted. You configure these conditions with the OR() function. Both conditions have restrictions, because each time, the formatting should only be applied up to a certain column or row. In this case, two conditions are valid and linked with the AND() function.

To highlight the result cell and insert leader lines into the data range, do the following:

1. Select the date range C9:J28 and select Conditional Formatting.

2. Select Formula and enter the formula

   `=C9=$G$4`

3. Select the format for the result cell, and click the Add button (or, in Excel 2007 and Excel 2010, the New Rule button).

4. Select Formula and enter the formula

   `=OR(AND($B9=$C$3,C$8<=$C$4),AND(C$8=$C$4,$B9<=$C$3))`

5. Select the format for the selected area, and confirm the format by clicking OK.

The order of the conditions is important. If the cell also corresponds to the result in the header, it should be highlighted as the result cell. Because this cell also meets condition 2, the formatting would never be displayed if the condition was the second condition.

Figure 5-17 shows the formulas for the conditions in the Conditional Formatting dialog box in Excel 2003.

Chapter 5

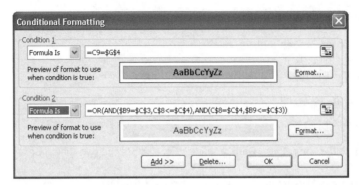

Figure 5-17 The first condition is for the result cell, and the second condition is for the leader lines.

> **Sample Files**
>
> Use the Credit worksheet in the Chapter05_CF.xls or Chapter05_CF.xlsx sample file. The sample files are found in the Chapter05 folder. For more information about the sample files, see the section titled "Using the Sample Files" on page xxiii.

Formatting Data Groups

Often large lists need to be sorted and separated. For example, a list containing information about several companies should be separated so that you can recognize associated groups quickly (see Figure 5-18). It is easy to do this manually, but can you do this dynamically, too?

	A	B	C	D	E	F
1	Company	City	Date	Country	Product nam	Sales
2	Alfreds Futterkiste	Berlin	01/05/10	Germany	Flatemysost	$ 1,961.00
3	Alfreds Futterkiste	Berlin	02/09/09	Germany	Mozzarella di	$ 1,729.00
4	Alfreds Futterkiste	Berlin	31/08/09	Germany	Röd Kaviar	$ 1,226.00
5	Alfreds Futterkiste	Berlin	03/10/09	Germany	Longlife Tofu	$ 1,012.00
6	Alfreds Futterkiste	Berlin	10/02/10	Germany	Rhönbräu	$ 1,950.00
7	Alfreds Futterkiste	Berlin	02/09/09	Germany	Lakkalikööri	$ 1,733.00
8	Alfreds Futterkiste	Berlin	02/11/09	Germany	Original	$ 1,871.00
9	Ana Trujillo Emparedados y	México D.F.	11/04/10	Mexico	Chai	$ -
10	Ana Trujillo Emparedados y	México D.F.	05/05/10	Mexico	Chang	$ 1,615.00
11	Ana Trujillo Emparedados y	México D.F.	18/03/10	Mexico	Aniseed Syrup	$ 1,771.00
12	Ana Trujillo Emparedados y	México D.F.	03/02/10	Mexico	Chef Anton's	$ 1,218.00
13	Antonio Moreno Taquería	México D.F.	03/07/10	Mexico	Röd Kaviar	$ 1,580.00
14	Antonio Moreno Taquería	México D.F.	15/11/09	Mexico	Longlife Tofu	$ 1,371.00
15	Antonio Moreno Taquería	México D.F.	08/11/09	Mexico	Rhönbräu	$ 1,637.00
16	Antonio Moreno Taquería	México D.F.	11/12/09	Mexico	Lakkalikööri	$ 1,604.00
17	Antonio Moreno Taquería	México D.F.	17/11/09	Mexico	Original	$ 1,369.00
18	Around the Horn	London	09/04/10	United Kingdom	Chai	$ -

Figure 5-18 Between each company, a separator line is inserted.

With conditional formatting, this task can be done dynamically:

1. Select the date range (the cells A2:F86 in this example).

2. Sort the data by company with the Data/Sort command.

3. Open the Conditional Formatting dialog box (New Rule).

4. In the dialog box, select Formula and enter the formula

   =$A2<>$A3

   in the formula field.

5. Click the Format button and select the bottom border on the Border tab.

6. Close the dialog boxes by clicking OK.

This formula checks whether the value in the line that follows is the same as the value in the current line. If it is different, a separator line is inserted between the groups.

Note
Even if you sort the data in descending order, the separator line is correctly inserted after a group change.

Sample Files
Use the Groups worksheet in the Chapter05_CF.xls or Chapter05_CF.xlsx sample file. The sample files are found in the Chapter05 folder. For more information about the sample files, see the section titled "Using the Sample Files" on page xxiii.

Formatting Subtotal Results

Suppose you have a list to which you have applied subtotals. Conditional formatting can be used to highlight the total lines (see Figure 5-19).

1 2 3		A	B	C
	1	**Agent**	**Date**	**Sales**
	2	Boldwin	09/27/2010	$ 22,611.00
	3	Boldwin	10/04/2010	$ 20,710.00
	4	Boldwin	10/16/2010	$ 20,063.00
	5	Boldwin	10/30/2010	$ 25,567.00
	6	**Boldwin Total**		$ **88,951.00**
	7	Fitzgerald	09/19/2010	$ 23,853.00
	8	Fitzgerald	10/12/2010	$ 17,592.00
	9	Fitzgerald	10/30/2010	$ 18,827.00
	10	**Fitzgerald Total**		$ **60,272.00**
	11	Jefferson	09/05/2010	$ 20,839.00
	12	Jefferson	10/21/2010	$ 10,382.00
	13	Jefferson	11/09/2010	$ 18,027.00
	14	**Jefferson Total**		$ **49,248.00**
	15	Myers	09/09/2010	$ 24,352.00
	16	Myers	10/04/2010	$ 14,817.00
	17	Myers	10/17/2010	$ 18,265.00
	18	**Myers Total**		$ **57,434.00**
	19	Miller	10/11/2010	$ 17,930.00
	20	Miller	12/21/2010	$ 13,415.00
	21	**Miller Total**		$ **31,345.00**
	22	Smith	10/30/2010	$ 27,933.00
	23	Smith	11/03/2010	$ 21,284.00
	24	Smith	12/15/2010	$ 13,287.00
	25	**Smith Total**		$ **62,504.00**
	26	Sussman	09/17/2010	$ 24,059.00
	27	Sussman	10/02/2010	$ 21,214.00
	28	Sussman	11/10/2010	$ 12,519.00
	29	**Sussman Total**		$ **57,792.00**
	30	**Grand Total**		$ **407,546.00**

Figure 5-19 The partial results are formatted in bold with a gray background and a border.

Perform the following steps to configure this format:

1. Use the Data/Sort command to sort the data by agent.

2. Select Data/Subtotal, and group the data by the Agent column.

3. Calculate the sum from Sales and click OK.

4. Select the data in the range A2:C30 and then select Conditional Formatting.

5. Enter the following formula:

    ```
    =ISNUMBER(FIND("Total",$A2))
    ```

    Note the mixed reference for cell $A2!

6. Specify the format, and confirm the formats by clicking OK.

> **Sample Files**
>
> Use the Subtotals worksheet in the Chapter05_CF.xls or Chapter05_CF.xlsx sample file.
> The sample files are found in the Chapter05 folder. For more information about the
> sample files, see the section titled "Using the Sample Files" on page xxiii.

Tips for Conditional Formatting in Excel 2003

In Excel 2007 and Excel 2010, the Conditional Formatting Rules Manager allows you to
handle and manage conditional formats in an intuitive and a comfortable way. This section
provides some hints for using conditional formats in Excel 2003 and previous versions.

Changing and Deleting Conditional Formats

To change a conditional format, select the cells you want to modify. Then open the Conditional Formatting dialog box and modify the setting for the individual conditions. Confirm
the format by clicking OK.

If you want to delete one or more conditions, select the corresponding cells and open the
Conditional Formatting dialog box. Click the Delete button to open the dialog box shown
in Figure 5-20. This dialog box contains three check boxes that you can select to indicate
the condition you want to delete. Click the OK button to delete the conditions according to
your settings.

Figure 5-20 The dialog box for deleting conditions.

Finding Cells Containing Conditional Formats

Sometimes you might not know exactly which cells or cell ranges on a worksheet or in a
workbook have conditional formats configured for them. In this case, Excel can help you
with a little-known option.

Chapter 5

1. Press the F5 key to open the Go To dialog box (or select the Edit/Go To menu item, or press Ctrl+G).

2. Click the Special button.

3. Select Conditional Formats and, under Data Validation, select All (see Figure 5-21).

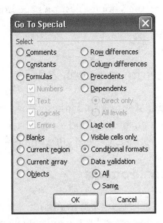

Figure 5-21 Finding cells that have conditional formats.

4. Start the operation by clicking OK.

With this approach, you can quickly delete or change the previously selected formats for all detected cells with conditional formats.

If you don't want to find all of the cells with conditional formats but only those cells with exactly the same conditional formats, select Same under Data Validation.

Using an Icon to Apply Conditional Formatting

You access the Conditional Format command in Excel 2003 from the menu options. To add this command as an icon to your toolbars, follow these steps. Steps 1–5 correspond to the number labels in Figure 5-22.

1. On the Tools menu, choose Customize. Click the Commands tab and select the Format category. On the right side of the list, you should see the Conditional Formatting command without an icon.

2. Drag the Conditional Formatting option onto one of the existing toolbars.

3. Right-click the new button to open the shortcut menu. Give the new button a new label, if required.

4. Click the Default Style menu option.

5. Click Change Button Image, and choose a picture.

6. Press the Enter key to confirm the changes.

7. Click Close in the Customize dialog box.

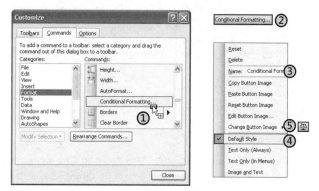

Figure 5-22 The new icon button gets a label.

Now you can click the new icon to quickly open the dialog box for conditional formatting.

Tips and Troubleshooting for Conditional Formatting

There are several reasons why a conditional format might not display correctly:

- If several conditions have been set, the conditions are applied sequentially, so a cell formatted by the first condition will never be considered for formatting by subsequent conditions.

- The other main source of confusion is determining exactly which ranges have been set to what conditions. A range may have been set to one scheme, and a second scheme may then have been set for a range that overlaps the first range. In this case, it is often simpler to remove all conditional formatting from a range and reset it.

- Finally, if formulas are used, check to make sure that the cell range has not been changed.

Functions for Validation

The validation features on the Data menu (Excel 2003) or the ribbon (Excel 2007 and Excel 2010) offer many possibilities for input control. Among other things, you can limit the input to certain data types and content. It gets really exciting if you use functions for validation—in other words, if you have calculated validation values.

Chapter 5

Cell Protection with Validation

The data validation options in Excel offer an invaluable facility for protecting data entry. This is different from the protection facilities that can limit changes to cells with password requirements. Data validation limits data input to a range of acceptable options. You can use data validation to protect cells by using the following technique. After you have entered text, values, and formulas into a worksheet, do the following:

1. Select the range of cells you want to protect.

2. Open the Data Validation dialog box.

3. Choose Custom in the Allow list, and enter this formula:

   `=LEN(A1)<1`

The entry is only valid if it is less than one character long. This prevents the cell from being accidentally directly overwritten. The data can still be removed with the Delete key, but this will help protect it from being overwritten.

Variable List Areas

You might want to specify lists for validation that are dependent on entries made in another cell. For example, assume that you want to configure validation for the selection of pay groups. The selection of the pay group is defined by the selection of the pay method (see Figure 5-23). The rules are listed in Table 5-1.

Table 5-1 **Pay Method Rules**

Pay Method	Pay Group From List
P (Piecework)	Pay
B (Bonus)	Pay
O (Overtime pay)	Pay
S (Salary)	Salary
SB (Salary with bonus)	Salary

As shown in Table 5-1, for piecework, bonus, and overtime pay, the selection is limited to the pay group Pay. For salaried staff, the selection is limited to the pay group Salary.

Start by typing in the list of Pay group options and Salary group options. Name the cell ranges **Pay** and **Salary**.

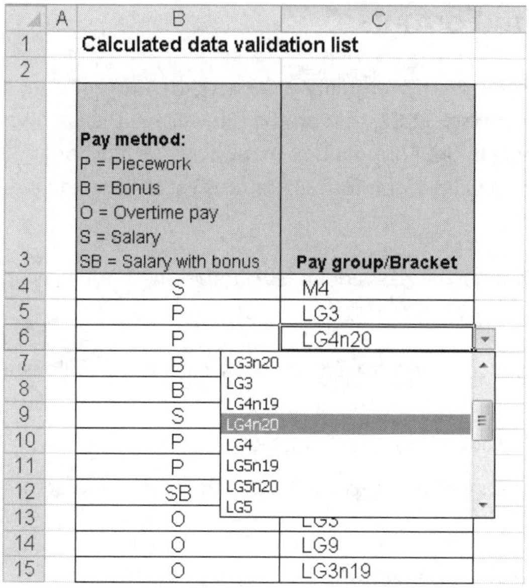

Figure 5-23 The selection list depends on the selected pay method.

The validation of the pay method in range B4:B15 is straightforward. You need only a fixed entry. In the Data Validation dialog box, click the Settings tab. On the Allow list, select List, and in the Source box, type these options:

`P,B,O,S,SB`

The validation for the pay group must consider the value in column B. On the Allow list, choose List, and enter the following formula as the source:

`=IF(OR($B4="S",$B4="SB"), Salary, Pay)`

This formula implements the rules (see Table 5-1, shown previously) and displays the applicable list depending on the selected pay method.

Sample Files

Use the Depending list worksheet in the Chapter05_DV.xls or Chapter05_DV.xlsx sample file. The sample files are found in the Chapter05 folder. For more information about the sample files, see the section titled "Using the Sample Files" on page xxiii.

Limiting Input with Formulas

If the list option does not provide the flexibility you need, the Custom option offers some further possibilities. When you select Custom on the Allow list in the Data Validation dialog box, you can enter a formula in the Formula box that will return TRUE or FALSE. If the formula returns TRUE, the data is valid. If the formula returns FALSE, the data is invalid and an error message is displayed.

When you use formulas, you have to consider a few limitations in the versions prior to Excel 2007:

- You cannot use references to external workbooks, such as the following (see Figure 5-24):

```
='C:\Functions\[Workbook.xlsx] Tab1'!$C$3=D7
```

  This is allowed in Excel 2007 and Excel 2010, but the external reference workbook must be open.

- You cannot use functions from add-ins. For instance, the NETWORKDAYS() function is only available in a table if the Analysis Functions add-in is installed. This function cannot be used directly for validation.

- You cannot use matrix constants.

- You cannot use formulas containing more than 255 characters.

Figure 5-24 The error message in Excel 2003 for using external functions and references.

To avoid these issues, enter the formula for validation in a table and use a reference to the cell containing the formula for validation.

Avoiding Duplicate Entries

A common problem with managing lists is duplicate entries. For example, maybe you have to avoid duplicate customer numbers in a customer list, or have to enter each date in a stock price list only once. This can be achieved by using a formula in the validation.

Assume that you want to make sure that each entry the range B2:B20 appears only once. If you try to enter a value more than once, an error message should be displayed.

To set the validation so that each entry can only be used once, do the following:

1. Select the test range B2:B20.

2. Open the Data Validation dialog box. On the Settings tab, select Custom on the Allow list.

3. Add the expression describing the allowed data in the Formula box. To avoid duplicate entries, use this formula (see Figure 5-25):

    `=COUNTIF($B$2:$B$20,B2)<=1`

4. Click the Error Alert tab and enter the error message.

5. Confirm your entry by clicking OK.

Figure 5-25 This formula checks how many entries exist in the input range.

Note that the search range is fixed at $B$2:$B$20, to define the range within which to find duplicates. The second argument of the COUNTIF() function is specified with a relative reference to point to a single input cell. If you look closely at how Excel enters the formula for validation for the range B2:B20, you will see the following:

- The data validation formula for Cell B2 is

    `=COUNTIF($B$2:$B$20;B2)<=1`

- The data validation formula for cell B3 is

    `=COUNTIF($B$2:$B$20;B3)<=1`

- The data validation formula for cell B4 is

    `=COUNTIF($B$2:$B$20;B4)<=1`

Chapter 5

The search range is always range B2:B20, whereas the Lookup_value always points to the active cell. For this validation, it doesn't matter if the entry consists of text or numbers. Each entry is checked independently of its data type.

> **Sample Files**
>
> Use the Duplicates worksheet in the Chapter05_DV.xls or Chapter05_DV.xlsx sample file. The sample files are found in the Chapter05 folder. For more information about the sample files, see the section titled "Using the Sample Files" on page xxiii.

Displaying Messages upon Field Completion

Formulas offer many possibilities. You can monitor a range and display a message after all data entry is complete.

Assume that you want to display a message if all fields in the range B2:B15 are filled out. To view the message when all fields are filled out, do the following:

1. Select the range B2:B15 and select Data/Validation or click the Data Validation button on the ribbon (in Excel 2007 and Excel 2010).

2. Choose Custom from the Allow list on the Settings tab, and enter this formula in the Formula field:

    `=COUNTBLANK($B$2:$B$15)>0`

    Pay attention to the absolute references.

3. Click the Error Alert tab, and select the Information style.

4. Enter a title, such as **Complete**, and enter the text in the Error Message field.

5. Confirm your entry by clicking OK.

When the last field is entered, a message appears telling the user that the data is complete.

> **Sample Files**
>
> Use the Completed worksheet in the Chapter05_DV.xls or Chapter05_DV.xlsx sample file. The sample files are found in the Chapter05 folder. For more information about the sample files, see the section "Using the Sample Files" on page xxiii.

Custom Functions

The numerous built-in math functions in Microsoft Excel allow you to perform complex calculations. But what happens if you cannot find the appropriate function or if you would rather use a simple syntax instead of a complicated formula? This chapter shows you the solution.

You could compare using Excel with driving a car. Until now you were comfortable sitting behind the wheel and using the built-in controls. Many controls were easily accessible on the dashboard, but others were hidden and could only be manipulated after opening a cover. However, everything you used was preinstalled at the factory.

If you want to use something that wasn't delivered with your car, you have to install it yourself. You have to get out, walk around your car, and open the hood. Then you need to use the proper tools to install the additional part. If you do it right, your car has one more valuable control.

Let's stay with this image: The driver's seat of your Excel program is the worksheet or chart view, and you surely recognize the menu and toolbar or ribbon as the dashboard—the logo is in the upper-left corner. But where is the engine compartment? The engine compartment (and here the comparison falls short) was sealed at the factory; you can enter only into an anteroom. However, you can access (nearly) all of the built-in controls. This anteroom is the Microsoft Visual Basic for Applications (VBA) development environment, also called the Visual Basic Editor: a module that was developed from the macro languages of previous Microsoft Office applications and the Basic programming language into a powerful tool. With this module you can develop all possible extensions for the various Office products, including Excel. The amount of knowledge about VBA you need depends on the difficulty of your project. The solution of mathematical problems does not require much VBA familiarity.

INSIDE OUT   Understand the value of using macros

A macro consists of a set of recorded or entered computer instructions that can be saved with a name and associated with a shortcut key combination. By using macros, you can simplify frequently recurring tasks with fixed instruction sequences. To run the instruction sequence, you only have to call the macro by its name or press the key combination. The macro will then run the instructions in the specified order.

In early macros, the instructions were simply executed one after the other. As computing advanced, macros were improved, and they can now respond to different conditions, system states, and user input. Entire macro languages were developed. However, each application had its own macro language. In the 1990s, the VBA programming language was introduced to unify these macro languages for the entire Office suite. Of course, application-specific differences still exist. For example, what would Microsoft Word do with the conditional formatting used in Excel?

Creating a Custom Function

With VBA you can automate worksheet and chart processes and also create custom functions. Functions generated with VBA procedures are similar to the built-in functions used in worksheets. A *function* consists of a unique name, parentheses, and usually one or more arguments separated by a comma. A function usually returns a single value as a result. The syntax is *Function Name(Arg1, Arg2,...)*. The number of arguments depends on the task and the use of the function. Custom functions are used from a cell in a worksheet, the same way you would use any built-in Excel function, such as SUM(*Number1, Number2,...*).

To create a function, you need the following:

- A function name

- The number of arguments and their names

- The algorithm to generate the result

Anyone can use the function with its name and arguments from the worksheet, but the algorithm is hidden from the user. However, a normal user is unlikely to care, as long as the function works properly.

A VBA procedure to create a function involves the following:

- The function is defined by the *function declaration*, which consists of the Function statement followed by the function's name, the arguments, and the Type statement.

- The result of a calculation or validation is assigned to the function name with the equal sign (=) operator.

- The end of the function is indicated by the End Function statement.

The part between the Function key word and the final End Function statement is called a *function block*. The remainder of this chapter presents a few examples to illustrate this process.

The AreaCircle() example explains the following:

- How to use the integrated development environment to create custom functions

- How to pass parameters as arguments to the function

- How to perform calculations with arguments and constants

- How to view the calculation result in a worksheet

By using the AreaQuad() example, you will learn the following:

- How to handle several arguments

- How to handle optional arguments

- How to evaluate conditions by using If statements

The AreaSect() function serves as an example for the following:

- How to use default values for missing optional arguments

- How to evaluate conditions by using If statements

By using the DigitSum() example, you will learn the following:

- How to use loops

- How to use VBA functions

- How to handle variables

Chapter 6

The AreaCircle1() example explains the following:

- How to use the built-in worksheet functions in custom functions

Finally, you learn how to use the Function Wizard and the Excel add-ins to create your own functions that you can use in your worksheets.

> **Note**
>
> For the following examples, you should open the Developer tab if you use Excel 2010 or Excel 2007. In Excel 2010, on the File tab, click Options and then Customize Ribbon. Select All Tabs or Main Tabs on the right, below the ribbon text. Select the Developer check box in the list. In Excel 2007, click the Office button and then Excel Options. Make sure that the Popular category is selected. Select the Show Developer Tab In The Ribbon check box. Click OK to display the Developer tab in the ribbon.

The AreaCircle() Function

The following nine steps include detailed instructions that explain how to create the custom function AreaCircle(*Radius*), which you can use to calculate the area of a circle. You have to pass the radius as a number, a calculated expression, or a cell reference as the argument for the function.

1. Press Alt+F11 to open the Visual Basic Editor (in all Excel versions).

   In Excel 2003 and previous versions, you can select Tools/Macro/Visual Basic Editor, and in the Excel 2010 and Excel 2007, you can click Visual Basic on the Developer tab.

   Like other typical windows in Windows, the Visual Basic Editor has a title bar, a menu bar, and toolbars. On the left side, you can see two subwindows: the Project Explorer window and the Properties window. The large gray area is the workspace, which is still empty (see Figure 6-1).

   You can see your Excel VBA projects in the Project Explorer (which is similar to the folder view in Windows Explorer). Each open Excel workbook has a folder with the name VBAProject followed by the name of the workbook in parentheses, such as Geometry.xlsm or Book1 if the workbook wasn't saved yet. By default, the Microsoft Excel Objects subfolder contains the objects ThisWorkbook, Sheet1, Sheet2, and

Sheet3. (The view of the Project Explorer in versions of Excel before Excel 2003 is slightly different.) The number and names of the subfolders vary depending on your project. In the next step, you will add a new subfolder named Modules that contains the object Module1.

The Properties window shows the properties and values of the selected VBA object. For the following practice, you don't need to understand the functionality of the Project Explorer and the Properties window.

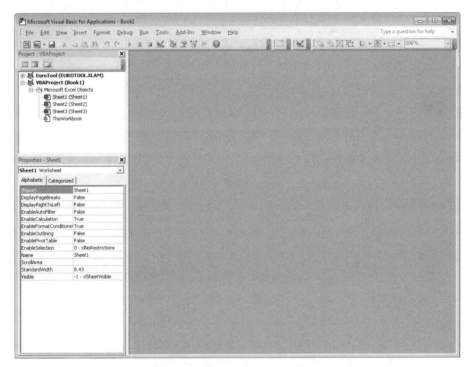

Figure 6-1 The Visual Basic Editor's opening screen (Excel 2010).

2. Select Insert/Module to prepare the workspace for the command code (see Figure 6-2).

If you are familiar with VBA, you know that there are other methods by which you can enter VBA procedures. These methods, however, are not suitable for custom functions.

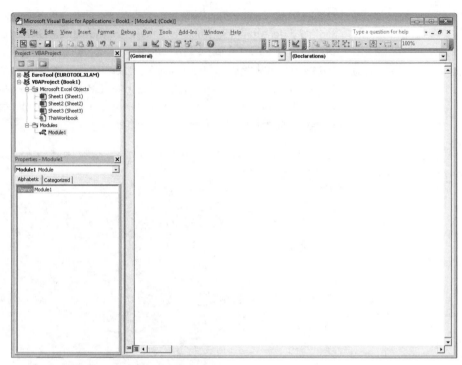

Figure 6-2 The Visual Basic Editor with a new but still empty module.

3. Select Insert/Procedure to open the dialog box shown in Figure 6-3, in which you can select the settings for the new function.

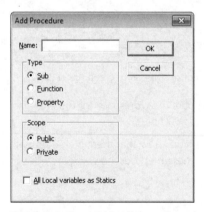

Figure 6-3 The Add Procedure dialog box with the default settings.

4. In the Add Procedure dialog box, enter **AreaCircle** in the Name field and select the Function option. You don't need to change any of the other options (see Figure 6-4).

Figure 6-4 The Add Procedure dialog box with the information required for the function declaration.

INSIDE OUT   Follow the function naming conventions

Functions follow several naming conventions that need to be observed. Function names cannot contain any of the Excel reserved characters, such as the math operators plus (+), minus (–), and division (/).

In the English version of Excel, you can use the following characters:

*   Letters a through z and A through Z

*   Digits 0 through 9

*   Underscore (_)

However, a function name must begin with a letter. Function names are not case-sensitive, and names only distinguished by uppercase or lowercase letters will not be recognized. Excel distinguishes function names from other names by the use of parentheses, so even if you are not using arguments, you must still use parentheses.

5. Click OK to add the procedure. You will see two lines in the workspace, with the cursor in an empty line. The Public keyword allows the module to be used in other modules. This is not necessary in this case, but for simplicity leave it there.

```
Public Function AreaCircle()
|
End Function
```

6. The AreaCircle function has a single argument, the radius. You need to declare the argument for this function in the procedure header. First enter the name of the argument. You can choose any name, but it should be descriptive, because this name will be displayed in the Function Wizard when you use the function in your Excel workbook. The argument type should also be declared. In this case, use **As Double**, indicating that the data type of the argument is Double, which is the standard number format of Excel worksheets. (This format, which is more precisely a floating-point number with double precision, is saved in 8 bytes in the range $-1.79769313486231 \times 10^{308}$ to $-4.94065645841247 \times 10^{-324}$ for negative values and $2.2250738585072 \times 10^{-308}$ to $1.79769313486232 \times 10^{308}$ for positive values.) Various other data types are available, including Variant, which will be explained later in this chapter.

```
Public Function AreaCircle(Radius As Double)
|
End Function
```

> **Tip Add a term to an expression**
>
> If you use keywords within your code, the Visual Basic Editor assists you by displaying relevant options as you type the code. Select a term in the list box and instead of pressing the Enter key, which will move to the next line and generate an error, press the Tab key or Ctrl+Enter to add the term to the expression. You can also ignore the list box and just keep typing.

7. It is also a good practice to assign a data type to the return value, which is the result of the function; otherwise, the Visual Basic Editor uses the Variant type by default. The Variant data type provides more flexible handling of data types but uses more memory and reduces the processing speed. Because our example uses only the standard Excel number format, enter **As Double** after the closing parenthesis.

```
Public Function AreaCircle(Radius As Double) As Double
|
End Function
```

8. Enter the actual procedure between these two lines; in other words, the executable code, as shown here.

```
Public Function AreaCircle(Radius As Double) As Double
AreaCircle = 3.14159265358979 * Radius ^ 2
End Function
```

9. The function calculates pi times the radius squared. Pi has been entered as a fixed constant. Press the Tab key to indent the code. This blocks and groups the lines of code and makes reading and understanding the procedure easier.

You have declared the custom AreaCircle() function with the argument Radius. To summarize:

● In step 4, you created the frame for the function block.

● In steps 5 through 7, you completed the function declaration.

● In step 8, you added the program code to the function. The function takes the number from the cell in the worksheet and assigns this to the Radius argument. It then passes the value over to the procedure, in which the area of the circle is calculated by the program code. The result is assigned to the function name with the equal sign. When you use this function name in the worksheet, the result is inserted into the cell by the program code and can be used for other operations. The function can be used repeatedly from anywhere in the workbook.

● You entered pi as a fixed number. We will deal with another possibility later in the AreaCircle1() example.

The completed AreaCircle() function appears in in the Visual Basic Editor as shown in Figure 6-5.

Tip   Use the apostrophe to indicate a comment

If you enter an apostrophe at any point in a line of code, the text that follows is considered to be a comment and is ignored by the Visual Basic Editor in terms of processing. You can enter comments to explain a particular code section.

Note that the text between the apostrophe and the end of the statement line should not include any executable expressions.

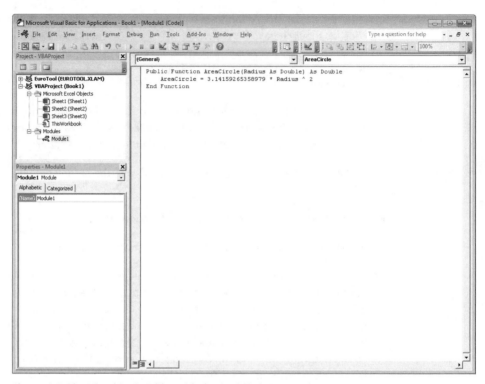

Figure 6-5 The Visual Basic Editor with the AreaCircle() procedure.

You probably want to know whether this function works. To test the function, switch back to the sheet view of Excel—use the taskbar or press Alt+F11. You can close the Visual Basic Editor without saving because the VBA module is part of your workbook and is saved together with the workbook.

1. Enter a number value for the radius into a cell (for example, enter **2** in cell A1).

2. Calculate the area of a circle with radius 2. Type in the formula

   `=AreaCircle(A1)`

   in another cell.

After you entered the formula, the result (the area of a circle with the radius specified in cell A1) 12.5663706 appears.

Every time you change the value in the cell referenced in the AreaCircle() function, Excel recalculates the sheet and therefore the function. The custom function behaves exactly like any built-in Excel function.

Custom functions and their arguments are also listed alphabetically in the Custom category and can be accessed from there:

- In Excel 2007 and Excel 2010: On the formula tab, click the Add Function button (the fx symbol).

- In Excel 2002 and Excel 2003: Select AutoSum/More Functions.

- In Excel 2000 and earlier: In the Function Wizard, click the fx symbol.

> **Sample Files**
> Use the Circle worksheet in the Geometry.xls or Geometry.xlsm sample file. The sample files are found in the Chapter06 folder. For more information about the sample files, see the section titled "Using the Sample Files" on page xxiii.

The AreaQuad() Function

The AreaQuad(*Length1,Length2,Height*) function calculates the area of a quadrilateral with at least two parallel sides (square, rectangle, parallelogram, or trapezoid). This example will not only simplify the use of geometry formulas but also introduce some new methods.

This function shows you how to handle the following in custom functions:

- Several arguments

- Optional arguments

- Logical conditions

Functions with Several Arguments

Although many functions need only one argument (such as the trigonometry functions and the AreaCircle() function from the previous example), there are also many functions that use two or more arguments to calculate the return value. To calculate the area of a trapezoid, three values have to be passed as arguments to the AreaQuad() function.

In the first line of the function block, you can enter several arguments separated by commas and enclosed in a pair of parentheses. You can enter the arguments in any order with one exception, mentioned later, in the section titled "Functions with Optional Arguments." To add the three arguments *Length1*, *Length2*, and *Height* to the AreaQuad() function, declare the function as follows:

```
Public Function AreaQuad(Length1, Length2, Height)
```

> ### Sample Files
>
> If you are unsure about formulas or area calculations, refer to the Fundamentals worksheet in the Geometry.xls or Geometry.xlsm sample file. This worksheet explains area calculations. The sample files are found in the Chapter06 folder. For more information about the sample files, see the section titled "Using the Sample Files" on page xxiii.

For this example, you don't always need three arguments for your function. This refers to the second bullet of the first enumeration of the AreaQuad() sample.

- Because all sides of a square have the same length, one argument is sufficient.

- For a rectangle or a parallelogram, you need to pass two arguments: the two sides for the rectangle; or the length of the parallels and their distance apart for the parallelogram.

- Only for the trapezoid do you need to pass three arguments.

Functions with Optional Arguments

Optional arguments are arguments that are not needed for all function calls. Because the calculation of the function in the worksheet doesn't impact the program code, you have to prepare for the case in which no values are passed to certain arguments at runtime as you create the function in the Visual Basic Editor. These optional arguments are identified by the keyword Optional preceding each name in the function declaration. The declaration must declare all required arguments before any optional ones.

Following these rules, a declaration for a function with two required and two optional arguments would be as follows:

```
Public Function DoItYourself(Always1, Always2, Optional Sometimes1, Optional
Sometimes2)
```

As you can see, you have to specify the keyword Optional for each optional argument. For the AreaQuad() function, enter the following declaration using the type Variant for the optional arguments:

```
Public Function AreaQuad(Length1 As Double, Optional Length2 As Variant, Optional
Height As Variant) As Double
```

This function declaration tells Excel that a custom function with the name AreaQuad, with the three arguments *Length1*, *Length2*, and *Height*, exists. Excel also knows that the first argument is required and is of type Double, whereas the last two arguments are optional.

INSIDE OUT   Split long code lines in VBA

When writing statements, you can usually fit them onto one line. However, for longer statements or when you want to split a statement to make the meaning clearer, you can continue onto subsequent lines. To continue a statement, enter a space and an underscore (_) at the end of the line. The Visual Basic Editor interprets all lines connected in this way as a single statement: Although the function declaration consists of two lines, it is one statement.

However, Excel doesn't know yet how to handle optional arguments without values. Therefore, you have to write the function in such a way that all possible combinations of used and not-used arguments are considered in the code. When you are using functions with optional arguments, you need to be able to establish whether an argument is passing a value. For this purpose, you can use the VBA IsMissing() function to check a special attribute of an optional argument. (This is a function that can be used only in the VBA module, not in a worksheet.)

What is the special attribute for? It isn't obvious whether the value passed by the argument of a function is actually passed or is missing. An argument will always have a value, and you cannot use the value of an argument to identify an argument as optional. This information has to be passed in addition to the value of the argument. However, you cannot accomplish this with "pure" data types; you must use only the Variant data type. Note, too, that optional arguments always require the data type Variant and cannot be declared as Double. Because Variant is the standard data type, you don't need an explicit declaration.

But how do you use a single function, AreaQuad(), to calculate the areas of a square, a rectangle, a parallelogram, and a trapezoid?

The VBA IsMissing() function is designed to solve this problem. Depending on the existence of an argument, the return value of this function is either TRUE or FALSE. If this function returns FALSE, the optional argument has a value and can be used in the calculation; otherwise, no value is passed. With this information and by using some logical VBA tests to branch, the solution is possible.

Chapter 6

Branches with Logical Conditions

To formulate a logical condition, you use the If-Then condition. For example, for the AreaQuad() function you could say, "If the Height argument is missing, then calculate the area of the square or rectangle; otherwise (else), calculate the area of the parallelogram or trapezoid." With the VBA IsMissing() function, the logical condition is If IsMissing(Height) Then, followed by the statements for the first calculation.

Next comes the Else keyword, which initiates the second calculation. End If completes the If block. A complete If block looks like the following example:

```
If condition Then
    Statement1
Else
    Statement2
End If
```

The condition is a logical expression that returns the logical value TRUE or FALSE. This expression could be a comparison, such as $x > 2$ or $Age <= 50$, or a function returning a logical value, such as IsMissing(). Depending on the logical value returned by the function, either Statement1 or Statement2 is used for the calculation.

Spacing and indenting the lines makes the code more readable. The following section provides an overview of the If statements in VBA and the options you can use to add branches to custom functions.

INSIDE OUT   Know how to use If statements in VBA

You can use the If statement in different ways. The simple version is:

```
If Age  >=  50 Then Feature = 1
```

Age and *Feature* are variables containing number values. If the *Age* variable contains a number greater than or equal to 50, the value 1 is assigned to the *Feature* variable. If the value of the *Age* variable is smaller than 50, the statement after Then is ignored and the next line after the If statement is used. The Then keyword can be followed by only one statement, because only one line is available. Therefore, the End If statement is not required and not possible for a one-line If statement.

The extended version is:

```
If Age >=  50 Then
    Feature = 1
End If
```

This statement is programmatically the same as the previous example. The code is easier to read but takes up more space. The statement is divided into multiple lines, allowing you to enter several statements after the Then keyword and the end of the If block, which in this case must be indicated by the End If statement.

The complete If block is:

```
If Age >=  50 Then
    Feature = 1
Else
    Feature = 2
End If
```

Here both options of the condition are used. If the condition *Age* >=50 is true, the *Feature* variable gets the value 1. If the condition is false, the value is 2. You can enter several statements between Then and Else as well as between Else and End If:

```
If Age >=  50 Then
    Feature = 1
    ID = "ID17"
Else
    Feature = 1
    ID = ""
End If
```

ID is a variable of the string data type that is used to store a string (a sequence of characters enclosed in quotation marks). The ID17 string is assigned to *ID* if the *Age* variable contains a number greater than or equal to 50. Otherwise, an empty string is assigned; in other words, nothing.

The ugly version:

```
If Age >= 50 Then Feature = 1 : ID = "ID17" Else Feature  = 1 : ID = ""
```

This version is not recommended but is shown only for the sake of completeness. The effect is the same as in the previous version. This is the shortest version, but the program is difficult to read. The colon allows you to write several statements in one line and indicates the end of a statement within a line.

The If statement allows you to evaluate the logical value returned by the IsMissing() function and to decide what action to take if an argument is missing.

But the example is a little more complicated. If you find out that the *Length2* argument is missing, the situation is still not clear, because the area of the square as well as the area of the parallelogram can be calculated without the *Length2* argument. The absence of the *Height* argument indicates that the area of a square is being calculated, because only one argument is needed; if the *Height* value is present, the area of a parallelogram is being calculated.

Even if the *Length2* argument is specified, you still have two alternatives: You could calculate the area of a rectangle or a trapezoid. The *Height* argument indicates whether the area of the rectangle or the trapezoid is calculated.

Therefore, two If blocks have to be nested in a parent If block. The different possibilities are shown in Table 6-1.

Table 6-1 **Type of Quadrilateral with Optional Arguments**

Length2 Argument	*Height* Argument	Quadrilateral
Missing	Missing	Square
Missing	Exists	Parallelogram
Exists	Missing	Rectangle
Exists	Exists	Trapezoid

The first If block checks whether the second argument, *Length2*, exists and branches into the appropriate statement blocks:

```
If IsMissing(Length2) Then
...         'these are the statements for the square and parallelogram
Else
...         'these are the statements for the rectangle and trapezoid
End If
```

Depending on the existence of the *Height* argument, the internal If block indicates whether the square or parallelogram (in the first case) or the rectangle or the trapezoid (in the second case) are calculated.

```
If IsMissing(Height) Then
   AreaQuad = Length1 ^ 2     'Square
Else
   AreaQuad = Length1 * Height      'Parallelogram
End If
```

Finally, the block checks for the existence of the *Height* parameter to evaluate the rectangle/trapezoid options.

```
If IsMissing(Height) Then
   AreaQuad = Length1 * Length2     'Rectangle
Else
   AreaQuad = (Length1 and Length2) /2 * Height       'Trapezoid
End If
```

The following summarizes the steps of the AreaQuad() function:

- In the function declaration, you specify the name AreaQuad and the three arguments *Length1*, *Length2* and *Height*. The last two arguments are optional. The function should return a value in the standard Excel number format.

- The first If statement addresses the optional *Length2* argument.

- If the *Length2* argument is missing, a further If test checks for the existence of the *Height* variable.

    ○ If the *Height* variable is missing, the square calculation is performed.

    ○ If it is not missing (Else), the parallelogram calculation is performed.

    ○ The End If statement is reached.

- Next, the case of the *Length2* argument being present is addressed in the Else branch of the first If statement.

    ○ If the *Height* variable is missing, the rectangle calculation is performed.

    ○ If it is not missing (Else), the Trapezoid calculation is performed.

    ○ The End If statement is reached.

- Complete the first If block with End If.

- With the End Function statement, you let the Visual Basic Editor know that your custom function is complete.

Here is the complete program code:

```
Public Function AreaQuad(Length1 As Double, Optional Length2, Optional Height) As
Double
If IsMissing(Length2) Then
   If IsMissing(Height) Then
         AreaQuad = Length1 ^ 2     'Square
   Else
         AreaQuad = Length1 * Height      'Parallelogram
   End If
Else
   If IsMissing(Height) Then
         AreaQuad = Length1 * Length2      'Rectangle
   Else
         AreaQuad = (Length1 and Length2) /2 * Height       'Trapezoid
   End If
End If
End Function
```

If the *Length1* argument is missing, the custom function returns the #VALUE! error. This alerts you to the fact that the required *Length1* argument is missing.

> **Sample Files**
>
> Use the Quadrilateral worksheet in the Geometry.xls or Geometry.xlsm sample file. The sample files are found in the Chapter06 folder. For more information about the sample files, see the section titled "Using the Sample Files" on page xxiii.

The AreaSect() Function

Many functions have optional arguments. However, many of these optional arguments shouldn't be ignored. These optional arguments have a specific value, and different values need to be used only in special cases. Therefore, default values are assigned to these optional arguments, and you need to make sure that if you do not specify a value for the optional argument, the default provided is appropriate. For this reason, the AreaSect() example in this section demonstrates the following:

- How to use default values for missing optional arguments

- How to evaluate conditions by using If statements

For example, the financial PMT() function calculates annuities and has five arguments. The last two of these arguments are optional: the time value *FV* and the *Type*. These arguments are required to calculate an annuity. However, you don't have to specify these arguments. Because a loan is usually repaid in full (*FV* = 0) and the interest payment is paid at the end of the corresponding payment period (*Type* = 0), these default values are predefined in the PMT() function. If you don't specify one of these arguments, the calculation uses the default value.

You can use the process described in this section in your custom functions.

Optional Arguments with Default Values

The syntax for functions with default values for optional arguments is:

```
Public Function DoItYourself(Always1, Always2, Optional Sometimes1, Optional Either_
Way = value)
```

This example includes two mandatory and two optional arguments. The default value *value* is assigned to the last optional argument. For this to work, you need to add only an equal sign and define the default value in the declaration for the optional *Either_Way* variable. The *Either_Way* argument in the formula will have either the value that is indicated when the function is defined in the worksheet or the default value specified in the function declaration.

This is illustrated in the example for AreaSect(*Radius,Phi,ADim*). This function is used to calculate the area of a segment of a circle based on the radius of the circle and the angle of the segment. In school, angles are usually measured in degrees. But in science and technology, radian measures are preferred. You want the AreaSect() function to be able to handle both measures. The optional *ADim* argument controls what angle measure is used. If you call the function without the *ADim* argument, the standard value is used in the function declaration, and the *ADim* argument used as a variable in the executable code has the value 1. In this case, the If statement is branched into the area calculation that uses degrees.

If *ADim* has any other value, the If statement initiates the calculation of the area with the angle *Phi* in radians. To do this, you have to enter a value other than 1 for the *ADim* argument in the worksheet formula.

```
Public Function AreaSect(Radius As Double, Phi As Double, Optional ADim = 1)
If ADim = 1 Then
    AreaSect = 3.14159265358979 * Radius ^ 2 * Phi / 360
Else
    AreaSect = Radius ^ 2 * Phi / 2
End If
End Function
```

Sample Files

Use the Sector of a circle worksheet in the Geometry.xls or Geometry.xlsm sample file. You'll also find more information in the Fundamentals worksheet in the same sample files. The sample files are found in the Chapter06 folder. For more information about the sample files, see the section titled "Using the Sample Files" on page xxiii.

The DigitSum() Function

With the example for DigitSum(Number), we leave geometry behind for a short time and turn to arithmetic. This example explains the following:

- How to use loops

- How to use VBA functions

- How to handle variables

To calculate the sum of the digits of a number, you add up the digits one by one:

1. Add the first digit of the number to the subtotal (currently zero).

2. Add the second digit of the number to the subtotal.

3. Add the third digit of the number to the subtotal.

4. Add the fourth digit of the number to the subtotal.

5. Continue until the end of the number is reached.

All programming languages include elements that allow you to run tasks repeatedly. The generic term for this is a *loop*.

Programming Loops

VBA recognizes several loop types:

- For...Next

- Do While...Loop/Do...Loop While

- Do Until...Loop/Do...Loop Until

> **Note**
> The two versions of the While and Until loops differ in when each determines whether the loop is to be performed. The Do While loop checks at the beginning of the loop, and the Do Until loop checks at the end.

Each loop consists of three parts:

1. The first statement handles the entry into the loop: This is the loop header.

2. The statements in the middle are processed during the loop iterations: This is the loop body.

3. The last statement indicates the end of the loop: This is the loop footer.

In the For...Next loop, the number of iterations is set by a counter. The While loop runs as long as a condition (specified after While) is true. The Until loop ends if the condition specified after Until is true.

You can use the For...Next loop to calculate the sum of digits, because the number of iterations is defined by the number of digits. The condition to end the loop is not determined during runtime but is set from the outset.

The following code shows the basic form of the For...Next loop:

```
Subtotal = 0
   For i = 1 To 10
           Subtotal = Subtotal   + i
   Next i
```

The first statement sets the *Subtotal* variable to zero. *Subtotal* is a variable that represents a number value that can be changed during runtime. These variables are used purely within the function evaluation code and are not visible in the worksheet. It is also good practice to declare a variable at the beginning of a function block and set the data type. The statement

```
Dim Subtotal As Long
```

specifies the data type Long for the variable *Subtotal*; that is, *Subtotal* is an integer in the range from –2,147,483,648 through 2,147,483,647. The loop header consists of the statement

```
For i = 1 To 10
```

The *i* is the counter that counts the number of iterations. This loop is iterated 10 times, and the counter *i* has the values 1 through 10 successively.

In the loop body, the counter also has another purpose: Each time the function loops, the counter is added to the current value of the subtotal.

```
Subtotal = Subtotal   + i
```

The loop footer with the Next keyword increases the counter by 1. If the end value indicated in the loop header is not exceeded, a new iteration starts. Otherwise, the iteration continues with the next statement after the loop.

These are all important elements that can be incorporated into the DigitSum() function.

```
Public Function DigitSum(Number As Double) As Long
Dim i As Integer
Dim S As String
   DigitSum = 0
   S = Str(Number)
         For i = 1 To Len(S)
                 DigitSum = DigitSum + Val(Mid(S, i, 1))
         Next i
End Function
```

The DigitSum() function is declared with the data type Long and the argument *Number* in the standard Excel number format. The next two statements declare two variables. The first variable *i* is the counter variable for the For...Next loop. The maximum value of this variable corresponds to the number of digits.

The second variable, *S*, is used as a string variable. This variable is going to be used to convert the number into a string by using the VBA function Str() so that you can determine the length of the string with the help of the VBA function Len() and pick out each digit from the number individually.

Within the loop, the VBA function Mid() returns the next digit in the number as a string. The VBA function Val() converts this back to a number, and this number can then be added to the *DigitSum* variable.

The loop cycles around, adding each digit of the number in turn.

The beginner might find the detour through the string variable and the use of the associated string functions Str(), Len(), Mid(), and Val() confusing. However, this is still the simplest solution and demonstrates how to use loops, variables, and VBA functions with only a few lines.

Sample Files

Use the DigitSum worksheet in the Geometry.xls or Geometry.xlsm sample file. The Special worksheet (also in those sample files) includes two other solutions you can use to calculate the number of digits. One of these solutions doesn't use VBA functions. The sample files are found in the Chapter06 folder. For more information about the sample files, see the section titled "Using the Sample Files" on page xxiii.

The AreaCircle1() Function

This function does basically the same thing that the AreaCircle() function described at the beginning of this chapter does, but the AreaCircle1() function will also show you how to use integrated worksheet functions.

The AreaCircle() function uses pi as a constant with the value 3.14159265358979 to calculate the area of a circle (by utilizing the maximum decimal places allowed in Excel). But you won't always have pi with all decimal places handy, in which case you will have to use additional handbooks with tables of mathematical constants.

An experienced Excel user could argue that Excel includes a Pi() function that calculates the area of a circle with sufficient accuracy (and speed). The custom functions described in this chapter show that the Excel worksheet and the VBA development environment aren't mutually incompatible. Numbers in worksheet cells can be passed to a VBA function, and the results returned by this function find their way back into the cell. Therefore, it is no surprise that worksheet functions can also be used in VBA.

Using Built-in Functions in Custom Functions

Excel includes more than 300 functions. It makes sense to make use of these functions in custom functions to save time. The process for using built-in functions in a VBA project might seem complicated and obscure for the beginner, but it isn't difficult. The complicated syntax is a consequence of object-oriented programming, which you don't need to know about to use worksheet functions in a VBA project.

Object-Oriented Programming

On the topic of object-oriented programming, consider this:

To handle the amount of programming elements in large applications, a hierarchy for these elements (known as *objects*) was introduced. To reference a subordinate object, you must indicate the entire path through the hierarchy.

If you are familiar with operating systems, you already know this. The path to a file includes the drive, folder, subfolders, and the file name—or, more precisely, the drive object, the folder object, and the file object.

However, programming languages use a period rather than a backslash to separate the elements.

The syntax for the Pi() function in VBA is:

```
Application.WorksheetFunction.Pi
```

This function call approach prompts the Visual Basic Editor to use the built-in pi function of Excel. (Unlike the formulas in a worksheet, VBA functions don't need the parentheses, because the term *WorksheetFunction* implies that the name is a function name.) A function call in the object-oriented manner is illustrated in the following simple example:

```
State.County.Town
```

Based on this statement, the town is located in the county, which is located in the state.

Now you can complete your enhanced AreaCircle() function. Instead of the constant for pi, you use the expression just shown with the Pi() function:

```
Public Function AreaCircle1(Radius As Double) As Double
    AreaCircle = Application.WorksheetFunction.Pi * Radius ^ 2
End Function
```

Chapter 6

Admittedly, the example of the pi function is quite simple. Usually you have to consider two things:

- You cannot use all built-in functions in VBA because VBA already includes functions that perform the same tasks.

- Some built-in function names are identical in VBA but return different results because of their definition (one example is the log function).

The list boxes of the Visual Basic Editor help you enter functions. While entering code, you can select function names in the lists even if you don't know the exact syntax (see Figure 6-6).

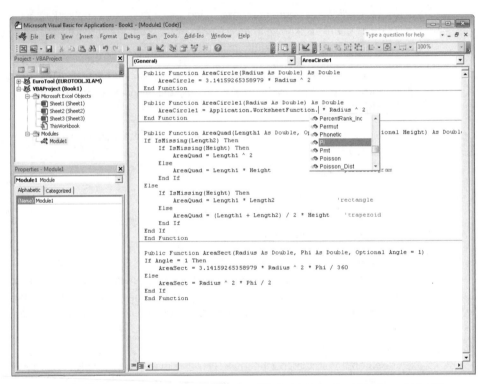

Figure 6-6 The list box in the Visual Basic Editor makes it easy to enter objects and identifiers.

Sample Files

Use the Circle worksheet in the Geometry.xls or Geometry.xlsm sample file. The sample files are found in the Chapter06 folder. For more information about the sample files, see the section titled "Using the Sample Files" on page xxiii.

The Functions in the Function Wizard

In Microsoft Excel 5.0 and Microsoft Excel 95, you could assign custom functions by using a category's object catalog in the Function Wizard. After Excel 97, this was no longer possible because the object catalog changed. Functions created with VBA are still assigned by using the Function Wizard.

Using Your Own Functions

All properly defined functions can be used in a worksheet. If cell A1 contains a positive number for the radius, you can calculate the area of the circle with the formula =AreaCircle(A1) in cell B1. For this to work, the module and the worksheet must exist in the same workbook, otherwise you will get the #NAME? error.

A custom function can also be used in another workbook. With the workbook open, extend the name of the function by using a pointer to the external reference.

```
=Geometry.xlsm!AreaCircle(A1)
```

If the workbook containing the function is not open, you must also enter the path:

```
=C:\Data\Geometry.xlsm!AreaCircle(A1)
```

> ### Tip   Select custom table functions
> If the workbook containing the custom functions is open, you can use the Function Wizard to enter table functions. Select Insert/Function to open the Insert Function dialog box, and select the function you want from the Custom category. The Function Wizard displays a dialog box you can use to enter arguments.

> ### Important
> If you share files that include custom functions, you must save these functions in the workbook. Alternatively, you can provide the file with the functions. If you don't do this, the calculations that use these functions cannot be performed, and the cells using custom functions display the #NAME? error.

Chapter 6

Saving Functions in Add-Ins

To share a custom function, you must first decide whether the user should be allowed to view the function code. Excel offers add-ins that allow you to hide the code of VBA functions. To create your own add-in, do the following:

1. Create the modules you want to save in the add-in.

2. Select the Debug/Compile VBAProject option in the Visual Basic Editor to compile the project, to ensure that no syntax errors exist.

3. Switch to the Excel window.

4. Select File/Save As (in Excel 2007, click the Office button and select Save As/Other Formats).

5. In all versions of Excel except Excel 2007, select the Excel Add-In (*.xlam) file format (in versions of Excel before Excel 2007, the extension appears as *.xla), and enter a name.

6. Switch back to the Visual Basic Editor.

7. In the Project Explorer, select This Workbook.

8. In the Properties window, set the IsAddin property to True. The included worksheets are now hidden.

9. Save your changes in the Visual Basic Editor.

> ## Important
>
> If you close Excel now, you can still create a backup copy. Excel offers the standard format again. But if you choose the standard format (*.xlsx), Excel will display a message box telling you that you are going to save your work as a macro-free workbook. You should click No and save your work as a macro-enabled file (*.xlsm).
>
> You can integrate the add-in with the Add-in Manager. If the file is open, it is displayed in the Project Explorer. You can select and edit the file.
>
> The worksheets of this file are hidden, but the included functions are displayed in the Function Wizard, in the Custom category.

This chapter describes the Microsoft Excel functions you can use to calculate date and time values. The functions are listed in Table 7-1. These functions also allow you to work with the system time of your computer, so make sure that the system time of your computer is set correctly.

Table 7-1 **Overview of the Date and Time Functions**

Function	Description
DATE()	Returns the Excel date sequential serial number for a given year, month, and day
DATEDIF()	Calculates the difference between a start and an end date in years, months, or days
DATEVALUE()	Converts a date as a text value into a date serial number (numeric value)
DAY()	Extracts the day from a date value
DAYS360()	Calculates the number of days between two dates based on a year with 360 days (twelve 30-day months)
EDATE()	Calculates the date a specified number of months before or after the start date
EOMONTH()	Returns the last date of the month a specified number of months before or after the start date

Function	Description
HOUR()	Extracts the hour from a time value
MINUTE()	Extracts the minute from a time value
MONTH()	Extracts the month from a date value
NETWORKDAYS()	Calculates the number of workdays between two dates
NETWORKDAYS.INTL()	Calculates the number of workdays between two days, allowing the weekend days to be defined (Excel 2010)
NOW()	Returns the current date and time (the system date and time of the computer)
SECOND()	Extracts the second from a time value
TIME()	Calculates a time value based on the indicated hours, minutes, and seconds
TIMEVALUE()	Converts a time formatted as text into a time value
TODAY()	Returns the current date (the system date of the computer)
WEEKDAY()	Converts a date value into a weekday numbered 1 through 7
WEEKNUM()	Returns the week number of a date value
WORKDAY()	Calculates the date before or after a specified number of workdays
WORKDAY.INTL()	Calculates the date before or after a certain number of workdays, allowing the weekend days to be defined (Excel 2010)
YEAR()	Extracts the year from a date value
YEARFRAC()	Calculates the fraction of the year between a start and an end date

DATE()

Syntax   DATE(*year,month,day*)

Definition   This function returns the serial number for a date indicated by the *year, month,* and *day* arguments.

Arguments

- ***year* (required)** The year, which can consist of one to four digits. Four digits is recommended.

- ***month* (required)** A number for the month of the year.

- ***day* (required)** A number for the day of the month.

Background   When calculating dates, you sometimes need to work with the component parts and might then want to return the value as a normal date. The DATE() function converts the parts of a date back into a (numeric) date expression that you can use in other date calculations. Excel interprets the year argument according to the date system being used by your computer. Excel for Windows uses the 1900 date system, and Excel for Mac uses the 1904 date system.

The following applies to the 1900 date system:

- For a year from 0 (zero) through 1899, Excel adds the value to 1900 to calculate the year.

- For a year from 1900 through 9999, Excel uses this value as year.

- If the year is less than 0 or greater than or equal to 10000, Excel returns the #NUMBER! error.

The following applies to the 1904 date system:

- For a year from 4 through 1899, Excel adds the value to 1900 to calculate the year.

- For a year from 1904 through 9999, Excel uses this value as the year.

- If the year is less than 4 or greater than or equal to 10000, or for a year from 1900 through 1903, Excel returns the #NUMBER! error.

For both systems, if the month is greater than 12, the number of months is added to the first month of the given year, and if the day is greater than the number of days in the given month, this number is added to the first day of the month.

See Also For more information about saving dates in Excel, see the section titled "The Excel Date System" on page 42 in Chapter 2, "Using Functions and PowerPivot."

Example   You might need to calculate the first and the last day of the month for a given date in an accounting application. The formula

```
=DATE(YEAR("07/23/2008"),MONTH("07/23/2008"),1)
```

returns 07/01/2008 as the first day of the month. The formula generates the number of the year and month from the given date with the day number 1. The formula

```
=DATE(YEAR("07/23/2008"),MONTH("07/23/2008")+1,1)-1
```

returns 07/31/2008 as the last day of the month. The formula generates the number of the year and the month increased by 1 (the following month) from the given date with the day number 1. If you subtract one day, you get the last day of the previous month.

Here are more examples:

- =DATE(108,1,2) returns 01/02/2008 (1900+108).

- =DATE(2008,1,2) returns 01/02/2008.

- =DATE(2008,14,2) returns 02/02/2009.

- =DATE(2008,1,35) returns 02/04/2008.

See Also TIME(), DATEVALUE(), TODAY(), YEAR(), MONTH(), DAY(), TIMEVALUE()

> **Sample Files**
>
> Use the DATE worksheet in the Date_Time.xls or Date_Time.xlsx sample file. The sample files are found in the Chapter07 folder. For more information about the sample files, see the section titled "Using the Sample Files" on page xxiii.

DATEDIF()

Syntax   DATEDIF(*start_date,end_date,unit*)

Definition   This function calculates the interval between a start and an end date (period) in years, months, or days.

Arguments

- *start_date* (**required**) The start date of the period.

- *end_date* (**required**) The end date of the period.

- *unit* (**required**) The unit type returned. The following units are available:

  - Y returns the number of whole years within the period.

  - M returns the number of whole months within the period.

  - D returns the number of days within the period.

  - MD returns the number of days between the two dates as if the dates were in the same month and year

  - YM returns the number of months between the two dates as if the dates were in the same year

  - YD returns the number of days between the two dates as if the dates were in the same year.

Background   This function calculates the interval between two dates (see Figure 7-1). You can enter all dates as strings enclosed in quotation marks, as serial numbers, or as the result of other formulas and functions.

Example   To calculate the employment period for employees up to a specified date, use the DATEDIF() function. For an employee hired on January 1, 2006, the calculation

```
=DATEDIF("01/01/2006","11/13/2011","Y")
```

returns 5 years for the period up to the date November 13, 2011. The formula

```
=DATEDIF("01/01/2006","11/30/2011","M")
```

calculates 70 months for the period up to November 13, 2011.

E6		f_x =DATEDIF(B6,C6,D6)		
A	B	C	D	E
1	**DATEDIF**			
2				
3	*Start date*	*End date*	*Basis*	Calculation
4	01/01/2006	11/11/2011	D	2140
5	01/01/2006	11/30/2011	M	70
6	01/01/2006	11/13/2011	Y	5
7	01/01/2006	11/14/2011	MD	13
8	01/01/2006	11/15/2011	YM	10
9	01/01/2006	11/16/2011	YD	319

Figure 7-1 Calculating the interval between dates.

See Also DAYS360(), EDATE(), EOMONTH(), NETWORKDAYS(), NETWORKDAYS.INTL()

Sample Files

Use the DATEDIF worksheet in the Date_Time.xls or Date_Time.xlsx sample file. The sample files are found in the Chapter07 folder. For more information about the sample files, see the section titled "Using the Sample Files" on page xxiii.

DATEVALUE()

Syntax   DATEVALUE(*date_text*)

Definition   This function converts a date formatted as text into a serial number based on the Excel date system.

Arguments

- *Date_text* **(required)**   A text value in an Excel date format

Background   If a date is formatted as text (for example, if it was imported in this format), use the DATEVALUE() function to convert the date into a serial number so that you can use the result for other calculations.

Most functions convert dates formatted as text automatically into serial numbers, but if you use imported data or worksheet functions from a third-party add-in, this might not always be true. To ensure that a date is converted, use the DATEVALUE() function.

For example, "12/12/2005" and "9/9/2001" are strings in quotation marks. If you use the standard Excel for Windows date system, the date string has to be a date from January 1, 1900, through December 31, 9999. If you use the standard Excel for Mac date system, the date string must be a date from January 1, 1904, through December 31, 9999. If the date string is a date out of range, the DATEVALUE() function returns the #VALUE! error.

If a date string doesn't include the year, the DATEVALUE() function uses the year from the system time of your computer. The time in the date string is ignored.

See Also   For more information about saving dates in Excel, see the section titled "The Excel Date System" on page 42 in Chapter 2.

Example   After the values are imported, they appear as text in a date column. In order for these dates to be usable in other calculations, the values have to be converted into numeric date values. The formula

```
=DATEVALUE("12/12/2008")
```

returns the date value 12/12/2008. This value is a serial date number in the Excel date system. Here are some more examples:

- =DATEVALUE("11/11") returns the date 11/11/2008 if the current year is 2008.

- =DATEVALUE("09/11/2001") returns the date 09/11/2001.

- =DATEVALUE("11/09/2006") returns the date 11/09/2006.

- =DATEVALUE("August 2007") returns the date 08/01/2007.

- =DATEVALUE("12/2008") returns the date 12/01/2008.

- =DATEVALUE("7/1999") returns the date 07/01/1999.

- =DATEVALUE("2008/11/22") returns the date 11/22/2008.

See Also NOW(), TIMEVALUE(), TODAY()

Sample Files

Use the DATEVALUE worksheet in the Date_Time.xls or Date_Time.xlsx sample file. The sample files are found in the Chapter07 folder. For more information about the sample files, see the section titled "Using the Sample Files" on page xxiii.

DAY()

Syntax   DAY(*serial_number*)

Definition   This function extracts the number of a day from a date. The DAY() function returns an integer from 1 through 31.

Arguments

- ***serial_number* (required)** The date for which the day number is calculated

Background   With this function, as with the YEAR() and MONTH() functions, you can extract a valid date and use its components for other calculations. Use the DAY() function to extract the day from a date.

Problems might occur if you enter dates as text. The values returned by the functions YEAR(), MONTH(), and DAY() correspond to the Gregorian calendar.

See Also For more information about saving dates in Excel, see the section titled "The Excel Date System" on page 42 in Chapter 2.

Example   You may want to use the Excel AutoFilter to look at the days in a birthday list. You can extract the day and put this in an auxiliary column. To do this, use the formula

=DAY(*date*)

Here are some more examples:

- =DAY("07/13/2008") returns 13.

- =DAY("11/14/1959") returns 14.

- =DAY("01/01/1900") returns 1.

- =DAY("12/31/1899") returns #VALUE!.

- =DAY("12/31/9999") returns 31.

- =DAY("01/01/10000") returns #VALUE!.

See Also DATE(), HOUR(), MINUTE(), MONTH(), SECOND(), TIME(), WEEKDAY(), YEAR()

Sample Files

Use the DAY worksheet in the Date_Time.xls or Date_Time.xlsx sample file. The sample files are found in the Chapter07 folder. For more information about the sample files, see the section titled "Using the Sample Files" on page xxiii.

DAYS360()

Syntax   DAYS360(*start_date,end_date,method*)

Definition   This function calculates the number of days between the start and end dates based on a year with 360 days.

Arguments

- *start_date* **(required)** The start date of the interval

- *end_date* **(required)** The end date of the interval

- *method* **(optional)** A logical value indicating whether the U.S. or European method is used for the calculation:

    - **FALSE or Omitted** U.S. (NASD) method. If the starting date is the last day of a month, the starting date becomes equal to the thirtieth day of the same month. If the ending date is the last day of a month and the starting date is earlier than the thirtieth day of a month, the ending date becomes equal to the first day of the next month; otherwise, the ending date becomes equal to the thirtieth day of the same month.

○ **TRUE** European method. Starting dates and ending dates that occur on the thirty-first day of a month become equal to the thirtieth day of the same month.

Background   If the start date is after the end date, the DAYS360() function returns a negative number and causes an incorrect result in interest calculations. Also, make sure to enter the interest rate in the Excel percent format.

To calculate interest, do the following: First, multiply the capital by the interest rate to calculate the interest amount for a year. Divide the result by 360 to determine the interest for one day. Multiply the result by the number of days you calculate with the DAYS360() function. This results in the following formula:

interest =capital x interest rate x DAYS360(start_date,end_date,TRUE)/360

If necessary, you can round the result to the second decimal place by using the ROUND() function (see Chapter 15 , "Financial Functions").

See Also For more information about saving dates in Excel, see the section titled "The Excel Date System" on page 42 in Chapter 2.

Example   Assume that you want to calculate the interest to date from November 22, 2010, (with the date in cell C12) through May 31, 2011 (in E12), for $250,000 (in C11), based on an interest rate of 5.25 percent (in E11). Make sure that you enter the percentage for the interest rate using the Excel format. You use the DAYS360() function to calculate the interest days.

=C11*E11*DAYS360(C12,E12,TRUE)/360

The result is $6,854.17. The partial calculation DAYS360(C12;E12;TRUE) returns 188 interest days (see Figure 7-2).

C14		f_x	=DAYS360(C12,E12,TRUE)	
A	B	C	D	E
1	**DAYS360**			
2				
9	**Charge interest on day**			
10				
11	Capital invested	$ 250,000.00	Interest rate	5.25%
12	Start date	11/22/2010	End date	05/31/2011
13				
14	Interest days	188	Interest	$ 6,854.17
15				

Figure 7-2 Calculating the interest to date with the DAYS360() function.

See Also DATEDIF(), EDATE(), EOMONTH(), NETWORKDAYS(), NETWORKDAYS.INTL()

Sample Files

Use the DAYS360 worksheet in the Date_Time.xls or Date_Time.xlsx sample file. The sample files are found in the Chapter07 folder. For more information about the sample files, see the section titled "Using the Sample Files" on page xxiii.

EDATE()

Note

In Excel 2003, this function is available as an add-in.

Syntax   EDATE(*start_date,months*)

Definition   This function returns the serial number of the date that is the indicated number of months before or after the start date.

Arguments

- *start_date* (required) The date that represents the start of the calculation.

- *months* (required) Indicates the number of months before or after the start date. A positive value for the months returns a future date, and a negative value returns a past date.

Background   The EDATE() function calculates the date for the specified number of months before or after the start date. Alternatively, you can use the YEAR(), MONTH(), and DAY() functions to divide the start date into three parts. Increase the month value as required, and then re-compile the three parts with the DATE() function to generate a regular date (serial number).

```
=DATE(YEAR(start_date),MONTH(start_date)+months,DAY(start_date))
```

If the start date is not a valid date, the EDATE() function returns the #VALUE! error. If a month is not an integer, the decimal places are truncated.

See Also   For more information about saving dates in Excel, see the section titled "The Excel Date System" on page 42 in Chapter 2.

Example　Assume that you want to calculate the end of an 18-month construction project. The formula

```
=EDATE("01/02/2010",18)
```

returns 07/02/2011 (see Figure 7-3).

Here are some further examples:

- =EDATE("01/02/2010",24) returns 01/02/2012.

- =EDATE("01/03/2010",0) returns 01/03/2010.

- =EDATE("01/04/2010",-5) returns 08/04/2009.

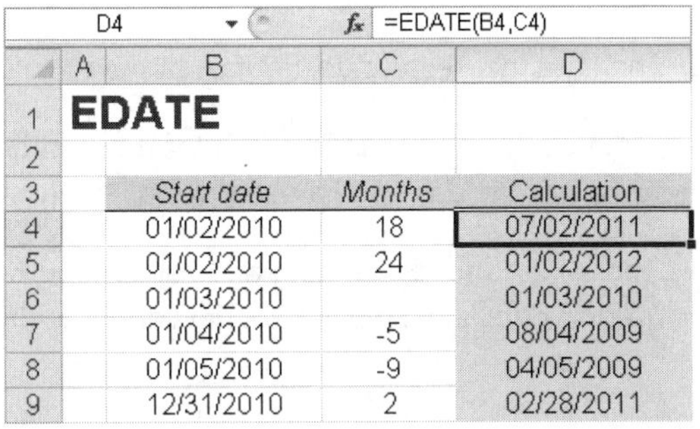

	D4	▾	*fx*	=EDATE(B4,C4)
	A	B	C	D
1		**EDATE**		
2				
3		*Start date*	*Months*	*Calculation*
4		01/02/2010	18	07/02/2011
5		01/02/2010	24	01/02/2012
6		01/03/2010		01/03/2010
7		01/04/2010	-5	08/04/2009
8		01/05/2010	-9	04/05/2009
9		12/31/2010	2	02/28/2011

Figure 7-3　Calculating the end date of projects.

See Also　DATE(), DATEDIF(), DAYS360(), EOMONTH(), NETWORKDAYS(), NETWORKDAYS.INTL(), WORKDAY(), WORKDAY.INTL()

> **Sample Files**
>
> Use the EDATE worksheet in the Date_Time.xls or Date_Time.xlsx sample file. The sample files are found in the Chapter07 folder. For more information about the sample files, see the section titled "Using the Sample Files" on page xxiii.

EOMONTH()

> **Note**
>
> In Excel 2003, this function is available as an add-in.

Syntax   EOMONTH(*start_date,months*)

Definition   This function returns the serial number of the last day of the month that is the indicated number of months before or after the start date.

Arguments

- ***start_date* (required)** The date that represents the start of the calculation.

- ***months* (required)** The number of months before or after the start date. A positive value for the months returns a future date, and a negative value returns a past date.

Background   This function is mostly used for accounting and banking purposes. The EOMONTH() function can be used to calculate a repayment date and due date on the last day of a month.

Alternatively, you can use the YEAR() and MONTH() functions to divide the start date into three parts. Increase the resulting value of *months* by 1 and then reconstruct the three component parts with the DATE() function to get a regular date (serial number). Subtract one day from this date to obtain the last day of the month.

```
=DATE(YEAR(start_date),MONTH(start_date)+months+1,1)-1
```

Problems might occur if you enter dates as text. If a month isn't an integer, the decimal places are truncated. If the start date isn't a valid date, the EOMONTH() function returns the #NUMBER! error. If the sum of the start date and *months* is an invalid date, the function returns the #NUMBER! error.

See Also For more information about saving dates in Excel, see the section titled "The Excel Date System" on page 42 in Chapter 2.

Example   Assume that you want to designate the last day of the month as the due date for a credit period 18 months from January 1, 2010. The formula

```
=EOMONTH("01/01/2010",18)
```

returns 07/31/2011 as the due date (see Figure 7-4).

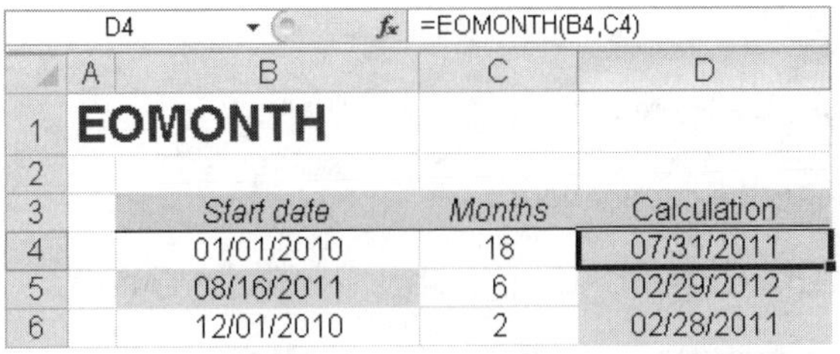

D4 =EOMONTH(B4,C4)

	A	B	C	D
1	EOMONTH			
2				
3		Start date	Months	Calculation
4		01/01/2010	18	07/31/2011
5		08/16/2011	6	02/29/2012
6		12/01/2010	2	02/28/2011

Figure 7-4 Calculating the due date of a loan.

See Also DATE(), DATEDIF(), DAYS360(), EDATE(), NETWORKDAYS(), NETWORKDAYS.INTL(), WORKDAY(), WORKDAY.INTL()

> **Sample Files**
>
> **Use the EOMONTH worksheet in the Date_Time.xls or Date_Time.xlsx sample file. The sample files are found in the Chapter07 folder. For more information about the sample files, see the section titled "Using the Sample Files" on page xxiii.**

HOUR()

Syntax HOUR(*serial_number*)

Definition This function extracts the hour from a serial number (a time with or without a date). The hour is returned as an integer from 0 through 23.

Arguments

- ***serial_number* (required)** A valid time (and a date, if applicable)

Background With this function, as with the MINUTE() and SECOND() functions, you can extract a valid time to use its components for other calculations.

You can enter times as strings enclosed in quotation marks (as in "06:43"), as decimal numbers (as in 0.27986111 for 06:43), or as a result of other formulas and functions.

Example If you want to extract the hours from a time value, you can use the formula

```
=HOUR("06:43")
```

which returns 6 hours.

Here are some more examples:

- `=HOUR("07/13/2008 20:48")` returns 20.

- `=HOUR(NOW())` returns the current hour.

See Also DAY(), MINUTE(), MONTH(), NOW(), SECOND(), TIME(), YEAR()

> **Sample Files**
>
> Use the HOUR worksheet in the Date_Time.xls or Date_Time.xlsx sample file. The sample files are found in the Chapter07 folder. For more information about the sample files, see the section titled "Using the Sample Files" on page xxiii.

MINUTE()

Syntax MINUTE(*serial_number*)

Definition This function extracts the minute from a serial number (a time with or without a date). The minute is returned as an integer from 0 through 59.

Arguments

- *serial_number* **(required)** A valid time (and a date, if applicable)

Background With this function, as well as with the HOUR() and SECOND() functions, you can determine a valid time and use its components for other calculations.

You can enter times as strings enclosed in quotation marks (as in "06:43"), as decimal numbers (as in 0.27986111 for 06:43), or as the result of other formulas and functions.

Example Assume that you need to calculate the minutes after the full hours.

Here are example formulas:

- `=MINUTE("06:43")` returns 43 minutes.

- `=MINUTE("12/24/2010 18:12")` returns 12.

- `=MINUTE(NOW())` returns the current minute.

See Also DAY(), HOUR(), MONTH(), SECOND(), WEEKDAY(), YEAR()

> **Sample Files**
> Use the MINUTE worksheet in the Date_Time.xls or Date_Time.xlsx sample file. The sample files are found in the Chapter07 folder. For more information about the sample files, see the section titled "Using the Sample Files" on page xxiii.

MONTH()

Syntax   MONTH(*serial_number*)

Definition   This function extracts the month number from a date. The calculated month numbers are in the range 1 (January) through 12 (December).

Arguments

- *serial_number* **(required)** The date for which the month number is calculated.

Background   With this function, as well as with the YEAR() and DAY()functions, you can extract a valid date and use the components for other calculations. Use the MONTH() function to group values by month. Note that problems might occur if you enter dates as text. The values returned by the YEAR(), MONTH(), and DAY() functions correspond to the Gregorian calendar.

See Also For more information about saving dates in Excel, see the section titled "The Excel Date System" on page 42 in Chapter 2.

Example   Assume that you want to enable the Excel AutoFilter for the months and need to calculate the month values from a date column by using an auxiliary column. To do this, use the formula

```
=MONTH(date_value)
```

Here are more examples:

- `=MONTH(TODAY())` returns 9 in September.

- `=MONTH("11/14/1959")` returns 11.

- `=MONTH("01/01/1900")` returns 1.

- `=MONTH("12/31/1899")` returns `#VALUE!`.

- `=MONTH("12/31/9999")` returns 12.

- `=MONTH("01/01/10000")` returns `#VALUE!`.

See Also DAY(), HOUR(), MINUTE(), SECOND(), WEEKDAY(), WEEKNUM(), YEAR()

Sample Files

Use the MONTH worksheet in the Date_Time.xls or Date_Time.xlsx sample file. The sample files are found in the Chapter07 folder. For more information about the sample files, see the section titled "Using the Sample Files" on page xxiii.

NETWORKDAYS()

Note

In Excel 2003, this function is available as an add-in.

Syntax NETWORKDAYS(*start_date,end_date,holidays*)

Definition This function returns the number of workdays within a given time interval.

Arguments

- *start_date* **(required)** The date that represents the start of the time interval.

- *end_date* **(required)** The date that represents the end of the time interval.

- *holidays* **(optional)** An array of one or more dates representing work-free days to exclude from the working calendar, such as federal holidays and floating holidays. The array can be a cell range containing the dates or an array constant with serial numbers for the dates.

Background With the NETWORKDAYS() function, you can calculate salaries based on the number of workdays.

The function excludes weekends (Saturdays and Sundays) by default. You can also enter your holiday list into a cell range and name this range free_days to exclude these dates from the calculation.

Problems might occur if you enter dates as text. If one of the arguments isn't a valid date, the NETWORKDAYS() function returns the #VALUE! error.

Remember that the function counts the day of the start date. If you compare this with the result from the WORKDAY() function, you will see that you have to pass one day fewer in the *days* argument to WORKDAY().

See Also For more information about saving dates in Excel, see the section titled "The Excel Date System" on page 42 in Chapter 2.

Example   Assume that a project is planned to extend over the period from December 12, 2008, through June 2, 2009. You have to calculate the number of workdays in this time-frame, excluding holidays. The formula

```
=NETWORKDAYS("12/12/10","06/02/11",{"12/25/10","01/01/11","01/17/11","02/21/11",
"05/30/2011","07/04/11"})
```

returns 121 workdays for the project. Note that in the preceding formula, holidays are enclosed in braces and not in parentheses. Figure 7-5 shows the calculation using cell references for the start date, end date, and holidays.

E8		f_x	=NETWORKDAYS(B8,C8,D8:D13)	
	A	B	C	D	E
1	**NETWORKDAYS**				
2					
3		*Start date*	*End date*	*Holidays*	Calculation
8		12/12/2010	06/02/2011	12/25/2010	121
9				01/01/2011	
10				01/17/2011	
11				02/21/2011	
12				05/30/2011	
13				07/04/2011	

Figure 7-5 Calculating billable workdays, taking weekends and holidays into consideration.

See Also DAYS360(), EDATE(), EOMONTH(), NETWORKDAYS(), NETWORKDAYS.INTL(), WORKDAY(), WORKDAY.INTL()

Sample Files

Use the NETWORKDAYS worksheet in the Date_Time.xls or Date_Time.xlsx sample file. The sample files are found in the Chapter07 folder. For more information about the sample files, see the section titled "Using the Sample Files" on page xxiii.

NETWORKDAYS.INTL()

Syntax   NETWORKDAYS.INTL(*start_date,end_date,weekend,holidays*)

Definition   This function returns the number of workdays within the given time interval. Weekend days and any days that are specified as holidays are not considered as workdays.

Arguments

- *start_date* **(required)** The date that represents the start of the time interval.

- *end_date* **(required)** The date that represents the end of the time interval.

- *weekend* **(optional)** A number or string indicating which days are weekends and should not be treated as workdays.

- *holidays* **(optional)** An array of one or more dates defining nonworking days to exclude from the calculation, such as federal holidays and floating holidays. The array can be a cell range containing the dates or an array with serial numbers for the dates.

Background   Refer also to the NETWORKDAYS() function discussed previously. The Excel 2010 NETWORKDAYS.INTL() function also allows you to specify which days are weekends and therefore are not counted. If you specify a number or string for the weekend, use the values shown in Table 7-2.

Table 7-2 Values for the NETWORKDAYS.INTL() Function

Number	Weekdays	String
1 (or no value)	Saturday, Sunday	0000011
2	Sunday, Monday	1000001
3	Monday, Tuesday	1100000
4	Tuesday, Wednesday	0110000
5	Wednesday, Thursday	0011000
6	Thursday, Friday	0001100
7	Friday, Saturday	0000110
11	Sunday	0000001
12	Monday	1000000
13	Tuesday	0100000
14	Wednesday	0010000
15	Thursday	0001000
16	Friday	0000100
17	Saturday	0000010

You can use any combination except 1111111. A 0 indicates a workday, and a 1 indicates a work-free day.

Example   Assume that a project is planned from December 12, 2008, through June 2, 2009. You have to calculate the number of workdays in this timeframe, excluding holidays. The formula

```
=NETWORKDAYS.INTL("12/12/10","06/02/11",1,{"12/25/10","01/01/11","01/17/11","02/21/11","05/30/2011","07/04/11"})
```

returns 121 workdays for the project. Note that in the formula, holidays are enclosed in braces and not in parentheses.

See Also DATEDIF(), DAYS360(), EDATE(), EOMONTH(), NETWORKDAYS(), WORKDAY(), WORKDAY.INTL()

> **Sample Files**
>
> Use the NETWORKDAYS.INTL worksheet in the Date_Time.xls or Date_Time.xlsx sample file. The sample files are found in the Chapter07 folder. For more information about the sample files, see the section titled "Using the Sample Files" on page xxiii.

NOW()

Syntax   NOW()

Definition   This function returns the serial number of the current date and time.

Arguments   None

The NOW() function returns the current date and the current time. Use this function if you need the current time for calculations. If you select the General option for the cell format before you enter the function, the result is formatted as a date.

Background   The related TODAY() function also returns the current date, but not the current time. If you use the NOW() function for calculations—for example, to calculate interest days—the returned time can be inconvenient. Therefore, use the TODAY() function to calculate date differences when only the days are important.

The results of both functions are not updated unless you open the workbook or update any information in the workbook that will automatically perform a recalculation of the sheet. To recalculate a sheet, press the F9 key.

The accuracy of both functions depends on your computer having the correct system time.

See Also For more information about saving dates in Excel, see the section titled "The Excel Date System" on page 42 in Chapter 2.

Example Suppose you want to include the current date and time in a form. Enter the NOW() function in a cell on the form. =NOW() returns the current date and time based on the system time of your computer. More examples (see Figure 7-6) include the following:

- =NOW()+1/24 returns the date and time one hour from now.

- =NOW()+12/24 returns the date and time 12 hours from now.

	C4	▾	f_x =NOW()	
⊿	A	B	C	D
1	**NOW**			
2				
3			Calculation	*Time (1-24 Hour)*
4		*Now*	08/16/2011 22:18	
5		*After one hour*	08/16/2011 23:18	
6		*After 12 hours*	08/17/2011 10:18	
7				
8		*Date/Time in other time zones in relation to* *(UTC+01:00) Amsterdam, Berlin, Bern, Rome, Stockholm, Vienna*		
9		*Lisbon*	08/16/2011 21:18	
10		*New York*	08/16/2011 16:18	
11		*Los Angeles*	08/16/2011 13:18	
12		*Sydney*	08/17/2011 6:18	
13		*Tokyo*	08/17/2011 5:18	
14		*Moscow*	08/17/2011 0:18	

Figure 7-6 In Excel 2007 and Excel 2010, you can use conditional formats to chart times.

See Also DATE(), DAY(), HOUR(), MINUTE(), MONTH(), SECOND(), WEEKDAY(), YEAR()

Sample Files

Use the NOW worksheet in the Date_Time.xls or Date_Time.xlsx sample file. The sample files are found in the Chapter07 folder. For more information about the sample files, see the section titled "Using the Sample Files" on page xxiii.

SECOND()

Syntax SECOND(*serial_number*)

Definition This function extracts the seconds from a serial number (a time with or without a date). The second is returned as an integer from 0 through 59.

Chapter 7

Arguments

- ***serial_number* (required)** A valid time (and a date, if applicable).

Background   With this function, as with the HOUR() and MINUTE() functions, you can extract a valid time to use its components for other calculations.

You can enter times as strings enclosed in quotation marks (as in "06:43"), as decimal numbers (as in 0.27986111 for 06:43), or as a result of other formulas and functions.

Examples   The following are examples where the function SECOND() extracts seconds from a date/time value:

- =SECOND("07/13/2008 20:48:31") returns 31.

- =SECOND("06:43:12") returns 12.

- =SECOND(NOW()) returns the current second.

See Also DAY(), HOUR(), MINUTE(), MONTH(), NOW(), TIME(), YEAR()

> ### Sample Files
> Use the SECOND worksheet in the Date_Time.xls or Date_Time.xlsx sample file. The sample files are found in the Chapter07 folder. For more information about the sample files, see the section titled "Using the Sample Files" on page xxiii.

TIME()

Syntax   TIME(*hour,minute,second*)

Description   This function returns the serial number for a time indicated by the arguments *hour*, *minute*, and *second*.

Arguments

- ***hour* (required)** A number from 0 through 32,767 indicating the hour. Each value greater than 23 is divided by 24, and the remainder is the hour value. For example, TIME(28,0,0) corresponds to TIME(4,0,0), which is 4:00 or 4/24 or 0.16667.

- ***minute* (required)** A number from 0 through 32,767 indicating the minute. Each value greater than 59 is divided by 24*60 and converted into hours and minutes. For example, TIME(150,0,0) corresponds to TIME(2,30,0), which is 2:30 or 0.1041667.

- *second* (**required**) A number from 0 through 32,767 indicating the second. Each value greater than 59 is divided by 24*60*60 and converted into hours, minutes, and seconds. For example, TIME(0,0,12011) corresponds to TIME(3,20,11), which is 3:20:11 or 0.139016204.

Background When calculating times, you sometimes have to deconstruct a time to add minutes. However, the result has to be returned as a normal time. The TIME() function converts the parts of a time back into a (numeric) time expression that you can use in other date calculations. The TIME() function is ideal for formulas.

The function returns a decimal number in the range of 0 through 0.99999999 and corresponds to a time from 00:00:00 through 23:59:59. If you select the General option for the cell format before entering the function, the result is formatted as time.

Examples For applications that include standard processing times in hours, minutes, and seconds, you might want to combine these to display a time value. To do this, use the formula

=TIME(*standard_hours*,*standard_minutes*,*standard_seconds*)

The following examples show possible results and exceptions if the 24-hour, 60-minute, or 60-second boundary is exceeded:

- =TIME(5,6,11) returns 05:06:11.

- =TIME(13,10,0) returns 13:10:00.

- =TIME(23,45,30) returns 23:45:30.

- =TIME(24,15,30) returns 00:15:30.

- =TIME(26,30,30) returns 02:30:30.

- =TIME(12,80,10) returns 13:20:10.

- =TIME(12,59,120) returns 13:01:00.

See Also DATE(), DAY(), HOUR(), MINUTE(), MONTH(), SECOND(), TIMEVALUE(), YEAR()

Sample Files

Use the TIME worksheet in the Date_Time.xls or Date_Time.xlsx sample file. The sample files are found in the Chapter07 folder. For more information about the sample files, see the section titled "Using the Sample Files" on page xxiii.

TIMEVALUE()

Syntax   TIMEVALUE(*time_text*)

Definition   This function converts a time formatted as text into a time value (serial number). The serial number is a value in the range of 0 through 0.99999999 and corresponds to a time from 00:00:00 through 23:59:59.

Arguments

- ***Time_text* (required)** A text value in any Excel time format. Dates in the time argument are ignored.

Background   If a time is formatted as text (for example, in values that have been imported), use the TIMEVALUE() function to convert the time into a serial number. You can use the result for other calculations.

Most functions convert times formatted as text automatically into serial numbers, but if you use imported data or worksheet functions from a third-party add-in, this might not always be true. To ensure that a date is converted, use the TIMEVALUE() function.

Example   Assume that after some values have been imported, they appear as text in a time column. So that they can be used in other calculations, the values have to be converted into numeric time values. The formula

```
=TIMEVALUE("06:00:00")
```

returns the time value 0.25 or 06:00, formatted in the number format *hh*:*mm*. This value is a time value in the Excel time system. Here are a few more examples:

- =TIMEVALUE("06:00 PM") returns 0.75.

- =TIMEVALUE("06:45:16") returns 0.281435185.

- =TIMEVALUE("12:00:00") returns 0.5.

See Also DATEVALUE(), HOUR(), MINUTE(), NOW(), SECOND(), TIME()

> **Sample Files**
>
> Use the TIMEVALUE worksheet in the Date_Time.xls or Date_Time.xlsx sample file. The sample files are found in the Chapter07 folder. For more information about the sample files, see the section titled "Using the Sample Files" on page xxiii.

TODAY()

Syntax   TODAY()

Definition   This function returns the serial number for the current date.

Arguments   None

Background   The TODAY() function returns the current date without the time. If you select the General option for the cell format before entering the function, the result is formatted as a date.

The related NOW() function returns both the current date and the time. The difference between TODAY() and NOW() is that TODAY() returns only the current date and NOW() returns the date and the time.

To calculate date differences from the current date, use the TODAY() function. You can use the TODAY() function to calculate the number of days since an invoice was issued. With the help of the calculated difference, you can see if deadlines were met or missed.

The results are updated only when you open a workbook or calculate a workbook. To recalculate at any time, press the F9 key.

The accuracy of this function depends on your computer having the correct system time.

See Also For more information about saving dates in Excel, see the section titled "The Excel Date System" on page 42 in Chapter 2.

Example   You might want to include the current date in an invoice form. The =TODAY() formula adds the current date to the form. More examples are listed here:

- =TODAY()+14 returns the date 14 days from today.

- =TODAY()+200 returns the date 200 days from today.

- =TODAY()-100 returns the date 100 days prior to today's date.

- =TODAY()-"11/14/1959" returns the current age in days for a person whose birthday is November 14, 1959.

See Also DATE(), DAY(), NOW()

Sample Files

Use the TODAY worksheet in the Date_Time.xls or Date_Time.xlsx sample file. The sample files are found in the Chapter07 folder. For more information about the sample files, see the section titled "Using the Sample Files" on page xxiii.

WEEKDAY()

Syntax   WEEKDAY(*serial_number;return_type*)

Definition   This function converts a date (serial number) into a weekday number. The weekday is returned as an integer from 1 (Sunday) through 7 (Saturday).

Arguments

- *serial_number* **(required)** The date for which the weekday number is calculated.

- *return_type* **(optional)** A number (1, 2, or 3) indicating the type of the return value. The types are defined as follows:

    - **1 (or no value)** 1 indicates Sunday, 2 indicates Monday, and so on, with 7 indicating Saturday.

    - **2** 1 indicates Monday, 2 indicates Tuesday, and so on, with 7 indicating Sunday.

    - **3** 0 indicates Monday, 1 indicates Tuesday, and so on, with 6 indicating Sunday.

    In Excel 2010, the return types are extended. You can choose these additional types:

    - **11** 1 indicates Monday, 2 indicates Tuesday, and so on, with 7 indicating Sunday.

    - **12** 1 indicates Tuesday, 2 indicates Wednesday, and so on, with 7 indicating Monday.

    - **13** 1 indicates Wednesday, 2 indicates Thursday, and so on, with 7 indicating Tuesday.

    - **14** 1 indicates Thursday, 2 indicates Friday, and so on, with 7 indicating Wednesday.

    - **15** 1 indicates Friday, 2 indicates Saturday, and so on, with 7 indicating Thursday.

    - **16** 1 indicates Saturday, 2 indicates Sunday, and so on, with 7 indicating Friday.

    - **17** 1 indicates Sunday, 2 indicates Monday, and so on, with 7 indicating Saturday.

Background   This function is useful for extracting the day of the week from a date.

Remember that you can use the TEXT() function (see Chapter 8, "Text and Data Functions") instead of the WEEKDAY() function to return a weekday as string:

`=TEXT(TODAY(),"dddd")`

See Also For more information about saving dates in Excel, see the section titled "The Excel Date System" on page 42 in Chapter 2.

Example You might want to format Sundays in a date column in red. To do this, use conditional formatting. Select the date column. In Excel 2003 and earlier, select the Format/ Conditional Formatting menu option and then select Formula in the list box. In Excel 2007 or Excel 2010, click the Conditional Formatting button in the Style group on the Start tab and select New Rule. Select Use A Formula To Determine Which Cells To Format as the rule type (see Figure 7-7).

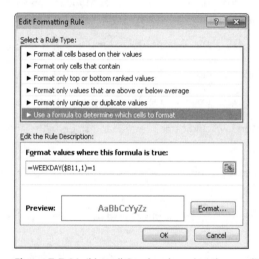

Figure 7-7 Marking all Sundays by using the conditional formats in Excel 2007 and Excel 2010.

Enter the formula

`=WEEKDAY($B11,1)=1`

and click the Format button to format the text (see Figure 7-8).

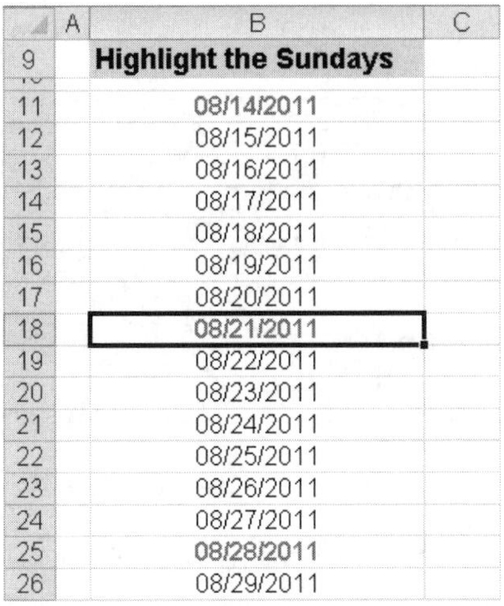

Figure 7-8 The Sundays in the date column are formatted in bold and red by using conditional formats.

The following examples show how the *type* parameter works:

- =WEEKDAY("08/03/2008",1) returns 1 (Sunday).

- =WEEKDAY("08/03/2008",2) returns 7.

- =WEEKDAY("08/03/2008",3) returns 6.

See Also DAY(), HOUR(), MINUTE(), MONTH(), SECOND(), TODAY(), WEEKNUM(), YEAR()

Sample Files

Use the WEEKDAY worksheet in the Date_Time.xls or Date_Time.xlsx sample file. The sample files are found in the Chapter07 folder. For more information about the sample files, see the section titled "Using the Sample Files" on page xxiii.

WEEKNUM()

> **Note**
> In Excel 2003, this function is available as an add-in.

Syntax   WEEKNUM(*serial_number,return_type*)

Definition   This function returns an integer for the week number for the given date.

Arguments

- **serial_number (required)** The date for which the week number is calculated.

- **return_type (optional)** A number indicating on what day the week begins. This argument has the different options depending on the version of Excel you are using. In Excel 2003 and earlier, there are two return types:

  - **1** System 1 (the default setting): The week begins on Sunday. The weekdays have the numbers 1 through 7, starting on Sunday.

  - **2** System 2: The week begins on Monday. The weekdays have the numbers 1 through 7, starting on Monday.

  In Excel 2010, the System 1 return type offers further options:

  - **1** System 1 (default setting): The week begins on Sunday.

  - **2** System 1: The week begins on Monday.

  - **11** System 1: The week begins on Monday.

  - **12** System 1: The week begins on Tuesday.

  - **13** System 1: The week begins on Wednesday.

  - **14** System 1: The week begins on Thursday.

  - **15** System 1: The week begins on Friday.

  - **16** System 1: The week begins on Saturday.

  - **17** System 1: The week begins on Sunday.

  - **21** System 2: The week begins on Monday.

Background   A year is divided into consecutively numbered weeks. There are two types of calculations in the WEEKNUM() function: In System 1, the week in which January 1 appears is considered as week number 1. In System 2, the week in which the first Thursday of the year appears is considered as week number 1. System 2 is the European week numbering system. The first day of week 1 is specified by the International Standards Organization (ISO) definition. System 2 is regulated by the ISO 8601 standard established in 1988.

See Also For more information about saving dates in Excel, see the section titled "The Excel Date System" on page 42 in Chapter 2.

Example   You may want to display the week number for each date in an operation schedule in Excel. To do this, use the formula

=WEEKNUM(*date*)

See Also DAY(), DAYS360(), MONTH(), WEEKDAY(); YEAR()

> ## Sample Files
> Use the WEEKNUM worksheet in the Date_Time.xls or Date_Time.xlsx sample file. The sample files are found in the Chapter07 folder. For more information about the sample files, see the section titled "Using the Sample Files" on page xxiii.

WORKDAY()

> ## Note
> In Excel 2003, this function is available as an add-in.

Syntax   WORKDAY(*start_date,days,holidays*)

Definition   This function returns the serial number of the date before or after an indicated number of workdays.

Arguments

- ***start_date* (required)** The start date for the calculation.

- ***days* (required)** The number of nonweekend and nonholiday days (workdays) before or after the start date. A positive value for the days returns a future date and a negative value a past date.

- ***holidays* (optional)** An array of one or more dates for work-free days to exclude from the working calendar, such as federal holidays and floating holidays.

Background   You might want to calculate a payment date based on a delivery time, or you might need to know the date 20 workdays after a particular date. If these calculations need to ignore nonworking days, use the WORKDAY() function.

This function doesn't count weekends and the days indicated in *holidays* as workdays. The *holidays* array can be a cell range containing the dates or an array of serial numbers for the dates.

The WORKDAY() function doesn't count the start date in the calculation, unlike the NETWORKDAYS() function, which would return one additional day.

Also note the following when working with this function:

- If one of the arguments is not a valid date, the WORKDAY() function returns the #VALUE! error.

- If the sum of the start date plus *days* is an invalid date, the WORKDAY() function returns the #NUMBER! error.

- If the number of the day is not an integer, the decimal places are truncated.

Example   To calculate the date of a payment 14 workdays after the current date, you would use the formula

`=WORKDAY(TODAY(),14)`

For example, this returns 08/03/2011 on July 14, 2011. This is the 14th workday after July 14, 2011. For a payment date of 10 days, the formula

`=WORKDAY("12/15/10",10)`

returns 12/29/2010 for the start date December 15, 2010. But taking the Christmas holidays into consideration and an interval of 15 days, the calculation

`=WORKDAY("12/15/10",15,{"12/25/2010","12/26/2010"})`

returns 01/05/2011. Note that in this last formula, holidays are enclosed in braces and not in parentheses.

See Also EDATE(), EOMONTH(), NETWORKDAYS(), NETWORKDAYS.INTL(), NOW(), TODAY(), WORKDAY.INTL()

> **Sample Files**
>
> Use the WORKDAY worksheet in the Date_Time.xls or Date_Time.xlsx sample file. The sample files are found in the Chapter07 folder. For more information about the sample files, see the section titled "Using the Sample Files" on page xxiii.

WORKDAY.INTL()

Syntax   WORKDAY.INTL()(*start_date,days,weekend,holidays*)

Definition   This function returns the serial number of the date before or after an indicated number of workdays and allows the weekend days to be defined.

Arguments

- **start_date (required)** The date that represents the start of the calculation.

- **days (required)** The number of nonweekend and nonholiday days (workdays) before or after the start date. A positive value for the days returns a future date, and a negative value returns a past date.

- **weekend (optional)** A number or string indicating which days are weekends and should not be treated as workdays.

- **holidays (optional)**   An array of one or more dates for work-free days to exclude from the working calendar, such as federal holidays and floating holidays.

Background   WORKDAY.INTL() has the same functionality as the WORKDAY() function with an additional feature that allows you to specify which days are weekends and therefore are not counted. You can specify a number or string for the weekend using the values in Table 7-3.

Table 7-3 Values for the WORKDAY.INTL() Function

Number	Weekend days	String
1 (or no value)	Saturday, Sunday	0000011
2	Sunday, Monday	1000001
3	Monday, Tuesday	1100000
4	Tuesday, Wednesday	0110000
5	Wednesday, Thursday	0011000

Number	Weekend days	String
6	Thursday, Friday	0001100
7	Friday, Saturday	0000110
8	Sunday	0000001
9	Monday	1000000
10	Tuesday	0100000
11	Wednesday	0010000
12	Thursday	0001000
13	Friday	0000100
14	Saturday	0000010

The string comprises seven characters, with each character representing a day of the week. A 0 indicates a workday, and a 1 indicates a work-free day. You can use any combination except 1111111.

Example   To calculate a payment date 14 days after the current date but not on a weekend date, use

`=WORKDAY.INTL(TODAY(),14)`

This would return 10/19/2010 from a start date of September 9, 2010.

To calculate the payment date 10 days after a start date, use the formula

`=WORKDAY.INTL("12/12/2011",10)`

This returns 12/26/2011, 10 working days from the start date of December 12, 2011.

When taking into consideration the Christmas holidays, the calculation

`=WORKDAY.INTL("12/12/2011",10,1,{"12/25/2011";"12/26/2011"})`

returns 12/27/2011. And to calculate a payment date 10 days after December 4, 2011, where Monday, Saturday, and Sunday are nonworking days,

`=WORKDAY.INTL("12/2/2011",10,"1000011")`

returns 12/21/2011. Note that in the last formula, holidays are enclosed in braces and not in parentheses.

See Also EDATE(), EOMONTH(), NETWORKDAYS(), NETWORKDAYS.INTL(), NOW(), TODAY(), WORKDAY()

> ### Sample Files
>
> Use the WORKDAY.INTL worksheet in the Date_Time.xlsx sample file. The sample files are found in the Chapter07 folder. For more information about the sample files, see the section titled "Using the Sample Files" on page xxiii.

YEAR()

Syntax   YEAR(*serial_number*)

Definition   This function extracts the four-digit year from a date. The YEAR() function returns an integer between 1900 and 9999.

Arguments

- *serial_number* **(required)** The date from which you want to extract the year.

Background   With this function, as well as with the MONTH() and DAY()functions, you can extract components for use in other calculations.

Take care not to enter the dates as text. The values returned by the functions YEAR(), MONTH(), and DAY() correspond to the Gregorian calendar.

See Also For more information about saving dates in Excel, see the section titled "The Excel Date System" on page 42 in Chapter 2.

Example   You might want to use the Excel AutoFilter to sort a set of data by year and need to calculate the year values from the date column by using an auxiliary column. To do this, use the formula

```
=YEAR(serial_number)
```

Here are a few more examples:

- `=YEAR(TODAY())` returns 2010 in the year 2010.

- `=YEAR("11/14/1959")` returns 1959.

- `=YEAR("01/01/1900")` returns 1900.

- =YEAR("12/31/1899") returns #VALUE!.

- =YEAR("12/31/9999") returns 9999.

- =YEAR("01/01/10000") returns #VALUE!.

See Also DAY(), HOUR(), MINUTE(), MONTH(), NOW(), SECOND(), TODAY(), WEEKDAY()

Sample Files

Use the YEAR worksheet in the Date_Time.xls or Date_Time.xlsx sample file. The sample files are found in the Chapter07 folder. For more information about the sample files, see the section titled "Using the Sample Files" on page xxiii.

YEARFRAC()

Note

In Excel 2003, this function is available as an add-in.

Syntax YEARFRAC(*start_date,end_date,basis*)

Definition This function converts the interval between the start date and the end date into a fraction of a year.

Arguments

- *start_date* **(required)** The date that represents the start of the calculation.

- *end_date* **(required)** The date that represents the end of the calculation.

- ***basis* (optional)** Indicates the basis on which the interval days are calculated. The following options are available:

    ○ **0 (or no value)** USA (NASD) 30/360

    ○ **1** Actual/Actual

    ○ **2** Actual/360

    ○ **3** Actual/365

    ○ **4** Europe 30/360

Background With the YEARFRAC() function, you can compare the duration of claims and liabilities. This function is related to the financial functions (see Chapter 15, "Financial Functions").

See Also For more information about saving dates in Excel, see the section titled "The Excel Date System" on page 42 in Chapter 2.

You need to pay attention to the following when working with this function:

- All arguments are truncated to integers by removing the decimal places.

- If the start or end date isn't a valid date, the YEARFRAC() function returns the #VALUE! error.

- If the basis is less than 0 or greater than 4, the YEARFRAC() function returns the #NUMBER! error.

Example For the credit period from January 1, 2008 through October 10, 2009, the formula

```
=YEARFRAC("01/01/2008","10/10/2009")
```

Chapter 7

calculates a duration of 1.775 years based on a month with 30 days and a year with 360 days. More examples (see Figure 7-9) include:

- =YEARFRAC("01/01/2010","10/10/2011",1) returns a value of 1.77260.

- =YEARFRAC("01/01/2010","10/10/2011",2) returns a value of 1.79722.

- =YEARFRAC("01/01/2010","10/10/2011",3) returns a value of 1.77260.

- =YEARFRAC("01/01/2010","10/10/2011",4) returns a value of 1.77500.

E4	▾	f_x =YEARFRAC(B4,C4)		
A	B	C	D	E
1	**YEARFRAC**			
2				
3	*Start date*	*End date*	*Basis*	Calculation
4	01/01/2010	10/10/2011		1.77500
5	01/01/2010	10/10/2011	1	1.77260
6	01/01/2010	10/10/2011	2	1.79722
7	01/01/2010	10/10/2011	3	1.77260
8	01/01/2010	10/10/2011	4	1.77500

Figure 7-9 The credit period calculated with YEARFRAC().

See Also EDATE(), EOMONTH(), NETWORKDAYS(), NETWORKDAYS.INTL(), NOW(), TODAY(), WORKDAY(), WORKDAY.INTL()

Sample Files

Use the YEARFRAC worksheet in the Date_Time.xls or Date_Time.xlsx sample file. The sample files are found in the Chapter07 folder. For more information about the sample files, see the section titled "Using the Sample Files" on page xxiii.

Text and Data Functions

This chapter describes the text and data functions in Microsoft Excel (see Table 8-1). The text and data functions provide all the tools you need to convert text or numbers and to edit and evaluate strings. When working with imported lists, you might need these functions so that you can divide, combine, or evaluate text.

Table 8-1 Overview of the Text and Data Functions

Function	Description
ASC()	Converts double-byte characters into single-byte characters
BAHTTEXT()	Converts a number into Thai text using the suffix "Baht"
CHAR()	Returns the character for a code
CLEAN()	Deletes all nonprintable characters from the text
CODE()	Returns the numeric code of the first character in a string
CONCATENATE()	Joins several strings into one string
DOLLAR()	Converts a number into a currency value
EXACT()	Checks whether two strings are exactly the same
FIND(), FINDB()	Finds a string within text
FIXED()	Rounds a number to a specified number of decimal places and returns the value as text

Function	Description
LEFT(), LEFTB()	Returns the number of characters starting at the beginning of the text string
LEN(), LENB()	Returns the number of characters in a string
LOWER()	Converts text into lowercase
MID(), MIDB()	Returns the number of characters starting at a certain position
PHONETIC()	Extracts the phonetic (Furigana) characters from a string
PROPER()	Converts the first letters of all words into uppercase
REPLACE(), REPLACEB()	Replaces a certain number of characters beginning at a given position
REPT()	Repeats a string parameter a given number of times
RIGHT(), RIGHTB()	Returns the number of characters in a text string starting at the end of the string
SEARCH(), SEARCHB()	Finds a string within the text, ignoring uppercase and lowercase distinctions
SUBSTITUTE()	Replaces a certain number of characters in the text
T()	Returns text strings
TEXT()	Converts numeric values into text
TRIM()	Deletes leading and trailing spaces from text
UPPER()	Converts a string into uppercase
VALUE()	Converts text (a number) into a numeric value

ASC()

Syntax   ASC(*text*)

Definition   This function converts double-byte characters into single-byte characters.

Arguments

- *text* **(required)** The text or the reference to a cell that contains the text you want to convert. If the text doesn't contain double-byte characters, the text is not changed.

Background   Use this function to convert double-byte characters into single-byte characters. Text data are saved, read, and transferred by using code pages. Each character is assigned a code (a numeric value). Single-byte code pages consist of only 256 characters. Double-byte code pages were developed to accommodate Asian languages, but this conversion function is of little relevance because most systems use the Unicode standards. *Unicode* is a universal character set for all known languages.

Note the following about this function:

- This function is not included in the Excel Function Wizard but is supported when entered manually.

- If an empty value is passed, ASC() also returns an empty value.

- ASC() returns numeric values as text.

- ASC() returns the first text from an array if an array is passed.

Example Because this function is not widely used, an example is not shown here. You will find an example of this function only in the sample files for this book.

See Also CHAR(), CODE()

Sample Files

Use the ASC worksheet in the Text_Data.xls or Text_Data.xlsx sample file. The sample files are found in the Chapter08 folder. For more information about the sample files, see the section titled "Using the Sample Files" on page xxiii.

BAHTTEXT()

Syntax BAHTTEXT(*number*)

Definition This function converts numeric values into numerals (in Thai text) and adds the suffix *Baht*.

Arguments

- *number* **(required)** A number converted into text, a reference to a cell that contains a number, or a formula that returns a number

Background The conversion of numeric values into the corresponding numerals is often used for checks or contracts, to protect against forgery and to avoid misunderstandings.

You can convert numeric values into Thai text but not into English text. There are, however, several downloads available on the Internet that provide this facility. Chapter 6, "Custom Functions," describes custom functions in more detail.

Example Unless you have downloaded English conversion tools, this is only of use for Thai conversions.

=BAHTTEXT(12)

The formula returns สิบสองบาทถ้วน

See Also ROMAN() (Math and Trigonometry), TEXT()

> **Sample Files**
> Use the BAHTTEXT worksheet in the Text_Data.xls or Text_Data.xlsx sample file. The sample files are found in the Chapter08 folder. For more information about the sample files, see the section titled "Using the Sample Files" on page xxiii.

CHAR()

Syntax   CHAR(*number*)

Definition   The CHAR() function returns the character corresponding to the code indicated by the number argument.

Arguments

- *number* **(required)** A number from 1 through 255 indicating the character

Background   Use the CHAR() function to convert the encoding in files created on other computers into characters. You can also use this function to insert nonprintable characters, such as line breaks, into calculated strings.

The CHAR() function is the counterpart of the CODE() function, which returns the code of a character. The character generated for a given code depends on the character set used by your computer.

Example   If you use special characters, such as quotation marks ("), the formula is more complicated. To replace an apostrophe (') with double quotation marks, use the following formula:

```
=SUBSTITUTE(E2,"'","""")
```

Example   Assume that cell A2 contains the text *The 'apostrophe'*. The formula results in The "apostrophe". Though you only had to put the word *apostrophe* in double quotation marks, you had to enter four double quotation marks instead of three in the third argument.

This is complicated because the double quotation mark is now the text. An alternative is:

```
=SUBSTITUTE(E2,CHAR(39),CHAR(34))
```

Decide for yourself which formula works better for you.

See Also CODE()

> ## Sample Files
> Use the CHAR worksheet in the Text_Data.xls or Text_Data.xlsx sample file. The sample files are found in the Chapter08 folder. For more information about the sample files, see the section titled "Using the Sample Files" on page xxiii.

CLEAN()

Syntax   CLEAN(*text*)

Definition   This function deletes all nonprintable characters from text.

Arguments

- ***text* (required)** The text to be cleaned

Background   Use the CLEAN() function for text imported from other applications that might include nonprintable characters. You can also use CLEAN() to delete code at the beginning and the end of a data file, or to remove unwanted characters such as line breaks.

The function removes mainly characters within the code range 1 through 31 (see the CODE() and CHARS() functions).

Example   Sometimes you might need to delete line breaks from data lists to export a list in a text format. Assume that cell A2 contains the following two text lines:

"August ¶

the Strong"

=CLEAN(A2) results in one line with the text "August the Strong", which you can export without any problems.

Another example is the formula

=CLEAN("inter"&CHARACTER(13)&"continental"&CHARACTER(32)&"flight")

which removes the line break (CHARACTER(13)) and keeps the space (CHARACTER(32)): intercontinental flight.

See Also CHAR(), CODE(), TRIM()

Sample Files

Use the CLEAN worksheet in the Text_Data.xls or Text_Data.xlsx sample file. The sample files are found in the Chapter08 folder. For more information about the sample files, see the section titled "Using the Sample Files" on page xxiii.

CODE()

Syntax   CODE(*text*)

Definition   This function returns the code of the first character in a string. The code corresponds to the character set used by your computer.

Arguments

- *text* **(required)** The text from which the code for the first character is returned

Background   Sometimes it is useful to know the code of a character, such as a special character. CODE() is the counterpart of CHAR(), which returns the character for a code value.

Because the function returns the code value for the first character of the text, you need to use only a single-letter argument. CODE("Excel"), CODE("Ergonomics") and CODE("E") all return 69 for the capital letter E.

To return the code for the second or third character, use the MID() function. The formula

```
=CODE(MID("Excel",2,1))
```

returns the code for the lowercase *x*: 120.

You can use this function to assign category numbers to the first names in a column. Assume that all first names beginning with A have the category number 1, all first names beginning with B have the number 2, and so on. Uppercase and lowercase characters should be treated the same. The formula uses another text function: UPPER().

```
=CODE(UPPER("torsten"))-64
```

The formula returns the value 20 (see Figure 8-1). This is the position of T in the alphabet. The UPPER() function changed the argument torsten to TORSTEN. Because the uppercase A has the code 65, you have to subtract 64 to get the correct position in the alphabet.

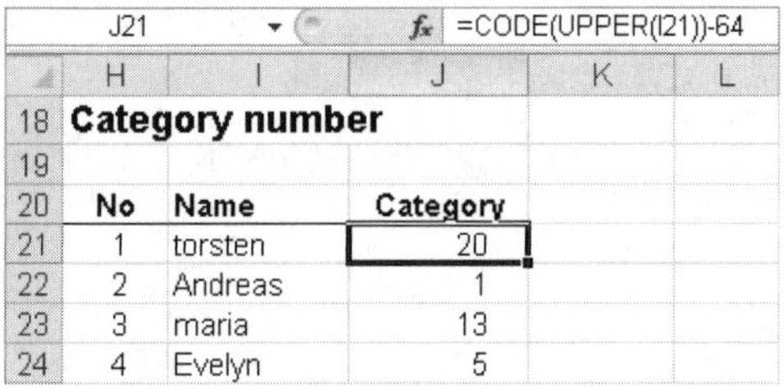

J21 =CODE(UPPER(I21))-64

	H	I	J	K	L
18	**Category number**				
19					
20	**No**	**Name**	**Category**		
21	1	torsten	20		
22	2	Andreas	1		
23	3	maria	13		
24	4	Evelyn	5		

Figure 8-1 Calculating the category number from the first letter.

See Also ASC(), CHAR()

Sample Files

Use the CODE worksheet in the Text_Data.xls or Text_Data.xlsx sample file. The sample files are found in the Chapter08 folder. For more information about the sample files, see the section titled "Using the Sample Files" on page xxiii. The CHAR worksheet also includes a code table.

CONCATENATE()

Syntax CONCATENATE(*text1*,*text2*,...)

Definition This function joins several strings into a single string.

Arguments

- ***text1,text2,...*up to 30 strings** The strings to be joined into a single text string. The arguments can be strings, numbers, or single-cell references.

The examples for the TEXT() function have already demonstrated a use for this function. With this function, you can create dynamic text combining static and calculated strings.

Keep in mind that arguments are combined without delimiters (spaces or commas). Include delimiters in the arguments or use them as separate arguments. To enter a space, enclose the space in quotation marks (" ") or use the CHAR(32) function. The value 32 for the CHAR() function returns a space.

Instead of the CONCATENATE() function, you can use the & operator to connect strings.

Example   If cell B22 contains the name *Counts*, cell C22 contains the first name *Robin*, and cell D22 contains the date of birth *12/06/1964*, the formula

```
=CONCATENATE(C22," ",B22," was born ",TEXT(D22,"MM/DD/YYYY"),". This was a
",TEXT(D22,"DDDD"),".")
```

returns `Robin Counts was born 12/06/1964. This was a Sunday.` (See Figure 8-2.)

	B24	▾ (●	ƒx	=CONCATENATE(C22," ",B22," was born ",TEXT(D22,"MM/DD/YYYY"),". This was a ",TEXT(D22,"DDDD"),".")			
⊿	A	B	C	D	E	F	G
20							
21		Name	First name	Birthday			
22		Counts	Robin	12/06/1964			
23							
24		Robin Counts was born 12/06/1964. This was a Sunday.					
25							

Figure 8-2   **The combination of text and calculations generates a sentence.**

See Also REPLACE(), REPT(), SUBSTITUTE()

Sample Files

Use the CONCATENATE worksheet in the Text_Data.xls or Text_Data.xlsx sample file. The sample files are found in the Chapter08 folder. For more information about the sample files, see the section titled "Using the Sample Files" on page xxiii.

DOLLAR()

Syntax   DOLLAR(*number,decimals*)

Definition   This function converts numbers into text and uses the currency format. The name of the function and the assigned currency symbol depend on the country settings. The decimal places are rounded according to the decimal places specified for the conversion. The default format is $#,##0.00;–$#,##0.00.

Arguments

- *number* **(required)** A numeric value, a reference to a cell that contains a number, or a formula that returns a number

- *decimals* **(optional)** The number of digits after the decimal point

  - ○ If the decimal places are negative, the number of digits to the left of the decimal point are rounded.

  - ○ If no decimal places are indicated, two decimal places are used.

Background   The difference between the Format/Cells command on the Number tab and the DOLLAR() function is that DOLLAR() converts a numeric value into text. A number formatted with the Format/Cells command is still a numeric value.

Despite this difference, you can use numbers converted with the DOLLAR() function in other formulas, because for calculations, Excel converts numbers displayed as text values into numeric values.

When you are using the DOLLAR() function to display numbers, it is important to remember that numbers displayed as text will extend into the next cell if the numbers are too large for the column width, or they might be truncated. Values that are formatted as numeric will display ### if the cell width is unable to accommodate the width of the number.

Example   Assume that you want to ensure that a price column used for a mail merge in Microsoft Word is not changed. For this reason, you use the DOLLAR() function to convert the values in the price column into the corresponding currency text in a calculated column. The calculated column is used for the mail merge process in Word. Here are some other examples:

- `=DOLLAR(12.56)` returns $12.56.

- `=DOLLAR(38612.60,-1)` returns $38,610.

- `=DOLLAR(12.56,0)` returns $13.

- `=DOLLAR(38612.60,-2)` returns $38,600.

- `=DOLLAR(12.46,0)` returns $12.

- `=DOLLAR(38612.60,-3)` returns $39,000.

- `=DOLLAR(PI(),3)` returns $3.142.

- `=DOLLAR(38612.60,-4)` returns $40,000.

See Also FIXED(), T(), TEXT(), VALUE()

> ## Sample Files
> Use the DOLLAR worksheet in the Text_Data.xls or Text_Data.xlsx sample file. The sample files are found in the Chapter08 folder. For more information about the sample files, see the section titled "Using the Sample Files" on page xxiii.

Chapter 8

EXACT()

Syntax EXACT(*text1*,*text2*)

Definition This function checks whether two strings are exactly the same and returns the logical value TRUE or FALSE.

Arguments

- ***text1* (required)** The first string to be compared.

- ***text2* (required)** The second string to be compared.

Background You can use the EXACT() function in an array expression to check whether a list contains certain strings. With EXACT(), you can also validate text entered into a form.

This function is case-sensitive but ignores formats.

Example Assume that after you have entered a list of data, you want to examine the array to check whether it contains a specific character string. The list is entered in the cell range B23:B48, and cell D22 contains the search string. Enter the following formula in a cell:

```
=OR(EXACT(D22,B23:B48))
```

and press Ctrl+Shift+Enter. The formula looks like this (see Figure 8-3):

```
{=OR(EXACT(D22,B23:B48))}
```

If you use the function as an array expression, you need the OR() function to return a single value from the list.

D23	▼	f_x {=OR(EXACT(D22,B23:B48))}		
⊿ A	B	C	D	
21	**Is search text in this list?**			
22	*List*	*Search text*	Find	
23	ASC	*Result*	FALSE	
24	BAHTTEXT			
25	CODE	*Search text*	FIND	
26	DOLLAR	*Result*	TRUE	
27	REPLACE			
28	FIXED			
29	FIND			
30	TRIM			
31	UPPER			
32	PROPER			
33	EXACT			
34	LOWER			
35	LEN			
36	LEFT			
37	PHONETIC			
38	RIGHT			
39	CLEAN			
40	SEARCH			
41	T			
42	MID			
43	TEXT			
44	CONCATENATE			
45	SUBSTITUTE			
46	VALUE			
47	REPT			
48	CHAR			

Figure 8-3 Using logical functions to determine whether a column contains a string.

Here are a few further examples:

- =EXACT("Microsoft Excel","Microsoft excel") returns FALSE.

- =EXACT("steamboat","steamboats") returns FALSE.

- =EXACT("gazelle","gazelle") returns TRUE.

- =EXACT("John Smith","Jeff Smith") returns FALSE.

See Also DELTA(), LEN(), SEARCH()

Sample Files

Use the EXACT worksheet in the Text_Data.xls or Text_Data.xlsx sample file. The sample files are found in the Chapter08 folder. For more information about the sample files, see the section titled "Using the Sample Files" on page xxiii.

FIND(), FINDB()

Syntax

- FIND(*find_text,within_text,start_num*)

- FINDB(*find_text,within_text,start_byte*)

Definition   This function returns the starting position of one text string within another text string. The function is case-sensitive.

Use FINDB() for double-byte characters.

Arguments

- ***find_text* (required)** The text you want to find.

- ***within_text* (required)** The text string to be searched.

- ***start_num/start_byte* (optional)** The character at which to start the search. The first character/byte has the value 1. If the argument is omitted, 1 is used.

Background   If you edit text, you often need to know the position of a certain character or string within the text; for example, you might need to remove or replace the characters. To do this, you use the functions FIND() or SEARCH().

> **Note**
> Unlike the SEARCH() and SEARCHB() functions, FIND() and FINDB() are case-sensitive and do not allow wildcard characters.

Use *start_num* to ensure that the search doesn't start at the first character but skips a specified number of characters. For example, if you want to know the position of the first *e* in the last part of the string *XLS2003_FormatCellProtection,* use 9 for *start_num* to skip the first part of the string. FIND() starts at the ninth character and returns the sixteenth character.

Also note the following when working with this function:

- If you search for an empty string (""), the FIND() function returns the value 1 or the value specified in *start_num*.

- The *find_text* argument cannot include placeholders. FIND() returns the #VALUE! error if it cannot find the string.

- FIND() returns the #VALUE! error if *start_num* is smaller than or equal to 0.

- FIND() returns the #VALUE! error if *start_num* is greater than the length of the string.

Example   Assume that you have a string that is separated into two parts by an underscore. If you want to locate the uppercase S in the second part of the string and find its position in the string, you will first need to determine the position of the underscore to ensure that the first part is not searched. Then you can perform the search in the remainder of the string. If cell C19 contains the string *XLS2003_FormatCellSecure*, the formula

```
=FIND("S",C19,FIND("_",C19)+1)
```

returns 19, because the *S* in the second part of the string is located in the nineteenth position (see Figure 8-4).

	F18			f_x	=FIND(C18,D18,E18)	
	C	D		E		F
3	Find_Text	Within_Text		Start_Num		Calculation
18	L	XLS2003_EditFillLeft		9		17

Figure 8-4 Cell E18 contains the formula =FIND("_",D18)+1, and the result is passed to the second argument.

If you had simply used

```
=FIND("S",C19)
```

the formula would have returned 3, which is the position of the *S* in the first part of the string.

See Also EXACT(), LEN(), MID(), REPLACE(), SEARCH(), SUBSTITUTE()

Sample Files

Use the FIND worksheet in the Text_Data.xls or Text_Data.xlsx sample file. The sample files are found in the Chapter08 folder. For more information about the sample files, see the section titled "Using the Sample Files" on page xxiii.

FIXED()

Syntax FIXED(*number,decimals,no_commas*)

Definition This function converts a numeric value into text with a fixed number of decimal places.

Arguments

- *number* **(required)** The numeric value you want to convert into text.

- *decimals* **(optional)** The number of digits to the right of the decimal point.

- *no_commas* **(optional)** A logical value. If *no_commas* is TRUE, the FIXED() function does not display commas in the returned text.

Background Like the DOLLAR() function, the FIXED() function rounds the number and converts it into text. The decimal places indicate whether a value is rounded or, if it is not, how many decimal places the value should have.

In Excel, numbers can have a maximum of 15 digit places. The maximum valid value for decimal places is 127. If the decimal places argument is a negative value, the value is rounded that number of digits to the left of the decimal point. If no decimal places are indicated, two decimal places are used. If you specify the logical value FALSE or nothing in the *no_commas* argument, the returned text contains commas.

The difference between the Format/Cells command on the Number tab and the FIXED() function is that FIXED() converts a numeric value into text. A number formatted with the Format/Cells command is still a numeric value. Despite this difference, you can use numbers converted with the FIXED() function in other formulas, because for calculations Excel converts numbers displayed as text values into numeric values.

Example Assume that you want to ensure that a column with number values that is used for a mail merge in Word is not changed. Use the FIXED() function to convert the values into text in a new column. This column can then be used for the mail merge in Word. Here are some more examples:

- =FIXED(12.56) returns 12.56.

- =FIXED(1234.56,-1,1) returns 1230.

- =FIXED(12.56,0) returns 13.

- =FIXED(1234.56,-2,TRUE) returns 1200.

- =FIXED(12.46,0) returns 12.

- `=FIXED(1234.56,-3,0)` returns 1,000.

- `=FIXED(PI(),3)` returns 3.142.

- `=FIXED(1234.56,-4,FALSE)` returns 0.

See Also DOLLAR(), ROUND(), TEXT(), VALUE()

> **Sample Files**
>
> Use the FIXED worksheet in the Text_Data.xls or Text_Data.xlsx sample file. The sample files are found in the Chapter08 folder. For more information about the sample files, see the section titled "Using the Sample Files" on page xxiii.

LEFT(), LEFTB()

Syntax

- LEFT(*text,num_chars*)

- LEFTB(*text,num_bytes*)

Definition   The LEFT() function returns the first characters of a string. The LEFTB() function is used for double-byte characters and returns the first bytes.

Arguments

- ***text* (required)** The string containing the characters you want to extract

- ***num_chars/num_bytes* (optional)** Specifies how many characters to extract

Background   Use the LEFT() function to extract the first part of a string. You can enter letters or numbers in the *text* argument. The functions LEFT(), RIGHT(), and MID() are especially useful if strings have a particular pattern, as in the case with ZIP Codes, locations, or ISBNs.

The *num_chars* argument has to be greater than or equal to 0. If the value of *num_chars* is greater than the value of the *text* argument, the LEFT() function returns the entire string. If the *num_chars* argument is not specified, the default value of 1 is used.

Example   A list of names is entered into a spreadsheet column with the first name separated from the last name with a space. Cell H4 contains a name. The following formula extracts the first name:

```
=LEFT(H4,SEARCH(" ",H4)-1)
```

You use the SEARCH() function to determine the position of the space between the first and last names (see Figure 8-5). If you subtract 1 from the result, you get the position of the last character of the first name (the number of characters from the left).

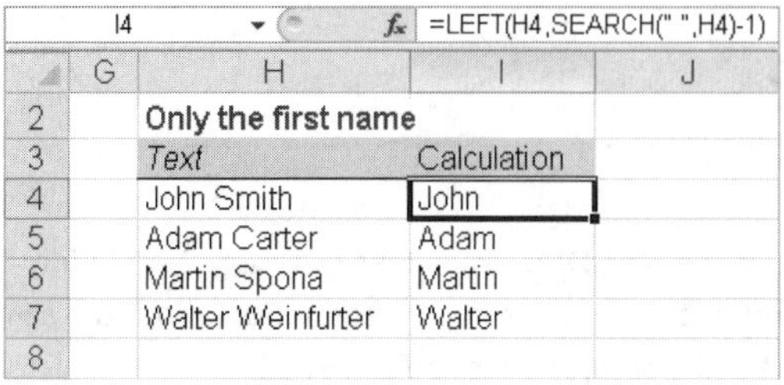

	14	▾ ⊙	*f_x* =LEFT(H4,SEARCH(" ",H4)-1)	
	G	H	I	J
2		Only the first name		
3		*Text*	Calculation	
4		John Smith	John	
5		Adam Carter	Adam	
6		Martin Spona	Martin	
7		Walter Weinfurter	Walter	
8				

Figure 8-5 Using the LEFT() function together with the SEARCH() function.

Here are some further examples:

- =LEFT("steamboat",5) returns steam.

- =LEFT("gazelle",4) returns gaze.

- =LEFT("Oliver Kiel",5) returns Oliver.

- =LEFT("Excel",1) returns E.

- =LEFT("Excel",2) returns Ex.

See Also MID(), RIGHT()

Sample Files

Use the LEFT worksheet in the **Text_Data.xls** or **Text_Data.xlsx** sample file. The sample files are found in the **Chapter08** folder. For more information about the sample files, see the section titled "Using the Sample Files" on page xxiii.

LEN(), LENB()

Syntax

- LEN(*text*)

- LENB(*text*)

Definition   The LEN() function returns the number of characters in a string. The LENB() function returns the number of bytes for the double-byte characters in a string.

Arguments

- ***text* (required)** The text whose length you want to determine.

Background   This function can be used for many tasks; for example, you could use the function together with other functions such as MID(), LEFT(), or RIGHT() to manipulate a string.

You can use this function to check whether an entry has a certain length. You can also check whether the content in text columns exceeds a given length. The function counts spaces and numerals as characters.

Example   Assume that you need to make sure that the interface descriptions in a column don't exceed 10 characters. To do this, you use the LEN() function. With the AutoFilter, you can quickly find and correct strings longer than 10 characters in the result column. Some other examples are listed here:

- `=LEN("CD")` returns 2.

- `=LEN("Excel 2007")` returns 10.

- `=LEN("Microsoft")` returns 9.

- `=LEN("No Panic!")` returns 9.

- `=LEN("")` returns 0.

- `=LEN(" ")` returns 1.

- `=LEN("1.345 $")` returns 7.

- `=LEN(TODAY())` returns 5.

See Also EXACT(), FIND(), SEARCH()

Sample Files

Use the LEN worksheet in the Text_Data.xls or Text_Data.xlsx sample file. The sample files are found in the Chapter08 folder. For more information about the sample files, see the section titled "Using the Sample Files" on page xxiii.

Chapter 8

LOWER()

Syntax LOWER(*text*)

Definition This function converts a string to lowercase.

Arguments

- **text (required)** The text you want to convert to lowercase

Background The LOWER() function is the counterpart of the UPPER() function that converts a string to uppercase. All uppercase letters are converted to lowercase letters. All other characters are left unchanged.

You can also use this function to compare non–case-sensitive strings.

If you pass a numeric value in the *text* argument, this value is converted to unformatted text. If you refer to this text in numeric calculations, Excel converts the text back to a number value so that you can still use the result for other calculations.

If you want to compare text and are not concerned about the comparison being case-sensitive, you can convert the entire text to lowercase (see Figure 8-6). The formula

```
=LOWER("Letters")="letters"
```

as well as

```
=LOWER("LETTERS")="letters"
```

returns TRUE.

	B	C	D
		D21	▾	*fx* =LOWER(B21)=C21
	Text	Inspection text	Identical
20	Text	Inspection text	Identical
21	Characters	characters	TRUE
22	characters	characters	TRUE
23	UppeRcase CharacTEr	uppercase character	TRUE
24	UppeRcase CharacTErs	uppercase character	FALSE

Figure 8-6 Text comparison independent of uppercase and lowercase, using the LOWER() function.

Here are some further examples:

- =LOWER("John Smith") results in john smith.

- =LOWER("Excel") results in excel.

- =LOWER("eXCEL") results in excel.

- =LOWER(TODAY()) returns 40450 on September 29, 2010.

See Also PROPER(), UPPER()

Sample Files

Use the LOWER worksheet in the Text_Data.xls or Text_Data.xlsx sample file. The sample files are found in the Chapter08 folder. For more information about the sample files, see the section titled "Using the Sample Files" on page xxiii.

MID(), MIDB()

Syntax

- MID(*text,start_num,num_chars*)

- MIDB(*text,start_num,num_bytes*)

Definition   The MID() function returns characters from the middle of a text string. The length of the character string is indicated by *num_chars*, and the starting position for the search is *start_num*. Use MIDB() for double-byte characters.

Arguments

- ***text* (required)** The string from which the characters are to be extracted

- ***start_num* (required)** The starting position for the character string to be extracted

- ***num_chars/num_bytes* (required)** Specifies how many characters/bytes to return from *text*

Background   Use the MID() function to return characters from the middle of a string. You can enter letters or numbers in the *text* argument. The MID(), LEFT(), and RIGHT() functions are especially useful if strings have a standard format, as with ZIP Codes, locations, or ISBNs.

Note the following when working with this function:

- MID() returns an empty string ("") if *start_num* is greater than the length of the string.

- MID() returns all characters to the end of the text if *start_num* is smaller than the length of the string but *start_num* plus *num_chars* exceeds the length of the string.

- MID() returns the #VALUE! error if *start_num* is less than or equal to 1.

- MID() returns the #VALUE! error if *start_num* is negative.

Example You might need to extract the product group from a column containing item numbers made up of 10 digits, where:

- The main product group is the first two digits.

- The product group is the next three digits.

- The product number is the remaining five digits.

So for an item number of 2301511290, you can use the MID() function to locate the product group, which starts at position 3 and is three digits long (see Figure 8-7). The formula

=MID("2301511290",3,3)

returns 015 as the product group.

	B	C	D	E
				E4 ▾ *fx* =MID(B4,C4,D4)
3	Text	Start_Num	Num_Chars	Calculation
4	2301511290	3	3	015
5	0811700678	3	3	117
6	1200301940	3	3	003

Figure 8-7 Extracting part of the item number.

Further examples:

- =MID("intercontinentalflight",1,5) returns inter.

- =MID("gazelle",1,4) returns gaze.

- =MID("gazelle",4,4) returns elle.

- =MID("Louis",2,3) returns oui.

- =MID("Excel",1,2) returns Ex.

- =MID("Excel",2,3) returns xce.

See Also CODE(), FIND(), LEFT(), RIGHT(), SEARCH()

Sample Files

Use the MID worksheet in the Text_Data.xls or Text_Data.xlsx sample file. The sample files are found in the Chapter08 folder. For more information about the sample files, see the section titled "Using the Sample Files" on page xxiii.

PHONETIC()

Syntax PHONETIC(*reference*)

Definition This function extracts the phonetic (Furigana) characters from a string.

Arguments

- ***reference* (required)** A string, or a reference to a cell or cell range containing a phonetic string. If a cell range is referenced, the phonetic string is returned in the upper-left cell of the range. If the range contains noncontiguous cells, the #NV error is returned.

Background The modern Japanese writing system uses three main scripts:

- **Kanji** Ideographs from Chinese characters

- **Kana** A pair of syllabaries, consisting of:

    o Hiragana, used for native Japanese words

    o Katakana, used for foreign words and names, loan words, onomatopoeia, scientific names, and sometimes to replace kanji or hiragana for emphasis

These fonts are used together in everyday text. The phonetic furigana spelling consists of small hiragana characters, which are used with kanji to indicate the pronunciation. This function extracts the furigana characters from Japanese strings. To use the PHONETIC() function, you must install Asian languages on your computer. The typical Excel user might not have a need for this function.

PROPER()

Syntax PROPER(*text*)

Definition This function converts the first character of all words in a string to uppercase and all other characters to lowercase.

Arguments

- ***text* (required)** The text string enclosed in quotation marks, a formula that returns text, or the reference to the cell that contains the text you want to convert to proper case

Background Many systems import data in uppercase. Using the PROPER() function allows you to convert the data to normal text.

Chapter 8

You can also use this function for names with a hyphen. If you pass numeric values, the PROPER() function works in the same way as the UPPER() function.

Examples   Assume that the text in an imported list consists of all uppercase letters. You want to convert the text to the correct casing (uppercase and lowercase).

- =PROPER("charles dickens") results in Charles Dickens.

- =PROPER("Excel") results in Excel.

- =PROPER("eXCEL") results in Excel.

- =PROPER("JEAN PHILIPPE BAGEL") results in Jean Philippe Bagel.

See Also LOWER(), UPPER()

> ## Sample Files
> Use the PROPER worksheet in the Text_Data.xls or Text_Data.xlsx sample file. The sample files are found in the Chapter08 folder. For more information about the sample files, see the section titled "Using the Sample Files" on page xxiii.

REPLACE(), REPLACEB()

Syntax

- REPLACE(*old_text,start_num,num_chars,new_text*)

- REPLACEB(*old_text,start_num,num_bytes,new_text*)

Definition   The REPLACE() function replaces the *old_text* string beginning at *start_num* and with the length indicated by *num_chars* with the new string in *new_text*.

Use REPLACEB() for double-byte characters.

Arguments

- ***old_text* (required)** The string containing the characters you want to replace

- ***start_num* (required)** The starting position for text replacement

- ***num_char/num_bytes* (required)** The number of characters/bytes beyond the start position in which to make replacements

- ***new_text* (required)** The text that will replace the characters in *old_text*

Background   Use this function to replace either specific characters or a specific string with a fixed length within a string. An example is a list that contains placeholders that you want to replace with fixed or calculated expressions.

REPLACE() differs from the SUBSTITUTE() function, which replaces a string within a piece of text. The REPLACE() function allows you to define which part of the text to search for replacement.

Assume that you want to replace the word *paragraph* with the § symbol in a list. Cell B25 contains the text *Paragraph 3, Sect. 4*. The formula

```
=REPLACE(B25,SEARCH("paragraph",B25),LEN("paragraph"),"§")
```

results in *§ 3, Sect. 4* (see Figure 8-8).

	A	B	C	D	E	F
F26		=REPLACE(B25,SEARCH("Paragraph",B25),LEN("Paragraph"),"§")				
3		Old_Text	Start_Num	Num_Chars	New_Text	Calculation
22						
23		Replace 'paragraph' with '§':				
24		The paragraph 92 U.S.C.	5	9	§	The § 92 U.S.C.
25		Paragraph 3, Sect. 4	1	9	§	§ 3, Sect. 4
26					In one formula:	§ 3, Sect. 4
27						

Figure 8-8 Replacing the word *paragraph* with §.

Assume now that you want to replace the word *date* with the current date in a list. If cell A2 contains the text *Seattle, date*, the formula

```
=REPLACE(A2,SEARCH("date",A2),LEN("date"),TEXT(TODAY(),"MM/DD/YYYY"))
```

results in Seattle, 12/24/2008 on December 24, 2008.

See Also MID(), SEARCH(), SUBSTITUTE(), TRIM()

Sample Files

Use the REPLACE worksheet in the Text_Data.xls or Text_Data.xlsx sample file. The sample files are found in the Chapter08 folder. For more information about the sample files, see the section titled "Using the Sample Files" on page xxiii.

REPT()

Syntax   REPT(*text,number_times*)

Definition   This function repeats *text* a given number of times.

Arguments

- *text* **(required)** The character or string you want to repeat

- *number_times* **(required)** A positive number indicating how often the text is repeated

Background   Use the REPT() function to fill a cell with a specified number of instances of a text string. You can also use this function for chart-like illustrations in worksheets.

Also note the following when working with this function:

- If *number_times* is 0, the REPT() function returns an empty string ("").

- If *number_times* is not an integer, the decimal places are truncated.

- If *number_times* is a negative number, the REPT() function returns the #VALUE! error.

- If the result exceeds 32,767 characters, the REPT() function returns the #VALUE! error.

Example   Assume that the cell range F6:F16 contains names, and the cell range G6:G16 contains scores. You want to show both the names and the scores in H6:H16, with the names on the left and the scores on the right. The cell width should be adjusted as necessary.

Create an auxiliary column (I) to calculate the maximum total length for the names and scores. Select the range I6:I16, and enter the following formula:

```
=MAX(LEN(F6:F16)+LEN(G6:G16))+1
```

Press Ctrl+Shift+Enter. The array formula enclosed in braces calculates the maximal necessary length for the names and scores in each line. Enter the formula

```
=F6&REPT(" ",I6-LEN(F6)-LEN(G6))&G6
```

in cell H6 (see Figure 8-9) and copy it into the cells below H6. Based on the maximal total length and the actual total length in the row, you can calculate the necessary space.

CAUTION

This example makes sense only when using nonproportional fonts (such as Courier), in which all characters are the same width.

H6	▼ (	*f_x* =F6&REPT(" ",I6-LEN(F6)-LEN(G6))&G6		

	F	G	H	I	J
3	*Column H should contain the left-aligned name and the right-aligned points.*				
4	*The width of all rows should be the maximum required.*				
5	**Name**	**Points**	**List**	(Help)	
6	Hansen	37	Hansen 37	14	
7	Zaki	123	Zaki 123	14	
8	Nixon	3	Nixon 3	14	
9	O'Neill	32	O'Neill 32	14	
10	Gray	2345	Gray 2345	14	
11	Rounthwaite	99	Rounthwaite 99	14	
12	Frost	134	Frost 134	14	
13	Miller	54	Miller 54	14	
14	Kiel	4	Kiel 4	14	
15	Timm	1204	Timm 1204	14	
16	Dickson	22	Dickson 22	14	

Figure 8-9 Using REPT() to fill in spaces.

See Also CONCATENATE(), REPLACE(), SUBSTITUTE()

> **Sample Files**
>
> Use the REPT worksheet in the Text_Data.xls or Text_Data.xlsx sample file. The sample files are found in the Chapter08 folder. For more information about the sample files, see the section titled "Using the Sample Files" on page xxiii.

RIGHT(), RIGHTB()

Syntax

- RIGHT(text;num_chars)

- RIGHTB(*text;num_bytes*)

Definition   The RIGHT() function returns the last characters of a string. The RIGHTB() function is used for double-byte characters and returns the last bytes.

Arguments

- ***text* (required)** The string from which to extract the characters

- ***num_chars/num_bytes* (optional)** Specifies how many characters to extract

Chapter 8

Background   Use the RIGHT() function to extract characters from the end of a string (see Figure 8-10). You can enter letters or numbers in the *text* argument. The functions RIGHT(), LEFT(), and MID() are especially useful for extracting information from strings with set formats, such as ZIP Codes, locations, or ISBNs.

	I4	▼	*fx*	=RIGHT(H4,LEN(H4)-SEARCH(" ",H4))	
	G	H		I	J
2		Only the last name			
3		*Text*		*Calculation*	
4		John Smith		Smith	
5		Adam Carter		Carter	
6		Martin Spona		Spona	
7		Walter Weinfurter		Weinfurter	
8					

Figure 8-10 Resolving text problems is not magic but is accomplished with text functions.

The *num_chars* argument must be greater than or equal to 0. If the value of *num_chars* is greater than the value of the *text* argument, the RIGHT() function returns the entire string. If the *num_chars* argument is not specified, the default value used is 1.

Example   In a spreadsheet column, the first name and last name are separated by a space. You want to extract the last name. Cell H4 contains the name. The following formula extracts the last name:

```
=RIGHT(H4,LEN(H4)-SEARCH(" ",H4))
```

You use the SEARCH() function to locate the space character. LEN() provides the total string length, and then the characters to the right of the space character can be extracted by using the RIGHT function.

See Also LEFT(), LEFTB(), MID()

Sample Files

Use the RIGHT worksheet in the Text_Data.xls or Text_Data.xlsx sample file. The sample files are found in the Chapter08 folder. For more information about the sample files, see the section titled "Using the Sample Files" on page xxiii.

SEARCH(), SEARCHB()

Syntax

- SEARCH(*find_text,within_text,start_num*)

- SEARCHB(*find_text,within_text,start_byte*)

Definition   The SEARCH() function returns the first occurrence at which a string is found. The search starts at the position indicated by the *start_num* argument. The function is not case-sensitive.

The SEARCHB() function returns the number of bytes of the characters. This function is used for double-byte strings.

Arguments

- ***find_text* (required)**   The string you are searching for

- ***within_text* (required)**   The text in which to search for *find_text*

- ***start_num/start_byte* (optional)**   The starting character from which to begin the search

Background   If you edit text, you often need to know the position of a certain character or string within the text—for example, when you want to remove or replace the character. To do this, you use the SEARCH() or FIND()function.

Important

Unlike FIND() and FINDB(), the SEARCH() and SEARCHB() functions are not case-sensitive and allow the wildcard characters * and ?.

The SEARCH() function returns the character number at the start of the located text. The search text can include the wildcard characters ? and *. The question mark (?) stands for a character, and the asterisk (*) stands for a string. If you enter ? or *, the search string must be preceded by a tilde (~).

Use *start_num* to begin the search a specified number of characters into the string. For example, if you want to know the position of the first *e* after the initial code in the string *XLS2003_FormatCellProtection*, use 9 for *start_num* to skip the first part of the string. SEARCH() starts at the ninth character and returns the sixteenth character.

Chapter 8

Note the following when working with this function:

- If you search for an empty string (""), the SEARCH() function returns the value 1 or the value specified in *start_num*.

- SEARCH() returns the #VALUE! error if it cannot find the string.

- If the *start_num* argument is not specified, the function uses the default value 1.

- SEARCH() returns the #VALUE! error if *start_num* is less than or equal to 0.

- SEARCH() returns the #VALUE! error if *start_num* is greater than the length of the string.

Example   If you want to know whether the text in a column contains letters or numbers enclosed by square brackets, you can use a calculated column with a wildcard character search, as shown in Figure 8-11. The formula

`=SEARCH(C25,D25)`

returns position 5. The search looks for a string of any characters enclosed in square brackets. The string *[small]* starts at position 5 in the search string.

	F25	▾ (	*fx* =SEARCH(C25,D25)		
	C	D		E	F
3	Find_Text	Within_Text		Start_Num	Calculation
25	[*]	The [small] haven in the sun			5
26	[*]	Here is only one open [square bracket.			#VALUE!
27	[*]	Here is no square bracket.			#VALUE!

Figure 8-11 The string is found or the search returns an error.

Here are some further examples:

- `=SEARCH("r","intercontinentalflight"1)` returns 5.

- `=SEARCH("R""intercontinentalflight"1)` returns 5.

- `=SEARCH("t""intercontinentalflight"1)` returns 3.

- `=SEARCH("I""intercontinentalflight"1)` returns 1.

- `=SEARCH("i""intercontinentalflight"1)` returns 1.

- `=SEARCH("I""intercontinentalflight"2)` returns 10.

See Also FIND(), FINDB(), MID(), MIDB(), REPLACE(), REPLACEB(), SUBSTITUTE()

Sample Files

Use the SEARCH worksheet in the Text_Data.xls or Text_Data.xlsx sample file. The sample files are found in the Chapter08 folder. For more information about the sample files, see the section titled "Using the Sample Files" on page xxiii.

SUBSTITUTE()

Syntax   SUBSTITUTE(*text,old_text,new_text,instance_num*)

Definition   The SUBSTITUTE() function replaces characters or strings with new text.

Arguments

- *text* **(required)** The text or the reference to a cell containing text in which you want to substitute characters

- *old_text* **(required)** The string you want to replace

- *new_text* **(required)** The string you want to replace *old_text* with

- *instance_num* **(optional)** Specifies which occurrence of *old_text* you want to replace with *new_text*. If you specify *instance_num*, only that occurrence of *old_text* is replaced; otherwise, every instance of *old_text* is replaced.

Background   Use this function to replace a string of text with alternative text. The replacement can be for a single or for multiple instances.

You can use the SUBSTITUTE() function to replace a specific string within text. Use the REPLACE() function to replace a string at a certain position within text.

Important

The SUBSTITUTE() function is case-sensitive when it is searching for *old_text*.

Example Suppose you want to replace German special characters; for example, *ä* with *ae*, *ö* with *oe*, and *ü* with *ue*. To do this, you nest the SUBSTITUTE() function three times:

```
=SUBSTITUTE(SUBSTITUTE(SUBSTITUTE("Dönerverkäuferprüfung","ä","ae"),"ö","oe"),"ü",
"ue")
```

This results in `Doenerverkaeuferpruefung`. Here are a few more examples:

- `=SUBSTITUTE("intercontinentalflight","flight","drive")` results in `intercontinentaldrive`.

- `=SUBSTITUTE("cell","l","t",2)` results in `celt`.

- `=SUBSTITUTE("vetter","tt","nt",1)` results in `venter`.

- `=SUBSTITUTE("canter","A","e")`results in `canter`.

- `=SUBSTITUTE("million","m","b")` results in `billion`.

See Also FIND(), REPLACE(), REPLACEB(), SEARCH(), TRIM()

Sample Files

Use the SUBSTITUTE worksheet in the Text_Data.xls or Text_Data.xlsx sample file. The sample files are found in the Chapter08 folder. For more information about the sample files, see the section titled "Using the Sample Files" on page xxiii.

T()

Syntax T(*value*)

Definition This function checks whether an entry is text and returns the text value. If the entry is not a text value, the return value is empty.

Arguments

- *value* **(required)** The expression (a number, text, a formula without an equal sign, a logical value, an error value, a reference, or a name) to check

Background The T() function is provided for compatibility with other spreadsheet software. You do not normally need to use the T() function in formulas, because Excel converts values as required.

When using this function, keep in mind that numbers are not converted into numerals; instead, the result is an empty string. The same applies to logical values. Error values are converted into error values, not into text.

See Also CELL(), DOLLAR(), FIXED(), N(), TEXT(), VALUE()

> ### Sample Files
>
> Use the T worksheet in the Text_Data.xls or Text_Data.xlsx sample file. The sample files are found in the Chapter08 folder. For more information about the sample files, see the section titled "Using the Sample Files" on page xxiii.

TEXT()

Syntax   TEXT(*value,format_text*)

Definition   This function converts a value into text in a specific number format.

Arguments

- *value* **(required)** A number, a formula that evaluates to a numeric value, or a reference to a cell containing a numeric value

- *format_text* **(required)** A number format, which is one of those in the Custom category box on the Number tab in the Format Cells dialog box

Background   You might need to convert numeric values to text to link static text with calculations. The TEXT() function not only converts numeric values to text but also allows you to use the number formats available in the Format Cells dialog box.

In the *format_text* argument you can specify custom formats. However, the formats have the following restrictions:

- Formats cannot contain an asterisks (*).

- The General number format is not allowed.

- Colors, such as red for negative values, are ignored.

The difference between the Format/Cells command and the TEXT() function is that TEXT() returns text. A number formatted with the Format/Cells command is still a numeric value. You can still use numbers converted with the TEXT() function in other formulas, because for calculations Excel converts numbers displayed as text values into numeric values.

Example   Assume that you want to include a dynamic date of payment in an invoice form, so that 14 days are added to the current date. The formula

```
=CONCATENATE("Please pay before ",TEXT(TODAY()+14,"MM/DD/YYYY"),".")
```

returns `Please pay before 12/15/2010` on December 1, 2010. The formula

```
=CONCATENATE("Please pay before ",TODAY()+14,".")
```

without the TEXT() function also works, but your customer probably wouldn't know what to do with `Please pay before 40527`.

On another form, assume that you want to show the current date in a sentence. The formula

```
="Today is "&TEXT(TODAY(),"DDDD")&", "&TEXT(TODAY(),"MMMM D. YYYY")&"."
```

results in `Today is Monday, December 1, 2010` on December 1, 2010.

See Also ASC(), DOLLAR(), FIXED(), T(), VALUE()

> **Sample Files**
>
> Use the TEXT worksheet in the Text_Data.xls or Text_Data.xlsx sample file. The sample files are found in the Chapter08 folder. For more information about the sample files, see the section titled "Using the Sample Files" on page xxiii.

TRIM()

Syntax   TRIM(*text*)

Definition   This function deletes the spaces in the text that are not used as delimiters between words.

Arguments

- **text (required)** The text containing the leading and trailing spaces you want to delete.

Background   You can use the TRIM() function for text imported from other applications that might contain unnecessary spaces. Redundant spaces at the beginning or end of text can be unhelpful, for example, for a mail merge or when searching for a string in a list.

If the string does not contain leading or trailing spaces, the result is the input string.

Assume that after you import a set of data, you notice that it contains trailing spaces. You need to remove these spaces to further process the data. You cannot use the Replace command (Ctrl+H), because you don't want to delete the spaces between words. You can use the TRIM() function to remove the redundant spaces. The following table shows some of the possible results for different input values:

Formula	Result
=TRIM("August")	The word *August* isn't changed.
=TRIM("August ")	The trailing space after *August* is removed.
=TRIM(" August ")	The two leading spaces before *August* are removed.
=TRIM(" August ")	The two leading spaces and the three trailing spaces are removed.
=TRIM(" August the Strong ")	The leading space and the trailing space are removed.

See Also CLEAN(), MID(), SUBSTITUTE()

Sample Files

Use the TRIM worksheet in the Text_Data.xls or Text_Data.xlsx sample file. The sample files are found in the Chapter08 folder. For more information about the sample files, see the section titled "Using the Sample Files" on page xxiii.

UPPER()

Syntax   UPPER(*text*)

Definition   The UPPER() function converts text to uppercase.

Arguments

- ***text* (required)** The text you want to convert to uppercase, which can be a reference or a string.

Background   This function provides a quick and easy method for converting text to uppercase.

You can also use this function to make non–case-sensitive comparisons.

If you pass a numeric value in the *text* argument, the value is converted to unformatted text. If you refer to this text in numeric calculations, Excel converts the text back to a number value so that you can still use the result for other calculations.

Example   If you want to compare text strings and are not concerned about the comparison being case-sensitive, you can convert the entire text to uppercase (see Figure 8-12). The formula

```
=UPPER("Letters")="LETTERS"
```

as well as

```
=UPPER("letters")="LETTERS"
```

returns TRUE.

	B	C	D
			D22 ▾ (f_x =UPPER(B22)=C22
21	*Text*	*Inspection text*	*Identical*
22	Characters	CHARACTERS	TRUE
23	characters	CHARACTERS	TRUE
24	LoweRcase CharacTEr	LOWERCASE CHARACTER	TRUE
25	LoweRcase CharacTErs	LOWERCASE CHARACTER	FALSE

Figure 8-12 Text comparison independent of uppercase and lowercase, using the UPPER() function.

Here are some further examples:

- =UPPER("Excel") returns EXCEL.

- =UPPER("eXCEL") returns EXCEL.

- =UPPER("1,232.56") returns 1232.56.

- =UPPER(TODAY()) returns 40450 on September 29, 2010.

See Also LOWER(), PROPER()

> ## Sample Files
>
> Use the UPPER worksheet in the Text_Data.xls or Text_Data.xlsx sample file. The sample files are found in the Chapter08 folder. For more information about the sample files, see the section titled "Using the Sample Files" on page xxiii.

VALUE()

Syntax   VALUE(*text*)

Definition   The VALUE() function converts the text into a number.

Arguments

- *text* **(required)** The text enclosed in quotation marks or the reference to the cell that contains the text you want to convert

Background   Excel converts numbers displayed as text values into numeric values. However, with data imported from third-party applications or with third-party add-ins, errors might occur.

Usually you do not need the VALUE() function within a formula, but you can convert a value list imported as text so that Excel can recognize and display the values:

1. Enter **1** in an empty cell.

2. Press Ctrl+C to copy the cell content into the Clipboard.

3. Select the range containing the "text" numbers, click the Paste arrow on the Home tab, and click Paste Special (Excel 2007 and Excel 2010). In Excel 2003, select the Edit/Paste Special command.

4. Select the Values and Multiply options in the Paste Special dialog box, and click OK.

All values in the selected range should be displayed as numbers instead of as text. Because you don't need the cell with the 1 anymore, you can delete this cell.

The content of the *text* argument can have any format supported by Excel for constants, dates, and times. VALUE() returns the #VALUE! error if the text has another format.

Example   You might need to ensure that imported numbers are passed as numeric values to further process numbers imported from text files. Here are a few more examples:

- =VALUE("1.234") returns 1234.

- =VALUE(1234) returns 1234.

- =VALUE("09/09/2008") returns 39700.

- =VALUE(TRUE) returns the #VALUE! error.

See Also DOLLAR(), FIXED(), N(), TEXT(), the information functions

Sample Files

Use the VALUE worksheet in the Text_Data.xls or Text_Data.xlsx sample file. The sample files are found in the Chapter08 folder. For more information about the sample files, see the section titled "Using the Sample Files" on page xxiii.

Logical Functions

T his chapter explains how to use the logical functions such as NOT(), AND(), and OR() in Microsoft Excel. Table 9-1 lists all the logical functions. Other functions, such as TRUE() and FALSE(), are less frequently used. All of these functions return logical values or use them as an integral part of the function. The IF() function evaluates logical expressions and implements appropriate branches. Comparison operators (=, <, >, <=, >=, and <>) are important when evaluating arguments. The IFERROR() function was introduced in Excel 2007.

Table 9-1 **Overview of the Logical Functions**

Function	Description
AND()	Returns the logical value TRUE if all arguments are true
FALSE()	Returns the logical value FALSE
IF()	Calculates alternatives (using then and else) corresponding to the logical results of a condition evaluation
IFERROR()	Calculates a specified output if an expression contains an error or returns the result of the expression
NOT()	Returns the opposite of the logical value specified in the parentheses
OR()	Returns the logical value TRUE if one of the arguments is true
TRUE()	Returns the logical value TRUE

AND()

Syntax AND(*logical1,logical2, ...*)

Definition This function returns the logical value TRUE only if all arguments are true. If the value of at least one argument is FALSE, the function returns FALSE.

Arguments

- **_logical1,logical2,..._** Up to 30 values (in Excel 2003) or up to 255 (in Excel 2007 or 2010), entered directly or resulting from conditions that can be evaluated to TRUE or FALSE

The arguments should be logical values (TRUE or FALSE), numbers, or values from arrays or references containing logical values or evaluated to logical values.

If an argument specified as an array or reference contains text or empty cells, these values are ignored if at least one of the arguments can be evaluated.

At least one of the arguments must be a logical value, a logical value resulting from a reference, or a logical value generated during the evaluation of logical expressions. Otherwise, the AND() function returns the #VALUE! error.

If arguments contain error values, the result is also an error.

Example   If you enter the word _text_ in cells H22 and H23, AND(H22,H23) returns the #VALUE! error, but AND(H22,H23,FALSE) and AND(H22,H23,0) each return FALSE. If you replace FALSE with TRUE and 0 or another number, the logical value TRUE is returned.

You get the same results if you enter the word _text_ in cells H25 and H27 and enter a logical value or a number in cell H26. When AND(H25:H27) is being evaluated, the cells containing text are ignored until one of the cells returns a logical value or a number.

The second example for the OR() function shows the connection between AND(), OR(), and NOT().

See Also NOT(), OR()

Sample Files

Use the Samples worksheet in the Logical_values.xls or Logical_values.xlsx sample file. The sample files are found in the Chapter09 folder. For more information about the sample files, see the section titled "Using the Sample Files" on page xxiii.

FALSE()

Syntax   FALSE()

Definition   This function returns the logical value (Boolean value) FALSE.

Arguments   None

Background   This function is seldom used, because you can just enter the word *false*. Excel interprets the result returned by the function as a logical value (in this case, FALSE). The interpretation forced by numeric operations is the number value 0. You can check this by entering the formula =3+FALSE in a cell.

However, if you compare two cells, and one cell contains FALSE and the other cell 0, the result is FALSE.

You can enter *false* (which is not case-sensitive) directly in a worksheet or formula. Excel recognizes this word as the logical value FALSE and formats the cell accordingly. To avoid this, do one of the following:

- Format the cell as text before you enter *false* (use Cells/Format/Format Cells on the Home tab in Excel 2007 and Excel 2010 and Format/Cells in earlier versions).

- Enter a space before the word *false*.

- Prefix the text with an apostrophe (').

Excel recognizes FALSE as a logical value even if you don't enter the parentheses. This is different from other functions; for example, an error is generated if the function TODAY() is entered without the parentheses.

Logical values can be useful when you are evaluating expressions using the logical operators AND and OR:

- The OR operator for two logical values is always TRUE unless both logical values are FALSE.

- The AND operator for two logical values is always FALSE unless both logical values are TRUE.

Example   If you are working with conditional formats in one or more cells, the conditions can get complex, and using logical values can help to maintain clarity.

For example, you might want to highlight the days at the end of a quarter. These can be defined as the days after the twentieth day in the months of March, June, September, and December. If you use the TODAY() function to enter the current date into cell B13 of your worksheet, the formula

`AND(MOD(MONTH(B13),3)=0,DAY(B13)>20`

defines the days that you want to highlight. If this function is true, format the background color as red; if the value is false, format the background green. The formula

`MOD(MONTH(B13),3)=0`

determines whether the month is the last month of a quarter—in other words, whether the month number is exactly divisible by 3. The formula

`DAY(B13)>20`

is TRUE if the number of the day is greater than 20. Therefore,

`=(AND(MOD(MONTH(B13),3)=0;DAY(B13)>20)=TRUE)`

selects the last days in each quarter, and

`=(AND(MOD(MONTH(B13),3)=0,DAY(B13)>20)=FALSE)`

returns the remaining days.

To enter the formulas, click New Rule in the Styles/Conditional Formatting menu on the Home tab, and select Use A Formula To Determine Which Cells To Format. In the dialog box that appears, you can change the existing rules (see Figure 9-1).

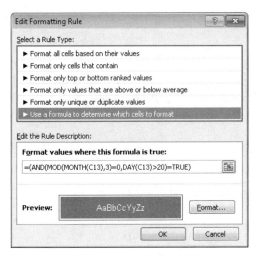

Figure 9-1 The Edit Formatting Rule dialog box (in Excel 2007 and Excel 2010).

In earlier Excel versions, select the Format/Conditional Formatting option to access the Conditional Formatting dialog box (see Figure 9-2).

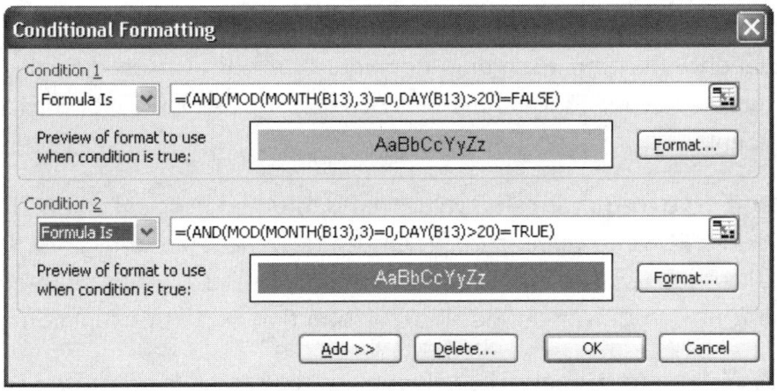

Figure 9-2   Conditional formats are perfect for logical functions. (This dialog box is in Excel 2003 and earlier.)

See Also AND(), NOT(), OR(), TRUE()

Sample Files

Use the Properties and Interpretation worksheet in the Logical_values.xls or Logical_values.xlsx sample file. The Properties and Interpretation worksheet reflects the background explanations. The sample files are found in the Chapter09 folder. For more information about the sample files, see the section titled "Using the Sample Files" on page xxiii.

IF()

Syntax   IF(*logical_test,value_if_true,value_if_false*)

Definition   This function checks a logical condition and performs the first action specified after the test argument if the condition is true and the second action if it is false.

Arguments

- *logical_test* **(required)** Any value or expression that can be evaluated to TRUE or FALSE

  This argument can use any comparison operator:

  ○ **Equal sign (=)** You can directly compare the content of a cell with a number (A1=7), or you can compare two cells (A1=B1).

  ○ **Greater than (>) or less than (<)** You can directly compare the content of a cell with a number (A1>7 or B1<8), or you can compare two cells (A1>B1 or C1<D1).

  ○ **Greater than or equal to (>=), less than or equal to, (<=), or not equal (<>)** The not equal sign (<>) is used like the other comparison operators.

  Evaluation with comparison operators returns a logical value. You can also use values returned by the logical functions AND(), OR(), and NOT() for the *logical_test* argument.

- *value_if_true* **(required)** The value that is returned if *logical_test* is TRUE. If *logical_test* is TRUE and *value_if_true* is empty, the function returns 0. To return the logical value TRUE, use TRUE or an expression that returns TRUE for this argument. The *value_if_true* argument can be an expression that uses other functions.

- *value_if_false* **(optional)** The value that is returned if *logical_test* is FALSE. If *logical_test* returns FALSE and *value_if_false* is not specified, the logical value FALSE is returned. If *value_if_false* is empty, the value 0 is returned. The *value_if_false* argument can be an expression that uses other functions.

Background   Use the IF() function to test values and formulas based on conditions.

The IF() function can be used with a preceding equal sign in a cell formula or as argument in another function.

More complicated conditions are restricted to seven nested IF() functions with *value_if_true* or *value_if_false* arguments. This limit was increased to 64 with Excel 2007.

After the *value_if_true* and *value_if_false* arguments are evaluated, the IF() function returns the value calculated by these instructions and determined by the *logical_test* argument. The function always evaluates both arguments even if it isn't required by the logical value of *logical_test*.

Examples   Excel Help contains the following statement (in Excel 2003, the term *matrix* was replaced by the term *array*):

If any of the arguments to IF are arrays, every element of the array is evaluated when the IF statement is carried out.

Consider the following examples that use arrays in the different arguments:

- The *logical_test* argument consists of a comparison with an array. Enter any numbers in cells B2 through B4. Select the adjacent cells C2 through C4, enter

  ```
  =IF(B2:B4>=0,"positive","negative")
  ```

  and press Ctrl+Shift+Enter. The result displays either *positive* or *negative* in the column to the right of the array of numbers.

- The *value_if_true* and *value_if_false* arguments contain references to arrays. Enter *red*, *green*, and *blue* in cells C6 through C8 and *black*, *red*, and *gold* in cells D6 through D8. Enter any number in cell B10. The mathematical sign of the number in B10 will determine whether the values from column C or column D are returned. Select the three cells and enter

  ```
  =IF(B10>0,C6:C8,D6:D8)
  ```

  Press Ctrl+Shift+Enter. If you change B10, cells C10 through C12 reflect the change.

- The *logical_test* argument as well as the *value_if_true* and *value_if_false* arguments contain references to one or more arrays. Enter any numbers in cells G2 through G5, enter

  ```
  =SUM(IF(G2:G5>0,G2:G5,0))
  ```

  in cell G6, and press Ctrl+Shift+Enter. Only the numbers greater than zero are added.

  This function is related to the SUMIF() function. In this case, the arguments for the function would be G2:G5,">0",G2:G5. There is a similar relationship between the COUNTIF() function and the COUNT() and IF() functions. In both cases, the IF() function provides more flexibility regarding the evaluated conditions, because they can be extended with AND() and OR().

Example   The following example shows how you can use the IF() function to evaluate calculations. Use sample numbers for the investment appraisal shown in Figure 9-3. The purchase prices for the two items in Model 1 and Model 2 are $80,000 and $90,000, respectively, and they earn the net income listed in the figure for the following years. The IRR() function calculates the internal rate of return for both models.

Chapter 9

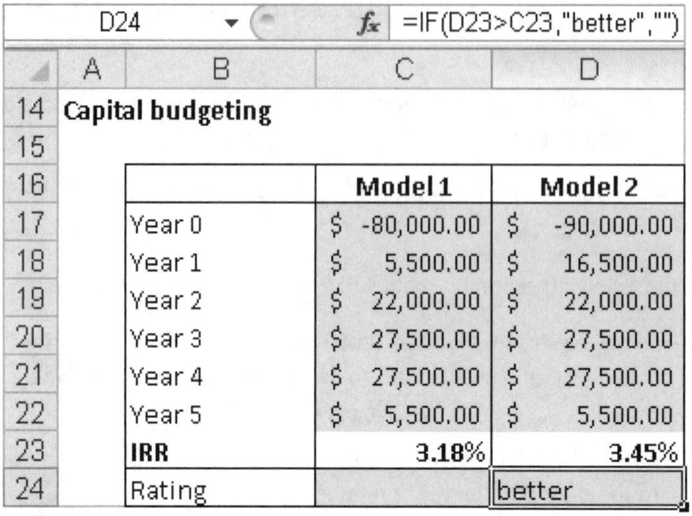

D24	▼	fx	=IF(D23>C23,"better","")

	A	B	C	D
14	Capital budgeting			
15				
16			Model 1	Model 2
17		Year 0	$ -80,000.00	$ -90,000.00
18		Year 1	$ 5,500.00	$ 16,500.00
19		Year 2	$ 22,000.00	$ 22,000.00
20		Year 3	$ 27,500.00	$ 27,500.00
21		Year 4	$ 27,500.00	$ 27,500.00
22		Year 5	$ 5,500.00	$ 5,500.00
23		IRR	3.18%	3.45%
24		Rating		better

Figure 9-3 An example of an investment appraisal.

In cell C24, enter the formula

```
=IF(C23>D23,"better","")
```

and in cell C25, enter the formula

```
=IF(D23>C23,"better","")
```

You can play with the numbers and display information in the evaluation line.

> **Tip**
>
> If the viewer is not concerned with the basic Excel IRR calculation, you can use conditional formatting instead of the evaluation line.

In this next example, a discount is calculated. Assume that a wholesaler offers the following discounts for a product with a basic price of $1.50: 5 percent for 10 items, 10 percent for 100 items, and 20 percent for 1,000 items (see Figure 9-4). The discount should apply to the entire batch and not only to the items above the minimum number.

A possible Excel solution uses the IF() function in a formula to calculate the total price of any number of items (cell C29 contains the item number):

```
=(1-IF(C29>=1000,20%,IF(C29>=100,10%,IF(C29>=10,5%,0))))*C29*1.5
```

However, this formula is not flexible. You should create a table displaying the minimum number of items and the discounts, and allocate a cell for the item price.

	A	B	C
27	Scale of discount		
28			
29		units	12
30		price per unit	$ 1.50
31			
32		10	5%
33		100	10%
34		1000	20%
35			
36		total	$ 17.10

Figure 9-4   The separation of input and output provides flexibility.

The formula

```
=(1-IF(C29>=B34,C34,IF(C29>=B33,C33,IF(C29>=B32,C32,0))))*C29*C30
```

is more complex but allows flexible item numbers, prices, and discounts.

Many nested IF() conditions can quickly become confusing and therefore error prone. You could also use the VLOOKUP() function:

```
=(1-VLOOKUP(C29,B32:C34,2,TRUE))*C29*C30
```

This formula requires cells B32 through B34 to contain the minimum item numbers and cells C32 through C34 to contain the discounts. The range B32:C34 is the array used in the VLOOKUP() function, and 2 is the number of the column that contains the return values. You search for the content of C29 in the first column of the array. The logical value TRUE indicates that the search doesn't need to return an exact match, and the value closest to the required value is returned.

See Also AND(), COUNTIF(), FALSE(), HLOOKUP(), LOOKUP(), NOT(), OR(), SUMIF(), TRUE(), VLOOKUP()

Sample Files

Use the IF worksheet in the Logical_values.xls or Logical_values.xlsx sample file. The Properties and Interpretation worksheet reflects the background explanations. The sample files are found in the Chapter09 folder. For more information about the sample files, see the section titled "Using the Sample Files" on page xxiii.

Chapter 9

IFERROR()

Syntax   IFERROR(*value,value_if_error*)

Definition   This function returns the second argument if the first argument results in an error. This function was introduced in Excel 2007.

Arguments

- *value* **(required)** Any value or expression

- *value_if_error* **(required)** The value that is returned if the value argument generates an error. The errors are #NA!, #VALUE!, #REF!, #DIV/0!, #NUM!, #NAME?, or #NULL!. If no error exists, the value of the first argument is returned.

Background   Use the IFERROR() function to test values and formulas based on conditions.

If the *value* or *value_if_error* argument refers to an empty cell, the function treats this cell as a cell containing an empty string ("").

If *value* is an array formula, the IFERROR() function returns a result array for each cell referred to by the *value* argument.

Because this function can be used instead of a combination of the IF() function and certain error functions, it results in shorter and clearer formulas.

Example   Assume that you have created a list with birthdays (or order numbers, address information, phone numbers, or something similar) and want to access this information using the VLOOKUP() function. Figure 9-5 shows an example.

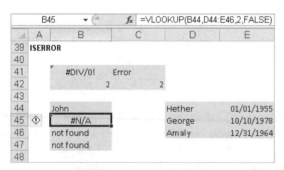

Figure 9-5 Generating an error explanation while searching lists.

If you enter the formula

```
=VLOOKUP(B44,D44:E46,2,FALSE)
```

in cell B45, you get the #N/A error that is especially annoying when you are printing. In this case, you can use the IF() function in B46 instead of the simpler formula in B45.

```
=IF(ISERROR(VLOOKUP(B44,D44:E46,2,FALSE)),"not found", VLOOKUP(B44,D44:E46,2,FALSE))
```

This formula is somewhat complicated because of the redundant portion.

```
VLOOKUP(B44,D44:E46,2,FALSE)
```

The formula

```
=IFERROR(VLOOKUP(B44,D44:E46,2,FALSE),"not found")
```

is much more concise. In other situations, you might want to use interim values and ignore errors.

See Also ERROR.TYPE(), ISERR(), ISERROR(), ISNA(), ISNUMBER(), ISTEXT()

Sample Files

Use the Samples worksheet in the Logical_values.xls or Logical_values.xlsx sample file. The sample files are found in the Chapter09 folder. For more information about the sample files, see the section titled "Using the Sample Files" on page xxiii.

NOT()

Syntax   NOT(*logical*)

Definition   This function reverses the logical value of your argument. Use the NOT() function if you want to incorporate the logical opposite of an expression in a calculation.

Arguments

- *logical* **(required)** A value or expression that can be evaluated to TRUE or FALSE

Background   If the logical argument is FALSE, the NOT() function returns TRUE. If the logical argument is TRUE, the NOT() function returns FALSE. In the example shown previously, for the FALSE() function, the formula

```
=(AND(MOD(MONTH(B13),3)=0,DAY(B13)>20)=TRUE)
```

checked whether the date fell at the end of a quarter, and

```
=(AND(MOD(MONTH(B13),3)=0,DAY(B13)>20)=FALSE)
```

checked for days that did not fall at the end of a quarter. You can shorten these conditions:

`=(AND(MOD(MONTH(B16),3)=0,DAY(B16)>20))`

or

`=NOT(AND(MOD(MONTH(B16),3)=0,DAY(B16)>20))`

Remember that NOT() is used to query the logical opposite. The shorter formulas take advantage of the fact that =(*expression*=TRUE) returns the same result as =(*expression*). The preceding formula could also read

`=(NOT(AND(MOD(MONTH(B16),3)=0,DAY(B16)>20))=TRUE)`

See Also AND(), OR()

> ## Sample Files
>
> Use the Samples worksheet in the Logical_values.xls or Logical_values.xlsx sample file. The sample files are found in the Chapter09 folder. For more information about the sample files, see the section titled "Using the Sample Files" on page xxiii.

OR()

Syntax   OR(*logical1,logical2,...*)

Definition   This function returns the logical value TRUE if at least one of the arguments is true. The OR() function returns the logical value FALSE only if all arguments are false.

Arguments

- **logical1,logical2,...** Up to 30 (and in Excel 2007 and Excel 2010 up to 255) logical values or conditions that can be evaluated to logical values (TRUE or FALSE)

Background   If you use arguments other than references and text, the OR() function returns the #VALUE! error. Except for the value of zero, all numbers are interpreted as TRUE. If an argument is omitted, as in

`=OR(TRUE)`

FALSE is returned.

Arguments from references or arrays should evaluate to logical values (TRUE or FALSE). There are exceptions: If at least one argument can be evaluated, other arguments containing text or containing references to empty cells are ignored. If arguments contain error values, the result is also an error.

Example   If you enter the word *text* in cells B22 and B23, OR(B22,B23) returns the #VALUE! error, but OR(B22,B23,FALSE) and OR(B22,B23,0) each return FALSE. If you replace FALSE with TRUE and zero with another number, the logical value TRUE is returned.

You get the same results if you enter the word *text* in cells B25 and B27 and enter a logical value or a number in cell B26. When you evaluate OR(B25:B27), the cells containing text are ignored.

The example for the NOT() function checked whether a day falls at the end of the quarter:

=(AND(MOD(MONTH(B16),3)=0,DAY(B16)>20))

or

=NOT(AND(MOD(MONTH(B16),3)=0,DAY(B16)>20))

With the calculation rules in mind, the formula directly preceding could also be entered as

=OR(NOT(MOD(MONTH(B16),3)=0),NOT(DAY(B16)>20))

or

=OR(MOD(MONTH(B19),3)>0,DAY(B19)<=20)

The AND() function was replaced by the OR() function. In Excel Help you can find the following statement:

You can use an OR array formula to check if an array contains a certain value. To enter an array formula press Ctrl+Shift+Enter.

To test this, enter 2 in cell B34, and enter 1, 2, and 3 in cells C34 through C36. In cell D34, enter

=OR(B34=C34:C36)

If you press the Ctrl+Shift+Enter key combination instead of the Enter key, the formula returns TRUE:

{=OR(B34=C34:C36)}

This checks whether any of the values in the range C34:C36 are the same as the value in cell B34. If you change the value in B34 to 4, the result is FALSE. Excel interprets the array formula as

=OR(B34=C34,B34=C35,B34=C36)

and the result is TRUE if one of the arguments returns TRUE—in other words, if the content in cell B34 is identical to one of the numbers in the C34:C36 column.

Chapter 9

If you use the array formula instead of the standard formula, you do not need to enter the arguments individually and are not restricted to 30 (in Excel 2003) or 255 (in Excel 2007 and Excel 2010) comparisons. You can force the comparison of B34 with (almost) any number of values, because OR(B34=*reference cells*) is used with only one argument.

See Also AND(), NOT()

Sample Files

Use the Samples worksheet in the Logical_values.xls or Logical_values.xlsx sample file. The sample files are found in the Chapter09 folder. For more information about the sample files, see the section titled "Using the Sample Files" on page xxiii.

TRUE()

Syntax   TRUE()

Definition   This function returns the logical value TRUE.

Arguments   None

Background   This function is seldom used because you can just enter the word *true*. Excel interprets the result returned by the function as a logical value (in this case, TRUE). The interpretation forced by numeric operations is the number value 1. You can check this by entering the formula =3+TRUE in a cell.

However, if you compare two cells, and one cell contains TRUE and the other cell contains 1, the result is FALSE.

Note

You can enter *true* (which is not case-sensitive) directly in a worksheet or formula. Excel recognizes this word as the logical value TRUE and formats the cell accordingly. To avoid this, do one of the following:

- Format the cell as text before you enter *true* (click Cells/Format/Format Cells on the Home tab in Excel 2007 or Excel 2010, and Format/Cells in earlier versions).

- Enter a space before the word *true*.

- Prefix the text with an apostrophe (').

Excel recognizes TRUE as a logical value even if you don't enter the parentheses. This is different from other functions; for example, the function TODAY() generates an error when the parentheses are missing.

Logical values can be useful when you are evaluating expressions using the logical operators AND and OR:

- The OR operator for two logical values is always TRUE unless both logical values are FALSE.

- The AND operator for two logical values is always FALSE unless both logical values are TRUE.

The second example for the FALSE() function illustrates how you can use logical values instead of the functions.

See Also AND(), FALSE(), NOT(), OR()

> ## Sample Files
> Use the Samples worksheet in the Logical_values.xls or Logical_values.xlsx sample file. The Properties and Interpretation worksheet reflects the background explanations. The sample files are found in the Chapter09 folder. For more information about the sample files, see the section titled "Using the Sample Files" on page xxiii.

Chapter 9

Lookup and Reference Functions

The lookup and reference functions or array functions in Microsoft Excel (see Table 10-1) are the some of the best Excel has to offer. The reference functions VLOOKUP(), LOOKUP(), and HLOOKUP(), as well as INDEX() and MATCH(), provide an amazing array of tools for searching and finding information in a spreadsheet. In combination, they can be used to enhance the way you work.

Some functions return general information about cells (COLUMN(), ROW(), and ADDRESS()), and other functions return specific information (OFFSET(), COLUMNS(), and ROWS()). Initially you might be confused by all the names and possibilities—but practice makes perfect.

> **Note**
>
> The Excel Function Wizard (in Microsoft Office Excel 2003 and earlier) provides the functions described in the following sections in the Lookup & Reference category. This category also includes the GETPIVOTDATA() function, which is explained in Chapter 13, "Database Functions", and thus is not covered in this chapter.

Table 10-1 **Overview of the Lookup and Reference Functions**

Function	Description
ADDRESS()	Converts a string into a cell reference
AREAS()	Returns the number of contiguous ranges

Function	Description
CHOOSE()	Returns the indexed value from a range
COLUMN()	Returns the column number of a reference
COLUMNS()	Returns the number of columns in a range
GETPIVOTDATA()	Calculates consolidated values from a Pivot range
HLOOKUP()	Returns a value from an array in the specified row for the column that meets a set criteria in the first row
HYPERLINK()	Creates a navigation link to files or web addresses
INDEX()	Returns the value of a cell for a specified number of rows and columns from the upper-left corner of a range
INDIRECT()	Returns the content of a cell specified by a text reference
LOOKUP()	Looks up a value in a range and returns the corresponding value from a second range
MATCH()	Returns the relative position of a value in an array that matches the criteria specified
OFFSET()	Returns the reference of a cell offset by a certain number of rows and columns from a fixed reference
ROW()	Returns the row number of a reference
ROWS()	Returns the number of rows in a range
RTD()	Queries data from a third-party application that supports COM automation
TRANSPOSE()	Transposes the specified array
VLOOKUP()	Returns a value from an array in the specified column for the row that meets a set criteria in the first column

ADDRESS()

Syntax   ADDRESS(*row_num,column_num,Abs,a1,sheet_text*)

Definition   This function converts arguments into a text cell reference.

Arguments

- ***row_num* and *column_num* (required)**   The coordinates of the address. These arguments can be any expression that can be evaluated to a number that will create a valid reference (values from 1 through 65,536 for *row_num* and from 1 through 256 for *column_num* in Excel 2003 and earlier, and a maximum of 1,048,476 for *row_num* and 16,384 for *column_num* in Excel 2007 and Excel 2010).

- ***Abs* (optional)** Indicates whether a reference is absolute or relative. Table 10-2 lists the valid arguments. The default value is 1.

Table 10-2 **Reference Style Numbers**

Reference Style	*Abs* Argument
Absolute row and column	1
Relative column, absolute row	2
Relative row, absolute column	3
Relative row and column	4

- ***a1* (optional)** A logical value specifying the reference style: a1 = 1 or TRUE; R1C1 = 0 or FALSE. If the argument is omitted, a1 is used as the default.

- ***sheet_text* (optional)** Puts a worksheet name and an exclamation point in front of the reference. The argument requires an expression that can be converted into text. If the argument is omitted, a simple cell reference is generated.

Background   You can use this function to generate the address of a cell in a worksheet. If the evaluation of the *row_num* and *column_num* arguments results in a positive fraction greater than 1, this value is truncated to the integer by removing the decimal places.

Addresses that include a sheet name do not verify that the sheet name exists.

Important

You cannot immediately use the result of the ADDRESS() function as a cell reference, because the result returned is a string. You can check this with the ISREF() function or by trying to add the string to a formula as a reference. The second example that follows shows how this problem can be solved.

Examples   The following examples show how this function is used.

Automatic Labels   Assume that you want to automatically label the columns in a table section that starts in column C with the letters A, B, and so on. You enter the formula

```
=LEFT(ADDRESS(1,COLUMN()-COLUMN($C$14)+1,4),1)
```

in the upper-left cell of the section and copy this formula into the columns to the right.

The COLUMN() function calculates the column number of the cell containing the formula. (The $C$14 argument in cell C14 doesn't generate a circular reference.) Subtract the column values and add 1 to ensure that A is always the starting point. If you add 2, the starting point is B, and so on. The LEFT() function with the second argument of 1 returns a single character.

Indirect Addressing   The formula =ADDRESS(6,2) returns $B$6 as a string. To use the content of cell B6 in other calculations, use the INDIRECT() function to convert the argument into a valid reference. The formula

```
=INDIRECT(ADDRESS(6,2))
```

returns the content of cell B6.

Find the Last Cell in a Range   Sometimes you might have to use the content of the last cell in a list (or in a range) without knowing how long the list is.

Assume that you have a list containing deposits and payments (see Figure 10-1).

	A	B	C	D
1	Date	Transaction	Amount	Total
2	08/01/2010	A	$ 12.00	$ 12.00
3	08/02/2010	B	$ 13.00	$ 25.00
4	08/03/2010	C	$ (17.00)	$ 8.00
5	08/04/2010	D	$ 29.75	$ 37.75

Figure 10-1 A small accounting list.

To use the account balance (here $37.75) at a different position in the worksheet or in a different worksheet, you enter a formula:

```
=INDIRECT(ADDRESS(COUNT(A:A)+1,4))
```

or

```
=INDIRECT(ADDRESS(COUNT(payments!A:A)+1,4,,,"payments"))
```

The COUNT() function calculates the number of the numeric values in column A (column A should contain only date values). You add 1 to take the title row into account, and the INDIRECT() function does everything else (as explained in the previous example).

The second formula assumes that the Payments worksheet contains your list (you pass this parameter to the ADDRESS() function).

INSIDE OUT   Use table names

In Excel 2007 and Excel 2010, you can name the payment table (for example, *Accounting*) and use this name in the formula:

```
=INDIRECT(ADDRESS(COUNT(Accounting[Date])+1,4))
```

The argument enclosed in square brackets points to the date column.

With the OFFSET() function, you can assign dynamic names (see the examples for the OFFSET() function later in this chapter).

See Also COLUMN(), OFFSET(), ROW()

Sample Files

Use the Misc, Payment, and Balance worksheets in the Address.xls or Address.xlsx sample file. The sample files are found in the Chapter10 folder. For more information about the sample files, see the section titled "Using the Sample Files" on page xxiii.

AREAS()

Syntax   AREAS(*reference*)

Definition   This function returns the number of contiguous ranges within a reference.

Arguments

- *reference* **(required)** Must evaluate to the reference for one or more cell ranges, otherwise Excel returns an error (preventing you from entering the formula) or an error value.

Background   If your argument consists of several references separated by a comma, you need to enter additional parentheses:

```
=AREAS((A1,A2))
```

or

```
=AREAS((A1:A2,B3))
```

If you don't enter the additional parentheses, the comma is treated as list separator and you will get an error message. If you try to calculate empty ranges, you will get the #NULL! error, as in this example, because there is no intersection between A1 and A2:

```
=AREAS(A1 A2)
```

Example   This function does not normally feature regularly in an Excel user's daily tasks; however, it can be useful if you have assigned a name to a dynamic list with the OFFSET() function, or if (in Excel 2007 or Excel 2010) you have formatted a list as a table. Assume that you want to fill this list by adding new cells below the title. You also want to make sure that the list doesn't contain more than 100 entries. If row 100 is reached, you need to be alerted by a change in the color of the title row.

The ranges that overlap when you are considering the named range list and cell A101 can be counted with

```
=Areas(List others!$A$101)
```

As soon as the value 1 is evaluated, indicating an overlap, the title row should change its color by using a conditional format. This fails because the Conditional Formatting dialog box doesn't allow intersection operations (cell references containing spaces).

You should therefore assign a name to the formula. Select Define Names on the Formula tab in the Defined Names group (in Excel 2007 or Excel 2010), or select Insert/Names/Define (in Excel 2003 and earlier), and enter the name you want to use as a reference (for example, *Formula*). Now you can enter the formula

```
=(Formula=1)
```

into the Formula field as a conditional format for the title row, and specify a color.

See Also   ADDRESS(), CELL(), COLUMN(), COLUMNS(), INDEX(), ROW(), ROWS()

Sample Files

Use the Misc worksheet in the References.xls or References.xlsx sample file. The sample files are found in the Chapter10 folder. For more information about the sample files, see the section titled "Using the Sample Files" on page xxiii.

CHOOSE()

Syntax   CHOOSE(*index,value1,value2,...*)

Definition   This function uses an index to return a value from the value argument list.

Arguments

- **_index_ (required)** Indicates the item that is selected from the _value_ arguments.

- **_value1,value2,..._ (the first value argument is required)** Value arguments divided by commas. These arguments can be numbers, cell references, defined names, formulas, functions, or text. In Excel 2007 and Excel 2010, the number of arguments is restricted to 254, and in earlier versions the limit is 29.

Background   The _index_ argument must evaluate to an integer from 1 through 29 or 1 through 254.

You can use a formula or reference to a cell returning such a number. If _index_ is smaller than 1 or greater than the number of value arguments in the list, the CHOOSE() function returns the #VALUE! error. If _index_ is a fraction, the decimal places are truncated before a value is returned.

You can use CHOOSE() in an array formula if you specify the index as an array. But take care to avoid errors: The formula

`{=CHOOSE({1;2},SUM(E41:G41),SUM(E42:G42))}`

returns the sum of E41 through G41 in the first cell, and the sum of E42 and G42 in the second cell. The formula

`{=SUM(CHOOSE({1;2},E41:G41,E42:G42))}`

returns the total of E41 through G42 in both cells. The formulas

`=SUM(CHOOSE(1,E41:G41,E42:G42))`

and

`=SUM(CHOOSE(2,E41:G41,E42:G42))`

return the correct results.

Example   Assume that you have entered the names of the days, starting with Sunday, in cells B42 through B48. The formula

`="Today is " & CHOOSE(WEEKDAY(D42),B42,B43,B44,B45,B46,B47,B48) & "."`

returns Today is [weekday name].

See Also INDEX()

Chapter 10

> **Sample Files**
>
> Use the Misc worksheet in the References.xls or References.xlsx sample file. The sample files are found in the Chapter10 folder. For more information about the sample files, see the section titled "Using the Sample Files" on page xxiii.

COLUMN()

Syntax   COLUMN(*reference*)

Definition   This function returns the column number of a reference.

Arguments

- *reference* **(optional)**   Must evaluate to a cell reference or cell range

Background   If you omit the *reference* argument, the function returns the column number corresponding to the cell containing the function.

If the reference is a cell range (which can also be specified with a name), you can use the function in array formulas. If the destination range includes fewer columns than the argument, the information that would be in the missing cells is truncated. If the destination range is greater than range of the argument, the excess cells display the #N/A error.

Example   Assume that you want to add up the numbers in a row with even (or odd) column numbers.

> **Note**
>
> You cannot use the ISEVEN() or ISODD() functions, because these functions don't accept references to multiple cells (they will give you a #VALUE! error).

A number is even if the formula

`(2*INT(A1/2)-A1)=0`

returns the logical value TRUE. In the case of

`((2*INT(A1/2)-A1)<>0)=TRUE`

the number is odd. If cells B21 through E21 contain numbers, the array formula

`{=SUM((INT(COLUMN(B21:E21)/2)*2-COLUMN(B21:E21)=0)*B21:E21)}` returns the sum of all columns with even column numbers. The formula

`{=SUM((INT(COLUMN(B21:E21)/2)*2-COLUMN(B21:E21)<>0)*B21:E21)}`

returns all columns with odd column numbers. This works because TRUE is interpreted as 1 and FALSE as zero.

See Also COLUMNS(), ROWS()

Sample Files

Use the Column-Row worksheet in the References.xls or References.xlsx sample file. The sample files are found in the Chapter10 folder. For more information about the sample files, see the section titled "Using the Sample Files" on page xxiii.

COLUMNS()

Syntax   COLUMNS(*array*)

Definition   This function returns the number of columns of an array or cell reference.

Arguments

- ***array* (required)** An array constant or a reference to a cell range

Background   If you try to use a discontiguous range as the argument, you will get the error message, "You've entered too many arguments to the function." If you enclose these arguments in additional parentheses, you get the #REF! error. If the range is defined by intersections and the intersection is empty, you get the #NULL! error.

Array constants are numbers or text that you must enclose in braces. Rows are separated by semicolons, and columns are separated by commas. The simple expression {1;2;3;4} is interpreted as a single column, as shown by the result of

`=COLUMNS({1;2;3;4})`

The expression {11,12,13;21,22,23} indicates three columns, as shown by the result of

`=COLUMNS({11,12,13;21,22,23})`

Example   With this function and the ROWS() function, you can access selected cells in a named range. This is especially useful if you use a dynamic range. You can find more examples in the section for the OFFSET() function later in this chapter.

Assume that a range has the name *MyRange*. In this case, the formula

`=INDEX(MyRange,ROWS(MyRange),COLUMNS(MyRange))`

returns a reference to the lower-right cell of the range.

See Also COLUMN(), ROWS()

> **Sample Files**
>
> Use the Column-Row worksheet in the References.xls or References.xlsx sample file. The sample files are found in the Chapter10 folder. For more information about the sample files, see the section titled "Using the Sample Files" on page xxiii.

GETPIVOTDATA()

This function is described in Chapter 13.

HLOOKUP()

Syntax HLOOKUP(*lookup_value,table_array,row_index_num,range_lookup*)

Definition This function looks for a value in the top row of a cell range or in an array constant. Depending on the passed arguments, the function returns an entry in the references table.

Arguments

- *lookup_value* **(optional)** Must evaluate as text, a number, or a logical value. This is the value you search for in the top row of the array.

> **Note**
>
> The search for text is not case-sensitive.

- *table_array* **(required)** A reference to a (named) cell range or an array constant (numbers and text must be in braces).

- *row_index_num* **(required)** Must evaluate to a positive integer not greater than the number of rows in *table_array*. This argument indicates the number of the row from which the information is returned.

- *range_lookup* **(optional)** Expects a logical value. The logical value determines whether an exact match should be found (=FALSE) or not (=TRUE or omitted) in the first row.

Background   The HLOOKUP() function begins by searching the first row in the table for the *lookup_value*. If the *range_lookup* has been set to FALSE, the function will search the first row for an exact match. If no match is found, you will get the #N/A error. The table does not need to be sorted.

If the *range_lookup* has been set to TRUE or has been omitted, the function will return an exact match if one exists. Otherwise it will return a value less than the *lookup_value*. This is used mainly to return values within ranges. In this case, it is important that the lookup table is sorted, so that if the first row displays the lower value in a range, the HLOOKUP() function will select the correct range for the lookup.

INSIDE OUT   Use HLOOKUP() with arrays

You can also pass the *table_array* argument as an array constant. An array constant consists of numbers or text enclosed in braces. Rows are separated by a semicolon, and columns by a comma. The array {1;2;3;4} consists of one column and four rows, and {11,12,13;21,22,23} consists of three columns and two rows. You can use HLOOKUP() to search the array constant as follows:

```
=HLOOKUP(B27,{11,12,13;21,22,23},2)
```

(if B27 contains the value 13, the function returns 23). The HLOOKUP() function is seldom used in this way, because entering arrays is time-consuming, error-prone, and inflexible.

Example   You might occasionally have to look for values in cross tables in the left column, based on the values in the header. Figure 10-2 shows an example that uses a time table. Assume that you want to calculate the minutes based on a bus stop and a time.

Chapter 10

C42	▼	f_x =HLOOKUP(C41,C32:G38,MATCH(C40,B33:B38,0)+1)				
	B	C	D	E	F	G
30	Time table					
31						
32		12:00 AM	6:00 AM	10:00 AM	4:00 PM	9:00 PM
33	A-street	3, 33	3, 18, 33, 48	3, 23, 43	3, 18, 33, 48	3, 33
34	B-street	8, 38	8, 23, 38, 53	8, 28, 48	8, 23, 38, 53	8, 38
35	C-street	12, 42	12, 27, 42, 57	12, 32, 52	12, 27, 42, 57	12, 42
36	E-street	13, 43	13, 28, 43, 58	13, 33, 53	13, 28, 43, 58	13, 43
37	F-street	15, 45	0, 15, 30, 45	15, 35, 55	0, 15, 30, 45	15, 45
38	G-street	18, 48	3, 18, 33, 48	18, 38, 58	3, 18, 33, 48	18, 48
39						
40	Bus Stop	G-street				
41	Time	7:15 AM				
42	Minutes	3, 18, 33, 48				
43						

Figure 10-2 Calculating departure times.

HLOOKUP() cannot do this by itself, because the row containing the stop has to be specified. The combined formula

```
=HLOOKUP(C41,C32:G38,MATCH(C40,B33:B38,0)+1)
```

returns the correct result. MATCH() finds the stop in C40 in the first column; adding 1 to this value includes the header in the search array.

> **Tip**
> To display a list box with the stops (the drop-down box), use a validation rule for C40 that allows only values from a list.

See Also INDEX(), LOOKUP(), MATCH(), VLOOKUP()

> **Sample Files**
> Use the HLOOKUP worksheet in the Lookups.xls or Lookups.xlsx sample file. The sample files are found in the Chapter10 folder. For more information about the sample files, see the section titled "Using the Sample Files" on page xxiii.

HYPERLINK()

Syntax   HYPERLINK(*link_location,friendly_name*)

Definition   This function creates a link to a document stored on your hard drive, on a network server, or on a server on an intranet or the Internet.

Arguments

- *link_location* **(required)** Expects an expression that can be evaluated to a string and specifies the name and path of the document to be opened.

- *friendly_name* **(optional)** The text displayed in the cell. You can use any expression that can be evaluated to text, a number, a logical value, or an error value. If this argument is omitted, the evaluation of the *link_location* argument is displayed.

Background   You can use this function to calculate dynamic links, instead of creating static links by pressing Ctrl+K.

> **Note**
> If the first argument can be evaluated as a valid address and the correct application (such as Microsoft Word or Windows Internet Explorer) is installed, the file opens in the application when you click the cell containing the function.

To edit the cell, click the cell and hold down the mouse button until the pointer changes into a cross.

If you don't enter a valid address in the first argument, you will get an error message.

> **Tip**
> You can click the Back button in a program with a web toolbar to go back to the worksheet.

Examples   The following examples show how this function is used.

Linking to Microsoft Office Online   The following entry opens Internet Explorer and displays the Office website from Microsoft:

```
=HYPERLINK("http://office.microsoft.com/en-us/default.aspx ","Internet test")
```

Chapter 10

The text `Internet test` is displayed in the cell as a link.

Accessing Word documents   The entry

```
=HYPERLINK("document#highlight","Word test")
```

opens the Word document (assuming that the document resides in the same folder as the worksheet), and the text `highlight` is selected. The text `Word test` is displayed in the cell as a link.

You can achieve almost the same effect if you select text in Word, copy this text into the Clipboard, and then insert the text in a worksheet by clicking Insert/Insert As Hyperlink (in Excel 2003) or Insert/Hyperlinks/Hyperlink (in Excel 2007 or Excel 2010). The content of the cell is displayed. The functionality of the hyperlink depends on the cell and can be changed by clicking the right mouse button.

> **Sample Files**
>
> Use the Misc worksheet in the References.xls or References.xlsx sample file. The sample files are found in the Chapter10 folder. The same folder includes Word files for tests. For more information about the sample files, see the section titled "Using the Sample Files" on page xxiii.

INDEX()

Syntax (Array Version)   INDEX(*array,row_num,column_num*)

Syntax (Reference Version)   INDEX(*reference,row_num,column_num,area_num*)

Definition   This function uses a row and/or column index to select one or more values from an array (multiple connected cells or expressions separated by a semicolon and enclosed in braces) or from a reference (which can contain one or more references to rectangular areas) based on index entries.

Arguments (Array Version)

- ***array* (required)** Must be a range of cells or an array constant.

- ***row_num* (optional)** Can be omitted if the array argument includes only one cell. This argument must evaluate to a positive integer and specifies the number of the row that holds the values to work with.

- ***column_num* (optional)** An expression that must evaluate to a positive integer. This argument specifies the number of the column that holds the values to choose and can be omitted if the array reference consists of only a single column.

Arguments (Reference Version)

- ***reference* (required)** Must evaluate to a reference to one or more cell ranges.

- ***row_num* and *column_num* (optional)** Same as for the array version, but these arguments indicate the number of the row or column that holds the values to choose, and therefore they don't have to evaluate to positive integers.

  If the reference argument consists of multiple parts, these parts are numbered in the order in which they are entered.

- ***area_num* (optional)** Selects a range specified in the *reference* argument pertaining to the order in which the ranges are defined.

> **Note**
> If the *reference* argument consists of only a single subarea, the *area_num* argument can be omitted. In this case, the reference version is identical to the array version.

Background   In the array version, the *row_num* and *column_num* arguments usually range from 1 through the number of rows or columns in the range or in a value list. If the range consists of only a single row (column), the *row_num* (*column_num*) argument can be omitted. To omit the *row_num* argument, enter two commas. If you omit several rows, you can reference the column specified in *column_num* with an array formula in the vertical cells. The same applies if you want to omit several columns.

If the *row_num* and *column_num* arguments exceed the range, you will get the #REF! error. The formula

```
=INDEX(B4:C6,3,2)
```

returns the element in C6 (third row, second column in the range B4:C6). Similarly, consider the following:

```
=INDEX({2;4;6;8},2,1)
```

(This isn't an array formula, so you have to enter the braces instead of pressing Ctrl+Shift+Enter.) The argument {2;4;6;8} is recognized as column, and the formula returns 4 (the second row in the column).

Chapter 10

Array constants that include multiple columns constitute a special situation, because rows are separated by semicolons, and columns are separated by commas. For example, {11,12,13;21,22,23} is recognized as

11	12	13
21	22	23

The formula

```
=INDEX({11,12,13;21,22,23},2,3)
```

returns 23 (second row, third column).

You can use the INDEX() function in an array formula as shown in the following example. If you enter

```
{=INDEX({11,12,13;21,22,23},0,3)}
```

or

```
{=INDEX({11,12,13;21,22,23},,3)}
```

as array formula in two vertical cells, the formula returns 13, 23. If you enter

```
{=INDEX({11,12,13;21,22,23},2,0)}
```

or

```
{=INDEX({11,12,13;21,22,23},2)}
```

as array formula in three horizontal cells, the formula returns 21, 22, 23. If the destination range is larger than the source range, the extra cells show the #N/A error.

In the reference version, the first argument must be a reference. If you want to use multiple ranges, each range must consist of contiguous cells. The *reference* argument for multiple references separated by semicolons must be enclosed in parentheses to ensure that Excel assigns the arguments correctly.

The order of the references in the argument is indicated by an integer, starting at 1, to identify the cell range in the *area_num* argument. The *row_num* and *column_num* arguments behave as in the array version.

If one of the *row_num*, *column_num* or *area_num* arguments exceeds the range, the function returns the #REF! error. The formula

```
=INDEX((B18:C20,E18:G19),3,2,1)
```

returns the reference to the element in the third row in the second column in the first range (C20).

INDEX() accepts named ranges in the *reference* argument. If you enter the name *first* for range B18:C20 (by selecting Defined Names/Define Name on the Formulas tab in Excel 2007 or Excel 2010 or Insert/Names/Define in earlier versions) and the name *second* for range E18 through G19, the formula

```
=INDEX((first,second),2,1,2)
```

returns a reference to the cell in the second row in the first column of the range named *second*: E19. You can also name all of the cells B18:C20,E18:G19 (in this order) with the name *both*. Then the formula

```
=INDEX(both,2,3,2)
```

returns the information in the third column in the second row of the second subarea: G19. You can omit the *row_num* or *column_num* argument or both (leaving the space between the commas empty) to reference columns or rows or an entire range. In this case, you have to use the formula as array formula or you will get the #VALUE! error unless the range consists of only one row or column.

> **Note**
>
> The *row_num*, *column_num*, and *area_num* arguments expect integers. If you pass decimal numbers, these numbers will not be rounded but truncated, and the decimal places will be removed.

Examples   The following examples show how this function is used.

Searching Lists   This example demonstrates the array version of the function. Assume that you have a product list with the product names in column 1 and the prices in column 2. You maintain this list on a special worksheet (or the information is imported from a database). On a different worksheet, you want to use a combo box (a form control) to access and select the product names as well as write the price into a cell.

1. Name the columns **PriceList** and **Products**.

2. Insert a combo box, and specify the value **Product** as the input range and **$B$28** as the cell range.

> **Tip**
>
> Position your combo box above the link cell to hide it.

3. In any cell, enter

    `=INDEX(PriceList,B28,1)`

    to display the product name.

4. In another cell, enter

    `=INDEX(PriceList,B28,2)`

    to display the associated price. Figure 10-3 shows an example.

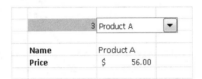

	3 Product A	▼
Name	Product A	
Price	$ 56.00	

Figure 10-3 The combo box should overlay the auxiliary linked cell.

> **Note**
>
> You can also create a combo box from the control toolbox (ActiveX Control on the Developer tab in Excel 2007 or Excel 2010). Unlike a form control, which displays the index of the entry in the linked cell, the combo box control displays the text of the entry in the linked cell.

Finding Information   This example demonstrates the reference version of the function. Assume that you have divided an advanced training course into three parts and offer single-unit or complete conference reservations. You also offer an early-bird discount for participants who book before a deadline. The details are shown in Figure 10-4.

	A	B	C	D	E
45					
46		Conference	Nr.	Early Bird	Normal
47		PreCon	1	$ 249.00	$ 274.00
48		MainCon	2	$ 899.00	$ 989.00
49		PostCon	3	$ 159.00	$ 175.00
50		Complete	4	$ 1,175.00	$ 1,295.00
51					
52		Deadline	12/01/2010		
53		Conference	PreCon		
54		Booking	11/01/2010		
55		Price	$ 249.00		
56					

Figure 10-4 Retrieving information with VLOOKUP(), INDEX(), and IF().

To calculate the price based on the elements booked and the reservation date, you use the following formula:

```
=INDEX((D47:D50,E47:E50),VLOOKUP(C53,B47:C50,2,FALSE),,IF(C54<C52,1,2))
```

You divide the price range into two parts (don't forget to put the reference in parentheses), calculate the course element with VLOOKUP(), and use this number as the row index. You don't need a column index, because each range includes only one column. The IF() function compares the booking date with the deadline to determine the range to be searched.

INSIDE OUT   Use the INDEX() function with large data lists

In this example, with the data ordered as it is now, you don't actually need the INDEX() function, because the formula

```
VLOOKUP(C53,B47:C50,2,FALSE)
```

returns the same result. However, VLOOKUP() fails if the regular prices and discounts are spread over the worksheet or are located on two different worksheets. This can happen with large data lists that are retrieved from different sources.

Working with Cells in Named Ranges   With INDEX(), you can address specific cells in a named range. This is especially useful for dynamic ranges. You can find more examples of this in the section for the OFFSET() function.

Assume that you want to add up the last cells in the lower-right corners of two ranges. The ranges are named *NumberOne* and *NumberTwo*, and their size is unknown. You can use the reference version

```
=INDEX((NumberOne,NumberTwo),ROWS(NumberOne),COLUMNS(NumberOne),1)+
    INDEX((NumberOne,NumberTwo),ROWS(NumberTwo),COLUMNS(NumberTwo),2)
```

as well as the array version

```
=INDEX(NumberOne,ROWS(NumberOne),COLUMNS(NumberOne))+
    INDEX(NumberTwo,ROWS(NumberTwo),COLUMNS(NumberTwo))
```

Tip

Data retrieved from external sources is automatically inserted into a named range. The INDEX(), ROW(), COLUMN(), and VLOOKUP() functions can be used for many purposes independent of the size of the data range.

See Also CHOOSE(), HLOOKUP(), LOOKUP(), MATCH(), VLOOKUP()

Sample Files

Use the Index worksheet in the References.xls or References.xlsx sample file. The sample files are found in the Chapter10 folder. For more information about the sample files, see the section titled "Using the Sample Files" on page xxiii.

INDIRECT()

Syntax   INDIRECT(*reference,A1*)

Definition   This function converts a text string into a reference.

Arguments

- **_reference_ (required)** Expects an expression that can be interpreted as a string. The function converts this string into a valid reference (a cell reference or named range).

- **_A1_ (optional)** Must be evaluated as a logical value. Defines whether the reference argument is in A1 syntax (if the argument returns TRUE or is omitted) or the R1C1 syntax (if the argument returns FALSE).

Background   If the *reference* argument cannot be evaluated to a valid reference or name, the function returns the #REF! error.

If you want to use an external reference to another workbook, the workbook must be open.

Example   The following examples show how this function is used.

Using Cell Addresses   The second example of the ADDRESS() function demonstrates how to use INDIRECT() to convert a string created with ADDRESS(*row_num,column_num*) into a reference.

Note

The explanation of the INDEX() function shows that

```
INDEX(A:Z,26,1)
```

does the same as

```
INDIRECT(ADDRESS(26,1))
```

Investment Analysis   Assume that you have an investment analysis that displays an optimal strategy for different investments with certain risk levels. The higher the estimated risk of a single investment, the higher the return will be. Figure 10-5 shows a simplified approach.

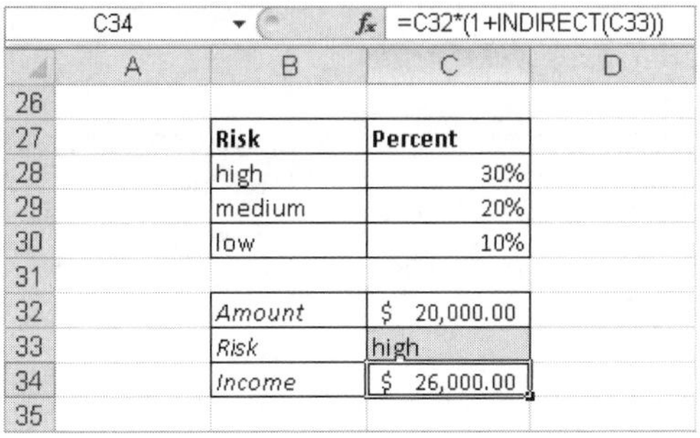

C34			fx	=C32*(1+INDIRECT(C33))	
	A	B	C	D	
26					
27		Risk	Percent		
28		high	30%		
29		medium	20%		
30		low	10%		
31					
32		Amount	$ 20,000.00		
33		Risk	high		
34		Income	$ 26,000.00		
35					

Figure 10-5 Investment analysis approach.

You want the user to only use the words *high*, *medium*, and *low* to see the expected yield of an investment. You give the name *high* to cell C28 (the first of the cells with assigned yield values in percent), cell C29 is *medium*, and cell C30 is *low*. With the investment capital in C32, the formula

```
=C32*(1+INDIRECT(C33))
```

returns the expected yield in C34. This works because INDIRECT() converts the string entered by the user in C33 into a name that is a valid reference.

> **Tip**
> With a validation rule (available on the Data tab, in Data Tools/Data Validation in Excel 2007 or Excel 2010 or Data/Validation in previous versions) you can add a dropdown box for cell C33.

See Also INDEX(), OFFSET()

> **Sample Files**
> Use the Misc worksheet in the References.xls or References.xlsx sample file. The sample files are found in the Chapter10 folder. For more information about the sample files, see the section titled "Using the Sample Files" on page xxiii.

LOOKUP()

Syntax

- **(Vector Version)** LOOKUP(*lookup_value,lookup_vector,result_vector*)

- **(Array Version)** LOOKUP(*lookup_value,array*)

Definition   This function finds values in an array (a cell range or an array constant). If the array consists of only one column or row, the vector version is used.

The vector version looks for a value in a vector and returns the value at the same position in the second vector.

The array version looks for a value in the first row or column of an array and returns the value at the same position in the last row or column of the same array.

Arguments (Vector Version)

- ***lookup_value* (required)** Must evaluate to a number, string, or logical value. This argument can be a reference to a cell containing the value.

- ***lookup_vector* (required)** A reference to a cell range consisting of one row or one column. The elements contained in the *lookup_vector* can be strings, numbers, or logical values.

- ***result_vector* (required)** Similar to the *lookup_vector* consisting of one row or one column. This argument must include the same number of elements as the *lookup_vector*. If this argument is omitted, the array version of the function and not the vector version is automatically assumed.

Arguments (Array Version)

- ***lookup_value* (required)** Must evaluate to a number, string, or logical value. This argument can be a reference to a cell containing the value.

- ***array* (required)** A reference to a cell range containing text, numbers, or logical values.

> **Note**
> You can use array constants instead of cell references. Array constants are values enclosed in braces. Rows are separated by a semicolon and columns by a comma. For example, {1;2;3;4} is a vector consisting of one column and four rows. {11,12,13;21,22,23} is an array consisting of three columns and two rows.

Background   In both the vector and array versions, the values you are searching must be arranged in ascending order; otherwise, LOOKUP() might return an unexpected or even wrong value. Unlike the VLOOKUP() and HLOOKUP() functions, with LOOKUP() you cannot further specify the search.

Strings (text) are not case-sensitive.

If the LOOKUP() function cannot find a value matching the search criteria, it uses the largest value in *lookup_vector* smaller than or equal to *lookup_value*. If *lookup_value* is smaller than the smallest value in *lookup_vector*, the LOOKUP() function returns the #N/A error.

In the array version, the size of the array determines the search range. If the array has more columns than rows, the function looks in the first row for the value. Otherwise, it looks in the first column. If no matching value is found, the largest value smaller than or equal to *lookup_value* is used. If *lookup_value* is smaller than all of the values, the function returns the #N/A error.

Example   The array version of LOOKUP() is similar to the HLOOKUP() and VLOOKUP() functions. The difference is that HLOOKUP() compares the first row and VLOOKUP() compares the first column; and LOOKUP() compares the row or column with *lookup_value*. With HLOOKUP() and VLOOKUP(), you can skip to a certain row or column by specifying an index. This is more flexible then the LOOKUP() function, which always returns the value in the last row or column.

For a dynamic list to which items might be added, there are usually fewer columns than rows, and you cannot search in the headers to get the information in the last row. For this situation, you can use HLOOKUP() together with ROWS() or, alternatively, MATCH() in combination with INDEX().

Excel is not a substitute for a database management system (such as Microsoft Access or Microsoft SQL Server). However, if you save data lists in worksheets, you can use the vector version of LOOKUP() instead of VLOOKUP() to search multiple contiguous ranges on different worksheets. For this to work, the lookup vectors must be sorted and the result vectors must match the lookup vectors.

See Also HLOOKUP(), INDEX(), MATCH(), VLOOKUP()

> ## Sample Files
>
> Use the LOOKUP worksheet in the Lookups.xls or Lookups.xlsx sample file. The sample files are found in the Chapter10 folder. For more information about the sample files, see the section titled "Using the Sample Files" on page xxiii.

Chapter 10

MATCH()

Syntax MATCH(*lookup_value*,*lookup_array*,*match_type*)

Definition This function searches for text, numbers, or logical values within a reference or an array and returns the position.

Arguments

- **lookup_value (required)** The number, a string, a logical value, or a reference to a cell containing a value.

- **lookup_array (required)** A contiguous range of cells consisting of one row or one column, or an array constant.

- **match_type (optional)** Must evaluate to a number (–1, 0, or 1). Determines how the *lookup_value* is matched in the search array. If this argument is omitted, Excel uses the value 1.

    The *match_type* argument is set as follows:

    o If *match_type* is –1, the MATCH() function returns the position of the smallest value greater than or equal to *lookup_value*. The elements in the search array should be sorted in descending order: numbers, letters, then logical values.

    o If *match_type* is 0, the MATCH() function returns the position of the first value equal to *lookup_value*. The elements in the search array do not need to be sorted.

    o If *match_type* is 1, the MATCH() function returns the position of the largest value smaller than or equal to *lookup_value*. The elements in the search array should be sorted in ascending order: first the numbers, then the letters in alphabetical order, and finally the logical values FALSE and TRUE.

Background Unlike the LOOKUP() function, the MATCH() function determines positions rather than values.

The function returns the #N/A error if no matching value is found. This error is also returned if the *lookup_value* argument does not correspond to a row or column. If you don't set the *match_type* parameter to correspond with the search array, this error is returned even if the value you search for exists in the list.

For a list containing strings, you usually set *match_type* to 0. In a list containing numbers in intervals (such as discounts, interest rates, or scores), the search array is ascending or descending.

If *match_type* is 0 and the *lookup_value* is a string, it can contain the * placeholder for any string and the ? for single characters. The MATCH() function is not case-sensitive.

Examples   The following examples show how this function is used.

Search in Multiple Columns   With the MATCH() function, you can quickly search multiple columns. Assume that you have a price list for clothing (see Figure 10-6).

	B	C	D	E	F
42	search in more than one column				
43					
44		product	color	price	
45		shirt	blue	$ 44.95	
46		shirt	yellow	$ 49.95	
47		pants	red	$ 89.95	
48		pants	brown	$ 84.95	
49					
50	search for:	pants	brown		
51	position:	4		price:	$ 84.95
52					
53	search for:	pants, red			
54	position:	3		price:	$ 89.95
55					

Figure 10-6 Searching multiple columns in a price list.

You can determine the position of the yellow shirt with the formula

`{=MATCH(C50 & D50,C45:C48 & D45:D48,0)}`

Because this is an array formula, you have to press Ctrl+Shift+Enter after entering the formula. The & links elements in the *lookup_value* and combines the two search columns into one column.

The INDEX() function returns the price:

`=INDEX(E45:E48,C51)`

Of course, you can combine both formulas into a single formula:

`{=INDEX(E45:E48,MATCH(C50 & D50,C45:C48 & D45:D48,0))}`

To enter the search criteria in a single row (C53 in Figure 9-9), use the following formula:

`{=MATCH(C53,C45:C48 & ", " & D45:D48,0)}`

This is also an array formula. The search columns are now combined.

You can use the placeholders to find the elements even if you know only part of their names. If you enter *pa* in C58 and *re* in D58, the formula

`{=MATCH("*" & C58 & "*" & D58 & "*",C45:C48 & D45:D48,0)}`

finds the row containing the red pants.

> **Note**
>
> Because such a formula can get quite complicated, you should consider using Advanced Filter. If you copy the table ranges to another location (instead of filtering the list in place), the copy is independent of the original table and not updated simultaneously.

Cross Tabulations in Practice Cross tabulations (the simplest form of PivotTable) are often used. These include tables such as time tables, distances between cities, and rate tables. Assume that you have a phone rate comparison table that tells you who the cheapest provider is at certain times of the day. Figure 10-7 shows an example.

C84		f_x =INDEX(C74:E74,1,MATCH(C83,OFFSET(C75:E79,C82-1,0,1,3),0))			
	B	C	D	E	F
72	crosstab				
73					
74		The Phone Company	Contoso, Ltd	City Power & Light	
75	12:00 AM	$ 0.08	$ 0.27	$ 0.18	
76	6:00 AM	$ 0.18	$ 0.07	$ 0.14	
77	9:00 AM	$ 0.27	$ 0.09	$ 0.18	
78	6:00 PM	$ 0.18	$ 0.10	$ 0.14	
79	9:00 PM	$ 0.11	$ 0.27	$ 0.18	
80					
81	search for:	7:00 AM			
82	found:	2			
83	minimum:	$ 0.07			
84	provider:	Contoso, Ltd			
85					

Figure 10-7 Navigating the phone rate complexity.

Looking for a time in the left column is a job for MATCH(). But what column contains the result? Use the MATCH() function to find the row, and the MIN() and OFFSET() functions to find the cheapest rate. Here is the MATCH() function:

`=MATCH(C81,B75:B79,1)`

And here are the MIN() and the OFFSET() functions:

`=MIN(OFFSET(C75:E79,C82-1,0,1,3))`

You can combine both formulas into one. Thus, the following formula locates the provider who offers the cheapest rate:

`=INDEX(C74:E74,1,MATCH(C83,OFFSET(C75:E79,C82-1,0,1,3),0))`

OFFSET() finds the correct row (with the first number being 0); C83 contains the cheapest rate returned by MATCH(), and INDEX() searches the header for the provider.

> ## Tip   Select a row using conditional formatting
>
> To select the row with the cheapest rate, use conditional formatting. In C75 enter the following formula:
>
> ```
> =AND(C75=MIN(OFFSET($C$75:$E$79,MATCH($C$81,$B$75:$B$79,1)-1,0,1,3)),
>     (ROW(C75)-ROW($C$75)+1)=$C$82)
> ```
>
> This formula checks whether the cell contains the cheapest rate in the correct row. Select a color, and copy the format by using Paste Format.

See Also HLOOKUP(), INDEX(), VLOOKUP()

> ## Sample Files
>
> Use the MATCH worksheet in the Lookups.xls or Lookups.xlsx sample file. The sample files are found in the Chapter10 folder. For more information about the sample files, see the section titled "Using the Sample Files" on page xxiii.

OFFSET()

Syntax   OFFSET(*reference,rows,columns,height,width*)

Definition   This function returns a cell reference that is a specified number of rows and columns from a given reference.

Arguments

- *reference* **(required)** The reference from which you want to base the offset, a reference to a single cell or to a range of adjacent cells. An argument with a different reference type causes the #VALUE! error.

  > ### Important
  >
  > If the argument is a named range, you need to press Ctrl+Shift+Enter after you enter the formula even if you enter the formula in a single cell. Otherwise you get an error.

Chapter 10

- *rows* **(required)** The number of rows that you want the upper-left cell of the range to be moved up or down.

- *columns* **(required)** An expression that can be evaluated to an integer. This argument indicates the number of columns you want the range to be moved to the left or right.

- *height* **(optional)** The height of the new reference in number of rows. If specified, this argument has to be evaluated to a positive integer. It defaults to the reference height.

- *width* **(optional)** Works like the *height* argument but indicates the number of columns.

Background   This function doesn't move cells on the worksheet; it moves the reference to a specified range. If you specify a value for the *rows* and *columns* arguments beyond the current sheet, the OFFSET() function returns the #REF! error.

The function expects integers for the four last arguments, and the last two integers must be positive. If the expressions in these arguments are evaluated to fractions, the decimal places are removed. No error occurs.

If you don't specify the *height* and *width* arguments, Excel assumes that the new reference has the same height and width as the initial reference.

If the *height* argument is smaller than the height of the destination range, the remaining cells display the #N/A error. The same applies to the *width* argument. If the value is 1, the corresponding rows and columns are repeated in the remaining cells. Figure 10-8 shows an example.

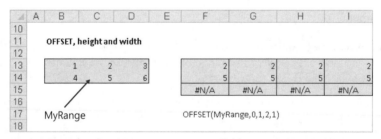

Figure 10-8 The *height* and *width* arguments.

The reference named MyRange has the dimensions two rows x three columns. The formula

`{=OFFSET(MyRange,0,1,2,1)}`

moves the target to the first cell in the range (B13) and offsets this by zero rows and one column, taking the starting point to cell C13. The *height* and *width* parameters extend the range to two rows and one column to target C13:C14. The destination range F13:I15 has the dimensions three rows x four columns. The destination range is filled with the values from C13:C14, repeating this four times across the destination range, but the remaining row (15) is filled with the error #N/A.

Examples   The following examples illustrate how the OFFSET() function is used.

Addressing Single Cells   Use this function to address single cells in the original named range. In this case, you don't move the entire range but only the upper-left corner of the range. If you specify the value 1 for the height and width, the result is a single cell.

Assume that your range, MyRange, includes cells B5 through D6. Cell D6 is the last cell in the range and can be addressed with the array formula

```
{=OFFSET(MyRange,1,2)}
```

To move the required reference to the right or down, start at the upper-left cell of the range: two cells to the right and one cell down.

This method is especially useful if you use dynamic ranges, which change over time (for example, a dynamic list, a manually entered list, or a list updated with a database). In this case, use the COUNT() or COUNTIF() function to specify the position. This is explained in the following examples.

Variable-Length Lists   Assume that you have a list like the one shown in Figure 10-9. You want to filter the information in the list using database functions. The list constantly changes because records are added or removed.

	A	B	C	D	E
1			Transactions	Category	Amount
2			2	English	$ 48.97
3			Transactions	Category	Amount
4			3	Drawing	$ 54.37
5					
6		Nr.	Transaction	Category	Amount
7		1	Notebooks	English	$ 12.99
8		2	Books	English	$ 35.98
9		3	Pencils	Drawing	$ 9.99
10		4	Tints	Drawing	$ 26.49
11		5	Brushs	Drawing	$ 17.89
12					

Figure 10-9 Evaluating lists with dynamic names.

Create the data list in a worksheet named *Calculations*. The titles of the columns don't have to match the list titles (for example, you could use *Category* instead of *Categories*).

Select the list titles. Select the Insert/Names/Define menu option (in Excel 2003 and earlier) or click Define Name in the Defined Names group on the Formula tab (Excel 2007 and Excel 2010). Enter the name *list* for the range defined by the following formula:

```
=OFFSET(Calculations!$B$6:$E$6,0,0,COUNT(Calculations!$B:$B)+1)
```

Based on the number of numeric entries in column B, the upper-left cell of the title range ($B$6:$E$6) is dynamically extended by the adjustable *height* argument. Remember that +1 is necessary to include the titles in the list.

You can now add up the invoice amounts in the English category using the following formula:

```
=DSUM(list,E6,D1:D2)
```

The DSUM() function takes the values identified by the list range and sums the values in the Amount column according to the criteria set in the range D1:D2 (Category, English). Other entries are evaluated with DCOUNT()

```
=DCOUNT(list,B6,D1:D2)
```

to return a count of the transaction. (The second argument can be empty.)

If you use Excel 2007 or Excel 2010 and format the list as a table, you don't have to specify the range name. If the table has the name Table1 (the default name), the formula is

```
=DCOUNT(Table1[#All],B6,D1:D2)
```

Dynamic Charts   You can use the method explained in the previous example to generate dynamic charts. Define a dynamic range name and use the named range to create the chart. Use a named range for the legend and data, as in these formulas:

```
=OFFSET(Charts!$C$4,0,Charts!$B$23)
```

```
=OFFSET(Charts!$C$5:$C$19,0,Charts!$B$23)
```

where the value in cell B23 defines which column should be selected to generate the chart.

Another Address Example   The third example for the ADDRESS() function returns the content of a cell with the ADDRESS() and INDIRECT() functions. You can also return the information by combining the first two examples in this section.

To use the sum from Figure 10-1, shown earlier, in a different cell on the Payments worksheet, give the dynamic range the name *Payments*:

```
=OFFSET(Payment!$A$1:$D$1,0,0,COUNT(Payment!$A:$A)+1)
```

The range (including its titles) is adjusted according to column A. You can obtain the reference to the lower-right cell of the range that contains the current sum with the following array formula:

```
{=OFFSET(Payment,ROWS(Payment)-1,3)}
```

Remember that the row and column numbers start with 0. If you have Excel 2007 or Excel 2010, you can use a table instead of a dynamic name:

```
{=OFFSET(Table2[#All],ROWS(Table2[#All])-1,3)}
```

See Also ADDRESS(), CHOOSE(), INDIRECT()

Sample Files

Use the Background, Samples, and Calculations worksheets in the Offset.xls or Offset.xlsx sample file. The sample files are found in the Chapter10 folder. For more information about the sample files, see the section titled "Using the Sample Files" on page xxiii.

ROW()

Syntax   ROW(*reference*)

Definition   This function returns the row number of a reference.

Arguments

- *reference* **(optional)** Must evaluate to a reference to one cell or to a cell range.

Background   If you omit the *reference* argument, the function returns the row number corresponding to the cell containing the function.

If the reference is a cell range (name), you can use the function in array formulas. If the destination range includes fewer rows than the argument, the information in the missing cells is truncated. If the destination range is larger than the reference range, the excess cells display the #N/A error.

Examples   The following examples explain how to use the ROW() function.

Consecutive Numbers   If you want to create consecutive numbers starting at cell A15, enter the formula

```
=ROW()-ROW($A$15)+1 & "."
```

in A15 and copy the formula into the cells below it.

Consecutive Numbers in a Range To create consecutive numbers in the first column of a named range, use the array formula

`{=ROW(Range)-ROW(OFFSET(Range,0,0,1))+1 & "."}`

This formula does not need the position of the range and doesn't create a circular reference.

See Also COLUMN(), ROWS()

> **Sample Files**
>
> Use the Column-Row worksheet in the References.xls or References.xlsx sample file. The sample files are found in the Chapter10 folder. For more information about the sample files, see the section titled "Using the Sample Files" on page xxiii.

ROWS()

Syntax ROWS(*array*)

Definition This function returns the number of rows of an array constant or a cell reference.

Arguments

- *array* **(required)** An array constant or a reference to a cell range

Background If you try to use a discontiguous range as the argument, you get the error message, "You've entered too many arguments for this function." If you enclose these arguments in additional parentheses, you will get the #REF! error. If the range is defined by intersections (created by including spaces between the cell references, as in the formula `=ROWS(B2:D4 E2:E4)` and the intersection is empty, you will get the #NULL! error.

Array constants are numbers or text enclosed in braces. Rows are separated by semicolons, and columns are separated commas. The simple expression {1;2;3;4} is interpreted as an array consisting of four rows, as shown by the result of

`=ROWS({1;2;3;4})`

The expression {11,12,13;21,22,23} indicates two rows, as shown by the result of

`=ROWS({11,12,13;21,22,23})`

Example To access the last cell in the lower-right corner of a named range, use the formula

```
=INDEX(MyRange,ROWS(MyRange),COLUMNS(MyRange))
```

MyRange is the name of the range.

See Also COLUMNS(), ROW()

> ## Sample Files
> Use the Column-Row worksheet in the References.xls or References.xlsx sample file. The sample files are found in the Chapter10 folder. For more information about the sample files, see the section titled "Using the Sample Files" on page xxiii.

RTD()

Syntax RTD(*progID,server,topic1,[topic2],...*)

Definition This function retrieves real-time data from a program that supports COM automation.

Arguments

- *progID* **(required)** A string specifying the class name (progID) of a registered COM automation add in.

- *server* **(optional)** The computer on which the add-in will run. This can be a local computer or a network computer.

- *topic1, [topic2],...* **(the first parameter is required)** Parameters that specify the requested real-time data.

> ## Note
> Strings have to be enclosed in quotation marks if they are not cell references.

Background If this function cannot find a valid real-time data server, it returns the #N/A error.

If the server is a local computer, you can omit this argument (enter a space between the commas) or specify an empty string. If you use this function in Microsoft Visual Basic for Applications (VBA), the empty string (vbNullString) is mandatory.

Note

The user of the workbook will need access to the COM add-in components on the network computer, and the DLL file must be locally registered.

With VBA, a real-time server can be accessed only by using the Microsoft Office Developer Edition (for versions of VBA before Office XP) and Visual Basic 6, or a programming language in Microsoft Visual Studio .NET until its 2010 version.

Example The exampleRTD.dll file is located in the Chapter10 folder with sample files. To register this file, click the Start button on the taskbar, type **cmd** to get the command line box, and type **regsvr32.exe *drive:\path\file name*** (the \u parameter will unregister the file). This DLL file returns the real-time data for the hour, minute, and second.

You can use the server with the following formulas:

```
=RTD("RealTime.clsRTDS",,"hour")
```

```
=RTD("RealTime.clsRTDS",,"minute")
```

or

```
=RTD("RealTime.clsRTDS",,"second")
```

INSIDE OUT   Use VBA to change the update behavior

After the DLL is installed, the real-time data are retrieved every two seconds. To change this interval, you have to use VBA. Run the following command:

```
Sub ChangeThrottleInterval() Application.RTD.ThrottleInterval = 1000
End Sub
```

This command reduces the frequency to one second. Experienced users can search the registry for RTDThrottleInterval to change this value.

> ## Tip   Add a clock to your worksheet
>
> Use the TIME() function to add a clock to your worksheet:
>
> ```
> =TIME(RTD("RealTime.clsRTDS",,"hour"),RTD("RealTime.clsRTDS",,"minute"),
>     RTD("RealTime.clsRT DS",,"second"))
> ```
>
> Unlike active macros, the real-time server doesn't affect changes you make on the current worksheet.

> ## Sample Files
>
> Use the worksheet in the exampleRTD.xls or exampleRTD.xlsm sample file. The sample files are found in the Chapter10 folder. This folder also includes the runtime library exampleRTD.dll. For more information about the sample files, see the section titled "Using the Sample Files" on page xxiii.

TRANSPOSE()

Syntax   TRANSPOSE(*array*)

Definition   This function transposes arrays.

Arguments

- *array* **(required)** A reference to a cell range or an array constant

Background   Use TRANSPOSE() as an array formula for a range that includes the same number of rows or columns as the initial array. The rows and columns are exchanged: The rows in the "old" array become the columns in the "new" array. The first row becomes the first column, the second row becomes the second column, and so on.

> ## Important
>
> The range with the initial array cannot contain empty cells; if it does, you will get the #VALUE! **error.**

If you don't use the necessary number of rows or columns in the destination range, the missing content is truncated. If you use too many rows or columns, the excess cells are filled with the #N/A error. When you use array constants (numbers or text in braces) in the expression

```
{=TRANSPOSE({11,12,13;21,22,23})}
```

the argument is interpreted as an array with two rows and three columns, and the result fits into an array with three rows and two columns. In the formula

```
{=TRANSPOSE({1;2;3;4})}
```

the argument is a single column that is converted into a row.

> **Note**
>
> Alternatively, you can transpose an array in the dialog box that appears after you copy the cell content into the Clipboard and select Clipboard/Paste Special on the Home tab in Excel 2007 or Excel 2010, or Edit/Paste Special in Excel 2003 or earlier. However, the result is separated from the original. The TRANSPOSE() function maintains the link between source and destination. The Paste option in Excel 2010 works in the same way.

Example Arrays and vectors are used for calculations in linear algebra, linear optimization, and decision theory. Vectors are always interpreted as column vectors. In this case, the scalar product of two vectors is the array multiplication of the first vector and the second transposed vector. For this purpose, Excel provides the MMULT() function for array multiplications.

The norm of the n-dimensional square array A can be calculated like this: Calculate the number resulting from the maximum of all scalar products between A and x if x iterates all vectors with the norm, 1 (the root from the scalar product of x with itself).

This is a task for the Solver, an Excel add-in that you must activate. Assume that this three-dimensional array includes B16 through D18. You use a placeholder for all vectors x in E16 through E18 (dynamic cells). You enter the scalar product of x with itself in G16 (a secondary condition):

```
{=MMULT(TRANSPOSE(E16:E18),E16:E18)}
```

You enter the formula that calculates the scalar product of Ax with x in G18:

```
=MMULT(TRANSPOSE(MMULT(B16:D18,E16:E18)),E16:E18)
```

You select cell G18 and call the Solver (on the Data tab, select Analysis/Solver in Excel 2007 or Excel 2010, and Tools/Solver in the previous versions), as shown in Figure 10-10.

Figure 10-10 Calculating the norm of arrays by using the Solver. (The Solver in Excel 2010 has a new user interface.)

As shown in Figure 10-10, you add the objective, constraint, and changing cells. If the Solver finds a solution, it displays the required norm.

See Also MDETERM(), MINVERSE(), MMULT()

Sample Files

Use the MTRANS worksheet in the References.xls or References.xlsx sample file. The sample files are found in the Chapter10 folder. For more information about the sample files, see the section titled "Using the Sample Files" on page xxiii.

Chapter 10

VLOOKUP()

Syntax   VLOOKUP(*lookup_value,table_array,col_index_num,range_lookup*)

Definition   This function looks for a value in the leftmost column of a table and returns a value in the row selected, as specified by the *col_index_num* argument. The *range_lookup* argument determines the type of match required.

Arguments

- *lookup_value* **(required)** Can be evaluated as text, a number, or a logical value. This is the value you search for in the first column of the table.

> **Note**
> The search for text is not case-sensitive.

- *table_array* **(required)** A reference to a cell range or an array constant (numbers and text must be in braces).

- *col_index_num* **(required)** Must evaluate to a positive integer and indicates the number of the column from which the information is returned. The leftmost column in the table is column 1.

- *range_lookup* **(optional)** A logical value. If this argument evaluates to TRUE (or is omitted), the function searches for the closest match for the *lookup_value*. FALSE requires an exact match.

Background   The VLOOKUP() function begins by searching the first column in the table for the *lookup_value*. If the *range_lookup* has been set to FALSE, the function will search the first column for an exact match. If no match is found, you will get the #N/A error. The table does not need to be sorted.

If the *range_lookup* has been set to TRUE or has been omitted, the function will return an exact match if one exists. Otherwise it will return a value less than the *lookup_value*. This is used mainly to return values within ranges. In this case, it is important that the lookup table is sorted, so that if the first column displays the lower value in a range, the VLOOKUP() function will select the correct range for the lookup.

INSIDE OUT   Use VLOOKUP() with arrays

You can also pass the *table_array* argument as an array constant. An array constant consists of numbers or text enclosed in braces. Rows are separated by a semicolon, and columns by a comma. The array {1;2;3;4} consists of one column and four rows, and {11,12,13;21,22,23} consists of three columns and two rows. You can use VLOOKUP() to search the array constant as follows:

```
=VLOOKUP(B27,{11,12,13;21,22,23},3)
```

(If B27 contains the value 21, the function returns 23.) The VLOOKUP() function is seldom used in this way, because entering arrays is time-consuming, error-prone, and inflexible.

Examples   The following examples illustrate how to use the VLOOKUP() function.

Combining with Other Functions   The second example of the INDEX() function uses the VLOOKUP() function to find an exact match for a value.

See Also The sections describing the ISERROR() and ISNA() functions in Chapter 11, "Information Functions," contain more examples. The examples for the IF() function in Chapter 9, "Logical Functions," include an example for discounts.

VLOOKUP() returns only the values to the right of the search column. If you want to locate values more generally across a table, use the INDEX() and MATCH() functions.

Assume that you have a list in which numbers are assigned to text (see Figure 10-11).

	F33		*fx*	=INDEX(Range,MATCH(F32,OFFSET(Range,0,1,,1),0),1)	
	A	B	C	D	E	F
30						
31		Number	Text			
32		-1	small		text searched	large
33		0	medium		number found	1
34		1	large			
35						

Figure 10-11 INDEX() and MATCH() simulate VLOOKUP().

Chapter 10

The range from B32 through C34 has the name *Range*. You want to determine the number assigned to *small*. You can also do the inverse, that is, find the word assigned to the number, which is no problem with VLOOKUP():

```
=VLOOKUP(-1,Range,2,FALSE)
```

This formula will search for –1 in the leftmost column and return small, but searching the other way around, for example, for the number associated with the text *large,* is more complicated. The following formula offers a solution:

```
=INDEX(Range,MATCH(F32,OFFSET(Range,0,1,,1),0),1)
```

With OFFSET(), you define the second column of the range as the column that is searched. MATCH() returns the row in the range containing the value in cell F32. INDEX() takes this row number and uses column number 1.

See Also HLOOKUP(), INDEX(), LOOKUP(), MATCH()

Sample Files

Use the VLOOKUP worksheet in the Lookups.xls or Lookups.xlsx sample file. The sample files are found in the Chapter10 folder. For more information about the sample files, see the section titled "Using the Sample Files" on page xxiii.

Information Functions

This chapter introduces the Microsoft Excel information functions (see Table 11-1), which return information about the content (text, values, or errors) and the format of cells. For example, the IS() functions allow you to use the IF() function and adjust and combine your calculations depending on the cell content. You can also base conditional formats and validation rules on the returned information. These functions are powerful tools and have many practical uses.

Table 11-1 **Overview of the Information Functions**

Function	Description
CELL()	Returns information about the format, location, and content of a cell
COUNTBLANK()	Returns the number of empty cells in a range
ERROR.TYPE()	Returns the error value for errors in formulas
INFO()	Returns information to the operating system and Excel
ISBLANK()	Returns TRUE if the value passed is empty
ISERR()	Returns TRUE if the value passed is an error (not #N/A)
ISERROR()	Returns TRUE if the value passed is an error
ISEVEN()	Returns TRUE if the number is even
ISLOGICAL()	Returns TRUE if the value is a logical value
ISNA()	Returns TRUE if the value is the #N/A error
ISNONTEXT()	Returns TRUE if the value is not text
ISNUMBER()	Returns TRUE if the value is a numeric value
ISODD()	Returns TRUE if the number is odd

Function	Description
ISREF()	Returns TRUE if the value passed is a valid cell reference
ISTEXT()	Returns TRUE if the value is text
N()	Converts a value to a number
NA()	Returns the error value #N/A
TYPE()	Returns a number for the data type

INSIDE OUT   The categorization of COUNTBLANK()

The Function Wizard in Excel 2003 and earlier versions locates the COUNTBLANK() function in the Statistical Functions category. However, this function is classified as an information function in Excel Help. In Excel 2007, the help was revised to match the Function Library group on the Formulas tab.

CELL()

Syntax   CELL(*info_type,reference*)

Definition   This function returns information about the formatting, location, or contents of the upper-left cell in the range specified by the reference argument.

Arguments

- *info_type* (**required**) An argument that specifies what type of information is returned.

- *reference* (**optional**) Identifies the cell you want information about. If you omit this argument, the function returns the information for the last cell that was changed.

Background   To use this function, you need to know the information types and the corresponding results. These are listed in Table 11-2.

Table 11-2 Arguments Passed as Strings to the CELL() Function

Argument (Text)	Returns
address	The absolute reference to the upper-left cell as text (can include the table or sheet name if the workbook is open).
width	Column width of the cell, rounded to an integer. Each unit of column width is equal to the width of one character in the default font size if all characters have the same width.

Argument (Text)	Returns
filename	Full path of the workbook including the table containing the cell (an empty string if the worksheet has not yet been saved).
color	Returns 1 if the cell is formatted in color for negative values; otherwise returns 0 (zero).
format	Returns a text value corresponding to the number format of the cell. The values for the various formats are shown in Table 11-3. Returns a hyphen (-) at the end of the text if the cell is formatted in color for negative values. Returns () at the end of the text if the cell is formatted with parentheses for positive or all values.
contents	Returns the value of the cell (not a formula).
parentheses	Returns 1 if the cell is formatted with parentheses for positive or all values; otherwise returns 0.
prefix	Returns a single quotation mark (') if the cell contains left-aligned text, a double quotation mark (") if the cell contains right-aligned text, a caret (^) if the cell contains centered text, a backslash (\) if the cell contains fill-aligned text, and an empty string ("") if the cell contains anything else.
protect	Returns 1 if the cell is locked and 0 if the cell is not locked.
col	Returns the column number of the cell.
type	Returns the data type of a cell: 1 is equal to text, b is equal to empty, w is equal to anything else.
row	Returns the row number of the cell.

> **Note**
>
> If the returned strings contain workbook names, table names, and/or cell addresses, the information structure is always the same:
>
> `Folder\[workbook name]worksheet!absolute address`
>
> **For example:**
>
> `F:\chapter 11\book\chp11\[Information.xls]cell`
>
> **is the path to the worksheet, and**
>
> `[Workbook2.xls]Table1!$A$1`
>
> **is the cell reference, including the workbook and worksheet information.**

The function returns some cryptic information that is explained in Table 11-3.

Table 11-3 **Number Formats, Encoded and in Plain Text**

Cell() Returns	Meaning
G	General
F0	0
0	#,##0
F2	0.00
,2	#,##0.00
C0	Currency without decimal places
C0-	Currency without decimal places; negative values are formatted in red
C2	Currency with two decimal places
C2-	Currency with two decimal places; negative values are formatted in red
P0	0%
P2	0.00%
S2	0.00E+00
G	# ?/? or # ??/??
D1	All dates have the format MM.DD.YY. The number of letters for M, D, and Y can be different.
D2	All dates have the format MM.DD. The number of letters for M and D can be different.
D3	All dates have the format MM.YY. The number of letters for M and Y can be different.
D4	All dates in which the order of the day and month was changed, as in DD/MM/YY.
D5	All dates without year number, in which the order of the day and month was changed, as in DD/MM.
D6	h:mm:ss AM/PM
D7	h:mm AM/PM
D8	h:mm:ss
D9	h:mm

Note

To ensure compatibility with other spreadsheet software, the CELL() function is made available and offers some interesting possibilities.

Important

The return value is not always current. If you save a workbook, the file name is not updated. If you change the color of negative numbers, this is not immediately shown with the value 1 or 0. To update, you have to recalculate, which can be done by pressing the F9 key.

Examples   The following examples illustrate how to use the CELL() function.

Making Changes Visible   You can use visual effects for cell changes made by the user. For example, the formula

```
=IF(CELL("address")="$C$63","Caution","OK")
```

shows in C64 that the adjacent cell C63 was changed. If you don't want to use another cell, enter the condition

```
=(CELL("address")="$C$63")
```

to format the cell in a color. This works because the reference in the CELL() function is missing.

This procedure doesn't protect the cell. If you edit another cell, everything except C63 is reset. If the user responds to the message by selecting Edit/Undo to reset the cell, the warning disappears only after another cell is changed.

Simplifying the Function   The CELL() function requires a string as the first argument. In versions of Excel earlier than Excel 2007, to use the function several times you create a list with the necessary terms. Instead of =CELL("type",B52), you can use =CELL($B$51,B52) if B51 contains the word *type*. In Excel 2007 and Excel 2010, IntelliSense helps you write formulas.

Formatting locked cells   Attempting to change a locked cell in a protected worksheet causes an annoying error message. You can format locked cells in a color to make them obvious for the user. It might also make sense to format editable cells in a color. The easiest way is to specify a conditional format for one cell and use the Format Painter for the other cells. Figure 11-1 shows an example.

Chapter 11

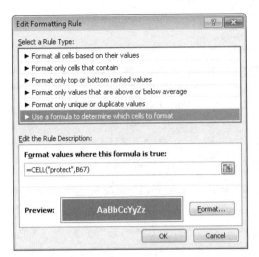

Figure 11-1 Using conditional formatting to distinguish locked cells.

The formula =CELL("protect",B67) instead of =(CELL("protect",B67)=1) works because it returns 1 if the cell is locked, and Excel interprets this as TRUE (0 would be recognized as FALSE).

Consecutive Numbers The formula

=CELL("row",C72)-71 & "."

creates consecutive numbers beginning at cell C72 with 1.

See Also All other information functions in this chapter

Sample Files

Use the Cell worksheet in the Information.xls or Information.xlsm sample file. The sample files are found in the Chapter11 folder. For more information about the sample files, see the section titled "Using the Sample Files" on page xxiii.

COUNTBLANK()

Syntax COUNTBLANK(*area*)

Definition This function counts the empty cells in a cell range.

Arguments

- ***area* (required)** The reference to the cells that you are testing for empty cells

Background This function counts not only the empty cells but also the cells containing empty strings. Cells containing the value 0 are not counted. This function is related to the COUNTIF() function. However, the COUNTIF() function evaluates numbers and text differently.

> **Note**
>
> The COUNTBLANK() function is also included in Chapter 12, "Statistical Functions."

Example Perform a few tests to get familiar with this function. Assume cells B2 through B8 contain a, b, ="", nothing, 0, 1, and 2:

- COUNTBLANK(B2:B8) returns 2 because the function counts B4 and B5 as empty cells.

- COUNTIF(B2:B8,">0") also returns 2, because two cells contain numbers greater than 0.

- COUNTIF(B2:B8,">""") returns 2 because the cells B2 and B3 contain non-empty strings.

- COUNTIF(B2:B8,"=0") returns 1 because only B6 contains 0.

However, COUNTIF(B2:B8,"=""") returns 0, and COUNTIF(B2:B8,"=") returns the expected value 1, because cell B5 is empty.

> **Note**
>
> The entry ="" is rarely used, but an empty string can be the result of the IF() function.

See Also COUNT(), COUNTA(), COUNTIF()

> **Sample Files**
>
> Use the Misc worksheet in the Information.xls or Information.xlsm sample file. The sample files are found in the Chapter11 folder. For more information about the sample files, see the section titled "Using the Sample Files" on page xxiii.

ERROR.TYPE()

Syntax   ERROR.TYPE(*error_value*)

Definition   This function returns a number corresponding to an error value in Excel. If no error exists in the cell or in the calculation, the function returns the #N/A error.

Arguments

- *error_value* **(required)** The error value (either the actual error value in a cell or the result of a calculation) for which you want to find the error code

Background   You can use this function in an IF() function to replace the error value with a string explaining the error. To do this, you need to be familiar with the relationship between error values and return values (see Table 11-4).

Table 11-4 Error Values and Results of the ERROR.TYPE Function

Error Value	Return Value
#NULL!	1
#DIV/0!	2
#VALUE!	3
#REF!	4
#NAME?	5
#NUM!	6
#N/A	7
No error	#N/A

> **Tip**
> To display the error value in a different format, use a custom function that you can program with Microsoft Visual Basic for Applications (VBA).

Examples   The following examples illustrate how to use the ERROR.TYPE() function.

Conditional Formatting   Assume that you want to use conditional formats to display the background of cells that contain error values in different colors. Figure 11-2 shows an example of the ISERROR() function that highlights cells with errors in a color defined by the user. The critical error caused by the division by zero (for which the ERROR.TYPE() function returns 2) is highlighted in a second color, such as red.

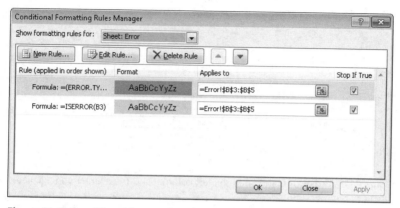

Figure 11-2 Conditional formats for error information.

Pay attention to the order of the conditions: If the ISERROR() check is performed first, the check for the divide-by-zero error will be ignored.

Custom Functions   If you repeatedly have to establish the relationship between error types (1 through 7) and error values (such as #DIV/0!), you can use a custom function to speed up and simplify this process. The following code shows a possible solution, and the implementation is shown in Figure 11-3.

```
Function ErrorDescription(Range As  Range)
   If WorksheetFunction.IsError(Range.Value) Then
      Select Case CStr(Range.Value)
         Case "Error 2000"
            ErrorDescription = "Intersection is empty"
         Case "Error 2007"
            ErrorDescription= "Division by zero"
         Case "Error 2015"
            ErrorDescription = "Noncalculable expression"
         Case "Error 2023"
            ErrorDescription = "Lost reference"
         Case "Error 2029"
            ErrorDescription= "Name not defined"
         Case "Error 2036"
            ErrorDescription = "Number cannot be shown"
         Case "Error 2042"
            ErrorDescription = "Nonexistent value"
      End Select
   Else
      ErrorDescription = "No error"
   End If
End Function
```

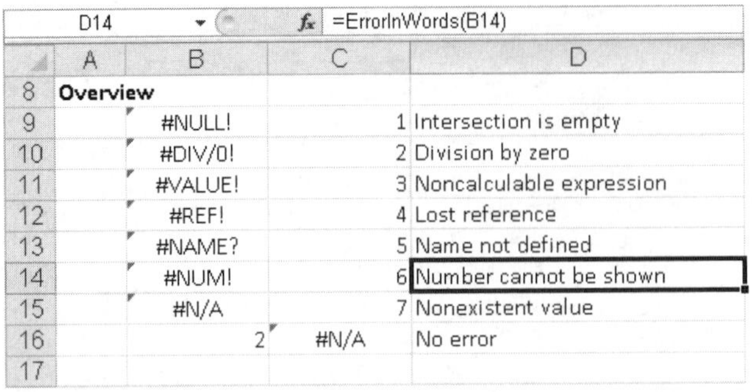

Figure 11-3 The error is shown in the left column, and the evaluation (calculated with a custom function) is in the right column.

> **Note**
> For VBA pros: Cell values in cells have the variant type. Error values have the error type and therefore have to be converted with CStr.

See Also ISERR(), ISERROR()

> **Sample Files**
> Use the Error worksheet in the Information.xls or Information.xlsm sample file. The sample files are found in the Chapter11 folder. For more information about the sample files, see the section titled "Using the Sample Files" on page xxiii.

INFO()

Syntax INFO(*type_text*)

Definition This function returns information about the operating system and Excel.

Arguments

- ***type_text*** (required) A string that specifies the type of information required

Background Table 11-5 shows the information returned by this function for different type arguments.

Table 11-5 **String Arguments and Their Meaning**

Argument	Return Value
memused	Memory used by Excel, in bytes.
memavail	Available memory, in bytes.
totmem	Total memory, in bytes, including the used memory.
recalc	Recalculation mode for the current workbook as specified in the Options dialog box: Automatic or Manual (text).
numfile	Number of active worksheets in the open workbooks and loaded add-ins.
system	Name of the operating system (pcdos for Windows and mam for Mac).
osversion	Version of the operating system (the cell content is formatted as text).
origin	Returns the absolute reference of the upper-left cell in the current window based on the current scrolling position. This argument has the prefix $A: (text).
version	The version of Excel as text.
directory	The path of the current directory or folder.

INSIDE OUT   Keep the results updated

The results of this function are not always automatically updated. After you switch into manual mode, you have to press the F9 key to recalculate the result.

The *directory* argument is more complex. If you open the Open File dialog box, the current directory changes. If you don't open a file in the dialog box (in other words, if you click Cancel), this change is applied only after the cell is recalculated.

Tip
The storage information refers to Excel and is not related to the information in the Windows Task Manager.

> **Note**
>
> **Excel Help in Excel 2007 and earlier versions contains the following safety note:**
>
> *Use this feature with caution. Sensitive or confidential information could be revealed to other users.*

Examples   The following examples show how this function is used.

XML Functionality   Assume that you want to create at note to alert the user that the functionality for XML lists is not available in Excel 2003 or previous versions. You can add a note to a cell (for example, on a cover sheet) by using INFO(version) within an IF() function.

Because the INFO() function returns text, a number comparison might fail. Alphabetically sorted, the string 11.0 is greater than 10.0 but smaller than 9.0! For this reason, the formula is more complex:

```
=IF(VALUE(REPLACE(INFO("version"),FIND(".",INFO("version"),1),1,","))<11, "Excel is
not XML-enabled.","You can use the XML function.")
```

The FIND() function returns the position of the period in the version number, and the REPLACE() function replaces the period with a comma. The VALUE() function converts the returned text into a number that is compared with the number 11.

Creating a Link   You can use the INFO() and HYPERLINK() functions to create a link to the current directory:

```
=HYPERLINK(INFO("directory"))
```

This works in Windows XP, but in Windows Vista you have to remove the last backslash if B11 contains the information:

```
=HYPERLINK(LEFT(B11,LEN(B11)-1))
```

The formula

```
=HYPERLINK(LEFT(INFO("directory"),LEN(INFO("directory"))-1))
```

doesn't work.

See Also CELL()

Sample Files

Use the Info worksheet in the Information.xls or Information.xlsm sample file. The sample files are found in the Chapter11 folder. For more information about the sample files, see the section titled "Using the Sample Files" on page xxiii.

ISBLANK()

Syntax   ISBLANK(*value*)

Definition   This function returns TRUE if the *value* argument refers to an empty cell. Otherwise, the function returns FALSE.

Arguments

- *value* **(required)** The expression (a number, text, a formula without an equal sign, a logical value, an error value, a reference, or a name) that you want to check

Background   This function is one of the nine IS() functions that return a logical value depending on the argument. The argument of the IS() functions is not converted for evaluation. This means that a string consisting of a number is interpreted as a string (not as a number).

IS() functions are often used together with the IF() function to pre-test the result of a calculation. The result returned by an IS() function can be used as the basis for conditional formats and validation rules.

The function returns the logical value FALSE not only for references to nonempty cells but also for arguments that are not valid references, such as text, numbers, logical values, and errors.

Example   Using cell references to display the values in a cell can cause unexpected results. In Figure 11-4, a reference to the cell in column G is created in column H. This figure shows the use of =G50 and so on in rows 50 through 52 and a formula returning the average of the three numbers in column H (0, 1, 2) in column I. This is wrong because column G doesn't contain the number 0.

Chapter 11

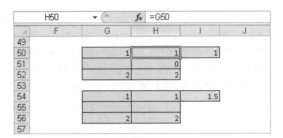

Figure 11-4 Solving the problem of calculating the average in cells containing references.

The correct solution is shown in cells 54 through 56. Here the values in column H have been pre-tested for blank cells and do not assume a 0 for a blank entry. The formula is

```
=IF(ISBLANK(G54),"",G54)
```

(with similar entries for rows 55 and 56). The result in I54 is the average of two numbers (1 and 2).

See Also ISERR(), ISERROR(), ISLOGICAL(), ISNA(), ISNONTEXT(), ISNUMBER(), ISREF(), ISTEXT()

Sample Files

Use the IS-functions worksheet in the Information.xls or Information.xlsm sample file. The sample files are found in the Chapter11 folder. For more information about the sample files, see the section titled "Using the Sample Files" on page xxiii.

ISERR()

Syntax   ISERR(*value*)

Definition   This function returns the logical value TRUE if the value is an error value. Otherwise, the function returns FALSE.

An exception is #N/A. Unlike the ISERROR() function, this function returns FALSE for the #N/A error value.

Arguments

- *value* **(required)** The expression (a number, text, a formula without an equal sign, a logical value, an error value, a reference, or a name) that you want to check

Background   This function is one of the nine IS() functions that return a logical value depending on the argument. The argument of the IS() functions is not converted for evaluation. This means that a string consisting of a number is interpreted as a string (not as a number). IS() functions are often used together with the IF() function to pre-test the result of a calculation. The result returned by an IS() function can be used as the basis for conditional formats and validation rules.

The examples for the ERROR.TYPE() function show how to locate errors in formulas.

Example   Assume that you want to calculate the average of a range (B26 through B28). You also want to check for and avoid an error if none of the cells within the range contains a number.

```
=IF(ISERR(AVERAGE(B26:B28)),"Check the input values.",AVERAGE(B26:B28))
```

See Also ERROR.TYPE(), ISBLANK(), ISERROR(), ISLOGICAL(), ISNA(), ISNONTEXT(), ISNUMBER(), ISREF(), ISTEXT()

> ## Sample Files
> Use the IS-functions worksheet in the Information.xls or Information.xlsm sample file. The sample files are found in the Chapter11 folder. For more information about the sample files, see the section titled "Using the Sample Files" on page xxiii.

ISERROR()

Syntax   ISERROR(*value*)

Definition   This function returns the logical value TRUE if the value is an error value. Otherwise, the function returns FALSE.

Unlike the ISERR() function, this function returns TRUE for the #N/A error value.

Arguments

- *value* **(required)** The expression (a number, text, a formula without an equal sign, a logical value, an error value, a reference, or a name) that you want to check.

Background   This function is one of the nine IS() functions that return a logical value depending on the argument. The argument of the IS() functions is not converted for evaluation. This means that a string consisting of a number is interpreted as a string (not as a number). IS() functions are often used together with the IF() function to pre-test the result of a calculation. The result returned by an IS() function can be used as the basis for conditional formats and validation rules.

The examples for the ERROR.TYPE() function show how to locate errors in formulas.

Example   Assume that you have created a list with birthdays (or order numbers, address information, or phone numbers) and want to access this information by using the VLOOKUP() function. Figure 11-5 shows an example.

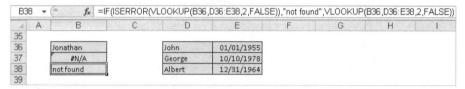

B38	▼	f_x	=IF(ISERROR(VLOOKUP(B36,D36:E38,2,FALSE)),"not found",VLOOKUP(B36,D36:E38,2,FALSE))					
	A	B	C	D	E	F	G	H	I
35								
36		Jonathan		John	01/01/1955			
37		#N/A		George	10/10/1978			
38		not found		Albert	12/31/1964			
39								

Figure 11-5 Error explanation for list searches.

If you enter the formula

```
=VLOOKUP(B36,D36:E38,2,FALSE)
```

in cell B37, you get the #N/A error, which is especially annoying when you are printing the worksheet. In other situations, you might want to use interim values and ignore errors.

In this case, you can use the IF() function in B38 instead of the simpler formula in B37:

```
=IF(ISERROR(VLOOKUP(B36,D36:E38,2,FALSE)),"not found"; VLOOKUP(B36,D36:E38,2,FALSE))
```

See Also ERROR.TYPE(), ISBLANK(), ISERR(), ISLOGICAL(), ISNA(), ISNONTEXT(), ISNUMBER(), ISREF(), ISTEXT()

Sample Files

Use the IS-functions worksheet in the Information.xls or Information.xlsm sample file. The sample files are found in the Chapter11 folder. For more information about the sample files, see the section titled "Using the Sample Files" on page xxiii.

ISEVEN()

Note

In Excel 2003, this function is available as an add-in.

Syntax   ISEVEN(*number*)

Definition   This function returns TRUE if the number argument is an even number. If the argument is an odd number, the function returns FALSE.

Arguments

- *number* **(required)** The expression to be checked

Background   You can pass any expression as an argument to this function. Integers are treated as expected. If you pass a decimal number, the decimal places are truncated and the resulting value is evaluated. =ISEVEN(2.4) returns TRUE, and =ISEVEN(-1.6) returns FALSE.

If the argument cannot be evaluated, the function returns the #VALUE! error for strings and logical values.

The ISEVEN() function is the counterpart to the ISODD() function:

```
ISEVEN(number)=NOT(ISODD(number))
```

Example   Assume that you want to assign a different background color to every other row in a worksheet. The obvious approach would be to use conditional formats and to check whether the ROW() function returns an even number. This could be done with the formula

```
=ISEVEN(ROW(cell))
```

However, if you use Excel 2003 or an earlier version and enter this formula in the Conditional Formatting dialog box, you will get an error message stating that functions from other workbooks are not allowed for conditional formats. The ISEVEN() function isn't a worksheet function like ISERROR() or SUM() but is included in the Analysis Toolpak add-in.

You can work around this by using the formula

```
=(INT(ROW(cell)/2)=ROW(cell)/2)
```

which returns the same logical value. You divide the result by two and truncate this result. If the result is the same as the division result, the number is even.

After you have entered the formula in cell A1, click Format Painter to copy the format into the other cells.

See Also EVEN(), ISODD(), ODD()

Chapter 11

> **Sample Files**
>
> Use the ISEVEN worksheet in the Information.xls or Information.xlsm sample file. The sample files are found in the Chapter11 folder. For more information about the sample files, see the section titled "Using the Sample Files" on page xxiii.

ISLOGICAL()

Syntax ISLOGICAL(*value*)

Definition This function returns TRUE if the *value* argument is evaluated to a logical value. Otherwise, the function returns FALSE.

Arguments

- **value (required)** The expression (a number, text, a formula without an equal sign, a logical value, an error value, a reference, or a name) that you want to check

Background This function is one of the nine IS() functions that return a logical value depending on the argument. The argument of the IS() functions is not converted for evaluation. This means that a string consisting of a number is interpreted as a string (not as a number). IS() functions are often used together with the IF() function to pre-test the result of a calculation. The result returned by an IS() function can be used as the basis for conditional formats and validation rules.

Examples The following examples show how this function can be used.

Logical Values as Messages With the IF() function, you can replace a logical value with text:

```
=IF(ISLOGICAL(H60),IF(H60=TRUE,"correct","not correct"),H60)
```

You could also hide cell H60. Here the ISLOGICAL() function is used to test whether a message makes sense. The second IF() function checks the logical value and translates it.

Visualizing Logical Values You can use conditional formats to display cells containing the two logical values differently (for example, green for TRUE and red for FALSE) and to match the font color to the background.

If you don't know which cells need to be formatted, you can start by selecting one of the possible cells and specifying the conditional format. Use the Format Painter to copy the format into the other cells in the range. Enter the following formulas:

```
=AND(ISLOGICAL(G63),G63)
```

for the green cells and

```
=AND(ISLOGICAL(G63),NOT(G63))
```

for the red cells (assuming that G63 is the first cell). In the first case, the condition is TRUE if the cell contains the logical value TRUE. The second formula checks whether the logical value FALSE exists. For all other results, no color is applied to the cells.

See Also ISBLANK(), ISERR(), ISERROR(), ISNA(), ISNONTEXT(), ISNUMBER(), ISREF(), ISTEXT()

> ## Sample Files
> Use the IS-functions worksheet in the Information.xls or Information.xlsm sample file. The sample files are found in the Chapter11 folder. For more information about the sample files, see the section titled "Using the Sample Files" on page xxiii.

ISNA()

Syntax　ISNA(*value*)

Definition　This function returns TRUE if the *value* argument is evaluated to the #N/A error. Otherwise, the function returns FALSE.

Arguments

- *value* **(required)** The expression (a number, text, a formula without an equal sign, a logical value, an error value, a reference, or a name) that you want to check.

Background　This function is one of the nine IS() functions that return a logical value depending on the argument. The argument of the IS() functions is not converted for evaluation. This means that a string consisting of a number is interpreted as a string (not as a number).

Example　If you use the VLOOKUP() or HLOOKUP() function, a search term might not be found in the first column (or row) of an array, and the #N/A error is returned. To avoid this, use the following formula:

```
=IF(ISNA(VLOOKUP(B76,D76:E78,2,FALSE)),"not found",VLOOKUP(B76,D76:E78,2,FALSE))
```

This ensures that only the #N/A error is replaced by a "not found" message and all other errors are displayed as usual.

See Also ISBLANK(), ISERR(), ISERROR(), ISLOGICAL(), ISNONTEXT(), ISNUMBER(), ISREF(), ISTEXT()

> ## Sample Files
>
> Use the IS-functions worksheet in the Information.xls or Information.xlsm sample file. The sample files are found in the Chapter11 folder. For more information about the sample files, see the section titled "Using the Sample Files" on page xxiii.

ISNONTEXT()

Syntax   ISNONTEXT(*value*)

Definition   This function returns TRUE if the *value* argument isn't a string. If the *value* argument is a string, the function returns FALSE.

Arguments

- *value* **(required)** The expression (a number, text, a formula without an equal sign, a logical value, an error value, a reference, or a name) that you want to check

Background   This function is one of the nine IS() functions that return a logical value depending on the argument. The argument of the IS() functions is not converted for evaluation. This means that a string consisting of a number is interpreted as a string (not as a number). IS() functions are often used together with the IF() function to pre-test the result of a calculation. The result returned by an IS() function can be used as the basis for conditional formats and validation rules.

This function always returns TRUE unless the argument contains text. The function also returns TRUE if the argument is a reference to an empty cell. If the reference points to a cell containing a reference to an empty cell in the cell with the reference, a 0 might be displayed, depending on the selected options.

The counterpart to this function is the ISTEXT() function:

```
ISNONTEXT(value)=NOT(ISTEXT(value))
```

Example   Strings longer than the cell width are only extended into the adjacent cell if that cell is empty. This can cause error messages if a string is generated by an evaluation.

You can assign a validation rule to a cell by entering the rule for that cell to the right of it. If a long string is entered into the cell (or information appears in it as a result of a function), the alert appears to the right of the cell.

Select the cell you want to lock (for example, H42). On the Data tab, select Data Tools/Data Validation/Data Validation (in Excel 2007 and Excel 2010) or Data/Validation (in earlier versions of Excel), and then select Custom in the Allow list on the Settings tab. In the Formula field, enter the following formula:

`=ISNONTEXT(G42)`

G42 is the reference to the cell containing the long text.

See Also ISBLANK(), ISERR(), ISERROR(), ISLOGICAL(), ISNA(), ISNUMBER(), ISREF(), ISTEXT()

> **Sample Files**
> Use the IS-functions worksheet in the Information.xls or Information.xlsm sample file. The sample files are found in the Chapter11 folder. For more information about the sample files, see the section titled "Using the Sample Files" on page xxiii.

ISNUMBER()

Syntax   ISNUMBER(*value*)

Definition   This function returns TRUE if the *value* argument is evaluated to a number (numeric value) without being converted. Otherwise, the function returns FALSE.

Arguments

- *value* **(required)** The expression (a number, text, a formula without an equal sign, a logical value, an error value, a reference, or a name) that you want to check

Background   This function is one of the nine IS() functions that return a logical value depending on the argument. The argument of the IS() functions is not converted for evaluation. This means that a string consisting of a number is interpreted as a string (not as a number). IS() functions are often used together with the IF() function to pre-test the result of a calculation. The result returned by an IS() function can be used as the basis for conditional formats and validation rules.

Note that this function returns FALSE if the value argument refers to an empty cell. But, if you create a reference to an empty cell, the cell containing the reference shows the value 0.

To avoid this, on the Advanced tab of the Excel Options dialog box, select Show A Zero In Cells That Have Zero Value (in Excel 2007 and Excel 2010), or select Tools/Options and select the Zero Values Disabled check box on the View tab (in previous versions of Excel). However, the calculation still uses 0.

Example In the example for the ISTEXT() function, the formula to calculate the sales tax was entered in column N (see Figure 11-6 later in this chapter):

```
=IF(ISTEXT(M42),,L42*M42)
```

If no sales tax is used, the value 0 is displayed. If you want to show an empty cell instead, enter the following formula:

```
=IF(ISTEXT(M42),"",L42*M42)
```

However, the formula

```
=L42+N42
```

to calculate the gross amount produces an error. To avoid this, use the ISNUMBER() function together with the IF() function:

```
=IF(ISNUMBER(N42),L42+N42,L42)
```

See Also ISBLANK(), ISERR(), ISERROR(), ISLOGICAL(), ISNA(), ISNONTEXT(), ISREF(), ISTEXT()

> **Sample Files**
> Use the IS-functions worksheet in the Information.xls or Information.xlsm sample file. The sample files are found in the Chapter11 folder. For more information about the sample files, see the section titled "Using the Sample Files" on page xxiii.

ISODD()

> **Note**
> In Excel 2003, this function is available as an add-in.

Syntax ISODD(*number*)

Definition This function returns TRUE if the *number* argument is an odd number. If the argument is an even number, the function returns FALSE.

Arguments

- *number* (required) The expression to be checked

Background   You can pass any expression as an argument to this function. Integers are treated as expected. If you pass a decimal number, the decimal places are truncated. =ISODD(2.4) returns FALSE, and =ISODD(-1.6) returns TRUE.

If the argument cannot be evaluated, the function returns the #VALUE! error for strings and logical values.

The counterpart to this function is the ISEVEN() function:

ISODD(number)=NOT(ISEVEN(number))

Example   You can use the example for the ISEVEN() function and format the rows with odd row numbers in a color. In Excel 2003 and earlier versions, you must replace the validation formula with

=NOT(INT(ROW(cell)/2)=ROW(cell)/2)

See Also ISEVEN(), EVEN(), ODD()

Sample Files

Use the ISODD worksheet in the Information.xls or Information.xlsm sample file. The sample files are found in the Chapter11 folder. For more information about the sample files, see the section titled "Using the Sample Files" on page xxiii.

ISREF()

Syntax   ISREF(*value*)

Definition   This function returns TRUE if the *value* argument is a valid cell reference (address or name). Otherwise, the function returns FALSE.

Arguments

- *value* (required) The expression (a number, text, a formula without an equal sign, a logical value, an error value, a reference, or a name) that you want to check

Background   This function is one of the nine IS() functions that return a logical value depending on the argument. The argument of the IS() functions is not converted for evaluation. This means that a string consisting of a number is interpreted as a string (not as a number). IS() functions are often used together with the IF() function to pre-test the result of a calculation. The result returned by an IS() function can be used as the basis for conditional formats and validation rules.

ISREF() checks whether an argument is a cell reference. Arguments such as B1 or Table1!$A$1 return TRUE even if Table1 doesn't exist in the workbook (although Excel tries to find this table). Arguments such as -B1, 12, or A1 return FALSE.

> **Note**
>
> If the reference type is R1C1, addresses are interpreted as references (for example, R2C3 or R(–1)C(–2)).

Example   The following examples illustrate how to use the ISREF() function.

Modified Error Messages   Assume that you have named a range in a workbook *ABC* and use this name for calculations in a cell outside the range. You want to prevent the name from being inadvertently deleted. The simple formula

```
=AVERAGE(ABC)
```

can be extended to

```
=IF(ISREF(ABC),AVERAGE(ABC),"The name ABC was deleted")
```

This formula displays the custom text instead of the #NAME? error.

> **CAUTION**
>
> The ISREF() function offers some surprises. For example
>
> ```
> =ISREF(A1)
> ```
>
> returns the logical value TRUE, but
>
> ```
> =ISREF(ADDRESS(1,1))
> ```
>
> returns FALSE. The reason for this is that ADDRESS() returns the text A1 instead of a reference, and text cannot be evaluated.

See Also   ISBLANK(), ISERR(), ISERROR(), ISLOGICAL(), ISNA(), ISNONTEXT(), ISNUMBER(), ISTEXT()

> **Sample Files**
>
> Use the IS-functions worksheet in the Information.xls or Information.xlsm sample file. The sample files are found in the Chapter11 folder. For more information about the sample files, see the section titled "Using the Sample Files" on page xxiii.

ISTEXT()

Syntax   ISTEXT(*value*)

Definition   This function returns TRUE if the *value* argument is not an empty string. Otherwise, the function returns FALSE.

Arguments

- *value* **(required)** The expression (a number, text, a formula without an equal sign, a logical value, an error value, a reference, or a name) that you want to check

Background   This function is one of the nine IS() functions that return a logical value depending on the argument. The argument of the IS() functions is not converted for evaluation. This means that a string consisting of a number is interpreted as a string (not as a number). The function also returns FALSE if the *value* argument refers to an empty cell. If the reference points to a cell containing a reference to an empty cell, a zero might be displayed depending on the selected options.

The counterpart to this function is the ISNONTEXT() function:

```
ISTEXT(value)=NOT(ISNONTEXT(value))
```

Example   If products are either exempt from sales tax or incur a 7 percent or a 19 percent rate, the gross value can be calculated. Create a list box containing the different sales tax rates, and enter 0% for *none*. You could also keep *none* and use a formula to check for text.

Assume you have a list like the one shown in Figure 11-6.

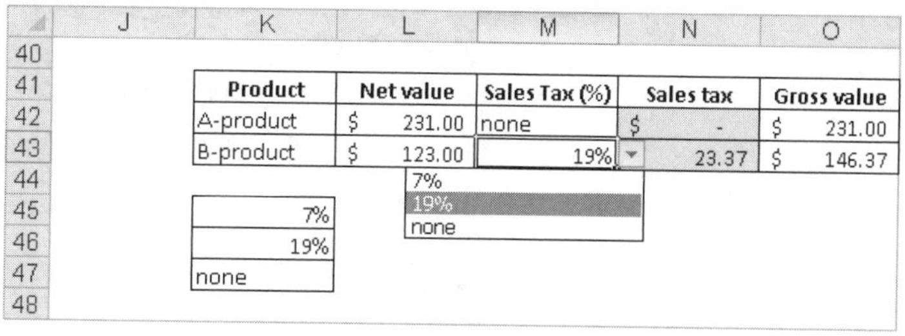

Figure 11-6 A simple sales tax calculation.

You can enter the percentages in column K in a different worksheet. It is important to use this list in the Validation Rules dialog box for column M.

For all calculations in column N, the same formula is used:

`=IF(ISTEXT(M42),,L42*M42)`

See Also ISBLANK(), ISERR(), ISERROR(), ISLOGICAL(), ISNA(), ISNONTEXT(), ISNUMBER(), ISREF()

> ### Sample Files
> Use the IS-functions worksheet in the Information.xls or Information.xlsm sample file. The sample files are found in the Chapter11 folder. For more information about the sample files, see the section titled "Using the Sample Files" on page xxiii.

N()

Syntax   N(*value*)

Definition   This function returns a value converted into a number.

Arguments

- *value* **(required)**   The expression (a number, text, a formula without an equal sign, a logical value, an error value, a reference, or a name) that you want to convert into a number

Background   Usually you don't have to use the N() function, because Excel converts values automatically if a number is required. The IS() functions are an exception. To provide compatibility with other spreadsheet software, this function is still available.

The N() function converts expressions as shown in Table 11-6.

Table 11-6 Conversion Results with the N() Function

Argument (Expression)	Return Value
Number	This number
Date	Consecutive number for the date
Time	Number for the time
TRUE	1
FALSE	0
Error value	This error value
Text or an empty cell	0

INSIDE OUT   Time basics

Excel saves dates as consecutive numbers. With the default setting, January 1, 1900, and also January 1, 1900, 12:00 AM have the value 1. Decimal numbers for days are saved in fractions of 1. The time 12:00 P.M. has the value 0.5; 6:00 P.M. has the value 0.75; and 3:46 A.M. has the value 0.15694444. Therefore, January 1, 1900, at 12:00 P.M. has the value 1.5; January 2, 1900, at 6:00 P.M. has the value 2.75; and so on. Decimal numbers without an integer part can be formatted as dates but are assigned the non-existent date of January 0, 1900, instead of December 31, 1899.

To change the default setting of the first day, on the Advanced tab of the Excel Options dialog box, select Use 1904 Date System (in Excel 2007 and Excel 2010) or select Tools/Options and then Use 1904 Date System (in previous versions of Excel). January 1, 1904, at 0:00 returns the value 0, and January 2, 1904, at 0:00 returns the value 1. Use this option with care, because all date values are changed.

Example   For examples of the use of this function, see the "Time Basics" Inside Out sidebar in this chapter.

See Also T()

Sample Files
Use the Misc worksheet in the Information.xls or Information.xlsm sample file. The sample files are found in the Chapter11 folder. For more information about the sample files, see the section titled "Using the Sample Files" on page xxiii.

NA()

Syntax   NA()

Definition   This function returns the #N/A error if a value doesn't exist.

Arguments   This function does not use arguments.

Background   Although this function doesn't use arguments, you have to enter the parentheses; otherwise, Excel recognizes the function as text.

Chapter 11

Similar to the TRUE() and FALSE() functions, in which you can enter the corresponding logical values, you can enter the #N/A error value for the NA() function to get the same result. The NA() function is provided for compatibility with other spreadsheet applications.

You can use this function or the result to explicitly mark empty cells. This ensures that empty cells are not used for other calculations. Formulas referring to these cells return the same error value. You should therefore use this function with care.

Example In the example for the ISBLANK() function, you checked whether empty cells existed so that you could exclude those cells from a calculation. If you used the NA() function instead, you wouldn't get the desired result (see Figure 11-7).

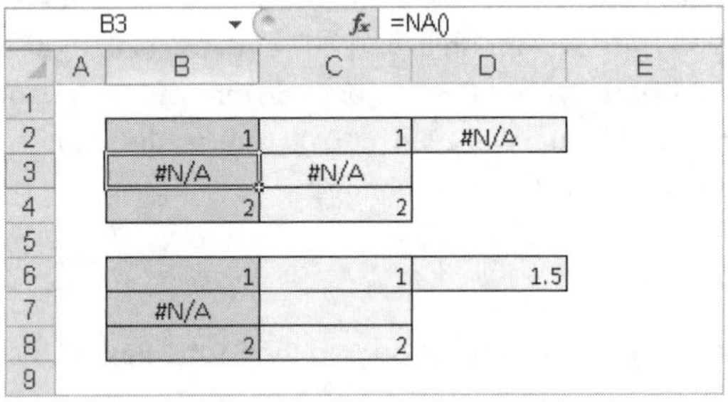

Figure 11-7 An alternative to the example shown in Figure 11-4.

Column C contains the references to column B, and the average should be calculated in cell D2. If C3 contained a 0, it wouldn't match column B. Therefore, you marked the empty cell in column B as empty (=NA() or #N/A). Unfortunately, the #N/A error value is used in all calculations.

```
=IF(ISNA(B7),"",B7)
```

This returns the correct result, which you would also get with the ISBLANK() function.

See Also The section "Using Information Functions" in Chapter 2, "Using Functions and PowerPivot," includes another interesting example for numbers in charts.

See Also ISBLANK(), ISERR(), ISERROR(), ISLOGICAL(), ISNA(), ISNONTEXT(), ISNUMBER(), ISREF(), ISTEXT()

Sample Files

Use the NA worksheet in the Information.xls or Information.xlsm sample file. The sample files are found in the Chapter11 folder. For more information about the sample files, see the section titled "Using the Sample Files" on page xxiii.

TYPE()

Syntax   TYPE(*value*)

Definition   This function returns a number indicating the data type of the *value* argument.

Arguments

- ***value* (required)** The expression (a number, text, a formula without an equal sign, a logical value, an error value, a reference, or a name) that you want to check

Background   This function is related to the IS() functions, which return a logical value depending on the argument.

This function is often used together with the IF() function to pre-test the result of a calculation. The result returned by an IS() function can be used as the basis for conditional formats and validation rules.

To use this function, you should be familiar with the mappings listed in Table 11-7.

Table 11-7 Types Mapped to Numbers

Argument	Return Value
Number	1
Text	2
Logical value	4
Error value	16
Array	64

With the exception of the last type, the results can be produced with the ISNUMBER(), ISTEXT(), ISNONTEXT(), ISLOGICAL(), and ISERROR() functions. For example:

```
ISNUMBER(B12)
```

and

```
TYPE(B12) = 1
```

have the same logical value.

The ISBLANK(), ISNA(), and ISREF() functions don't work with the TYPE() function, along with ISERR(), which does not recognize #N/A as an error.

Chapter 11

Tip   Use TYPE() or IF() to test for a condition

There is no general rule for choosing between TYPE() and an IS() function to test for a condition (IF() or conditional formatting). If you use an IS() function, you have to nest after the IS() function when using it in an IF() function. If you use the TYPE() function, you nest after the type function. The same information is returned from

```
=IF(ISERROR(F26),"error",IF(ISNUMBER(F26),"number",IF(ISTEXT(F26),"text")))
```

and

```
=IF(TYPE(F26)=16,"error",IF(TYPE(F26)=1,"number",IF(TYPE(F26)=2,"text")))
```

You cannot use the TYPE() function to find out whether a cell contains a formula. If the cell contains a formula, the TYPE() function returns the type of the formula result.

You will not get the value 64 if the cell contains an array formula. To get 64, you have to specify a range as the TYPE() argument and press Ctrl+Shift+Enter.

Examples   The following examples illustrate how to use the TYPE() function.

Producing IS() Functions   You can use the TYPE() function in the examples for the IS() functions. The second condition, =ISERROR(B3), in the example shown earlier in Figure 11-2, is now

```
=(TYPE(B3)=16)
```

For the example in Figure 11-6 (also shown earlier), you can use

```
=IF(TYPE(M42)=2,,L42*M42)
```

instead of

```
=IF(ISTEXT(M42),,L42*M42)
```

And in the second example for the ISLOGICAL() function, the identification of the cells containing logical values with colors can be done with

```
=AND(TYPE(G63)=4,G63)
```

for the red cells and with

```
=AND(TYPE(G63)=4,NOT(G63))
```

for the green cells.

Creating a Custom Function   If you often use information from a value type for text, you can create a custom function. The following code checks whether the cell contains an error. If the cell doesn't contain an error, it checks whether the cell value is TRUE or FALSE. If the cell contains a different value, it checks whether the value is a numeric value.

```
Function TypeInWords(myRange As Range) As String
    Dim var As Variant
    var = myRange.Value
    If Not IsEmpty(var) Then
        If IsError(var) Then
            TypeInWords = "Error"
        Else
            If var = True Or var = False And Not IsEmpty(var) Then
                TypeInWords = "Logical value"
            Else
                If IsNumeric(var) Then
                    TypeInWords = "Number"
                Else
                    TypeInWords = "Text"
                End If
            End If
        End If
    Else
        TypeInWords = ""
    End If
End Function
```

> **Tip**
>
> For VBA pros: Unfortunately, not all worksheet functions have a counterpart in the object model. Therefore, you sometimes have to enter formulas manually.

See Also ISBLANK(), ISERR(), ISERROR(), ISLOGICAL(), ISNA(), ISNONTEXT(), ISNUMBER(), ISREF(), ISTEXT()

> **Sample Files**
>
> Use the Misc worksheet in the Information.xls or Information.xlsm sample file. The modFunction module in this workbook contains the code shown in this section. The sample files are found in the Chapter11 folder. For more information about the sample files, see the section titled "Using the Sample Files" on page xxiii.

Chapter 11

CHAPTER 12
Statistical Functions

This chapter explains the statistical functions and their use in Microsoft Excel. The functions are described in Table 12-1. You might, however, need some statistical knowledge to interpret and use these functions.

Statistics addresses the following questions:

- How is data presented?

- What conclusions can be drawn from this data?

Statistical evaluations address extensive and complex data analyses with regard to:

- Summarizing data with key measures.

- Defining models to explain data patterns (such as correlation, regression, and multivariate analyses).

- Defining underlying distributions to explain deviations and errors in data (such as binomial and Poisson distributions for random events and normal distribution—the Gaussian distribution curve—for measurement errors).

- Comparing samples and populations to test hypotheses.

- Evaluating observations to test whether they are random.

- Defining models to allow for errors.

Table 12-1 **Overview of the Statistical Functions**

Function (Excel 2010, Excel 2007, and Excel 2003)	Description
AVEDEV()	Returns the average absolute deviation of data points from their mean
AVERAGE()	Returns the average
AVERAGEA()	Returns the average, including numbers, text, and logical values
AVERAGEIF()	Average (arithmetic average) of all cells in a range that meet a specified criterion
AVERAGEIFS()	Returns the average (arithmetic average) of all cells in a range that meet several criteria
BETA.DIST() (2010)/BETADIST()	Returns the values of the cumulative beta distribution function
BETA.INV() (2010)/BETAINV()	Returns the inverse of the cumulative beta distribution
BINOM.DIST() (2010)/ BINOMDIST()	Returns the probabilities of a binomial distributed random variable
BINOM.INV() (2010)/ CRITBINOM()	Returns the smallest value from the cumulative binomial distribution
CHI.DIST() (2010)	Returns the right-tailed, chi-squared distribution value
CHISQ.DIST.RT() (2010)/ CHIDIST()	Returns the chi-squared distribution value
CHISQ.INV() (2010)	Returns the inverse of the chi-squared distribution
CHISQ.INV.RT() (2010)/ CHIINV()	Returns the inverse of a right-tailed, chi-squared distribution
CHISQ.TEST() (2010)/ CHITEST()	Returns the independent test statistic of a chi-squared distribution
CONFIDENCE.NORM() (2010)/ CONFIDENCE()	Returns the confidence interval for a normal distribution
CONFIDENCE.T() (2010)	Returns the confidence interval for a t-distribution
CORREL()	Returns the correlation coefficient between two data sets
COUNT()	Counts the numbers in an argument list
COUNTA()	Counts the values in an argument list
COUNTBLANK()	Returns the number of empty cells in a range
COUNTIF()	Counts the cells in a range that meet a certain criterion
COUNTIFS()	Counts the cells of a range that meet several criteria

Function (Excel 2010, Excel 2007, and Excel 2003)	Description
COVARIANCE.P()/COVAR()	Returns the covariance of a population
COVARIANCE.S() (2010)	Returns the covariance of a sample
DEVSQ()	Returns the sum of the squared deviations
EXPON.DIST() (2010)/ EXPONDIST()	Returns the probabilities of an exponential distribution
F.DIST() (2010)	Returns the values of the F-distribution
F.DIST.RT() (2010)/FDIST()	Returns the right-tailed values of the F-distribution
F.INV() (2010)	Returns the inverse of the F-distribution
F.INV.RT() (2010)/FINV()	Returns the right-tailed inverse of the F-distribution
F.TEST() (2010)/FTEST()	Returns the test statistics of an f-test
FISHER()	Returns the Fisher transformation
FISHERINV()	Returns the inverse of the Fisher transformation
FORECAST()	Returns the estimated value for a linear trend
FREQUENCY()	Returns a frequency distribution as a single-column matrix
GAMMA.DIST() (2010)/ GAMMDIST()	Returns the probabilities of a gamma-distributed random variable
GAMMA.INV() (2010)/ GAMMAINV()	Returns the inverse of the gamma distribution
GAMMALN()	Returns the natural logarithm of the gamma function
GAMMALN.PRECISE() (2010)	Returns the natural logarithm of the gamma function with 15 places
GEOMEAN()	Returns the geometric mean
GROWTH()	Returns values based on an exponential trend
HARMEAN()	Returns the harmonic mean
HYPGEOM.DIST() (2010)/ HYPGEOMDIST()	Returns the probabilities of a hypergeometric distribution
INTERCEPT()	Returns the intersection of a linear regression line
KURT()	Returns the kurtosis of a data set
LARGE()	Returns the k-th highest value of a data group
LINEST()	Returns the parameters of a linear trend
LOGEST()	Returns the parameters of an exponential trend
LOGNORM.DIST() (2010)/ LOGNORMDIST()	Returns the lognormal distribution
LOGNORM.INV() (2010)/ LOGNORMINV()	Returns the inverse of the lognormal distribution

Function (Excel 2010, Excel 2007, and Excel 2003)	Description
MAX()	Returns the largest value from an argument list
MAXA()	Returns the largest value from an argument list, including numbers, text, and logical values
MEDIAN()	Returns the median
MIN()	Returns the smallest value from an argument list
MINA()	Returns the smallest value from an argument list, including numbers, text, and logical values
MODE.SNGL() (2010)/MODE()	Returns the most frequent value occurring in a data set
MODE.MULT() (2010)	Returns a vertical array of the most frequent or repeated values in an array or a data set
NEGBINOMDIST()	Returns the probabilities of a negative binomial distributed random variable
NORM.DIST() (2010)/ NORMDIST()	Returns the probabilities of a normal distributed random variable
NORM.INV() (2010)/ NORMINV()	Returns the inverse of the normal distribution
NORM.S.DIST() (2010)/ NORMSDIST()	Returns the probabilities of a standard normal distributed random variable
NORM.S.INV() (2010)/ NORMSINV()	Returns the inverse of the standard normal distribution
PEARSON()	Returns the Pearson correlation coefficient
PERCENTILE()	Returns a percentile of a data set
PERCENTILE.EXC()	Returns the k-quantile of a data group where k is between 0 and 1, excluding 0 and 1
PERCENTILE.INC()	Returns the k-quantile of a data group where k can be between 0 and 1, including 0 and 1
PERCENTRANK()	Returns the rank of a percentile as a percentage
PERCENTRANK.EXC() (2010)	Returns the rank of a percentile as a percentage, excluding 0.1
PERCENTRANK.INC() (2010)	Returns the percentage rank of a value
PERMUT()	Returns the number of permutations for the specified number of objects
POISSON.DIST() (2010)/ POISSON()	Returns the probabilities of a Poisson distributed random variable
PROB()	Returns the probability that values in a range lie between two limits
QUARTILE()	Returns the quartile of a data set
QUARTILE.EXC() (2010)	Returns the quartile of a data set based on percentiles, excluding 0.1

Chapter 12

Function (Excel 2010, Excel 2007, and Excel 2003)	Description
QUARTILE.INC() (2010)	Returns the quartile of a data set based on percentiles, including 0.1
RANK()	Returns the rank of a number within a list of numbers
RANK.AVG (2010)	Returns the rank of a number within a list of numbers: the relative value to other values within the list is important; if several values have the same rank, the average rank is returned
RANK.EQ() (2010)	Returns the rank of a number within a list of numbers: the value is relative to other values in the list; if several values have the same rank, the top rank of this group of values is returned
RSQ()	Returns the square of the Pearson correlation coefficient
SKEW()	Returns the skewness of a distribution
SLOPE()	Returns the slope of a linear regression line
SMALL()	Returns the k-th lowest value of a data group
STANDARDIZE()	Returns a normalized value
STDEV.P() (2010)/STDEVP()	Calculates the standard deviation based on the population
STDEV.S (2010)/STDEV()	Estimates the standard deviation based on a sample
STDEVA()	Estimates the standard deviation based on a sample, including numbers, text, and logical values
STDEVPA()	Calculates the standard deviation based on the population, including numbers, text, and logical values
STEYX()	Returns the standard error of the predicted y-values for each x-value in a regression
T.DIST() (2010)	Returns the left-tailed Student's t-distribution
T.DIST.RT() (2010)	Returns the right-tailed Student's t-distribution
T.DIST.2T() (2010)/TDIST()	Returns the two-tailed Student's t-distribution
T.INV() (2010)	Returns the left-tailed inverse of a Student's t-distribution
T.INV.2T() (2010)/TINV()	Returns the two-tailed inverse of a Student's t-distribution
T.TEST() (2010)/TTEST()	Returns the test statistics of a Student's t-test
TREND()	Returns values based on a linear trend
TRIMMEAN()	Returns the mean of a data group, excluding the values from the top and bottom of the data set
VAR.P() (2010)/VARP()	Calculates the variance based on the population

Function (Excel 2010, Excel 2007, and Excel 2003)	Description
VAR.S() (2010)/VAR()	Calculates the variance based on a sample
VARA()	Estimates the variance based on a sample, including numbers, text, and logical values
VARPA()	Calculates the variance based on the population, including numbers, text, and logical values
WEIBULL.DIST() (2010)/ WEIBULL()	Returns the probabilities of a Weibull-distributed random variable
ZTEST()	Returns the one-tailed probability test value for a Gauss (normal) distribution

New in Excel 2007   The following functions from Table 12-1 were introduced in Excel 2007:

- AVERAGEIF()

- AVERAGEIFS()

- COUNTIFS()

CAUTION

Many statistical functions were revised for Excel 2010. The accuracy and performance of these functions was enhanced in response to user feedback. The number and type of parameters, as well as the usage, is in some cases different from that of the previous versions. The names of some functions have also been changed to keep them in line with current naming convention.

To maintain compatibility with previous versions of Excel, the original functions are still available (in the new Compatibility category). The names of the modified functions were changed to include a period in the function name. However, the names don't indicate which category a function belongs to or whether the name changed or the algorithm or function is new. The following lists will help you determine the function category.

This book focuses on the functions in Excel 2010. The older versions of functions are not explained in detail but only referenced.

New in Excel 2010   The following functions are available only in Excel 2010:

- CHISQ.DIST()
- CHISQ.INV
- CONFIDENCE.T()
- COVARIANCE.P()
- COVARIANCE.S()
- F.DIST
- F.INV()
- GAMMALN.PRECISE()
- MODE.MULT()
- PERCENTILE.EXC()

- PERCENTILE.INC()
- PERCENTRANK.EXC()
- PERCENTRANK.INC()
- QUARTILE.EXC()
- QUARTILE.INC()
- RANK.AVG()
- RANK.EQ()
- T.DIST()
- T.DIST.RT()
- T.INV()

The accuracy and processing speed of the following functions were improved:

- BETA.DIST()
- BETA.INV()
- BINOM.DIST()
- BINOM.INV()
- CHISQ.INV.RT()
- CHISQ.TEST()
- F.DIST.RT()
- F.INV.RT()
- GAMMA.DIST()
- GAMMA.INV()
- GAMMALN()
- GEOMEAN()
- HYPGEOM.DIST()

- LOGNORM.INV()
- LOGNORM.DIST()
- NEGBINOM.DIST()
- NORM.DIST()
- NORM.INV()
- NORM.S.DIST()
- POISSON.DIST()
- LINEST()
- STDEV.S()
- T.DIST.RT()
- T.DIST.2T()
- T.INV.2T()
- VAR.S()

> **Note**
> The functions with name changes only are listed in Table 12-1.

One example is used to illustrate most of the functions in this chapter and to show how the functions address the two questions about Statistics posed at the beginning of the chapter.

> **Note**
> Different examples are used for some of the functions, such as the probability functions.

Scenario   A small software company markets its products over the Internet through its website as well as through direct sales. The company regularly monitors its product sales over the web, as well as the general traffic to its website. Because the webpages serve different purposes, the company can capture valuable information about the visitors and their interests. The following data is available:

- Daily visits to the website

- Visits to the webpages (for general information, information about products and events, and so on)

- Total sales per day for each product

- Number of clicks after a newsletter has been sent

- Cost and time required to maintain the website

- Sales calls of each field representative per day

- Sales of each field representative per month

> **Sample Files**
> Use the Web access and evaluation worksheets in the WEBACCESS.xls or WEBCCESS.xlsx sample file. The sample files are found in the Chapter12 folder. For more information about the sample files, see the section titled "Using the Sample Files" on page xxiii.

AVEDEV()

Syntax   AVEDEV(*number1,number2,...*)

Definition   This function returns the average of the absolute deviation of data points from their mean. The function calculates the arithmetic mean of the deviations of a data set based on the average, excluding the sign. AVEDEV() is a measure of the variance in a data set.

Arguments

- *number1 (required)* and *number2 (optional)*   At least one and up to 255 arguments (30 in Excel 2003 and earlier versions) for which you want to calculate the absolute deviation. You can also use a single array or a reference to an array instead of arguments separated by commas.

> **Note**
>
> Arguments can be numbers, names, arrays, or references containing numbers. If an array or a reference argument contains text, logical values, or empty cells, those values are ignored. However, cells with the value 0 are included.
>
> AVEDEV() is influenced by the unit of measurement in the input data.

Background   To calculate the deviation of sales or, as in our example, the monthly website visits related to the mean, use the AVEDEV() function. AVEDEV() is a measure of the variance in a data set.

In a sense, measures of dispersion are a quality criterion for the measure of central tendency. These measures indicate the accuracy of a measure of central tendency. Variance parameters refer to the difference between the following:

- Location values (range, quartile, or semiquartile distance)

- Individual values and a mean (average linear deviation, variance, standard or deviation)

Although the measure for the average deviation is easy to calculate, the standard deviation and variance are most commonly used. The equation for the average deviation is:

$$\frac{1}{n}\sum \left| x - \overline{x} \right|$$

Example   The marketing department of the software company wants to analyze the customers' website visits. The visits to the various website areas in the past 18 months are recorded in an Excel table (see Figure 12-1).

C23			f_x =AVEDEV(C4:C21)					
	B	C	D	E	F	G	H	I
3	Date	ADVENT	DOWNLOAD	EVENT	TRAINING	KNOWHOW	PRODUCTS	ALL (SUM)
4	Jan-07		6		19	43	22	90
5	Feb-07		498	38	1319	3000	1170	6025
6	Mar-07		1401	119	2233	6116	1545	11414
7	Apr-07		1076	16	1903	2860	1168	7023
8	May-07		1563	15	1589	3126	1139	7432
9	Jun-07		1790	1853	2428	6682	5083	17836
10	Jul-07		1367	1622	1559	3311	3609	11468
11	Aug-07		1138	2170	1502	3317	4810	12937
12	Sep-07		1352	2611	1628	3542	5581	14714
13	Oct-07	1	1343	538	1440	2971	5506	11799
14	Nov-07	272	1430	1254	2255	4735	11786	21732
15	Dec-07	1874	1140	631	1583	2652	6227	14107
16	Jan-08	42	1421	1515	2224	4837	9500	19539
17	Feb-08	32	1508	1433	1418	4006	12000	20397
18	Mar-08	10	2137	3114	1298	3128	8000	17687
19	Apr-08	10	1948	2347	1085	3575	8208	17173
20	May-08	9	1521	848	765	2139	7739	13021
21	Jun-08		426	440	123	768	778	2535
22	Average	281.25	1281.39	1209.65	1465.06	3378.22	5215.06	12607.17
23	Mean deviation	398.2	378.3	827.3	472.6	1093.9	3067.9	4785.7

Figure 12-1   Mean value and average deviation for the website visits.

Because the average deviation refers to the mean values in the data sets, the marketing department calculates the mean value for each website area by using the AVERAGE() function. Afterwards, the marketing department calculates the average deviation for each data set. The AVEDEV() function returns the results—the arithmetic mean of the deviation from the mean value.

Now the mean values and average deviations can be compared and analyzed. The following statements can be made from this result: The AVEDEV() function is a measure of the variance in a data set where the variance parameters refer to the differences between single values and mean values. The average deviation for the DOWNLOAD area is 378.3 for each month. This means that, compared with the calculated mean value, the visits of the DOWNLOAD area vary by 378.3 per month.

See Also AVERAGE(), AVERAGEA(), DEVSQ(), STDEV.S(), STDEVP(), VAR.P(), VAR.S()

Sample Files

Use the AVEDEV worksheet in the Variance.xls or Variance.xlsx sample file. The sample files are found in the Chapter12 folder. For more information about the sample files, see the section titled "Using the Sample Files" on page xxiii.

AVERAGE()

Syntax AVERAGE(*number1,number2,...*)

Definition This function returns the average (arithmetic mean) of the arguments. To calculate the average, the interval-scaled variables are added and then divided by their number.

Arguments

- *number1* **(required) and** *number2* **(optional)** At least one and up to 255 arguments (30 in Excel 2003 and earlier versions) for which you want to calculate the average

> **Note**
> Arguments can be numbers, names, arrays, or references containing numbers. If an array or a reference argument contains text, logical values, or empty cells, those values are ignored. However, cells with the value 0 are included.

Background The arithmetic mean is the best known mean value and is widely accepted among nonstatisticians. Because the mean value can easily be calculated based on all values, it plays an important role in inferential statistics.

To calculate the mean value, the values in a range are added and the sum is divided by the number of values. The calculation of the arithmetic mean requires the interval scale. The formula to calculate the arithmetic mean is:

$$\bar{x} = \frac{X_1 + X_2 + ...X_n}{n} = \frac{1}{n}\sum Xj$$

The common mean can be calculated from the arithmetic mean of two data sets.

The biggest disadvantage of the arithmetic mean is that extreme values are important because all values are included. Also, the central tendency might be at a location with only a few or no observed values.

For grouped values, the arithmetic mean is only an estimate and cannot be calculated for continuous variables when no additional information regarding the estimate of the central tendency exists.

Although the calculation of the arithmetic mean requires a metric scale, the mean values for ordinal scaled data can also be calculated. This includes sets of data such as those that consist of the answers to questions regarding customer satisfaction with certain services. This is allowed because a normal distribution of the data can be assumed if the samples are sufficient and a confidence interval is indicated by the actual mean value of a distribution. The mean value and variance of a sufficient sample ($n > 30$) are required.

For data that allows the calculation of the arithmetic mean, the mode and median can also be calculated. The best of the three measures of central tendency to use depends on the question. Mean value, mode, and median use different information and usually also have different number values. Although the arithmetic mean is the most common measure of central tendency, it might be necessary to use the mode or median because of the low scale or outliers.

Example   You are the marketing manager of the software company and have to calculate the average visits per webpage in 2007. Based on this evaluation, the company is able to see which areas are visited the most and to improve the areas that have fewer visitors.

Assume that you have imported the data from your system into an Excel file. With a Pivot-Table, you can easily calculate and analyze the visits of the individual areas. You are interested in the Products, Publications, Team, Training, and Knowledge areas as well as in the overall result. You calculate the average visits for each area by using the AVERAGE() function to see the popularity of the single areas. As you can see in Figure 12-2, the Products area has far more visits than the Publications area.

	C16	f_x	=AVERAGE(C4:C15)				
	B	C	D	E	F	G	H
3	CLICKS 2007	PRODUCTS	PUBLICATIONS	TEAM	TRAINING	KNOWHOW	OVERALL RESULT
4	January	22	2	19	19	43	105
5	Febuary	1,170	356	505	1,319	3,000	6,350
6	March	1,545	756	1,307	2,233	6,116	11,957
7	April	1,168	518	884	1,903	2,860	7,333
8	May	1,139	684	835	1,589	3,126	7,373
9	June	5,083	1,678	820	2,428	6,682	16,691
10	July	3,609	844	276	1,559	3,311	9,599
11	August	4,810	622	365	1,502	3,317	10,616
12	September	5,581	893	309	1,628	3,542	11,953
13	October	5,506	724	259	1,440	2,971	10,900
14	November	11,786	1,046	447	2,255	4,735	20,269
15	December	6,227	339	234	1,583	2,652	11,035
16	Average	3,971	705	522	1,622	3,530	10,348

Figure 12-2 Calculating the average visits per website area with AVERAGE().

Note
If you used the TRIMMEAN() function instead of AVERAGE(), the result for the average visits of the Products area would be higher because a certain percentage of the values might not be used in the calculation of the mean value of the data set. This percentage is subtracted from the beginning and the end of the data set.

Chapter 12

You can also calculate the average website visits for all areas within a year to get an overview of the entire website's activity. If you have the comparative values from the previous year, you can further analyze the data.

> **Note**
>
> To calculate the mean value from discontiguous ranges, separate the ranges with a comma, as in AVERAGE(*range1,range2,...range n*).
>
> Remember that a function can have a maximum of 255 arguments (30 in Excel 2003). To select multiple discontiguous ranges, hold down the Ctrl key while clicking the cells.

See Also AVEDEV(), AVERAGEA(), AVERAGEIF(), AVERAGEIFS(), GEOMEAN(), HARMEAN(), MEDIAN(), MODE.SNGL(), TRIMMEAN()

> **Sample Files**
>
> Use the AVERAGE worksheet in the Average.xls or Average.xlsx sample file. The sample files are found in the Chapter12 folder. For more information about the sample files, see the section titled "Using the Sample Files" on page xxiii.

AVERAGEA()

Syntax AVERAGEA(*value1,value2,...*)

Definition This function calculates the average of the values in an argument list. Not only numbers but also text and logical values (TRUE and FALSE) are included in the calculation.

Arguments

- **value1 (required) and value2 (optional)** At least one and up to 255 arguments (30 in Excel 2003 and earlier versions) for which you want to calculate the average

> **Note**
>
> The arguments can be numbers, names, arrays, or references.

Tip   Show a zero in cells with zero values

Remember that empty cells are treated differently from cells with the value 0. Empty cells are not counted, but 0 values are. If you activate the zero values option for cells with the value 0, you can see which cells are really empty and which contains the value 0. To do this in Excel 2003, click Tools, select Options, and click the Zero Values check box on the View tab of the Options dialog box. In Excel 2007, click the Office button and select Excel Options (in Excel 2010, click the File tab and then select the Options button). In the Excel Options dialog box, click Advanced. Under "Display options for this worksheet," select the "Show a zero in cells that have zero value" check box (see Figure 12-3).

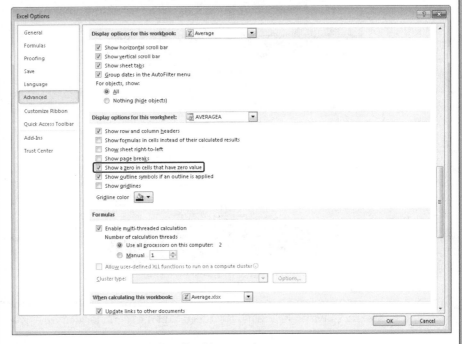

Figure 12-3 Displaying a zero in cells with zero values.

Background   You will find more information about the average in the definition of AVERAGE().

The following applies to the AVERAGEA() function:

- If arguments containing text are specified as arrays or references, they evaluate as 0.

- Arguments that contain TRUE evaluate as 1, and arguments that contain FALSE evaluate as 0.

Chapter 12

If you do not want to include text values as part of the calculation, use the AVERAGE() function.

Example   You work in the controlling department of the software company and create an Excel table containing the sales for the past twelve months. Because the list also includes text and logical values, you calculate the average sales with the AVERAGEA() function.

In the first column, you enter the text *Closed* for February (see Figure 12-4). Because the AVERAGEA() function converts text automatically into the value 0, all 12 values are added, and the sum is divided by 12. The result is $916.67.

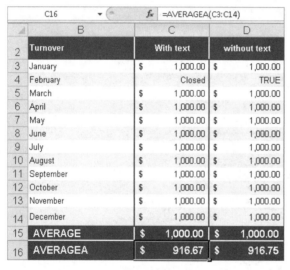

Figure 12-4   The calculation of AVERAGEA() includes text and logical values.

The second column contains TRUE instead of *Closed*. This logical value is evaluated as 1. Therefore, again all 12 values are added, and the sum is divided by 12. The result is $916.75.

If you used the AVERAGE() function, the text values wouldn't be included; only 11 values would be added, and the sum divided by 11. In this case, the result would be $1,000.00.

See Also AVERAGE()

Sample Files

Use the AVERAGEA worksheet in the Average.xls or Average.xlsx sample file. The sample files are found in the Chapter12 folder. For more information about the sample files, see the section titled "Using the Sample Files" on page xxiii.

AVERAGEIF()

Syntax   AVERAGEIF(*range,criteria,average_range*)

> **Note**
>
> The AVERAGEIF() function was new in Excel 2007.

Definition   This function calculates the average of all cells in a range that meet a specified criterion.

Arguments

- *range* **(required)** One or more cells to average, including numbers, names, arrays, or references that contain numbers.

- *criteria* **(required)** The criteria—in the form of a number, an expression, a cell reference, or text—that define which cells are averaged.

- *average_range* **(optional)** The actual set of cells to average. If *average_range* is not specified, *range* is used.

> **Note**
>
> Cells in *range* that contain TRUE or FALSE are ignored.
>
> If a cell in *average_range* is an empty cell, AVERAGEIF() ignores it. If *range* is empty or is a text value, AVERAGEIF() returns the #DIV0! error.
>
> If a cell in *criteria* is empty, AVERAGEIF() treats it as a 0 value. If no cells in the range meet the criteria, AVERAGEIF() returns the #DIV0! error.
>
> You can use the wildcard characters ? (question mark) and * (asterisk) as criteria. The question mark stands for a character and the asterisk for a string. If you want to search for an actual question mark or asterisk, enter a tilde (~) before the character.
>
> *Average_range* does not have to be the same size and shape as *range*. The actual cells that are averaged are determined by using the upper-left cell in *average_range* as the beginning cell and then including cells that correspond in size and shape to *range*.

Background You will find more information about the average in the description of AVERAGE().

The AVERAGEIF() function measures the central tendency that is the location of the center of a group of numbers in a statistical distribution. For the AVERAGEIF() function, you can specify a criterion that is determinative for the calculation of the mean value.

The three most common measures of a central tendency are:

- Average: the arithmetic mean of the distribution

- Median: the middle value in a group of numbers

- Mode: the most frequently occurring number in a group of numbers

For a symmetrical distribution of a group of numbers, these three measures of a central tendency are identical. For a skewed distribution of a group of numbers, the measures can be different.

Example As a software company, your company has to market its software. Among other things, you send regular email messages with information about your products. Usually you promote your software by sending a newsletter for each product, to reduce the content and to evaluate the click rate on your website after a mailing is sent.

Assume that you have collected the data for the past 30 months and have a list with the number of clicks and the mailing types for each month (see Figure 12-5).

	B		C	D
1	Month		Email Campaign	Clicks on Website
2	January	2006	Software A	15355
3	February	2006	Software B	1316
4	March	2006	Software C	1398
5	April	2006	General	7015
6	May	2006	Software A	15805
7	June	2006	Software B	14596
8	July	2006	Software C	7596
9	August	2006	General	7889
10	September	2006	Software A	4369
11	October	2006	Software B	1314
12	November	2006	Software C	13067
13	December	2006	General	2381

Figure 12-5 List with the number of clicks and mailings.

You want to know the average click rate on your website after the different mailings. The question is: What is the mean value of the click rate for the Software B mailing? For this you use the AVERAGEIF() function.

As you can see in Figure 12-6, the formula uses the following arguments:

- *criteria*: This is cell range C2:C30 because this column contains the criteria on which the evaluation is based.

- *range*: Software B is specified as *range,* because you only want to know the mean value of the click rate after this mailing was sent.

- *average_range*: This is cell range D2:D30 because for these cells the mean value is calculated based on the specified criterion.

	D31	▼		*fx*	=AVERAGEIF($C$2:$C$30,"Software B",$D$2:$D$30)	
	B		C		D	E
1	Month		Email Campaign		Clicks on Website	
2	January	2006	Software A		15355	
3	February	2006	Software B		1316	
4	March	2006	Software C		1398	
5	April	2006	General		7015	
6	May	2006	Software A		15805	
7	June	2006	Software B		14596	
8	July	2006	Software C		7596	
9	August	2006	General		7889	
10	September	2006	Software A		4369	
11	October	2006	Software B		1314	
12	November	2006	Software C		13067	
13	December	2006	General		2381	
14	January	2007	Software A		13997	
15	February	2007	Software B		2612	
16	March	2007	Software C		4116	
17	April	2007	General		13003	
18	May	2007	Software A		5865	
19	June	2007	Software B		15632	
20	July	2007	Software C		14135	
21	September	2007	General		12012	
22	October	2007	Software A		17162	
23	November	2007	Software B		3381	
24	December	2007	Software C		14468	
25	January	2008	General		21506	
26	February	2008	Software A		17677	
27	March	2008	Software B		11252	
28	April	2008	Software C		5876	
29	May	2008	General		5928	
30	June	2008	Software A		11333	
31					7157.57	

Figure 12-6 Calculating the average click rate after the Software B mailing.

You can make the following statements from the results: For the past 30 months, the average click rate after the Software B mailing is 7157.57. If you calculate the average click rate for the Software A, Software C, and General mailings, as well as the normal mean value, the result shows that the average click rate after the Software A mailing is the highest (see Figure 12-7). This means that your customers are most interested in this software.

Chapter 12

	B	D
32	Software A	12695.38
33	Software B	7157.57
34	Software C	8665.14
35	General	9962.00
36	Overall average	9726.07

Figure 12-7 Calculating all mean values.

See Also AVERAGE(), AVERAGEIFS(), COUNTIF(), MEDIAN(), MODE.SNGL()

Sample Files

Use the AVERAGEIF worksheet in the Average.xls or Average.xlsx sample file. The sample files are found in the Chapter12 folder. For more information about the sample files, see the section titled "Using the Sample Files" on page xxiii.

AVERAGEIFS()

Syntax AVERAGEIFS(*average_range,criteria_range1,criteria1,criteria_range2,criteria2,...*)

Note

The AVERAGEIFS() function was new in Excel 2007.

Definition This function returns the average of all cells that meet several criteria.

Arguments

- *average_range* **(required)** One or more cells to average, including numbers, names, arrays, or references that contain numbers

- *criteria_range1* **(required)** The range in which to evaluate the associated criteria

- *criteria1* **(required)** The criteria in the form of a number, an expression, a cell reference, or text that defines which cells will be averaged

- *criteria_range2* **(optional)** At least one and up to 127 ranges containing the criteria to be evaluated

- *criteria2* **(optional)** At least one and up to 127 criteria in the form of a number, an expression, a cell reference, or text that defines which cells will be averaged

> **Note**
>
> If *average_range* is empty or is a text value, AVERAGEIFS() returns the #DIV0! error.
>
> If a cell in a criteria range is empty, AVERAGEIFS() treats it as a 0 value. Cells in a range that contain TRUE evaluate as 1. Cells in a range that contain FALSE evaluate as 0.
>
> Each cell in *average_range* is used in the calculation only if all of the criteria specified are true for that cell.
>
> Unlike the range and criteria arguments of the AVERAGEIF() function, the *criteria_range* for AVERAGEIFS() has to be the same size and shape as *average_range*.
>
> If a cell in *average_range* cannot be converted into a number, AVERAGEIFS() returns the #DIV0! error.
>
> If no cells in the range meet the criteria, AVERAGEIFS() returns the #DIV0! error.
>
> You can use the wildcard characters ? (question mark) and * (asterisk) as criteria. The question mark stands for a character and the asterisk for a string. If you want to search for an actual question mark or asterisk, enter a tilde (~) before the character.

Background   You will find more information about the average in the description of AVER-AGE(). Like the AVERAGEIF() function, the AVERAGEIFS() function measures the central tendency.

For the AVERAGEIFS() function, you can specify criteria that are determinative for the calculation of the mean value. You will find more information in the description of AVERAGEIF().

Example   Let's stay with the example of the mailing. You wanted to know the average click rate on your website after a mailing. Now you want to specify another criterion to include only click rates higher than 10,000 in the calculation of the mean value. This way you can ensure that the result is not impacted by outliers.

As you can see in Figure 12-8, the formula uses the following arguments:

- *average_range*: This is cell range D2:D30 because this column contains the values from which the mean value is calculated.

- *criteria_range1*: This is cell range C2:C30 because these cells contain criteria on which the evaluation is based.

- *criteria1*: Software A is specified, because you only want to know the mean value of the click rate after this mailing was sent.

Chapter 12

- *criteria_range2*: This is cell range D2:D30 because these cells contain criteria on which the evaluation is based.

- *criteria2*: """>10000" is specified because you only want to know the mean value of the click rates higher than 10,000.

You can make the following statement from these results: For the past 30 months, the average click rate after the Software A mailing was 15,221.50.

	D31			*fx*	=AVERAGEIFS(D2:D30,C2:C30,"Software A",D2:D30,">10000")		

	B		C	D	E	F
1	Month		Email Campaign	Clicks on Website		
2	January	2006	Software A	15355		
3	February	2006	Software B	1316		
4	March	2006	Software C	1398		
5	April	2006	General	7015		
6	May	2006	Software A	15805		
7	June	2006	Software B	14596		
8	July	2006	Software C	7596		
9	August	2006	General	7889		
10	September	2006	Software A	4369		
11	October	2006	Software B	1314		
12	November	2006	Software C	13067		
13	December	2006	General	2381		
14	January	2007	Software A	13997		
15	February	2007	Software B	2612		
16	March	2007	Software C	4116		
17	April	2007	General	13003		
18	May	2007	Software A	5865		
19	June	2007	Software B	15632		
20	July	2007	Software C	14135		
21	September	2007	General	12012		
22	October	2007	Software A	17162		
23	November	2007	Software B	3381		
24	December	2007	Software C	14468		
25	January	2008	General	21506		
26	February	2008	Software A	17677		
27	March	2008	Software B	11252		
28	April	2008	Software C	5876		
29	May	2008	General	5928		
30	June	2008	Software A	11333		
31				15221.50		

Figure 12-8 Calculating the average with AVERAGEIFS().

If you calculate the average click rate for the Software B and Software C mailings, the result shows that the average click rate after the Software A mailing is the highest, as shown in Figure 12-9.

D32	▾	f_x	=AVERAGEIFS(D3:D31,C3:C31,"Software B",D3:D31,">10000")		
	B	C	D	E	F
31	Software A > 10000		15221.50		
32	Software B > 10000		13826.67		
33	Software C > 10000		13890.00		

Figure 12-9 Calculating additional mean values by using different criteria.

See Also AVERAGE(), AVERAGEIF(), COUNTIF(), MEDIAN(), MODE.SNGL()

Sample Files

Use the AVERAGEIFS worksheet in the Average.xlsx sample file. The sample files are found in the Chapter12 folder. For more information about the sample files, see the section titled "Using the Sample Files" on page xxiii.

BETA.DIST()/BETADIST()

Syntax   BETA.DIST(*x;alpha;beta;cumulative;A;B*)

Definition   This function returns the values of the cumulative beta distribution function. The beta distribution is usually used to examine the variance of processes across samples. For example, you can calculate the percentage of time people spend every day on their computers.

Arguments

- *x* **(required)** The value between *A* and *B* at which to evaluate the function

- *alpha* **(required)** A parameter of the distribution

- *beta* **(required)** A parameter of the distribution

- *cumulative* **(required)** The logical value that represents the type of the function

- *A* **(optional)** The lower limit of the interval for *x*

- *B* **(optional)** The upper limit of the interval for *x*

> **Note**
>
> If one of the arguments isn't a numeric value, the BETA.DIST() function returns the #VALUE! error. If *alpha* or *beta* is less than or equal to 0, the BETA.DIST() function returns the #NUM! error.
>
> If x is smaller than *A* or greater than *B*, or *A* equals *B*, the BETA.DIST() function returns the #NUM! error.
>
> If you don't enter values for *A* and *B*, the BETA.DIST() function uses the standard distribution, *A* = 0 and *B* = 1.

Background   BETA.DIST() calculates the probability of a value (*x*) given the beta distribution shape parameters (see Figure 12-10). The value *x* should lie between 0 and 1 unless upper and lower values are given. Either the probability or the cumulative probability will be returned.

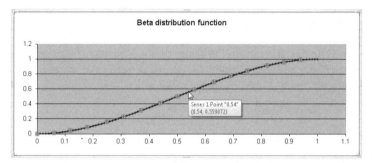

Figure 12-10 The BETA.DIST() function returns the y-value of the distribution function.

See Also You will find more information about beta distributions in the discussion of the BETA.INV()/BETAINV() function.

Example   To practice calculating BETA.DIST(), use the following values:

- 2 = the value at which to evaluate the function
- 8 = parameter of the distribution
- 10 = parameter of the distribution
- TRUE = cumulative, the logical value of the function
- 1 = lower limit
- 3 = upper limit

Figure 12-11 shows the calculation of BETA.DIST().

	E9	▼	f_x	=BETA.DIST(E3,E4,E5,TRUE,E7,E8)	
	B	C	D	E	F
2	**Meaning**			**Parameter**	
3	Value for which the function should be analyzed			2	
4	Parameter of distribution			8	
5	Parameter of distribution			10	
6	Logical value (cumulative)			TRUE	
7	Upper limit			1	
8	Lower limit			3	
9	**BETA.DIST()**			**0.685470581**	

Figure 12-11 Calculating BETA.DIST().

The BETA.DIST() function is described by the shape parameters 8 and 10. In the range 1 to 3, what is the cumulative probability of a value of 2? The BETA.DIST() function returns a value of 0.68547.

See Also BETA.INV(), BETAINV()

Sample Files

Use the BETADIST or BETA.DIST worksheet in the Probability.xls or Probability.xlsx sample file. The sample files are found in the Chapter12 folder. For more information about the sample files, see the section titled "Using the Sample Files" on page xxiii.

The sample files also include a table you can use to specify the *alpha* and *beta* parameters. Enter the parameters to change the density and distribution functions.

BETA.INV()/BETAINV()

Syntax   BETA.INV(*probability,alpha,beta,A,B*)

Definition   This function returns the inverse of a beta distribution. If probability = BETADIST(x,...), then BETAINV(probability,...) = *x*. BETA.INV() is the inverse function of BETA.DIST().

The beta distribution can be used in project planning to model completion times based on the expected completion time and variance. The inverse of the function returns the value *x* (completion time) for a given probability of the beta cumulative frequency distribution.

Arguments

- **_probability_ (required)** A probability associated with the beta distribution

- **_alpha_ (required)** A parameter of the distribution (describes the shape)

- **_beta_ (required)** A parameter of the distribution (describes the shape)

- **_A_ (optional)** The lower limit of the interval for _x_

- **_B_ (optional)** The upper limit of the interval for _x_

The alpha and beta arguments describe the shape of the beta distribution. The lower and upper limits transcribe the values for 0 and 1. If _A_ is supplied, then _B_ must also be supplied.

> ## Note
>
> If one of the arguments isn't a numeric value, the BETA.INV() function returns the #VALUE! error.
>
> If _alpha_ or _beta_ is less than or equal to 0, the BETA.INV() function returns the #NUM! error.
>
> If _probability_ is less than or equal to 0 or greater than 1, the BETA.INV() function returns the #NUM! error.
>
> If you don't enter values for _A_ and _B,_ the BETAINV() function uses the standard distribution, _A_ = 0 and _B_ = 1.
>
> If _probability_ has a value, BETA.INV() looks for the value x so that BETA.DIST(_x, alpha, beta, A, B_) = _probability_. Therefore, the accuracy of BETA.INV() depends on the accuracy of BETA.DIST(). BETA.INV() uses an iterative search technique. If the search has not converged after 100 iterations, the function returns the #N/A error.

Background   Beta distribution is a continuous probability distribution indicating the probability that a random variable _x_ has a certain value in the interval [0,1].

Beta distribution is defined by the probability density (see Figure 12-12):

$$f(x) = \frac{1}{B(p;q)} x^{p-1} (1-x)^{q-1}$$

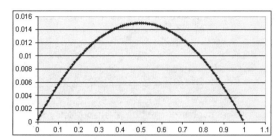

Figure 12-12 The beta density function in an interval of [0.1] with *p* and *q* = 1.

Outside the interval [0,1], it is continued with f(x)=0. The parameters are *p* and *q*. To ensure standardization, *p,q* has to be greater than 0. The prefactor 1/B(*p;q*) ensures the correct standardization (the normalization to a value range from 0 through 1). The expression

$$B(p;q) = \frac{\Gamma(p)\Gamma(q)}{\Gamma(p+q)} = \int_0^1 u^{p-1}(1-u)^{q-1}\,du$$

stands for the beta function. $\Gamma(p)$ is the gamma function.

The beta function (or Euler's beta function) is a mathematical function of two positive real numbers or two complex numbers *x* and *y*, defined by the following formula:

$$\beta(x,y) = \int_0^1 t^{x-1}(1-t)^{y-1}\,dt$$

The formula is often denoted with B(x,y). Excel uses the cumulative distribution (see Figure 12-13).

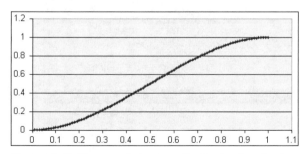

Figure 12-13 The cumulative beta distribution function in an interval of [0.1] with *p* and *q* = 1.

The following equations demonstrate the expected value and variance of the cumulative beta distribution:

$$E(X) = \frac{p}{p+q} \text{ and } V(X) = \frac{pq}{(p+q+1)(p+q)^2}$$

The BETA.INV() function returns the inverse of the beta distribution.

Example To practice calculating BETA.INV(), use the following example values:

- 0.685470581 = the probability associated with the beta distribution

- 8 = parameter of the distribution

- 10 = parameter of the distribution

- 1 = lower limit

- 3 = upper limit

With these parameters, the BETA.INV() function returns the quantile 2 for the given beta distribution.

You have described the shape of the cumulative beta distribution with the distribution parameters 8 and 10. You want to know what value you could expect with a probability of 0.6854. The result would be returned in the range 0 to 1, but because you are using lower and upper limits of 1 and 3 respectively, the answer is converted to this range, resulting in 2 (see Figure 12-14).

	B	C	D	E	F
2	Meaning			Parameter	
3	Probability of beta distribution			0.685470581	
4	Parameter of distribution			8	
5	Parameter of distribution			10	
6	Upper limit			1	
7	Lower limit			3	
8	BETA.INV()			2	
9				=BETA.INV(E3,E4,E5,E6,E7)	

Figure 12-14 Calculation of BETA.INV().

See Also BETA.DIST(), BETADIST()

> **Sample Files**
>
> Use the BETA.INV worksheet in the Probability.xls or Probability.xlsx sample file. The sample files are found in the Chapter12 folder. For more information about the sample files, see the section titled "Using the Sample Files" on page xxiii.
>
> The sample files also include a table you can use to specify the *alpha* and *beta* parameters. Enter the parameters to change the density and distribution functions.

BINOM.DIST()/BINOMDIST()

Syntax   BINOM.DIST(*number_s;trials;probability_s;cumulative*)

Definition   This function returns the probabilities of a binomial distributed random variable. Use the BINOM.DIST() function for problems with a fixed number of tests or trials when the results of a trial are only success or failure, when trials are independent, and when the probability of success is constant throughout all trials. For example, you can use the BINOM.DIST() function to calculate the probability that 50 of 100 people in a restaurant support a smoking ban.

Arguments

- *number_s* **(required)** The number of successes in trials.

- *trials* **(required)** The number of independent trials.

- *probability_s* **(required)** The probability for the success of each trial.

- *cumulative* **(required)** The logical value that represents the type of the function. Use TRUE for the cumulative distribution, otherwise use FALSE for the probability mass distribution.

> **Note**
>
> The *number_s* and *trials* arguments are rounded to integers.
>
> If *number_s*, *trials*, or *probability_s* isn't a numeric value, the BINOM.DIST() function returns the #VALUE! error.
>
> If *number_s* is less than 0 or greater than *trials*, the function returns the #NUM! error.
>
> If *probability_s* is less than 0 or greater than 1, the function returns the #NUM! error.

Background In general, the probability can be defined as the likelihood that an event will occur when running a random trial where none of the given events is favored.

For example, how high is the probability that 30 packages will be damaged when producing 2,000 pills if it is assumed that 2 percent of the packages will be damaged?

Random trials for which a random variable can fall in one of two categories are usually called *Bernoulli experiments*, named for the Swiss mathematician Jakob Bernoulli (1654–1705).

The random variable (Bernoulli variable) x has the value $x=1$ with probability p (success) and the value $X=0$ with probability $q=1-p$ (failure). The probability p is also called the *success rate*.

You often encounter events where the outcome can be divided into two categories. Therefore, a series of n Bernoulli experiments exists. The probability that the random variable $x=1$ occurs in k cases is calculated with the following Bernoulli formula:

$$P(X = k) = \binom{n}{k} p^k q^{n-k}$$

The distribution

$$F_B : kaP(X \le k) = F_B(k; n, p) = \sum_{i=0}^{k} f_b(i; n, p)$$

of the random variable is called *binomial distribution,* with the binomial coefficient

$$\binom{n}{k}$$

—that's *n* over *k*.

Binomial distribution is one of the most important probability distributions and is a special case of the multinomial distributions. Binomial distribution describes the results from Bernoulli processes, which in turn are defined as multiple Bernoulli experiments run under consistent conditions (for example, the toss of a coin).

If you toss a coin, the probability of success and failure is the same. However, if you toss the coin 12 times, you get 2^{12} possible results.

Example The result of seven "heads" means that seven of the 12 results have "heads" as a single result. Choosing seven objects out of 12 is possible in many ways:

$$\binom{12}{7}$$

Therefore, the probability for seven heads results equals

$$\frac{\binom{12}{7}}{2^{12}}$$

Excel provides the BINOM.DIST() function to calculate the probability of a binomial distrib-uted random variable. Figure 12-15 shows an example of a binomial distribution.

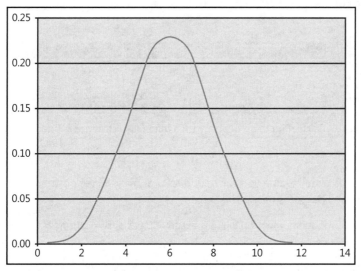

Figure 12-15 Binomial distribution for $p=0.5$ and $n=12$.

The density function of the binomial distribution is

$$b(x;n,p) = \binom{n}{x} p^x (1-p)^{n-x}$$

where

$$\binom{n}{x}$$

is COMBIN($n;x$). The distribution function of the binomial distribution is

$$B(x,n,p) = \sum_{y=0}^{x} b(y;n,p)$$

Examples

Vacation Directions You are on vacation in a foreign city and ask a passerby for directions to a certain location. The question "Do you know the way?" can be answered only with *yes* or *no*. This means that there is a probability of 50 percent that the answer will be yes. Therefore, *p* is 0.5.

You want to know the probability that 66 of the 100 respondents (2/3) will answer yes. Figure 12-16 shows the calculation of the probability for the binomial distributed random variable 66.

	B	C	D	E
3	**Arguments**	**Example**	**Formula**	
4	Number of successful answers	66		
5	Attempts	100		
6	Probability of success	0.5		
7	Cumulative Yes	TRUE	0.9996	=BINOM.DIST(C4,C5,C6,C7)
8	Cumulative No	FALSE	0.0005	=BINOM.DIST(C4,C5,C6,C8)

Figure 12-16 Calculating the probability for a binomial distributed random variable.

Here are the results:

- The probability that you will get up to or at most 66 yes answers from 100 interviewed people is nearly 100 percent.

- The probability that you will get exactly 66 yes answers from 100 interviewed people is 0.05 percent.

In this way you can calculate many different probabilities.

Damaged Packages Let's use the example for the BINOM.DIST() function. The question in that example was: How high is the probability that 30 packages will be damaged when producing 2,000 pills if it is assumed that 2 percent of the packages will be damaged? Figure 12-17 shows the result.

	B	C	D	E
17	**Arguments**	**Example**	**Formula**	
18	Number of successful answers	30		
19	Attempts	2000		
20	Probability of success	0.02		
21	Cumulative Yes	TRUE	0.0598	=BINOM.DIST(C18,C19,C20,C21)
22	Cumulative No	FALSE	0.0181	=BINOM.DIST(C18,C19,C20,C22)

Figure 12-17 BINOM.DIST() returns the probability for a binomial distributed random variable.

Here's what you have discovered:

- The probability that a maximum of 30 packages will be damaged is 6 percent.

- The probability that exactly 30 packages will be damaged is 1.8 percent.

See Also BINOM.INV(), COMBIN(), CRITBINOM(), FACT(), HYPGEOM.DIST(), NEGBINOM.DIST(), PERMUT(), PROB()

> **Sample Files**
>
> Use the BINOMDIST or BINOM.DIST worksheet in the Probability.xls or Probability.xlsx sample file. The sample files are found in the Chapter12 folder. For more information about the sample files, see the section titled "Using the Sample Files" on page xxiii.

BINOM.INV()/CRITBINOM()

Syntax   BINOM.INV(*trials;probability_s;alpha*)

Definition   This function returns the smallest value for which the cumulative binomial distribution is greater than or equal to the specified probability. Use this function for quality assurance applications. For example, use the BINOM.INV() function to determine the largest number of defective parts that are allowed to come off an assembly line run without rejecting the entire lot.

Arguments

- **trials (required)** The number of Bernoulli trials

- **probability_s (required)** The probability for the success of each trial

- **alpha(required)** The cumulative binomial probability

> **Note**
>
> If one of the arguments isn't a numeric value, the BINOM.INV() function returns the #VALUE! **error.**
>
> If *trials* isn't an integer, the decimal places are truncated. If *trials* is less than 0, the BINOM.INV() function returns the #NUM! **error.**
>
> If *probability_s* is less than 0 or greater than 1, the BINOM.INV() function returns the #NUM! **error.**
>
> If *alpha* is less than 0 or greater than 1, the BINOM.INV() function returns the #NUM! **error.**

Background   The BINOM.INV() function returns the smallest value for a cumulative binomial distribution not exceeding the specified probability.

BINOM.INV() calculates how often an event can occur based on the probability p in a sample with n repetitions before its cumulative probabilities have a value greater than or equal to the cumulative binomial probability *alpha*.

This function can only be used for binomial distributions. Therefore, the events have to be independent and can return only two results: an event either occurs or doesn't occur.

BINOM.INV() is the inverse function of BINOM.DIST().

See Also You will find more information about binomial distributions in the section that discusses the BINOM.DIST()/BINOMDIST() function.

Example   We use the example from the BINOM.DIST() function to explain the BINOM.INV() function. Assume that you are on vacation in a foreign city and ask 100 people (*n* trial) for directions. This question can be answered only with *yes* or *no*. This means there is a probability of 50 percent that the answer is yes. Therefore, *p* is 0.5.

You use the BINOM.DIST() function to calculate the probability that 66 of the 100 respondents (2/3) answer *yes*. Then you calculate with BINOM.INV() how often the answer is *yes* based on the probability $p = 0.5$ in a sample with $n = 100$ repetitions before the cumulative probability has a value greater than or equal to the criteria *alpha*. Figure 12-18 shows the result.

D7		f_x	=BINOM.INV(D4,D5,D6)					
B	C	D	E	F	G	H	I
4 Size of sample n		100	100	100	100	100	100
5 Probability of success p		50%	50%	50%	50%	50%	50%
6 Probability of limit (~Alpha Risk)		0.1%	0.2%	0.4%	0.6%	0.8%	1.0%
7 BINOM.INV		35	36	37	37	38	38

Figure 12-18 Calculation with the BINOM.INV() function.

Based on the probability of 0.1 percent, a maximum of 35 people should answer *yes* before the cumulative probability has a value greater than or equal to the probability criteria *alpha*.

The BINOM.INV() function calculates the maximum number of characteristics within the sample based on the given probability criteria *alpha*.

See Also BINOM.DIST(), COMBIN(), FACT(), HYPGEOM.DIST(), NEGBINOM.DIST(), PERMUT(), PROB()

Sample Files

Use the CRITBINOM or BINOM.INV worksheet in the Probability.xls or Probability.xlsx sample file. The sample files are found in the Chapter12 folder. For more information about the sample files, see the section titled "Using the Sample Files" on page xxiii.

CHISQ.DIST()

Syntax   CHISQ.DIST(*x,degrees_freedom,cumulative*)

Definition   This function returns the values of the chi-squared distribution. The chi-squared distribution is often used to examine the variance across samples. For example, you can calculate the percentage of time people spend every day watching TV.

Arguments

- *x* **(required)** The value (quantile) for which you want to calculate the probability (1-alpha).

- *degrees_freedom* **(required)** The number of degrees of freedom.

- *cumulative* **(required)** The logical value. If *cumulative* is TRUE, the cumulative distribution is returned; otherwise, the probability density function is returned.

Note

If one of the arguments isn't a numeric value, the CHISQ.DIST() function returns the #VALUE! **error.**

If *x* is negative, CHISQ.DIST() returns the #NUM! error value.

If *degrees_freedom* isn't an integer, the decimal places are truncated. If *degrees_freedom* is less than 1 or greater than or equal to 1010, the function returns the #NUM! error.

Background   The CHISQ.DIST.RT() function describes the right distribution function, and the CHISQ.DIST() function describes the left distribution of a chi-square distributed random variable.

See Also You will find more information about chi-tests and significance levels in the description of CHISQ.TEST().

Chapter 12

The CHISQ.INV() function is the inverse function of CHISQ.DIST().

Example   See the example for the CHISQ.DIST.RT() function.

See Also CHISQ.DIST.RT(), CHISQ.TEST()

Sample Files

Use the CHIDIST or CHISQ.DIST worksheet in the Probability.xls or Probability.xlsx sample file. The sample files are found in the Chapter12 folder. For more information about the sample files, see the section titled "Using the Sample Files" on page xxiii.

CHISQ.DIST.RT()/CHIDIST()

Note

In Excel 2010, the CHIDIST() function was replaced with the CHISQ.DIST.RT() function, and the CHISQ.DIST() function was added to increase the accuracy of the results. To ensure the backward compatibility of CHISQ.DIST.RT(), the CHIDIST() function is still available.

Syntax   CHISQ.DIST.RT(*x,degrees_freedom*)

Definition   This function returns the values of the right-tailed probability of chi-square distribution. The χ^2 c^2-distribution is required for a c^2-test. Use this test to compare observed and expected values. For example, an experiment might hypothesize that the regular use of vitamins reduces the risk of colds. By comparing the observed results with the expected results, you can validate this hypothesis.

Arguments

- *x* **(required)** The probability value at which you want to evaluate the distribution

- *degrees_freedom* **(required)** The number of degrees of freedom

> **Note**
>
> If one of the arguments isn't a numeric value, the CHISQ.DIST.RT() function returns the #VALUE! error. If x is negative, CHISQ.DIST.RT() returns the #NUM! error value.
>
> If *degrees_freedom* isn't an integer, the decimal places are truncated. If *degrees_freedom* is less than 1 or greater than or equal to 1010, the function returns the #NUM! error.
>
> CHISQ.DIST.RT() is calculated as CHISQ.DIST.RT = $P(X>x)$, where x is a c^2 random variable.

Background   The CHISQ.DIST.RT() function calculates the right-tailed probability of the chi-square distribution.

See Also You will find more information about chi-tests and significance levels in the description of the CHISQ.TEST() function.

The CHISQ.INV.RT() function is the inverse function of CHISQ.DIST.RT().

Example   Assume that you are a manufacturer of vitamins and want to prove that the regular use of Vitamin C reduces the risk of catching colds. You took two samples from the same population, where 22 of the 936 participants had a cold. The first sample contains the expected values, and the second sample contains the observed values. The goal is to prove your assumption that Vitamin C protects against colds (the null hypothesis) is correct.

You have already calculated the critical value c with a given probability (significance level a) of 2.5 percent, as well as the degrees of freedom and v as measure for the total deviation.

See Also The descriptions of the CHISQ.TEST() and CHISQ.INV.RT() functions explain how to calculate these components.

Until now, because of the results of your statistical calculations, you have had to reject the null hypothesis—the assumption that Vitamin C protects against colds.

Therefore, you want to perform one last test to confirm the null hypothesis. You use the CHISQ.DIST.RT() function to calculate the probability for v, to compare the significance level and the calculated probability value.

Figure 12-19 shows how the probability for v is calculated.

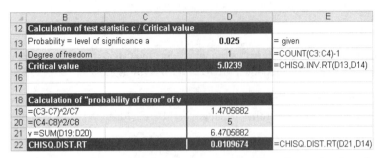

	B	C	D	E
12	Calculation of test statistic c / Critical value			
13	Probability = level of significance a		0.025	= given
14	Degree of freedom		1	=COUNT(C3:C4)-1
15	Critical value		5.0239	=CHISQ.INV.RT(D13,D14)
16				
17				
18	Calculation of "probability of error" of v			
19	=(C3-C7)^2/C7		1.4705882	
20	=(C4-C8)^2/C8		5	
21	v =SUM(D19:D20)		6.4705882	
22	CHISQ.DIST.RT		0.0109674	=CHISQ.DIST.RT(D21,D14)

Figure 12-19   CHISQ.DIST.RT() returns the probability of error for the value *v*.

If you compare CHISQ.DIST.RT() for *v*, you can see that *v* is smaller than the significance level. As a consequence, the null hypothesis is confirmed.

See Also CHISQ.INV(), CHISQ.INV.RT(), CHISQ.TEST()

> ## Sample Files
> Use the CHIDIST or CHISQ.DIST.RT worksheet in the Probability.xls or Probability.xlsx sample file. The sample files are found in the Chapter12 folder. For more information about the sample files, see the section titled "Using the Sample Files" on page xxiii.

CHISQ.INV()

Syntax   CHISQ.INV(*probability,degrees_freedom*)

Definition   This function returns the percentile of the left χ^2-distribution. If *probability* = CHISQ.DIST(*x*,...) then CHISQ.INV(*probability*,...) = *x*. Use this function to compare the observed results with the expected results in order to decide whether your original hypothesis is valid.

Arguments

- *probability* **(required)** A probability associated with the χ^2-distribution

- *degrees_freedom* **(required)** The number of degrees of freedom

Note

If one of the arguments isn't a numeric value, the CHISQ.INV() function returns the #VALUE! error.

If *probability* is less than 0 or greater than 1, the CHISQ.INV() function returns the #NUM! error. If *degrees_freedom* isn't an integer, the decimal places are truncated. If *degrees_freedom* is less than 1 or greater than or equal to 1010, the function returns the #NUM! error.

If *probability* has a value, CHISQ.INV() looks for the value *x* so that CHISQ.DIST(*x*, *degrees_freedom*) = *probability*. Therefore, the accuracy of CHISQ.INV() depends on the accuracy of CHISQ.DIST(). CHISQ.INV() uses an iterative search technique. If the search has not converged after 100 iterations, the function returns the #N/A error.

Background   The CHISQ.INV.RT() function describes the percentile of the right χ^2-distribution and CHISQ.INV() describes the left χ^2-distribution.

See Also   You will find more information about chi-squared distributions in the discussion of the CHISQ.TEST() function.

Example   The CHISQ.DIST() function is the inverse function of CHISQ.INV(). See the example for the CHISQ.INV.RT() function to see the use of this function.

See Also   CHISQ.INV(), CHISQ.INV.RT(), CHISQ.TEST()

Sample Files

Use the CHI.INV or CHISQ.INV worksheet in the Probability.xls or Probability.xlsx sample file. The sample files are found in the Chapter12 folder. For more information about the sample files, see the section titled "Using the Sample Files" on page xxiii.

CHISQ.INV.RT()/CHIINV()

Note

In Excel 2010, the CHIINV() function was replaced with the CHISQ.INV.RT() function, and the CHISQ.INV() function was added to increase the accuracy of the results. To ensure the backward compatibility of CHISQ.INV.RT(), the CHIINV() function is still available.

Syntax CHISQ.INV.RT(*probability,degrees_freedom*)

Definition This function returns the inverse of the right-tailed probability of the chi-square distribution. If *probability* = CHISQ.DIST.RT($x,...$) then CHI.INV(*probability,...*) = x. Use this function to compare the observed results with the expected results in order to decide whether your original hypothesis is valid.

Arguments

- *probability* **(required)** A probability associated with the χ^2-distribution

- *degrees_freedom* **(required)** The number of degrees of freedom

> **Note**
>
> If one of the arguments isn't a numeric value, the CHISQ.INV.RT() function returns the #VALUE! error.
>
> If *probability* is less than 0 or greater than 1, the CHISQ.INV.RT() function returns the #NUM! error. If *degrees_freedom* isn't an integer, the decimal places are truncated. If *degrees_freedom* is less than 1 or greater than or equal to 1010, the function returns the #NUM! error.
>
> If *probability* has a value, CHISQ.INV.RT() looks for the value x so that CHISQ.DIST.RT(x, *degrees_freedom*) = *probability*. Therefore, the accuracy of CHISQ.INV.RT() depends on the accuracy of CHISQ.DIST.RT(). CHISQ.INV.RT() uses an iterative search technique. If the search has not converged after 100 iterations, the function returns the #N/A error.

Background The CHISQ.INV.RT() function returns the test statistic c for the confidence interval of a chi-square distributed random variable. The test statistic c is also called a *critical value*.

See Also You will find more information about chi-squared distributions in the discussion of the CHISQ.TEST() function.

For a given probability, this function finds the value x such that CHISQ.DIST.RT($x,degrees\_freedom$) = *probability*. The *degrees_freedom* argument in the χ^2 test is based on the number of trials decreased by 1. A statistical test is possible only if at least one degree of freedom exists. The CHISQ.DIST.RT() function is the inverse function of CHISQ.INV.RT().

Example   Assume that you are a manufacturer of vitamins and want to prove that the regular use of Vitamin C reduces the risk of catching colds. You took two samples from the same population where 22 of the 936 participants had a cold.

The first sample contains the expected values, and the second sample contains the observed values. The goal is to prove that your assumption that Vitamin C protects against colds (the *null hypothesis*) is correct.

Therefore, you calculate the critical value for the random variable with a given probability of 2.5 percent (see Figure 12-20).

	B	C	D	E
13	Calculation of test statistic c / Critical value			
14	Probability = level of significance a		0.025	= given
15	Degree of freedom		1	=COUNT(C3:C4)-1
16	Critical value		5.0239	=CHISQ.INV.RT(D14,D15)

Figure 12-20 Calculating the critical value with the CHISQ.INV.RT() function.

The critical value calculated by the CHISQ.INV.RT() function is 5.0239 with a significance level of 2.5 percent and 1 degree of freedom.

If *v* (the measure for the total variance) falls below this statistic, the null hypothesis is assumed and your statement that Vitamin C protects against colds is confirmed.

To calculate *v*, the differences between the observed and expected frequencies are squared and divided by the expected frequency (see Figure 12-21).

	B	C	D
19	Calculation of test statistic v / Dimension of total variance		
20	=(C3-C7)^2/C7		1.4705882
21	=(C12-C16)^2/C16		5
22	v=SUM(D20:D21)		6.4705882

Figure 12-21 The check sum *v* is calculated to compare the value with the critical value.

Because *v* is above the critical value, the null hypothesis cannot be assumed. This means that your statement that Vitamin C protects against colds cannot be confirmed.

See Also CHISQ.INV(), CHISQ.INV.RT(), CHISQ.TEST()

Sample Files

Use the CHIINV or CHISQ.INV.RT worksheet in the Probability.xls or Probability.xlsx sample file. The sample files are found in the Chapter12 folder. For more information about the sample files, see the section titled "Using the Sample Files" on page xxiii.

CHISQ.TEST()/CHITEST()

Syntax   CHISQ.TEST(*actual_range,expected_range*)

Definition   This function returns the test statistic of a χ^2-test for independence. CHISQ.TEST() returns the value from the chi-squared (χ^2) distribution for the statistic and the appropriate degrees of freedom. You can use c^2-tests to determine whether hypothesized results are verified.

Arguments

- *actual_range* (**required**) The range of data that contains observations to test against expected values

- *expected_range* (**required**) The range of expected observations

> **Note**
>
> If *actual_range* and *expected_range* have a different number of data points, the function CHISQ.TEST() returns the #N/A error.
>
> The c^2-test first calculates a c^2-statistic by using the following formula:
>
> $$x^2 = \sum_{j=1}^{i} \sum_{j=1}^{c} \frac{\left(A_{ij} - E_{ij}\right)^2}{E_{ij}}$$
>
> where
>
> > A_{ij} = actual frequency in the *i*-th row, *j*-th column
> >
> > E_{ij} = expected frequency in the *i*-th row, *j*-th column
> >
> > $\sum$ = number of rows
> >
> > $\sum$ = number of columns
>
> A low value of *i* c^2 is an indicator of independence. As you can see in the formula, c^2 is always positive or 0 and is 0 only if $A_{ij} = E_{ij}$ for every *i,j*.
>
> CHISQ.TEST() returns the probability that a value of the c^2-distribution that is at least as high as the value calculated by the preceding formula could have happened by chance, assuming independence.

To calculate this probability, the CHISQ.TEST() function uses the c^2-distribution with the appropriate number of degrees of freedom (*df*):

- If *r* is greater than 1 and *c* is greater than 1, then $df = (r - 1)(c - 1)$.

- If *r* is equal to 1 and *c* is greater than 1, then $df = c - 1$.

- If *r* is greater than 1 and *c* is equal to 1, then $df = r - 1$.

- $r = c = 1$ is not allowed and #N/A is returned.

The CHISQ.TEST() function is most useful when expected values are not too small. Some statisticians suggest that each E_{ij} should be greater than or equal to 5.

Background   The chi-square test provides a method for testing the association of variables in a two-way table. The null hypothesis assumes that there is no association, whereas the alternative hypothesis assumes that some association exists, although that alternative hypothesis is not any more specific than this. The chi-square test measures the divergence of the observed values in the two-way table from those that would be expected using the null hypothesis (no association). The two-way table of expected values can be calculated from the row and column totals.

The CHISQ.TEST() function returns the test for independence, comparing the existing values with the expected values.

The significance level, with a number value from 0 through 100 percent, indicates the level of confidence in the hypothesis test. A significance of 90 percent doesn't mean that:

- The probability for the existing data to be random is only 10 percent.

- A certain fact has a probability of 90 percent to be true.

The significance level indicates the percentage of allowed errors for a sample to still be considered random.

Example   You are a manufacturer of vitamins and want to test whether the regular use of Vitamin C reduces the risk of catching colds. You took two samples from the same population, where 22 of the 936 participants had a cold. The first sample contains the expected values, and the second sample contains the observed values.

In the first step, you want to determine the significance level of the values to check whether the samples are random and the values are similar. You use the CHISQ.TEST() function, as shown in Figure 12-22.

	C12	▼	f_x	=CHISQ.TEST(C5:C6,C9:C10)	
	B	C	D	E	F
3	**Values**	**Cold**	**No cold**	**Sum**	
4	**Observed values**				
5	Vitamin C	12	704	716	=SUM(C5:D5)
6	No Vitamin C	10	210	220	=SUM(C6:D6)
7	**Sum**	22	914	**936**	=SUM(E5:E6)
8	**Expected values**				
9	Vitamin C	17	699	716	=SUM(C9:D9)
10	No Vitamin C	5	215	220	=SUM(C10:D10)
11	**Sum**	22	914	**936**	=SUM(E9:E10)
12	**CHISQ.TEST**			0.0109674	

Figure 12-22 Calculating CHISQ.TEST() with observed and expected values.

The calculated significance level of 1 percent indicates that the observed and existing incidence numbers in 99 percent (100 minus 1) of the cases show comparable characteristics. This suggests that the samples are random; that is, that the sample taken does not differ significantly from what you would expect with the level of colds and the incidence of Vitamin C use in the population.

The value calculated by CHISQ.TEST() can also indicate the probability for a calculated v. The variable v is a statistical indicator that characterizes a measure of the total deviation.

To calculate the variable, use the following formula:

$$CHI - Formel\ r = 1 - \frac{6 \sum\limits_{1=i}^{n} D_i^2}{n_{(n^2-1)}}$$

If the value for the statistic n is very high, the null hypothesis is rejected. If the probability for v is lower than the corresponding significance level, the difference is significant. This means that the alternative hypothesis is assumed. If the probability for v is higher, the difference is not significant and the null hypothesis is assumed.

See Also CHISQ.DIST(), CHISQ.DIST.RT(), CHISQ.INV(), CHISQ.INV.RE()

Sample Files

Use the CHITEST or CHISQ.TEST worksheet in the Probability.xls or Probability.xlsx sample file. The sample files are found in the Chapter12 folder. For more information about the sample files, see the section titled "Using the Sample Files" on page xxiii.

CONFIDENCE.NORM()/CONFIDENCE()

> **Note**
>
> In Excel 2010, the CONFIDENCE() function was replaced with the CONFIDENCE.NORM()
> function, and the CONFIDENCE.T() function was added to increase the accuracy
> of the results. To ensure the backward compatibility of CONFIDENCE.NORM() and
> CONFIDENCE.T(), the CONFIDENCE() function is still available.

Syntax   CONFIDENCE(*alpha,standard_dev,size*)

Definition   This function returns a value used to create a confidence interval for the expected value of a random variable. The confidence interval is a range of values. The sample mean x is at the center of this range, and the range is $x \pm$ CONFIDENCE.NORM().

For example, if x is the sample mean of delivery times for products ordered through the mail, $x \pm$ CONFIDENCE.NORM() is a range of expected values of a random variable. For any expected value of a random variable μ_0 in this range, the probability of obtaining a sample mean further from μ_0 than x is greater than *alpha*. For any expected value of a random variable μ_0 not in this range, the probability of obtaining a sample mean further from μ_0 than x is less than *alpha*.

Assume you use x, *standard_dev*, and *size* to construct a two-tailed test at significance level *alpha* for the hypothesis that the expected value of a random variable is μ_0. Then you will not reject that hypothesis if μ_0 is in the confidence interval and will reject that hypothesis if μ_0 is not in the confidence interval.

The confidence interval does not allow you to infer that there is a probability of $1 - alpha$ that your next package will take a delivery time that is in the confidence interval.

Arguments

- *alpha* **(required)** The probability of error used to calculate the confidence interval. The confidence interval equals $100*(1 - alpha)\%$, which means that an *alpha* of 0.05 indicates a 95-percent confidence level.

- *standard_dev* **(required)** The standard deviation of the population. The argument *standard_dev* is assumed to be known.

- *size* **(required)** The size of the sample.

> **Note**
>
> If one of the arguments isn't a numeric value, the CONFIDENCE.NORM() function returns the #VALUE! error.
>
> If *alpha* is less than or equal to 0 or greater than or equal to 1, CONFIDENCE.NORM() returns the #NUM! error.
>
> If *standard_dev* is less than or equal to 0, the function returns the #NUM! error.
>
> If *size* isn't an integer, the decimal places are truncated. If *size* is less than 1, the function returns the #NUM! error.
>
> If *alpha* equals 0.05, you have to calculate the area under the standard normal distribution that equals (1 – *alpha*) or 95 percent. This value is ± 1.96. Therefore, the confidence interval is:
>
> $$\overline{x} \pm 1.96 \left(\frac{\sigma}{\sqrt{n}} \right)$$

Background   In statistics, confidence intervals are a commonly used method to indicate the accuracy of estimated values. The higher the confidence interval, the less accurate the information is. A lower confidence interval is more likely to return the accurate value.

For this reason, the standard deviation for the variance or the confidence interval is usually specified in addition to the calculated mean.

The CONFIDENCE.NORM() function determines the 1 *alpha* confidence interval for the expected value (mean) of a probability distribution. *alpha* is the probability of error or the *alpha risk*. Only values within the interval [0..1] are valid (0 to 100 percent). If *alpha* is 0.05 (5 percent), the probability that the mean is outside the interval calculated by CONFIDENCE.NORM() is 5 percent. In other words, the probability for the mean of the population to be in the calculated interval is 95 percent. This is called a 95-percent confidence interval.

A sample from a normal distributed population with a known standard deviation and mean is used to calculate the confidence interval. The CONFIDENCE.NORM() function returns half the confidence interval of the arithmetic mean for the sample. This means that the 1 *alpha* confidence interval is a symmetrical area around the mean of a sample containing the population mean with a probability of 1 *alpha*.

Example   We will use the example of the software company to explain CONFIDENCE.NORM(). The company sells all its products through its internal website. You are the marketing manager and want to further analyze the numbers of the past four years. You have entered the number of website visits and online orders per month in Excel (see Figure 12-23).

B	C	D
	Independant = x-values	Dependent = y-values
	Web access	Orders
January 2005	89	None
February 2005	65	4
March 2005	198	65
April 2005	358	38
May 2005	287	48
June 2005	896	25
July 2005	965	89
August 2005	735	198
September 2005	1,398	376
October 2005	653	234
November 2005	498	76
December 2005	1,673	456
January 2006	236	6
February 2006	1,221	17
March 2006	1,563	456
April 2006	2,682	544
May 2006	4,569	349
June 2006	6,848	854
July 2006	8,463	427
August 2006	10,157	337
September 2006	11,837	899
October 2006	12,987	1,011
November 2006	13,739	720
December 2006	14,376	1,069
January 2007	15,739	1,070
February 2007	16,123	967
March 2007	16,548	1,401
April 2007	17,352	1,076
May 2007	17,986	1,563
June 2007	18,234	1,485
July 2007	18,769	1,367
August 2007	19,736	1,138
September 2007	20,333	1,352
October 2007	20,987	1,343
November 2007	21,323	1,430
December 2007	21,999	1,375
January 2008	22,786	1,421
February 2008	23,784	1,508
March 2008	24,574	1,876
April 2008	25,111	1,948
May 2008	25,789	2,094
June 2008	26,948	2,134
July 2008	15,635	1,673

Figure 12-23 The numbers of website visits and online orders.

You have also already calculated the sample mean and the standard deviation of the population for both areas. Because you use only one sample, you calculate a 95-percent confidence interval for the population mean (see Figure 12-24).

F	G	H
Calculations	Web access	orders
Average (SP)	11,308	870
Standard deviation (GG)	9379.89	658.52
Probability of error Alpha	0.05	0.05
Size of sample	43	42

Figure 12-24 Calculating the average, standard deviation, and sample size.

Because you want a 95-percent confidence level, *alpha* = 0.05 (5 percent).

Figure 12-25 shows the calculation of the confidence interval for the average of the website visits and the average of the online orders.

	F	G	H
	G13	▾	f_x =CONFIDENCE.NORM(G5,G4,G6)

	F	G	H
12		Web access	Orders
13	CONFIDENCE()	2803.57	199.16
14		=CONFIDENCE.NORM(G5,G4,G6)	=CONFIDENCE.NORM(H5,H4,H6)
15			
16		Lower limit	Upper limit
17		Average-CONFIDENCE	Average+CONFIDENCE
18	Interval for web access visits	8504.54	14111.69
19		=G3-G13	=G3+G13
20			
21			
22		Lower limit	Upper limit
23		Average-CONFIDENCE	Average+CONFIDENCE
24	Interval for orders	670.34	1068.66
25		=H3-H13	=H3+H13

Figure 12-25 CONFIDENCE.NORM() calculates the 1 *alpha* confidence interval.

For website visits, the CONFIDENCE.NORM() function returns 2,803.57 (half the confidence interval of the arithmetic average for the sample).

To determine the lower and upper limits of the interval, the sample mean plus CONFIDENCE.NORM() as well as the sample mean minus CONFIDENCE.NORM() were calculated.

The result for the lower limit is 8504.54, and the result for the upper limit is 14,111.69.

Statements   You expected *alpha* to be 0.05 and draw the following conclusions based on the result:

- The population mean for the website visits is in the range from 8504.54 through 14,111.69, with a 95-percent confidence interval.

- Because the sample size is only 43, the confidence interval is inaccurate. The larger the sample, the more accurate the confidence interval is—and the population mean is also more accurate.

See Also CONFIDENCE.T(), Z.TEST()

Sample Files

Use the CONFIDENCE or CONFIDENCE.NORM worksheet in the Probability.xls or Probability.xlsx sample file. The sample files are found in the Chapter12 folder. For more information about the sample files, see the section titled "Using the Sample Files" on page xxiii.

CONFIDENCE.T()

Syntax   CONFIDENCE.T(*alpha,standard_dev,size*)

Definition   This function returns the confidence interval for the expected value of a random variable by using a Student's t-test.

Arguments

- *alpha* **(required)** The probability of error used to calculate the confidence interval. The confidence interval equals 100*(1 – *alpha*)%, which means that an *alpha* of 0.05 indicates a 95-percent confidence level.

- *standard_dev* **(required)** The standard deviation of the population. The argument *standard_dev* is assumed to be known.

- *size* **(required)** The size of the sample.

> **Note**
>
> If one of the arguments isn't a numeric value, the CONFIDENCE.T() function returns the #VALUE! error.
>
> If *alpha* is less than or equal to 0 or greater than or equal to 1, the CONFIDENCE.T() function returns the #NUM! error.
>
> If *standard_dev* is less than or equal to 0, the function returns the #NUM! error.
>
> If *size* isn't an integer, the decimal places are truncated. If *size* is equal to 1, the function returns the #DIV/0! error.

Background   See the background information for the CONFIDENCE.NORM() function.

Example   See the example for the CONFIDENCE.NORM() function.

See Also   CONFIDENCE(), CONFIDENCE.NORM(), T.TEST(), Z.TEST()

> **Sample Files**
>
> Use the CONFIDENCE.T worksheet in the Probability.xlsx sample file. The sample files are found in the Chapter12 folder. For more information about the sample files, see the section titled "Using the Sample Files" on page xxiii.

CORREL()

Syntax   CORREL(*array1,array2*)

Definition   This function returns the correlation coefficient of a two-dimensional random variable with values in the cell ranges *array1* and *array2*. Use the correlation coefficient to determine the relationship between two properties.

For example, you can examine the relationship between the number of website visits and online orders.

Arguments

- *array1* **(required)** A cell range of values

- *array2* **(required)** A second cell range of values

> **Note**
>
> If an array or reference argument contains text, logical values, or empty cells, those values are ignored. However, cells with the value 0 are included.
>
> If *array1* and *array2* have a different number of data points, CORREL() returns the #N/A error. If either *array1* or *array2* is empty or if *s* (the standard deviation) of their values equals 0, CORREL() returns the #DIV/0! error.

Background   Is there any correlation between two variables? This question often comes up when data is analyzed or interpreted. To answer this question, you can use correlation analysis.

Using the correlation coefficient, you can determine the relation between two properties. The result is a value from 1 (perfect correlation) to −1 (the absolute contrary effect). The sign indicates the direction of the correlation.

The correlation analysis provides an important method for determining the linear correlation between two variables (in the example later in this section, these will be the website visits and the online orders).

The following formula calculates the equation:

$$p_{xy} = \frac{Cov(x,y)}{\sigma_x * \sigma_y}$$

where

$$-1 \leq p_{xy} \leq 1$$

and where

$$Cov(x, y) = \frac{1}{n} \sum_{j-1}^{n} (x_j - \mu_x)(y_j - \mu_y)$$

Statements   The following apply to the correlation coefficient:

- If the value is smaller than 0.3, the correlation between the two variables is minor.

- If the value is from 0.3 through 0.5, the correlation is moderate.

- If the value is from 0.5 through 0.7, the correlation is distinct.

- If the value is from 0.7 through 0.9, the correlation is close.

- If the value is greater than 0.9, the correlation is very close.

Example   A software company sells all of its products through its website. The company regularly sends out newsletters to inform existing and potential customers about new and updated products and to draw attention to its website.

Last year, the orders through the website significantly increased. The management wants to know the reason. Is the increase in sales attributable to marketing or to advertising? Did the increased website visits cause the increase in sales?

This means that the company wants to know the correlation between the website visits and the online orders. The CORREL() function provides the evidence (see Figure 12-26).

> **Note**
>
> If the result is a correlation coefficient close to +1, the correlation between the two variables is positive. This means that the greater the value of variable *x* (orders), the greater the value of variable *y* (website visits).
>
> The correlation coefficient 0 indicates that the two variables are independent of each other.
>
> The correlation coefficient –1 indicates a negative correlation between *x* (orders) and *y* (website visits).

C22		f_x =CORREL(D4:D21,C4:C21)	
	B	C	D
3	**Month**	**Web access**	**Orders**
4	January 2007	236	98
5	February 2007	11593	8000
6	March 2007	18491	6000
7	April 2007	11743	8587
8	May 2007	11452	7985
9	June 2007	26651	18968
10	July 2007	16287	9753
11	August 2007	17750	7857
12	September 2007	19985	13986
13	October 2007	17285	6875
14	November 2007	30369	22765
15	December 2007	19674	9465
16	January 2008	28464	19875
17	February 2008	25000	15987
18	March 2008	24574	9653
19	April 2008	23141	12986
20	May 2008	17700	8543
21	June 2008	3702	1654
22	**Coefficient of correlation**		0.89201155

Figure 12-26 Calculating the correlation coefficient with the CORREL() function.

Figure 12-27 shows the dependency between the website visits and the orders without the correlation coefficient.

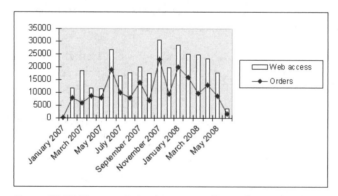

Figure 12-27 The correlation between online orders and website visits.

The correlation coefficient of 0.89 indicates a positive, close correlation between the two variables. This means that if the number of website visits increases because of marketing activities, the number of online orders also increases.

See Also COVAR(), COVARIANCE.P(), COVARIANCE.S(), FISHER(), FISHERINV()

Sample Files

Use the CORREL worksheet in the Probability.xls or Probability.xlsx sample file. The sample files are found in the Chapter12 folder. For more information about the sample files, see the section titled "Using the Sample Files" on page xxiii.

COUNT()

Syntax   COUNT(*value1,value2,...*)

Definition   This function calculates how many numbers are included in an argument list. The COUNT() function calculates the number of entries in a number field that is in a range or array of numbers.

Arguments

- *value1* **(required) and** *value2* **(optional)**   At least one and up to 255 arguments (30 in Excel 2003 and earlier versions). The arguments can contain or refer to different types of data, but only numbers are counted.

Background   The COUNT() function performs a simple task but can save a lot of time. Especially for tables containing a large number of values, the task of manual counting would be very time consuming. If you need to count the values in a table, this function does the work for you.

Note

All arguments that are numbers (including zero), dates, or text representations of numbers are counted. Arguments that are error values or text that cannot be converted into numbers are not counted.

If an argument is an array or a reference, only numbers in that array or reference are counted. Empty cells, logical values, text, or error values in the array or reference are ignored. If you want to count logical values, text, or error values, use the COUNTA() function.

Example Figure 12-28 shows an example table with the sales from January 2007 through November 2008 that were entered by the sales representatives of the software company.

You are the manager of the sales department and use the COUNT() function to find the number of months over a two-year period in which sales were made. You specify the range C3:C25 in the function COUNT(C3:C25), and the formula returns 19.

	C28		f_x	=COUNT(C3:C25)
	B		**C**	
1	**In how many months were sales made?**			
2	**Month**		**Sales**	
3	January-07	$	17,500.00	
4	February-07	$	17,867.00	
5	March-07	$	10,966.00	
6	April-07			
7	May-07	$	12,838.00	
8	June-07	$	14,888.00	
9	July-07	$	14,245.00	
10	August-07	$	16,292.00	
11	September-07	$	11,689.00	
12	October-07			
13	November-07	$	18,560.00	
14	December-07	$	15,697.00	
15	January-08	$	16,022.00	
16	February-08		closed	
17	March-08	$	12,556.00	
18	April-08	$	18,681.00	
19	May-08	$	14,643.00	
20	June-08			
21	July-08	$	18,172.00	
22	August-08	$	19,710.00	
23	September-08	$	17,182.00	
24	October-08	$	11,045.00	
25	November-08	$	18,494.00	
27	**=COUNT(C3:C25)**			
28	*Result*		19	

Figure 12-28 The table contains the sales for certain dates in the range C3:C25.

Tip   Display number arguments in the status bar

If the data is selected, the number arguments are also displayed in the status bar. Right-click the status bar and select Numerical Count on the menu (see Figure 12-29).

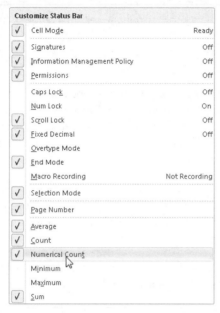

Figure 12-29 Part of the shortcut menu for the Excel status bar.

The information for the selected argument is displayed in the status bar (see Figure 12-30).

Average: $15,634.05   Count: 20   Numerical Count: 19   Sum: $297,047.00

Figure 12-30 A range of options are available in the Excel status bar.

See Also AVERAGE(), COUNTA(), DCOUNT(), DCOUNTA(), SUM()

Sample Files

Use the COUNT worksheet in the Count.xls or Count.xlsx sample file. The sample files are found in the Chapter12 folder. For more information about the sample files, see the section titled "Using the Sample Files" on page xxiii.

COUNTA()

Syntax   COUNTA(*value1,value2,...*)

Definition   This function calculates how many values are included in an argument list. Use the COUNTA() function if you want to know how many cells in a range or an array contain data.

Arguments

- *value1* **(required) and** *value2* **(optional)**   At least one and up to 255 arguments (30 in Excel 2003 and earlier versions) indicating the values to be counted. A value can be any information, including an empty string (""). However, empty cells are not counted. If an argument is an array or a reference, the empty cells in the array or for the reference are ignored. If you want to exclude logical values, text, or error values, use the COUNT() function.

Background   Like the COUNT() function, this function can save you time when you are counting the values in an argument list. The only difference is that the COUNTA() function also counts text, logical values, and error values.

Example   For the cell range shown earlier in Figure 12-3, the COUNTA() function returns 20 because the word *closed* in the cell range is counted.

> **Tip**
> To display the number of entries in the cell range in the status bar, right-click the status bar and select Count (see Figure 12-4, in the discussion of the COUNT() function).

See Also   AVERAGE(), COUNT(), DCOUNT(), DCOUNTA(), PRODUCT(), SUM()

> **Sample Files**
> Use the COUNTA worksheet in the Count.xls or Count.xlsx sample file. The sample files are found in the Chapter12 folder. For more information about the sample files, see the section titled "Using the Sample Files" on page xxiii.

COUNTBLANK()

Syntax   COUNTBLANK(*range*)

Definition   This function counts the empty cells in a cell range.

Arguments

- *range* **(required)**   The range for which you want to count the blank cells

Background   Like the COUNT() and COUNTA() functions, this function is especially useful when you work with large sets of data.

> ## Note
> Cells with formulas that return empty strings ("") are also counted. Cells with zero values are not counted.

Example   If you use the COUNTBLANK() function in the example used for the COUNT() function, COUNTBLANK() returns 3 for the cell range C3:C25. The table in Figure 12-3 in the discussion of the COUNT() function contains three cells without numbers or text.

See Also COUNTIF()

> ## Sample Files
> Use the COUNTBLANK worksheet in the Count.xls or Count.xlsx sample file. The sample files are found in the Chapter12 folder. For more information about the sample files, see the section titled "Using the Sample Files" on page xxiii.

COUNTIF()

Syntax   COUNTIF(*range,criteria*)

Definition   This function counts the cells within a range whose content matches the search criteria.

Arguments

- *range* **(required)** The cell range from which you want to count the cells meeting the search criteria.

- *criteria* **(required)** The criteria in the form of a number, an expression, or text. The criteria determine which cells will be counted. Criteria can be expressed as numbers (such as 2000), text (such as *none*), or a cell reference (such as B5).

Background   You can analyze your data based on a condition. However, it is not obvious why this function is categorized as a statistic function and not as a math and trigonometry function.

The COUNTIF() function can use only a precise value as search criterion. The attempt to search for cells with values less than 0 fails. You can use < and > only if you enclose these signs and the corresponding value in quotation marks or if you enclose < or > in quotation marks and precede the value with &.

Examples

Example 1   The following example again uses the table with the sales of the past two years from the software company. The goal was to raise the sales to more than $200,000 per month. Now you have to check how often this goal was reached in the last 24 months.

You want to calculate the result by using the COUNTIF() function. For *range* you enter C3:C26, and for *criteria* you specify *>200000*. As shown in Figure 12-31, the result is 15 sales over $200,000.

Tip   Specify several conditions for a data set

Although COUNTIF() works only with one condition, you can specify several conditions for a data set. To use two conditions, you enter one COUNTIF() function for each condition and link these functions with a + (plus sign). In this example, you can search for the values between $180,000 and $200,000 where the first condition is greater than $180,000 and the second condition is less than $200,000.

Enter a COUNTIF() function for each of the two conditions, link the functions with +, and enclose this part of the formula in quotation marks. Then subtract the number of all values in this range from the result to return the numbers greater than 180,000 and less than 200,000.

E3	▾	fx	=COUNTIF(C3:C26,">200000")		
	B		C	D	E
1	Sales higher than 200,000?				
2	Month		Sales		Result
3	Jan-07	$	107,629.00		15
4	Feb-07	$	185,385.00		
5	Mar-07	$	180,807.00		
6	Apr-07	$	124,328.00		
7	May-07	$	146,215.00		
8	Jun-07	$	185,675.00		
9	Jul-07	$	210,169.00		
10	Aug-07	$	221,729.00		
11	Sep-07	$	234,187.00		
12	Oct-07	$	237,947.00		
13	Nov-07	$	210,088.00		
14	Dec-07	$	207,791.00		
15	Jan-08	$	201,097.00		
16	Feb-08	$	222,460.00		
17	Mar-08	$	208,585.00		
18	Apr-08	$	206,387.00		
19	May-08	$	218,951.00		
20	Jun-08	$	95,642.00		
21	Jul-08	$	126,895.00		
22	Aug-08	$	654,988.00		
23	Sep-08	$	126,874.00		
24	Oct-08	$	524,985.00		
25	Nov-08	$	346,852.00		
26	Dec-08	$	236,985.00		

Figure 12-31 How many table cells match the criterion ">200000"?

Example 2 You can also use placeholders with COUNTIF(). Assume that you are the head of the Human Resources department of the software company and create a list for the employees to enter their vacation and flextime. You want to count the flextime days but the employees entered *Flexible time day*, *Flex day*, *Flex*, and *FL*.

You can enter placeholders because the COUNTIF() function accepts placeholders as search criteria. As shown in Figure 12-32, the * (asterisk) placeholder together with *f* returns all values beginning with *f*. In this case, it returns six entries and therefore six flextime days the employees applied for in two days.

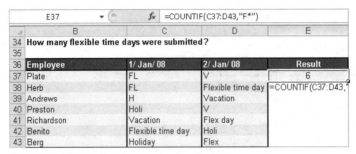

Figure 12-32 Placeholders as search criteria.

See Also COUNTBLANK(), COUNTIFS(), SUMIF()

Sample Files

Use the COUNTIF worksheet in the Count.xls or Count.xlsx sample file. The sample files are found in the Chapter12 folder. For more information about the sample files, see the section titled "Using the Sample Files" on page xxiii.

COUNTIFS()

Note

The COUNTIFS() function was new in Excel 2007.

Syntax COUNTIFS(*criteria_range1,criteria1,criteria_range2,criteria2,...*)

Definition This function counts the number of cells in a range meeting several criteria.

Arguments

- ***criteria_range1* (required)** The range in which to evaluate the associated criteria. The cells in the range have to be cell names, cell arrays, or references to cells containing numbers. Empty cells and text values are ignored.

- ***criteria1* (required)** The criteria in the form of numbers, expressions, cell references, or text that define which cells will be counted.

- ***criteria_range2* (optional)** One to 127 ranges in which the criteria has to be evaluated. The cells in the ranges have to be cell names, cell arrays, or references to cells containing numbers. Empty cells and text values are ignored.

- *criteria2* **(optional)**   One to 127 criteria in the form of numbers, expressions, cell references, or text that define which cells will be counted.

> ## Note
>
> The cells in a range are counted only if all specified criteria for a cell are met.
>
> If the one of the criteria arguments reference an empty cell, the COUNTIFS() function treats the empty cell as a 0 value.
>
> You can use the wildcard characters ? (question mark) and * (asterisk) as criteria. The question mark stands for a character, and the asterisk for a string. If you search for an actual question mark or asterisk, enter a tilde (~) before the character.

Background   The COUNTIFS() function is an extension of the COUNTIF() function. The advantage of COUNTIFS() is that it calculates the number of cells that meet multiple conditions and criteria. You will find more information about the COUNTIF() function in the description of COUNTIF().

Example   The following example again uses the table with the sales of the past two years from the software company (see Figure 12-33).

	B	C	D
2	**Month**	**Year**	**Sales**
3	January	2007	$ 175,000.00
4	Feburary	2007	$ 178,670.00
5	March	2007	$ 109,660.00
6	April	2007	$ 109,660.00
7	May	2007	$ 128,380.00
8	June	2007	$ 148,880.00
9	July	2007	$ 142,450.00
10	August	2007	$ 162,920.00
11	September	2007	$ 116,890.00
12	October	2007	$ 116,890.00
13	November	2007	$ 185,600.00
14	December	2007	$ 156,970.00
15	January	2008	$ 160,220.00
16	Feburary	2008	$ 160,220.00
17	March	2008	$ 125,560.00
18	April	2008	$ 186,810.00
19	May	2008	$ 146,430.00
20	June	2008	$ 146,430.00
21	July	2008	$ 181,720.00
22	August	2008	$ 197,100.00
23	September	2008	$ 171,820.00
24	October	2008	$ 110,750.00
25	November	2008	$ 184,940.00
26	December	2008	$ 158,760.00

Figure 12-33 Part of the sales table for 2007 and 2008.

Chapter 12

The goal was to raise the sales to more than $150,000 per month. Now you have to check how often this goal was reached in the past 24 months. To calculate the entire time period, you can use the COUNTIF() function.

However, you want to compare the two years. Therefore, you search for the number of months with sales greater than $150,000 in the years 2007 or 2008.

You use the COUNTIFS() function because this function allows you to specify multiple criteria. In this case, the criteria are *>150,000* and *2007* or *2008*. Figure 12-34 shows the result:

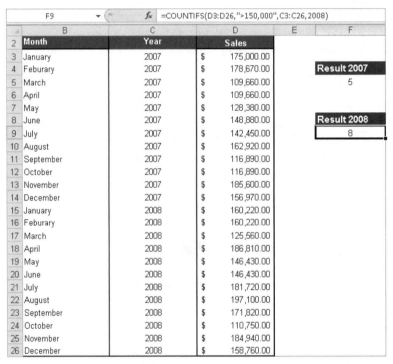

Figure 12-34 Calculating the number of sales over 150,000 by year.

As you can see in Figure 12-34, the number of months with sales over $150,000 increased by eight in 2008.

See Also COUNTIF(), SUMIF()

Sample Files

Use the COUNTIFS worksheet in the Count.xlsx sample file. The sample files are found in the Chapter12 folder. For more information about the sample files, see the section titled "Using the Sample Files" on page xxiii.

COVAR()

> **Note**
>
> In Excel 2010, the COVAR() function was replaced with the COVARIANCE.P() and COVARIANCE.S() functions to increase the accuracy of the results. To ensure the backward compatibility of COVARIANCE.P() and COVARIANCE.S(), the COVAR() function is still available.

Syntax   COVAR(*array1,array2*)

Definition   This function returns the covariance of two value pairs. Use the covariance to determine the relationship between two data sets. For example, you can examine whether the increase in online orders is related to the number of website visits. To calculate the covariance, the deviations of all value pairs between the actual value and the mean is multiplied and the mean is formed.

Arguments

- *array1* **(required)** The first cell range of integers

- *array2* **(required)** The second cell range of integers

> **Note**
>
> The arguments must be numbers, names, arrays, or references that contain numbers. If an array or reference argument contains text, logical values, or empty cells, those values are ignored. However, cells with the value 0 are included.
>
> If *array1* and *array2* have a different number of data points, COVAR() returns the #N/A error. If *array1* or *array2* is empty, the function returns the #DIV/0! error.

Background   The covariance describes the correlation between the two characteristics x and y with the terms positive and negative. This means that the direction of the dependency between the two characteristics is indicated. The covariance can have any real value.

What conclusions can you draw after the covariance is calculated?

- If the covariance is positive, the correlation between x and y is concordant linear. This means that if x has a high value, the value of y is also high. The same applies to low values.

- If the covariance is negative, the correlation between x and y is reverse linear. This means that the high values of one random variable are associated with low values of the other random variable.

- If the result is 0, there is no correlation between the two variables x and y.

Although the covariance indicates the direction of a correlation between two variables, there is no indication of the strength of the correlation. The reason for this is the dependency of the calculated covariance on the values of variables x and y. If the covariance of two variables is 5.2 meters, the covariance for the same values is 520 centimeters.

> **Note**
>
> The covariance as a measure for the stochastic correlation is not very descriptive and is difficult to compare. To make a correlation comparable, the covariance can be standardized. This way you get a correlation between two or more quantitative statistical variables with a value of +1 (perfect linear correlation), 0 (no linear correlation), and –1 (perfect reverse linear correlation).

You can derive the following important general correlations from the covariance and the two standard deviations:

- If n value pairs (x_1, y_1), (x_2, y_2), ... , (x_n, y_n) with the standard deviations s_x and s_y and the covariance sxy are given, then the maximum size of the covariance is the product of the standard deviations.

- The upper limit is reached when the dependency between x_i and y_i is linear with the fixed numbers a and b.

The covariance is calculated as follows:

$$COVAR(X,Y) = \frac{1}{n}\sum_{i-1}^{n}\left(x_i - \mu_y\right)\left(y_i - \mu_y\right)$$

Values x and y are the sample means AVERAGE(*array1*) and AVERAGE(*array2*), and n is the sample size.

Example   Let's use the example of the software company that sells its products through its website and sends out newsletters to boost the sales. Last year, the orders through the website significantly increased. To understand the reason for the increased sales, you calculate the correlation coefficient. Now you want to know the direction of the correlation between website visits and online orders and calculate the covariance. Figure 12-35 shows the result.

	D25		f_x	=COVAR(D4:D21,C4:C21)	
	B		C		D
3	**Month**		**Web access**		**Orders**
4	**January 2007**		236		98
5	**February 2007**		11593		8000
6	**March 2007**		18491		6000
7	**April 2007**		11743		8587
8	**May 2007**		11452		7985
9	**June 2007**		26651		18968
10	**July 2007**		16287		9753
11	**August 2007**		17750		7857
12	**September 2007**		19985		13986
13	**October 2007**		17285		6875
14	**November 2007**		30369		22765
15	**December 2007**		19674		9465
16	**January 2008**		28464		19875
17	**February 2008**		25000		15987
18	**March 2008**		24574		9653
19	**April 2008**		23141		12986
20	**May 2008**		17700		8543
21	**June 2008**		3702		1654
22	**Coefficient of correlation**				0.89201155
23	**Average**		18005.39		10502.06
24	**Standard deviaton**		8079.11		5978.92
25	**Covariance**				40694286.37

Figure 12-35   The COVAR() function calculates the direction of the dependency between two variables.

The positive result for the covariance indicates that the correlation between the x and y values (website visits and orders) is concordant linear. If x has high values, y also has high values. If x has low values, y has also low values. The positive covariance is confirmed by the correlation coefficient, 0.89, because this indicates a close linear correlation.

Figure 12-36 shows how you can get the same result by using the formula presented in the "Background" section of this function without the COVAR() function.

	B	C	D
29	**Variable X**	**Variable Y**	
30	**Web access**	**Orders**	**Product x*y**
31	-17769.38889	-10404.05556	184873709.2
32	-6412.388889	-2502.055556	16044153.24
33	485.6111111	-4502.055556	-2186248.201
34	-6262.388889	-1915.055556	11992822.63
35	-6553.388889	-2517.055556	16495243.91
36	8645.611111	8465.944444	73193263.35
37	-1718.388889	-749.0555556	1287168.744
38	-255.3888889	-2645.055556	675517.7994
39	1979.611111	3483.944444	6896855.133
40	-720.3888889	-3627.055556	2612890.522
41	12363.61111	12262.94444	151614276.2
42	1668.611111	-1037.055556	-1730442.423
43	10458.61111	9372.944444	98027980.91
44	6994.611111	5484.944444	38365053.35
45	6568.611111	-849.0555556	-5577115.756
46	5135.611111	2483.944444	12756572.69
47	-305.3888889	-1959.055556	598273.7994
48	-14303.39	-8848.06	126557179.5
49	=C21-$C$23	=D21-$D$23	=B48*C48
50	=Amount of web access visits in June (C21) minus the average of the sum of all web accesses (C23)	=Amount of orders in June (D21) minus the average of the sum of all orders (D23)	=Product of the results in the red marked cells below web access and orders
51			**40694286.37**
52			=AVERAGE(D31:D48)

Figure 12-36 Calculating the covariance by using a mathematical formula.

See Also CORREL(), COVARIANCE.P(), COVARIANCE.S(), FISHER(), FISHERINV()

Sample Files

Use the COVAR worksheet in the Regression.xls or Regression.xlsx sample file. The sample files are found in the Chapter12 folder. For more information about the sample files, see the section titled "Using the Sample Files" on page xxiii.

COVARIANCE.P()

Syntax   COVARIANCE.P(*array1,array2*)

Definition   This function returns the covariance of a population, which is the average of the products of deviations for each data-point pair.

Use the covariance to determine the relationship between two data sets. For example, you can determine whether a higher income is based on education.

Arguments

- *array1* **(required)** The first cell range of integers

- *array2* **(required)** The second cell range of integers

> **Note**
>
> The arguments must be numbers, names, arrays, or references that contain numbers. If an array or a reference argument contains text, logical values, or empty cells, those values are ignored. However, cells with the value 0 are included.
>
> If *array1* and *array2* have a different number of data points, COVARIANCE.P() returns the #N/A error. If *array1* or *array2* is empty, the function returns the #DIV/0! error.

See Also You will find more information about covariances in the description of COVAR().

See Also CORREL(), COVAR(), COVARIANCE.S(), FISHER(), FISHERINV()

> **Sample Files**
>
> Use the COVARIANCE.P worksheet in the Regression.xls or Regression.xlsx sample file. The sample files are found in the Chapter12 folder. For more information about the sample files, see the section titled "Using the Sample Files" on page xxiii.

COVARIANCE.S()

Syntax COVARIANCE.S(*array1,array2*)

Definition This function returns the covariance of a sample, which is the average of the products of deviations for each data-point pair.

Arguments

- *array1* **(required)** The first cell range of integers

- *array2* **(required)** The second cell range of integers

> **Note**
>
> The arguments must be numbers, names, arrays, or references that contain numbers. If an array or reference argument contains text, logical values, or empty cells, those values are ignored. However, cells with the value 0 are included.
>
> If *array1* and *array2* have a different number of data points, COVARIANCE.S() returns the #N/A error. If *array1* or *array2* is empty, the function returns the #DIV/0! error.

See Also You will find more information about covariances in the description of COVAR().

See Also CORREL(), COVAR(), COVARIANCE.P(), FISHER(), FISHERINV()

> **Sample Files**
>
> Use the COVARIANCE.S worksheet in the Regression.xls or Regression.xlsx sample file. The sample files are found in the Chapter12 folder. For more information about the sample files, see the section titled "Using the Sample Files" on page xxiii.

DEVSQ()

Syntax DEVSQ(*number1,number2,...*)

Definition This function returns the sum of squares of deviations of data points from their sample mean.

Arguments

- *number1* **(required) and** *number2* **(optional)** At least one and up to 255 arguments (30 in Excel 2003 and earlier versions) for which you want to calculate the sum of squared deviations. You can also use a single array or a reference to an array instead of arguments separated by commas.

> **Note**
>
> Arguments can be numbers, array names, or references to cells containing numbers.
>
> If an array or a reference argument contains text, logical values, or empty cells, those values are ignored. However, cells with the value 0 are included.

Background   In general, correlations between variables are defined by coefficients. Based on the regression calculation, you can also estimate models for interval-scaled variables. A model is the mathematical core of a theory. A model allows the prediction of the dependent variable based on the independent variable. In this way, linear correlations can be defined. This means that the higher the count of the x-values is, the higher (or lower) the y-values. The correlation x to y can also be illustrated with a straight line. More complex models are also possible.

The quality of the regression is usually described by r^2.

See Also You will find more information about r^2 in the descrpiton of RSQ().

The average is the best y forecast value regarding the quality of the regression. The deviation from the average is also called *forecast error*. To calculate the average deviation, you can use the VAR.S() function.

The DEVSQ() function calculates the sum of the squared deviations from the sample mean. The equation for the sum of the squared deviation is:

$$DEVSQ = \sum \left(x - \overline{x}\right)^2$$

Example   You are still busy with analyzing the website and want to further calculate the correlation between the website visits and the online orders. You work on the website visits—the independent variable y. You want to calculate the sum of the squared deviations from the sample mean and use the DEVSQ() function. Figure 12-37 shows the solution.

	C21		f_x	=DEVSQ(C3:C20)
	B		C	
1			Independent variable	
2	**Month**		**Web access**	
3	January 2007		236	
4	February 2007		11593	
5	March 2007		18491	
6	April 2007		11743	
7	May 2007		11452	
8	June 2007		26651	
9	July 2007		16287	
10	August 2007		17750	
11	September 2007		19985	
12	October 2007		17285	
13	November 2007		30369	
14	December 2007		19674	
15	January 2008		28464	
16	February 2008		25000	
17	March 2008		24574	
18	April 2008		23141	
19	May 2008		17700	
20	June 2008		3702	
21	**DEVSQ**		1109624270	

Figure 12-37 The sum of the squared deviations from the sample mean.

Chapter 12

The DEVSQ() function returns 1,109,624,270 for the website visits. This value matches the sum of the squared deviations from the sample mean.

See Also AVEDEV(), STDEV.S(), STDEVP(), VAR.P(), VAR.S()

> **Sample Files**
>
> Use the DEVSQ worksheet in the Regression.xls or Regression.xlsx sample file. The sample files are found in the Chapter12 folder. For more information about the sample files, see the section titled "Using the Sample Files" on page xxiii.

EXPON.DIST()/EXPONDIST()

Syntax EXPON.DIST(*x,lambda,cumulative*)

Definition This function returns the probabilities of an exponential distributed random variable. Use EXPON.DIST() to model the time between events. For example, you can calculate the probability that a call center will receive a call after three minutes, although the hourly average for incoming calls is three minutes.

Arguments

- *x* **(required)** The value of the function.

- *lambda* **(required)** The value that is passed.

- *cumulative* **(required)** The logical value. If *cumulative* is TRUE, the cumulative distribution is returned; otherwise, the probability density function is returned.

> **Note**
>
> If *x* or *lambda* isn't a numeric value, the EXPON.DIST() function returns the #VALUE! error.
>
> If *x* is less than 0, the function returns the #NUM! error.
>
> If *lambda* is less than or equal to 0, the function returns the #NUM! error.

Background   These functions have a special characteristic: Over equal intervals, the function value changes by the same factor. These functions are useful for describing growth and decaying processes for which the value changes by the same factor in equal time intervals. The inverse functions are called *logarithms*. The exponential function $x = e^x$ with Euler's number e is the basis (see Figure 12-38).

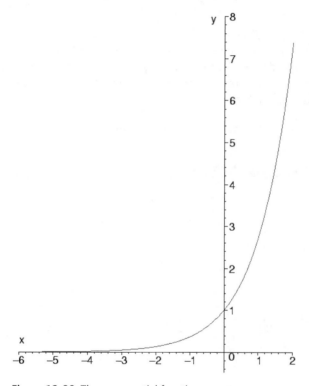

Figure 12-38 The exponential function $y = e^x$.

As mentioned previously, the EXPON.DIST() function returns the probabilities of independent events, such as the time it takes an ATM machine to disperse money or other waiting times.

Here is another example: If a support call center receives a call every three minutes, you can use this function to calculate the probability that the phone will ring after only one minute. This is called an *exponential random variable*, because the ringing of the phone and the time are independent from each other. The EXPON.DIST() function calculates the probability that this will happen.

The equation for the probability density is:

$$f(x;\lambda) = \lambda e^{-\lambda x}$$

The equation for the distribution function is:

$$F(x;\lambda) = 1 - e^{-\lambda x}$$

Example   Let's use with the example of the call center. Assume that you operate a call center for a printer manufacturer. The call center is open 24 hours a day, seven days a week. You want to analyze the call pattern and count the incoming calls every hour over one day. This means that the time interval is 60 minutes.

The recorded calls result in the statistics shown in Figure 12-39.

	B	C
3	time interval = 1 hour	Calls
4	Hour 1	8
5	Hour 2	9
6	Hour 3	10
7	Hour 4	20
8	Hour 5	18
9	Hour 6	22
10	Hour 7	34
11	Hour 8	32
12	Hour 9	42
13	Hour 10	37
14	Hour 11	25
15	Hour 12	20
16	Hour 13	23
17	Hour 14	26
18	Hour 15	31
19	Hour 16	21
20	Hour 17	28
21	Hour 18	20
22	Hour 19	21
23	Hour 20	38
24	Hour 21	13
25	Hour 22	2
26	Hour 23	4
27	Hour 24	1
28	**Number of calls**	505
29	Average	21.04

Figure 12-39 Incoming calls.

After you have calculated the average of all incoming calls, you can make the following statements:

- Every hour, an average of 21 calls come in.

- This means that, on average, every three minutes a customer calls.

Now you want to know the probability that a customer will call after two minutes. To find out, you use the EXPON.DIST() function. What information do you have to enter for the arguments?

- $x = 2$, because we want to calculate the probability for a call after 2 minutes.

- *Lambda* = 3, because this is the mean value of events per interval and therefore the passed value.

- *cumulative* = TRUE, because in our example the cumulative distribution should be returned.

Figure 12-40 shows the result from the calculation of the probability with the EXPON.DIST() function.

F19		f_x	=EXPON.DIST(F16,F17,F18)		
	E	F	G	H	I
15	Caluculation				
16	x (Minutes)	2	1	0.5	0.2
17	Lambda	3	3	3	3
18	Cumulative	TRUE	TRUE	TRUE	TRUE
19	EXPON.DIST()	0.9975	0.9502	0.7769	0.4512
20		=EXPON.DIST(F16,F17,F18)			

Figure 12-40 EXPON.DIST() returns the probability for the value.

The probability for a call coming in after two minutes is 99 percent.

As you can see in Figure 12-40, the probability decreases as the time interval decreases. This means that the probability for a call to come in after 0.2 minutes (12 seconds) is only 45 percent.

See Also GAMMA.DIST(), POISSON()

Sample Files

Use the EXPONDIST or EXPON.DIST worksheet in the Probability.xls or Probability.xlsx sample file. The sample files are found in the Chapter12 folder. For more information about the sample files, see the section titled "Using the Sample Files" on page xxiii.

F.DIST()

Syntax   F.DIST(*x,degrees_freedom1,degrees_freedom2,cumulative*)

Definition   This function returns the values of a distribution function (1 alpha) of a left F-distributed random variable. Use this function to determine whether two data sets have different variances.

For example, you can examine the test scores of men and women taking a recruitment test and determine whether the variance for the females is different from the variance for the males.

Arguments

- *x* **(required)** The value at which to evaluate the function.

- *degrees_freedom1* **(required)** The degrees of freedom in the numerator.

- *degrees_freedom2* **(required)** The degrees of freedom in the denominator.

- *cumulative* **(required)** The logical value that represents the type of the function. If cumulative is TRUE, the F.DIST() function returns the value of the distribution function. If cumulative is FALSE, the F.DIST() function returns the value of the density function.

> **Note**
>
> If one of the arguments isn't a numeric expression, the F.DIST() function returns the #VALUE! error.
>
> If *x* is negative, F.DIST() returns the #NUM! error value.
>
> If *degrees_freedom1* or *degrees_freedom2* isn't an integer, the decimal places are truncated. If *degrees_freedom1* is less than 1, F.DIST() returns the #NUM! error. If *degrees_freedom2* is less than 1, F.DIST() returns the #NUM! error.

Background   The F.DIST.RT() function describes the quantile of the right F-distribution, and the F.DIST() function describes the left quantile.

Example   Compare the example for the F.DIST.RT() function.

See Also F.DIST.RT(), F.TEST()

F.DIST.RT()/FDIST()

Note

In Excel 2010, the FDIST() function was replaced with the F.DIST.RT() function, and the F.DIST.RT() function was added to increase the accuracy of the results. To ensure the backward compatibility of F.DIST.RT(), the FDIST() function is still available.

Syntax   F.DIST.RT(*x,degrees_freedom1,degrees_freedom2*)

Definition   This function returns the values of a distribution function (1 alpha) of a right F-distributed random variable. Use this function to determine whether two data sets have different variances. For example, you can compare the survey results of three equal employee groups to determine whether the variance or results are different.

Arguments

- *x* **(required)** The value at which to evaluate the function

- *degrees_freedom1* **(required)** The degrees of freedom in the numerator

- *degrees_freedom2* **(required)** The degrees of freedom in the denominator

Note

If one of the arguments isn't a numeric value, the F.DIST.RT() function returns the #VALUE! error.

If *x* is negative, F.DIST.RT() returns the #NUM! error value.

If *degrees_freedom1* or *degrees_freedom2* isn't an integer, the decimal places are truncated. If *degrees_freedom1* is less than 1 or *degrees_freedom2* is greater than or

> equal to 10^{10}, the function returns the #NUM! error. If *degrees_freedom2* is less than 1 or *degrees_freedom2* is greater than or equal to 10^{10}, the function returns the #NUM! error.
>
> F.DIST.RT() is calculated as F.DIST.RT = $P(F>x)$ where F is an F-distributed random variable with *degrees_freedom1* and *degrees_freedom2*.

Background   The F.DIST.RT() function returns the significance level based on a value. The F.DIST.RT() function calculates the probability—that is, the significance level—for the critical values calculated by F.INV.RT().

The F.INV.RT() function calculates the critical F-value based on the probability and degrees of freedom and requires the *probability* argument.

Example   Let's use the example for F.INV.RT(). In a survey, 15 employees had to answer 10 questions. Each question had three possible answers, as shown in Figure 12-41.

	B	C	D	E	F
3	**Group I**	**Group II**	**Group III**		
4	4	2	2		
5	2	1	1		
6	1	4	6		
7	5	7	4		
8	2	5	7		
9					
10	**Summary**				
11	**Group**	**Number**	**Sum**	**Average**	**Variance**
12	Group I	5	14	2.8	2.7
13	Group II	5	19	3.8	5.7
14	Group III	5	20	4.0	6.5

Figure 12-41 Summary of the survey results.

The null hypothesis indicates that there is no difference between the three groups. However, the alternative hypothesis assumes the opposite. A simple variance analysis returns the results shown in Figure 12-42.

H19	f_x	=F.INV.RT(0.05,D19,D20)				
	B	C	D	E	F	G	H
17	**Cause of spread**	**Square sum (SS)**	**Degree of freedom (df)**	**Average square sum (AS)**	**Test statistic (F)**	**P-Value**	**critical F-value**
18	Differences						
19	- between the groups	4.13	2	2.07	0.416107	0.67	**3.89**
20	- in the groups	59.60	12	4.97			=F.INV.RT(0.05,D19,D20)
21	**Total**	63.73	14				

Figure 12-42 The results of the unifactorial variance analysis.

With the F.INV.RT() function and a significance level (probability) of 0.05, you calculate a critical F-value of 3.89. The F.DIST.RT() function returns a significance level of 0.05.

The example uses the values shown in Figure 12-43 to calculate F.DIST.RT().

Wanted = Level of significance	?
Degree of freedom 1 (between the groups)	2
Degree of freedom 2 (in the groups)	12
Fcrit	3.89

Figure 12-43 The values for calculating the significance level.

The calculation of the significance level for *F* returns the result shown in Figure 12-44.

	H8	▾	f_x	=F.DIST.RT(H6,H4,H5)	
	F		G		H
3	Wanted = Level of significance				?
4	Degree of freedom 1 (between the groups)				2
5	Degree of freedom 2 (in the groups)				12
6	Fcrit				3.89
7	Test statistic F				0.41
8	F.DIST.RT for Fcrit (level of significance)				**0.05**
9	F.DIST.RT for test statistic F				

Figure 12-44 Calculating the significance level with the F.DIST.RT() function.

The F.DIST.RT() function returns a probability of 0.67 (67 percent) for statistic F = 0.4161 (see Figure 12-45).

	H9	▾	f_x	=F.DIST.RT(H7,H4,H5)	
	F		G		H
3	Wanted = Level of significance				?
4	Degree of freedom 1 (between the groups)				2
5	Degree of freedom 2 (in the groups)				12
6	Fcrit				3.89
7	Test statistic F				0.41
8	F.DIST.RT for Fcrit (level of significance)				0.05
9	F.DIST.RT for test statistic F				0.67

Figure 12-45 F.DIST.RT() returns the significance level for statistic F.

Because the significance level *a* is greater than the statistic *F*, the null hypothesis is confirmed. This means that you can assume that there is no significant difference between the two groups.

See Also F.INV.RT(), F.TEST()

> ## Sample Files
> Use the FDIST or F.DIST.RT worksheet in the Probability.xls or Probability.xlsx sample file. The sample files are found in the Chapter12 folder. For more information about the sample files, see the section titled "Using the Sample Files" on page xxiii.

F.INV()

Syntax   F.INV(*probability,degrees_freedom1,degrees_freedom2*)

Definition   This function returns the quantile of the left F-distribution.

Arguments

- ***probability* (required)** The probability associated with the F-distribution

- ***degrees_freedom1* (required)** The degrees of freedom in the numerator

- ***degrees_freedom2* (required)** The degrees of freedom in the denominator

> **Note**
>
> If one of the arguments isn't a numeric expression, the F.INV() function returns the #VALUE! error.
>
> If *probability* is less than 0 or greater than 1, the F.INV() function returns the #NUM! error.
>
> If *degrees_freedom1* or *degrees_freedom2* isn't an integer, the decimal places are truncated. If *degrees_freedom1* is less than 1 or *degrees_freedom2* is less than 1, the F.INV() function returns the #NUM! error.

Background   The F.INV.RT() function describes the quantile of the right F-distribution, and the F.INV() function describes the left quantile.

See Also You will find more information about ANOVA analyses and F-distributions in the description of F.INV.RT()/FINV().

Example   Compare the example for the F.INV.RT() function.

See Also   F.INV.RT(), F.TEST()

> **Sample Files**
>
> Use the F.INV worksheet in the Probability.xls sample file. The sample files are found in the Chapter12 folder. For more information about the sample files, see the section titled "Using the Sample Files" on page xxiii.

F.INV.RT()/FINV()

> **Note**
>
> In Excel 2010, the FINV() function was replaced with the F.INV.RT() function, and the F.INV() function was added to increase the accuracy of the results.
>
> To ensure the backward compatibility of F.INV.RT(), the FINV() function is still available.

Syntax   F.INV.RT(*probability,degrees_freedom1,degrees_freedom2*)

Definition   The F.INV.RT() function returns the inverse of the right F-distribution. If p = F.DIST.RT(x,...) then F.INV.RT(p,...) = x.

The F-distribution can be used in an f-test to compare the variances in two data sets. For example, you can analyze income distributions in the United States and Canada to determine whether the two countries have similar income diversity.

Arguments

- *probability* **(required)** The probability associated with the F-distribution

- *degrees_freedom1* **(required)** The degrees of freedom in the numerator

- *degrees_freedom2* **(required)** The degrees of freedom in the denominator

> **Note**
>
> If one of the arguments isn't a numeric value, the F.INV.RT() function returns the #VALUE! error.
>
> If *probability* is less than 0 or greater than 1, the F.INV.RT() function returns the #NUM! error.
>
> If *degrees_freedom1* or *degrees_freedom2* isn't an integer, the decimal places are truncated. If *degrees_freedom1* is less than 1 or *degrees_freedom2* is greater than or equal to 10^{10}, the function returns the #NUM! error. If *degrees_freedom2* is less than 1 or *degrees_freedom2* is greater than or equal to 10^{10}, the function returns the #NUM! error.

F.INV.RT() can be used to return critical values from the F-distribution. For example, the output of an ANOVA (analysis of variance) calculation often includes data for the F-statistic, F-probability, and critical F-value at the 0.05 significance level. To calculate the critical value of *F*, pass the significance level as the probability argument to F.INV.RT().

If *probability* has a value, F.INV.RT() looks for the value *x* so that F.INV.RT(*x, degrees_freedom1,degrees_freedom2*) = *probability*. Therefore, the accuracy of F.INV.RT() depends on the accuracy of F.DIST.RT(). The function F.INV.RT() uses an iterative search technique. If the search has not converged after 100 iterations, the function returns the #N/A error.

Background   As already mentioned, the output of an ANOVA calculation often includes data for the F-statistic, F-probability, and critical F-value at the 0.05 significance level. This function performs a simple variance analysis to evaluate the hypothesis that the means of two or more samples are equal. The function can also test the significance of the differences in the arithmetic means of these groups to check if the variance between means is random.

The F.INV.RT() function calculates the critical value of a distribution. To calculate the critical value, pass the significance level as the *probability* argument to F.INV.RT().

The calculation of F.INV.RT() allows you to draw a conclusion regarding the null hypothesis. The arguments of the F.INV.RT() function are *probability* (for example, significance level *a*), *degrees_freedom1*, and *degrees_freedom2*.

Example   You work as an occupational therapist and want to find out to what extent employees identify with a company. You have selected 15 employees. Each employee answered 10 questions on other subject areas. For each question, the employees could choose between three answers.

You have already summarized the answers (see Figure 12-46).

	B	C	D	E	F
3	Group I	Group II	Group III		
4	4	2	2		
5	2	1	1		
6	1	4	6		
7	5	7	4		
8	2	5	7		
9					
10	Summary				
11	Group	Number	Sum	Average	Variance
12	Group I	5	14	2.8	2.7
13	Group II	5	19	3.8	5.7
14	Group III	5	20	4.0	6.5

Figure 12-46 The results of the survey.

The null hypothesis is that there is no difference between the three groups. The alternative hypothesis assumes the opposite. The significance level is 0.05 percent. Figure 12-47 shows the result of the univariate variance analysis.

	B	C	D	E	F	G	H
17	Cause of spread	Square sum (SS)	Degree of freedom (df)	Average square sum (AS)	Test statistic (F)	P-Value	critical F-value
18	Differences						
19	- between the groups	4.13	2	2.07	0.416107	0.67	**3.89**
20	- in the groups	59.60	12	4.97			=F.INV.RT(0.05,D19,D20)
21	Total	63.73	14				

Figure 12-47   Calculating the univariate variance analysis and the critical F-value.

The result distinguishes the differences between the groups and the differences within groups, because not only are the three groups different but also the results of the employees within a group are different.

The differences between the groups correspond to the evaluated difference, and the differences within a group are random.

The number of degrees of freedom 1 (degrees of freedom within the groups) is calculated based on the size of the three groups minus 1 ($5 - 1 + 5 - 1 + 5 - 1 = 12$). The number of degrees of freedom 2 (degrees of freedom between the groups) is calculated based on the number of groups minus 1 ($3 - 1 = 2$).

The value for statistic F is 0.42 (cell F19). When you compare this value with the critical F-value calculated by F.INV.RT(), you can draw a conclusion regarding the null hypothesis. If the value of the calculated statistic F is greater than or equal to the critical F-value, the null hypothesis is rejected. In this example, the null hypothesis is accepted, because there is no significant difference between the three groups.

See Also   F.INV(), F.TEST()

Sample Files

Use the FINV or F.INV.RT worksheet in the Probability.xls or Probability.xlsx sample file. The sample files are found in the Chapter12 folder. For more information about the sample files, see the section titled "Using the Sample Files" on page xxiii.

F.TEST()/FTEST()

Syntax   F.TEST(*array1,array2*)

Definition   This function returns the test statistics of an f-test. An f-test returns the one-tailed probability that the variances in *array1* and *array2* are not significantly different.

Arguments

- *array1* **(required)** The first array or range of data

- *array2* **(required)** The second array or range of data

> **Note**
>
> Arguments can be numbers, names, arrays, or references containing numbers.
>
> If an array or reference argument contains text, logical values, or empty cells, those values are ignored. However, cells with the value 0 are included.
>
> If the number of data points in *array1* or *array2* is less than 2 or if the variance of *array1* or *array2* is 0, F.TEST() returns the #DIV/0! error value.

Background   Use this function to determine whether two samples have different variances. For example, given test scores from public and private schools, you can test whether these schools have different levels of test score diversity. You want to know whether the variance of the test scores is different.

F.TEST() calculates the significance level that indicates whether two samples are identical. The question answered by F.TEST() is: Are the two variances of the given samples equal or not?

The calculation of the significance level uses the entire value range of the samples. The values of the first sample are *array1*, and the values of the second sample are *array2*. F.TEST() calculates the significance level based on *array1* and *array2* without calculating the sample variances first.

The calculated significance level is a percentage from 0 through 100. This value indicates the accuracy for statistical hypothesis tests. Often the accuracy is 90 or 95 percent

What does the result returned by F.TEST() mean? If the result for the significance level is 90 percent, the existing random numbers will match in only 100 minus 90 = 10 percent of the cases. This means that the probability that the data are 90 percent significant is 10 percent.

Therefore, a significance of 90 percent doesn't indicate that the existing data with a probability of 10 percent is random and the probability that a certain fact is true is 90 percent.

Example   The compatibility of a medicine was examined in a clinical study. You have the test results as well as some explanations.

One test group took the normal daily dosage, and the other test group took an increased dosage at the beginning of the study. The goal was to determine whether the increased dosage accelerated the healing process. The duration of treatment was calculated in days.

The null hypothesis indicates that there is no difference in the two test groups regarding the success of treatment. The alternative hypothesis indicates that the second group recovered faster because this method of treatment is more efficient than the usual treatment.

You have to analyze the test results to determine whether the null hypothesis can be accepted or has to be rejected. Because you weren't present during the test and don't have all the background information, you want to calculate the probability that the variances of the two samples are equal by using the F.TEST() function. This means that you want to know the difference in the variances of the test results. What does the result of 0.89 returned by F. TEST(), seen in Figure 12-48, mean?

B14		f_x	=F.TEST(B2:B11,C2:C11)
	B	**C**	
1	**Group 1 x_1**	**Group 2 x_2**	
2	7	8	
3	8	4	
4	8	8	
5	9	5	
6	6	6	
7	8	9	
8	4	5	
9	7	6	
10	6	3	
11	3	8	
12			
13	**Result for F.TEST**		
14	0.890719801		

Figure 12-48 F.TEST() calculates the significance for the sample variance.

The result of 89 percent for the significance level means that the existing random numbers will match only in 100 minus 90 = 10 percent of the cases. This means that the probability that the data are 90 percent significant is 10 percent.

The calculation of the significance with F.TEST() indicates a probability of 89 percent that the variances of the two samples are not different. If you calculate the variance for both samples, this result is confirmed.

As you can see in Figure 12-49, the variances for both samples are only slightly different. The result returned by F.TEST() is confirmed with a significance of 89 percent.

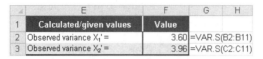

Figure 12-49 The variance calculated for *array1* and *array2*.

See Also F.DIST.RT()

> **Sample Files**
>
> Use the FTEST or F.TEST worksheet in the Probability.xls or Probability.xlsx sample file. The sample files are found in the Chapter12 folder. For more information about the sample files, see the section titled "Using the Sample Files" on page xxiii.

FISHER()

Syntax   FISHER(*x*)

Definition   This function returns the Fisher transformation for *x*. This transformation produces a function that is normally distributed with a skewness of about 0. Use this function to test the hypothesis for the correlation coefficient.

Arguments

- *x* **(required)** The numeric value you want to transform

> **Note**
>
> If *x* isn't a numeric value, the FISHER() function returns the #VALUE! error. If *x* is less than or equal to –1, or greater than or equal to 1, the FISHER() function returns the #NUM! error.

Background   Whereas the *regression* describes the type and covariance of the correlation between two characteristics, the *correlation* is the term for their relation.

The following provides an overview of the product-moment correlation (Pearson):

- The correlation describes the linear correlation of two variables.

- The correlation is the standardized covariance or the covariance.

- The correlation doesn't change with the linear transformation of the values.

- The correlation coefficient r has values between -1 and $+1$ and a two-tailed limit.

- The coefficient is calculated for interval-scaled variables.

- The coefficient depends on the variance of the two characteristics.

- A causal relationship cannot be derived from a correlation.

The *Fisher transformation* (Fisher z-transformation) was developed by Sir Ronald Aylmer Fisher (1890–1962), one of the most renowned geneticists, evolutionary modelers, and statisticians of the 20th century.

This type of transformation was developed to average correlations. Because the correlation coefficient is not interval-scaled—that is, the distance between $r = .20$ and $r = .40$ is not identical with the distance between $r = .40$ and $r = .60$—the average between different correlations cannot be calculated.

The solution is the Fisher transformation, which converts correlations into interval-scaled variables.

The average of multiple correlations is calculated as follows:

1. Convert all correlation coefficients to be averaged into Fisher values.

2. Average the z-values.

3. Retransform the averaged z-values into correlation coefficients.

The transformed value can be calculated with the FISHER() function or generated with the following formula:

$$z = \frac{1}{2}\ln\left(\frac{1+x}{1-x}\right)$$

The z-transformation transforms the correlation coefficient in its value range (-1 to $+1$) into an approximately normal distribution—that is, the correlation coefficient is asymptotic normal distributed to perform tests based on the normal distribution. This includes significance calculations.

Chapter 12

The formula for the expected value and the variance of the z-transformed correlation coefficient is:

$$E(x) = \frac{1}{2}\ln\left(\frac{1+p}{1-p}\right) \text{ and } Variance = \frac{1}{(n-3)}$$

Example   A software company sells all of its products through the company website. The company regularly sends out newsletters to inform existing and potential customers about new and updated products and to draw attention to its website. The company was founded in 2005.

The marketing department wants to analyze the website visits as well as the online orders in the last four years to determine the dependency between the orders and the website visits. You have already calculated the correlation coefficient for each year to see the correlation between the two variables (see Figure 12-50).

	B	C	D	E	F	G	H
1		Independent = x-value	Dependent = y-value			Independent = x-value	Dependent = y-value
2	Month	Web access	Orders		Month	Web access	Orders
3	January 2005	89	-		January 2006	236	6
4	February 2005	65	4		February 2006	1,221	17
5	March 2005	198	65		March 2006	1,563	456
6	April 2005	358	38		April 2006	2,682	544
7	May 2005	287	48		May 2006	4,569	349
8	June 2005	896	25		June 2006	6,848	854
9	July 2005	965	89		July 2006	8,463	427
10	August 2005	735	198		August 2006	10,157	337
11	September 2005	1,398	376		September 2006	11,837	899
12	October 2005	653	234		October 2006	12,987	1,011
13	November 2005	498	76		November 2006	13,739	720
14	December 2005	1,673	456		December 2006	14,376	1,069
15	Coefficient of correlation		0.856291674		Coefficient of correlation		0.786671098
18							
19		Independent = x-value	Dependent = y-value			Independent = x-value	Dependent = y-value
20	Month	Web access	Orders		Month	Web access	Orders
21	January 2007	15,739	1,070		January 2008	22,786	1,421
22	February 2007	16,123	967		February 2008	23,784	1,508
23	March 2007	16,548	1,401		March 2008	24,574	1,876
24	April 2007	17,352	1,076		April 2008	25,111	1,948
25	May 2007	17,986	1,563		May 2008	25,789	2,094
26	June 2007	18,234	1,485		June 2008	26,948	2,134
27	July 2007	18,769	1,367		July 2008	15,635	1,673
28	August 2007	19,736	1,138		August 2008	10,157	337
29	September 2007	20,333	1,352		September 2008	11,837	899
30	October 2007	20,987	1,343		October 2008	12,987	1,011
31	November 2007	21,323	1,430		November 2008	13,739	720
32	December 2007	21,999	1,375		December 2008	14,376	1,069
33	Coefficient of correlation		0.44987926		Coefficient of correlation		0.90305595

Figure 12-50 The correlation coefficient shows the correlations.

Now you want to calculate the average correlation for the last four years. Because the correlation coefficient is not interval-scaled, you cannot calculate the average from different correlations.

Therefore, you use the FISHER() function to transform all correlation coefficients into Fisher values. You specify the correlation coefficient for the *x* argument of the FISHER() function.

Figure 12-51 shows the result of the calculation with the FISHER() function.

	B	C	D	E	F	G	H
1		Independent = x-value	Dependent = y-value			Independent = x-value	Dependent = y-value
2	Month	Web access	Orders		Month	Web access	Orders
3	January 2005	89	-		January 2006	236	6
4	February 2005	65	4		February 2006	1,221	17
5	March 2005	198	65		March 2006	1,563	456
6	April 2005	358	38		April 2006	2,682	544
7	May 2005	287	48		May 2006	4,569	349
8	June 2005	896	25		June 2006	6,848	854
9	July 2005	965	89		July 2006	8,463	427
10	August 2005	735	198		August 2006	10,157	337
11	September 2005	1,398	376		September 2006	11,837	899
12	October 2005	653	234		October 2006	12,987	1,011
13	November 2005	498	76		November 2006	13,739	720
14	December 2005	1,673	456		December 2006	14,376	1,069
15	Coefficient of correlation		0.856291674		Coefficient of correlation		0.786671098
16	z-transformed value		1.2793		z-transformed value		1.0626
17	=FISHER(C15)				=FISHER(G15)		
18							
19		Independent = x-value	Dependent = y-value			Independent = x-value	Dependent = y-value
20	Month	Web access	Orders		Month	Web access	Orders
21	January 2007	15,739	1,070		January 2008	22,786	1,421
22	February 2007	16,123	967		February 2008	23,784	1,508
23	March 2007	16,548	1,401		March 2008	24,574	1,876
24	April 2007	17,352	1,076		April 2008	25,111	1,948
25	May 2007	17,986	1,563		May 2008	25,789	2,094
26	June 2007	18,234	1,485		June 2008	26,948	2,134
27	July 2007	18,769	1,367		July 2008	15,635	1,673
28	August 2007	19,736	1,138		August 2008	10,157	337
29	September 2007	20,333	1,352		September 2008	11,837	899
30	October 2007	20,987	1,343		October 2008	12,987	1,011
31	November 2007	21,323	1,430		November 2008	13,739	720
32	December 2007	21,999	1,375		December 2008	14,376	1,069
33	Coefficient of correlation		0.44987926		Coefficient of correlation		0.90305595
34	z-transformed value		0.4845		z-transformed value		1.4885
35	=FISHER(C33)				=FISHER(G33)		

Figure 12-51 Calculating the transformed correlation coefficient with the FISHER() function.

Figure 12-52 shows how you can calculate the average from the *z*-values returned by FISHER().

Average of single z-values	
Z-value 1 for 2005	1.2793
Z-value 1 for 2006	1.0626
Z-value 1 for 2007	0.4845
Z-value 1 for 2008	1.4885
Average	1.0788

Figure 12-52 Calculating the average from the *z*-values.

To retransform the average calculated from the *z*-values into a correlation coefficient, use the FISHERINV() function.

Chapter 12

You have to retransform the calculated average into a correlation coefficient to get the correlation between the website visits and the online orders in the last four years. As you can see in Figure 12-53, the correlation coefficient calculated from the average is 0.7927.

Average of single z-values	
Z-value 1 for 2005	1.2793
Z-value 1 for 2006	1.0626
Z-value 1 for 2007	0.4845
Z-value 1 for 2008	1.4885
Average	**1.0788**
Coefficient of correlation	**0.7927**
=FISHERINV(C43)	

Figure 12-53 Transforming the average (calculated from the z-values) into a correlation coefficient.

The following statements can be made:

- The correlation coefficient of 0.7927 indicates a positive correlation. The closer the correlation coefficient is to 1, the closer the correlation. This means that the website visits and online orders are linear interdependent.

- If the number of website visits increases because of marketing activities, the number of online orders also increases.

- This proves that in the last four years the online orders were dependent on the number of website visits.

See Also   CORREL(), COVAR(), FISHERINV()

Sample Files

Use the FISHER worksheet in the Probability.xls or Probability.xlsx sample file. The sample files are found in the Chapter12 folder. For more information about the sample files, see the section titled "Using the Sample Files" on page xxiii.

FISHERINV()

Syntax   FISHERINV(*y*)

Definition   This function returns the inverse of the Fisher transformation. Use this transformation when analyzing correlations between ranges or arrays of data.

If *y* = FISHER(*x*), then FISHERINV(*y*) = *x*.

Arguments

- **y (required)** The value for which you want to invert the transformation

> **Note**
> If *y* isn't a numeric value, the FISHERINV() function returns the #VALUE! error.

Background   The FISHERINV() function is the inverse function of FISHER(). This means that this function returns the inverse of the Fisher transformation.

FISHERINV() calculates the initial x-value of the Fisher-transformed *z*-value. Use this transformation when analyzing correlations between ranges or arrays of data. The equation for the inverse of the Fisher transformation is:

$$x = \frac{e^{2y} - 1}{e^{2y} + 1}$$

See Also You will find more information about Fisher transformations in the description of FISHER().

Example   You will find more information about the functionality of FISHERINV() in the description of FISHER().

See Also   CORREL(), COVAR(), FISHER()

> **Sample Files**
> Use the FISHER.INV worksheet in the Probability.xls or Probability.xlsx sample file. The sample files are found in the Chapter12 folder. For more information about the sample files, see the section titled "Using the Sample Files" on page xxiii.

Chapter 12

FORECAST()

Syntax FORECAST(*x,known_y's,known_x's*)

Definition This function returns the estimated value for a linear trend. The predicted value is a y-value for a given x-value. The known values are existing x-values and y-values, and the new value is predicted by using a linear regression. You can use this function to predict future sales, inventory requirements, or consumer trends.

Arguments

- **x (required)** The data point for which you want to predict a value

- **known_y's (required)** The dependent array or range of data

- **known_x's (required)** The independent array or range of data

> **Note**
>
> If *x* isn't a numeric expression, the FORECAST() function returns the #VALUE! error.
>
> If *known_y's* and *known_x's* are empty or contain a different number of data points, the FORECAST() function returns the #N/A error.
>
> If the variance of *known_x's* equals 0, then FORECAST() returns the #DIV/0! error.
>
> The equation for FORECAST() is *a+bx*, where
>
> $$a = \bar{a} - b\bar{x}$$
>
> and
>
> $$b = \frac{\sum(x - \bar{x})(y - \bar{y})}{\sum(x - \bar{x})^2}$$
>
> The *x* and *y* are the sample means AVERAGE(*known_x's*) and AVERAGE(*known y's*).

Background For extensive trend analyses, use the TREND() and GROWTH() functions. However, those functions are complex and require an array to return the calculated values.

See Also You will find more information about these function in the descriptions of TREND() and GROWTH().

To quickly calculate the prognosis for a certain value in a number series or a range, use the FORECAST() function. The FORECAST() function returns the estimated value for a linear trend. This means that the function calculates a trend based on given data and the "future number" for the specified x-value. In the following example, the estimated website visits for July 2008 (the x-value) are returned.

Example   You are the marketing director of a software company and want to create a forecast table. The forecast is to be calculated for the next nine months (July 2008 to March 2009) and includes the number of website visits as well as the number of online orders.

You assume that between January 2006 and June 2008 the data are linear. You have already calculated a line you could also use to create a prognosis (see Figure 12-54). However, you decide to calculate the forecast with the FORECAST() function.

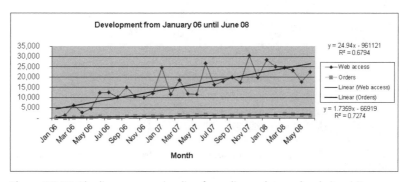

Figure 12-54 The linear regression line for online orders and website visits.

First you want to calculate the expected number of website visits for July 2008. You enter the following arguments for the FORECAST() function (see Figure 12-55):

- **x = cell B40 (July 2008)** This is the cell for which you want to calculate the expected number of website visits.

- **known_y's = cell range C10:C39** The number of website visits from January 2006 through June 2008 are the dependent y-values.

- **known_x's = cell range B10:B39** The months between January 2006 and June 2008 are the independent x-values.

Figure 12-55 shows how to enter the arguments for the trend in cell C32.

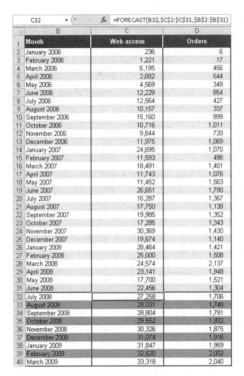

Figure 12-55 The FORECAST() function calculates the website visits for July 2008.

Note

Make sure you enter the absolute path for the *known_y's* and *known_x's* arguments. Press the F4 key after you have selected the cells. The $ sign is displayed in the formula bar. Because you entered the absolute path, you can copy the formula into cells C33:C40.

When you copy the formula, the cell containing the *x* argument (the estimated number of website visits) is automatically adjusted to the corresponding cell because the path is relative.

By copying the formula from cell C32 into the cells C33:C40, you get the trend for the website visits from July 2008 through March 2009.

You can use the FORECAST() function in the same way to create a prognosis for the online orders depending on the calculated website visits. To calculate the estimated online orders, enter the following arguments:

- **x = cell C32 (number of the online orders in July 2008)** This is the cell for which you want to calculate the expected number of online orders.

- **known_y's = cell range D2:D31** The number of online orders from January 2005 through June 2008 are the dependent y-values.

- **known_x's = cell range C2:C31** The online orders between January 2005 and June 2008 are the independent x-values.

Figure 12-56 shows the result and the formula for the FORECAST() function for calculating the expected number of online orders.

D32		f_x =FORECAST(C32,$D$2:$D$31,$C$2:$C$31)	
	B	C	D
1	Month	Web access	Orders
32	July 2008	27,258	1,706
33	August 2008	28,031	1,748
34	September 2008	28,804	1,791
35	October 2008	29,552	1,832
36	November 2008	30,326	1,875
37	December 2008	31,074	1,916
38	January 2009	31,847	1,959
39	February 2009	32,620	2,002
40	March 2009	33,318	2,040

Figure 12-56 The prognosis for online orders calculated with the FORECAST() function.

If you enter the absolute path for the *known_y's* and *known_x's* arguments, you can copy the function from cell D32 into the cells D33:D40 to calculate the trend for the other months depending on the number of website visits.

See Also GROWTH(), LINEST(), LOGEST(), TREND()

> ## Sample Files
> Use the FORECAST worksheet in the Regression.xls or Regression.xlsx sample file. The sample files are found in the Chapter12 folder. For more information about the sample files, see the section titled "Using the Sample Files" on page xxiii.

FREQUENCY()

Syntax   FREQUENCY(*data_array,bins_array*)

Definition   This function returns a frequency distribution as single-column matrix. For example, use FREQUENCY() to count the sales in a certain area. Because FREQUENCY() returns an array of values, it must be entered as an array formula.

Arguments

- *data_array* **(required)** An array of or a reference to a set of values for which you want to count frequencies. If *data_array* contains no values, FREQUENCY() returns an array of zeros.

- *bins_array* **(required)** An array of or reference to intervals into which you want to group the values in *data_array*. If *bins_array* contains no values, FREQUENCY() returns the number of elements in *data_array*.

Background   To reduce the quantitative data, the existing data are categorized into classes for which the frequency is calculated. Remember the following:

- If you have too many classes, you will have more information but less of an overview. The opposite is true for not enough classes.

- The classes don't need to have the same size.

The FREQUENCY() function counts the numeric data for given intervals. Unlike with the COUNTIF() function, you don't need to enter the FREQUENCY() function in each result cell, but you can enter the function in all cells at once. FREQUENCY() is an array function, and it returns an array. In the example, the array consists of four numbers.

> **Note**
>
> Select the cell range to display the results and enter FREQUENCY() as array formula.
>
> FREQUENCY() ignores empty cells and text.

Example   For FREQUENCY(), we will use the example of the software company again. A sales representative has entered his sales every month for the last two years in an Excel table. His manager wants to know the sales up to $15,000, up to $17,000, up to $19,000, and more than $19,000. Therefore, four classes are needed.

Cell range C3:C26 contains the data to be classified (see Figure 12-57). The four classes are specified in the Class column. The frequency of the data within a class is calculated based on this column.

		F6			f_x {=FREQUENCY($C$3:$C$26,E3:E5)}		

	B	C	D	E	F
2	**Month**	**Sales (data)**		**Category**	**Result**
3	January-07	$ 17,500.00		15000	9
4	February-07	$ 17,867.00		17000	5
5	March-07	$ 10,966.00		19000	7
6	April-07	$ 25,948.00			3
7	May-07	$ 12,838.00			
8	June-07	$ 14,888.00		=FREQUENCY($C$3:$C$26,E3:E5)	
9	July-07	$ 14,245.00			
10	August-07	$ 16,292.00			
11	September-07	$ 11,689.00			
12	October-07	$ 12,587.00			
13	November-07	$ 18,560.00			
14	December-07	$ 15,697.00			
15	January-08	$ 16,022.00			
16	February-08	$ 16,589.00			
17	March-08	$ 12,556.00			
18	April-08	$ 18,681.00			
19	May-08	$ 14,643.00			
20	June-08	$ 15,698.00			
21	July-08	$ 18,172.00			
22	August-08	$ 19,710.00			
23	September-08	$ 17,182.00			
24	October-08	$ 11,075.00			
25	November-08	$ 18,494.00			
26	December-08	$ 21,534.00			

Figure 12-57 The sales are divided into classes to calculate the frequency.

Because FREQUENCY() is an array function, select the four result cells (F3:F6) in the result column to get the result as an array.

Tip   Use analysis functions in Excel 2003

Excel provides numerous analysis functions that you can access by selecting Tools/ Analysis Functions (Excel 2003). With analysis functions, you can easily calculate a frequency distribution.

To use the analysis functions in Excel 2003, you must first activate the Analysis Function add-in. Select Tools/Add-Ins and select the Analysis Functions check box.

To calculate a frequency, select Tools/Analysis Functions and then select Historgram. You can also select the chart view to graphically evaluate your data.

Tip   Use analysis functions in Excel 2007 and Excel 2010

In Excel 2007 and Excel 2010, the analysis functions are located in the Analysis group on the Data tab. If the functions are not available, you must first activate them. In Excel 2010, click File and then select Options. In Excel 2007, click the Office button and select Excel Options. See Figure 12-58.

Figure 12-58 Accessing the Excel Options dialog box to select an add-in.

In the Excel Options dialog box, click Add-Ins, select Excel-Add-Ins in the Manage list, and then click Go (see Figure 12-59).

Figure 12-59 Selecting an add-in in Excel 2010.

Select the Analysis ToolPak check box in the Add-Ins dialog box, and click OK (see Figure 12-60).

Figure 12-60 Activating the analysis functions.

After the analysis functions have been installed, they are available on the Data tab (see Figure 12-61).

Figure 12-61 The analysis functions on the Data tab.

See Also COUNT(), DCOUNT()

Sample Files

Use the FREQUENCY worksheet in the Count.xls or Count.xlsx sample file. The sample files are found in the Chapter12 folder. For more information about the sample files, see the section titled "Using the Sample Files" on page xxiii.

GAMMA.DIST()/GAMMADIST()

Syntax   GAMMA.DIST(*x,alpha,beta,cumulative*)

Definition   This function returns the probabilities of a gamma-distributed random variable. Use this function to examine variables that have a skewed distribution. The gamma distribution is commonly used in queuing analyses.

Arguments

- ***x* (required)** The value (quantile) for which you want to calculate the probability (1-*alpha*).

- ***alpha* (required)** A parameter of the distribution.

- ***beta* (required)** A parameter of the distribution. If *beta* = 1, GAMMA.DIST() returns the standard gamma distribution.

- *cumulative* **(required)** The logical value that represents the type of the function. If *cumulative* is TRUE, GAMMA.DIST() returns the value of the distribution function that is the probability that the number of random events is between 0 and *x*. If *cumulative* is FALSE, the GAMMA.DIST() function returns the value of the density function.

> ## Note
>
> If *x*, *alpha*, or *beta* isn't a numeric expression, the GAMMA.DIST() function returns the #VALUE! error.
>
> If *x* is less than 0, the function returns the #NUM! error.
>
> If *alpha* or *beta* is less than or equal to 0, the GAMMA.DIST() function returns the #NUM! error.
>
> The density function for the standard gamma distribution is:
>
> $$f(x, \alpha) = \frac{x^{\alpha-1}e^{-x}}{\Gamma(\alpha)}$$
>
> If *alpha* = 1, GAMMA.DIST() returns the exponential distribution with the following:
>
> - For a positive integer *n*, when *alpha* = *n*/2, *beta* = 2, and *cumulative* = TRUE, GAMMA.DIST() returns the same result as (1 – CHIDIST(x)) with *n* degrees of freedom.
>
> - If *alpha* is a positive integer, the gamma distribution is also called the *Erlang distribution*.

Background   The gamma distribution is a continuous probability distribution of positive real numbers (see Figure 12-62). The gamma distribution is defined by the probability density with *x* greater than 0.

$$f(x) = \frac{b^p}{\Gamma(p)} x^{p-1} e^{-bx}$$

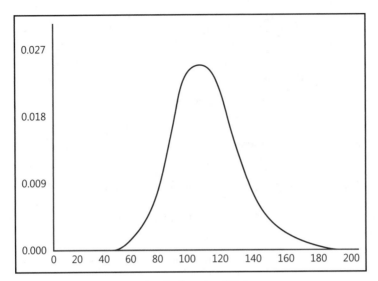

Figure 12-62 The gamma density function (25.4).

For other values, the gamma density function is continued with f(x)=0. The parameters are p and q (*alpha* and *beta*). To ensure standardization p,q has to be greater than 0. The prefactor bp/Γ(p) ensures that the standardization is correct. The expression Γ(p) is the gamma function.

The following shows the expected value and variance of the gamma distribution:

$$E(x) = \frac{p}{b} \text{ and } V(x) = \frac{p}{b^2}$$

The gamma distribution is reproductive.

> **Note**
>
> The reproductivity of a probability distribution indicates that the sum of independent random variables is distributed based on the distribution type.
>
> The normal distribution, the Poisson distribution, the gamma distribution, and the Cauchy distribution are examples of a reproductive distribution.

The sum of the stochastically independent random variables x and y, gamma-distributed with the parameters b and px or py, is gamma-distributed with the parameters b and px + py.

The gamma distribution creates a *family* for several theoretical distribution functions:

- The chi-square distribution with k degrees of freedom is a gamma distribution using the parameters $p = k/2$ and $b = \frac{1}{2}$.

- The exponential distribution with the parameter λ is a gamma distribution using the parameters $p = 1$ and $b = \lambda$. According to this, the Erlang distribution with the parameter λ and n degrees of freedom corresponds to a gamma distribution with the parameters $p = n$ and $b = \lambda$.

- The quotient $X/(X + Y)$ from the stochastically independent random variables x and y gamma-distributed with the parameters b and px or py is beta-distributed with the parameters px and py.

Alternatively, the parameters are as follows:

$$\alpha = a, \beta = \frac{1}{b}$$

The density and moments are changed accordingly (for example, the expected value would be $\alpha\beta$). Because this parameterization is commonly used in the English-speaking world, it can often be found in technical literature. To avoid misunderstandings, it is recommended that you explicitly specify the moments—for example, the expected value ab and variance ab^2—for a gamma distribution (see Figure 12-63).

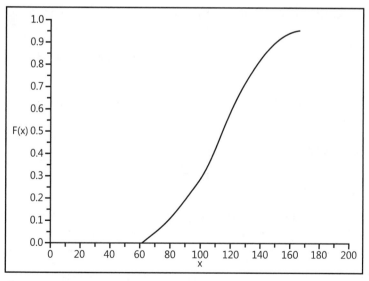

Figure 12-63 The gamma distribution function (25.4).

The GAMMA.DIST() function is a mathematical distribution function with two parameters (*alpha* and *beta*) based on the gamma function. GAMMA.DIST() is the inverse function of GAMMA.INV.

Example   Use the following values to calculate GAMMA.DIST():

- 10 = value (quantile) for which you want to calculate the probability

- 2.70 = *alpha* parameter of the distribution

- 2 = *beta* parameter of the distribution

Figure 12-64 shows the calculation of GAMMA.DIST().

	B	C	D	E	F
2	**Meaning**			**Parameter**	
3	x= Value (quantile) for which the probability should be calculated			10	
4	Parameter Alpha for the distriubution			2.70	
5	Parameter Beta for the distribution			2	
6	Cumulative = true			TRUE	
7	Cumulative = false			FALSE	
8	**GAMMA.DIST() (cumulative = TRUE)**			**0.90679**	
9				=GAMMA.DIST(E3,E4,E5,E6)	
10	**GAMMA.DIST() (cumulative = FALSE)**			**0.03364**	
11				=GAMMA.DIST(E3,E4,E5,E7)	

Figure 12-64 Calculating GAMMA.DIST()

With the parameters shown in Figure 12-42, the GAMMA.DIST() function returns the following results:

- 0.90679 = probability of the gamma distribution based on the data provided and *cumulative* = TRUE

- 0.03364 = probability of the gamma distribution based on the data provided and *cumulative* = FALSE

See Also CHISQ.DIST.RT(), EXPON.DIST(), GAMMA.INV()

Sample Files

Use the GAMMADIST or GAMMA.DIST worksheet in the Probability.xls or Probability.xlsx sample file. The sample files are found in the Chapter12 folder. For more information about the sample files, see the section titled "Using the Sample Files" on page xxiii.

The sample files also include a table you can use to specify the *alpha* and *beta* parameters. Enter the parameters to change the density and distribution functions.

GAMMA.INV()/GAMMAINV()

Syntax   GAMMA.INV(*probability,alpha,beta*)

Definition   This function returns the quantile of the gamma distribution. If *p* = GAMMA.DIST(*x*,...) then GAMMA.INV(*p*,...) = *x*.

Use this function to examine a variable whose distribution may be skewed.

Arguments

- **probability (required)** A probability associated with the gamma distribution.

- **alpha (required)** A parameter of the distribution.

- **beta (required)** A parameter of the distribution. If *beta* = 1, GAMMA.INV() returns the standard gamma distribution.

> **Note**
>
> If one of the arguments isn't a numeric expression, the GAMMA.INV() function returns the #VALUE! error.
>
> If *probability* is less than 0 or greater than 1, the GAMMA.INV() function returns the #NUM! error.
>
> If *alpha* or *beta* is less than or equal to 0, the GAMMA.INV() function returns the #NUM! error.
>
> If *probability* has a value, GAMMA.INV() looks for the value *x* so that GAMMA.DIST(*x*, *alpha*, *beta*, TRUE) = *probability*. Therefore, the accuracy of GAMMA.INV() depends on the accuracy of GAMMA.DIST(). GAMMA.INV() uses an iterative search technique. If the search has not converged after 100 iterations, the function returns the #N/A error.

Background   GAMMA.INV() is the inverse function of GAMMA.DIST() and can be used to monitor a gamma distribution. The *alpha* and *beta* arguments correspond to the values for the GAMMA.DIST() function. The probability can be any value from 0 through 100 percent. GAMMA.INV() calculates the position of *x* on the horizontal axis that matches the cumulative area ratio of the gamma distribution.

See Also You will find more information about gamma distributions in the description of GAMMA.DIST().

Example   Use the values in Figure 12-65 to calculate GAMMA.INV(). The figure also shows the calculation of GAMMA.INV().

Chapter 12

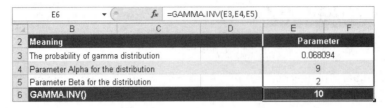

Figure 12-65 Calculating GAMMA.INV().

The GAMMA.INV() function returns the quantile 10 for the gamma distribution based on the parameters shown.

> **See Also** GAMMA.DIST()

Sample Files

Use the GAMMAINV or GAMMA.INV worksheet in the Probability.xls or Probability.xlsx sample file. The sample files are found in the Chapter12 folder. For more information about the sample files, see the section titled "Using the Sample Files" on page xxiii.

The sample files also include a table you can use to specify the *alpha* and *beta* parameters. Enter the parameters to change the density and distribution functions.

GAMMALN()

Syntax   GAMMALN(*x*)

Definition   This function returns the natural logarithm of the gamma function ($\Gamma(x)$).

Arguments

- **x (required)** The value for which you want to calculate GAMMALN()

Note

If *x* isn't a numeric expression, the GAMMALN() function returns the #VALUE! error. If *x* is less than or equal to 0, the function returns the #NUM! error.

The number *e* raised to the GAMMALN(*i*) power, where *i* is an integer, returns the same result as ($i - 1$).

Background The GAMMALN() function returns the natural logarithm of the gamma function.

See Also You will find more information about gamma distributions in the description of GAMMA.DIST().

The logarithm of a number is the exponent by which a fixed number, the base, has to be raised to produce that number. The following logarithms exist:

- Natural logarithm to base e (Euler's number = 2.72)

- Logarithm to base 10

- Logarithm to base 2

The logarithm (to base b) of a number y is the number by which base b has to be raised to produce number y. Therefore, the logarithm is an exponent, and the logarithm function is the inverse function of the exponential function (see Figure 12-66).

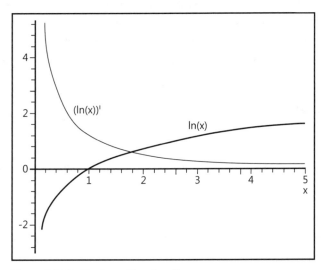

Figure 12-66 The logarithm function.

GAMMALN() is calculated as follows:

$$GAMMALN = LN\left(\Gamma(x)\right)$$

where

$$\Gamma(x) = \int_0^\infty e^{-u} u^{x-1} du$$

Example   Assume that you want to calculate GAMMALN() given the value 4. Figure 12-67 shows the calculation of GAMMALN().

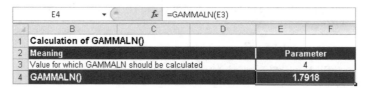

	B	C	D	E	F
	E4		f_x =GAMMALN(E3)		
1	Calculation of GAMMALN()				
2	Meaning			Parameter	
3	Value for which GAMMALN should be calculated			4	
4	GAMMALN()			1.7918	

Figure 12-67 Calculating GAMMALN().

The GAMMALN() function returns the natural logarithm, 1.7918, for the gamma function based on the parameters shown in Figure 12-67.

See Also FACT(), GAMMA.DIST()

> **Sample Files**
>
> Use the GAMMALN worksheet in the Probability.xls or Probability.xlsx sample file. The sample files are found in the Chapter12 folder. For more information about the sample files, see the section titled "Using the Sample Files" on page xxiii.

GAMMALN.PRECISE()

Syntax   GAMMALN.PRECISE(*x*)

Definition   This function returns the natural logarithm of the gamma function ($\Gamma(x)$) calculated to 15 places.

Arguments

- **x (required)** The value for which you want to calculate GAMMALN.PRECISE()

> **Note**
>
> If *x* isn't a numeric expression, the GAMMALN.PRECISE() function returns the #VALUE! error. If *x* is less than or equal to 0, the function returns the #NUM! error. The number *e* raised to the GAMMALN.PRECISE(*i*) power, where *i* is an integer, returns the same result as ($i - 1$).

Background   See the background information for the GAMMALN() function.

See Also You will find more information about gamma distributions in the description of GAMMA.DIST().

Example   For an example that shows the use of the GAMMALN functions, see the example for the GAMMALN() function.

See Also FACT(), GAMMA.DIST(), GAMMALN()

> ## Sample Files
> Use the GAMMALN.PRECISE worksheet in the Probability.xls or Probability.xlsx sample file. The sample files are found in the Chapter12 folder. For more information about the sample files, see the section titled "Using the Sample Files" on page xxiii.

GEOMEAN()

Syntax   GEOMEAN(*number1,number2,...*)

Definition   This function returns the geometric mean of a set of positive numbers. For example, you can use GEOMEAN() to calculate the average growth rate for an interest calculation with variable rates.

The geometric mean is calculated as the *n*-th root from the product of all values where *n* is the number of values.

Arguments

- *number1* **(required) and** *number2* **(optional)** At least one and up to 255 arguments (30 in Excel 2003 and earlier versions) for which you want to calculate the geometric mean. You can also use a single array or a reference to an array instead of arguments separated by commas.

> ## Note
> Arguments can be numbers, names, arrays, or references containing numbers.
>
> If an array or a reference argument contains text, logical values, or empty cells, those values are ignored. However, cells with the value 0 are included. If one of the numbers is less than or equal to 0, the function returns the #NUM! error.
>
> The equation for the geometric mean is:
>
> $$GM_{\bar{y}} = \sqrt[n]{y_1 y_2 y_3 \ldots y_n}$$

Background   The geometric mean is mostly used for increase and decrease processes where the increase (or decrease) is not a fixed value but rather a percentage.

If you use the arithmetic average to examine a sales trend over a certain amount of time, the results won't be sufficient. In this case, the geometric mean is the better choice.

Example   You are the executive manager of the controlling department of a software company and want to know whether sales have increased. If they have, you also want to know the average percentage of the sales increase.

You use the GEOMEAN() function because the arithmetic average would return the wrong result, as shown in Figure 12-68.

	B	C	D	E	F
3	Annual turnover in 2008		Changes compared		
4	Month	Amount	to previous month		
5	January-08	$ 13,332,315.00	X		
6	February-08	$ 11,038,333.00	0.827938209		
7	March-08	$ 7,031,695.00	0.637025083		
8	April-08	$ 12,335,681.00	1.754296937		
9	May-08	$ 4,476,739.00	0.362909757		
10	June-08	$ 9,609,594.00	2.146561146		
11	July-08	$ 7,136,415.00	0.742634392		
12	August-08	$ 12,626,557.00	1.769313724		
13	September-08	$ 15,515,165.00	1.228772420		
14	October-08	$ 8,466,178.00	0.545671155		
15	November-08	$ 15,991,765.00	1.888900163	=GEOMEAN(D6:D16)	0.967157
16	December-08	$ 9,233,586.00	0.577396304	=AVERAGE(D6;D16)	1.134674

Figure 12-68 Calculating the geometric mean from the sales data.

First you calculate the monthly growth factor by dividing the monthly results by the results of the previous month. Then you calculate the geometric mean based on these results to get an average indicating the percentage of the sales of the previous month over the entire time period. The result is the average growth factor of the sales increase.

If you calculate the arithmetic average and the geometric mean, you get two results that don't seem to be very different. The difference becomes clear if you try to derive a general definition from these values. The geometric mean indicates an average of 97 percent for the sales of the previous month since January 2008, and the arithmetic average shows an average of 113 percent. This means that there was no average increase but a decrease of 1 minus 0.967157.

See Also   AVERAGE(), HARMEAN(), MEDIAN(), MODE(), TRIMMEAN()

> ## Sample Files
> Use the GEOMEAN worksheet in the Average.xls or Average.xlsx sample file. The sample files are found in the Chapter12 folder. For more information about the sample files, see the section titled "Using the Sample Files" on page xxiii.

GROWTH()

Syntax   GROWTH(*known_y's;known_x's;new_x's;const*)

Definition   This function returns values from an exponential trend. GROWTH() returns the y-values for a series of new x-values that you specify by using existing x-values and y-values. You can also use the GROWTH() function to calculate an exponential curve for the existing x-values and y-values.

Arguments

- **known_y's (required)** The y-values you already know from the relationship
  $y = b * m^x$

  - If the *known_y's* array consists of a single column, then each column in the *known_x's* array is interpreted as a separate variable.

  - If the *known_y's* array consists of a single row, then each row in the *known_x's* array is interpreted as a separate variable.

- **known_x's (optional)** The x-values you already know from the relationship
  $y = b * m^x$

  - The *known_x's* array can include one or more sets of variables. If only one variable is used, *known_y's* and *known_x's* can be ranges of any shape as long as they have equal dimensions. If more than one variable is used, *known_y's* must be a vector (a range consisting of a single row or column).

  - If *known_x's* is not specified, it is assumed to be the array {1,2,3,...} containing the same number of elements as *known_y's*.

  - The *known_y's* and *known_x's* arguments must have the same number of rows or columns. If the number of rows (columns) is different, you get the #REF! error. If one of the y-values is 0 or negative, you get the #NUM! error.

- **new_x's (optional)** The new x-values for which you want to return the corresponding y-values

  - Like *known_x's*, the *new_x's* argument must include a column (or row) for each independent variable. The *known_x's* and *new_x's* arguments must have the same number of columns if *known_y's* is in a single column. If *known_y's* is in a single row, *known_x's* and *new_x's* must have the same number of rows.

  - If *new_x's* is not specified, it is assumed to be the same as *known_x's*.

  - If both *known_x's* and *new_x's* are omitted, they are assumed to be the array {1,2,3,...} that contains the same number of elements as *known_y's*.

Chapter 12

- ● **const (optional)** A logical value specifying whether to force the constant b to equal 1

    - ○ If *const* is TRUE or omitted, b is calculated normally.

    - ○ If *const* is FALSE, b is set equal to 1 and the m-values are adjusted so that $y = m^x$.

Note

Formulas that return arrays must be entered as array formulas after you have selected the correct number of cells. When entering an array constant instead of an argument (such as *known_x's*), use commas to separate values in the same row and colons to separate rows.

Background   Whereas the TREND() function calculates the linear trend—future values—from existing values, you can also calculate the exponential trend because not all models follow a linear trend.

See Also You will find more information about trends in the description of TREND().

An exponential trend exists if a value always changes by the same factor or percentage. The exponential trend fits an exponential curve to existing data. Use the GROWTH() function to calculate an exponential trend model.

Example   Let's use the same example as for TREND(). You are the marketing manager of a software company and analyze the website. Recently the website visits as well as the online orders have increased significantly. Figure 12-69 shows the exponential increase in website visits and online orders.

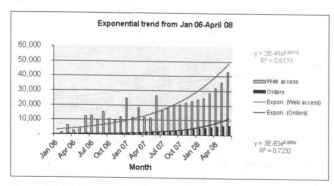

Figure 12-69 The exponential trend lines for website visits and online orders.

You know the number of website visits and online orders between January 2007 and June 2008. Now you want to create a prognosis for both components. You use the GROWTH() function to calculate the exponential trend. The website visits and orders through June 2008 are shown in Figure 12-70.

	B	C	D
2	Month	Web access	Orders
3	January 2006	236	6
4	February 2006	1,221	17
5	March 2006	6,195	456
6	April 2006	2,682	544
7	May 2006	4,569	349
8	June 2006	12,229	854
9	July 2006	12,564	427
10	August 2006	10,157	337
11	September 2006	15,160	899
12	October 2006	10,716	1,011
13	November 2006	9,844	720
14	December 2006	11,975	1,069
15	January 2007	24,695	1,070
16	February 2007	11,593	1,284
17	March 2007	18,491	1,572
18	April 2007	11,743	1,874
19	May 2007	11,452	2,098
20	June 2007	26,651	2,284
21	July 2007	16,287	2,534
22	August 2007	17,750	2,764
23	September 2007	19,985	2,987
24	October 2007	20,543	3,173
25	November 2007	21,958	3,587
26	December 2007	22,645	3,982
27	January 2008	23,954	4,620
28	February 2008	24,932	4,912
29	March 2008	28,743	5,374
30	April 2008	31,948	5,729
31	May 2008	35,928	6,046
32	June 2008	42,943	6,439

Figure 12-70 Website visits and online orders through June 2008.

Now you want to know the trend of the website visits and online orders from July 2008 through March 2009. The GROWTH() function provides the following arguments to calculate the website visits in the next nine months:

- *known_y's* = website visits between January 2008 and June 2008

- *known_x's* = months (January 2006 to June 2008)

- *new_x's* = months from July 2008 to March 2009

- *const* = TRUE (the constant *b* of the equation $y = mx + b$ is calculated normally)

Figure 12-71 shows the result.

C33	▾ (	f_x	=GROWTH(C3:C32,B3:B32,B33:B41,TRUE)}

	B	C	D
2	**Month**	**Web access**	**Orders**
3	January 2006	236	6
4	February 2006	1,221	17
5	March 2006	6,195	456
6	April 2006	2,682	544
7	May 2006	4,569	349
8	June 2006	12,229	854
9	July 2006	12,564	427
10	August 2006	10,157	337
11	September 2006	15,160	899
12	October 2006	10,716	1,011
13	November 2006	9,844	720
14	December 2006	11,975	1,069
15	January 2007	24,695	1,070
16	February 2007	11,593	1,284
17	March 2007	18,491	1,572
18	April 2007	11,743	1,874
19	May 2007	11,452	2,098
20	June 2007	26,651	2,284
21	July 2007	16,287	2,534
22	August 2007	17,750	2,764
23	September 2007	19,985	2,987
24	October 2007	20,543	3,173
25	November 2007	21,958	3,587
26	December 2007	22,645	3,982
27	January 2008	23,954	4,620
28	February 2008	24,932	4,912
29	March 2008	28,743	5,374
30	April 2008	31,948	5,729
31	May 2008	35,928	6,046
32	June 2008	42,943	6,439
33	July 2008	53,742	
34	August 2008	59,183	
35	September 2008	65,175	
36	October 2008	71,551	
37	November 2008	78,796	
38	December 2008	86,504	
39	January 2009	95,263	
40	February 2009	104,908	
41	March 2009	114,457	

Figure 12-71 Calculating the values for the exponentially increasing website visits.

> **Note**
>
> Remember, the GROWTH() function is an array function when calculating the values for cell range C33:C41. This means that the function immediately returns the result for all months. Therefore, you have the select cell range C33:C41, enter the formula, and press Ctrl+Page Up+Enter. You can recognize array functions by the braces in the formula bar.

Using the same procedure, you calculate the values for the online orders based on the calculated trend values for website visits. Figure 12-72 shows the result and the arguments of the GROWTH() function.

	B	C	D
2	Month	Web access	Orders
33	July 2008	53,742	104,183
34	August 2008	59,183	201,298
35	September 2008	65,175	415,757
36	October 2008	71,551	899,527
37	November 2008	78,796	2,161,947
38	December 2008	86,504	5,496,234
39	January 2009	95,263	15,866,575
40	February 2009	104,908	50,993,886
41	March 2009	114,457	161,983,212

D33 =GROWTH(D3:D32,C3:C32,C33:C41,TRUE)}

Figure 12-72 Calculating exponential trend values for online orders.

With the GROWTH() function, Excel allows for a good prognosis of the website visits and online orders as long as the previous exponential trend continues.

See Also FORECAST(), LINEST(), LOGEST(), TREND()

> **Sample Files**
>
> Use the GROWTH worksheet in the Regression.xls or Regression.xlsx sample file. The sample files are found in the Chapter12 folder. For more information about the sample files, see the section titled "Using the Sample Files" on page xxiii.

HARMEAN()

Syntax   HARMEAN(*number1,number2,...*)

Definition   This function returns the harmonic mean of a data set. The *harmonic mean* is the reciprocal of the arithmetic average of reciprocals.

Arguments

- *number1* **(required) and** *number2* **(optional)**   At least one and up to 255 arguments (30 in Excel 2003 and earlier versions) for which you want to calculate the harmonic mean. You can also use a single array or a reference to an array instead of arguments separated by commas.

> **Note**
>
> Arguments can be numbers, names, arrays, or references containing numbers. If an array or a reference argument contains text, logical values, or empty cells, those values are ignored. However, cells with the value 0 are included. If one of the numbers is less than or equal to 0, the function returns the #NUM! error.

Background   Statistics use different means including the geometric, arithmetic, square, and harmonic mean. The harmonic mean is mostly used to calculate the mean of quotients and when the observed values are defined as ratios or references. A typical example is the averaging of speeds; in other words, the calculation of the quotient of distance/time, assuming that the distance is known.

The equation for the harmonic mean is:

$$\frac{1}{H_y} = \frac{1}{n} \Sigma \frac{1}{y_i}$$

Important

The harmonic mean is always less than the geometric mean, which is always less than the arithmetic average.

Example   To explain how the harmonic mean is calculated, use the previously mentioned example of speed and time. A bicyclist travels 300 miles through the Alps. The distance is divided into five legs, for which he measures the speed of each.

Now the bicyclist wants to calculate the average speed from the speeds reached in each leg. The result should show the consistent speed at which he could have traveled the same distance in the same time (see Figure 12-73).

D9		f_x =HARMEAN(D6:H6)					
B	C		D	E	F	G	H
4 Road section No.			1	2	3	4	5
5 Length in miles			60	60	60	60	60
6 Speed in mph			20	15	25	23	30
7 Arithmetic mean in mph					22.60		
8 Geometric mean in mph					22.02		
9 Harmonic mean in mph					21.42		

Figure 12-73 Calculating the average speed with HARMEAN().

To get a better overview, he also calculated the arithmetic average and the geometric mean.

To find out what calculation returns the best result, he transforms the results of the arithmetic, geometric, and harmonic means in meters/seconds and then calculates the time it would take to travel the 300 miles at the average speed (see Figure 12-74).

	B	C	D	E	F	G
12	**Arithmetic mean in kilometers per sec.**		**Geometric mean in kilometers per sec.**		**Harmonic mean in kilometers per sec.**	
13	22.6 kilometers	1 h	22.02 kilometers	1h	21.42 kilometers	1 h
14	22600 meters	3600 s	22020 meters	3600 s	21420 meters	3600 s
15	**6.27 meters**	**1 s**	**6.12 meters**	**1 s**	**5.95 meters**	**1 s**
16						
17	**Arithmetic mean: time taken to ride 300 kilometers (in seconds)**		**Geometric mean: time taken to ride 300 kilometers (in seconds)**		**Harmonic mean: time taken to ride 300 kilometers (in seconds)**	
18	6.27 meters	1 s	6.12 meters	1 s	5.95 meters	1 s
19	0.00627 kilometers	1 s	0.00612 kilometers	1 s	0.00595 kilometers	1 s
20	**300 kilometers**	**47846 s**	**300 kilometers**	**49019 s**	**300 kilometers**	**50420 s**

Figure 12-74 The time in seconds to ride 300 miles calculated for the arithmetic, geometric, and harmonic means.

This calculation also confirms that the geometric mean is smaller than the harmonic mean, and the arithmetic mean is smaller than the geometric mean.

Next, you prove that the harmonic mean returns the best result. First you have to calculate speed v in m/s for the actual miles travelled at speed v for each leg in an hour. At a steady speed, the cyclist could have traveled 20 miles per hour in the first leg. If you divide 20 miles by 3,600 seconds, you get the speed v (see Figure 12-75).

The formula is:

$$v = \frac{s}{t}$$

	B	C	D	E	F	G
25		**Way in meters with constant speed for road section 1**	**Way in meters with constant speed for road section 2**	**Way in meters with constant speed for road section 3**	**Way in meters with constant speed for road section 4**	**Way in meters with constant speed for road section 5**
26		20000	15000	25000	23000	30000
27	**Time (1 hour) in seconds (s)**	3600	3600	3600	3600	3600
28	**Speed in meters per second**	5.56	4.17	6.94	6.39	8.33

Figure 12-75 Calculating the speed v in m/s based on the original leg.

Then you use the result for the speed in m/s in the same formula for t (time) to calculate the time for each leg in seconds. The formula is:

$$t = \frac{s}{v}$$

Figure 12-76 shows the result.

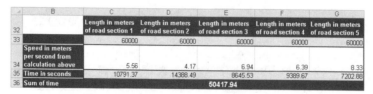

B	C	D	E	F	G
32	Length in meters of road section 1	Length in meters of road section 2	Length in meters of road section 3	Length in meters of road section 4	Length in meters of road section 5
33	60000	60000	60000	60000	60000
34 Speed in meters per second from calculation above	5.56	4.17	6.94	6.39	8.33
35 Time in seconds	10791.37	14388.49	8645.53	9389.67	7202.88
36 Sum of time	50417.94				

Figure 12-76 Time for the legs in seconds and as sum.

The sum of the times in seconds for the legs shows that the value is approximately the same as the harmonic mean. The difference of three seconds is based on the rounded values.

The comparison of the actual result of 50,417.94 seconds with the calculated results of the different means shows that the harmonic mean returns the best result.

See Also   AVERAGE(), GEOMEAN(), MEDIAN(), MODE(), TRIMMEAN()

> **Sample Files**
>
> Use the HARMEAN worksheet in the Average.xls or Average.xlsx sample file. The sample files are found in the Chapter12 folder. For more information about the sample files, see the section titled "Using the Sample Files" on page xxiii.

HYPGEOM.DIST()/HYPGEOMDIST()

Syntax   HYPGEOM.DIST(*sample_s,number_sample,population_s,number_ population,cumulative*)

Definition   This function returns the probabilities of a hypergeometric distributed random variable. HYPGEOM.DIST() calculates the probability of a certain number of observations in a sample.

The following information is required:

- Number of successes in the sample

- Size of the sample

- Number of possible successes in the population

- Size of the population

- Logical value for the function

Arguments

- *sample_s* **(required)** The number of successes in the sample

- *number_sample* **(required)** The size of the sample

- *population_s* **(required)** The number of successes in the population

- *number_population* **(required)** The size of the population

- *cumulative* **(required)** The logical value that represents the type of the function

> ### Note
>
> All arguments are truncated to integers by removing the decimal places. If one of the arguments isn't a numeric expression, the HYPGEOM.DIST() function returns the #VALUE! error.
>
> If *sample_s* is less than 0 or greater than the lesser value of *number_sample* or *population_s*, HYPGEOM.DIST() returns the #NUM! error. If *sample_s* is less than the larger value of 0 or (*number_sample – number_population + population_s*), HYPGEOM.DIST() returns the #NUM! error.
>
> If *number_sample* is smaller than 0 or greater than *number_population*, HYPGEOM. DIST() returns the #NUM! error.
>
> If *population_s* is less than 0 or greater than *number_population*, HYPGEOM.DIST() returns the #NUM! error.
>
> If *number_population* is less than 0, HYPGEOM.DIST() returns the #NUM! error.
>
> Use HYPGEOM.DIST() to take samples from a finite population without replacing these samples.

Background   The hypergeometric distribution answers the question, "What is the probability of finding *x* characteristics in a sample?" Because a random sample is taken from an entire population, you cannot use binomial distribution. The equation for the hypergeometric distribution is:

$$P(X = x) = h(x, n, M, N) = \frac{\binom{M}{x}\binom{N-M}{n-x}}{\binom{N}{n}}$$

where

- $x = sample\_s$

- $n = number\_sample$

- $M = population\_s$

- $N = number\_population$

Use HYPGEOM.DIST() for problems with a finite population where each observation is either a success or a failure and where each subset of a given size is chosen with equal likelihood.

Example   A simple example for explaining the HYPGEOM.DIST() function is a game of luck. The HYPGEOM.DIST() function provides a simple method to calculate the chances of winning the lottery.

The following list defines the arguments for the lottery example:

- The *sample_s* argument is the number of successes in the sample. For example, a drawing can consist of up to six winning numbers. Therefore, *sample_s* = 6.

- The *number_sample* argument is the size of the sample. Therefore, *number_sample* = 6.

- The *population_s* argument is the number of possible successes in the population — the number of winning balls. Therefore, *population_s* = 6.

- The *number_population* argument is the size of the population: 49 balls. Therefore, *number_population* = 49.

- The *cumulative* argument is FALSE and indicates the logical value for the function.

What is the probability of having six winning numbers? Figure 12-77 shows the answer.

	B	C	D
	C7	f_x =HYPGEOM.DIST(C3,C4,C5,C6,FALSE)	
	B	C	D
3	Sample_S	6	
4	Number_Sample	6	
5	Population_S	6	
6	Number_Population	49	
7	Chance of winning	0.000007%	

Figure 12-77 HYPGEOM.DIST() calculates the probability of selecting six winning numbers.

The probability of winning big is miniscule. Of course, you can use the HYPGEOM.DIST() function to calculate the probability for five, four, or three numbers if you settle for smaller winnings. Figure 12-78 shows the result.

C7		*fx*	=HYPGEOM.DIST(C3,C4,C5,C6,FALSE)					
B	C	D	E	F	G	H	I
3 Sample_S	6	5	4	3	2	1	0
4 Number_Sample	6	6	6	6	6	6	6
5 Population_S	6	6	6	6	6	6	6
6 Number_Population	49	49	49	49	49	49	49
7 Chance of winning	0.000007%	0.0018%	0.10%	1.77%	13.24%	41.30%	43.60%

Figure 12-78 Calculating the probability of different characteristics.

See Also BINOM.DIST(), COMBIN(), FACT(), NEGBINOM.DIST(), PERMUT()

> **Sample Files**
>
> Use the HYPGEOMDIST or HYPGEOM.DIST worksheet in the Probability.xls or Probability.xlsx sample file. The sample files are found in the Chapter12 folder. For more information about the sample files, see the section titled "Using the Sample Files" on page xxiii.

INTERCEPT()

Syntax INTERCEPT(*known_y's,known_x's*)

Definition This function returns the intersection of the regression line (see Figure 12-124, in the discussion of the SLOPE() function).

The function calculates the point at which a line will intersect the y-axis by using existing x-values and y-values. The intercept point is based on the best-fit regression line drawn through the known x-values and known y-values.

Arguments

- *known_y's* **(required)** The dependent set of observations or data

- *known_x's* **(required)** The independent set of observations or data

> **Note**
>
> Arguments can be numbers, names, arrays, or references containing numbers. If an array or a reference argument contains text, logical values, or empty cells, those values are ignored. Note that cells with the value zero are included.

If *known_y's* and *known_x's* contain a different number of data points or no data points, the INTERCEPT() function returns the #N/A error value.

Background   Regression analysis is one of the most commonly used multivariate analysis methods. When single-regression is used, the relationship between dependent and independent variables is analyzed. Correlations must be determined in a linear function. The function finds a straight line between the two sets of values such that the sum of the squared deviations of values from this line is minimized.

This straight line is referred to as a *regression line* or *level* and provides information about statistical relations between variables and the proportionality factor. So the regression line determines the direction of the relation between the dependent and the independent variables. Furthermore, it shows the degree of the proportional changes in the dependent variable if the independent variable is increased or reduced by one unit.

The INTERCEPT() function calculates the y-axis intercept of the regression line—where the x-value is 0. This is the value *b* in the equation of the line:

$$y = mx + b$$

The equation can be rearranged to express the intercept *b* as:

$$b = y - mx$$

where the slope *m* is calculated as:

$$m = \frac{\sum(x - \bar{x})(y - \bar{y})}{\sum(x - \bar{x})^2}$$

In this equation, *x* and *y* are the average values of a sample AVERAGE(*X_values*) and AVERAGE(*Y_values*).

See Also You will find more information about regression analysis in the discussion of the LINEST() function.

Example   The INTERCEPT() function is easy to use. Assume that a software company wants to analyze its website traffic. The marketing department has imported the website visit and order data for January 2007 through June 2008 into an Excel table.

The company wants to investigate whether the number of orders placed is dependent upon the number of visits to the website. A graph of the data can be drawn and the intercept of the line of best fit calculated. The intercept defines the intersection of the regression line with the y-axis (orders) (see Figure 12-79).

Month	Web access	Orders
January 2007	236	6
February 2007	11593	17
March 2007	18491	456
April 2007	11743	544
May 2007	11452	349
June 2007	26651	854
July 2007	16287	427
August 2007	17750	337
September 2007	19985	899
October 2007	17285	1011
November 2007	30369	720
December 2007	19674	1069
January 2008	28464	1070
February 2008	25000	498
March 2008	24574	1401
April 2008	23141	1076
May 2008	17700	1563
June 2008	3702	1790
Axis intercept		524.0479792

Figure 12-79 Calculating the intercept of the regression line.

The orders (dependent y-values), website visits (independent x-values), and intercept (b) are illustrated in Figure 12-80.

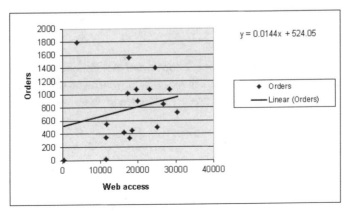

Figure 12-80 The regression line with the calculated intercept of 524.05.

If you plot the orders against the web visits in a scatter plot and then insert a linear trend line for the data points, the equation of the line of best fit will automatically provide the intercept with the value 524.05, the value that was calculated by the INTERCEPT() function.

> **Tip**
>
> To display the trend line equation, click Format Trend Line on the shortcut menu for the trend line, and select the Display Equation On Chart check box on the Options tab of the Format Trend Line dialog box.

See Also   FORECAST(), GROWTH(), LINEST(), LOGEST(), PEARSON(), RSQ(), SLOPE(), STEYX(), TREND()

> **Sample Files**
>
> Use the INTERCEPT worksheet in the Regression.xls or Regression.xlsx sample file. The sample files are found in the Chapter12 folder. For more information about the sample files, see the section titled "Using the Sample Files" on page xxiii.

KURT()

Syntax   KURT(*number1,number2,...*)

Definition   This function returns the kurtosis of a data set. The *kurtosis* characterizes the relative peakedness or flatness of a distribution compared with the normal distribution. A positive kurtosis indicates a relatively peaked distribution, and a negative kurtosis indicates a relatively flat distribution.

Arguments

- *number1* **(required) and** *number2* **(optional)**   At least one and up to 255 arguments (30 in Excel 2003 and earlier versions) for which you want to calculate the kurtosis. You can also use an array or a reference to an array instead of arguments separated by commas.

> **Note**
>
> Arguments can be numbers, names, arrays, or references containing numbers. If an array or a reference argument contains text, logical values, or empty cells, those values are ignored. However, cells with the value 0 are included.
>
> If there are fewer than four data points or the sample standard deviation is 0, KURT() returns the #DIV/0! error.

Background   The kurtosis indicates whether the distribution (curve) of observed values is peaked or flat compared with a normal distribution. A normal distribution has the kurtosis 0.

See Also You will find more information about normal distributions in the description of NORM.DIST().

The kurtosis indicates whether the empirical distribution is more peaked than the normal distribution. In this case, the kurtosis is positive. A kurtosis is defined as follows:

$$\left\{ \frac{n(n+1)}{(n-1)(n-2)(n-3)} \Sigma \left(\frac{x_i - \overline{x}}{s} \right)^4 \right\} - \frac{3(n-1)^2}{(n-2)(n-3)}$$

s is the standard deviation of the sample.

The kurtosis and the skewness characterize the form and the degree of symmetry of a distribution. Both calculations are important for finding the correct distribution to be used to further evaluate the data.

See Also You will find more information about skewness in the description of SKEW().

The kurtosis of a statistical distribution is defined as follows:

$$\frac{m_4(\mu)}{\sigma^4} - 3$$

$m_4(\mu)$ is the fourth central moment, and σ is the standard deviation. As already mentioned, the kurtosis describes the deviation of the given probability distribution compared with the normal distribution.

Example We will use the example of the software company to explain the KURT() function. The marketing department wants to evaluate the download area as well as the entire website and to calculate the kurtosis of the website clicks in the download area.

To illustrate the probability distribution compared to the normal distribution for the download area as well as for the entire website, you create charts (see Figures 12-81 and 12-82).

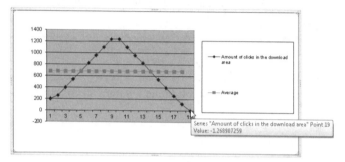

Figure 12-81 Calculating the kurtosis for the download area and the average clicks of the entire website.

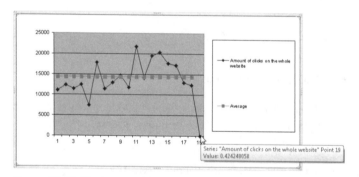

Figure 12-82 The kurtosis for the entire website.

Statements The negative kurtosis of –1.27 for the download area (as shown in Figure 12-81) indicates a relative flat distribution compared to the normal distribution. The values for the empirical distribution are dispersed further around the mean than for the normal distribution.

The positive kurtosis of 0.42 for the entire website indicates the relative peaked distribution compared to the normal distribution. The values for the empirical distribution are dispersed closer around the mean than for the normal distribution.

See Also SKEW(), STDEV(), STDEVP(), VAR(), VARP()

> ### Sample Files
>
> Use the KURTOSIS worksheet in the Symmetry.xls or Symmetry.xlsx sample file. The sample files are found in the Chapter12 folder. For more information about the sample files, see the section titled "Using the Sample Files" on page xxiii.

LARGE()

Syntax   LARGE(*array*,*k*)

Definition   This function returns the largest *k*-value in a data set. Use this function to select a value based on its relative size. For example, you can use LARGE() to calculate the top three sales in a table.

Arguments

- **array (required)** The array or range of data for which you want to determine the largest *k*-value

- **k (required)** The position of the element in the array or cell range to return

Background   The MIN() and MAX() functions find the smallest or largest value in a cell range, but if you need the second-largest or third-smallest value, use the LARGE() and SMALL() functions.

LARGE() returns the largest values, and SMALL() returns the smallest values from a range.

Note the following:

- If *array* is empty, LARGE() returns the #NUM! error value.

- If *k* is less than or equal to 0 or greater than the number of data points, the function returns the #NUM! error.

- If *n* is the number of data points in a range, then LARGE(*array*,1) returns the largest value and LARGE(*array*,*n*) returns the smallest value.

Examples

Simple Example   The following example explains the formula LARGE(*array*,*k*).

If cell range B1:B100 contains your values, LARGE(B1:B100;1) returns the largest value in the array.

> **Note**
>
> The following formula returns the sum of the largest, second-largest, and third-largest value:
>
> `=LARGE(B1:B100;1)+LARGE(B1:B100;2)+LARGE(B1:B100;3)`
>
> If you use an array formula, you can use a shorter formula:
>
> `=SUM(LARGE(B1:B100;{1,2,3}))`
>
> After you have entered an array formula, press Ctrl+Page Up+Enter. The formula is automatically enclosed in braces.
>
> Although the second formula is shorter than the formula containing the + operator, you have to enter the parameters for all values manually.

Software Company Example Assume that the software company has a table with the sales of the last two years and wants to know the three highest sales without having to sort the data. The LARGE() function finds and returns the three largest values, as shown in Figure 12-83.

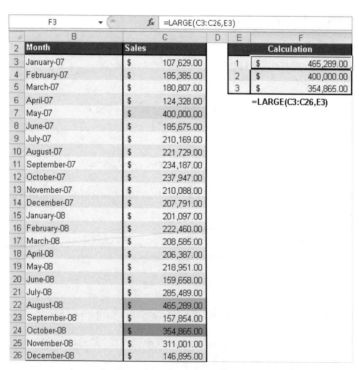

Figure 12-83 Finding the three largest values in a table.

INSIDE OUT   Use conditional formats for Excel 2007

If you use conditional formats together with the LARGE() function, you can highlight the values in color (see Figure 12-84).

Excel 2007 offers many new formats. Open the menu on the Conditional Formatting button and select a format.

Figure 12-84 Selecting one of the numerous formats.

The formats are applied according to the size of the values (see Figure 12-85).

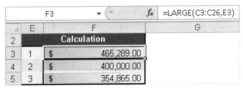

Figure 12-85 Formats as applied in Excel 2007.

See Also PERCENTILE(), PERCENTRANK(), QUARTILE(), SMALL()

Sample Files

Use the LARGE worksheet in the Count.xls or Count.xlsx sample file. The sample files are found in the Chapter12 folder. For more information about the sample files, see the section titled "Using the Sample Files" on page xxiii.

Chapter 12

LINEST()

Syntax LINEST(*known_y's,known_x's,const,stats*)

Definition This function calculates the statistics for a line using the smallest squares to calculate a straight line appropriate for the data and then returns an array describing a line. Because this function returns an array of values, it must be entered as an array formula.

The equation for the line is:

$$y = mx + b$$

or, if there are multiple ranges of x-values:

$$y = m1x1 + m2x2 + ... + b$$

The dependent y-values are a function of the independent x-values. The *m*-values are coefficients corresponding to each x-value, and *b* is a constant value. Note that *y*, *x*, and *m* can be vectors. The array that the LINEST() function returns is {mn,mn-1,...,m1,b}. LINEST() can also return additional regression statistics (see Table 12-2 later in this section).

Arguments

- **known_y's (required)** The y-values you already know from the relationship *y = mx + b*

  ○ If the *known_y's* array consists of a single column, then each column of the *known_x's* array is interpreted as a separate variable.

  ○ If the *known_y's* array consists of a single row, then each row of the *known_x's* array is interpreted as a separate variable.

- **known_x's (optional)** The x-values you already know from the relationship *y = mx + b*

  ○ The *known_x's* array can include one or more sets of variables. If only one variable is used, *known_y's* and *known_x's* can be ranges of any shape, as long as they have equal dimensions. If more than one variable is used, *known_y's* must be a vector (a range consisting of a single row or column).

  ○ If *known_x's* is not specified, it is assumed to be the array {1,2,3,...} containing the same number of elements as *known_y's*.

- **_const_ (optional)** A logical value specifying whether to force the constant _b_ to equal 0

    o   If _const_ is TRUE or omitted, _b_ is calculated normally.

    o   If _const_ is FALSE, then _b_ is set equal to 0 and the _m_-values are adjusted to $y = m$.

- **_stats_ (optional)** A logical value specifying whether to return additional regression statistics

    o   If _stats_ is TRUE, the LINEST() function returns the additional regression statistics and the returned array is: `{mn;mn-1;...;m1;b.sen;sen-1;...;se1;seb.r2; sey.F;df.ssreg;ssresid}`.

    o   If _stats_ is FALSE or not specified, the LINEST() function returns only the _m_-coefficients and the constant _b_.

Table 12-2 describes the additional regression statistics.

Table 12-2 Overview of the Regression Statistics

Statistic	Description
se1,se2,...,sen	The standard error values for the coefficients _m1,m2,...,mn_.
seb	The standard error value for constant _b_ (se_b = #N/A when _const_ is FALSE).
_r2_	The coefficient of determination. Compares calculated and actual y-values and ranges in value from 0 to 1. If this coefficient is 1, there is a perfect correlation in the sample; there is no difference between the calculated y-value and the actual y-value. At the other extreme, if the coefficient of determination is 0, the regression equation is not helpful in predicting a y-value. You will find more information about the calculation of y^2 in the description of RSQ().
sey	The standard error for the estimated y-value.
_F_	The f-statistic (or the calculated f-value). Use the f-statistic to determine whether the observed relation between the dependent and independent variables occurs by chance.
_df_	The degrees of freedom. Use the degrees of freedom to find critical f-values in a statistical table. Compare the values you find in the table to the f-statistic returned by LINEST() to determine a confidence level for the model.
ssreg	The regression sum of squares.
ssresid	The residual sum of squares.

Chapter 12

> **Note**
>
> You can describe any straight line with the slope and the y-intercept:
>
> - **Slope (*m*):** To find the slope of a line (often written as *m*), take two points on the line, (*x1,y1*) and (*x2,y2*); the slope is equal to (*y2 – y1*)/(*x2 – x1*).
>
> - ***y*-intercept (*b*):** The y-intercept of a line (often written as *b*) is the value of *y* at the point where the line crosses the y-axis.
>
> You will find more information about slopes and intercepts in the descriptions of SLOPE() and INTERCEPT().

The equation for a straight line is $y = mx + b$. When you know the values of *m* and *b*, you can calculate any point on the line by inserting the y-value or x-value into the equation. You can also use the TREND() function.

Background   The correlation examines whether the variables are interrelated and expresses this interrelation with a single number. The regression analysis compares the dependent variables (for instance, the online orders in the software company example) with the independent variables (the website visits).

A regression analysis is used to explain a characteristic with one characteristic (dependent variable) with one or more other characteristics (independent variables). It is assumed that the dependent variable is increased or decreased according to the independent variable. Therefore, it determines a one-tailed dependency. You have to specify which of the two variables is dependent or independent.

If only one independent x-variable exists, you can calculate the slope and the y-intercept with the following formula:

- Slope: =INDEX(LINEST(*known_y's;known_x's*);1)

- *y* intercept: =INDEX(LINEST(*known_y's;known_x's*);2)

The accuracy of a line calculated with LINEST() depends on the data variance. The more linear the data, the more accurate is the model calculated by LINEST(). LINEST() uses the smallest squares to calculate the best fit for the data. If only one independent x-variable exists, calculate *m* and *b* with the following formula:

$$m = \frac{\sum \left(x - \overline{x}\right)\left(y - \overline{y}\right)}{\sqrt{\sum \left(x - \overline{x}\right)^2}}$$

The values x and y are the sample means: x = AVERAGE(*known_x's*) and y = AVERAGE(*known_y's*).

The regression functions LINEST() (linear regression) and LOGEST() (exponential regression) calculate the coefficient for the optimal line based on the given data. However, you have to decide which of the two results is a better fit for your data.

In a regression analysis, Excel calculates the square of the difference for each point between the y-value of a point and the actual y-value. The sum of the squared differences is called a *residual sum of squares (ssresid)*. Then Excel calculates the total sum of the squares (*sstotal*). If *const* = TRUE or not specified, the total sum of the squares equals the sum of the squared differences between the actual y-values and the average of the y-values. If *const* = FALSE, the total sum of the squares equals the sum of the squares of the actual y-values.

The regression sum of squares (*ssreg*) is calculated as follows:

ssreg = *sstotal* – *ssresid*

The smaller the residual sum of squares is in relation to the total sum of the deviation squares, the greater is the value of the coefficient of determination (r^2) that indicates how well the relation between the variables is defined by the equation resulting from the regression analysis.

$$r^2 = \frac{SS_{reg}}{SS_{total}}$$

Sometimes one or more x columns (assuming that the x-values and y-values are specified in columns) aren't useful for calculating the estimated values together with the other x columns. In other words, if you exclude these x columns, the y-values are still accurate.

In this case, you should remove the redundant x columns from the regression model. This phenomenon is called *collinearity* because each redundant x column can be defined as the sum of the multiple of the nonredundant x columns. LINEST() checks for collinearity and excludes all redundant x columns from the regression model.

In the output of the LINEST() function, the coefficient and the *se*-values of an excluded x column equal 0. The exclusion of one or more columns impacts the *df* because the *df* depends on the number of x columns used to calculate the estimated values. If the value of *df* changes because redundant x columns are removed, the values of *sey* and *f* are also impacted. Collinearity does not occur very often.

If no x column is excluded, the *df* is calculated as follows: If k columns exist and *const* = TRUE or not specified:

$$df = n - k - 1$$

If *const* = FALSE:

$$df = n - k$$

In both cases, for each *x* column that is excluded, the *df* is increased by 1.

If you specify an array constant (such as *values_x*) as an argument, you have to divide the values in a row with colons and the rows with commas.

> **Tip**
> Note that if you use a regression equation, the predicted y-values may be invalid because they reside outside of the y-value range you used for the equation.

Example A software company sells all its products through its website. The company regularly sends out newsletters to inform existing and potential customers about new and updated products and to draw attention to its website.

Last year, the orders through the website significantly increased. The management wants to know the reason. Is the increase in sales attributable to marketing or advertising? Did the increased website visits cause the increase in sales? This means that the company wants to know the correlation between the website visits and the online orders. The website manager has given you information about the users and their activities. The marketing department is asked to perform an analysis and creates an Excel list to compare the website visits and the online orders of the past 18 months. The marketing department performs a regression analysis by using the LINEST() function (see Figure 12-86).

	B	C	D
3	Month	Web access	Orders
4	January 2007	236	98
5	February 2007	11593	8000
6	March 2007	18491	6000
7	April 2007	11743	8587
8	May 2007	11452	7985
9	June 2007	26651	18968
10	July 2007	16287	9753
11	August 2007	17750	7857
12	September 2007	19985	13986
13	October 2007	17285	6875
14	November 2007	30369	22765
15	December 2007	19674	9465
16	January 2008	28464	19875
17	February 2008	25000	15987
18	March 2008	24574	9653
19	April 2008	23141	12986
20	May 2008	17700	8543
21	June 2008	3702	1654
22	Gradient		0.660130798

Figure 12-86 Comparing the website visits with the online orders.

Figure 12-87 shows how the LINEST() function returns the results.

	B		C	D	E
33	b		m_1	0.660130798	-1383.85617
34	se_b		se_1	0.083627684	1642.68237
35	R^2		se_y	0.795684605	2785.72374
36	F		d_f	62.31030061	16
37	ss_{reg}		ss_{resid}	483543930.9	124164108

Figure 12-87 Regression analysis using the LINEST() function.

CAUTION

Formulas that return an array as a result have to be entered as array formulas. Because LINEST() can calculate all 10 regression values simultaneously and returns an array, the formula or the arguments have to be entered in a certain way.

Select the cell range D39:E43 and then enter the arguments for LINEST() in cell D39. After you are finished, press the F2 key and Ctrl+Page Up+Enter.

See Also GROWTH(), LOGEST(), TREND()

Sample Files

Use the LINEST worksheet in the Regression.xls or Regression.xlsx sample file. The sample files are found in the Chapter12 folder. For more information about the sample files, see the section titled "Using the Sample Files" on page xxiii.

LOGEST()

Syntax   LOGEST(*known_y's,known_x's,const,stats*)

Definition   This function calculates the exponential curve in regression analyses and returns a value array describing this curve. Because this function returns an array of values, it must be entered as an array formula.

Arguments

- ***known_y's* (required)** The y-values you already know from the relationship $y = b * m^x$

    ○ If the *known_y's* array consists of a single column, then each column in the *known_x's* array is interpreted as a separate variable.

    ○ If the *known_y's* array consists of a single row, then each row in the *known_x's* array is interpreted as a separate variable.

- ***known_x's* (optional)** The x-values you already know from the relationship $y = b * m^x$

    ○ The *known_x's* array can include one or more sets of variables. If only one variable is used, *known_y's* and *known_x's* can be ranges of any shape as long as they have equal dimensions. If more than one variable is used, *known_y's* must be a range of cells consisting of a single row or column (which is also known as a *vector*).

    ○ If *known_x's* is not specified, it is assumed to be the array {1,2,3,...} containing the same number of elements as *known_y's*.

- ***const* (optional)** A logical value specifying whether to force the constant *b* to equal 1

    ○ If *const* is TRUE or omitted, *b* is calculated normally.

    ○ If *const* is FALSE, *b* is set equal to 1 and the *m*-values are adjusted so that $y = m^x$.

- ***stats* (optional)** A logical value specifying whether to return additional regression statistics

    ○ If *stats* is TRUE, the LOGEST() function returns the additional regression statistics and the returned array is:

    `{mn.mn-1. ... .m1.b;sen.sen-1. ... .se1.seb;r 2.sey;F.df.ssreg.ssresid}`

    ○ If *stats* is FALSE or not specified, the LOGEST() function returns only the *m*-coefficients and the constant *b*.

See Also You will find more information about regression statistics in the description of LINEST().

Background Unlike the LINEST() function, the LOGEST() function describes the dependent y-values and the independent x-values by calculating a exponential curve with the following common formula:

$$y = b \times m^x$$

where *y* and *x* can be vectors:

$$y = \left(b \times \left(m_1^{x^1}\right) \times \left(m_2^{x^2}\right) \times \left(m_n^{x^n}\right)\right)$$

Each basis has an associated exponent *x*. This means that the references or values must have the same number of elements.

Like the LINEST() function, LOGEST() returns an array that describes the relation between the values. The difference is that the LOGEST() function adjusts the data to an exponential curve whereas LINEST() uses a straight line.

If only one independent *x*-variable exists, you can calculate the slope *m* and the *y*-intercept with the following formulas:

- Slope *m*: =INDEX(LOGEST(*known_y's;known_x's*);1)

- *y*-intercept *b*: =INDEX(LOGEST(*known_y's;known_x's*);2)

Use the equation $y = b*m^x$ to estimate future y-values. To estimate the values, you can also use the GROWTH() function.

If you specify an array constant (such as *values_x*) as an argument, you have to divide the values in a row with colons, and the rows with commas.

> **Tip**
> Note that if you use a regression equation, the predicted y-values may be invalid because they reside outside of the y-value range you used for the equation.

Example To explain how the regression values are calculated, use the example for the LINEST() function. Last year the orders through the company website significantly increased. The management wants to know the reason. Is the increase in sales attributable to market-ing or advertising? Did the increased website visits cause the increase in sales? This means that the company wants to know the correlation between the website visits and the online orders.

The marketing department is asked to perform an analysis and creates an Excel list to com-pare the website visits and the online orders of the past 18 months. The marketing depart-ment performs a regression analysis using the LOGEST() function (see Figure 12-88).

	B	C	D
3	**Month**	**Web access**	**Orders**
4	January 2007	236	485
5	February 2007	11593	5948
6	March 2007	18491	6000
7	April 2007	11743	7465
8	May 2007	11452	8364
9	June 2007	26651	9486
10	July 2007	16287	10837
11	August 2007	17750	11937
12	September 2007	19985	12847
13	October 2007	17285	13857
14	November 2007	30369	14827
15	December 2007	19674	15736
16	January 2008	28464	16837
17	February 2008	25000	17483
18	March 2008	24574	18938
19	April 2008	23141	19524
20	May 2008	17700	20492
21	June 2008	3702	21938

Figure 12-88 Comparing the website visits with the online orders.

A chart illustrates the orders compared to the website visits, as shown in Figure 12-89.

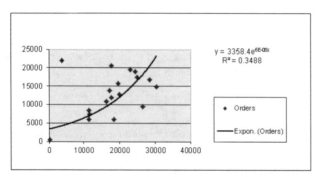

Figure 12-89 Orders as an exponential trend line.

As you can see in Figure 12-89, the online orders show an exponential growth depending on the website visits. Therefore, it can be assumed that the orders increase depending on the website visits.

In this case, use the LOGEST() function to calculate the regression values. This function returns the results shown in Figure 12-90.

	B	C	D	E
25	**b**	**m_1**	1.00006366	3358.432538
26	**se_b**	**se_1**	2.17467E-05	0.427166435
27	**R^2**	**se_y**	0.348768458	0.724405218
28	**F**	**d_f**	8.568834519	16
29	**ss_{reg}**	**ss_{resid}**	4.496606619	8.396206712

Figure 12-90 The results of the exponential regression analysis.

CAUTION

Formulas that return an array as a result have to be entered as array formulas. Because LOGEST() can calculate all 10 regression values simultaneously and returns an array, the formula or the arguments have to be entered in a certain way.

Select the cell range D31:E43 and then enter the arguments for LOGEST() in cell D31. After you are finished, press the F2 key and Ctrl+Page Up+Enter.

See Also   FORECAST(), GROWTH(), LINEST(), TREND()

Sample Files

Use the LOGEST worksheet in the Regression.xls or Regression.xlsx sample file. The sample files are found in the Chapter12 folder. For more information about the sample files, see the section titled "Using the Sample Files" on page xxiii.

LOGNORM.DIST()/LOGNORMDIST()

Syntax   LOGNORM.DIST(*x,mean,standard_dev,cumulative*)

Definition   This function returns the values of the distribution function of a lognormal distributed random variable where ln(*x*) is normally distributed with the parameters *mean* and *standard_dev*. Use this function to analyze data that has been logarithmically transformed.

Arguments

- ***x* (required)** The value at which to evaluate the function

- ***mean* (required)** The mean of the lognormal distribution

- ***standard_dev* (required)** The standard deviation of the lognormal distribution

- ***cumulative* (required)** The logical value that represents the type of the function

> ### Note
>
> If one of the arguments isn't a numeric expression, the **LOGNORM.DIST()** function returns the #VALUE! error.
>
> If *x* is less than or equal to 0, or *standard_dev* is greater than or equal to 0, the **LOG-NORM.DIST()** function returns the #NUM! error.

Background The LOGNORM.DIST() function returns the probabilities of a logarithmically normal distributed random variable. Use this function to evaluate probability distributions where the natural logarithm instead of the random variable is normal distributed.

The lognormal distribution is similar to the normal distribution but has a logarithm in the exponent. The lognormal distribution is right skewed (see Figure 12-72 later in this section). If a random variable is lognormal distributed, its logarithm is also normal distributed. For example, incomes are often lognormal distributed. The reason for this is the usual percentage increase. Large incomes increase a lot, and smaller incomes increase only a little. Over time, the small incomes remain small, and the large incomes become bigger. Therefore, the distribution is right skewed. The logarithmic function transforms the multiplicative structure into an additive structure. Then the logarithmized values are normal distributed.

Another reason for the lognormal distributed income structure is the lack of high-salaried jobs. The salary for the majority of jobs is small, but extremely low incomes are less common. Most lognormal distributions are based on this fact.

The lognormal distribution with the μ and σ2 parameters for positive real numbers is defined by the following probability density:

$$f(x) = \frac{1}{\sigma\sqrt{2\pi}}\frac{1}{x}e^{-\frac{(\ln(x)-\mu)^2}{2\sigma^2}}$$

Figure 12-91 shows the probability density of the lognormal distribution.

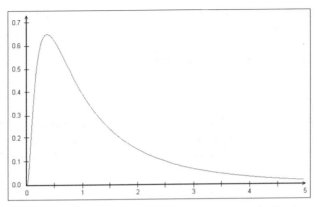

Figure 12-91 Probability density of the lognormal distribution with μ = 0 and σ = 1.

The equation for the distribution function of a lognormal distribution is:

$$LOGNORM.DIST(x, \mu, \sigma) = NORM.DIST\left(\frac{\ln(x) - \mu}{\sigma}\right)$$

Example   Use the following values to calculate LOGNORM.DIST():

- 4 = the value at which to evaluate the function (*x*)

- 3.5 = the mean of ln(*x*) (*mean*)

- 1.2 = the standard deviation of ln(*x*) (*standard_dev*)

- TRUE = the logical value that represents the type of the function

Figure 12-92 shows the calculation of LOGNORM.DIST().

	E7		f_x	=LOGNORM.DIST(E3,E4,E5,TRUE)	
	B	C	D	E	F
1	**Calculation of LOGNORM.DIST()**				
2	Meaning			**Parameter**	
3	Value for which the function should be analyzed			4	
4	Mean of ln(x)			3.5	
5	Standard deviation of ln(x)			1.2	
6	Cumulative			TRUE	
7	**LOGNORM.DIST()**			0.039083556	

Figure 12-92 Calculating LOGNORM.DIST().

Chapter 12

The LOGNORM.DIST() function returns the cumulative lognormal distribution of 0.039084 based on the parameters shown in Figure 12-72.

See Also EXP(), LN(), LOG(), LOG10(), LOGNORM.INV()

Sample Files

Use the LOGNORMDIST or LOGNORM.DIST worksheet in the Probability.xls or Probability.xlsx sample file. The sample files are found in the Chapter12 folder. For more information about the sample files, see the section titled "Using the Sample Files" on page xxiii.

LOGNORM.INV()/LOGINV()

Syntax LOGNORM.INV(*probability,mean,standard_dev*)

Definition This function returns the quantile of the lognormal distribution of *x*, where ln(*x*) is normally distributed with the parameters *mean* and *standard_dev*. If p = LOGNORM.DIST(*x*,...) then LOGNORN.INV(*p*,...) = *x*. If the probability is *p*, you can calculate the quantile of the lognormal distribution.

Use the lognormal distribution to analyze logarithmically transformed data.

Arguments

- ***probability* (required)** A probability associated with the lognormal distribution

- ***mean* (required)** The mean of the lognormal distribution

- ***standard_dev* (required)** The standard deviation of the lognormal distribution

---

Note

If one of the arguments isn't a numeric expression, the LOGNORM.INV() function returns the #VALUE! error.

If *probability* is less than 0 or greater than 1, the LOGNORM.INV() function returns the #NUM! error.

If *standard_dev* is less than or equal to 0, the function returns the #NUM! error.

Background   The inverse of the lognormal distribution function is:

$$LOGNORM.INV\left(p,\mu,\sigma\right)=e^{\left[\mu+\sigma x\left(NORM.INV\left(p\right)\right)\right]}$$

See Also You will find more information about lognormal distributions in the description of LOGNORM.DIST().

Example   Use the following values to calculate LOGNORM.INV():

- 0.039084 = the probability associated with the lognormal distribution (*probability*)

- 3.5 = the mean of ln(x) (*mean*)

- 1.2 = the standard deviation of ln(x) (*standard_dev*)

Figure 12-93 shows the calculation of LOGNORM.INV().

	E6			fx	=LOGNORM.INV(E3,E4,E5)	
	B	C	D		E	F
1	Calculation of LOGNORM.INV()					
2	Meaning				Parameter	
3	Probability of lognormal distribution				0.039084	
4	Mean of ln(x)				3.5	
5	standard deviation of ln(x)				1.2	
6	LOGNORM.INV()				4.000025	

Figure 12-93 Calculating LOGNORM.INV().

The LOGNORM.INV() function returns the quantile 4.000025 of the lognormal distribution based on the parameters shown in Figure 12-93.

See Also EXP(), LN(), LOG(), LOG10(), LOGNORM.DIST()

Sample Files

Use the LOGINV or LOGNORM.INV worksheet in the Probability.xls or Probability.xlsx sample file. The sample files are found in the Chapter12 folder. For more information about the sample files, see the section titled "Using the Sample Files" on page xxiii.

MAX()

Syntax MAX(*number1,number2,...*)

Definition This function returns the largest value in an argument list.

Arguments

- **number1 (required) and number2 (optional)** At least one and up to 255 arguments (30 in Excel 2003 and earlier versions) for which you want to find the maximum value

Background Use the MIN() and MAX() functions to find the smallest or largest value in a data set.

Arguments can be numbers, empty cells, logical values, and numbers as text. Arguments that are error values or text that cannot be converted into numbers cause errors.

If an argument is an array or a reference, only numbers in that array or reference are used. Empty cells, logical values, or text in the array or reference are ignored. If you want to include logical values and text representations of numbers, use the MAXA() or MINA() function.

If the arguments contain no numbers, MAX() and MIN() return 0.

Example You are the head of accounting and want to display the highest value in a table containing the sales of the past two years. The MAX() function returns the highest value from an unsorted data set, as shown in Figure 12-94.

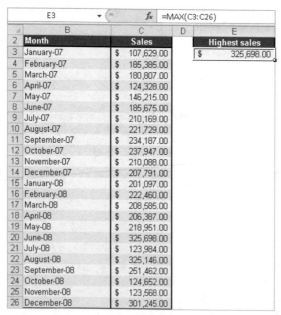

Figure 12-94 The MAX() function finds the highest value in a table.

> **Tip**
> To display the corresponding month, use conditional formats or the MATCH() and INDEX() functions.

See Also DMAX(), MAXA(), MIN(), MINA()

> **Sample Files**
> Use the MAX&MIN worksheet in the Count.xls or Count.xlsx sample file. The sample files are found in the Chapter12 folder. For more information about the sample files, see the section titled "Using the Sample Files" on page xxiii.

MAXA()

Syntax　MAXA(*value1,value2,...*)

Definition　This function returns the largest value in an argument list. Not only numbers but also text and logical values (TRUE and FALSE) are compared.

Arguments

- *value1* **(required)** and *value2* **(optional)** At least one and up to 255 arguments (30 in Excel 2003 and earlier versions) for which you want to find the largest value

Background　In a table containing not only number values but also text and logical values, you can calculate the greatest and smallest value with the MAXA() or MINA() function.

The arguments for MAXA() and MINA() can be numbers, empty cells, logical values, and text representations of numbers. Incorrect values in the arguments cause errors. If an argument is an array or a reference, this range uses only numbers. Empty cells and text representations of numbers are ignored.

Logical values are evaluated as follows:

- TRUE = 1

- FALSE = 0 (including arguments containing text)

If the arguments contain no values, MAXA() and MINA() return 0.

> **Note**
> If you want to exclude logical values and text, use the MAX() or MIN() function.

Example To show how MAXA() evaluates logical values (TRUE or FALSE) to 0 or 1, we used numbers between 0 and 1 in the example table (see Figure 12-95).

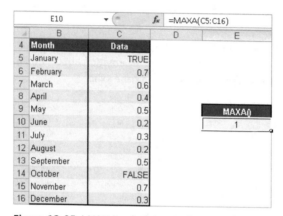

	E10		▼	f_x	=MAXA(C5:C16)	
	B	C		D	E	
4	**Month**	**Data**				
5	January	TRUE				
6	February	0.7				
7	March	0.6				
8	April	0.4				
9	May	0.5			**MAXA()**	
10	June	0.2			1	
11	July	0.3				
12	August	0.2				
13	September	0.5				
14	October	FALSE				
15	November	0.7				
16	December	0.3				

Figure 12-95 MAXA() calculates the largest value in a data set containing text and logical values.

MAXA() returns 1 because the largest value is the logical value TRUE.

See Also DMAX(), MINA()

> **Sample Files**
> Use the MAXA&MINA worksheet in the Count.xls or Count.xlsx sample file. The sample files are found in the Chapter12 folder. For more information about the sample files, see the section titled "Using the Sample Files" on page xxiii.

MEDIAN()

Syntax MEDIAN(*number1,number2,...*)

Definition The *median* is the number in the middle of a set of numbers. This means that half of the numbers have values that are greater than the median, and half of the numbers have values that are smaller than the median. Therefore, the number of the median within a sorted data set equals half of the elements.

Arguments

- ***number1* (required) and *number2* (optional)** At least one and up to 255 arguments (30 in Excel 2003 and earlier versions) for which you want to calculate the median.

> **Note**
>
> Arguments can be numbers, names, arrays, or references containing numbers. All numbers associated with a reference or array argument are evaluated. If an array or reference argument contains text, logical values, or empty cells, those values are ignored. However, cells with the value 0 are included.
>
> If there is an even number of values in the data set, MEDIAN() calculates the mean of the two numbers in the middle.

Background   The median is the mean value in a data set.

If there is an odd number of values in the data set, the median is an observed value. If there is an even number of values in the data set, the MEDIAN() function calculates the average of the two numbers in the middle.

If the data set contains classified values, the median is in the class in which the sum function exceeds 0.5. In this case, the median has to be estimated or calculated with a linear interpolation. To calculate the median, the ordinal scale is required and the observed values have to be sorted by size.

Although the median is easy to understand, it is not as common as the arithmetic mean or the mode. The formula for the median is:

$$\bar{x} = x_{j-1} + \frac{b_j}{n_j}\left(\frac{n}{2} - N_{j-1}\right)$$

Contrary to the mean, the median doesn't depend on outliers. For example, you can use the median to calculate the average duration of study without taking career students and other outliers into account.

The median is especially useful when marginal values are of little importance or might lead to false interpretations when using the arithmetic mean. The median also returns a better result than the average if there is a low number of characteristics to be evaluated.

Another feature of the median is its low sensitivity. You can replace values in the given data set with other values without affecting the median.

Chapter 12

You can calculate the common median of two statistical distributions by combining the medians of both data sets. You have to merge the data sets, sort the data sets, and recalculate the median.

A generalization of the median is the quantile. The median divides the distribution in half, and the *quantile* divides the distribution in several equal parts. Most common is the quartile (four parts). As for the median, the ordinal scale is required, and the observed values have to be sorted by size.

Example   Suppose you are the manager of the software company's marketing department and you want to evaluate the website for the past year. The evaluation includes all clicks in all website areas. Now you want to calculate the median to get the mean value in this data set for the website visits in the past twelve months.

This example calculates the median from the two mean values in the data sets, because the number of elements is even (see Figure 12-96).

	B	C	D	E	F	G	H	I
		Events	Publications	Team	Training	Know-how	Overall result	Average
4 January		22	2	19	19	43	105	21
5 Febuary		1,170	356	505	1,319	3,000	6,350	1,270
6 March		1,545	756	1,307	2,233	6,116	11,957	2,391
7 April		1,168	518	884	1,903	2,860	7,333	1,467
8 May		1,139	684	835	1,589	3,126	7,373	1,475
9 June		5,083	1,678	820	2,428	6,682	16,691	3,338
10 July		3,609	844	276	1,559	3,311	9,599	1,920
11 August		4,810	622	365	1,502	3,317	10,616	2,123
12 September		5,581	893	309	1,628	3,542	11,953	2,391
13 October		5,506	724	259	1,440	2,971	10,900	2,180
14 November		11,786	1,046	447	2,255	4,735	20,269	4,054
15 December		6,227	339	234	1,583	2,652	11,035	2,207
16 Median		4,210	704	406	1,586	3,219	10,758	2,152
17 Average		3,971	705	522	1,622	3,530	1,622	2,070
18 Total Median			1380	1609				

Cell D18: fx =MEDIAN(C4:G15)

Figure 12-96 Calculating the median and the mean for the website visits.

If you sort the events, you can see that the means are July (3,609) and August (4,810). These two values are added by the MEDIAN() function and divided by 2. The result is a median of 4,210. If the example included a 13th month, the median would be the seventh value in the sorted data set.

> **Note**
> The comparison with the mean value shows that the outliers in January and November are of no consequence.

See Also   AVERAGE(), AVERAGEIF(), AVERAGEIFS(), COUNT(), COUNTA(), DAVERAGE(), MODE.SNGL(), SUM()

MIN()

Syntax MIN(*number1,number2,...*)

Definition This function returns the smallest value in an argument list.

Arguments

- *number1* **(required)** and *number2* **(optional)** At least one and up to 255 arguments (30 in Excel 2003 and earlier versions) for which you want to find the minimum value

Background The MIN() and MAX() functions as well as the arguments were already explained in detail in the description of MAX().

Tip Calculate the smallest value using a condition

When calculating the smallest value, the value 0 often has to be excluded.

To calculate the smallest value using a condition, use the following formula:

```
=MIN(IF(array<>0;array;""))
```

Enter this formula as an array formula by pressing Ctrl+Page up+Enter.

Example The software company wants to find the smallest number of sales in a given period in a sales table. MIN() returns $107,629 for January from the unsorted data set (see Figure 12-97).

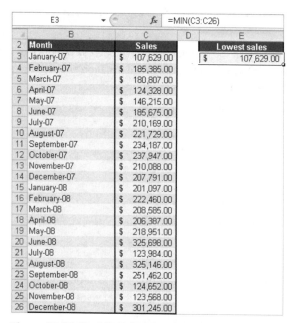

Figure 12-97 The MIN() function finds the smallest value in a table.

See Also DMIN(), MAX(), MAXA(), MINA()

Sample Files

Use the MAX&MIN worksheet in the Count.xls or Count.xlsx sample file. The sample files are found in the Chapter12 folder. For more information about the sample files, see the section titled "Using the Sample Files" on page xxiii.

MINA()

Syntax   MINA(*value1,value2,...*)

Definition   This function returns the smallest value in an argument list. Not only numbers but also text and logical values (TRUE and FALSE) are compared.

Arguments

- ***value1*** **(required) and** ***value2*** **(optional)** At least one and up to 255 arguments (30 in Excel 2003 and earlier versions) for which you want to find the smallest value

Background   The MINA() and MAXA() functions as well as their arguments were already explained in detail in the description of MAXA().

Example   Using the same example as for MAXA(), the MINA() function returns 0 because the smallest value is the logical value FALSE (see Figure 12-98).

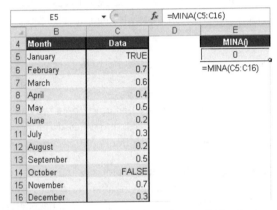

Figure 12-98 MINA() calculates the smallest value in a data set containing text and logical values.

See Also DMIN(), MAXA()

Sample Files

Use the MAXA&MINA worksheet in the Count.xls or Count.xlsx sample file. The sample files are found in the Chapter12 folder. For more information about the sample files, see the section titled "Using the Sample Files" on page xxiii.

MODE.SNGL()/MODE()

Syntax   MODE.SNGL(*number1,number2,...*)

Definition   This function returns the most frequent value of a data group. The result of the function is the characteristic that most often occurs in a data set.

Arguments

- **number1 (required) and number2 (optional)** At least one and up to 255 arguments (30 in Excel 2003 and earlier) for which you want to calculate the mode. You can also use an array or a reference to an array instead of arguments separated by commas.

Background   The MODE.SNGL() function returns the most frequently occurring or repetitive value in an array.

Assume that two ranges contain certain data where half of the data has a low value and the other half has a high value. In this case, the AVERAGE() and MEDIAN() functions return the mean value, whereas MODE.SNGL() returns the most frequently occurring value.

Example   You are the sales manager of the software company and want to evaluate the number of visits your sales representatives made in different regions numbered 1 through 5: Texas, Virginia, California, Oregon, and Washington. You have already created a table (see Figure 12-99).

	C12		f_x	=MODE.SNGL(C5:G10)		
	B	C	D	E	F	G
3	Number of visits of sales representative					
4		Region 1	Region 2	Region 3	Region 4	Region 5
5	Monday	4	3	6	4	4
6	Tuesday	7	3	4	4	3
7	Wednesday	2	2	4	6	7
8	Thursday	4	4	4	4	5
9	Friday	1	1	4	7	8
10	Saturday	2	3	4	6	6
11						
12		4		=MODE.SNGL(C5:G10)		
13		12		=COUNTIF(C5:G10,C12)		

Figure 12-99 Calculating the mode from a data list.

You want to know how many visits were usually necessary before a contract was signed. For this you use the MODE.SNGL() function.

Most of the time, it took four visits to get to the point where the customer signed the con-tract. If you nest the COUNTIF() and MODE.SNGL() functions, you can also count the num-ber of modes in the range.

You can format the cells that contain a mode by using conditional formats. In Excel 2003, select range C5:G10 and then select Format/Conditional Formatting; in Excel 2007 or Excel 2010, click the Conditional Formatting button in the Styles group on the Home tab (see Figure 12-100).

Figure 12-100 Conditional formatting in Excel 2007 and Excel 2010.

Select Formula Is For Condition 1, and enter the formula =MODE.SNGL($C$5:$G$10)=C5. Note that absolute and relative references are mixed. Click the Format button, select a color, and click OK. The modes in the range are displayed in the selected color.

See Also   AVERAGEA(), AVERAGEIF(), AVERAGEIFS(), GEOMEAN(), HARMEAN(), MEDIAN(), TRIMMEAN()

> ## Sample Files
> Use the MODE or MODE.SNGL worksheet in the Average.xls or Average.xlsx sample file. The sample files are found in the Chapter12 folder. For more information about the sample files, see the section titled "Using the Sample Files" on page xxiii.

MODE.MULT()

Syntax   MODE.MULT(*number1,number2,...*)

Definition   The MODEMULT() function is new in Excel 2010 and returns a vertical array of the most frequent or repeated values in an array or a data range. Use the function TRANSPOSE(MODE.MULT(*number1,number2,...*)) for a horizontal array.

If there are multiple mode values, the function returns several results. Because this function returns an array of values, it must be entered as an array formula.

Arguments

- **number1 (required)** The first numeric argument for which you want to calculate the mode.

- **number2 (optional)** At least two and up to 254 arguments (30 in Excel 2003 and earlier versions) for which you want to calculate the mode. You can also use an array or a reference to an array instead of arguments separated by commas.

> **Note**
>
> Arguments can be numbers, names, arrays, or references containing numbers. If an array or a reference argument contains text, logical values, or empty cells, those values are ignored. However, cells with the value 0 are included.
>
> Arguments that are error values or text that cannot be converted into numbers cause errors.
>
> If the data set contains no duplicate data points, MODE.MULT() returns the #N/A error.

Background   For more information about the mode, see the description of MODE.SNGL().

Example   Compare the example for the MODE.SNGL() function.

See Also   AVERAGEA(), AVERAGEIF(), AVERAGEIFS(), GEOMEAN(), HARMEAN(), MEDIAN(), TRIMMEAN()

> **Sample Files**
>
> Use the MODE.MULT worksheet in the Average.xlsx sample file. The sample files are found in the Chapter12 folder. For more information about the sample files, see the section titled "Using the Sample Files" on page xxiii.

NEGBINOM.DIST()/NEGBINOMDIST()

Syntax   NEGBINOM.DIST(*number_f,number_s,probability_s*)

Definition   This function returns the probabilities of a negative binomial distributed random variable. NEGBINOM.DIST() calculates the probability that there will be *number_f* failures before the last *number_s* when the constant probability of a success is *probability_s*.

Arguments

- *number_f* **(required)** The number of failures

- *number_s* **(required)** The number of successes

- *probability_s* **(required)** The probability of a success

> **Note**
>
> *Number_f* and *number_s* are truncated to integers. If one of the arguments isn't a numeric expression, the NEGBINOM.DIST() function returns the #VALUE! error.
>
> If *probability_s* is less than 0 or greater than 1, the NEGBINOM.DIST() function returns the #NUM! error.
>
> If *number_f* is less than 0 or *number_s* is less than 1, the NEGBINOM.DIST() function returns the #NUM! error.

Background   This function is similar to the binomial distribution except that the number of successes is fixed and the number of trials is variable. This is called a *negative binomial distribution*. As with the binomial distribution, trials are assumed to be independent.

See Also You will find more information about binomial distributions in the description of BINOM.DIST().

In a random experiment with independent repetitions and only two possible results (success or failure), the negative binomial distribution (or *Pascal distribution*) returns the probability of a fixed number of failures before the *x*-th success. The equation for a negative binomial distribution is

$$nb(x,r,p) = \binom{x+r-1}{r-1} p(1-p)^x$$

where

- x equals *number_f*

- r equals *number_s*

- p equals *probability_s*

Example You are on vacation in a foreign city and ask a passerby for directions. This question can be answered only with *yes* or *no*. This means that there is a probability of 50 percent that the answer is *yes*. Therefore, *p* is 0.5.

After you have asked a few people and nobody can tell you the way, you buy a map. Now you want to know the probability that you will find five people who know the way or how many "No, I'm sorry" responses you will get before you meet five people who do know the way. You calculate the probability with the NEGBINOM.DIST() function, as shown in Figure 12-101.

F7		f_x =NEGBINOMDIST(F4,F5,F6)						
B		C	D	E	F	G	H	I
3 **Arguments for the function**					Examples			
4 NumberFailure		15	10	8	6	4	2	0
5 NumberSuccess		5	5	5	5	5	5	5
6 Probability of success		0.5	0.5	0.5	0.5	0.5	0.5	0.5
7 NEGBINOMDIST()		0.37%	3.05%	6.04%	10.25%	13.67%	11.72%	3.13%

Figure 12-101 Calculating the probability with the NEGBINOM.DIST() function.

You can make the following statements from this result: Regarding *number_f* = 6 in Figure 12-89, the probability of you asking six people who don't know the way before you ask five people who do know is 10.25 percent.

See Also BINOM.DIST(), BINOM.INV(), COMBIN(), FACT(), HYPGEOM.DIST(), PERMUT(), PROB()

Sample Files

Use the NEGBINOM.DIST worksheet in the _Probability.xls or Probability.xlsx sample file. The sample files are found in the Chapter12 folder. For more information about the sample files, see the section titled "Using the Sample Files" on page xxiii.

NORM.DIST()/NORMDIST()

Syntax   NORM.DIST(*x,mean,standard_dev,cumulative*)

Definition   This function returns the normal distribution for an average value and a standard variance. This function has a very wide range of applications in statistics, including hypothesis testing.

Arguments

- ***x* (required)** The distribution value (quantile) for which you want to calculate the probability.

- ***mean* (required)** The arithmetic mean of the distribution.

- ***standard_dev* (required)** The standard deviation of the distribution.

- ***cumulative* (required)** The logical value that represents the type of the function. If *cumulative* is TRUE, the NORM.DIST() function returns the value of the distribution function (cumulative density function). If *cumulative* is FALSE, the NORM.DIST() function returns the value of the density function.

> **Note**
>
> If *mean* or *standard_dev* isn't a numeric expression, the NORM.DIST() function returns the #VALUE! error. If *standard_dev* is less than or equal to 0, the function returns the #NUM! error.
>
> If *mean* = 0, *standard_dev* = 1, and *cumulative* = TRUE, NORM.DIST() returns the standard normal distribution.

Background   Excel offers numerous functions to calculate distributions and to evaluate hypotheses. One example is the NORM.DIST() function. In general, distributions help to answer questions regarding probabilities. An example is a coin toss that has only two probabilities: heads or tails.

As already mentioned, the NORM.DIST() function returns the normal distribution of given values. The normal distribution is the most important continuous probability distribution that indicates the probability of a value for a random variable *x*. The probability density is also called the *Gaussian function, Gaussian curve, Gaussian bell,* or *bell curve* and is shown in Figure 12-102.

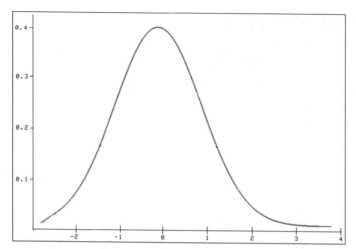

Figure 12-102 Different density functions for normal distributed random variables.

The special meaning of the normal distribution is based on the central limit theorem that states that a sum of n independent identical distributed random variables is normal distributed at the limit.

The normal distribution explains many scientific processes exactly or approximately—especially processes that work independently of each other in different directions.

Unlike the binomial distribution, the normal distribution is symmetrical (as shown in Figure 12-95). This means that the normal distribution is similar to a bell curve where the smallest and largest value have the lowest probability and the mean value has the highest probability.

Note the following for a normal distribution:

- It is bell-curved.

- It is unimodal.

- It comes asymptotically close to the x axis.

- It is symmetrical.

The following statements are also true:

- The maximum is at the arithmetic mean.

- Each 50 percent of the range is two-tailed to the arithmetic mean.

- The arithmetic mean and median are congruent.

- The mode, median, and arithmetic mean are congruent.

- The inflection points are at the mean value plus standard deviation and at the mean value minus standard deviation.

Excel offers two functions for most distributions. A function that calculates a distribution and ends in *DIST* calculates the probability for a certain value. The associated inverse function, ending in *INV*, calculates the value for a certain probability.

> **Note**
> The NORM.INV() function accepts a probability, a standard deviation, and a mean value as arguments.

The equation for the density function of the normal distribution (*cumulative* = FALSE) is:

$$f(x, \mu, \sigma) = \frac{1}{\sqrt{2\pi\sigma}} e^{-\left(\frac{(x-\mu)^2}{2\sigma^2}\right)}$$

If *cumulative* = TRUE, the formula returns the integral of the given formula from negative infinity to *x*.

Example   You are a light bulb manufacturer and want to analyze the performance of light bulbs. You also have calculated the average life cycle and the associated standard deviation. You want to know the probability for the light bulbs to last longer or less long when used daily. For this calculation, you use the NORM.DIST() function. The life cycle of your light bulbs is normal distributed with:

- An average of 2,000 working hours = *arg-hour average*

- A standard deviation of 579 hours = *argument StdDev*

To calculate the distribution function, you specify the logical value TRUE for the *cumulative* argument. If you want to calculate the density function, use the logical value FALSE.

You ask the following question: How high is the probability for a light bulb to work up to 2,600 hours or only up to 1,400 hours? And how high is the probability that exactly these hours will be reached?

The values 2,600 hours and 1,400 hours are indicated by the *x* argument. They are the values within the distribution that you want to calculate the probability for. Figure 12-103 shows the results.

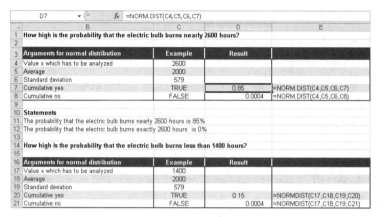

Figure 12-103 Calculating the probability for different performances.

What conclusions can you draw from these results?

● The probability for a light bulb to work up to 2,600 hours is 85 percent.

● The probability for a light bulb to work exactly 2,600 hours is 0.04 percent.

● The probability for a light bulb to work only 1,400 hours is 15 percent.

● The probability for a light bulb to work exactly 1,400 hours is 0.04 percent.

In this way you, can perform numerous calculations, test hypotheses, and specify the probabilities for characteristics in intervals.

See Also NORM.INV(), NORM.S.DIST(), NORM.S.INV(), STANDARDIZE(), Z.TEST()

Sample Files

Use the NORMDIST or NORM.DIST worksheet in the Probability.xls or Probability.xlsx sample file. The sample files are found in the Chapter12 folder. For more information about the sample files, see the section titled "Using the Sample Files" on page xxiii.

NORM.INV()/NORMINV()

Syntax   NORMINV(*probability,mean,standard_dev*)

Definition   This function returns the quantile of the normal distribution.

Arguments

- *probability* **(required)**   A probability associated with the standard normal distribution

- *mean* **(required)**   The arithmetic mean of the distribution

- *standard_dev* **(required)**   The standard deviation of the distribution

> **Note**
>
> If one of the arguments isn't a numeric expression, the NORM.INV() function returns the #VALUE! error.
>
> If *probability* is less than 0 or greater than 1, the NORM.INV() function returns the #NUM! error.
>
> If *standard_dev* is less than or equal to 0, the function returns the #NUM! error. If *mean* = 0 and *standard_dev* = 1, NORM.INV() uses the standard normal distribution (see the description of NORM.S.INV()).

Background   A standardized normal distribution is a normal distribution with the mean value 0 and the standard deviation 1. Each normal distribution can be transformed into a standard normal distribution by subtracting the mean from the x_i values and dividing the difference by the standard deviation.

Because the standard normal distribution is standardized, you can calculate the range for the normal distribution from the *z*-values by using the following formula:

$$z_i = \frac{x_i - \overline{x}}{s}$$

See Also   You will find more information about normal distributions in the description of NORM.DIST().

For the density function of the standard normal distribution, the intervals are 1, 2, and 3 standard deviations from the expected value 0 (see Figure 12-104). These ranges are about 68 percent, 95.5 percent, and 99.7 percent of the bell curve. The same percentages apply for all normal distributions regarding the expected values and the standard deviations.

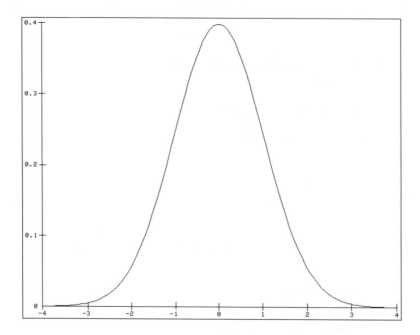

Figure 12-104 The density function of the standard normal distribution.

Example   You are a light bulb manufacturer and want to analyze the performance of light bulbs. You also have calculated the average life cycle and the associated standard deviation. Now you want to know the performance of 85 percent and 15 percent of your light bulbs based on the mean values and the standard deviation.

For this calculation, you use the NORM.INV() function with the following arguments:

- *probability* = 85 percent (15 percent); that is, you calculate the performance of 85 percent (15 percent) of the light bulbs

- *mean* = 2,000 hours (calculated from the population *n*)

- *standard_dev* = 579 hours (calculated from the population)

Figure 12-105 shows the results.

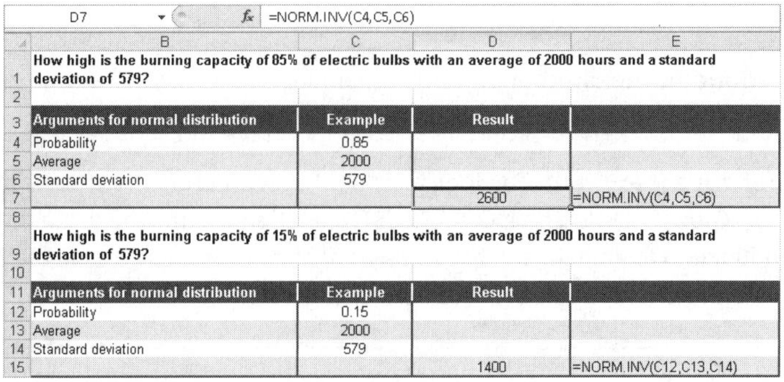

D7 =NORM.INV(C4,C5,C6)

How high is the burning capacity of 85% of electric bulbs with an average of 2000 hours and a standard deviation of 579?

Arguments for normal distribution	Example	Result	
Probability	0.85		
Average	2000		
Standard deviation	579		
		2600	=NORM.INV(C4,C5,C6)

How high is the burning capacity of 15% of electric bulbs with an average of 2000 hours and a standard deviation of 579?

Arguments for normal distribution	Example	Result	
Probability	0.15		
Average	2000		
Standard deviation	579		
		1400	=NORM.INV(C12,C13,C14)

Figure 12-105 NORM.INV() returns the performance of 85 percent or 15 percent of the light bulbs.

You can make the following statements from these results:

- 85 percent of the light bulbs have a performance of up to 2,600 hours.
- 15 percent of the light bulbs have a performance of up to 1,400 hours.

See Also NORM.DIST(), NORM.S.DIST(), NORM.S.INV(), STANDARDIZE(), Z.TEST()

Sample Files

Use the NORM.INV worksheet in the Probability.xls or Probability.xlsx sample file. The sample files are found in the Chapter12 folder. For more information about the sample files, see the section titled "Using the Sample Files" on page xxiii.

NORM.S.DIST()/NORMSDIST()

Syntax NORM.S.DIST(*z,cumulative*)

Definition This function returns the values or probabilities of the distribution function of a standard normal distributed random variable. The standard normal distribution has a mean of 0 and a standard deviation of 1. Use this function instead of a table containing the values of the distribution function of a standard normal distribution.

Arguments

- **z (required)** The distribution value (quantile) for which you want to calculate the probability

- **cumulative (required)** The logical value that represents the type of the function. If *cumulative* is TRUE, the NORM.S.DIST() function returns the value of the distribution function (cumulative density function). If *cumulative* is FALSE, the NORM.S.DIST() function returns the value of the density function.

> **Note**
>
> If *z* isn't a numeric expression, the NORM.S.DIST() function returns the #VALUE! error.

Background   The NORM.S.DIST() function returns the probabilities of a standard normal distributed random variable. The standard normal distribution is a normal distribution with the arithmetic mean $\mu = 0$ and the standard deviation $\acute{o} = 1$. The equation for the density function of the standard normal distribution is:

$$f(z) = \frac{1}{\sqrt{2\pi}} e^{-\frac{z^2}{2}}$$

See Also You will find more information about normal distributions in the descriptions of NORM.DIST() and STANDARDIZE().

Example   To explain the example of the NORM.S.DIST() function, we will use the same example as for the STANDARDIZE() function. You are a light bulb manufacturer and want to analyze the performance of light bulbs. You have already entered the measurements in an Excel table. You also calculated the average life cycle and the associated standard deviation. You calculated the standard distribution values with the STANDARDIZE() function.

Now you want to use the NORM.S.DIST() function to calculate the values or probabilities of all standard normal distributed variables of the distribution. What arguments does this function require?

- z = the distribution value (quantile) for which you want to calculate the probability. In this case, this is the performance in the form of the standard normal distributed z-value.

- *cumulative* = the logical value that represents the type of the function.

Figure 12-106 shows the results.

	E2		f_x	=NORM.S.DIST(D2,TRUE)	
	B	C	D	E	
1	Test electric bulbs	Measured burning capacity in hours (=X)	Standardization =z-values	Probability of distribution	
2	1	1000	-1.728	0.042	
3	2	1100	-1.555	0.060	
4	3	1200	-1.382	0.083	
5	4	1300	-1.209	0.113	
6	5	1400	-1.037	0.150	
7	6	1500	-0.864	0.194	
8	7	1600	-0.691	0.245	
9	8	1700	-0.518	0.302	
10	9	1800	-0.346	0.365	
11	10	1900	-0.173	0.431	
12	11	2000	0.000	0.500	

Figure 12-106 Calculating the probability of standard normal distributed variables.

You can make the following statement from the results: The probability for the standard normal distributed value –1.728 (cell D2) is 4.2 percent (cell E2).

See Also   NORM.DIST(), NORM.INV(), NORM.S.INV(), STANDARDIZE(), Z.TEST()

Sample Files

Use the NORMSDIST or NORM.S.DIST worksheet in the Probability.xls or Probability.xlsx sample file. The sample files are found in the Chapter12 folder. For more information about the sample files, see the section titled "Using the Sample Files" on page xxiii.

NORM.S.INV()/NORMSINV()

Syntax   NORM.S.INV(*probability*)

Definition   This function returns the quantile of the standard normal distribution. The standard normal distribution has a mean of 0 and a standard deviation of 1.

Arguments

- ***probability* (required)** A probability associated with the standard normal distribution

> **Note**
>
> If *probability* isn't a numeric expression, the NORM.S.INV() function returns the #VALUE! error.
>
> If *probability* is less than 0 or greater than 1, the NORM.S.INV() function returns the #NUM! error. If *probability* has a value, NORM.S.INV() looks for the value *z* so that NORMSDIST(*z*) = *probability*.
>
> Therefore, the accuracy of NORM.S.INV() depends on the accuracy of NORM.S.DIST(). NORM.S.INV() uses an iterative search technique. If the search has not converged after 100 iterations, the function returns the #N/A error.

Background   The NORM.S.INV() function is the inverse function of the NORM.S.DIST() function and returns a standard normal distributed random variable or the *z*-value of a standard normal distribution associated with a probability.

NORM.S.INV() calculates the position of *z* on the horizontal axis that matches the cumulative area ratio of the standard normal distribution.

See Also You will find more information about (standard) normal distributions in the descriptions of NORM.DIST(), STANDARDIZE(), and NORM.S.DIST().

Example   For NORM.S.INV() we use the same example as for STANDARDIZE() and NORM.S.DIST(). You are a light bulb manufacturer and want to analyze the performance of light bulbs. You already entered the measurements in an Excel table. You also calculated the average life cycle and the associated standard deviation, as well as the probabilities for all calculated performance values (see Figure 12-107).

	B	C	D
1	Test electric bulbs	Measured burning capacity in hours (=X)	Probability of distribution
2	1	1000	4.20%
3	2	1100	6.00%
4	3	1200	8.35%
5	4	1300	11.33%
6	5	1400	15.00%
7	6	1500	19.38%
8	7	1600	24.48%
9	8	1700	30.21%
10	9	1800	36.48%
11	10	1900	43.14%
12	11	2000	50.00%
13	12	2100	56.86%
14	13	2200	63.52%
15	14	2300	69.79%
16	15	2400	75.52%
17	16	2500	80.62%
18	17	2600	85.00%
19	18	2700	88.67%

Figure 12-107 The performances with the associated probabilities.

You want to calculate the standard normal distributed x-values (variables) for the probabilities with the NORM.S.INV() function. What arguments does this function require?

- *probability* = the probability associated with the standard normal distribution (column D)

Figure 12-108 shows the result.

E17		f_x	=NORM.S.INV(D17)	
	B	C	D	E
1	Test electric bulbs	Measured burning capacity in hours (=X)	Probability of distribution	z-values
2	1	1000	4.20%	-1.7277
3	2	1100	6.00%	-1.5550
4	3	1200	8.35%	-1.3822
5	4	1300	11.33%	-1.2094
6	5	1400	15.00%	-1.0366
7	6	1500	19.38%	-0.8639
8	7	1600	24.48%	-0.6911
9	8	1700	30.21%	-0.5183
10	9	1800	36.48%	-0.3455
11	10	1900	43.14%	-0.1728
12	11	2000	50.00%	0.0000
13	12	2100	56.86%	0.1728
14	13	2200	63.52%	0.3455
15	14	2300	69.79%	0.5183
16	15	2400	75.52%	0.6911
17	16	2500	80.62%	0.8639
18	17	2600	85.00%	1.0366
19	18	2700	88.67%	1.2094

Figure 12-108 Calculating the standard normal distributed variables with NORM.S.INV().

Chapter 12

The NORM.S.INV() function calculates the standard normal distributed values of the distribution based on a given probability.

> **Note**
>
> You can also use the STANDARDIZE() function to calculate the standard normal distributed values. For this function, you have to specify the *x*, *mean*, and *standard_dev* arguments. You will find more information about this function in the description of STANDARDIZE().

See Also   NORM.DIST(), NORM.INV(), NORM.S.DIST(), STANDARDIZE(), Z.TEST()

> **Sample Files**
>
> Use the NORMSINV or NORM.S.INV worksheet in the Probability.xls or Probability.xlsx sample file. The sample files are found in the Chapter12 folder. For more information about the sample files, see the section titled "Using the Sample Files" on page xxiii.

PEARSON()

Syntax   PEARSON(*array1,array2*)

Definition   This function returns the Pearson correlation coefficient r. This coefficient is a dimensionless index that ranges from −1.0 to 1.0 inclusive and reflects the extent of a linear relationship between two data sets.

Arguments

- *array1* **(required)** A set of independent values

- *array2* **(required)** A set of dependent values

> **Note**
>
> Arguments can be numbers, names, arrays, or references containing numbers.
>
> If an array or a reference argument contains text, logical values, or empty cells, those values are ignored. However, cells with the value 0 are included.
>
> If *array1* and *array2* are empty or have a different number of data points, the PEARSON() function returns the #N/A error value.

Background The correlation coefficient provides a quantitative measure for the extent of the correlation between metric characteristics.

In Excel, the correlation coefficient is calculated with the PEARSON() function. You can enter the two data sets in the arguments *array1* and *array2*. The first data set represents the values of the independent variable *x*, and the second data set represents the values of the dependent variable *y*.

The result returned by PEARSON() for *r* is between –1 and +1. But what do the results mean?

- *r* = –1 indicates a negative correlation—the data sets are independent from each other.

- *r* = +1 indicates a positive correlation—the data sets are dependent on each other.

- A value close to *r* = 0 indicates that there is no linear correlation.

The correlation between the two characteristics has to be linear because the PEARSON() function doesn't calculate nonlinear correlations. For this reason, the variance has to be taken into account when calculating the correlation coefficient *r*. Otherwise, the result might indicate that there is no correlation for *r* even though a nonlinear (for example, an exponential) correlation exists.

The value of a correlation coefficient calculated by PERSON() or CORREL() doesn't indicate the direction of the correlation between two variables. For a statistical correlation, you might also have to determine whether the correlation is unreal or real. Unreal correlations often occur in time series if both variables have the same trend. In general, a high correlation should only be considered as an indication that a correlation might exist.

The equation for the Pearson correlation coefficient *r* is:

$$r = \frac{\sum (x - \bar{x})(y - \bar{y})}{\sqrt{\sum (x - \bar{x})^2 \sum (y - \bar{y})^2}}$$

The values *x* and *y* are the sample means AVERAGE(*array1*) and AVERAGE(*array2*).

> **Note**
>
> The difference between the CORREL() and PEARSON() function is that PEARSON() assumes a linear dependent correlation between two variables. Therefore, the arguments for the function are independent values (*array1*) and dependent values (*array2*). This means that PEARSON() calculates the extent of an already obvious dependency.

Chapter 12

> The CORREL() function doesn't assume a linear correlation. The values for the correlation are treated as two independent variables. Therefore, the arguments for the function are cell ranges containing values. This means that CORREL() calculates a probable correlation that doesn't have to exist.

Example A software company sells all its products through its website. The company regularly sends out newsletters to inform existing and potential customers about new and updated products and to draw attention to its website. Last year, the orders through the website significantly increased. The management wants to know the reason. Is the increase in sales attributable to marketing or advertising? Did the increased website visits cause the increase in sales?

This means that the company wants to know the correlation between the website visits and the online orders. A scatter diagram and a linear trend line already show a linear correlation between the variables *x* (website visits) and *y* (online orders) (see Figure 12-109).

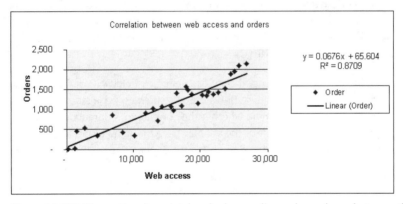

Figure 12-109 The scatter diagram already shows a linear dependency between the variables.

> **Note**
> If the scatter diagram doesn't show a linear correlation between the two variables, you have to use the CORREL() function instead of the PEARSON() function.

The calculation of the correlation coefficient *r* with the PEARSON() function proves that a linear dependency exists (see Figure 12-110).

D33		f_x	=PEARSON(C3:C32,D3:D32)	

	B	C	D
1		Independent = x-value	Dependent = y-value
2	**Month**	**Web access**	**Order**
3	January 2006	236	6
4	February 2006	1,221	17
5	March 2006	1,563	456
6	April 2006	2,682	544
7	May 2006	4,569	349
8	June 2006	6,848	854
9	July 2006	8,463	427
10	August 2006	10,157	337
11	September 2006	11,837	899
12	October 2006	12,987	1,011
13	November 2006	13,739	720
14	December 2006	14,376	1,069
15	January 2007	15,739	1,070
16	February 2007	16,123	967
17	March 2007	16,548	1,401
18	April 2007	17,352	1,076
19	May 2007	17,986	1,563
20	June 2007	18,234	1,485
21	July 2007	18,769	1,367
22	August 2007	19,736	1,138
23	September 2007	20,333	1,352
24	October 2007	20,987	1,343
25	November 2007	21,323	1,430
26	December 2007	21,999	1,375
27	January 2008	22,786	1,421
28	February 2008	23,784	1,508
29	March 2008	24,574	1,876
30	April 2008	25,111	1,948
31	May 2008	25,789	2,094
32	June 2008	26,948	2,134
33	**Coefficient of correlation from Pearson**		0.933231423

Figure 12-110 This PEARSON() function returns the value for the correlation coefficient r.

The correlation coefficient of 0.933 indicates an almost perfect positive correlation. This means that the website visits and online orders are linear interdependent. This was already assumed based on the scatter diagram (shown previously in Figure 12-97).

In other words, the correlation coefficient of 0.933 indicates that the number of online orders increases simultaneously with the number of website visits.

See Also CORREL(), INTERCEPT(), LINEST(), LOGEST(), RSQ(), STEYX()

Sample Files

Use the PEARSON worksheet in the Regresson.xls or Regression.xlsx sample file. The sample files are found in the Chapter12 folder. For more information about the sample files, see the section titled "Using the Sample Files" on page xxiii.

PERCENTILE()

> **Note**
> In Excel 2010, the PERCENTILE() function was replaced with the PERCENTILE.EXC() and the PERCENTILE.INC() functions to increase the accuracy of the results. To ensure the backward compatibility of PERCENTILE.EXC() and PERCENTILE.INC(), the PERCENTILE() function is still available.

Syntax PERCENTILE(*array,alpha*)

Definition This function returns the *alpha* quantile of a data set. You can use this function to establish a threshold of acceptance. For example, you can decide to invite only the customers with sales above the 80th percentile to a festivity.

In statistics, the *p* percent quantile for a probability function is the value of the event range with the value *p* percent of the density function. *p* percent of the observations or the population are smaller than the *p* percent quantile.

Arguments

- *array* **(required)** The array or range of data that defines the relative standing of the data

- *alpha* **(required)** A value between 0 and 1 inclusive

> **Note**
> If *array* is empty or contains more than 8,191 data points, PERCENTILE() returns the #NUM! error. If *alpha* isn't a numeric expression, the PERCENTILE() function returns the #VALUE! error. If *alpha* is less than 0 or greater than 1, the PERCENTILE() function returns the #NUM! error. If *alpha* isn't a multiple of $1/(n - 1)$, PERCENTILE() interpolates to determine the value at the *alpha* quantile.

Background A quantile is a defined part of a data set sorted by size. Quantiles (except the median) are values that define the variance of a data set. Some of the most important quantiles are the decile, the quartile, and the median. The median matches the 50 percent quantile.

In other words, the *p* quantile of a distribution indicates what value separates the lower $p*100$ percent of the data values from the upper $100-p*100$ percent. If you specify the 0.65

quantile of a distribution, then 65 percent of the data are less than or equal to the data value, and 35 percent of the data are greater than or equal to this value.

Sometimes no value in the data set matches the corresponding value. A rule for quantile calculations is (n = number of data values): If $n*p$ isn't an integer, the next integer is used as the ordinal number for the quantile value. If $n*p$ is an integer, the quantile is a value between $n*p$ and $n*p+1$.

When 16 data values exist, the 0.25 quantile (the first quartile) has the ordinal number 4 (16*0.25). The 0.25 quantile or the first quartile should be located between the lower 25 and the upper 75 percent. Therefore, it makes sense to define a value between the fourth and the fifth value of the sorted data set. The first decile can be defined by the ordinal number for $n*p$ = 1.6. In this example, this is the second value in the data set. At least 10 percent of the data is less than or equal to this value, and 90 percent of the data is greater than or equal to this value.

Example   Let's use the example of the software company again. You are the manager of the controlling department and generate the sales numbers for the different business units for an entire year. Now you want to separate the data to further analyze it. The goal is to generate the sales values that exceed the 0.6 quantile (60th percentile).

With Excel you can calculate any p percent quantile. For the *alpha* argument, you have to enter the percentage as a decimal number. You calculate the results in 10-percent increments.

As you can see in Figure 12-111, the results are sorted in ascending order. Now you can analyze all sales that are greater than or equal to the 0.6 quantile.

G25		f_x =PERCENTILE(G$4:G$15,1)				
B	C	D	E	F	G	
Sales	**EVENTS**	**PUBLICATIONS**	**TEAM**	**TRAINING**	**KNOWHOW**	
January	$ 1,127	$ 1,141	$ 1,049	$ 1,339	$ 1,060	
February	$ 1,407	$ 945	$ 938	$ 1,014	$ 1,230	
March	$ 1,334	$ 1,388	$ 902	$ 1,153	$ 805	
April	$ 981	$ 1,353	$ 897	$ 1,441	$ 1,398	
May	$ 1,223	$ 813	$ 1,464	$ 1,481	$ 861	
June	$ 1,322	$ 1,358	$ 1,385	$ 1,166	$ 1,081	
July	$ 1,316	$ 982	$ 892	$ 1,015	$ 1,424	
August	$ 1,168	$ 896	$ 1,000	$ 1,035	$ 1,094	
September	$ 1,212	$ 1,243	$ 1,050	$ 1,077	$ 848	
October	$ 1,218	$ 1,088	$ 998	$ 1,446	$ 1,108	
November	$ 1,311	$ 945	$ 1,222	$ 828	$ 1,465	
December	$ 1,421	$ 903	$ 1,087	$ 854	$ 1,189	
Quantile 0.1	$ 1,131	$ 897	$ 898	$ 870	$ 849	
Quantile 0.2	$ 1,177	$ 911	$ 909	$ 1,014	$ 901	
Quantile 0.3	$ 1,214	$ 945	$ 956	$ 1,021	$ 1,066	
Quantile 0.4	$ 1,220	$ 960	$ 999	$ 1,052	$ 1,086	
Quantile 0.5	$ 1,267	$ 1,035	$ 1,025	$ 1,115	$ 1,101	
Quantile 0.6	$ 1,314	$ 1,120	$ 1,050	$ 1,161	$ 1,157	
Quantile 0.7	$ 1,320	$ 1,212	$ 1,076	$ 1,287	$ 1,218	
Quantile 0.8	$ 1,332	$ 1,331	$ 1,195	$ 1,421	$ 1,364	
Quantile 0.9	$ 1,400	$ 1,358	$ 1,369	$ 1,446	$ 1,421	
Quantile 0.10	$ 1,421	$ 1,388	$ 1,464	$ 1,481	$ 1,465	

Figure 12-111 The quantiles are calculated in 10-percent increments.

The 0.6 quantile indicates that 60 percent of the values in the original data are less than the value, and 40 percent are greater than or equal to this value.

See Also LARGE(), MAX(), MEDIAN(), MIN(), PERCENTRANK(), SMALL()

> **Sample Files**
>
> Use the PERCENTILE worksheet in the Average.xls or Average.xlsx sample file. The sample files are found in the Chapter12 folder. For more information about the sample files, see the section titled "Using the Sample Files" on page xxiii.

PERCENTILE.EXC()

Syntax   PERCENTILE.EXC(*array,k*)

Definition   This function returns the k-quantile of the values in a range where k is between 0 and 1.

Arguments

- *array* **(required)** The range of data that defines the relative standing of the data

- *k* **(required)** A value between 0 and 1 exclusive

> **Note**
>
> If *array* has no data points, the function returns the #NUM! error.
>
> If k isn't a numeric expression, the PERCENTILE.EXC() function returns the #VALUE! error. For $k \leq 0$ or $k \geq 1$, the PERCENTILE.EXC() function returns the #NUM! error. If k isn't a multiple of $1/(n-1)$, PERCENTILE.EXC() interpolates to determine the value at the k quantile.
>
> PERCENTILE.EXC() interpolates when the value for the given quantile is between two values in the range. If the quantile cannot be interpolated and k is specified, Excel returns the #NUM! error.

Example   You will find more information about the use of this function in the description of PERCENTILE().

See Also LARGE(), MAX(), MEDIAN(), MIN(), PERCENT.INC(), PERCENTRANK(), SMALL()

PERCENTILE.INC()

Syntax   PERCENTILE.INC(*array,k*)

Definition   This function returns the *k*-quantile of the values in a range where *k* is between 0 and 1.

You can use this function to establish a threshold of acceptance. For example, you can decide to examine candidates who score above the 90th percentile.

Arguments

- *array* **(required)** The range of data that defines the relative standing of the data

- *k* **(required)** A value between 0 and 1 inclusive

Note

If *array* has no data points, the function returns the #NUM! error.

If *k* isn't a numeric expression, the PERCENTILE.INC() function returns the #VALUE! error. If *k* is less than 0 or greater than 1, the PERCENTILE.INC() function returns the #NUM! error. If *k* isn't a multiple of 1/(*n* – 1), PERCENTILE.INC() interpolates to determine the value at the *k* quantile.

Background   You will find more information about the use of this function in the description of PERCENTILE().

See Also LARGE(), MAX(), MEDIAN(), MIN(), PERCENT.EXC(), PERCENTRANK(), SMALL()

Chapter 12

PERCENTRANK()

> **Note**
>
> In Excel 2010, the PERCENTRANK() function was replaced with the PERCENTRANK.EXC() and PERCENTRANK.INC() functions to increase the accuracy of the results. To ensure the backward compatibility of PERCENTRANK.EXC() and PERCENTRANK.INC(), the PERCENTRANK() function is still available.

Syntax PERCENTRANK(*array,x,significance*)

Definition This function returns the rank of a value (*alpha*) as a percentage.

This function can be used to evaluate the relative position of a value within a data set. For example, you can use PERCENTRANK() to evaluate the position of an aptitude test score among all scores for the test.

Arguments

- *array* **(required)** The array or range of data with numeric values that defines the relative position of the data.

- *x* **(required)** The value for which you want to know the rank.

- *significance* **(optional)** A value that identifies the number of decimal places for the returned percentage value. If *significance* is not specified, PERCENTRANK() uses three decimal places (0.*xxx*).

> **Note**
>
> If *array* is empty, PERCENTRANK() returns the #NUM! error. If *significance* is less than 1, PERCENTRANK() returns the #NUM! error. If *x* does not match one of the values in the array, PERCENTRANK() interpolates to return the correct percentage rank.

Background PERCENTRANK() is the inverse function of PERCENTILE(). This function calculates the relative position a of value *x* in a value set. You will find more information about quantiles in the description of PERCENTILE().

Example   You are the manager of the controlling department and want to analyze the total sales of all business units for the past year. The goal is to find the position of a sale in a given month within all sales on a scale from 1 to 100 to calculate the variance of the monthly sales compared to all sales. Therefore, you use the PERCENTRANK() function.

Based on the sales of $4,656.00 in January and the calculated quantile rank of 0.55, you can draw the following conclusion: The sales of $4,656.00 in January calculated from the total sales is ranked 55 on a scale from 1 to 100. This means that 55 percent of the values are less than or equal to the value, and 45 percent of the values are greater than or equal to $4,656.00 (see Figure 12-112).

	EVENTS	PUBLICATIONS	TEAM	TRAINING	OVERALL RESULT	PERCENTRANK
Sales						
January	$ 1,127.00	$ 1,141.00	$ 1,049.00	$ 1,339.00	$ 4,656.00	0.55
February	$ 1,407.00	$ 945.00	$ 938.00	$ 1,014.00	$ 4,304.00	0.27
March	$ 1,334.00	$ 1,388.00	$ 902.00	$ 1,153.00	$ 4,777.00	0.82
April	$ 981.00	$ 1,353.00	$ 897.00	$ 1,441.00	$ 4,672.00	0.64
May	$ 1,223.00	$ 813.00	$ 1,464.00	$ 1,481.00	$ 4,981.00	0.91
June	$ 1,322.00	$ 1,358.00	$ 1,385.00	$ 1,166.00	$ 5,231.00	1.00
July	$ 1,316.00	$ 982.00	$ 892.00	$ 1,015.00	$ 4,205.00	0.09
August	$ 1,168.00	$ 896.00	$ 1,000.00	$ 1,035.00	$ 4,099.00	-
September	$ 1,212.00	$ 1,243.00	$ 1,050.00	$ 1,077.00	$ 4,582.00	0.45
October	$ 1,218.00	$ 1,088.00	$ 998.00	$ 1,446.00	$ 4,750.00	0.73
November	$ 1,311.00	$ 945.00	$ 1,222.00	$ 828.00	$ 4,306.00	0.36
December	$ 1,421.00	$ 903.00	$ 1,087.00	$ 854.00	$ 4,265.00	0.18

H15 =PERCENTRANK($G$4:$G$15,G15)

Figure 12-112 Percentile rank for the monthly sales of different business units.

See Also LARGE(), MAX(), MEDIAN(), MIN(), PERCENTILE(), PERCENTILE.EXC(), PERCENTILE.INC(), QUARTILE(), QUARTILE.INC(), QUARTILE.EXC(), SMALL()

Sample Files
Use the PERCENTRANK worksheet in the Average.xls or Average.xlsx sample file. The sample files are found in the Chapter12 folder. For more information about the sample files, see the section titled "Using the Sample Files" on page xxiii.

PERCENTRANK.EXC()

Syntax   PERCENTRANK.EXC(*array,x,significance*)

Definition   This function returns the rank of a value (*alpha*) in a data set as a percentage (0 to 1, exclusive).

Arguments

- ● **array (required)** The array or range of data with numeric values that defines the relative position of the data.

- ● **x (required)** The value for which you want to know the rank.

- ● **significance (optional)** A value that identifies the number of decimal places for the returned percentage value. If *significance* is not specified, PERCENTRANK.EXC() uses three decimal places (0.*xxx*).

> **Note**
>
> If *array* is empty, PERCENTRANK.EXC() returns the #NUM! error value.
>
> If *significance* is less than 1, PERCENTRANK.EXC() returns the #NUM! error value.
>
> If *x* does not match one of the values in the array, PERCENTRANK.EXC() interpolates to return the correct percentage rank.

Background   PERCENTRANK.EXC() and PERCENTRANK.INC() are the inverse functions of PERCENTILE.EXC() and PERCENTILE.INC(). This function calculates the relative position a of value *x* in a value set.

You will find more information about quantiles in the description of PERCENTILE().

Example   You find more information about the use of this function in the description of PERCENTRANK().

See Also LARGE(), MAX(), MEDIAN(), MIN(), PERCENT.EXC(), PERCENT.INC(), QUARTILE.EXC(), QUARTILE.INC(), SMALL()

> **Sample Files**
>
> Use the PERCENTRANK.EXC worksheet in the Average.xlsx sample file. The sample files are found in the Chapter12 folder. For more information about the sample files, see the section titled "Using the Sample Files" on page xxiii.

PERCENTRANK.INC()

Syntax PERCENTRANK.INC(*array,x,significance*)

Definition This function returns the rank of a value (*alpha*) in a data set as a percentage (0 to 1 inclusive).

This function can be used to evaluate the relative position of a value within a data set. For example, you can use PERCENTRANK.INC() to evaluate the position of an aptitude test score among all scores for the test.

Arguments

- *array* **(required)** The array or range of data with numeric values that defines the relative position of the data.

- *x* **(required)** The value for which you want to know the rank.

- *significance* **(optional)** A value that identifies the number of decimal places for the returned percentage value. If *significance* is not specified, PERCENTRANK.INC() uses three decimal places (0.*xxx*).

> **Note**
>
> If *array* is empty, PERCENTRANK.INC() returns the #NUM! error value.
>
> If *significance* is less than 1, PERCENTRANK.INC() returns the #NUM! error value.
>
> If *x* does not match one of the values in the array, PERCENTRANK.INC() interpolates to return the correct percentage rank.

Background PERCENTRANK.EXC() and PERCENTRANK.INC() are the inverse functions of PERCENTILE.EXC() and PERCENTILE.INC(). This function calculates the relative position a of value *x* in a value set.

You will find more information about quantiles in the description of PERCENTILE().

Example You will find more information about the use of this function in the description of PERCENTRANK().

See Also LARGE(), MAX(), MEDIAN(), MIN(), PERCENT.EXC(), PERCENT.INC(), QUARTILE.EXC(), QUARTILE.INC(), SMALL()

Chapter 12

Sample Files

Use the PERCENTRANK.INC worksheet in the Average.xlsx sample file. The sample files are found in the Chapter12 folder. For more information about the sample files, see the section titled "Using the Sample Files" on page xxiii.

PERMUT()

Syntax   PERMUT(*number;number_chosen*)

Definition   This function returns the number of permutations to query *k* elements from *n* elements. A permutation is a set of elements or events where the internal order is significant.

Arguments

- *number* **(required)** The number of elements

- *number_chosen* **(required)** Specifies the number of elements for a permutation

Note

Both arguments are truncated to integers.

If *number* or *number_chosen* isn't a numeric value, the PERMUT() function returns the #VALUE! error. If *number* is less than or equal to 0, the PERMUT() function returns the #NUM! error. If *number* is less than *number_chosen*, the PERMUT() function returns the #NUM! error.

Background   The PERMUT() function belongs to combinatorics that determine the number of possible orders for objects. The PERMUT() function is different from the COMBIN() function, for which the internal order is not significant. This means that for PERMUT(), the order of the elements cannot be subsequently changed—for COMBIN(), this is immaterial. For example, the PERMUT() function calculates the probabilities for the first three places in a race with ten participants, whereas with the COMBIN() function you can calculate lottery-style probabilities. The difference: Although the order of the lottery numbers can be changed, the runners would protest if you sorted the first to third places by the first letter of the last names.

The PERMUT() function calculates the number of ordered samples of k elements from n elements. The equation to calculate the number of permutations is:

$$P_{k,n} = \frac{n!}{(n-k)!}$$

Example   Let's use the example of the race. Ten runners participate in the race. The first three runners get a prize, and the other runners get nothing. You want to know the number of possible variations for the first three places. Therefore, you use the PERMUT() function.

What values are specified for the n and k arguments?

- $n = 10$ (the number of elements equals the number of runners)

- $k = 3$ (the permutation consists of three elements—the first three places)

Figure 12-113 shows the result.

	B	C
	C15	f_x =PERMUT(B12,C12)
1	Participant	Example
2	Runner 1	Place 1
3	Runner 2	Place 2
4	Runner 3	Place 3
5	Runner 4	
6	Runner 5	
7	Runner 6	
8	Runner 7	
9	Runner 8	
10	Runner 9	
11	Runner 10	
12	10	3
13	=COUNTA(B2:B11)	
14		
15	Variations	720

Figure 12-113 Calculating the possible winners.

The PERMUT() function returns 720 different possibilities for the winners of the three places.

See Also BINOM.DIST(), BINOM.INV(), COMBIN(), FACT(), HYPGEOM.DIST(), NEGBINOM.DIST()

Sample Files

Use the PERMUT worksheet in the Probability.xls or Probability.xlsx sample file. The sample files are found in the Chapter12 folder. For more information about the sample files, see the section titled "Using the Sample Files" on page xxiii.

POISSON.DIST()/POISSON()

Syntax   POISSON.DIST(*x,mean,cumulative*)

Definition   This function returns the probabilities of a Poisson distributed random variable. A common application of the Poisson distribution is the prediction of the number of events over a specific time period such as the number of calls a call center receives within an hour.

Arguments

- *x* **(required)** The number of events.

- *mean* **(required)** The expected numeric value.

- *cumulative* **(required)** The logical value that represents the type of the function. If *cumulative* is TRUE, POISSON.DIST() returns the cumulative Poisson probability that the number of random events occurring will be between zero and *x* inclusive. If *cumulative* is FALSE, the function returns the probability that the number of events occurring will be exactly *x*.

> **Note**
> If *x* isn't an integer, the decimal places are truncated. If *x* or *mean* isn't a numeric expression, the POISSON.DIST() function returns the #VALUE! error. If *x* is less than 0, the function returns the #NUM! error. If *mean* is less than or equal to 0, the function returns the #NUM! error.

Background   The POISSON.DIST() function (named after Denis Poisson, 1781–1840) returns the probabilities of a Poisson-distributed random variable. The Poisson distribution predicts the frequency of independent similar events from a large number of elements.

An example is the number of customers arriving at a plaza or the number of incoming phone calls.

The Poisson distribution is especially useful for probability distributions with many results from a sample and a low probability for the event to occur. In this case, the Poisson distribution is similar to the binomial distribution. Unlike the binomial distribution, the Poisson distribution (in addition to *x*) requires only one parameter—the expected value or the *mean* argument.

For low probabilities, the binomial distribution approximates the Poisson distribution. This means that the distribution applies if the average number of events is the result of a large number of event possibilities and a low number of event probabilities. Radioactive decay is often used as example. In a very large number of atoms, only a very small amount of atoms decay within a time interval. The decay is random and independent from the already decayed atoms. This is an important requirement for the Poisson distribution.

The Poisson distribution assumes that the event occurs rarely within a certain time interval. However, the distribution depends only on the length of the interval and is independent of the position on the time axis. Therefore, you can use the Poisson distribution to calculate the error probability or one event per interval.

The POISSON.DIST() function calculates the following formulas:

- For *cumulative* = FALSE:

$$POISSON.DIST = \frac{e^{-\lambda}\lambda^{x}}{x!}$$

- For *cumulative* = TRUE:

$$CUMPOISSON = \sum_{k=0}^{x}\frac{e^{\lambda}\lambda^{x}}{k!}$$

For these formulas, the POISSON.DIST() function replaces *x* with the number of events and *mean* with the expected number value. The *cumulative* argument indicates whether the mean is reached exactly (*cumulative* = FALSE) or at the most (*cumulative* = TRUE).

Example You are a tire dealer and sell your own brand. You have analyzed the quality of your brand over a long time period. It has turned out that with your tires, an average of four incidents of tire damage per 100,000 miles occur (see Figure 12-114).

	B	C
1		Tire damage within 100,000 miles
2	Test vehicle 1	5
3	Test vehicle 2	3
4	Test vehicle 3	6
5	Test vehicle 4	2
6	Test vehicle 5	3
7	Test vehicle 6	5
8	Test vehicle 7	4
9	Test vehicle 8	2
10	Test vehicle 9	3
11	Test vehicle 10	4
12	Test vehicle 11	5
13	Test vehicle 12	6
14	Test vehicle 13	3
15	Test vehicle 14	7
16	Test vehicle 15	2
17	**Average**	**4**

Figure 12-114 The analysis of the tires indicates an error rate of four per 100,000 miles.

Compared with the interval of 100,000 miles, these four events are rare events. Therefore you use the Poisson distribution. You ask the following question: How high is the probability for only three tire-damage incidents per 100,000 miles to occur?

You enter the following values for the arguments required by the POISSON.DIST() function:

- $x = 3$ (number of events you want to evaluate)

- *mean* = 4 (number of expected events)

- *cumulative* = FALSE (because you want to calculate the probability of *x* events to occur)

Figure 12-115 shows the result.

	H11	▼	f_x	=POISSON.DIST(H8,H9,H10)
	E	F	G	H
8	x = Number of "desired" events			3
9	Average = Number of expected events			4
10	Cumulative			FALSE
11	**POISSON.DIST()**			**19.54%**

Figure 12-115 Calculating the probability for exactly three events.

The POISSON() function returns a probability of 19.54 percent that three tire damage incidents per 100,000 miles will occur. To calculate the probability of 0 to *x* tire damage incidents per 100,000 miles, specify the logical value TRUE for the *cumulative* argument (see Figure 12-116).

	H22	▼	f_x	=POISSON.DIST(H19,H20,H21)
	E	F	G	H
19	x = Number of "desired" events			3
20	Average = Number of expected events			4
21	Cumulative			TRUE
22	**POISSON.DIST()**			**43.35%**

Figure 12-116 Calculating the probability of 0 to 3 events.

The POISSON.DIST() function returns a probability of 43.35 percent for 0 to 3 tire damage incidents per 100,000 miles to occur.

See Also EXPON.DIST()

Sample Files

Use the POISSON or POISSON.DIST worksheet in the Probability.xls or Probability.xlsx sample file. The sample files are found in the Chapter12 folder. For more information about the sample files, see the section titled "Using the Sample Files" on page xxiii.

PROB()

Syntax   PROB(*x_range,prob_range,lower_limit,upper_limit*)

Definition   This function returns the probability for an interval between two values. If *upper_limit* is not specified, the function calculates the probability that the values in *x_range* are equal to *lower_limit*.

Arguments

- ***x_range* (required)** The range of random variable realizations that have associated probabilities

- ***prob_range* (required)** A set of probabilities associated with values in *x_range*

- ***lower_limit* (required)** The lower limit of the values for which the probability is calculated

- ***upper_limit* (optional)** The upper limit of the values for which the probability is calculated

> ## Note
>
> If any value in *prob_range* is less than or equal to 0 or greater than 1, the function returns the #NUM! error.
>
> If the sum of the values in *prob_range* is greater than 1, PROB() returns the #NUM! error.
>
> If *upper_limit* is not specified, PROB() returns the probability for *lower_limit*.
>
> If *x_range* and *prob_range* contain a different number of data points, PROB() returns the #N/A error.

Background   The PROB() function calculates the probability of a value interval where the single probabilities are known. In other words, the function adds up the probabilities of the values within this interval. The values correspond to the *x_range* argument (the values to be examined), and the probabilities correspond to the *prob_range* argument (the probabilities associated with the values). All probabilities have to be greater than or equal to 0 (0 percent) and less than or equal to 1 (100 percent), and the sum has to be 1.

Example   You are a doctor and offer a free health check for your patients that includes weighing. Five of your patients have been weighed. Based on previous weighings, you were able to associate probabilities with the current values. You entered the values and their probabilities into a table (see Figure 12-117).

	C	D	E
1	**Person**	**Weight in pounds**	**Probability**
2	1	60	10%
3	2	80	15%
4	3	100	20%
5	4	120	25%
6	5	140	30%

Figure 12-117 The values and their associated probabilities.

As Patient 6 enters the examination room you ask yourself the following questions:

1. How high is the probability that the weight of Patient 6 matches value 4 and the patient weighs 120 pounds?

2. How high is the probability that the weight of Patient 6 is between values 4 and 5 and the patient weighs between 120 and 140 pounds?

The PROB() function answers these questions (see Figure 12-118).

D8		f_x	=PROB(D2:D6,E2:E6,D5,D6)
	C	D	E
1	**Person**	**Weight in pounds**	**Probability**
2	1	60	10%
3	2	80	15%
4	3	100	20%
5	4	120	25%
6	5	140	30%
7	**PROB 1**	**0.25**	**25%**
8	**PROB 2**	**0.55**	**55%**

Figure 12-118 Calculating probabilities by using the PROB() function.

The answers to these questions are:

1. The probability that Patient 6 will weigh 120 pounds is 25 percent.

2. The probability that Patient 6 will weigh between 120 and 140 pounds is 55 percent.

As you can see in Figure 12-118, the optional *upper_limit* argument wasn't specified to answer question 1. This means that the PROB() function calculated the probability for *lower_limit* (in this example, 120 pounds).

To get an answer to question 2, both arguments (*lower_limit* and *upper_limit*) had to be specified. This means that the PROB() function calculated the probability for value *x* within an interval (in this example, 120 to 140 pounds).

See Also BINOM.DIST(), BINOM.INV()

Sample Files

Use the PROB worksheet in the Probability.xls or Probability.xlsx sample file. The sample files are found in the Chapter12 folder. For more information about the sample files, see the section titled "Using the Sample Files" on page xxiii.

QUARTILE()

Note

In Excel 2010, the QUARTILE() function was replaced with the QUARTILE.EXC() and QUARTILE.INC() functions to increase the accuracy of the results. To ensure the backward compatibility of QUARTILE.EXC() and QUARTILE.INC(), the QUARTILE() function is still available.

Syntax   QUARTILE(*array,quart*)

Definition   This function returns the quartile of a data set. Quartiles are often used in sales and survey data to divide populations into groups. For example, you can use QUARTILE() to find the top 25 percent of incomes in a population.

The *quart* argument indicates which value to return. Table 12-3 lists the values for this argument.

Arguments

- **array (required)** The array or cell range of numeric values for which you want the quartile value

- **quart (required)** Indicates which value to return

> **Note**
>
> If *array* is empty, QUARTILE() returns the #NUM! error value. If *quart* isn't an integer, the decimal places are truncated. If *quart* is less than 0 or greater than 4, the QUARTILE() function returns the #NUM! error.
>
> MIN(), MEDIAN(), or MAX() return the same value as QUARTILE() if the quartile is 0, 2, or 4, respectively.

Background   By using quantiles and quartiles, you can calculate the distribution of data. Whereas the median divides the distribution in half, the quantile divides the distribution into several equal parts, and the quartile divides the distribution into four equal parts.

The QUARTILE() function requires the *array* argument indicating the range to be evaluated and the *quart* argument indicating the quartile to be returned. This can be any value from 0 through 4. Table 12-3 lists the values for the *quart* argument.

Table 12-3 **The Values for the *quart* Argument**

Value	Result
0	Smallest value (minimum)
1	Lower quartile (25 percent quantile)
2	Median (50 percent quantile)
3	Upper quartile (75 percent quantile)
4	Largest value (maximum)

If quartile 0 is the minimum, quartile 4 the maximum, and quartile 2 the median, then quartiles 1 and 3 can be easily calculated.

Example   A pharmaceutical company that produces pills for headaches and sells these pills throughout the entire country wants to evaluate the pill sales in different regions numbered 1 through 5 (Texas, Virginia, California, Oregon, and Washington) for every 100,000 residents in each state. The goal is to calculate how much of the sales is 25 percent of the sales in a state in one year (see Figure 12-119). You know the sales for a year (12 values) per state. To calculate the quartile, you have to sort the values in ascending order.

	B	C	D	E	F	G
	G20	▾	f_x	=QUARTILE(G4:G15,4)		
1	Sales of headache tablets per 100,000 inhabitants					
2						
3	Month	Region 1	Region 2	Region 3	Region 4	Region 5
4	January	$ 800.00	$ 236.00	$ 189.00	$ 987.00	$ 1,563.00
5	February	$ 1,190.00	$ 356.00	$ 505.00	$ 1,319.00	$ 3,000.00
6	March	$ 1,545.00	$ 756.00	$ 1,307.00	$ 2,233.00	$ 6,116.00
7	April	$ 1,168.00	$ 518.00	$ 884.00	$ 1,903.00	$ 2,860.00
8	May	$ 1,139.00	$ 684.00	$ 835.00	$ 1,589.00	$ 3,126.00
9	June	$ 5,083.00	$ 1,678.00	$ 820.00	$ 2,428.00	$ 6,682.00
10	July	$ 3,609.00	$ 844.00	$ 276.00	$ 1,559.00	$ 3,311.00
11	August	$ 4,810.00	$ 622.00	$ 365.00	$ 1,502.00	$ 3,317.00
12	September	$ 5,581.00	$ 893.00	$ 309.00	$ 1,628.00	$ 3,542.00
13	October	$ 5,506.00	$ 724.00	$ 259.00	$ 1,440.00	$ 2,971.00
14	November	$ 11,786.00	$ 1,046.00	$ 447.00	$ 2,255.00	$ 4,735.00
15	December	$ 6,227.00	$ 339.00	$ 234.00	$ 1,583.00	$ 2,652.00
16	Quartile 0 = Min	800	236	189	987	1,563
17	Quartile 1	1,185	478	272	1,487	2,943
18	Quartile 2 =Median	4,210	704	406	1,586	3,219
19	Quartile 3	5,525	856	824	1,986	3,840
20	Quartile 4 = Max	11,786	1,678	1,307	2,428	6,682

Figure 12-119 For a better overview, the yearly sales in the states are divided into quartiles.

The sales for Region 1 indicate that the smallest value is the minimum, the largest value is the maximum, and quartile 2 (50 percent and the median) is 4,210.

How can you calculate the second quartile without using the QUARTILE() function? Because the number of values is even, the 50 limit has to be between the fifth and sixth value. If you add both values and divide the result by 2, you get the median. If there were 13 values, the median or the second quartile would be the seventh value.

You already have the following quartiles:

Quartile 0 = 800

Quartile 2 = 4,210

Quartile 4 = 11,786

Now you still need quartile 1 and quartile 3 (the 25 percent and 75 limit percentile). Therefore, you have to find the values at position 0.25 and 0.75 based on the original data. You need to calculate the values for which 25 percent of the observations are smaller than or equal to the value (the first quartile) and 75 percent of the observations are greater than or equal to it (the third quartile).

You have 12 number values (*n*). If you multiply *n* by 0.25 and 0.75, you find out that the first quartile is between the third and fourth values and the third quartile is between the ninth and tenth values of the sorted original data.

The QUARTIL() function returns the following results for the first and the third quartile:

Quartile 1 = 1,185

Quartile 3 = 5,525

The first quartile is between the third and the fourth values but not in the middle and more towards the fourth value.

Now you can draw the following conclusions:

- In Region 1, 25 percent of the sales are up to $1,185.00.

- In Region 5, 75 percent of the sales are up to $3,840.00.

See Also LARGE(), MAX(), MEDIAN(), MIN(), PERCENTILE(), PERCENTILE.EXC(), PERCENTILE.INC(), PERCENTRANK(), PERCENTRANK.EXC(), PERCENTRANK.INC(), SMALL()

Sample Files

Use the QUARTILE worksheet in the Average.xls or Average.xlsx sample file. The sample files are found in the Chapter12 folder. For more information about the sample files, see the section titled "Using the Sample Files" on page xxiii.

QUARTILE.EXC()

Syntax   QUARTILE.EXC(*array*,*quart*)

Definition   This function returns the quartile of a data group only based on 0 to 1 exclusive.

Arguments

- *array* **(required)** The array or cell range of numeric values for which you want the quartile value

- *quart* **(required)** Indicates which value to return

> **Note**
>
> If *array* is empty, QUARTILE.EXC() returns the #NUM! error value.
>
> If quart isn't an integer, the decimal places are truncated. If *quart* is 0 or 4, the QUAR-TILE.EXC() function returns the #NUM! error. MIN(), MEDIAN(), or MAX() return the same value as QUARTILE.EXC() if the quartile is 0, 2, or 4.

Background   You will find more information in the description of QUARTILE().

Example   You will find more information about the use of this function in the description of QUARTILE().

See Also   LARGE(), MAX(), MEDIAN(), MIN(), PERCENTILE(), PERCENTILE.EXC(), PERCENTILE.INC(), PERCENTRANK(), PERCENTRANK.EXC(), PERCENTRANK.INC(), SMALL()

> **Sample Files**
>
> Use the QUARTILE.EXC worksheet in the Average.xlsx sample file. The sample files are found in the Chapter12 folder. For more information about the sample files, see the section titled "Using the Sample Files" on page xxiii.

QUARTILE.INC()

Syntax   QUARTILE.INC(*array,quart*)

Definition   This function returns the quartile of a data set only based on 0 to 1 inclusive.

Arguments

- *array* **(required)** The array or cell range of numeric values for which you want the quartile value

- *quart* **(required)** Indicates which value to return

> **Note**
>
> If *array* is empty, QUARTILE.INC() returns the #NUM! error value.
>
> If *quart* isn't an integer, the decimal places are truncated. If *quart* is smaller than 0 or greater than 4, the QUARTILE.INC() function returns the #NUM! error.
>
> MIN(), MEDIAN(), or MAX() return the same value as QUARTILE.INC() if the quartile is 0, 2, or 4.

Background   You will find more information in the description of QUARTILE().

Example   You will find more information about the use of this function in the description of QUARTILE().

See Also LARGE(), MAX(), MEDIAN(), MIN(), PERCENTILE(), PERCENTILE.EXC(), PERCENTILE.INC(), PERCENTRANK(), PERCENTRANK.EXC(), PERCENTRANK.INC(), SMALL()

> **Sample Files**
>
> Use the QUARTILE.INC worksheet in the Average.xlsx sample file. The sample files are found in the Chapter12 folder. For more information about the sample files, see the section titled "Using the Sample Files" on page xxiii.

RANK()

> **Note**
>
> In Excel 2010, the RANK() function was replaced with the RANK.EQ() and RANK.AVG() functions to increase the accuracy of the results. To ensure the backward compatibility of RANK.EQ() and RANK.AVG(), the RANK() function is still available.

Syntax   RANK(*number,ref,order*)

Definition   This function returns the rank of a number within a list of numbers.

The rank of a number is its size relative to other values in a list. If you were to sort the list, the rank of the number would be its position.

Arguments

- ***number* (required)** The value for which you want to know the rank.

- ***ref* (required)** An array of or a reference to a list of numbers. Nonnumeric values in *ref* are ignored.

- ***order* (required)** A number specifying how to rank numbers. If *order* is 0 or not specified, the number is ranked as if *ref* were a list sorted in descending order. If *order* is a nonzero value, the number is ranked as if *ref* were a list sorted in ascending order.

Background   This function is especially useful if you work with large amounts of data, because manually ranking values is difficult and time-consuming.

Note that RANK() gives duplicate numbers the same rank and skips the subsequent rank. For some purposes, you might want to use a definition of rank that takes identical values into account. This can be done by adding the following correction factor to the value returned by RANK(). This correction factor is appropriate when the rank is calculated in descending order (order = 0 or omitted) or ascending order (order = nonzero value).

The correction factor for tied ranks is:

[COUNT(*reference*) + 1 − RANK(*number, reference*, 0) − RANK(*number, reference*, 1)]/2

> **Note**
> To calculate the second-largest or second-smallest value, use the LARGE() or SMALL() functions.

Example   The software company has created a table with the sales of the past two years. Because the manager wants to know the ranks of the months, you have to rank the sales (see Figure 12-120).

| | D3 | | ▼ | | f_x | =RANK(C3,$C$3:$C$26) |

	B		C	D
2	Month		Sales	Rank
3	January-07	$	107,629.00	24
4	February-07	$	185,385.00	18
5	March-07	$	180,807.00	19
6	April-07	$	124,328.00	22
7	May-07	$	146,215.00	21
8	June-07	$	185,675.00	17
9	July-07	$	210,169.00	11
10	August-07	$	221,729.00	9
11	September-07	$	234,187.00	7
12	October-07	$	237,947.00	6
13	November-07	$	210,088.00	12
14	December-07	$	207,791.00	14
15	January-08	$	201,097.00	16
16	February-08	$	222,460.00	8
17	March-08	$	208,585.00	13
18	April-08	$	206,387.00	15
19	May-08	$	218,951.00	10
20	June-08	$	365,425.00	5
21	July-08	$	542,896.00	2
22	August-08	$	365,478.00	4
23	September-08	$	165,845.00	20
24	October-08	$	642,598.00	1
25	November-08	$	432,695.00	3
26	December-08	$	123,458.00	23

Figure 12-120 The RANK() function returns the ranks of the sales.

The Rank column contains the ranks 1 through 24 for the sales of the corresponding month. Because all sales were different, all ranks are used.

Sample Files

Use the RANK worksheet in the Count.xls sample file. The sample files are found in the Chapter12 folder. For more information about the sample files, see the section titled "Using the Sample Files" on page xxiii.

RANK.AVG()

Syntax   RANK.AVG(*number,ref,order*)

Definition   This function returns the rank of a number within a list of numbers. The rank of a number is its size relative to the other values in a list. If several values have the same rank, the average rank is returned.

Definition   This function returns the rank of a number within a list of numbers.

The rank of a number is its size relative to other values in a list. If you were to sort the list, the rank of the number would be its position.

Arguments

- *number* **(required)** The value for which you want to know the rank.

- *ref* **(required)** An array of or a reference to a list of numbers. Nonnumeric values in *ref* are ignored.

- *order* **(required)** A number specifying how to rank numbers. If *order* is 0 or not specified, the number is ranked as if *ref* were a list sorted in descending order. If *order* is a nonzero value, the number is ranked as if *ref* were a list sorted in ascending order.

Background   This function is especially useful if you work with large amounts of data, because manually ranking values is difficult and time-consuming.

Note that RANK() gives duplicate numbers the same rank and skips the subsequent rank. For some purposes, you might want to use a definition of rank that takes identical values into account. This can be done by adding the following correction factor to the value returned by RANK(). This correction factor is appropriate when the rank is calculated in descending order (order = 0 or omitted) or ascending order (order = nonzero value).

The correction factor for tied ranks is:

[COUNT(*reference*) + 1 − RANK(*number, reference*, 0) − RANK(*number, reference*, 1)]/2

> **Note**
> To calculate the second-largest or second-smallest value, use the LARGE() or SMALL() functions.

Example   The software company has created a table with the sales of the past two years. Because the manager wants to know the ranks of the months, you have to rank the sales (see Figure 12-120).

Figure 12-120 The RANK() function returns the ranks of the sales.

The Rank column contains the ranks 1 through 24 for the sales of the corresponding month. Because all sales were different, all ranks are used.

> **Sample Files**
>
> Use the RANK worksheet in the Count.xls sample file. The sample files are found in the Chapter12 folder. For more information about the sample files, see the section titled "Using the Sample Files" on page xxiii.

RANK.AVG()

Syntax   RANK.AVG(*number,ref,order*)

Definition   This function returns the rank of a number within a list of numbers. The rank of a number is its size relative to the other values in a list. If several values have the same rank, the average rank is returned.

Arguments

- *number* **(required)** The value for which you want to know the rank.

- *ref* **(required)** An array of or a reference to a list of numbers. Nonnumeric values in *ref* are ignored.

- *order* **(required)** A number specifying how to rank numbers. If *order* is 0 or not specified, the number is ranked as if *ref* were a list sorted in descending order. If *order* is a nonzero value, the number is ranked as if *ref* were a list sorted in ascending order.

Background   You will find more information in the description of RANK().

Example   For information about the use of the RANK.AVG() function, see the example for the RANK() function.

> ### Sample Files
>
> Use the RANK.AVG worksheet in the Count.xlsx sample file. The sample files are found in the Chapter12 folder. For more information about the sample files, see the section titled "Using the Sample Files" on page xxiii.

RANK.EQ()

Syntax   RANK.EQ(*number,ref,order*)

Definition   This function returns the rank of a number within a list of numbers. The rank of a number is its size relative to the other values in a list. If you were to sort the list, the rank of the number would be its position.

Arguments

- *number* **(required)** The value for which you want to know the rank.

- *ref* **(required)** An array of or a reference to a list of numbers. Nonnumeric values in *ref* are ignored.

- *order* **(required)** A number specifying how to rank numbers. If *order* is 0 or not specified, the number is ranked as if *ref* were a list sorted in descending order. If *order* is a nonzero value, the number is ranked as if *ref* were a list sorted in ascending order.

Background   You will find more information in the description of RANK().

Example   For information about the use of the RANK.EQ() function, see the example for the RANK() function.

> ## Sample Files
>
> **Use the RANK.EQ worksheet in the Count.xlsx sample file. The sample files are found in the Chapter12 folder. For more information about the sample files, see the section titled "Using the Sample Files" on page xxiii.**

RSQ()

Syntax   RSQ(*known_y's;known_x's*)

Definition   This function returns the square of the Pearson correlation coefficient based on a set of data points *known_y's* and *known_x's*. The r^2 value can be interpreted as the proportion of the variance in *y* attributable to the variance in *x*.

See Also   The Pearson correlation coefficient is explained in more detail in the section discussing the PEARSON() function.

Arguments

- *known_y's* **(required)**   An array or a range of data points

- *known_x's* **(required)**   An array or a range of data points

> ## Note
>
> Arguments can be numbers or names, arrays, or references containing numbers. If an array or a reference argument contains text, logical values, or empty cells, those values are ignored. However, cells with the value 0 are included.
>
> If *known_y's* and *known_x's* are empty or have a different number of data points, the RSQ() function returns the #N/A error value.

Background   RSQ() calculates the coefficient of determination and is the square of the simple correlation coefficient. It is an indication of the strength of the relationship between the two sets of values.

> **Note**
> The correlation coefficient is a measure of association between two quantitative characteristics. The value ranges between −1 and +1 with the sign indicating whether the association is positive or negative; values closer to +1 or −1 indicate a stronger association. The value 0 indicates that no linear correlation exists.

The coefficient of determination ranges between 0 and +1 and is a measure of the variance in the y attributable to the variance in x. Thus, an r^2 value of −0.0354 suggests that only 3.5 percent of the variation is attributable to the association between the two sets of data.

A coefficient of determination of 1 suggests a linear relationship, but care should be taken that a causal effect is not assumed. The equation for the Pearson correlation coefficient r is:

$$r = \frac{\sum(x - \bar{x})(y - \bar{y})}{\sqrt{\sum(x - \bar{x})^2 \sum(y - \bar{y})^2}}$$

The values x and y are the average values of a sample AVERAGE(x_values) and AVERAGE(y_values).

RSQ() returns r^2, which is the square of this correlation coefficient.

Example   The software company is still busy evaluating its website. The marketing department wants to know the extent of the association between the online orders and the website visits. The marketing department calculates the coefficient of determination for the two interdependent variables to assess any association between the two (see Figure 12-121).

Month	Web access	Order
January 2007	236	6
February 2007	11593	17
March 2007	18491	456
April 2007	11743	544
May 2007	11452	349
June 2007	26651	854
July 2007	16287	427
August 2007	17750	337
September 2007	19985	899
October 2007	17285	1011
November 2007	30369	720
December 2007	19674	1069
January 2008	28464	1070
February 2008	25000	498
March 2008	24574	1401
April 2008	23141	1076
May 2008	17700	1563
June 2008	3702	1790
Coefficient of determination		0.053481332

Figure 12-121 Calculating the coefficient of determination to show the association between online orders and website visits.

Chapter 12

The online orders are compared with the website visits.

Then the RSQ() function calculates the association between the two and returns 5.35 percent.

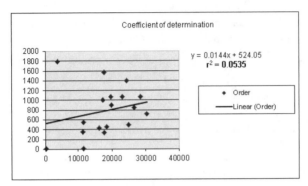

Figure 12-122 The association between online orders and website visits.

The illustration of the association of the online orders and the website visits in a chart returns the same result for r^2 (see Figure 12-122).

> **Tip**
>
> To display the coefficient of determination r^2, click Format Trend Line on the shortcut menu for the trend line, and then on the Options tab of the format Trent Line dialog box, select the Display R-Squared Value On Chart check box.

The calculation of the coefficient of determination and the result $r^2 = 0.0535$ shows that only 5.35 percent of the association between website visits and orders can be explained by a linear relationship.

See Also CORREL(), COVAR(), INTERCEPT(), LINEST(), LOGEST(), PEARSON(), SLOPE(), STEYX(), TREND()

> **Sample Files**
>
> Use the RSQ worksheet in the Regression.xls or Regression.xlsx sample file. The sample files are found in the Chapter12 folder. For more information about the sample files, see the section titled "Using the Sample Files" on page xxiii.

SKEW()

Syntax   SKEW(*number1,number2,...*)

Definition   This function returns the skewness of a distribution. The *skewness* characterizes the degree of asymmetry of a distribution around its mean. A *positive skewness* indicates a distribution with an asymmetric tail extending toward more positive values. This distribution is also called *left-skewed distribution*. *Negative skewness* indicates a distribution with an asymmetric tail extending toward more negative values.

Arguments

- ***number1* (required) and *number2* (optional)** At least one and up to 255 arguments (30 in Excel 2003 and earlier versions) for which you want to calculate the skewness. You can also use a single array or a reference to an array instead of arguments separated by commas.

> **Note**
>
> Arguments can be numbers or names, arrays, or references containing numbers.
>
> If an array or reference argument contains text, logical values, or empty cells, those values are ignored. However, cells with the value 0 are included.
>
> If there are fewer than three data points or the sample standard deviation is zero, SKEW() returns the #DIV/0! error value.

Background   SKEW() returns the skewness or the degree of asymmetry of a unimodal frequency distribution around the mean. The skewness and the kurtosis characterize the form and the degree of the symmetry of a distribution. The skew heavily relies on extreme values (outliers).

Because the Gaussian normal distribution has a skewness of 0 and is always symmetrical to the mean, the skewness is useful in comparing a distribution with the normal distribution.

The normal distribution has the following properties: average, median, and mode. The variance is symmetrical around the arithmetic mean. The first inflection point is the average minus the standard deviation, and the third inflection point is the average plus standard deviation. About 66 percent of the values are between the mean minus standard deviation, and the mean plus standard deviation.

In practice, skewed distribution occurs often. For skewed distributions, the average, median, and mode are not at the same point.

The formula to calculate the skewness is:

$$\frac{n}{(n-1)(n-2)} \sum \left(\frac{x_i - \overline{x}}{s} \right)^3$$

In statistics, the skewness is defined as follows:

$$v = \frac{m^3(\mu)}{\sigma^3}$$

In this equation, $m3(\mu)$ is the third middle moment, and σ is the standard deviation. If $v > 0$, the distribution is right skewed; if $v < 0$, the distribution is left skewed.

Example   We use the example of the software company to explain the SKEW() function. The marketing department wants to evaluate the download area as well as the entire website. The marketing department also wants to calculate the asymmetrical distribution of the website clicks. The result is a value that can be used to analyze the unimodal frequency distribution of the values around the average (see Figure 12-123).

		C22		f_x	=SKEW(C4:C21)	
	B		C	D	E	F
3	Date		Amount of clicks in the download area	Average	Amount of clicks on the whole website	Average
4	Jan-07		5000	1725	13987	15163
5	Feb-07		1000	1725	17645	15048
6	Mar-07		1076	1725	13435	15048
7	Apr-07		1521	1725	14424	15048
8	May-07		1790	1725	15000	15048
9	Jun-07		3908	1725	17875	15048
10	Jul-07		1138	1725	16049	15048
11	Aug-07		1352	1725	16734	15048
12	Sep-07		1343	1725	15039	15048
13	Oct-07		1430	1725	23424	15048
14	Nov-07		1140	1725	8974	15048
15	Dec-07		1421	1725	15049	15048
16	Jan-08		1508	1725	15874	15048
17	Feb-08		2137	1725	15987	15048
18	Mar-08		1948	1725	4980	15048
19	Apr-08		1521	1725	1600	15048
20	May-08		426	1725	23424	15048
21	Jun-08		1384	1725	23442	15048
22	Skew		2.23		-0.73	

Figure 12-123 Calculating the skew for the download area and the entire website.

The frequency distributions for the download area and the entire website are illustrated in charts (see Figures 12-124 and 12-125).

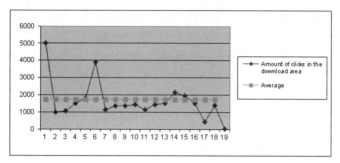

Figure 12-124 The distribution of the clicks in the download area around the mean.

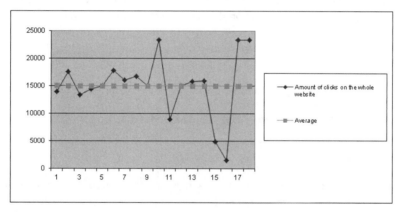

Figure 12-125 The distribution of the clicks in the entire website around the mean.

The following statements can be made based on these results:

- The positive skewness of 2.23 for the download area indicates that the distribution tends to the values greater than the mean (left skewed distribution). This distribution is also called *left modal* because the highest point of the distribution is left; that is, the measurement data extend in a positive direction (as shown in Figure 12-124).

- The negative skewness of -0.73 for the entire website indicates that the distribution tends to the values smaller than the mean (right skewed distribution). This distribution is also called *right modal* because the highest point of the distribution is right; that is, the measurement data extend in a negative direction (as shown in Figure 12-125).

See Also KURT(), STDEV.S(), STDEVP(), VAR.P(), VAR.S()

Chapter 12

Sample Files

Use the SKEW worksheet in the Symmetry.xls or Symmetry.xlsx sample file. The sample files are found in the Chapter12 folder. For more information about the sample files, see the section titled "Using the Sample Files" on page xxiii.

SLOPE()

Syntax   SLOPE(*known_y's,known_x's*)

Definition   This function returns the slope of the regression line through data points in *known_y's* and *known_x's*. The slope is the vertical distance divided by the horizontal distance between any two points on the line, which is the rate of change along the regression line.

Arguments

- *known_y's* **(required)** An array or cell range of numeric dependent data points

- *known_x's* **(required)** A set of independent data points

Note

Arguments can be numbers, names, arrays, or references containing numbers. If an array or reference argument contains text, logical values, or empty cells, those values are ignored. However, cells with the value 0 are included.

If *known_y's* and *known_x's* are empty or have a different number of data points, the SLOPE() function returns the #N/A error value.

Background   Most often a slope is calculated for regression analyses.

See Also You will find more information about regression analysis in the description of LINEST().

An example of a linear function is:

$$yt_i = a + bx_i$$

The variables are defined as follows:

- a = y-intercept of the function (intercept with the y-axis)

- b = slope of the function (tangent of the gradient angle)

- x_i = values on the x-axis ($i=1,2,...,n$)

- yt_i = values on the y-axis ($i=1,2,...,n$)

Figure 12-126 shows a linear function.

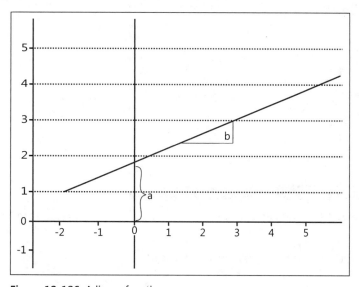

Figure 12-126 A linear function.

If the y-intercept a and the slope b are given, a linear function in the intercept is defined. For example, in

yt_i = 2 + 0.4 * x_i

the function has the y-intercept a = 2 and the slope b = 0.4. The value 0.4 indicates that the function increases by 0.4 y-units if x increases by 1 unit.

The equation to calculate the slope of a regression line is:

$$b = \frac{\sum\left(x-\overline{x}\right)\left(y-\overline{y}\right)}{\sqrt{\sum\left(x-\overline{x}\right)^2}}$$

The values x and y are the sample means AVERAGE(known_x's) and AVERAGE(known y's).

Use the SLOPE() function to calculate the slope of a regression line or a trend line.

Example   You are the marketing manager of the software company and want to thoroughly analyze the internal website. After you compare the number of online orders in the past 18 months with the number of website visits, you want to calculate the slope of the linear trend line for the orders. The goal is to find out how the regression line changes per unit (see Figure 12-127).

C22		f_x	=SLOPE(D4:D21,C4:C21)

	B	C	D
3	**Month**	**Web access**	**Orders**
4	January 2007	236	6
5	February 2007	11593	17
6	March 2007	18491	456
7	April 2007	11743	544
8	May 2007	11452	349
9	June 2007	26651	854
10	July 2007	16287	427
11	August 2007	17750	337
12	September 2007	19985	899
13	October 2007	17285	1011
14	November 2007	30369	720
15	December 2007	19674	1069
16	January 2008	28464	1070
17	February 2008	25000	498
18	March 2008	24574	1401
19	April 2008	23141	1076
20	May 2008	17700	1563
21	June 2008	3702	1790
22	**Gradient**		**0.014360319**

Figure 12-127 Calculating the slope of the regression line for the orders depending on the website visits.

Figure 12-128 shows the regression line in a chart.

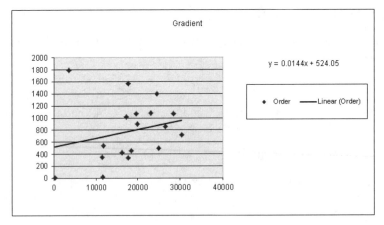

Figure 12-128 The regression line with a slope of 0.0144.

The result indicates that the orders increase by 0.0144 per website visit (click). In other words, the function increases by 0.0144 *y*-units if *x* increases by 1 unit.

See Also INTERCEPT(), LINEST(), LOGEST(), PEARSON(), RSQ(), STEYX(), TREND()

> **Sample Files**
>
> Use the SLOPE worksheet in the Regression.xls or Regression.xlsx sample file. The sample files are found in the Chapter12 folder. For more information about the sample files, see the section titled "Using the Sample Files" on page xxiii.

SMALL()

Syntax   SMALL(*array,k*)

Definition   This function returns the smallest *k*-value in a data set. Use this function to return values with a certain relative size in a data set.

Arguments

- ***array* (required)** The array or range of data for which you want to determine the smallest *k*-value

- ***k* (required)** The position of the element in the array or cell range to return

Background   The SMALL() function is the counterpart to the LARGE() function and returns the smallest value in a table. Note the following about the SMALL() function:

- If *array* is empty, SMALL() returns the #NUM! error value.

- If *k* is less than or equal to 0 or greater than the number of data points, the function returns the #NUM! error.

- If *n* is the number of data points in a range, then SMALL(*array*, 1) returns the smallest value and SMALL(*array,n*) returns the largest value.

Example   A football league has recorded the number of visitors watching football games in an Excel file. Now the league wants to know the days with the least visitors without having to sort the data. Figure 12-129 shows the result of the SMALL() function.

> ## Tip
> If you want to know what days are associated with the results of the SMALL() function, use conditional formats or return the number of the entry by using the MATCH() function. Use this number and the INDEX() function to find the corresponding day.

▲	B	C	D	E	F
2	Day of event	Amount of visitors		Calculation of lowest amount of visitors	
3	Day 1	107,629		1	107,629
4	Day 2	185,385		2	124,328
5	Day 3	180,807		3	146,215
6	Day 4	124,328		=SMALL(VISITOR,E5)	
7	Day 5	146,215			
8	Day 6	185,675			
9	Day 7	210,169			
10	Day 8	221,729			
11	Day 9	234,187			
12	Day 10	237,947			
13	Day 11	210,088			
14	Day 12	207,791			
15	Day 13	201,097			
16	Day 14	222,460			
17	Day 15	208,585			
18	Day 16	206,387			
19	Day 17	218,951			

Figure 12-129 Finding the smallest value from the number of visitors watching the games.

See Also LARGE(), MAX(), MEDIAN(), MIN(), PERCENTILE.INC(), PERCENTILE.EXC(), PERCENTRANK.EXC(), PERCENTRANK.INC(), QUARTILE.EXC(), QUARTILE.INC()

> ## Sample Files
> Use the SMALL worksheet in the Count.xls or Count.xlsx sample file. The sample files are found in the Chapter12 folder. For more information about the sample files, see the section titled "Using the Sample Files" on page xxiii.

STANDARDIZE()

Syntax   STANDARDIZE(*x,mean,standard_dev*)

Definition   This function returns the standardized value of a distribution characterized by an average value and a standard variance.

Arguments

- *x* **(required)** The value you want to standardize

- *mean* **(required)** The arithmetic mean of the distribution

- *standard_dev* **(required)** The standard deviation of the distribution

> **Note**
> If *standard_dev* is less than or equal to 0, the function returns the #NUM! error.

Background   In statistics, the *standardization* is the transformation of differently scaled number values in a consistent value range from 0 to 1 to compare distributed values.

The standard normal distribution is a type of continuous probability distribution. The special meaning of the normal distribution is based on the central limit theorem that states that a sum of *n* independent identical distributed random variables is normal distributed at the limit.

See Also   You will find more information about (standard) normal distributions in the description of NORM.DIST().

A standardized normal distribution has the mean 0 and the standard deviation 1. The STANDARDIZE() function returns the standardized value *x* of a normal distribution with a known mean and standard deviation. The equation for a standardized value is:

$$Z = \frac{x - \mu}{\sigma}$$

Example   You are a light bulb manufacturer and want to analyze the performance of light bulbs. You have already entered the measurements in an Excel table (see Figure 12-130).

	D2	▼	f_x =STANDARDIZE(C2,$F$6,$G$6)	

	B	C	D
1	Test electric bulbs	Measured burning capacity in hours (=X)	Standardization =z-values
2	1	1000	-1.728
3	2	1100	-1.555
4	3	1200	-1.382
5	4	1300	-1.209
6	5	1400	-1.037
7	6	1500	-0.864
8	7	1600	-0.691
9	8	1700	-0.518
10	9	1800	-0.346
11	10	1900	-0.173
12	11	2000	0.000
13	12	2100	0.173
14	13	2200	0.346
15	14	2300	0.518
16	15	2400	0.691
17	16	2500	0.864
18	17	2600	1.037
19	18	2700	1.209
20	19	2800	1.382
21	20	2900	1.555
22	21	3000	1.728
23	22	2900	1.555

Figure 12-130 The measurement results.

You have also calculated the average life cycle and the associated standard deviation, as shown in Figure 12-131.

Average	Standard deviation
2000	579

Figure 12-131 Mean and standard deviation of the performance.

You use the STANDARDIZE() function to standardize all measured values. What arguments does this function require?

- x = distribution values (measured performance)

- *mean* = 2000 (F6)

- *standard_dev* = 579 (G6)

Figure 12-132 shows the results.

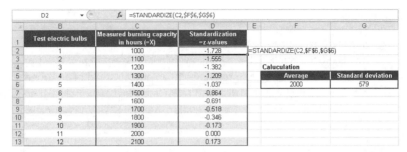

Figure 12-132 Calculating the standardized values with the STANDARDIZE() function.

Using the STANDARDIZE() function, you generated all standardized distribution values.

> **Tip**
>
> If you specify absolute cell references for the *mean* and *standard_dev* arguments, you have to enter the formula only once for any distribution value. Then you can copy the formula for the other values. To specify an absolute cell reference, press the F4 key.

See Also   NORM.DIST(), NORM.INV(), NORM.S.DIST(), NORM.S.INV(), Z.TEST()

> **Sample Files**
>
> Use the STANDARDIZE worksheet in the Probability.xls or Probability.xlsx sample file. The sample files are found in the Chapter12 folder. For more information about the sample files, see the section titled "Using the Sample Files" on page xxiii.

STDEV.P()/STDEVP()

Syntax   STDEV.P(*number1,number2,...*)

Definition   This function calculates the standard deviation based on the population. All values have to be specified as arguments. The standard deviation is a measure of how widely values are dispersed from the average value (the mean).

Arguments

- **_number1_ (required) and _number2_ (optional)** At least one and up to 255 arguments (30 in Excel 2003 and earlier versions) corresponding to a population. You can also use a single array or a reference to an array instead of arguments separated by commas. Logical values (TRUE and FALSE) and text are ignored. If you want to include logical values and text in the calculation, use the STDEVA.P() function.

> **Note**
>
> The STDEV.P() function assumes that its arguments are the entire population. If your data represents a sample of the population, calculate the standard deviation with STDEV.S(). For large sample sizes, the STDEV.S() and STDEV.P() functions return approximately equal values.
>
> The calculated standard deviation for a sample isn't an estimate of the standard deviation of the population. This means that it is divided by n instead of by $n-1$.

Background   Because the only difference between STDEV.P() and STDEV.S() is that STDEV.P() doesn't calculate the standard deviation based on a sample but based on the entire population, this example focuses on STDEV.P().

See Also You will find more information about standard deviations in the description of STDEV.S().

STDEV.P() uses the following formula:

$$\sqrt{\frac{\sum\left(x-\bar{x}\right)^2}{n}}$$

The value x is the sample mean AVERAGE(_number1,number2,..._), and n is the sample data set.

Example   Let's get back to the website evaluation of the software manufacturer (see Figure 12-133).

> **Note**
>
> The data to be evaluated includes the entire population. This means that the website has been available for only 18 months and that all of the visits of the past 18 months are recorded. The calculation with STDEV.P() and STDEV.S() is based on the population of the data from January 2007 to June 2008.

C28		f_x	=STDEV.P(C5:C22)					
	B	C	D	E	F	G	H	I
4	Date	ADVENT	DOWNLOAD	EVENT	TRAINING	KNOWHOW	PRODUCTS	ALL (SUM)
5	Jan-07		6		19	43	22	90
6	Feb-07		498	38	1319	3000	1170	6025
7	Mar-07		1401	119	2233	6116	1545	11414
8	Apr-07		1076	16	1903	2860	1168	7023
9	May-07		1563	15	1589	3126	1139	7432
10	Jun-07		1790	1853	2428	6682	5083	17836
11	Jul-07		1367	1622	1559	3311	3609	11468
12	Aug-07		1138	2170	1502	3317	4810	12937
13	Sep-07		1352	2611	1628	3542	5581	14714
14	Oct-07	1	1343	538	1440	2971	5506	11799
15	Nov-07	272	1430	1254	2255	4735	11786	21732
16	Dec-07	1874	1140	631	1583	2652	6227	14107
17	Jan-08	42	1421	1515	2224	4837	9500	19539
18	Feb-08	32	1508	1433	1418	4006	12000	20397
19	Mar-08	10	2137	3114	1298	3128	8000	17687
20	Apr-08	10	1948	2347	1085	3575	8208	17173
21	May-08	9	1521	848	765	2139	7739	13021
22	Jun-08		426	440	123	768	778	2535
23	Sum	2250	23065	20564	26371	60808	93871	226929
24	Average	281.25	1281.39	1209.65	1465.06	3378.22	5215.06	12607.17
25	Mean deviation	398.2	378.3	827.3	472.6	1093.9	3067.9	4785.7
26	Variance (VAR.S())	369515	263885	909327	419645	2419493	13563385	35319311
27	STDEV.S()	649.85	528.59	982.93	666.58	1600.57	3789.62	6115.30
28	STDEV.P()	607.88	513.70	953.59	647.80	1555.47	3682.85	5943.01

Figure 12-133 Based on a population, the STDEV.P function returns a different result than the STDEV.S function that assumes a sample of the population.

Therefore, the STDEV.P() and STDEV.S() functions, which use different formulas, also return different results.

If you take a closer look at the PRODUCTS area, you can make the following statement: The result of 3,682.85 indicates the variance around the mean. This means that the clicks are higher or lower by 3,682.85 than the mean.

If you square the value calculated by STDEV.P(), you get the result from VAR.P().

See Also   DSTDEV(), DSTDEVP(), STDEV.S(), STDEVA(), STDEVPA()

Sample Files

Use the STDEV.P worksheet in the Variance.xls or Variance.xlsx sample file. The sample files are found in the Chapter12 folder. For more information about the sample files, see the section titled "Using the Sample Files" on page xxiii.

STDEV.S()/STDEV()

Syntax STDEV.S(*number1,number2,...*)

Definition This function estimates the standard deviation based on a sample. The *standard deviation* is a measure of how widely values are dispersed from the average value (the mean).

Arguments

- *number1* **(required) and** *number2* **(optional)** At least one and up to 255 arguments (30 in Excel 2003 and earlier versions) corresponding to a sample of the population. You can also use a single array or a reference to an array instead of arguments separated by commas.

> **Note**
>
> The STDEV.S() function assumes that its arguments are a sample of the entire population. If the data passed as arguments are a population, calculate the standard deviation with the STDEV.P() function.
>
> The calculated standard deviation is an estimate of the standard deviation of the sample from a population. This means that it is divided by $n-1$ instead of by n.
>
> Logical values (TRUE and FALSE) and text are ignored. If you want to include logical values and text in the calculation, use the STDEVA() function.

Background The standard deviation is the square root of the variance. The standard deviation indicates the variance in the measure for the characteristic.

See Also You will find more information about variances in the definition of VAR.S().

Both measures are used in inferential statistics for the equation of the normal distribution. These measures are also used in descriptive statistics because they are considered more reliable than linear deviations.

The height of the variance and the standard deviation depend on the measure containing the characteristic. This factor has to be taken into account when comparing different distributions, especially for variables that also refer to different property dimensions.

In these cases, the variance coefficient is used. The variance coefficient is calculated by dividing the standard deviation by the arithmetic mean and the relative spreads. The higher the variance coefficient, the higher the variance relative to other distributions. To calculate the variance coefficient, the ratio scale is required.

The standard deviation is one of the most important spreads. Like the variance, the standard deviation describes the deviation from the mean. However, unlike the variance, the standard deviation is calculated based on the square of the difference.

In other words: The standard deviation is the square root of the arithmetic mean of the squared deviation of the values from the arithmetic mean. Therefore, the standard deviation is the root of the variance. STDEV() uses the following formula:

$$\sqrt{\frac{\sum\left(x-\bar{x}\right)^{2}}{(n-1)}}$$

The value x is the sample mean AVERAGE(*number1,number2,...*) and n is the sample data set.

Example   You are the manager of the marketing department and already know a lot about statistics and the possible evaluations. Now you want to use the STDEV.S() function to create detailed evaluations of the website visits. The goal is to calculate the standard deviation based on a sample to evaluate the variance of the visits around the mean.

> **Note**
> The data to be evaluated is a sample. This means that although the website has existed for a long time, the calculation of the standard deviation with STDEV.S() and STDEV.A() is based on the data from 18 months (January 2007 to June 2008).

You have already created an Excel file containing the number of visits per months for different areas of the website. In addition to the standard deviation, you also calculated the variance, the average deviation, and the mean for each data set.

To calculate the variance, square the lower standard deviation by the returned value (see Figure 12-134).

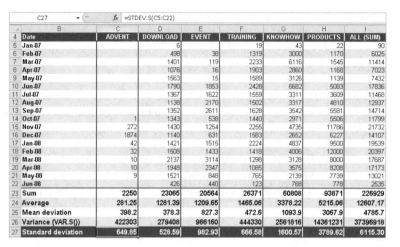

	C27	▾	*fx*	=STDEV.S(C5:C22)				
	B	C	D	E	F	G	H	I
4	Date	ADVENT	DOWNLOAD	EVENT	TRAINING	KNOWHOW	PRODUCTS	ALL (SUM)
5	Jan-07		6		19	43	22	90
6	Feb-07		498	38	1319	3000	1170	6025
7	Mar-07		1401	119	2233	6116	1545	11414
8	Apr-07		1076	16	1903	2860	1168	7023
9	May-07		1563	15	1589	3126	1139	7432
10	Jun-07		1790	1853	2428	6682	5083	17836
11	Jul-07		1367	1622	1559	3311	3609	11468
12	Aug-07		1138	2170	1502	3317	4810	12937
13	Sep-07		1352	2611	1628	3542	5581	14714
14	Oct-07	1	1343	538	1440	2971	5506	11799
15	Nov-07	272	1430	1254	2255	4735	11786	21732
16	Dec-07	1874	1140	631	1583	2652	6227	14107
17	Jan-08	42	1421	1515	2224	4837	9500	19539
18	Feb-08	32	1508	1433	1418	4006	12000	20397
19	Mar-08	10	2137	3114	1298	3128	8000	17687
20	Apr-08	10	1948	2347	1085	3575	8208	17173
21	May-08	9	1521	848	765	2139	7739	13021
22	Jun-08		426	440	123	768	778	2535
23	Sum	2250	23065	20564	26371	60808	93871	226929
24	Average	281.25	1281.39	1209.65	1465.06	3378.22	5215.06	12607.17
25	Mean deviation	398.2	378.3	827.3	472.6	1093.9	3067.9	4785.7
26	Variance (VAR.S())	422303	279408	966160	444330	2561816	14361231	37396918
27	Standard deviation	649.85	528.59	982.93	666.58	1600.57	3789.62	6115.30

Figure 12-134 The variance is calculated by squaring the result.

If you take a closer look at the PRODUCTS area, you can make the following statement: The result of 3,789.62 indicates that the website visits (clicks) scatter in height of 3,789.62 around the mean of 5,215.06.

The ALL (SUM) column contains the standard deviation for all areas and months of the sample period and indicates that they scatter in height of 6,115.3 clicks around the mean.

See Also DSTDEV(), DSTDEVP(), STDEV.A(), STDEVP(), STDEVPA()

> **Sample Files**
>
> Use the STEDV or STEDV.S worksheet in the Variance.xls or Variance.xlsx sample file. The sample files are found in the Chapter12 folder. For more information about the sample files, see the section titled "Using the Sample Files" on page xxiii.

STDEVA()

Syntax STDEVA(*value1,value2,...*)

Definition This function estimates the standard deviation based on a sample. The standard deviation is a measure of how widely values are dispersed from the average value (the mean). The STDEVA function includes text and logical values (TRUE and FALSE).

Arguments

- ***value1* (required) and *value2* (optional)** At least one and up to 255 value arguments (30 in Excel 2003 and earlier versions) corresponding to a sample of the population. You can also use a single array or a reference to an array instead of arguments separated by commas.

> **Note**
>
> The STDEVA() function assumes that its arguments are a sample from the entire population. If your data represents a population, calculate the standard deviation with STDEVPA().
>
> Unlike STDEV.S(), the STDEVA() function includes text and logical values. Arguments that contain TRUE evaluate to 1, and arguments that contain text or FALSE evaluate to 0. If you do not want to include logical values and text in the calculation, use the STDEV.S() function.
>
> The calculated standard deviation is an estimate of the standard deviation of the sample from a population. This means that it is divided by $n-1$ instead of by n.

Background Because the only difference between STDEVA() and STDEV.S() is that STDEVA() includes text and logical values, this example focuses on STDEVA().

See Also You will find more information about standard deviations in the description of STDEV.S().

STDEVA() uses the same formula as STDEV.S().

$$\sqrt{\frac{\sum\left(x-\overline{x}\right)^2}{(n-1)}}$$

The value x is the sample mean AVERAGE(*value1*,*value2*,...), and n is the sample data set.

Example Let's look again at the evaluation of the website visits. Because in the past 18 months several website problems occurred, the visits could not be counted in all months. The company had the following problems:

- In March 2007 and September 2007, a problem with website hosting occurred and in both months the website was not available. These months are marked with the string "hostingproblems".

- In February 2008, the content pages of the training area were changed to include the entire area. Because external access to the training area wasn't possible, this month is marked with the logical value FALSE.

- For May 2008, the website visits were not counted. Because the website was accessed, this month has the logical value TRUE.

As you can see in Figure 12-135, the STDEVA() function returns a different result than STDEV.S(). This happens because STDEVA() includes text and logical values. The text values and the logical value FALSE were set to 0, and the logical value TRUE was set to 1.

C28	▼	f_x =STDEVA(C5:C22)						
B	C	D	E	F	G	H	I
4 Date	ADVENT	DOWNLOAD	EVENT	TRAINING	KNOWHOW	PRODUCTS	ALL (SUM)
5 Jan-07		6		19	43	22	90
6 Feb-07		498	38	1319	3000	1170	6025
7 Mar-07	Hostingproblems	Hostingproblems	Hostingproblems	Hostingproblems	Hostingproblems	Hostingproblems	Hostingproblems
8 Apr-07		1076	16	1903	2860	1168	7023
9 May-07		1563	15	1589	3126	1139	7432
10 Jun-07		1790	1853	2428	6682	5083	17836
11 Jul-07		1367	1622	1559	3311	3609	11468
12 Aug-07		1138	2170	1502	3317	4810	12937
13 Sep-07	Hostingproblems	Hostingproblems	Hostingproblems	Hostingproblems	Hostingproblems	Hostingproblems	Hostingproblems
14 Oct-07	1	1343	538	1440	2971	5506	11799
15 Nov-07	272	1430	1254	2255	4735	11786	21732
16 Dec-07	1874	1140	631	1583	2652	6227	14107
17 Jan-08	42	1421	1515	2224	4837	9500	19539
18 Feb-08	FALSE	FALSE	FALSE	FALSE	FALSE	FALSE	FALSE
19 Mar-08	10	2137	3114	1298	3128	8000	17687
20 Apr-08	10	1948	2347	1085	3575	8208	17173
21 May-08	TRUE	TRUE	TRUE	TRUE	TRUE	TRUE	TRUE
22 Jun-08		426	440	123	768	778	2535
23 Sum	2209	17283	15553	20327	45005	67006	167383
24 Average	368.17	1234.50	1196.38	1451.93	3214.64	4786.14	11955.93
25 Mean deviation	501.9	446.1	846.2	489.7	1024.2	2975.8	5331.4
26 Variance (VAR.S())	554909	353161	1010192	495586	2594171	13504340	43314992
27 STDEV.S()	744.92	594.27	1005.08	703.98	1610.64	3674.83	6581.41
28 STDEVA()	586.84	740.85	1015.46	874.44	1968.42	3810.32	7699.47

Figure 12-135 Because text and logical values are included, the STDEVA() function returns a different result than the STDEV.S() function.

If you take a closer look at the PRODUCTS area, you can make the following statement: The result of 3,810.32 indicates the variance around the mean. This means that the clicks are higher or lower by 3,810.32 than the mean.

See Also DSTDEV(), DSTDEVP(), STDEV.P(), STDEV.S(), STDEVPA()

Sample Files

Use the STDEVA worksheet in the Variance.xlsx sample file. The sample files are found in the Chapter12 folder. For more information about the sample files, see the section titled "Using the Sample Files" on page xxiii.

STDEVPA()

Syntax   STDEVPA(*value1,value2,...*)

Definition   This function calculates the standard deviation based on a population indicated as arguments, including text and logical values. The standard deviation is a measure
of how widely values are dispersed from the average value (the mean).

Arguments

- *value1* **(required) and** *value2* **(optional)** At least one and up to 255 values (30 in
  Excel 2003 and earlier versions) corresponding to a population. You can also use a
  single array or a reference to an array instead of arguments separated by commas.

> **Note**
>
> The STDEVPA() function assumes that its arguments are the entire population. If your
> data represents a sample of the population, calculate the standard deviation with
> STDEVA().
>
> Arguments that contain TRUE evaluate to, 1 and arguments that contain text or FALSE
> evaluate to 0. If you do not want to include logical values and text in the calculation,
> use the STDEV.P() function.
>
> For large sample sizes, STDEVA() and STDEVPA() return equal values.
>
> The calculated standard deviation for a sample isn't an estimate of the standard devia-
> tion of the population. This means that it is divided by *n* instead of by *n*–1.

Background   Because the standard deviation was already explained in detail in the
description of STDEV(), this section focuses on the example.

STDEVPA() uses the same formula as STDEV.P():

$$\sqrt{\frac{\sum\left(x-\overline{x}\right)^{2}}{n}}$$

X is the sample mean AVERAGE(*value1,value2,...*) and *n* is the sample data set.

Example   For STDEVPA() we use the same example as for the STDEVA() function. In this example, the software company had the following problems with its website:

- In March 2007 and September 2007, a problem with website hosting occurred and in both months the website was not available. These months are marked with the string "hostingproblems".

- In February 2008, the content pages of the training area were changed to include the entire area. Because external access to the training area wasn't possible, this month is marked with the logical value FALSE.

- For May 2008, the website visits were not counted. Because the website was accessed, this month has the logical value TRUE.

> **Note**
>
> As for STDEV.P(), the data to be evaluated includes the entire population. This means that the website is only available for 18 months and all of the visits of the last 18 months are recorded.

As you can see in Figure 12-136, the STDEVPA() function returns a different result than STDEV.P(). This happens because STDEVPA() includes text and logical values. In this example, the text values and the logical value FALSE are set to 0, and the logical value TRUE is set to 1.

	C28	▼	*fx*	=STDEVPA(C5:C22)			
	B	C	D	E	F	G	H	I
4	Date	ADVENT	DOWNLOAD	EVENT	TRAINING	KNOWHOW	PRODUCTS	ALL (SUM)
5	Jan-07		6		19	43	22	90
6	Feb-07		498	38	1319	3000	1170	6025
7	Mar-07	Hostingproblems	Hostingproblems	Hostingproblems	Hostingproblems	Hostingproblems	Hostingproblems	Hostingproblems
8	Apr-07		1076	16	1903	2860	1168	7023
9	May-07		1563	15	1589	3126	1139	7432
10	Jun-07		1790	1853	2428	6682	5083	17836
11	Jul-07		1367	1622	1559	3311	3609	11468
12	Aug-07		1138	2170	1502	3317	4810	12937
13	Sep-07	Hostingproblems	Hostingproblems	Hostingproblems	Hostingproblems	Hostingproblems	Hostingproblems	Hostingproblems
14	Oct-07	1	1343	538	1440	2971	5506	11799
15	Nov-07	272	1430	1254	2255	4735	11786	21732
16	Dec-07	1874	1140	631	1583	2652	6227	14107
17	Jan-08	42	1421	1515	2224	4837	9500	19539
18	Feb-08	FALSE	FALSE	FALSE	FALSE	FALSE	FALSE	FALSE
19	Mar-08	10	2137	3114	1298	3128	8000	17687
20	Apr-08	10	1948	2347	1085	3575	8208	17173
21	May-08	TRUE	TRUE	TRUE	TRUE	TRUE	TRUE	TRUE
22	Jun-08		426	440	123	768	778	2535
23	Sum	2209	17283	15553	20327	45005	67006	167383
24	Average	368.17	1234.50	1196.38	1451.93	3214.64	4786.14	11955.93
25	Mean deviation	501.9	446.1	846.2	489.7	1024.2	2975.8	5331.4
26	VARPA()	309942	518360	970510	722160	3659402	13711984	55988426
27	STDEV.P()	680.02	572.66	965.65	678.37	1552.05	3541.15	6342.01
28	STDEVPA()	556.72	719.97	985.14	849.80	1,912.96	3,702.97	7,482.54

Figure 12-136 Because text and logical values are included, the STDEVPA()function returns a different result than the STDEV.P() function.

If you take a closer look at the PRODUCTS area, you can make the following statement: The result of 3,702.97 indicates the variance around the mean based on a population and including text and logical values. This means that the clicks are higher or lower by 3,702.97 than the mean.

See Also   DSTDEV(), DSTDEVP(), STDEV.P(), STDEV.S(), STDEVA()

Sample Files

Use the STDEVPA worksheet in the Variance.xlsx sample file. The sample files are found in the Chapter12 folder. For more information about the sample files, see the section titled "Using the Sample Files" on page xxiii.

STEYX()

Syntax   STEYX(*known_y's,known_x's*)

Definition   This function returns the standard error of the predicted y-values for each *x* in the regression. The standard error is a measure of the amount of error in the prediction of a y-value associated with an x-value.

Arguments

- *known_y's* **(required)** An array or a range of dependent data points

- *known_x's* **(required)** An array or a range of independent data points

---

Note

Arguments can be numbers, names, arrays, or references containing numbers.

If an array or a reference argument contains text, logical values, or empty cells, those values are ignored. However, cells with the value 0 are included.

If *known_y's* and *known_x's* are empty or have a different number of data points, the STEYX() function returns the #N/A error value.

Background   The standard error is the variance of the sample values around the actual value of the calculated parameter in the population. The higher the standard error is, the larger the confidence interval containing the parameter with a given probability will be.

Chapter 12

The size of the standard error depends on the variance of the values in the population. The lower the variance is, the lower the standard errors in the sample will be. In general, the standard error decreases proportional to the square root of the sample size. This means that you have to quadruple the sample size to divide a standard error in half.

The STEYX() function returns the estimated standard error of a linear regression and indicates the reliability of the linear regression. The higher the standard error is, the higher the deviation of the estimated values will be from the values in the population.

Usually you specify a cell range for the *known_y's* and *known_x's* arguments. The *known_y's* argument contains dependent variables, and the *known_x's* argument contains independent variables.

This function expects *known_y's* first and then *known_x's*—not the other way around.

If the population is normal distributed with μ and σ, the following is true for the estimate function from the means of multiple samples *n*:

- It is normal distributed.

- The mean is μ.

- The variance of the sample distribution in a standard deviation is called the *standard error of the mean*.

The standard error defines the standard deviation of all sample means from the assumed mean of the population. If the variance of different sample means is approximately 0, the standard error is also approximately 0. If the variance is large, the standard error will also be large. The larger the sample size, the lower the standard error.

The equation to calculate the standard error of an expected y-value is:

$$\sqrt{\left(\frac{1}{n-2}\right)\left[\sum\left(y-\overline{y}\right)^2 - \frac{\left[\sum\left(x-\overline{x}\right)\left(y-\overline{y}\right)\right]^2}{\sum\left(x-\overline{x}\right)^2}\right]}$$

The values *x* and *y* are the sample means AVERAGE(*array1*) and AVERAGE(*array2*), and *n* is the sample size.

Example   We use the example of the software company to explain the STEYX() function. The company sells all its products through its internal website. The company was founded

10 years ago. Although the website and online order are also available for 10 years, the number of website visits has been recorded only for the past eight years. The online orders are not recorded in a separate database.

You are the marketing manager and have the numbers for the last 2.5 years. You want to further analyze this data. You have entered the number of website visits and online orders per month in Excel.

The online orders depend on the website visits. The means that the higher the number of website visits the more online orders are placed. You also calculated the mean for both components. For the dependent online orders (y-values), the mean is 1,121 between July 2007 and June 2008 (see Figure 12-137).

	B	C	D
2	**Month**	**Web access**	**Orders**
3	January 2006	236	20
4	February 2006	1,221	387
5	March 2006	1,563	456
6	April 2006	2,682	544
7	May 2006	4,569	349
8	June 2006	6,848	854
9	July 2006	8,463	427
10	August 2006	10,157	337
11	September 2006	11,837	899
12	October 2006	12,987	1,011
13	November 2006	13,739	720
14	December 2006	14,376	1,069
15	January 2007	15,739	1,070
16	February 2007	16,123	967
17	March 2007	16,548	1,401
18	April 2007	17,352	1,076
19	May 2007	17,986	1,563
20	June 2007	18,234	1,485
21	July 2007	18,769	1,367
22	August 2007	19,736	1,138
23	September 2007	20,333	1,352
24	October 2007	20,987	1,343
25	November 2007	21,323	1,430
26	December 2007	21,999	1,375
27	January 2008	22,786	1,421
28	February 2008	23,784	1,508
29	March 2008	24,574	1,876
30	April 2008	25,111	1,948
31	May 2008	25,789	2,094
32	June 2008	26,948	2,134
33	**Average**	**15,427**	**1,121**

Figure 12-137 The calculated mean for the website visits and the online orders.

Now you want to know how realistic the calculated sample mean is for the expected online orders. The question is: How high is the standard error of the estimated online orders for all website visits? To answer this, you use the STEYX() function. Figure 12-138 shows the result.

	C34	▼	f_x	=STEYX(D3:D32,C3:C32)

⊿	B	C	D
1		Independent = x-value	Dependent = y-value
2	**Month**	**Web access**	**Orders**
3	January 2006	236	20
4	February 2006	1,221	387
5	March 2006	1,563	456
6	April 2006	2,682	544
7	May 2006	4,569	349
8	June 2006	6,848	854
9	July 2006	8,463	427
10	August 2006	10,157	337
11	September 2006	11,837	899
12	October 2006	12,987	1,011
13	November 2006	13,739	720
14	December 2006	14,376	1,069
15	January 2007	15,739	1,070
16	February 2007	16,123	967
17	March 2007	16,548	1,401
18	April 2007	17,352	1,076
19	May 2007	17,986	1,563
20	June 2007	18,234	1,485
21	July 2007	18,769	1,367
22	August 2007	19,736	1,138
23	September 2007	20,333	1,352
24	October 2007	20,987	1,343
25	November 2007	21,323	1,430
26	December 2007	21,999	1,375
27	January 2008	22,786	1,421
28	February 2008	23,784	1,508
29	March 2008	24,574	1,876
30	April 2008	25,111	1,948
31	May 2008	25,789	2,094
32	June 2008	26,948	2,134
33	**Average**	**15,427**	**1,121**
34	**Standard error**	210.07	

Figure 12-138 STEYX() returns the standard error for the y-values associated with the x-values.

As you can see in the figure, the standard error is 210.07.

Based on these results, you can draw the following conclusion: The result of 210.07 indicates that the sample mean of the online orders for all website visits is dispersed by 210 orders around the mean.

The result of 210.07 is the size of the error of the expected online orders depending on the website visits.

See Also INTERCEPT(), LINEST(), LOGEST(), PEARSON(), RSQ(), SLOPE()

Sample Files

Use the STEYX worksheet in the Probability.xls or Probability.xlsx sample file. The sample files are found in the Chapter12 folder. For more information about the sample files, see the section titled "Using the Sample Files" on page xxiii.

T.DIST()

Syntax   T.DIST(*x,degrees_freedom,cumulative*)

Definition   This function returns the Student's t-distribution. The *t-distribution* is used to test hypotheses for small sample data sets. Use this function instead of a table of critical values for the t-distribution.

Arguments

- *x* **(required)** The numeric value at which to evaluate the distribution.

- *degrees_freedom* **(required)** An integer indicating the number of degrees of freedom.

- *cumulative* **(required)** The logical value that represents the type of the function. If *cumulative* is TRUE, the T.DIST() function returns the accumulated distribution function. If *cumulative* is FALSE, the T.DIST() function returns the value of the density function.

> **Note**
>
> If one of the arguments isn't a numeric expression, the T.DIST() function returns the #VALUE! error.
>
> If *degrees_freedom* < 1, the function returns the #NUM! error.
>
> If $x < 0$, the function returns the #NUM! error.

Background   You will find more information about t-distributed random variables in the description of T.TEST().

Example   You will find more information about the use of this function in the description of T.DIST.2T().

See Also T.INV(), T.INV.2T, T.TEST()

> **Sample Files**
>
> Use the TDIST or T.DIST worksheet in the Probability.xls or Probability.xlsx sample file. The sample files are found in the Chapter12 folder. For more information about the sample files, see the section titled "Using the Sample Files" on page xxiii.

Chapter 12

T.DIST.RT()

Syntax   T.DIST.RT(*x,degrees_freedom*)

Definition   This function returns the Student's t-distribution of the right tail. The t-distribution is used to test hypotheses for small sample data sets. Use this function instead of a table of critical values for the t-distribution.

Arguments

- ***x* (required)** The numeric value at which to evaluate the distribution

- ***degrees_freedom* (required)** An integer indicating the number of degrees of freedom

> **Note**
>
> If one of the arguments isn't a numeric expression, the T.DIST.RT() function returns the #VALUE! error.
>
> If *degrees_freedom* < 1, the function returns the #NUM! error.
>
> If $x < 0$, the function returns the #NUM! error.

Background   You will find more information about t-distributed random variables in the description of T.TEST().

Example   You will find more information about the use of this function in the description of T.DIST.2T().

See Also   T.INV(), T.INV.2T, T.TEST()

> **Sample Files**
>
> Use the T.DIST.RT worksheet in the Probability.xls or Probability.xlsx sample file. The sample files are found in the Chapter12 folder. For more information about the sample files, see the section titled "Using the Sample Files" on page xxiii.

T.DIST.2T()/TDIST()

> **Note**
>
> In Excel 2010, the TDIST() function was replaced with the T.DIST.2T() function and the T.DIST() and T.DIST.RT() functions were added to increase the accuracy of the results. To ensure the backward compatibility of T.DIST.2T(), the TDIST() function is still available.

Syntax   T.DIST.2T(*x,degrees_freedom*)

Definition   This function returns the values of a distribution function (1 alpha) of a Student's t-distributed random variable. The t-distribution is used to test hypotheses for small sample data sets. Use this function instead of a table of critical values for the t-distribution.

Arguments

- ***x* (required)** The distribution value (quantile) for which you want to calculate the probability

- ***degrees_freedom* (required)** An integer indicating the number of degrees of freedom

> **Note**
>
> If one of the arguments isn't a numeric expression, the T.DIST.2T() function returns the #VALUE! error.
>
> If *degrees_freedom* < 1, the function returns the #NUM! error. If *x* < 0, the function returns the #NUM! error.

Background   The T.DIST.2T() function calculates the significance level (alpha risk) of a t-distributed random variable. The probability of a hypothesis is evaluated based on the significance level.

See Also You will find more information about t-distributed random variables in the description of T.TEST().

The calculation of the significance level gets interesting if you calculate the critical value for the sample and then calculate the significance level for this critical value by using the T.DIST.2T() function. Using the result returned by the T.DIST.2T() function, you can determine if the null hypothesis is valid.

Example   The compatibility of a drug is examined in a clinical study. One test group takes the normal daily dosage and the other test group takes an increased dosage at the beginning of the study. One person has to cancel the test early for private reasons. The goal is to determine whether the increased dosage accelerates the healing process. The duration of treatment is calculated in days.

The null hypothesis indicates that there is no difference in the two test groups regarding the success of treatment. The alternative hypothesis indicates that the second group recovered faster because the method of treatment is more efficient than the usual treatment.

You run a two-tailed, type 2 t-test; that is, you compare the mean of two independent samples. You want to calculate the significance level for the critical value of the samples to evaluate the hypotheses based on the result. Therefore you use the T.DIST.2T() function. Figure 12-139 shows the calculation of T.DIST.2T().

B17	▾	f_x =T.DIST.2T(F9,F7)			
	B	C	D	E	F
1	Group 1 x₁	Group 2 x₂		Calculated/given values	Wert
2	7	2		Observed average X₁' =	6.60
3	8	4		Observed average X₂' =	4.33
4	8	3		Level of significance α=	
5	9	5		Size of sample N₁=	10
6	6	2		Size of sample N₂=	9
7	8	9		Degree of freedom = N₁+N₂-2 =	17
8	4	5		Test statistic t	2.39049197
9	7	6		Critical value	1.739606716
10	6	3			
11	3				
12					
13	**Result for T.TEST**				
14	0.01433616	=T.TEST(B9:B18;C9:C18;1;2)			
15					
16	**Result for T.DIST.2T**				
17	0.100000002	=T.DIST.2T(F9,F7)			

Figure 12-139 T.DIST.2T() returns the significance level for the critical value.

Because T.DIST.2T() returns a probability value, the result is 10 percent. Now you can assume with a 10 percent probability that the null hypothesis is valid. Because the probability is minor, the null hypothesis has to be rejected.

See Also   T.INV(), T.INV.2T, T.TEST()

Sample Files

Use the TDIST or T.DIST.2T worksheet in the Probability.xls or Probability.xlsx sample file. The sample files are found in the Chapter12 folder. For more information about the sample files, see the section titled "Using the Sample Files" on page xxiii.

T.INV()

Syntax   T.INV(*probability,degrees_freedom*)

Definition   This function returns the left quantile of a Student's t-distribution.

Arguments

- ***probability* (required)** The probability associated with the two-tailed Student's t-distribution

- ***degrees_freedom* (required)** The number of degrees of freedom with which to characterize the distribution

---

Note

If one of the arguments isn't a numeric expression, the T.INV() function returns the #VALUE! error.

If *probability* is less than 0 or greater than 1, the T.INV() function returns the #NUM! error.

If *degrees_freedom* isn't an integer, the decimal places are truncated. If *degrees_freedom* is less than 1, the function returns the #NUM! error.

Background   You will find more information about t-values or critical values in the description of T.INV.2T().

Example   You will find more information about the use of this function in the description of T.INV.2T().

See Also   T.DIST.2T(), T.TEST()

Sample Files

Use the TINV or T.INV worksheet in the Probability.xls or Probability.xlsx sample file. The sample files are found in the Chapter12 folder. For more information about the sample files, see the section titled "Using the Sample Files" on page xxiii.

Chapter 12

T.INV.2T()/TINV()

> **Note**
>
> In Excel 2010 the TINV() function was replaced with the T.INV.2T() function, and the T.INV() function was added to increase the accuracy of the results. To ensure the backward compatibility of T.INV.2T(), the TINV() function is still available.

Syntax   T.INV.2T(*probability,degrees_freedom*)

Definition   This function returns the t-value of the t-distribution as a probability and degrees of freedom.

Arguments

- *probability* **(required)** The probability associated with the two-tailed Student's t-distribution

- *degrees_freedom* **(required)** The number of degrees of freedom with which to characterize the distribution

> **Note**
>
> If one of the arguments isn't a numeric expression, the T.INV.2T() function returns the #VALUE! error.
>
> If *probability* is less than 0 or greater than 1, the T.INV.2T() function returns the #NUM! error.
>
> If *degrees_freedom* isn't an integer, the decimal places are truncated. If *degrees_freedom* is less than 1, the function returns the #NUM! error.
>
> T.INV.2T returns the value t, such that $P(|X| > t) = probability$ where X is a random variable that follows the t-distribution and $P(|X| > t) = P(X < -t \text{ or } X > t)$.
>
> A quantile of the t-distribution can be interpreted as the t-value of a one-tailed confidence interval. Because of the symmetry of the t-distribution, the t-value for a one-tailed confidence interval can be calculated by replacing the *probability* argument with 2*probability.

> For a probability of 0.05 and 10 degrees of freedom, the t-value for a two-tailed confidence interval is calculated with =T.INV.2T()(0.05,10). The result is 2.28139.
>
> The t-value for a one-tailed confidence interval for the same probability and the same number of degrees is calculated with =T.INV.2T() (2*0.05,10). The result is 1.812462.
>
> If *probability* has a value, T.INV.2T() looks for the value *x* such that T.DIST.2T(*x,degrees_freedom*,2) = *probability*. Therefore, the accuracy of T.INV.2T() depends on the accuracy of T.DIST.2T(). T.INV.2T() uses an iterative search technique. If the search has not converged after 100 iterations, the function returns the #N/A error.

Background   The t-value returned by the T.INV.2T() function is also called the *critical value* and is used as a statistic for the prepared hypotheses.

Based on this statistic, you can run additional tests to evaluate the validity of the null hypothesis.

The arguments for this function are the probability and the degrees of freedom. The *probability* argument indicates the significance level you can calculate with the T.DIST.2T() function. For a one-tailed t-test, the significance level is doubled. The degrees of freedom are calculated based on the sum of the two samples minus 2.

See Also You will find more information about t-tests in the description of T.DIST.2T().

Example   The compatibility of a drug is examined in a clinical study. One test group takes the normal daily dosage, and the other test group takes an increased dosage at the beginning of the study. One person has to cancel the test early for private reasons. The goal is to determine whether the increased dosage accelerates the healing process. The duration of treatment is calculated in days.

The null hypothesis indicates that there is no difference in the two test groups regarding the success of treatment. The alternative hypothesis indicates that the second group recovered faster because the method of treatment is more efficient than the usual treatment.

You use a one-tailed t-test type 2: You compare the mean of two independent samples, and use a significance level of 0.05. Now you want to calculate the critical value of the sample with the T.INV.2T() function. Figure 12-140 shows the calculation of T.INV.2T().

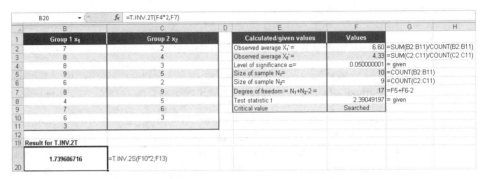

Figure 12-140 T.INV.2T() returns the t-value (critical value).

The t-value for the evaluated samples based on a probability is 1.7396. This critical value is a statistic and can be used to evaluate the null hypothesis.

> **Note**
>
> The t-value is listed in the t-tables in statistics books.

See Also   T.DIST.2T(), T.TEST()

> **Sample Files**
>
> Use the T.INV or T.INV.2T worksheet in the Probability.xls or Probability.xlsx sample file. The sample files are found in the Chapter12 folder. For more information about the sample files, see the section titled "Using the Sample Files" on page xxiii.

T.TEST()/TTEST()

Syntax   T.TEST(*array1,array2,tails,type*)

Definition   This function returns the test statistic of a Student's t-test. Use TTEST() to check whether two samples are likely to have come from the same two populations that have the same mean.

Arguments

- *array1* **(required)** The first data set.

- *array2* **(required)** The second data set.

- **tails (required)** Specifies the number of distribution tails. If *tails* = 1, the T.TEST() function uses the one-tailed distribution. If *tails* = 2, the T.TEST() function uses the two-tailed distribution.

- **type (required)** The type of t-test to perform:

  - If *type* equals 1, the test is paired.

  - If *type* equals 2, the two-sample equal variance (homoscedastic) test is performed.

  - If *type* equals 3, the two-sample unequal variance (heteroskedastic) test is performed.

Note

If *array1* and *array2* have a different number of data points and *type* = 1 (paired), T.TEST() returns the #N/A error.

The *tails* and *type* arguments are truncated to integers. If *tails* or *type* isn't a numeric value, the T.TEST() function returns the #VALUE! error.

If *tails* is any value other than 1 or 2, T.TEST() returns the #NUM! error.

The T.TEST() function uses the data in *array1* and *array2* to calculate a nonnegative t-statistic value. If *tails* = 1, T.TEST() returns the probability of a higher value of the t-statistic value under the assumption that *array1* and *array2* are samples from populations with the same mean. The value returned by T.TEST() when *tails* = 2 is double that returned when *tails* = 1 and corresponds to the probability of a higher absolute value of the t-statistic under the "same population means" assumption.

Background   The t-distribution functions indicate whether one or two samples correspond to the normal distribution. For example, you can test whether a treatment method is better than another.

The t-distribution belongs to the probability distributions and was developed in 1908 by William Sealey Gosset (alias "Student"). William Gosset found out that standardized normal distributed data are no longer normal distributed if the variance of the characteristic is unknown and the sample variance has to be used for an estimate.

The t-distribution is independent from the mean μ and the standard deviation *s* and only depends on the degrees of freedom.

Chapter 12

> **Note**
>
> The t-distribution is similar to the standard normal distribution. Like the standard normal distribution, the t-distribution is consistent, symmetrical, and bell-shaped, and has a variance range from plus/minus infinity.

Because the normal distribution applies only to a large amount of data, it usually has to be corrected. This uncertainty is observed in a t-distribution by the symmetrical distribution. If there are high degrees of freedom, the t-distribution transitions into the normal distribution.

The lower the degrees of freedom, the further away are the integral limits from the mean based on a given probability and fixed standard deviation such that for a two-tailed test, the interval is greater than 1.96 (for $P = 0.95$).

The t-distribution describes the distribution of a term:

$$t_m = \frac{N(0,1)}{\sqrt{\dfrac{\chi_m^2}{m}}}$$

$N(0.1)$ is a standard normal distributed random variable and a χ^2-distributed with m degrees of freedom. The counter variable has to be independent from the denominator variable. The density function of the t-distribution is symmetrical based on the expected value 0 (see Figure 12-141).

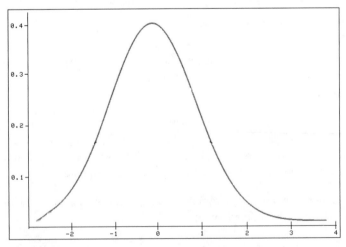

Figure 12-141 The density function of a t-distributed random variable.

The t-test allows hypotheses for smaller samples if the population shows a normal distribution, a certain mean is assumed, and the standard deviation is unknown.

There are three types of t-tests:

- **Comparison of the means from the sample with the mean from the population** An example is the comparison of the average age of the population in New York with that of the population in the entire United States.

- **Mean comparison from independent samples** An example is the comparison of the average income of men and women in New York. Because the variances of the two populations from which the samples were obtained are unknown, the variances from the sample are estimated. The *t*-distribution is followed by a t-test with *k* degrees of freedom.

> **Note**
>
> If the variances of the populations from which the samples were obtained are known, the test statistic is normal distributed.

- **Comparison of the sample means from interdependent samples** An example is the comparison of the education of spouses. A characteristic of a sample is evaluated twice and tested if the second value is higher (or lower) than the first value. The t-distribution is followed by a t-value with $n - 1$ degrees of freedom. *N* is the number of the value pairs.

The question the t-test answers is: What is the probability that the difference between the means is random? And what is the probability for an alpha error if, based on the different means in the sample, you assume that this difference also exists in the population?

> **Note**
>
> The alpha error (also called *alpha risk*) is the probability that a characteristic of the data is random. The alpha error is often 10 percent, 5 percent, or less than 5 percent (significance level) and seldom larger than 10 percent.

In other words, the t-test evaluates the (error) probability of a thesis based on samples–that is, it evaluates the probability for an alpha error.

Types of t-Tests   There are two general distinctions between the different t-test types::

- **One-tailed t-test** For a one-tailed t-test, directional hypotheses are prepared. Where H_0 and H_1:

  H_0: $\mu_1 - \mu_2$ *less than or equal to 0*

  H_1: $\mu_1 - \mu_2$ *greater than 0*

  To reach a conventional alpha level (significance level) of 5 percent, *t* has to be positioned on the predicted side of the t-distribution in the 5 percent range (see Figure 12-142).

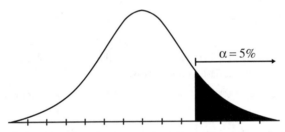

Figure 12-142 Graph of a one-tailed t-test.

- **Two-tailed t-test** For a two-tailed t-test, nondirectional hypotheses are prepared. Where H_0 and H_1:

  H_0: $\mu_1 - \mu_2 = 0$

  H_1: $\mu_1 - \mu_2 ? 0$

  To reach an overall alpha level (significance level) of 5 percent, *t* has to be positioned in the lower or upper 2.5 percent range (see Figure 12-143).

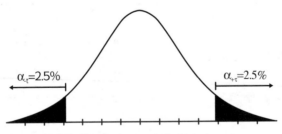

Figure 12-143 Graph of a two-tailed t-test.

The following is true for one-tailed t-tests versus two-tailed t-tests:

- For a two-tailed test, *t* has to have a higher value to be significant (α=0.05).

- For a two-tailed test, *t* is assigned a higher error probability than for a one-tailed test.

- x_1–x_2 is more likely to be significant in a one-tailed test than in a two-tailed test.

- A one-tailed test has a higher test performance.

For a two-tailed test, usually the t-value is assigned double the p-value that is assigned for a one-tailed test. This p-value can be converted into the p-value for a one-tailed test (and vice versa).

This results in the following formulas:

$$P_{two-tailed} = 2 \times P_{one-tailed}$$

$$P_{one-tailed} = \frac{1}{2} P_{two-tailed}$$

Example   The compatibility of a drug was examined in a clinical study. You have the test results as well as some explanations. One test group took the normal daily dosage, and the other test group took an increased dosage at the beginning of the study. One person had to cancel the test early for private reasons. The goal was to determine whether the increased dosage accelerates the healing process. The duration of treatment was calculated in days.

The null hypothesis indicates that there is no difference in the two test groups regarding the success of treatment. The alternative hypothesis indicates that the second group recovered faster because the method of treatment is more efficient than the usual treatment. You have to analyze the test results to determine whether the null hypothesis can be accepted or has to be rejected.

Because you weren't present during the test and don't have all the background information, you want to calculate the probability that the means of the two samples are equal by using the T.TEST() function. By comparing the result with the significance level, you can draw a conclusion about the null hypothesis.

You run a one-tailed, type 2 t-test; that is, you compare the mean of two independent samples. The significance level is 5 percent. The following formula calculates the statistic *t*:

$$t = \frac{\overline{X}_1 - \overline{X}_2}{\sqrt{\dfrac{\left[\sum X_2^1 - \dfrac{\left(\sum X_1\right)^2}{N_1}\right] + \left[\sum X_2^2 - \dfrac{\left(\sum X_2\right)^2}{N_2}\right]}{N_1 + N_2 - 2} \times \left(\dfrac{N_1 + N_2}{N_1 \times N_2}\right)}}$$

The x-values are the means of Group 1 and Group 2; N_1 and N_2 indicate the size of the two samples. Figure 12-144 shows the result of the study.

	B	C	D	E	F
	B14			f_x =T.TEST(B2:B11,C2:C11,1,2)	
	B	**C**	**D**	**E**	**F**
1	**Group 1 x₁**	**Group 2 x₂**		**Calculated/given values**	**Value**
2	7	2		Observed average X₁' =	6.60
3	8	4		Observed average X₂' =	4.33
4	8	3		Level of significance α=	0.05
5	9	5		Size of sample N₁=	10
6	6	2		Size of sample N₂=	9
7	8	9		Degree of freedom = N₁+N₂-2 =	17
8	4	5		Test statistic t	2.39049197
9	7	6			
10	6	3			
11	3				
12					
13	**Result for T.TEST**				
14	0.01433616	=T.TEST(B2:B11,C2:C11,1,2)			

Figure 12-144 Are the means of both samples equal? T.TEST() is used to calculate the result.

Because T.TEST() returns a probability value, the result is 1.4 percent. Now you can assume with a 1.4 percent probability that the sample means are not equal. In other words: You can say with 1.4 percent certainty that the samples are unequal. This is already shown in cells F2 and F3 in Figure 12-144. However, these are only estimated values based on samples.

Because the result for T.TEST() is < α, the null hypothesis has to be rejected. This means that the statement that there is no difference in the two test groups regarding the success of treatment is disregarded.

See Also T.DIST(), T.DIST.2T(), T.DIST.RT(), T.INV(), T.INV.2T

Sample Files

Use the T.TEST worksheet in the Probability.xls or Probability.xlsx sample file. The sample files are found in the Chapter12 folder. For more information about the sample files, see the section titled "Using the Sample Files" on page xxiii.

TREND()

Syntax   TREND(*known_y's;known_x's;new_x's;const*)

Definition   This function returns values along a linear trend. TREND() fits a straight line (using the method of least squares) to the *known_y's* and *known_x's* arrays. The function returns the y-values along that line for the specified array of *new_x's*.

Arguments

- ***known_y's* (required)** The y-values you already know from the relationship $y = mx + b$:

    - If the *known_y's* array consists of a single column, then each column in the *known_x's* array is interpreted as a separate variable.

    - If the *known_y's* array consists of a single row, then each row in the *known_x's* array is interpreted as a separate variable.

- ***known_x's* (optional)** The x-values you already know from the relationship $y = mx + b$:

    - The *known_x's* array can include one or more sets of variables. If only one variable is used, *known_y's* and *known_x's* can be ranges of any shape as long as they have equal dimensions. If more than one variable is used, *known_y's* must be a vector (a range consisting of a single row or column).

    - If *known_x's* is not specified, it is assumed to be the array {1,2,3,...} containing the same number of elements as *known_y's*.

    - The *known_y's* and *known_x's* arguments must have the same number of rows or columns. If the number of rows (columns) is different, you get the #REF! error. If one of the y-values is 0 or negative, you get the #NUM! error.

- ***new_x's* (optional)** The new x-values for which you want to return the corresponding y-values:

    - Like *known_x's*, the *new_x's* argument must include a column (or row) for each independent variable. The *known_x's* and *new_x's* arguments must have the same number of columns if *known_y's* is in a single column. If *known_y's* is in a single row, *known_x's* and *new_x's* must have the same number of rows.

    - If *new_x's* is not specified, it is assumed to be the same as *known_x's*.

    - If both *known_x's* and *new_x's* are omitted, they are assumed to be the array {1,2,3,...} that contains the same number of elements as *known_y's*.

- **_const_ (optional)** A logical value specifying whether to force the constant _b_ to equal 1:

  - If _const_ is TRUE or omitted, _b_ is calculated normally.

  - If _const_ is FALSE, _b_ is set equal to 1 and the m-values are adjusted so that $y = m^x$.

Note

You can use TREND() for polynomial curve fitting by regressing against the same variable raised to different powers. For example, suppose column A contains y-values and column B contains x-values. You can enter $x2$ in column C, $x3$ in column D, and so on, and then regress columns B through D against column A.

Formulas that return an array as a result have to be entered as array formulas.

When entering an array constant instead of an argument (such as _known_x's_), use commas to separate values in the same row and colons to separate rows.

Background   If you know that different values are interdependent, you can make a prediction based on the known values.

Excel provides numerous statistical functions you can use to calculate trends. Statistical functions calculate a line or curve based on known values. If you extend the time axis, you can view the future values. The known values are analyzed and described with a formula that allows extrapolation of the values. However, the data set has to be sufficient to compensate for seasonal variation. Other unforeseeable factors that impact the trend can also cause problems.

For example, consider the case in which a competitor realizes huge sales with a new product in your region. Because the regression analysis assumes that the data can be approximated with a mathematical function, Excel provides many of these functions, including TREND().

Use the TREND() function to calculate a linear trend or to analyze known values. The values are entered into a formula and allow you to predict future trends.

The y-values and x-values are the values from $y = mx + b$ where the intercept b indicates the intercept of the line with the y-axis and slope m indicates by how much the y-value changes if an x-value changes.

If values always change by a certain value, a linear trend exists.

Example   You are the marketing manager of a software company and analyze the company's website. Recently the website visits as well as the online orders have increased significantly. Because you want to know the future trend of the two components, you use the TREND() function to calculate the future values to predict the estimated number of website visits and online orders.

The website visits and orders until June 2008 are shown in Figure 12-145.

Month	Web access	Order
January 2006	236	6
February 2006	1,221	17
March 2006	6,195	456
April 2006	2,682	544
May 2006	4,569	349
June 2006	12,229	854
July 2006	12,564	427
August 2006	10,157	337
September 2006	15,160	899
October 2006	10,716	1,011
November 2006	9,844	720
December 2006	11,975	1,069
January 2007	24,695	1,070
February 2007	11,593	498
March 2007	18,491	1,401
April 2007	11,743	1,076
May 2007	11,452	1,563
June 2007	26,651	1,790
July 2007	16,287	1,367
August 2007	17,750	1,138
September 2007	19,985	1,352
October 2007	17,285	1,343
November 2007	30,369	1,430
December 2007	19,674	1,140
January 2008	28,464	1,421
February 2008	25,000	1,508
March 2008	24,574	2,137
April 2008	23,141	1,948
May 2008	17,700	1,521
June 2008	22,456	1,304

Figure 12-145 Website visits and online orders until June 2008.

You create a chart from the values generated so far to view the linear trend of the website visits and the online orders, including the equations and the value calculated for r^2 (see Figure 12-146).

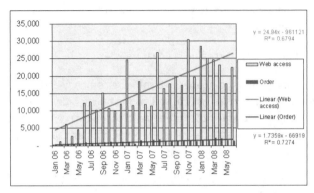

Figure 12-146 Chart of the website visits and online orders.

The linear trend line and the associated function indicate that the orders increase by 52.872 per month. This means about 53 new orders per month. Now you want to know the trend of the website visits and online orders from July 2008 through March 2009.

The TREND() function provides the following arguments to calculate the website visits in the next nine months:

- *known_y's* = website visits between January 2008 and June 2008

- *known_x's* = months (January 2006 through June 2008)

- *new_x's* = months from July 2008 through March 2009

- *const* = TRUE (the constant *b* of the equation *y* = *mx* + *b* is calculated normally)

Figure 12-147 shows the result.

Note

Remember, the TREND() function is an array function when it is calculating the values for cell range C33:C41. This means that the function immediately returns the result for all months. Therefore, you have the select cell range C33:C41, enter the formula, and press Ctrl+Page Up+Enter.

You can recognize array functions by the braces in the formula bar (see Figure 12-147).

	B	C	D
		C33	▾	fx	{=TREND(C3:C32,B3:B32,B33:B41,TRUE)}
2	Month	Web access	Order
3	January 2006	236	6
4	February 2006	1,221	17
5	March 2006	6,195	456
6	April 2006	2,682	544
7	May 2006	4,569	349
8	June 2006	12,229	854
9	July 2006	12,564	427
10	August 2006	10,157	337
11	September 2006	15,160	899
12	October 2006	10,716	1,011
13	November 2006	9,844	720
14	December 2006	11,975	1,069
15	January 2007	24,695	1,070
16	February 2007	11,593	498
17	March 2007	18,491	1,401
18	April 2007	11,743	1,076
19	May 2007	11,452	1,563
20	June 2007	26,651	1,790
21	July 2007	16,287	1,367
22	August 2007	17,750	1,138
23	September 2007	19,985	1,352
24	October 2007	17,285	1,343
25	November 2007	30,369	1,430
26	December 2007	19,674	1,140
27	January 2008	28,464	1,421
28	February 2008	25,000	1,508
29	March 2008	24,574	2,137
30	April 2008	23,141	1,948
31	May 2008	17,700	1,521
32	June 2008	22,456	1,304
33	July 2008	27,258	
34	August 2008	28,031	
35	September 2008	28,804	
36	October 2008	29,552	
37	November 2008	30,326	
38	December 2008	31,074	
39	January 2009	31,847	
40	February 2009	32,620	
41	March 2009	33,318	

Figure 12-147 Calculating the future website visits using the TREND() function.

By using the same procedure, you can calculate the values for the online orders based on the calculated trend values for website visits. Figure 12-148 shows the result and the arguments of the TREND() function. With the TREND() function, Excel allows for a good prognosis of the website visits and online orders, assuming that the previous exponential trend continues.

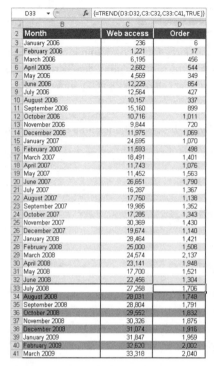

Figure 12-148 Calculating the trend values for online orders.

See Also   FORECAST(), GROWTH(), LINEST(), LOGEST()

> **Sample Files**
>
> Use the TREND worksheet in the Regression.xls or Regression.xlsx sample file. The sample files are found in the Chapter12 folder. For more information about the sample files, see the section titled "Using the Sample Files" on page xxiii.

TRIMMEAN()

Syntax   TRIMMEAN(*array,percent*)

Definition   This function returns the average value of a data group, excluding the values from the top and bottom of the data set. TRIMMEAN() calculates the average of a subset of data points excluding the smallest and largest values of the original data points based on the percentage. Use this function to exclude outlying data from your analysis.

Arguments

- ***array* (required)** The array or range of values to trim and average.

- ***percent* (required)** The percentage of data points to exclude from the calculation. For example, if *percent* = 0.2, four points are trimmed from a data set of 20 points (20 x 0.2): two from the top and two from the bottom of the set.

> **Note**
>
> If *percent* is less than 0 or greater than 1, the TRIMMEAN() function returns the #NUM! error.
>
> TRIMMEAN() rounds the number of excluded data points down to the nearest multiple of 2. If *percent* = 0.1 (10 percent), three of 30 data points are excluded. For symmetry, TRIMMEAN() excludes a single value from the top and bottom of the data set.

Background   Usually all values in a data set are used to calculate the mean. However, you might want to exclude the marginal areas to calculate a mean without outliers to get a trimmed mean.

If the data contains outliers—that is, a few values that are to high or to low—sort the observed values in ascending order, trim the values at the beginning and at the end, and calculate the mean from the remaining values.

To get a mean trimmed by 10 percent, omit 5 percent of the values at the beginning and 5 percent at the end.

Example   You are the executive manager of the controlling department of a software company and have compiled the sales for the past 17 months, from January 2007 to May 2008. You want to calculate the average sales and exclude outliers because you want to sort the sales in ascending order.

If you use the AVERAGE() function, the result is not meaningful because the outliers are included in the calculation and impact the result. The MEDIAN() function also doesn't return the correct result. Therefore, you use the TRIMMEAN() function.

As you can see in Figure 12-149, the calculation of the average sales returns a higher value because of the outliers.

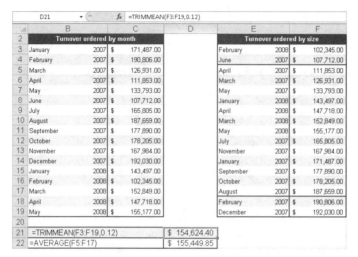

Figure 12-149 Calculating the trimmed mean from the sales of the past 17 months.

You specify 0.12 for the *percent* argument. This means that 5 percent of the original values are excluded from the calculation. The trimmed mean returns an average sale of $154,624.40.

See Also   AVERAGE(), GEOMEAN(), HARMEAN(), MEDIAN(), MODE()

Sample Files

Use the TRIMMEAN worksheet in the Average.xls or Average.xlsx sample file. The sample files are found in the Chapter12 folder. For more information about the sample files, see the section titled "Using the Sample Files" on page xxiii.

VAR.P()/VARP()

Syntax   VAR.P(*number1,number2,...*)

Definition   This function calculates the variance based on the population.

Arguments

- *number1* (required) and *number2* (optional)   At least one and up to 255 arguments (30 in Excel 2003 and earlier versions) corresponding to a population

> **Note**
>
> The VAR.P() function assumes that its arguments are the entire population. If your data represents a sample of the population, calculate the variance with VAR.S() or VARA().
>
> Logical values (TRUE and FALSE) and text are ignored. If you want to include logical values in the calculation, use the VARPA() function.

Background   Because the only difference between VAR.P() and VAR.S() is that VAR.P() doesn't calculate the variance based on a sample but based on the entire population, this example focuses on VAR.P(). You will find more information about variances in the description of VAR.S().

VAR.P() uses the following formula:

$$\frac{\sum \left(x - \overline{x} \right)^2}{n}$$

The value x is the sample mean AVERAGE(*number1,number2,...*), and n is the sample data set.

Example   Let's get back to the website evaluation of the software company (see Figure 12-150).

> **Note**
>
> Note that the data to be evaluated includes the entire population. This means that the website has been available for only 18 months and that all the visits of the past 18 months have been recorded. The calculation with VAR.P() and VARPA() is based on the population of the data from January 2007 to June 2008.

Therefore, the VAR.P() and VAR.S() functions, which use different formulas, also return different results (see Figure 12-150). If you take a closer look at the DOWNLOAD area, you can make the following statement: The average squared deviation of the values from the arithmetic mean based on the population is 263,885.

	C26	▾	(	*f*x	=VAR.P(C4:C21)			
	B	C	D	E	F	G	H	I
3	Date	ADVENT	DOWNLOAD	EVENT	TRAINING	KNOWHOW	PRODUCTS	ALL (SUM)
4	Jan-07		6		19	43	22	90
5	Feb-07		498	38	1319	3000	1170	6025
6	Mar-07		1401	119	2233	6116	1545	11414
7	Apr-07		1076	16	1903	2860	1168	7023
8	May-07		1563	15	1589	3126	1139	7432
9	Jun-07		1790	1853	2428	6682	5083	17836
10	Jul-07		1367	1622	1559	3311	3609	11468
11	Aug-07		1138	2170	1502	3317	4810	12937
12	Sep-07		1352	2611	1628	3542	5581	14714
13	Oct-07	1	1343	538	1440	2971	5506	11799
14	Nov-07	272	1430	1254	2255	4735	11786	21732
15	Dec-07	1874	1140	631	1583	2652	6227	14107
16	Jan-08	42	1421	1515	2224	4837	9500	19539
17	Feb-08	32	1508	1433	1418	4006	12000	20397
18	Mar-08	10	2137	3114	1298	3128	8000	17687
19	Apr-08	10	1948	2347	1085	3575	8208	17173
20	May-08	9	1521	848	765	2139	7739	13021
21	Jun-08		426	440	123	768	778	2535
22	Sum	2250	23065	20564	26371	60808	93871	226929
23	Average	281.25	1281.39	1209.65	1465.06	3378.22	5215.06	12607.17
24	Mean deviation	398.2	378.3	827.3	472.6	1093.9	3067.9	4785.7
25	VAR.S()	422303	279408	966160	444330	2561816	14361231	37396918
26	VAR.P()	369515	263885	909327	419645	2419493	13563385	35319311

Figure 12-150 Unlike VAR.S(), the calculation with the VAR.P() function includes the entire population.

See Also   DVAR(), DVARP(), VAR.S(), VARA(), VARPA()

Sample Files

Use the VARP or VAR.P worksheet in the Variance.xls or Variance.xlsx sample file. The sample files are found in the Chapter12 folder. For more information about the sample files, see the section titled "Using the Sample Files" on page xxiii.

VAR.S()/VAR()

Syntax   VAR.S(*number1,number2,...*)

Definition   This function estimates the variance based on a sample. VAR.S() indicates how the data are distributed around the mean.

Arguments

- *number1* **(required) and** *number2* **(optional)**   At least one and up to 255 arguments (30 in Excel 2003 and earlier versions) corresponding to a sample of the population

> **Note**
>
> The VAR.S() function assumes that its arguments are a sample of the entire population. If the data passed as arguments is a population, calculate the associated variance with the VAR.P() function.
>
> Logical values (TRUE and FALSE) and text are ignored. If you want to include logical values and text in the calculation, use the VARA() function.

Background   The most commonly used spreads in statistics are the variance and the standard deviation. The *variance* indicates the deviation of a random variable x from the expected value $E(x)$. In other words, the variance is the average of the squared deviation of a single value divided by the number of values. The result is also called *empirical variance*.

The following variances exist:

- **Variance of a random variable** The average squared deviation of characteristics in the population. The function to use is VAR.P().

- **Sample variance** Variance of observed values from a sample of a population. This variance is used in descriptive statistics to measure the spread of data. In inferential statistics, this variance estimates the unknown variance in a population. The function to use is VAR.S().

If the evaluated data is a sample, the sum of the squared deviations is not divided by the number of values (n) but by the number minus one ($n - 1$). VAR.S() uses the following formula:

$$\frac{\sum \left(x - \overline{x}\right)^2}{(n-1)}$$

The value x is the sample mean AVERAGE(*number1,number2,...*), and n is the sample data set. Note that because of the squaring, the extreme value might have a higher weight.

The disadvantage of the variance is that it uses a unit other than the data (squared units). Therefore, the standard deviation defined as the square root of the variance is often used.

Example   Because the sample variance measures the spread of data, it is often used in descriptive statistics. The marketing department of the software company uses the VAR.S() function to create a detailed evaluation of the website visits. The goal is to get more accurate information and to improve the individual areas.

Chapter 12

Note that the data to be evaluated is a sample. This means that although the website has existed for a long time, the calculation with VAR.S() and VARA() is based on the data from 18 months (January 2007 through June 2008).

As you can see in Figure 12-151, the marketing department calculated the variance as well as the mean and the average deviation.

Date	ADVENT	DOWNLOAD	EVENT	TRAINING	KNOWHOW	PRODUCTS	ALL (SUM)
Jan-07		6		19	43	22	90
Feb-07		498	38	1319	3000	1170	6025
Mar-07		1401	119	2233	6116	1545	11414
Apr-07		1076	16	1903	2860	1168	7023
May-07		1563	15	1589	3126	1139	7432
Jun-07		1790	1853	2428	6682	5083	17836
Jul-07		1367	1622	1559	3311	3609	11468
Aug-07		1138	2170	1502	3317	4810	12937
Sep-07		1352	2611	1628	3542	5581	14714
Oct-07	1	1343	538	1440	2971	5506	11799
Nov-07	272	1430	1254	2255	4735	11786	21732
Dec-07	1874	1140	631	1583	2652	6227	14107
Jan-08	42	1421	1515	2224	4837	9500	19539
Feb-08	32	1508	1433	1418	4006	12000	20397
Mar-08	10	2137	3114	1298	3128	8000	17687
Apr-08	10	1948	2347	1085	3575	8208	17173
May-08	9	1521	848	765	2139	7739	13021
Jun-08		426	440	123	768	778	2535
Sum	2250	23065	20564	26371	60808	93871	226929
Average	281.25	1281.39	1209.65	1465.06	3378.22	5215.06	12607.17
Mean deviation	398.2	378.3	827.3	472.6	1093.9	3067.9	4785.7
VAR.S()	422303	279408	966160	444330	2561816	14361231	37396918

Figure 12-151 VAR.S() calculates the distribution of the data around the mean based on a sample.

If you take a closer look at the DOWNLOAD area, you can make the following statement: The average squared deviation of the values from the arithmetic mean is 279,408 for the DOWNLOAD area.

Note
If the deviations aren't squared, the sum of the deviations is 0 and is useless.

See Also DVAR(), DVARP(), VAR.P(), VARA(), VARPA()

Sample Files
Use the VAR or VAR.S worksheet in the Variance.xls or Variance.xlsx sample file. The sample files are found in the Chapter12 folder. For more information about the sample files, see the section titled "Using the Sample Files" on page xxiii.

VARA()

Syntax VARA(*value1,value2,...*)

Definition This function estimates the variance based on a sample. Not only numbers but also text and logical values (TRUE and FALSE) are included in the calculation.

Arguments

- *value1* **(required) and** *value2* **(optional)** At least one and up to 255 value arguments (30 in Excel 2003 and earlier versions) corresponding to a sample of the population.

> **Note**
>
> The VARA() function assumes that its arguments are a sample of the entire population. If your data represents the entire population, calculate the variance with VARPA().
>
> The difference between VAR.S() and VARA() is that VARA() evaluates arguments with the value TRUE to 1 and arguments with text, or FALSE to 0. If you do not want to include logical values and text in the calculation, use the VAR.S() function.

Background Because the only difference between VARA() and VAR.S() is that VARA() includes text and logical values, this example focuses on VARA().

See Also You will find more information about variances in the description of VAR.S().

VARA() uses the same formula as VAR.S():

$$\frac{\sum \left(x - \overline{x} \right)^2}{(n-1)}$$

The value *x* is the sample mean AVERAGE(*value1,value2,...*), and *n* is the sample data set.

Example Let's look again at the evaluation of the website visits. Because in the past 18 months several website problems occurred, the visits could not be counted in all months. The company had the following problems:

- In May 2007 and August 2007, a problem with website hosting occurred, and in both months the website was not available. These months are marked with the string "hostingproblems".

- In March 2008, the content pages of the product area were changed to include the entire area. Because external access to the product area wasn't possible, this month is marked with the logical value FALSE.

As you can see in Figure 12-152, the VARA() function returns a different result than VAR.S(). This happens because VARA() includes text and logical values. Because this example uses text and the logical value FALSE, both values are set to 0.

	C27		fx	=VARA(C5:C22)				
	B	C	D	E	F	G	H	I
4	Date	ADVENT	DOWNLOAD	EVENT	TRAINING	KNOWHOW	PRODUCTS	ALL (SUM)
5	Jan-07		6		19	43	22	90
6	Feb-07		498	38	1319	3000	1170	6025
7	Mar-07		1401	119	2233	6116	1545	11414
8	Apr-07		1076	16	1903	2860	1168	7023
9	May-07	Hostingproblems	Hostingproblems	Hostingproblems	Hostingproblems	Hostingproblems	Hostingproblems	Hostingproblems
10	Jun-07		1790	1853	2428	6682	5083	17836
11	Jul-07		1367	1622	1559	3311	3609	11468
12	Aug-07	Hostingproblems	Hostingproblems	Hostingproblems	Hostingproblems	Hostingproblems	Hostingproblems	Hostingproblems
13	Sep-07		1352	2611	1628	3542	5581	14714
14	Oct-07	1	1343	538	1440	2971	5506	11799
15	Nov-07	272	1430	1254	2255	4735	11786	21732
16	Dec-07	1874	1140	631	1583	2652	6227	14107
17	Jan-08	42	1421	1515	2224	4837	9500	19539
18	Feb-08	32	1508	1433	1418	4006	12000	20397
19	Mar-08	FALSE	FALSE	FALSE	FALSE	FALSE	FALSE	FALSE
20	Apr-08	10	1948	2347	1085	3575	8208	17173
21	May-08	9	1521	848	765	2139	7739	13021
22	Jun-08		426	440	123	768	778	2535
23	Sum	2240	18227	15265	21982	51237	79922	188873
24	Average	320	1215.13	1090.36	1465.47	3415.80	5328.13	12591.53
25	Mean deviation	444.0	390.6	714.6	545.2	1277.7	3189.6	5038.2
26	VAR.S()	478672	275154	714102	536355	3099980	15672494	41646292
27	VARA()	343008	443737	763784	757527	4268761	17081614	57612639

Figure 12-152 Calculating the variance with the VARA() function, including text and logical values.

If you take a closer look at the DOWNLOAD area, you can make the following statement: The average squared deviation of the values from the arithmetic mean based on text and logical values is 443,737 for the DOWNLOAD area.

See Also   DVAR(), DVARP(), VAR.P(), VAR.S(), VARPA()

Sample Files

Use the VARA worksheet in the Variance.xls or Variance.xlsx sample file. The sample files are found in the Chapter12 folder. For more information about the sample files, see the section titled "Using the Sample Files" on page xxiii.

VARPA()

Syntax   VARPA(*value1,value2,...*)

Definition   This function calculates the variance based on the population. Not only numbers but also text and logical values (TRUE and FALSE) are included in the calculation.

Arguments

- *value1* **(required) and** *value2* **(optional)**   At least one and up to 255 value arguments (30 in Excel 2003 and earlier versions) corresponding to a population

> **Note**
>
> The VARPA() function assumes that its arguments are the entire population. If your data represents a sample of the population, you have to calculate the variance with VARA().
>
> Arguments that contain TRUE evaluate to 1, and arguments that contain text or FALSE evaluate to 0. If you do not want to include logical values and text in the calculation, use the VARP() function.

Background   Because the variance was already explained in detail in the description of VAR.S(), this section focuses on the example.

VARPA uses the same formula as VAR.P():

$$\frac{\sum \left(x - \overline{x}\right)^2}{n}$$

The value x is the sample mean AVERAGE(*value1,value2,...*), and n is the sample data set.

Example   For VARPA() we use the same example as for the VARA() function. In this example, the software company had the following problems with its website:

- In May 2007 and August 2007, a problem with website hosting occurred, and in both months the website was not available. These months are marked with the string "hostingproblems".

- In March 2008, the content pages of the product area were changed to include the entire area. Because external access to the product area wasn't possible, this month is marked with the logical value FALSE.

As you can see in Figure 12-153, the VARPA() function returns a different result than VAR.P(). This happens because VARPA() includes text and logical values. Because this example uses text and the logical value FALSE, both values are set to 0.

Note

As for VAR.P(), the data to be evaluated includes the entire population. This means that the website has been available for only 18 months and that all the visits of the last 18 months are recorded.

	C26		f_x =VARPA(C4:C21)					

	B	C	D	E	F	G	H	I
3	Date	ADVENT	DOWNLOAD	EVENT	TRAINING	KNOWHOW	PRODUCTS	ALL (SUM)
4	Jan-07		6		19	43	22	90
5	Feb-07		498	38	1319	3000	1170	6025
6	Mar-07		1401	119	2233	6116	1545	11414
7	Apr-07		1076	16	1903	2860	1168	7023
8	May-07	Hostingproblems	Hostingproblems	Hostingproblems	Hostingproblems	Hostingproblems	Hostingproblems	Hostingproblems
9	Jun-07		1790	1853	2426	6682	5083	17836
10	Jul-07		1367	1622	1559	3311	3609	11468
11	Aug-07	Hostingproblems	Hostingproblems	Hostingproblems	Hostingproblems	Hostingproblems	Hostingproblems	Hostingproblems
12	Sep-07		1352	2611	1628	3542	5581	14714
13	Oct-07	1	1343	538	1440	2971	5506	11799
14	Nov-07	272	1430	1254	2255	4735	11786	21732
15	Dec-07	1874	1140	631	1583	2652	6227	14107
16	Jan-08	42	1421	1515	2224	4837	9500	19539
17	Feb-08	32	1508	1433	1418	4006	12000	20397
18	Mar-08	FALSE	FALSE	FALSE	FALSE	FALSE	FALSE	FALSE
19	Apr-08	10	1948	2347	1085	3575	8208	17173
20	May-08	9	1521	848	765	2139	7739	13021
21	Jun-08		426	440	123	768	778	2535
22	Sum	2240	18227	15265	21982	51237	79922	188873
23	Average	320	1215.13	1090.36	1465.47	3415.80	5328.13	12591.53
24	Mean deviation	444.0	390.6	714.6	545.2	1277.7	3189.6	5038.2
25	VAR.P()	410290	256810	663094	500598	2893314	14627661	38869873
26	VARPA()	308707	419085	718856	715442	4031608	16132635	54411937

Figure 12-153 Calculating the variance based on the entire population, including text and logical values.

If you take a closer look at the DOWNLOAD area, you can make the following statement: The average squared deviation of the values from the arithmetic mean based on the population and including text and logical values is 419,085 for the DOWNLOAD area.

See Also   DVAR(), DVARP(), VAR.P(), VAR.S(), VARA()

Sample Files

Use the VARPA worksheet in the Variance.xls or Variance.xlsx sample file. The sample files are found in the Chapter12 folder. For more information about the sample files, see the section titled "Using the Sample Files" on page xxiii.

WEIBULL.DIST()/WEIBULL()

Syntax   WEIBULL.DIST(*x;alpha;beta;cumulative*)

Definition   This function returns the probabilities of a Weibull-distributed random variable. Use this distribution in a reliability analysis (for example, to calculate a device's mean time to failure).

Arguments

- ***x* (required)** The value at which to evaluate the function.

- ***alpha* (required)** A parameter of the distribution.

- ***beta* (required)** A parameter of the distribution.

- ***cumulative* (required)** The logical value that represents the type of the function. If *cumulative* is TRUE, then WEIBULL.DIST() returns the value of the distribution function that is the probability that the number of random events is between 0 and *x*. If *cumulative* is FALSE, the WEIBULL.DIST() function returns the value of the density function.

> **Note**
>
> If *x*, *alpha*, or *beta* isn't a numeric expression, the WEIBULL.DIST() function returns the #VALUE! error.
>
> If *x* is less than 0, the function returns the #NUM! error.
>
> If *alpha* or *beta* is less than or equal to 0, the WEIBULL.DIST() function returns the #NUM! error.

Background   The Weibull distribution is also a statistical distribution. Among other things, the Weibull distribution is used to examine the life cycle of devices based on the fatigue of brittle material or the mean time to failure of electronic parts.

The Weibull distribution is named after Waloddi Weibull (1887–1979). The Weibull analysis is considered a classic reliability analysis or classic life cycle chart and is commonly used in the auto industry. The so called "Weibull net" shows the typical life cycle and the failure probability for parts and other components.

Chapter 12

In general, a Weibull distribution is an exponential distribution. The Weibull distribution is used for different purposes:

- Many distribution forms can be defined with the Weibull distribution.

- The Weibull function is easy to calculate.

- Time-dependent failure methods are displayed as straight lines.

See Also You will find more information about exponential distributions in the description of EXPON.DIST().

The WEIBULL.DIST() function calculates the density and the distribution function of the Weibull distribution.

To calculate the density function, specify the logical value FALSE for the *cumulative* argument. The density function is the first derivation of the distribution function based on a random variable (such as the time for the failure density function). In other words, the differential change of the relative frequency per scale unit is calculated.

To calculate the distribution function, specify the logical value TRUE for the *cumulative* argument. The distribution function F(x) indicates the relative cumulative frequency of events.

The distribution function F(x) indicates the probability that the random variable *y* doesn't exceed value *x* (see Figure 12-154).

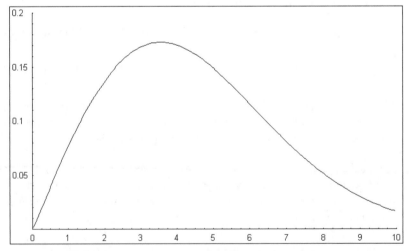

Figure 12-154 A Weibull distribution with the arguments *x*, *alpha*=5, *beta*=2, and *cumulative* = FALSE.

The equation for the distribution function of a Weibull distribution is:

$$F(x, \alpha, \beta) = 1 - e^{-(x/\beta)^{\alpha}}$$

The equation for the density function of a Weibull distribution is:

$$f(x, \alpha, \beta) = \frac{\alpha}{\beta^{\alpha}} x^{\alpha-1} e^{-(x/\beta)^{\alpha}}$$

If *alpha* = 1, WEIBULL.DIST() returns the exponential distribution with:

$$\lambda = \frac{1}{\beta}$$

The failure ratio depends on the parameter β:

- 1 > β means that the rate is monotonically increasing.

- 1 = β means that it is consistent and is an exponential distribution.

- 1 < β means that the rate is monotonically decreasing.

Example   Use the following values to calculate WEIBULL.DIST():

- 105 = the value at which to evaluate the function (*x*)

- 20 = *alpha* parameter of the distribution (alpha)

- 100 = *beta* parameter of the distribution (beta)

- TRUE = *cumulative*

- FALSE = *cumulative*

Figure 12-155 shows the calculation of WEIBULL.DIST().

E8		f_x	=WEIBULL.DIST(E3,E4,E5,E6)	
	B	C	D	E	F
1	Calculation of WEIBULL.DIST()				
2	Meaning			Parameter	
3	Value for which the function has to be analyzed			105	
4	Alpha-parameter of distribution			20	
5	Beta-parameter of distribution			100	
6	Cumulative			TRUE	
7	Cumulative			FALSE	
8	WEIBULL.DIST() for cumulative = TRUE			0.929581	
9	WEIBULL.DIST() for cumulative = FALSE			0.035589	

Figure 12-155 Calculating WEIBULL.DIST().

The WEIBULL.DIST() function returns the following results using the parameters shown in Figure 12-155:

- For *cumulative* = TRUE, the WEIBULL.DIST() function returns the distribution function of a Weibull distribution with the value 0.929581.

- For *cumulative* = FALSE, the WEIBULL.DIST() function returns the density function of a Weibull distribution with the value 0.035589.

See Also EXPON.DIST()

> **Sample Files**
>
> Use the WEIBULL or WEIBULL.DIST worksheet in the Probability.xls or Probability.xlsx sample file. The sample files are found in the Chapter12 folder. For more information about the sample files, see the section titled "Using the Sample Files" on page xxiii.

Z.TEST()/ZTEST()

Syntax   Z.TEST($array, \mu_0, sigma$)

Definition   This function returns the one-tailed probability value for a Gauss test (normal distribution). For the expected value of a random variable (μ_0), the Z.TEST() function returns the probability that the sample mean would be greater than the average of observations in the data set (array)—that is, the observed sample mean.

Arguments

- *array* **(required)** The array or range of data against which to test μ_0.

- μ_0 **(required)** The value to test.

- *sigma* **(optional)** The known standard deviation of the population. If this argument is not specified, the standard deviation of the sample is used.

Note

If *array* is empty, the Z.TEST() function returns the #N/A error.

Z.TEST() is calculated as follows when *sigma* is specified:

$$Z.TEST\left(Matrix, x\right) = 1 - NORM.DIST\left(\frac{\mu - x}{\sigma \div \sqrt{n}}\right)$$

or when *sigma* is omitted:

$$Z.TEST\left(Array, \mu_0\right) = 1 - NORM.S.DIST\left(\left(\bar{x} - \mu_0\right) \div \left(\frac{S}{\sqrt{n}}\right)\right)$$

where:

- *x* is the sample mean AVERAGE(*array*).

- *s* is the sample standard deviation STDEV.S(*array*).

- *n* is the number of observations in the sample COUNT(*array*).

Z.TEST() indicates the probability that the sample mean is greater than the observed value AVERAGE(*array*) when the underlying expected value of a random variable is μ_0.

Because of the symmetry of the normal distribution, if AVERAGE(*array*) is smaller than μ_0, Z.TEST() returns a value greater than 0.5.

The following Excel formula can be used to calculate the two-tailed probability that the sample mean is further from μ_0 (in either direction) than AVERAGE(*array*) when the underlying expected value of a random variable is μ_0:

=2 * MIN(Z.TEST(*array*,μ_0,*sigma*), 1 – Z.TEST(*array*,μ_0,*sigma*))

Background   The Gaussian test (named after the mathematician Carl Friedrich Gauss) is a statistical test based on the standard normal distribution. This test is used to examine the significance of a value from a normal distributed population where the expected value and the standard deviation have to be known.

Example   Use the following values to calculate Z.TEST():

- Data = the data range against which you want to test μ_0

- 4 = the value of the random variable μ_0 to test

- 6 = the value of the random variable μ_0 to test

Figure 12-156 shows the calculation of Z.TEST().

	B	C	D	E
1	Data	Random variable	Results for ZTEST()	In percent
2	3	4	0.090574197	9.06%
3	6		=Z.TEST(B2:B11,C2)	
4	7	6	0.863043389	86.30%
5	8		=Z.TEST(B2:B11,C4)	
6	6			
7	5			
8	4			
9	2			
10	1			
11	9			

Figure 12-156 Calculating Z.TEST().

The Z.TEST() function returns the one-tailed probability value for a Gaussian test by using the parameters shown in Figure 12-45. The following results were calculated:

- For an expected value of 4 for a random variable, the result is a one-tailed probability value of 0.09057 = 9.06 percent.

- For an expected value of 6 for a random variable, the result is a one-tailed probability value of 0.86304 = 86.30 percent.

See Also CONFIDENCE(), NORM.DIST(), NORM.INV(), NORM.S.DIST(), NORM.S.INV(), STANDARDIZE()

Sample Files

Use the ZTEST or Z.TEST worksheet in the Probability.xls or Probability.xlsx sample file. The sample files are found in the Chapter12 folder. For more information about the sample files, see the section titled "Using the Sample Files" on page xxiii.

Database Functions

This chapter describes the database functions. The Microsoft Excel database functions can be used to evaluate information held in a set of data stored in a spreadsheet.

A database in Excel consists of a list of information with labels (*field names*) and data rows (*data records*), as shown In Figure 13-1. The field names describe the information in the fields below them, such as sales or company names. The information in a column is the field content.

	A	B	C	D	E	F
1	Company	City	Date	Country/Region	Product	Sales
5458	Save-a-lot Markets	Boise	3/26/08	USA	Laughing Lumberjack Lager	$ 1,976.00
5459	Save-a-lot Markets	Boise	6/9/08	USA	Scottish Longbreads	$ 1,116.00
5460	Save-a-lot Markets	Boise	1/19/08	USA	Gudbrandsdalsost	$ 1,571.00
5461	Save-a-lot Markets	Boise	9/1/07	USA	Outback Lager	$ 1,598.00
5462	Save-a-lot Markets	Boise	10/24/07	USA	Fløtemysost	$ 1,238.00
5463	Save-a-lot Markets	Boise	6/9/08	USA	Mozzarella di Giovanni	$ 1,997.00
5464	Save-a-lot Markets	Boise	6/21/08	USA	Röd Kaviar	$ 1,616.00
5465	Save-a-lot Markets	Boise	1/25/08	USA	Longlife Tofu	$ 1,401.00
5466	Save-a-lot Markets	Boise	2/9/08	USA	Rhönbräu Klosterbier	$ 1,631.00
5467	Save-a-lot Markets	Boise	8/16/08	USA	Lakkalikööri	$ 1,747.00
5468	Save-a-lot Markets	Boise	8/20/08	USA	Original Frankfurter grüne Soße	$ 1,465.00
5469	Seven Seas Imports	London	11/8/07	Great Britain	Chai	$ 1,473.00
5470	Seven Seas Imports	London	7/14/08	Great Britain	Chang	$ 1,247.00
5471	Seven Seas Imports	London	12/12/07	Great Britain	Aniseed Syrup	$ 1,087.00

Figure 13-1 The database range consists of field names and field contents.

Excel recognizes a table like the one in Figure 13-1 as a database. The structure of a database is important. Field names should be unique, the labels must be entered in the top row, and the database range should not contain any blank rows or blank columns within the data set.

The Excel database functions are not as commonly known as other functions, but they provide powerful and effective analysis tools.

> **Note**
> The database functions are applicable only to Excel databases.

You can also create PivotTables or apply data filters to generate additional results. Excel also provides database functions for queries based on criteria to evaluate specified data ranges.

In Microsoft Office Excel 2003 and earlier, the use of database functions was limited to data lists of up to 65,536 rows. In Excel 2007, this limit was extended, and now a data list can have up to 1,048,576 rows.

Arguments in Database Functions

Because all database functions—except the GETPIVOTDATA() function—have the same arguments, these functions will be explained at the beginning of this chapter. For database functions, you have to specify three arguments:

- *database* The *database* argument specifies the cell range that makes up the list or database. In the example used in this chapter, the range A1:F7008 has been given the range name Database.

- *field* The *field* argument indicates which column is to be used in the function. Enter the column label enclosed in quotation marks, as in "country/region", "sales", or "company". You can also enter a number that represents the position of the column within the list, such as 1 for the first column or 2 for the second column.

> **Tip**
> Specifying names for the *field* argument to make the function easier to understand is recommended as is always specifying this argument even though it is not strictly a required field.

- *criteria* The *criteria* argument indicates a cell range containing the field names and the filter criteria that will be used for the function. You can specify any search criteria for this argument. However, the argument has to include at least one column label and at least one cell below the column label in which you specify a condition for the column.

Note

You cannot enter criteria as array expressions directly into the function. You need to set up an area in the spreadsheet where the criteria range is specified, and reference this range as the argument in the database function.

An example of search criteria and their functionality is outlined in the example that follows.

Sample Files

Use the Raw data worksheet in the DBFUNCTION empty.xls or DBFUNCTION empty.xlsx sample file. The sample files are found in the Chapter13 folder. For more information about the sample files, see the section titled "Using the Sample Files" on page xxiii.

In the database example, for simplicity, the examples are set up to the side of the raw data.

Assume that you want to evaluate sales for particular articles within different countries:

1. Set up the criteria definitions to the right of the data set. You need the three field names Country/Region, Product, and Sales. To ensure that you have exactly what has been typed in the database, copy the column headings and paste them to the right of the table.

2. Below the field names, enter a condition. A field could be quoted as text together with the column heading in quotation marks, such as in *"USA"*, *"1500"* or *"U*"*; as well as logical operators and expressions such as *">k"* or *"<2000"*. For countries and products, you can again copy and paste from entries in the database to ensure that you have typed the entry correctly.

3. Use the range containing the field names and the filter conditions in the database functions. The following example outlines the use of the criteria ranges.

Note

In the search criteria, the asterisk (*) is used as a wildcard for any characters, and the question mark (?) is used as wildcard for a single character.

Figure 13-2 specifies the search criteria: Country/Region is Mexico AND the product is Geitost AND the Sales value is greater than $1,500.

Country/Region	Product	Sales
Mexico	Geitost	>1500

Figure 13-2 Search criteria using AND conditions.

You can also use OR conditions by entering the criteria in multiple rows (see Figure 13-3).

Country/Region	Product	Sales
Mexico	Geitost	>1500
Mexico	Pavlova	>1500

Figure 13-3 Search criteria using the OR condition.

In this example, the criteria specifies Mexico Geitost orders greater than $1500 or Mexico Pavlova orders greater than $1,500.

> **Note**
> If you specify the search criterion *cha*, all records with the item name *chai* and *chang* and similar are selected. For an exact match, put the criteria in quotation marks and enter an equal sign: "=chai" only finds the items for the product Chai.

Working with Databases and Records

You will find the following pointers helpful to remember when you are working with databases and records.

Watch Out for Spaces   Excel is very tolerant regarding capitalization rules. However, Excel behaves differently with spaces at the end of an entry. If you don't find any records, the filter might contain an unintended space. A space can cause problems in a record or criteria. If you are sure there are data matching the criteria but no data is returned, use a question mark or an asterisk as a wildcard to select data with trailing blanks, or use the TRIM() and CLEAN() functions (described in Chapter 8, "Text and Data Functions") to clean the data.

Include All Records with or without Content   To include all records with a field entry in a calculation, use < > as the criterion for the field. For example, if you use this string for the product, all records with an entry in the product field are included.

To include all records with an empty field, specify = as the criterion. In other words, just type an equal sign and then press the Enter key.

Calculated Criteria   To specify multiple conditions, add a further row to the criteria range specifying the additional conditions. You can also specify calculated criteria. You cannot use field names as labels for calculated criteria.

Overview of Operators and Wildcards   The operators and wildcards are explained in Table 13-1 and Table 13-2.

Table 13-1 Overview of the Operators

Operator	Example	Returns All Records in the Selected Column...
> (greater than)	> 5000	... greater than 5,000.
< (less than)	< 5000	... less than 5,000.
> = (greater than or equal to)	> = 5000	... greater than or equal to 5,000.
< = (less than or equal to)	< = 5000	... less than or equal to 5,000.
< > (unequal)	< > 5000	... different from 5,000.
= (equals)	= 5000	... exactly 5,000. You don't have to enter the equal sign in search criteria.

Table 13-2 Overview of the Wildcards

Wildcard	Example	Returns All Records in the Selected Column...
* (any number of characters)	D*	... starting with D.
=* (any number of characters in combination with an exact string)	="=*and"	... starting with one or more characters and ending in *and*, such as *land* or *wand*. *Candy* is not displayed because it has another character after *and*.
? (a single character)	?and	... starting with any character and followed by *and*, such as *candy*. *Stand* is not displayed because it has other characters before *and*.
=? (single character in combination with an exact string)	="=?and"	... starting with any character and ending in *and*, such as *land* or *wand*. *Stand* and *candy* are not displayed.

If you use wildcards in combination with an exact string, you have to enclose the search term in quotation marks because Excel expects a formula after the equal sign (=) unless the equal sign is followed by a string in quotation marks. You also need to enter the equal sign, otherwise Excel would look for the string "?and".

Using Controls

Controls can be buttons, list boxes, check boxes, option buttons, and more. They are part of the integrated dialog boxes in Excel. If you use Microsoft Visual Basic for Applications (VBA), you can work with them in user-defined dialog boxes.

Excel uses controls in worksheets. For example, the AutoFilter uses list boxes for filter criteria.

AutoFilter in Excel 2007 and Excel 2010   To set the AutoFilter in Excel 2007 or Excel 2010, follow these steps:

1. Click the Data tab.

2. Click the Filter button in the Sort & Filter group. The filter is added automatically and can be used to filter for certain criteria (see Figure 13-4).

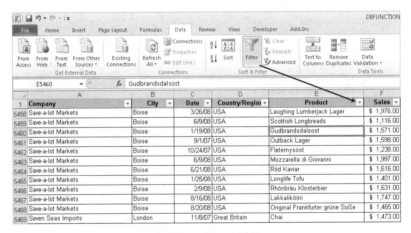

Figure 13-4 AutoFilter in Excel 2007 and Excel 2010.

AutoFilter in Excel 2003   In Excel 2003, you select Data/Filter/AutoFilter to set the AutoFilter. You can also use custom controls in a worksheet.

Overview of the Database Functions

This section gives you an overview of the individual database functions and how to use them, as described in Table 13-3.

Table 13-3 **Overview of the Database Functions**

The Function...	Returns...
DAVERAGE()	... the mean of the values matching the condition(s).
DCOUNT()	... the number of fields matching the condition(s).
DCOUNTA()	... the number of nonempty fields matching the condition(s).
DGET()	... a single value matching the condition(s).
DMAX()	... the largest value matching the condition(s).
DMIN()	... the smallest value matching the condition(s).
DPRODUCT()	... the product of the values matching the condition(s).
DSTDEV()	... the estimated standard deviation of the values from a sample matching the condition(s).
DSTDEVP()	... the standard deviation of the values matching the condition(s).
DSUM()	... the sum of the values matching the condition(s).
DVAR()	... the estimated variance of the values from a sample matching the condition(s).
DVARP()	... the variance of the values matching the condition(s).
GETPIVOTDATA()	... the values from a PivotTable report.

Functions in This Chapter

The database functions and a sample of each are described in the rest of this chapter.

The following scenario is used: You are a wholesaler selling 76 different products to a variety of countries. The database records sales orders showing the date of the order, customer, city and country/region, product sold, and order value. You can use the database functions to analyze your sales.

DAVERAGE()

Syntax   DAVERAGE(*database,field,criteria*)

Definition   This function returns the arithmetic mean for the values in a list or database column that match the specified conditions.

Arguments

- *database* **(required)** The cell range that makes up the list or database

- *field* **(optional)** Indicates which column is used in the function

- *criteria* **(required)** The cell range containing the field names and the filter criteria

Background The arithmetic mean is the best known mean value. Because it can easily be calculated, it plays an important role in summarizing and analyzing data.

To calculate the mean, the values in a range are added and the sum is divided by the number of values.

See Also You will find more information about the mean in the description of AVERAGE() in Chapter 12, "Statistical Functions."

Use the DAVERAGE() function to calculate the mean for selected database records.

Example It is the end of the year and you want to analyze the sales. More specifically, you want to look at the average sales of products within different countries. You can use the DAVERAGE() function to calculate these values.

To calculate the average sales for Chang in the United States, you specify the country/region *USA* and the item name *Chang*. Because you want to know the average sales, you use *Sales* as the database field. DAVERAGE() returns $1,522.85 (see Figure 13-5).

	D5		f_x	=DAVERAGE(Database,C4,A4:B5)	
	A	B		C	D
3	Search criteria			Field in database	Result
4	Country/Region	Product		Sales	
5	USA	Chang			1522.85

Figure 13-5 DAVERAGE() returns the average sales for Chang in the United States.

You also want to calculate the overall average sales for Chang. To calculate the average sales for Chang in all countries and regions, don't specify the country/region as a search criterion. This means that all countries and regions are included in the calculation. DAVERAGE() returns $1,560.02 as the average sales order value (see Figure 13-6).

	D12		f_x	=DAVERAGE(Database,C11,A11:B12)	
	A	B		C	D
10	Search criteria			Field in database	Result
11	Country/Region	Product		Sales	
12		Chang			1560.02

Figure 13-6 DAVERAGE() returns the average sales for the item Chang.

By using the DGET() function, you can compare the average sales for products in different countries.

See Also AVERAGE(), MEDIAN()

DCOUNT()

Syntax   DCOUNT(*database,field,criteria*)

Definition   This function counts the number of records containing numbers in the field column that match the specified conditions.

Arguments

- *database* **(required)** The cell range that identifies the list or database.

- *field* **(optional)** Indicates which column is used in the function. Enter the column label enclosed in quotation marks, such as "country/region", "sales", or "company". You can also enter a number that represents the position of the column within the list: 1 for the first column, 2 for the second column, and so on.

- *criteria* **(required)** The cell range containing the field names and the filter criteria. You can use any range for the *criteria* argument as long as the argument includes at least one column label and at least one cell below the column label in which you specify a condition for the column.

Background   The DCOUNT() function performs a simple task but can save a lot of time, especially when you work with databases and have to count many records. To count records containing numbers that match certain criteria in a database, use the DCOUNT() function.

Note

The DCOUNT() function counts all values that are numbers, 0, dates, or a text representation of numbers. Values that are error values or text that cannot be converted into numbers are not counted.

Example   You are a wholesaler and want to know how many deliveries have been invoiced. This means that you want to return all sales greater than 0.

Open a new worksheet and define the criteria range as the Sales field from the original data. Then specify the search criterion *>0*.

Now use the DCOUNT() function to calculate the number of sales that are more than zero in the database (see Figure 13-7).

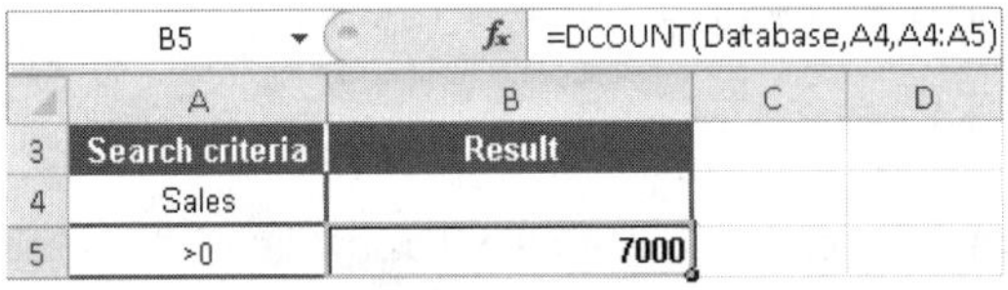

	A	B	C	D
	B5	*fx* =DCOUNT(Database,A4,A4:A5)		
3	Search criteria	Result		
4	Sales			
5	>0	7000		

Figure 13-7 Calculating the number of sales greater than zero.

Specify the named range *Database* for the database argument, this is A1:F7008. In this example, the cell range has the dynamic name Database so that you can avoid having to type in the cell range A1:F7008 each time you enter the database range.

As you can see in Figure 13-8, you get the same result if you enter the name SEARCH1 for the *criteria* range (A11:A12 in the figure) and specify "Sales" instead of cell A11 for the *field* argument. Remember to enclose the field name, Sales, in quotation marks. As shown in Figure 13-8, the result is still 7,000.

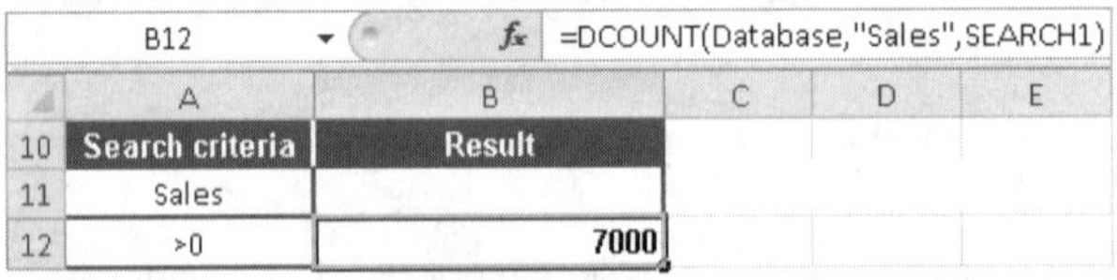

	A	B	C	D	E
	B12	*fx* =DCOUNT(Database,"Sales",SEARCH1)			
10	Search criteria	Result			
11	Sales				
12	>0	7000			

Figure 13-8 Different arguments for the DCOUNT() function.

This means that the database contains 7,000 records for sales greater than zero. In the same way, you can quickly count the sales greater than 1,500.

See Also COUNT(), COUNTA(), COUNTBLANK(), COUNTIF(), DCOUNTA()

> **Sample Files**
>
> Use the DCOUNT worksheet in the DBFUNCTION2.xls or DBFUNCTION2.xlsx sample file. The sample files are found in the Chapter13 folder. For more information about the sample files, see the section titled "Using the Sample Files" on page xxiii.

DCOUNTA()

Syntax DCOUNTA(*database,field,criteria*)

Definition This function counts the number of cells in a column, list, or database that are not empty and match the specified conditions.

Arguments

- *database* **(required)** The cell range that makes up the list or database

- *field* **(optional)** Indicates which column is used in the function

- *criteria* **(required)** The cell range containing the field names and the filter criteria

Background DCOUNTA() counts nonempty cells, in contrast to DCOUNT(), which counts number values.

Example Because your business is relatively new, you want to know how many invoices were sent to companies within the United States. You also want to know the total number of invoices in the database so that you can calculate the percentage of the invoices for companies within the United States.

You open a new worksheet and define the criteria range (the Country/Region field from the original data). Then you specify the search criterion *USA* (see Figure 13-9).

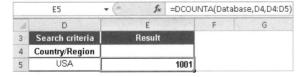

Figure 13-9 Calculating the number of records containing USA as the country/region.

Because the DCOUNTA() function counts text, it returns the number of records matching the criterion *USA*.

Specify the cell range containing the database for the database argument, such as A1:F7008. In this example, that cell range has the dynamic name Database.

You get the same result if you enter the name SEARCH2 for the *criteria* range (A4:A5 in this example) and enter *"country/region"* instead of cell A4 in the *field* argument. Remember to enclose the field name, country/region, in quotation marks.

The result is still 1001; the database contains 1,001 records matching the criterion USA: 1,001 invoices were sent to companies in the United States (see Figure 13-10).

Figure 13-10 Different arguments for the DCOUNTA() function.

> ## Note
>
> The calculation of the invoices in the United States does not consider the sales values. Although it is very unlikely that invoices were issued for orders without sales, you can take this into account by adding the sales field to the *criteria* range and specifying the conditions and formula shown in Figure 13-11.
>
>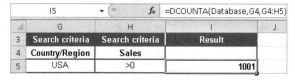
>
> **Figure 13-11** Although there are probably no invoices issued for sales with the value 0, you can add a second filter criterion to ensure that you get the correct number of invoices.

Now you calculate the total number of issued invoices in the same way. The search range doesn't change. Refer the search criterion to an empty cell to count all records in the search range country (see Figure 13-12).

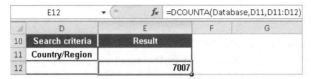

Figure 13-12 DCOUNTA() calculates the total number of invoices issued.

After you have calculated a total of 7,007 for all invoices, you can calculate the percentage of the invoices for companies within the United States. As you can see in Figure 13-13, you can calculate the percentage with the DCOUNTA() function.

	A16	▾	f_x =B5/E12				
	A	B	C	D	E	F	G
15	Number of invoices within the United States as a percentage of all invoices						
16	14.29%	=B5/E12					
17	14.29%	=DCOUNTA(Database,"Country/Region",SEARCH2)/DCOUNTA(Database,"Country/Region",SEARCH3)					

Figure 13-13 The percentage of the invoices.

Although this method is tedious, it is possible. You know that 14 percent of your invoices go to companies in the United States. The rest of the invoices are sent to companies outside the United States.

See Also COUNT(), COUNTA(), COUNTBLANK(), COUNTIF(), DCOUNT()

> ### Sample Files
> Use the DCOUNTA worksheet in the DBFUNCTION2.xls or DBFUNCTION2.xlsx sample file. The sample files are found in the Chapter13 folder. For more information about the sample files, see the section titled "Using the Sample Files" on page xxiii.

DGET()

Syntax DGET(*database,field,criteria*)

Definition This function extracts a value from a column in a list or database that matches the specified conditions.

Arguments

- *database* **(required)** The cell range that makes up the list or database

- *field* **(optional)** Indicates which column is used in the function

- *criteria* **(required)** The cell range containing the field names and the filter criteria

> **Note**
> If no record matches the criteria, the DGET() function returns the #VALUE! error. If more than one record matches the criteria, the DGET() function returns the #VALUE! error.

Background   To find a value within a database where a field matches a specific criteria, use the DGET() function.

See Also You will find more information about search criteria in the section titled "Arguments in Database Functions" earlier in this chapter.

Example   You are a wholesaler and receive a complaint from one of your customers, Old World Delicatessen. This customer ordered tofu that they say is moldy. To be able to send a complaint to the manufacturer and to ask if there are known production issues, you want to know the date you sold the tofu to Old World Delicatessen. You can use the DGET() function to do this. Because Old World Delicatessen has ordered the tofu, you are sure the DGET() function will return a result.

DGET() returns 12/3/2007 based on the company name, country/region, and item number criteria (B4:D5 as shown in Figure 13-14). Using the DGET() function, you can quickly return values from the database even if you specify several search criteria.

E5		f_x =DGET(Database,D4,A4:C5)		
	A	B	C	D	E
1	On which date was the Longlife Tofu sold to the US company Old World Delicatessen?				
2					
3	Search criteria			Search field	Result
4	Company	Country/Region	Product	Date	
5	Old World Delicatessen	USA	Longlife Tofu		12/3/2007

Figure 13-14 DGET() returns the delivery date for the moldy tofu.

See Also DMAX(), DMIN()

> **Sample Files**
> Use the DGET worksheet in the DBFUNCTION2.xls or DBFUNCTION2.xlsx sample file. The sample files are found in the Chapter13 folder. For more information about the sample files, see the section titled "Using the Sample Files" on page xxiii.

DMAX()

Syntax   DMAX(*database,field,criteria*)

Definition   This function returns the largest number from a column in a list or database that matches the specified conditions.

Arguments

- *database* **(required)** The cell range that makes up the list or database

- *field* **(optional)** Indicates which column is used in the function

- *criteria* **(required)** The cell range containing the field names and the filter criteria

Background   Use the DMIN() and DMAX() functions to find the smallest or largest value in a database based on certain criteria. DMAX() returns a value from a database, such as the highest production volume for a product within the past five years.

Example   As a wholesaler, you have many customers to whom you sell a range of the products you offer. You want to analyze your customers, sales, and products. First you want to know the product and customer with the highest sales based on orders within the United States. For this you can use the DMAX() function.

The DMAX function looks for the largest sales value for orders from the United States (see Figure 13-15). Because you want to know only the highest sales within the United States, you specify *USA* as a search criterion (B5). You don't specify the product because you want to include all products in the search.

	A	B	C	D
	D5		*fx* =DMAX(Database,C4,A4:B5)	
3	**Search criteria**		**Search field**	**Result**
4	Product	Country/Region	Sales	
5		USA		2000

Figure 13-15 DMAX() returns the greatest value from a list based on certain criteria.

DMAX() returns 2000; that is, the highest order placed in the United States was for $2,000.

If you also want to know which company placed this order and what product the company bought, you can perform additional calculations with the DGET() function. Figure 13-16 shows a possible solution.

⊿	A	B	C	D
8	Which company placed an order for $2,000?			
9				
10	Search criteria		Search field	Result
11	Country/Region	Sales	Company	
12	USA	2000		Save-a-lot Markets
13				=DGET(Database,C11,A11:B12)
14				
15	For what product was this order placed?			
16				
17	Search criteria		Search field	Result
18	Company	Sales	Product	
19	Save-a-lot Markets	2000		Côte de Blaye
20				=DGET(Database,C18,A18:B19)

Figure 13-16 The DGET() function is used for additional calculations.

With the DMAX() function, you can quickly analyze your sales and customers.

See Also DMIN(), MAX(), MIN()

Sample Files

Use the DMAX worksheet in the DBFUNCTION2.xls or DBFUNCTION2.xlsx sample file. The sample files are found in the Chapter13 folder. For more information about the sample files, see the section titled "Using the Sample Files" on page xxiii.

DMIN()

Syntax DMIN(*database,field,criteria*)

Definition This function returns the smallest number from a column in a list or database that matches the specified conditions.

Arguments

- *database* **(required)** The cell range.that makes up the list or database

- *field* **(optional)** Indicates which column is used in the function

- *criteria* **(required)** The cell range containing the field names and the filter criteria

Background Use the DMIN() and DMAX() functions to find the smallest or largest value, respectively, in a database based on certain criteria. DMIN() returns a value from a database, such as the smallest sales for a product within the past five years.

Example Your wholesale company is doing well and the sales are high. However, you want to know which product has the lowest sales so that you can consider changing the product or offering a different product. You want to return the product with the lowest sales for a particular customer. You can use the DMIN() function to do this.

The DMIN() function returns the order value for the Save-a-lot Markets company (see Figure 13-17). Because the database contains sales of $0, you have to specify >0.

C4		f_x =DMIN(Database,B3,A3:B4)	
	A	B	C
3	Company	Sales	Result
4	Save-a-lot Markets	>0	1020

Figure 13-17 DMIN() returns the lowest sales for your customer, Save-a-lot Markets.

DMIN() returns the lowest sales of $1,020 for your customer, Save-a-lot Markets. You can also use the DGET() function to determine which product this sale was for. Figure 13-18 shows the solution.

D11		f_x =DGET(Database,C10,A10:B11)		
	A	B	C	D
8	For what product was this sale made?			
9				
10	Sales	Company	Product	Result
11	1020	Save-a-lot Markets		Steeleye Stout

Figure 13-18 DGET() returns the relevant product.

In this way, you can analyze each customer and the products with the smallest sales to change your product line.

See Also DMAX(), MAX(), MIN()

Sample Files

Use the DMIN worksheet in the DBFUNCTION2.xls or DBFUNCTION2.xlsx sample file. The sample files are found in the Chapter13 folder. For more information about the sample files, see the section titled "Using the Sample Files" on page xxiii.

DPRODUCT()

Syntax DPRODUCT(*database,field,criteria*)

Definition This function multiplies the values in a column in a list or database that match the specified conditions.

Arguments

- *database* **(required)** The cell range that makes up the list or database

- *field* **(optional)** Indicates which column is used in the function

- *criteria* **(required)** The cell range containing the field names and the filter criteria

Background Use the DPRODUCT() function to multiply the values in a list based on specified criteria.

Example The wholesaler example used previously does not provide any useful data to demonstrate this function, so we will use a different example.

> ## Note
> It was not easy to find an example of this function that makes sense, because database fields are not normally multiplied. There is an example in Excel Help, but it is not obvious what the product of the crops of apple trees with a height between 4.5 and 7.5 meters is used for. Other publications also struggle to find meaningful examples. The following simple example is similarly challenged.

Assume that you are a real estate agent and create a database for the apartments you are trying to sell (see Figure 13-19).

	A	B	C	D
3	**Apartment**	**Rooms**	**Dimension for**	**Measurements in meters**
4	Welcome Street 5	1	Length	3.50
5	Welcome Street 5	1	Width	2.10
6	Welcome Street 5	2	Length	5.20
7	Welcome Street 5	2	Width	2.45
8	Welcome Street 5	3	Length	3.60
9	Welcome Street 5	3	Width	4.10
10	Welcome Street 5	4	Length	4.70
11	Welcome Street 5	4	Width	3.30
12	Parklane 23	1	Length	3.50
13	Parklane 23	1	Width	2.10
14	Parklane 23	2	Length	5.20
15	Parklane 23	2	Width	2.45
16	Parklane 23	3	Length	3.60
17	Parklane 23	3	Width	4.10
18	Apple Street 134	1	Length	4.70
19	Apple Street 135	1	Width	3.30
20	Apple Street 136	2	Length	3.50
21	Apple Street 137	2	Width	2.10
22	Apple Street 138	3	Length	5.20
23	Apple Street 139	3	Width	2.45
24	Apple Street 140	4	Length	3.60
25	Apple Street 141	4	Width	4.10
26	Apple Street 142	5	Length	4.70
27	Apple Street 143	5	Width	3.30
28	Apple Street 144	6	Length	3.50
29	Apple Street 145	6	Width	2.10

Figure 13-19 The real estate database sorted by rooms.

You have entered the dimensions of each room in the apartments and want to calculate the area of each room to be able to give this information to your customers. You use the DPRODUCT() function to calculate the square meters. Figure 13-20 shows a possible solution.

I5		f_x	=DPRODUCT(A3:D29,H4,F4:G5)	
	F	G	H	I
1	**How many square meters is each room?**			
2				
3	**Search criteria**		**Field in database**	**Result**
4	**Apartment**	**Rooms**	**Measurements in meters**	
5	Welcome Street 5	1		7.35

Figure 13-20 Calculating the area based on the selected criteria.

The following arguments were used for this solution:

- Specify the cell range A3:D29 for the *database* argument.

- The street name and one of the rooms are used as the *criteria* fields F4:G5.

- Specify cell H4 to identify the *field* argument.

The function returns 7.35 square meters for room 1 in the apartment on Welcome Street. If you change the value in cell G5 or the street name, you can calculate the area of other rooms in selected apartments.

See Also DSUM(), PRODUCT(), SUMIF()

> ### Sample Files
>
> **Use the DPPRODUCT worksheet in the DBFUNCTION2.xls or DBFUNCTION2.xlsx sample file. The sample files are found in the Chapter13 folder. For more information about the sample files, see the section titled "Using the Sample Files" on page xxiii.**

DSTDEV()

Syntax   DSTDEV(*database,field,criteria*)

Definition   This function estimates the standard deviation of a population based on a sample of data in a column in a list or database that match the specified conditions.

Arguments

- ***database* (required)** The cell range that makes up the list or database

- ***field* (optional)** Indicates which column is used in the function

- ***criteria* (required)** The cell range containing the field names and the filter criteria

Background   The standard deviation is an important measure of spread and describes the deviation from the arithmetic mean. It is a measure of dispersion where the more spread out the data is around the mean, the higher the standard deviation. The standard deviation is the square root of the variance.

See Also You will find more information about the standard deviation and variance in the descriptions of STDEV.P() and VARA() in Chapter 12.

Example   You are a wholesaler and have analyzed your sales data by using several functions. Now you want to use the DSTDEV() function to look at the dispersion of the sales. Specifically, you want to know how widely the sales orders for a particular product in a country vary around the mean order value.

> **Note**
> The data to be evaluated is a sample. More sales took place, but only a sample is used for the evaluation.

In Figures 13-21 and 13-22, the standard deviation is calculated for orders of Longlife Tofu in the United States. The result shows a standard deviation of $301.13 around the mean of $1,617.38. Figure 13-22 shows the calculation of the average.

D4	fx	=DSTDEV(Database,C3,A3:B4)	
A	B	C	D
1 What is the standard deviation of sales orders for Longlife Tofu in the United States?			
2			
3 Country/Region	Product	Sales	Result
4 USA	Longlife Tofu		301.13

Figure 13-21 Calculating the standard deviation based on a sample.

D10	fx	=DAVERAGE(Database,C9,A9:B10)	
A	B	C	D
9 Country/Region	Product	Sales	Result
10 USA	Longlife Tofu		1617.38

Figure 13-22 The mean of the sales of the product, Longlife Tofu, in the United States.

See Also DSTDEVP(), STDEV.P(), STDEVA(), STDEVPA()

> **Sample Files**
> Use the DSTDEV worksheet in the DBFUNCTION2.xls or DBFUNCTION2.xlsx sample file. The sample files are found in the Chapter13 folder. For more information about the sample files, see the section titled "Using the Sample Files" on page xxiii.

DSTDEVP()

SyntaxDSTDEVP(*database,field,criteria*)

Definition   This function calculates the standard deviation of a population based on the numbers in a column in a list or database that match the specified criteria.

Arguments

- *database* **(required)** The cell range that makes up the list or database

- *field* **(optional)** Indicates which column is used in the function

- *criteria* **(required)** The cell range containing the field names and the filter criteria

Background   The only difference between DSTDEVP() and DSTDEV() is that the DSTDEVP() calculation is based on the entire population and is not an estimate of the population value based on a sample.

See Also You will find more information about standard deviations in the description of STDEV.P() in Chapter 12 and in the description of the DSTDEV() function in this chapter.

Example   You are a wholesaler and need to analyze your sales orders. You have already calculated the standard deviation for the sales of a product based on a sample by using the DSTDEV() function. Now you want to calculate the standard deviation based on the entire population.

Calculate the standard deviation based on the population of sales orders for a particular product in a certain country (see Figure 13-23).

> **Note**
> The data to be evaluated includes the entire population. The two functions DSTDEV() and DSTDEVP() will return different results if applied to the same data, because the sample DSTDEV() function will make an adjustment to estimate the population value.

Figure 13-23 Calculating the standard deviation based on a population.

To evaluate your findings, it is helpful to calculate the mean (see Figure 13-24).

D9		fx	=DAVERAGE(Database,C8,A8:B9)
	A	B	C	D
6	What is the mean sales value for orders of Longlife Tofu in the United States?			
7				
8	Country/Region	Product	Sales	Result
9	USA	Longlife Tofu		1617.38

Figure 13-24 The mean of the sales of the product Longlife Tofu in the United States.

The calculation of the standard deviation based on the population and several criteria returns 289.32. This means that the sales of Longlife Tofu in the United States spread around the mean ($1,617.38) by $289.32.

See Also DSTDEV(), STDEV.S(), STDEVA(), STDEVPA()

> **Sample Files**
> Use the DSTDEVP worksheet in the DBFUNCTION2.xls or DBFUNCTION2.xlsx sample file. The sample files are found in the Chapter13 folder. For more information about the sample files, see the section titled "Using the Sample Files" on page xxiii.

DSUM()

Syntax   DSUM(*database,field,criteria*)

Definition   This function adds the numbers in a column in a list or database that match the specified conditions.

Arguments

- *database* **(required)** The cell range that makes up the list or database

- *field* **(optional)** Indicates which column is used in the function

- *criteria* **(required)** The cell range containing the field names and the filter criteria

Background   Use the DSUM() function to sum a list of values matching a specific criteria. DSUM() can calculate the sum of data with criteria matching a lot of conditions.

Example   The sales order database contains many orders for your wholesale company. Suppose you want to know the total sales of orders for a particular product in a particular country that are larger than the average. You start by calculating the average sales for Chai in the United States by using the DAVARAGE() function, as shown in Figure 13-25.

D18	▾	fx	=DAVERAGE(Database,C17,A17:B18)	
	A	B	C	D
15	What is the average sales for Chai in the United States?			
16				
17	Country/Region	Product	Sales	Result
18	USA	Chai		1473.54

Figure 13-25 The average sales for Chai in the United States.

See Also You will find more information about the mean in the description of AVERAGE() in Chapter 12.

You can use the DSUM() function to calculate the sum of the sales orders with values greater than the mean. This means that you calculate the sum of the sales based on the following criteria:

- Country/Region = USA

- Item name = Chai

- Sales = >$1473.54

Figure 13-26 shows the solution.

D4	▾	fx	=DSUM(Database,C3,A3:C4)	
	A	B	C	D
1	What is the sum of sales above $ 1473.54 for the product Chai in the United States?			
2				
3	Country/Region	Product	Sales	Result
4	USA	Chai	>1473.54	11966.00

Figure 13-26 Calculating the sum of the sales based on certain criteria.

The database argument uses the dynamic range A1:F7008, which has the name Database.

See Also Dynamic names are explained in detail in the section titled "Dynamic Database Names" in Chapter 2.

You get the same result if you enter the name *SEARCH5* for the *criteria* range (A10:C11 in Figure 13-27) and specify *"Sales"* instead of cell C10 for the *field* argument. Remember to enclose the field name, Sales, in quotation marks.

D11		fx =DSUM(Database,"Sales",SEARCH5)	
A	B	C	D
8 What is the sum of sales above $ 1473.54 for the product Chai in the United States? (Calculation with database names)			
9			
10 Country/Region	Product	Sales	Result
11 USA	Chai	>1473.54	11966.00

Figure 13-27 Calculating the sum of the sales using names.

Until now you have used only the AND condition for the criteria, but you can also specify the OR condition. Assume that you want to calculate the standard deviation for the total sales of Chai in the United States based on a sample (see Figure 13-28).

See Also You will find more information about standard deviations in the description of STDEVP() in Chapter 12.

D25		fx =DSTDEV(Database,C24,A24:B25)	
A	B	C	D
24 Country/Region	Product	Sales	Result
25 USA	Chai		284.50

Figure 13-28 The standard deviation for the sales of Chai in the United States.

The sales of Chai in the United States has a standard deviation of $284.50 around the mean ($1,473.54).

Now you want to calculate the sum of the sales outside the mean plus or minus one standard deviation. You are calculating the sum of the sales orders at the extremes of the distribution, both at the top end and the bottom end.

So you want to add the sales that are either above the mean plus one standard deviation or below the mean minus one standard deviation. The following conditions have to be met:

- Country/Region = USA AND
- Item name = Chai AND
- Sales = >1758.04 $ (mean plus standard deviation)

OR

- Country/Region = USA AND
- Item name = Chai AND
- Sales = <1189.04 $ (mean minus standard deviation)

Figure 13-29 shows the result.

D32	▾ (	fx	=DSUM(Database,C30,A30:C32)

	A	B	C	D
28	What is the sum of sales for Chai in the United States that are higher than $ 1758.04 and lower than $ 1189.04?			
29				
30	Country/Region	Product	Sales	Result
31	USA	Chai	>1758.04	
32	USA	Chai	<1189.04	7745

Figure 13-29 Calculating the sum with an OR condition.

If you investigate this further, you can see that there are only five sales of Chai in the United States that match the specified criteria, which summed to the value of $7,745.00 (see Figure 13-30).

J7011	▾ (	fx			

	A	B	C	D	E	F
1	Company ▾	City ▾	Date ▾	Country/ ▾	Product ▾	Sales ▾
5719	Let's Stop N Shop	San Francisco	8/8/07	USA	Chai	$ 1,615.00
5815	Rattlesnake Canyon	Albuquerque	9/15/07	USA	Chai	$ 1,766.00
5864	Lazy K Kountry Store	Walla Walla	10/3/07	USA	Chai	$ 1,250.00
5879	Hungry Coyote Import	Elgin	10/9/07	USA	Chai	$ 1,090.00
5979	Save-a-lot Markets	Boise	11/8/07	USA	Chai	$ 1,714.00
6000	The Big Cheese	Portland	11/14/07	USA	Chai	$ 1,211.00
6176	Great Lakes Food Market	Eugene	1/13/08	USA	Chai	$ 1,872.00
6221	Split Rail Beer & Ale	Lander	1/23/08	USA	Chai	$ 1,233.00
6403	Lonesome Pine	Portland	6/1/08	USA	Chai	$ 1,592.00
6534	Trail's Head Gourmet	Kirkland	7/12/08	USA	Chai	$ 1,150.00
6575	White Clover Markets	Seattle	7/25/08	USA	Chai	$ 1,256.00
6608	Old World Delicatessen	Anchorage	8/7/08	USA	Chai	$ 1,540.00
6663	The Cracker Box	Butte	8/21/08	USA	Chai	$ 1,867.00
7010						
7011						$ 7,745.00

Figure 13-30 Comparison with the original data.

Database functions allow you to analyze the sales based on criteria linked with an AND or OR condition.

See Also SUM(), SUMIF()

> **Sample Files**
>
> Use the DSUM worksheet in the DBFUNCTION2.xls or DBFUNCTION2.xlsx sample file. The sample files are found in the Chapter13 folder. For more information about the sample files, see the section titled "Using the Sample Files" on page xxiii.

Chapter 13

DVAR()

Syntax   DVAR(*database,field,criteria*)

Definition   This function estimates the variance of a sample based on the numbers in a column in a list or database that match the specified conditions.

Arguments

- ***database* (required)** The cell range that makes up the list or database

- ***field* (optional)** Indicates which column is used in the function

- ***criteria* (required)** The cell range containing the field names and the filter criteria

Background   The most commonly used spreads in statistics are the variance and the standard deviation. The *variance* is the sum of the squared deviation of each value from the mean divided by the number of values with an adjustment for the sample.

See Also You will find more information about the variance in the description of VARA() in Chapter 12.

Example   Because the sample variance measures the spread of data, it is often used in descriptive statistics.

Assume that you are a wholesaler and want to use the DVAR() function to explain variation in your sales orders. Let's use the example for the DSTDEV() function. The goal here is to calculate the variance instead of the standard deviation based on a sample with criteria defining the product and country/region selection (see Figure 13-31).

> **Note**
> The data to be evaluated is a sample. More sales took place, but only a sample is evaluated.

D4		*fx*	=DVAR(Database,C3,A3:B4)
A	B	C	D
1 What is the variance in relation to sales for Longlife Tofu in the United States based on a sample?			
2			
3 Country/Region	Product	Sales	Result
4 USA	Longlife Tofu		90680.92

Figure 13-31 Calculating the variance based on a sample.

To analyze the data, you need to calculate the mean, as shown in Figure 13-32.

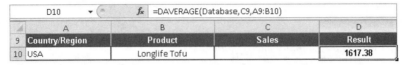

	A	B	C	D
D10		f_x	=DAVERAGE(Database,C9,A9:B10)	
9	Country/Region	Product	Sales	Result
10	USA	Longlife Tofu		1617.38

Figure 13-32 The mean of the sales of Longlife Tofu in the United States.

The result of the variance calculation based on a sample and the set criteria shows an average squared deviation of $90,680.52 from the arithmetic mean. If you take the square root of the variance, the result is the standard deviation (see the DSTDEV() function, described earlier in this chapter).

See Also DVARP(), VAR.P(), VAR.S(), VARA(), VARPA()

Sample Files

Use the DVAR worksheet in the DBFUNCTION2.xls or DBFUNCTION2.xlsx sample file. The sample files are found in the Chapter13 folder. For more information about the sample files, see the section titled "Using the Sample Files" on page xxiii.

DVARP()

Syntax   DVARP(*database,field,criteria*)

Definition   This function calculates the variance of the entire population based on the numbers in a column in a list or database that match the specified conditions.

Arguments

- *database* **(required)** The cell range that makes up the list or database

- *field* **(optional)** Indicates which column is used in the function

- *criteria* **(required)** The cell range containing the field names and the filter criteria

Background   The only difference between DVARP() and DVAR() is that the DVARP() function calculates the value based on the entire population.

See Also You will find more information about standard deviations in the description of STDEV.P() in Chapter 12 and in the description of the DVAR() function earlier in this chapter.

Example   You have already calculated the variance for the sales of a product based on a sample by using the DVAR() function. Now you want to calculate the variance based on the entire population (see Figure 13-33).

> **Note**
>
> The data to be evaluated includes the entire population. The two functions DVAR() and DVARP() will return different results, because DVAR() will make an adjustment to estimate the population variance.

	D4		f_x	=DVARP(Database,C3,A3:B4)	
	A	B		C	D
1	What is the variance in relation to sales for Longlife Tofu in the United States based on a population?				
2					
3	Country/Region	Product		Sales	Result
4	USA	Longlife Tofu			83705.47

Figure 13-33 Calculating the variance based on a population.

To put this in context, you need to calculate the mean, as shown in Figure 13-34.

	D10		f_x	=DAVERAGE(Database,C9,A9:B10)	
	A	B		C	D
9	Country/Region	Product		Sales	Result
10	USA	Longlife Tofu			1617.38

Figure 13-34 The mean of the sales of Longlife Tofu in the United States.

The variance calculation based on a population meeting the criteria is $83,705.47. If you take the square root of the calculated variance, the result is the standard deviation based on a population (see the DVAR() function, described earlier in this chapter).

See Also DVAR(), VAR.P(), VAR.S(), VARA(), VARPA()

> **Sample Files**
>
> Use the DVARP worksheet in the DBFUNCTION2.xls or DBFUNCTION2.xlsx sample file. The sample files are found in the Chapter13 folder. For more information about the sample files, see the section titled "Using the Sample Files" on page xxiii.

GETPIVOTDATA()

Syntax   GETPIVOTDATA(*data_field,pivot_table,field1,item1,field2,item2,...*)

Definition   This function returns data from a PivotTable report. You can use GETPIVOT-DATA() to retrieve summary data from a PivotTable report as long as the summary data is visible in the report.

> **Tip**
> You can quickly enter a simple GETPIVOTDATA() formula by typing = in the cell to which you want to return the value and then clicking the cell in the PivotTable report that contains the data you want to return.

Arguments

- **data_field** (required) The name, enclosed in quotation marks, for the data field that contains the data that you want to retrieve.

- **pivot_table** (required) A reference to a cell, cell range, or named cell range in a PivotTable report. This information is used to determine which PivotTable report contains the data that you want to retrieve.

- **field1**, **item1**, **field2**, **item2** At least 1 and up to 14 pairs of field names and item names that describe the data you want to retrieve. The pairs can be in any order. Field names and item names other than dates and numbers are enclosed in quotation marks. For OLAP (online analytical processing, which is one type of analytical information system) PivotTable reports, the items can contain the source name of the dimension as well as the source name of the item. A field and item pair for an OLAP PivotTable might look like this:

  `"[Product]","[Product].[All Products].[Foods].[Baked Goods]"`

> **Note**
>
> Calculated fields or items and custom calculations are included in GETPIVOTDATA() calculations.
>
> If *pivot_table* is a range that includes two or more PivotTable reports, the data is retrieved from the range that was created most recently.
>
> If the field and item arguments describe a single cell, the value of that cell is returned regardless of whether it is a string, a number, an error, or anything else.
>
> If an element contains a date, the value must be specified as a serial number or generated by using the DATE() function so that the value will be retained if the worksheet is opened in a different location. You can enter times as decimal numbers or with the TIME() function.
>
> If *pivot_table* is not a range in which a PivotTable report is found, the GETPIVOTDATA() function returns the #REF! error.
>
> If the arguments do not describe a visible field or include a page field that is not displayed, the GETPIVOTDATA() function returns the #REF! error.

Background   The PivotTable in Excel is a powerful tool for data analyses. In a PivotTable, you can sort the data from a database and display summary information. You can group, hide, filter, or evaluate your data without changing the Excel table of raw data.

PivotTables are particularly powerful because you can change the data view in seconds, and there are many layout options available to create different views of your data.

A PivotTable is useful only for databases and lists that contain similar elements that can be summarized on different criteria. For example, if five sales were made in Seattle and three sales in Chicago, you can summarize these cities to view the number of orders and the sum of the sales. If there was only one sale for each city, a summary would not be useful because you could retrieve this data directly from the database.

The GETPIVOTDATA() function allows you to retrieve the data summarized in a PivotTable report. You can refer to all results from a PivotTable in the current workbook or another workbook.

Example   At the end of a business year, you want to create a PivotTable and use the GETPIVOTDATA() function to identify the product with the highest sales.

First, you select Data/Pivot Table And Pivot Chart Report to create a PivotTable (see Figure 13-35).

	A	B	C	D	E	F	G	H	I
1									
2	Country/Region	(All)							
3	City	(All)							
4	Company	(All)							
5									
6	**Sum of Sales**	Column Labels							
7	**Row Labels**	Jan	Feb	Mar	Jun	Jul	Aug	Sep	Oct
8	Alice Mutton	$12,223.00	$7,452.00	$10,838.00	$9,673.00	$13,063.00	$29,589.00	$16,361.00	$12,943.00
9	Aniseed Syrup	$2,954.00	$10,747.00	$20,232.00	$14,195.00	$11,334.00	$28,269.00	$8,438.00	$8,620.00
10	Boston Crab Meat	$12,310.00	$12,320.00	$5,844.00	$15,109.00	$11,120.00	$32,652.00	$6,049.00	$17,797.00
11	Camembert Pierrot	$21,890.00	$7,940.00	$12,308.00	$16,797.00	$19,201.00	$15,135.00	$14,476.00	$14,445.00
12	Carnarvon Tigers	$9,986.00	$8,938.00	$5,986.00	$23,850.00	$21,600.00	$23,682.00	$13,632.00	$10,666.00
13	Chai	$15,530.00	$7,766.00	$11,717.00	$7,574.00	$15,856.00	$24,586.00	$11,089.00	$4,862.00
14	Chang	$9,727.00	$8,034.00	$3,023.00	$13,620.00	$12,699.00	$33,150.00	$16,200.00	$15,063.00
15	Chartreuse verte	$9,137.00	$9,772.00	$21,561.00	$10,772.00	$14,346.00	$32,163.00	$6,083.00	$9,913.00
16	Chef Anton's Cajun Seasoning	$12,281.00	$8,853.00	$14,727.00	$12,356.00	$14,408.00	$28,779.00	$6,175.00	$7,395.00
17	Chef Anton's Gumbo Mix	$13,747.00	$6,492.00	$11,174.00	$18,042.00	$15,790.00	$17,960.00	$18,189.00	$7,807.00
18	Chocolade	$4,322.00	$20,457.00	$11,040.00	$7,769.00	$9,108.00	$33,836.00	$14,755.00	$15,920.00
19	Côte de Blaye	$4,372.00	$16,668.00	$14,591.00	$3,607.00	$12,301.00	$24,182.00	$20,073.00	$13,613.00
20	Escargots de Bourgogne	$8,682.00	$14,089.00	$11,037.00	$11,612.00	$14,292.00	$17,652.00	$9,567.00	$18,755.00
21	Filo Mix	$12,532.00	$17,029.00	$5,817.00	$15,316.00	$13,274.00	$14,671.00	$13,237.00	$16,304.00
22	Fløtemysost	$14,419.00	$10,367.00	$7,927.00	$5,980.00	$16,322.00	$26,786.00	$13,170.00	$16,012.00
23	Geitost	$5,263.00	$20,888.00	$7,884.00	$17,327.00	$18,543.00	$33,033.00	$11,385.00	$7,955.00

Figure 13-35 A PivotTable created from original data.

> **Note**
> For the GETPIVOTDATA() function, the order of the data isn't important.

Figure 13-36 illustrates how the GETPIVOTDATA() function can be used. A combo box allows the user to select a product, and the table below it displays the sales figures for each month for the selected product.

Month	Sales
1	9,727.00 $
2	8,034.00 $
3	3,023.00 $
4	0.00 $
5	0.00 $
6	13,620.00 $
7	12,699.00 $
8	33,150.00 $
9	16,200.00 $
10	15,063.00 $
11	13,626.00 $
12	16,820.00 $

Combo box selection:
Chang
Chartreuse verte
Chef Anton's Cajun Seasoning
Chef Anton's Gumbo Mix
Chocolade
Côte de Blaye
Escargots de Bourgogne
Filo Mix

Figure 13-36 The sales for the months of January through December for all countries/regions is displayed.

After you select a product from the combo box, you want to display all sales for all countries that took place within the year. Open a new worksheet and click a cell. To test the GETPIVOTDATA() function, you enter an equal sign (=) in the selected cell and click any cell in the PivotTable you created.

> ## Note
>
> You must ensure that this option is activated in the Pivot Table tools. Click into the PivotTable. On the PivotTable Tools Options tab, select Options from the PivotTable group. Make sure that Generate GetPivotData is selected (see Figure 13-37).
>
>
>
> **Figure 13-37** Activate the PivotTable function.

The GETPIVOTDATA() function is applied automatically (see Figure 13-38).

	B11		*fx*	=GETPIVOTDATA("Sales",'Pivot from raw data'!$A$6,"Date",1,"Product",$A$1)		

	A	B	C	D	E	F	G
1							
2	Country	(All)					
3	City	(All)					
4	Company	(All)					
5							
6	**Sum of Sales**	Column Labels					
7	**Row Labels**	Jan	Feb	Mar	Jun	Jul	Aug
8	Alice Mutton	$12,22?.00	$7,452.00	$10,838.00	$9,673.00	$13,063.00	$29,589.00
9	Aniseed Syrup	$2,95?.00	$10,747.00	$20,232.00	$14,195.00	$11,334.00	$28,269.00
10	Boston Crab Meat	$12,31?.00	$12,320.00	$5,844.00	$15,109.00	$11,120.00	$32,652.00
11	Camembert Pierrot	$21,890.00	$7,940.00	$12,308.00	$16,797.00	$19,201.00	$15,135.00
12	Carnarvon Tigers	$9,986.00	$8,938.00	$5,986.00	$23,850.00	$21,600.00	$23,682.00
13	Chai	$15,530.00	$7,766.00	$11,717.00	$7,574.00	$15,856.00	$24,586.00

Figure 13-38 The GETPIVOTDATA() function is activated by clicking in the PivotTable.

If you confirm the selected cell (cell B11 in the figure) by pressing the Enter key, the value $21,890 appears in the worksheet (see Figure 13-39).

	D5		*fx*	=GETPIVOTDATA("Sales",'Pivot from raw data'!$A$6,"Date",1,"Product","Camembert Pierrot")		

	B	C	D	E	F	G	H
5			21890				
6							

Figure 13-39 The PivotTable data are assigned to cell D5.

Here are the arguments for the GETPIVOTDATA() function:

```
=GETPIVOTDATA("Sales",'Pivot from raw data'!$A$6,"Date",1,"Product","Camembert
Pierrot")
```

- **"Sales"** The required data field containing the data to be retrieved—in this case, the sales.

- **'Pivot from original data'!$A$6** The reference to cell A6 (or a cell range) within the PivotTable containing the data you want to retrieve.

- **"Date",1** The first field name of the field/item pair. This means that the sales for January are returned. 1 indicates January, 2 indicates February, and so on.

- **"Product","Chai"** The first item name of the field/item pair. This means that the sales for the product Chai are returned.

After you have familiarized yourself with the GETPIVOTDATA() function, you decide that you want to create a sales overview. Copy all item names from the original data list and insert them into the new worksheet (see Figure 13-40).

Product from raw data
Alice Mutton
Aniseed Syrup
Boston Crab Meat
Camembert Pierrot
Carnarvon Tigers
Chai
Chang
Chartreuse verte
Chef Anton's Cajun Seasoning
Chef Anton's Gumbo Mix
Chocolade
Côte de Blaye
Escargots de Bourgogne
Filo Mix
Fløtemysost

Figure 13-40 The item names copied from the original data.

Next, add a combo box to allow a selection to be made from this product list. If the Developer tab is not displayed, you need to activate it. To display the Developer tab in Excel 2007, click the Microsoft Office Button, click Excel Options, click Popular, and then under Top Options For Working With Excel, select the Show Developer Tab In The Ribbon check box. In Excel 2010, click Options on the File tab, and then select Customize Ribbon. Select Developer in the Main Tabs section and click OK (see Figure 13-41).

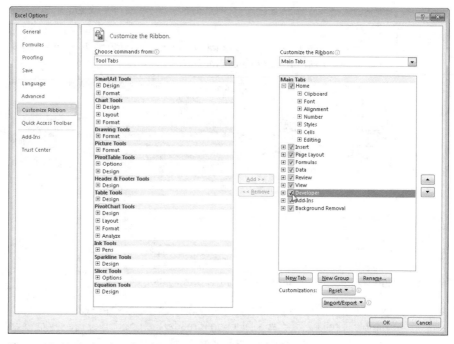

Figure 13-41 Activating the developer tools in Excel 2010.

The Developer tab is displayed. Click the Insert button in the Controls group and add a combo box from the Active X controls (see Figure 13-42).

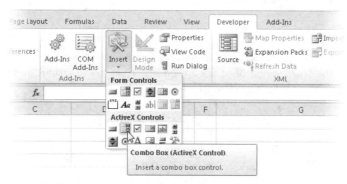

Figure 13-42 The developer tools provide form fields.

To add a combination field in Excel 2003 and previous versions, right-click the menu bar and select Form to activate the Form toolbar. The Form toolbar opens. You can drag a combination field from the Form toolbar into the worksheet and open the properties. For Input Range, select the copied item names, and for Cell Link, assign an empty cell to the form.

> **Note**
>
> In this example we assigned a range name to the products. In Figure 13-43, we use the name PRODUCT instead of a cell range.

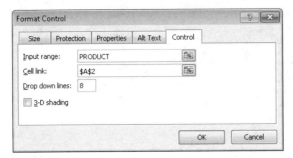

Figure 13-43 Setting properties for the combination field.

If you click the arrow in the combo box, all item names are available. The cell link in this example is cell A2, and as a selection is made, the position of the selected entry in the list is displayed in this cell (see Figure 13-44).

Figure 13-44 Chang is the seventh entry in the combination field.

By using the INDEX() function, you can display the text value associated with the selection rather than the position number. Click any empty cell in the worksheet and specify the arguments for the INDEX() function (see Figure 13-45).

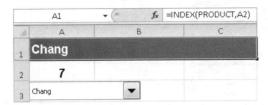

Figure 13-45 The INDEX() function creates a label for the evaluation.

The following arguments are specified for the INDEX() function:

- *array* = This is the list of the product names.

- *row* = A2 indicates the row or cell position to be returned.

- *column* = This argument doesn't have to be specified because the row argument is used.

No matter what product you select in the combo box, the selection is displayed as a label in cell A1.

To display the sales for each month, create a table with the two columns Month and Sales. Enter *1* through *12* in the Month column and click the sales cell for month 1 (January). Enter an equal sign in this cell and click a cell under January in the PivotTable. Press the Enter key to confirm.

> **Note**
> You can select any product because the function generated will be amended to reference the selection made by the combo box.

Figure 13-46 shows the first entry in the sales cell for January.

Figure 13-46 The sales for the product "Chang" in January, February, and March.

Now you only have to change the formula for the GETPIVOTDATA() function.

The formula generated displays the sales in January for the product Alice Mutton. Replace this with a reference to cell A1 to dynamically display the January sales for whatever product is selected in the combo box (see Figure 13-47).

> **Important**
> After you have changed the reference to A1, press the F4 key to create an absolute reference and press the Enter key to confirm.

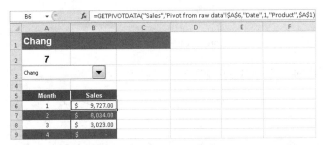

Figure 13-47 The sales displayed depend on the selected product.

Now you only have to drag the formula in cell B6 to the month of December to get the sales for all months depending on the product selected in the combo box.

The GETPIVOTDATA() function allows you to create neatly arranged summary tables.

Sample Files

Use the GETPIVOTDATA worksheet in the DBFUNCTION2.xls or DBFUNCTION2.xlsx sample file. The sample files are found in the Chapter13 folder. For more information about the sample files, see the section titled "Using the Sample Files" on page xxiii.

Cube Functions

Cube functions were introduced in Microsoft Excel 2007. They are used with connections to external SQL data sources and provide analysis tools. Data cubes are multidimensional sets of data that can be stored in a spreadsheet, providing a means to summarize information from the raw data source. A cube is different from queries in Microsoft Access or Microsoft SQL Server because the data in a cube is already grouped in hierarchies, and calculated measures are saved in the cube. This offers two advantages to the user: Summary information is readily available, and most of the heavy-duty calculations are performed on the server. The user does not have to spend much time consolidating the data in Excel. However, you cannot use calculated fields or elements for a PivotTable.

To use cube functions, you must be working with data that is available in one of these two forms:

- Through a connection to a SQL Server Analysis Services data source

- In an offline cube in the user's local file system

These conditions limit the usefulness of cube functions. So that you will be able to work through some examples, the sample files accompanying this book include offline cube and data connection files for the example outlined in Chapter 2, "Using Functions and PowerPivot."

> **Note**
>
> You can create and change an offline cube (a file with the extension .cub) in Excel.
>
> First, you must establish a connection to the Analysis Services by using Microsoft Query (on the Data Tab, Query External Data/From Other Source/From Microsoft Query), or by using the Data Connection Assistant (on the Insert Tab, select PivotTable/Use External Data Source). Then click the OLAP Tools button, as shown in Figure 14-1, to open the

Offline OLAP Settings dialog box. (OLAP stands for *online analytical processing*.) Click the Create Offline Data File button to create the cube, and follow the step-by-step instructions.

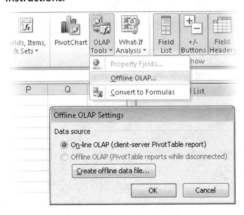

Figure 14-1 Creating an offline cube.

However, you will have to change the sample data connection files (they have either the extension .odc for a workbook connection, or .oqy for Microsoft Query) because the path to a database must be the full path. Use Windows Notepad to change the paths as follows:

```
Data Source='X:\Documents\Chp14\Book\CubeTest.cub';
    Location='X:\Documents\Chp14\Book\CubeTest.cub';
```

Sample Files

Use the offline cubeTest.xlsx sample file. This sample file and the additional files are found in the Chapter14 folder. For more information about the sample files, see the section titled "Using the Sample Files" on page xxiii.

The prepared sample workbook serves as a guide. To avoid unnecessary errors when modifying this sample, perform the following steps to create your own workbook:

1. On the Insert tab, select PivotTable/Use External Data Source. (You can search for additional elements and use the existing data connection files.)

2. Create the layout and include the content from the data source.

3. Use the cube functions.

When you open a workbook with data connections and use the default Excel settings, you have to explicitly allow these connections (click the Enable Content button, as shown in Figure 14-2). When you activate a document in Excel 2010, the document is trusted and you don't have to confirm the activation again until the trusted document is reset in the Trust Center.

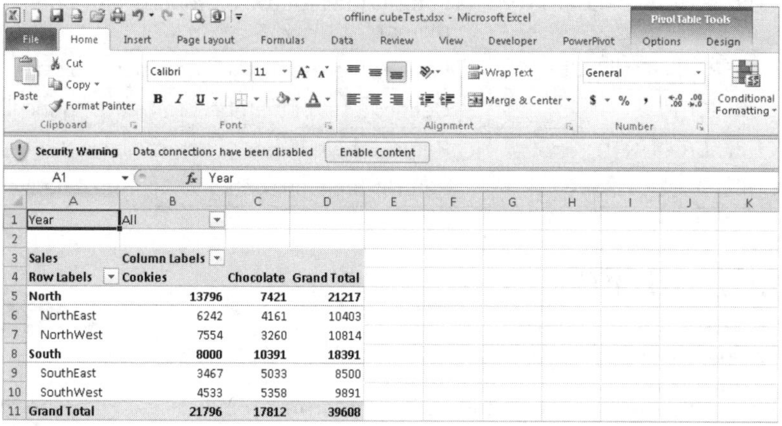

Figure 14-2 The security warning that is shown when Excel is accessing external data.

> **Note**
>
> If you select Convert To Formulas from the OLAP Tools menu (see Figure 14-1, shown earlier in this chapter), Excel converts part of the PivotTable or the entire PivotTable into an unformatted table with the same content as the PivotTable. The advantage of this is that the entire layout (columns and rows) is fixed. You can also include filters.
>
> If you are familiar with formulas, you can create individual structures similar to Pivot-Tables that allow for flexible data evaluation.

The descriptions of the functions throughout the rest of this chapter refer to the example in Chapter 2. The example uses two store groups named North and South, which sell sweets (chocolate and cookies) from the years 2008 through 2011. Each store group consists of two stores. Table 14-1 describes the functions.

Table 14-1 **Overview of the Cube Functions**

Function	Description
CUBEKPIMEMBER()	Returns the requested property for a Key Performance Indicator (KPI) of a cube
CUBEMEMBER()	Returns a member of the cube
CUBEMEMBERPROPERTY()	Returns the requested property (attribute) for a cube member
CUBERANKEDMEMBER()	Returns the *n*-th ranked member of a set
CUBESET()	Defines a set of members to create a subcube
CUBESETCOUNT()	Returns the number of items in a set
CUBEVALUE()	Returns the aggregated value from a data cube

CUBEKPIMEMBER()

Syntax   CUBEKPIMEMBER(*connection,kpi_name,kpi_property,caption*)

Definition   This function returns a Key Performance Indicator (KPI) property and displays the KPI name in the cell.

Arguments

- ***connection* (required)** A string with the name of the workbook connection to the cube. After you enter the first quotation mark, the existing context-sensitive data connections are displayed (see Figure 14-4, shown later in this chapter in the description of CUBEMEMBER()).

- ***kpi_name* (required)** Specifies the name of the KPI in the cube.

- ***kpi_property* (required)** A KPI consists of several components that are specified by using an integer (see Table 14-2).

Table 14-2 **Integers for the Third Argument of the CUBEKPIMEMBER() Function**

Integer	MDX expression	Description
1	*[KPIValue]*	Actual value
2	*[KPIGoal]*	Target value
3	*[KPIStatus]*	State of the KPI at a specific moment in time
4	*[KPITrend]*	Measure of the value over time
5	*[KPIWeight]*	Relative importance assigned to the KPI
6	*[KPICurrentTimeMember]*	Temporal context for the KPI

- ***caption* (optional)** A string displayed in the cell instead of the caption of the KPI components in the cube.

Background

> **Note**
>
> In the cell containing the function, the message #GETTING_DATA temporarily appears while the data is being queried.

Error values and messages provide information about incorrect or missing entries:

- If the connection name is not a valid workbook connection, the CUBEKPIMEMBER() function returns the #NAME? error.

- If the OLAP server (or the offline cube) is not available, you get an error message. The content of the affected cell doesn't change.

- CUBEKPIMEMBER() returns the #N/A error value when *kpi_name* or *kpi_property* is invalid.

- CUBEKPIMEMBER() might return the #N/A error when the connection to the data source is interrupted and cannot be re-established

You can combine CUBEKPIMEMBER() with CUBEVALUE(). Specify CUBEKPIMEMBER() as the second argument or reference for CUBEVALUE().

Example   In this example, a KPI named *average* is saved in the cube. This cube calculates the average of the sales and the total number of sales as integers. Both values are also saved as measures in the cube but cannot be used to calculate fields in the PivotTable. The target value (goal) is $1,500. Figure 14-3 shows the example for cookies.

	A	B	C	D
1	Year	All		
2				
3	**Sales**	**Column Labels**		
4	**Row Labels**	**Cookies**	Chocolate	Grand Total
5	**North**	13796	7421	21217
6	NorthEast	6242	4161	10403
7	NorthWest	7554	3260	10814
8	**South**	**8000**	**10391**	**18391**
9	SouthEast	3467	5033	8500
10	SouthWest	4533	5358	9891
11	**Grand Total**	**21796**	**17812**	**39608**
12				

Figure 14-3 The KPI average.

The formula

```
=CUBEKPIMEMBER("offline","average",1)
```

displays the word *average*. The formula

```
=CUBEVALUE("offline",CUBEKPIMEMBER("offline","average",1))
```

returns 1453 (the rounded average of all sales). In the second formula, you can enter a reference to the cell containing the first formula as the second argument. To get the target value of the average, use the formula

```
=CUBEVALUE("offline",CUBEKPIMEMBER("offline","average",2))
```

The value of 2 in the last argument is important, because it indicates, in this case, the target value.

You can use the cell containing the formula to create cell captions. The real content of the cell is more informative, as shown by using the CUBEVALUE() function.

See Also All other cube functions, GETPIVOTDATA()

CUBEMEMBER()

Syntax CUBEMEMBER(*connection,member_expression,caption*)

Definition This function returns a member (cell) from a cube. Use CUBEMEMBER() to validate that the member exists and to pass the member to other functions through a cell reference.

Arguments

- *connection* **(required)** The text string name of the workbook connection to the cube, in quotation marks. When you are entering the connection, after you type the first quotation mark, existing context-sensitive data connections are displayed (see Figure 14-4).

Figure 14-4 Context sensitivity helps you enter formulas.

- *member_expression* **(required)** Defines the position of a member in the cube based on a multidimensional expression (MDX). The expression can be entered directly or it can be referenced in a cell. You can also use tuples in expressions.

- *caption* **(optional)** A string displayed in the cell instead of the caption of the member in the cube. If a tuple is used, the function returns the caption of the last member in the tuple.

Background   When you use CUBEMEMBER() as an argument for another cube function, the MDX expression instead of the displayed value is used in the argument.

> ## Note
> In the cell containing the function, the message #GETTING_DATA temporarily appears while the data is being queried.

Error values and messages provide information about incorrect or missing entries:

- If the connection name is not a valid workbook connection, the CUBEMEMBER() function returns the #NAME? error.

- If the OLAP server (or the offline cube) is not available, you get an error message. The content of the affected cell doesn't change.

- If at least one member within the tuple is invalid, the CUBEMEMBER() function returns the #VALUE! error.

- If *member_expression* is longer than 255 characters, the CUBEMEMBER() function returns the #VALUE! error.

- CUBEMEMBER() returns the #N/A error when:

  - The *member_expression* syntax is incorrect.

  - The member specified in the MDX query doesn't exist in the cube.

  - The tuple is invalid because there is no intersection for the specified values.

  - The set contains at least one member with a different dimension from the other members.

- CUBEMEMBER() may also return the #N/A error when the connection to the data source is interrupted and cannot be re-established.

Chapter 14

Example So that you can gain a better understanding of the use of the functions in this section, take a close look at the PivotTable in Figure 14-5.

	A	B	C	D	E
1	Year	All ▾			
2					
3		Column Labels ▾			
4		Cookies			
5	Row Labels ▾	Sales	Sales Count	Average	Average Goal
6	**North**	**13796**	**8**	**1724**	**1500**
7	NorthEast	6242	4	1560	1500
8	NorthWest	7554	4	1888	1500
9	**South**	**8000**	**7**	**1143**	**1500**
10	SouthEast	3467	3	1156	1500
11	SouthWest	4533	4	1133	1500
12	**Grand Total**	**21796**	**15**	**1453**	**1500**
13					

Figure 14-5 The candy sales PivotTable used to demonstrate the cube functions.

The formula

```
=CUBEMEMBER("offLine","[Products].[Product].[All].[Cookies]")
```

looks for a single cell and returns the Cookies member which has the caption we looked for. If you use the tuple

```
=CUBEMEMBER("offLine",
    "([Stores].[Store].[All].[NorthEast],[Products].[All].[Cookies],
    [Years].[2009])")
```

the result is 2009 (the cookie sales in the year 2009 in the NorthEast store). If you use

```
=CUBEMEMBER("offLine",
    "([Stores].[Group].[All].[North],[Stores].[Store].[All].[NorthEast]")
```

to find an empty intercept, you get the #N/A error. To display the word *total*, enter

```
=CUBEMEMBER("offLine","[Products].[Product].[All]","total")
```

You can use the cell containing the formula to create cell captions. The actual content of the cell is more informative if it refers to the cells with the CUBEMEMBER() entries.

See Also All other cube functions, GETPIVOTDATA()

CUBEMEMBERPROPERTY()

Syntax   CUBEMEMBERPROPERTY(*connection,member_expression,property*)

Definition   This function returns the property of a member from the cube. Use CUBEMEM-BERPROPERTY() to validate that a member exists within the cube and to return the property for this member as a value.

Arguments

- *connection* **(required)** A string with the name of the workbook connection to the cube. After you enter the first quotation mark, the existing context-sensitive data connections are displayed (see Figure 14-4, shown earlier).

- *member_expression* **(required)** Defines the position of a member in the cube based on an MDX. The expression can be entered directly or can be in a cell that is referenced. You can also use tuples in expressions.

- *property* **(required)** The name of the property for which you want to return the value.

> **Note**
> For a PivotTable that retrieves data from a cube, use the PivotTable tools to find out whether a member has properties (see Figure 14-6).

Figure 14-6 Checking whether cube members have properties—not all members do.

Background   In the example in this section, the stores have the Group property with the possible values North or South (shown previously in Figure 14-5).

In the cell containing the function, the message #GETTING_DATA temporarily appears while the data is being queried.

Error values and messages provide information about wrong or missing entries:

- If the connection name is not a valid workbook connection, the CUBEMEMBERPROPERTY() function returns the #NAME? error.

- If the OLAP server (or the offline cube) is not available, you get an error message. The content of the affected cell doesn't change.

- If the *member_expression* syntax is incorrect, or if the member specified by *member_expression* doesn't exist in the cube, the CUBEMEMBERPROPERTY() function returns the #N/A error.

- CUBEMEMBERPROPERTY() might return the #N/A error when the connection to the data source is interrupted and cannot be re-established

Example As previously mentioned, the stores in the PivotTable have the Group properties North and South. The formula

```
=CUBEMEMBERPROPERTY("offline","[Stores].[Store].[All].[NorthEast]","group")
```

returns North, and the formula

```
=CUBEMEMBERPROPERTY("offline","[Stores].[Store].&[3]","group")
```

returns South. This example uses the position number of the store in the list instead of the store name.

See Also All other cube functions, GETPIVOTDATA()

CUBERANKEDMEMBER()

Syntax CUBERANKEDMEMBER(*connection,set_expression,rank,caption*)

Definition This function returns the *n*-th member in a set.

Arguments

- ***connection* (required)** A string with the name of the workbook connection to the cube. After you enter the first quotation mark, the existing context-sensitive data connections are displayed (see Figure 14-4, shown earlier).

- ***set_expression* (required)** Defines the number of members in the cube based on an MDX. The expression can be entered directly or can be in a cell that is referenced. You can also use tuples in expressions.

- ***rank* (required)** An integer indicating the position of a member in the set.

- ***caption* (required)** A string displayed in the cell instead of the caption of the member in the cube. If a tuple is used, the function returns the caption of the last member in the tuple.

Background

> **Note**
>
> In the cell containing the function, the message #GETTING_DATA temporarily appears while the data is being queried.

Error values and messages provide information about incorrect or missing entries:

- If the connection name is not a valid workbook connection, the CUBERANKEDMEM-BER() function returns the #NAME? error.

- If the OLAP server (or the offline cube) is not available, you get an error message. The content of the affected cell doesn't change.

- If *set_expression* is longer than 255 characters, the CUBERANKEDMEMBER() function returns the #VALUE! error.

- CUBERANKEDMEMBER() returns the #N/A error when:

  o The *set_expression* syntax is incorrect.

  o The set specified in the MDX query doesn't exist in the cube.

- CUBERANKEDMEMBER() might return the #N/A error when the connection to the data source is interrupted and cannot be re-established.

Example   If you reference a cell in the formula

```
=CUBERANKEDMEMBER("offline",B9,1)
```

that returns the store set with

```
=CUBESET("offline","[Stores].[Store].Children", "all store
   sales",2,"[Measures].[Sale]")
```

the result is NorthEast. This store has the most sales for all products and in all years. The nested formula

```
=CUBERANKEDMEMBER("offLine",CUBESET("offLine","([Stores].[Store].[All].[NorthEast],
   [Years].Children)","all sales",2;"[Measures].[Sales]"),3)
```

calculates the year with the least sales for this store (position 3): 2011.

See Also All other cube functions, GETPIVOTDATA()

CUBESET()

Syntax CUBESET(*connection,set_expression,caption,sort_order,sort_by*)

Definition This function returns a calculated set of members by sending a set expression to the cube on the server, which creates the set and then returns that set to Excel. The content of the cell and the actual value of the cell are different.

Arguments

- ***connection* (required)** A string with the name of the workbook connection to the cube. After you enter the first quotation mark, the existing context-sensitive data connections are displayed (see Figure 14-4, shown earlier).

- ***set_expression* (required)** Defines the number of elements in the cube based on an MDX. The expression can be entered directly or can be in a cell that is referenced. You can also use tuples in expressions.

- ***caption* (optional)** A string displayed in the cell instead of the caption of the member in the cube. If a tuple is used, the function returns the caption of the last member in the tuple.

- ***sort_order* (optional)** The type of sorting; the values are integers that affect the treatment of the fifth argument, *sort_by* (see Table 14-3). The formulas are context-sensitive (see Figure 14-7).

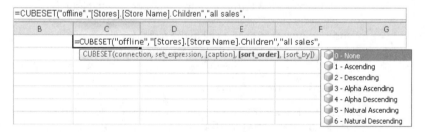

Figure 14-7 Tooltips show the choices for the CUBESET() function.

Table 14-3 Integers for the Fourth Argument of the CUBESET() Function

Integer	Description	Impact on the Fifth Argument
0	Leaves the set in the existing order in the cube	Ignored
1	Sorts the set in ascending order by *sort_by*	Required
2	Sorts the set in descending order by *sort_by*	Required
3	Sorts the set in ascending alphabetical order	Ignored

Integer	Description	Impact on the Fifth Argument
4	Sorts the set in descending alphabetical order	Ignored
5	Sorts the set in natural ascending order	Ignored
6	Sorts the set in natural descending order	Ignored

The default value of the fourth argument is 0. An alphabetical sorting for a set of tuples is based on the last element in the tuple. You will find more information about the different sort orders in the SQL Analysis Services Help.

- **sort_by (optional)** The *sort_by* argument depends on the fourth argument and defines the values in the set that is sorted. If *sort_by* is not provided but *sort_order* requires *sort_by*, the function returns the #VALUE! error.

Background   When you use CUBESET() as an argument for another cube function, the set instead of the displayed value is used in the argument.

> **Note**
>
> In the cell containing the function, the message #GETTING_DATA temporarily appears while the data is being queried.

Error values and messages provide information about incorrect or missing entries:

- If the connection name is not a valid workbook connection, the CUBESET() function returns the #NAME? error.

- If the OLAP server (or the offline cube) is not available, you get an error message. The content of the affected cell doesn't change.

- If *set_expression* is longer than 255 characters, the CUBESET() function returns the #VALUE! error.

- CUBESET() returns the #N/A error when:

  - The *set_expression* syntax is incorrect.

  - The set specified in the MDX query doesn't exist in the cube.

  - The set contains at least one member with a different dimension from the other members.

- CUBESET() might return the #N/A error when the connection to the data source is interrupted and cannot be re-established.

Example The formula

```
=CUBESET("offline","[Stores].[Store].Children",
  "all store sales",2,"[Measures].[Sale]")
```

returns the sorted set of all stores based on the sales (all products and years). The store with the largest sale is listed first.

You can use the cell containing the formula to create cell labels. The actual content of the cell is more informative if it refers to the cells with the CUBESET() entries.

See Also All other cube functions, GETPIVOTDATA()

CUBESETCOUNT()

Syntax CUBESETCOUNT(*set*)

Definition This function returns the number of members in a set.

Argument

- *set* **(required)** A set defined with the CUBESET() function or a reference to the cell containing members of the cube

Background The result of this function is an integer. If the argument causes an error, this error is also returned as the result.

> **Note**
> In the cell containing the function, the message #GETTING_DATA temporarily appears while the data is being queried.

Example In the CUBESETCOUNT() function, if you reference a cell that returns the sorted set of the stores like

```
=CUBESET("offline","[Stores].[Store].Children", "all store sales",2,"[Measures].
[Sale]")
```

the result will be 4. You get the same result if you pass this formula as an argument. The keyword *Children* is not context sensitive.

See Also All other cube functions, GETPIVOTDATA()

CUBEVALUE()

Syntax   CUBEVALUE(*connection,member_expression1,member_expression2,...*)

Definition   This function returns the value of a member (cell) from a cube.

Arguments

- *connection* **(required)** A string with the name of the workbook connection to the cube. After you enter the first quotation mark, the existing context-sensitive data connections are displayed (see Figure 14-4, shown earlier).

- *member_expression1* **(required) and** *member_expression2* **(optional)** At least one and up through 255 expressions that define the position of a member in the cube based on an MDX. The expression can be entered directly or can be in a cell that is referenced. You can also use tuples in expressions. Alternatively, *member_expression* can be a set defined with the CUBESET() function. If no measure is specified in *member_expression*, the default measure for that cube is used.

  Because the argument can be repeated, you can define intersections. You can also use tuples.

Background   When you use CUBEVALUE() as an argument for another cube function, the MDX expression instead of the displayed value is used in the argument.

> **Note**
> In the cell containing the function, the message #GETTING_DATA temporarily appears while the data is being queried.

Error values and messages provide information about wrong or missing entries:

- If the connection name is not a valid workbook connection, the CUBEVALUE() function returns the #NAME? error.

- If the OLAP server (or the offline cube) is not available, you get an error message. The content of the affected cell doesn't change.

- If at least one member within the arguments or the tuple is invalid, the CUBEVALUE() function returns the #VALUE! error.

- If *member_expression* is longer than 255 characters, the CUBEVALUE() function returns the #VALUE! error.

Chapter 14

- CUBEVALUE() returns the #N/A error when:

  ○ The *member_expression* syntax is incorrect.

  ○ The member specified in the MDX query doesn't exist in the cube.

  ○ The tuple is invalid because there is no intersection for the specified values.

  ○ The set contains at least one member with a different dimension from the other members.

- CUBEVALUE() might return the #N/A error when the connection to the data source is interrupted and cannot be re-established

The formula

```
=CUBEVALUE("offLine","[Measures].[GrossSales]","[Stores].[Store].[All].
   [NorthEast]"," [Years].[Year].[All].[2009]","[Products].[Product].
   [All].[Cookies]")
```

calculates the gross sales for cookies in the store NorthEast in the year 2009: $1,856.40. You get the same result if you use a tuple (the arguments of the previous formula are enclosed in parentheses):

```
=CUBEVALUE("offline","([Measures].[GrossSales],[Stores].[Store].[All].[NorthEast],
   [Years].[Year].[All].[2009],[Products].[Product].[All].[Cookies])")
```

If you enter the formula

```
=CUBEMEMBER("offLine","[Products].[Product].[All].[Cookies]")
```

in cell B3, the formula

```
=CUBEVALUE("offline",B3)
```

returns the total sales for cookies: $21,796.

You can also use the examples for the CUBEKPIMEMBER() function. The formula

```
=CUBEVALUE("offline",CUBERANKEDMEMBER("offline",CUBESET("offline","[Stores]
   .[Store].Children","all store sales",2;"[Measures].[sale]"),1))
```

returns $10,814 for the total sales of the best store (NorthEast).

See Also All other cube functions, GETPIVOTDATA()

Sample Files

Use the offline cubeTest.xlsx sample file. This sample file and the additional files are found in the Chapter14 folder. For more information about the sample files, see the section titled "Using the Sample Files" on page xxiii.

Financial Functions

The basic financial calculations in Microsoft Excel can be divided into the following areas:

- **Simple interest calculation** Simple interest calculation is characterized by the fact that the interest is not added to the capital at the due date. This kind of calculation is mostly used for periods shorter than a year (sometimes only a few days).

  Financial mathematics recognizes many different interest terms. In every case, the interest is the price for borrowed (borrowing rate) or lent (loan interest) capital. The price is based on the interest rate for 100 monetary units or one monetary unit. The interest rate always relates to a certain period (usually an entire year). To denote a period of a year, p.a. (*per annum*) is added.

  You will encounter two different basic interest calculations over and over in this chapter: anticipative interest yield and interest yield in arrears.

  Anticipative interest yield is paid for the capital due at the end, calculated based on the interest rate and paid at the beginning of the period. For *interest yield in arrears*, the interest is calculated and paid at the end of the interest period for the capital it started with.

- **Compound interest calculation** In this case, interest is added to the capital at maturity. This results in *compound interest*. Because Excel formulas are used frequently, it is assumed that the interest rate doesn't change in the entire given period.

- **Annuity calculation** An *annuity* is a periodic payment of the same amount. All functions available in Excel assume that the payment date for the annuity is the same as the interest date. The only difference is between anticipative annuities and annuities in arrears, which are paid at the end of the period.

- **Repayment calculation** Financial mathematics uses at least three basic forms for the repayment of a loan: repayment via a single payment at the end, repayment via installments in the same amounts, and repayment via annuity payments for which the repayment amount plus interest stays the same. The last type is basically a type of annuity calculation.

  The Excel functions for calculating repayments refer only to the first and the third type. This does not mean that you cannot reproduce other situations on worksheets by using many different means without using functions.

- **Price calculation** Calculations of the price and yield and the overall return on an investment are an especially complex area of financial mathematics. Many of the integrated functions focus on these areas. The *exchange rate* is always defined as the relative cash value of future payments after the accrued interest is subtracted, if necessary. The rate of return is the figure (as an interest rate) that implements an actual market interest rate.

- **Investment calculation** Investments are often calculated with a static or dynamic investment analysis. This might include cost/revenue comparisons as well as the amortization calculation. These are based on cost and payment calculations. Dynamic methods consider the compound interest and evaluate deposits and disbursements. Excel provides several functions for dynamic investment calculations (capital value method and internal interest rate method).

- **Amortization calculation** This is important for understanding financial mathematics processes: Payments are not only defined by the amount but also by the payment date. It makes a difference whether a debtor pays his debt today or a year from today. The longer it takes to pay the debt back, the higher the amount due; interest is added to the debt. Sometimes this principle can be defined the other way around: Late money is worth little. This has nothing to do with inflation. From a financial point of view, it is irrelevant whether $110 is repaid in a year or $100 is repaid today (based on an annual interest rate of 10 percent).

  Therefore, amortization calculations are not really part of financial mathematics. Traditionally, amortization calculations are discussed in textbooks, and Excel provides the corresponding functions in a separate group. The meaning of the depreciation methods provided by Excel varies according to country/region because depreciation is regulated by the country's specific tax laws.

> ## Important
>
> In the standard Microsoft Office Excel 2003 installation, most financial mathematics functions are not easily accessible. Before you can use the Analysis Functions group, you need to enable it by selecting Tools/Add-Ins in the Add-Ins dialog box (see Figure 15-1). This does not apply to Excel 2007 and Excel 2010.

When it comes to financial functions (see Table 15-1), the descriptions in Excel Help are not always the descriptions of the financial functions themselves. Therefore, you should compare it to the background information in this chapter and, if necessary, use the examples and consult additional literature for clarification.

Chapter 15

Figure 15-1 In the Add-Ins dialog box, you need to enable the Analysis ToolPak.

Table 15-1 Overview of the Financial Functions

Function	Description
ACCRINT()	Calculates the accrued interest of a debt due in full intra-annually or the accrued interest of a fixed-interest security with periodic interest payments
ACCRINTM()	Calculates the accrued interest of a debt due in full intra-annually or the accrued interest of a fixed-interest security with one interest payment per year
AMORDEGRC()	Calculates the depreciation amount based on the French accounting system
AMORLINC()	Calculates the linear depreciation amount for assets
COUPDAYBS()	Determines the number of days that have passed between the last interest payment and the change of ownership of a fixed-interest security with regular coupon dates
COUPDAYS()	Determines the number of days of the interest period into which the change of ownership of a fixed-interest security with regular coupon dates falls
COUPDAYSNC()	Determines the number of days between the day on which the change of ownership of a fixed-interest security with regular coupon dates took place and the next coupon date
COUPNCD()	Determines the date of the first coupon interest payment after a fixed-interest security with regular coupon dates has changed ownership
COUPNUM()	Determines the number of interest payments (coupon dates) that the new owner is facing after buying a fixed-interest security with regular coupon dates

Function	Description
COUPPCD()	Determines the date of the latest interest payment before the change of ownership of a fixed-interest security with regular coupon dates
CUMIPMT()	Calculates the accrued interest that is paid between two points in time when a loan is repaid as an annuity loan
CUMPRINC()	Calculates the part of the repayment that is paid between two points in time when a loan is repaid as an annuity loan
DB()	Calculates the depreciation amounts using a geometrically degressive depreciation method
DDB()	Calculates the depreciation amounts by using a multiple-rate depreciation method
DISC()	Calculates the anticipative interest rate of a given cash value or final value and given duration
DOLLARDE()	Converts the decimal places of a number that is interpreted as the numerator of a fraction into a decimal number, if the denominator is given
DOLLARFR()	Converts the decimal places of a decimal number into the numerator of a fraction with a given denominator and displays it in the decimal places
DURATION()	Calculates the (average) capital commitment of a fixed-interest security
EFFECT()	Calculates the equivalent effective annual interest rate from a nominal interest rate that is equally divided into several periods of the same length within one year
FV()	Calculates the final value of a regular payment flow, taking into consideration possible single payments at the beginning of the period in question, according to the finance mathematical benefit principle
FVSCHEDULE()	Calculates the final value for capital with variable period interest rates
INTRATE()	Determines the repayment amount of a deposit resulting from a simple anticipative deduction of accrued interest
IPMT()	Determines the part of an annuity that is used for the interest payment of a loan that is repaid according to the principle of annuity repayment
IRR()	Calculates a par value of the dynamic investment calculation: the internal interest rate
ISPMT()	Calculates the sum of interest that accrues for a certain part of the year with a given annual interest rate and simple yield in arrears
MDURATION()	Calculates the figure known as *modified duration* for fixed-interest securities
MIRR()	Calculates the internal yield of an investment while evaluating the negative period surpluses with a different interest rate as positive

Function	Description
NOMINAL()	Calculates the nominal interest rate that in a finance mathematically correct way leads to equivalence from a given effective interest rate
NPER()	Determines the duration of a process of the compound interest rate, annuity calculation, or repayment calculation
NPV()	Calculates the net cash value of future surplus periods (cash flow) of an investment based on a given interest rate used for the calculation
ODDFPRICE()	Calculates the price of a fixed-interest security while considering a first interest period
ODDFYIELD()	Calculates the yield of a fixed-interest security for the duration from the settlement day to the due date
ODDLPRICE()	Calculates the price of a fixed-interest security in a final interest period
ODDLYIELD()	Calculates the return of a fixed-interest security in a final interest period
PMT()	Returns the annuity amount of a process mapped to the annuity calculation or, in a repayment calculation, the annuity for a loan with annuity repayment
PPMT()	Determines the part of an annuity that is used for the repayment of a loan
PRICE()	Calculates the price of a fixed-interest security
PRICEDISC()	Calculates the disbursement amount of a simply discounted security with anticipative interest yield
PRICEMAT()	Returns the price (as a percent based on a nominal value) of a security that has a simple interest yield in arrears
PV()	Calculates the cash value of a regular payment flow, taking into consideration possible single payments at the end of the period in question, according to the finance mathematical benefit principle
RATE()	Determines the applicable interest rate for compound interest and annuity calculation
RECEIVED()	Calculates the equivalent interest rate in arrears for a security that has received a markdown (discount, disagio) for an intra-annual duration
SLN()	Calculates the depreciation amounts of capital assets by using the linear depreciation method
SYD()	Determines the depreciation amounts of an asset according to the arithmetic-degressive method
TBILLEQ()	Calculates the equivalent annual interest rate in arrears based on 365 days for a given anticipative annual interest rate based on 360 days
TBILLPRICE()	Returns the price of a discounted security as a percent, as if the value was 100 monetary units
TBILLYIELD()	Returns the yield of a discounted security as an annual interest rate in arrears

Function	Description
VDB()	Calculates the depreciation amounts for assets using the geometrically degressive depreciation method
XIRR()	Returns the internal interest rate for a series of not-necessarily periodic payments in the intra-annual scope
XNPV()	Returns the capital value for a series of not-necessarily periodic surpluses (as the difference between deposits and disbursements) in the intra-annual scope
YIELD()	Determines the yield of a fixed-interest security (loan/bond)
YIELDDISC()	Calculates the annual yield (as an interest rate in arrears) for a security that has received a markdown (discount, disagio) for an intra-annual duration
YIELDMAT()	Calculates the annual yield of a fixed-interest security in the intra-annual scope (without compound interest)

ACCRINT()

Syntax   ACCRINT(*Issue,First_Interest_Date,Settlement,Nominal_Interest,Par_Value, Frequency,Basis,Calculation_Method*)

Definition   The function ACCRINT() calculates the accrued interest of a debt due in full intra-annually or the accrued interest of a fixed-interest security with periodic interest payments.

Arguments

- *Issue* **(required)** Specifies the date of the loan agreement or the issue of the security.

- *First_Interest_Date* **(required)** Identical to the due date if it is intra-annual; otherwise, results from the number of periods, which is defined by the frequency.

- *Settlement* **(required)** The date when the ownership of the security changes.

- *Nominal_Interest* **(required)** The agreed-upon yearly interest rate (coupon interest rate) of the debt instrument/loan/bond.

- *Par Value* **(optional)** The nominal value of the security. If this argument is not specified, Excel calculates with 1000 monetary units (contrary to the information provided in Excel Help in Excel 2003 and earlier versions).

- *Frequency* **(required)** Specifies the number of interest payments within a year. Valid values are the integers 1 = annual; 2 = biannual; 4 = quarterly.

- *Basis* **(optional)** Defines the method you want to use for determining the days in the year according to Table 15-2, shown in the section titled "AMORDEGRC()." If this argument is omitted, Excel calculates with Basis = 0.

- *Calculation method* **(optional)** A logical value that decides whether the interest is calculated for the duration up to this point (TRUE or omitted) or whether only the interest since the last interest payment is specified (FALSE).

All function arguments that call for a date use the date without the time. In other words, fractions are rounded. The *Frequency* and *Basis* arguments also require integers and truncate decimal places.

If invalid dates are used or no numbers are entered where required, the function returns the error #VALUE!. If invalid numbers are entered for non-date arguments, the function returns the #NUMBER! error.

Important

To avoid unnecessary errors, please be aware of the following note from Excel Help:

"Dates should be entered with the DATE() function or as results of other formulas or functions. Problems might occur if dates are entered as text."

Background   Interest for fixed-interest loans/bonds is paid once or several times a year depending on the *Frequency* argument. If the security changes ownership between interest deadlines, the buyer must pay the seller the interest rate as well as the accrued interest up to that date (which makes up the purchase price). If there is more than one interest date within the year, the accrued interest is calculated by dividing the nominal interest by the number of interest dates. With this (*relative*) interest rate, the days of the starting interest period are then calculated by using the day counting method specified in the *Basis* argument.

Example   A debt of $1,000.00, which is due in full with a nominal interest rate of 4 percent p.a. and a repayment by December 1, 2010, has been agreed upon on June 1, 2010. On August 9, 2010, there is a change in creditors. At this date, a real interest rate of 4.5 percent p.a. for the outstanding time until repayment is customary. What price does the person who takes over the debt pay?

To come to the point right away: You can simply determine the result with the functions PRICEMAT() and ACCRINT(). However, if you want to recreate what these functions are doing, think about the following:

- How much interest has accrued up to today and must be paid to the creditor? The answer of $7.56 (after rounding) is

  =ACCRINT(C2,C4,C3,4%,1000,1,4)

  if cell C2 contains the date June 1, 2010; C3 the date August 9, 2010; and C4 the date December 1, 2010. You can test this by counting the days that have passed since the debt agreement (68, as also proven with DAYS360() and COUPDAYBS()) and determining the interest part with 1000*68/360*4%.

- What is the value of the disbursement of $1,000.00 plus interest (of 4%/2 for 1000, because of the difference of only half a year) on December 1, 2010, with the given real rate of interest on August 9, 2010? This is calculated by discounting the future value of $1,020.00 to the day of August 9, 2010. To do so, you can determine that there are 112 days (with *Basis* = 4) between the two dates. DAYS360() can help here, as can the function COUPDAYSNC(), which recognizes counters other than 30/360 days. The cash value is $1,005.92.

- You get the same cash value (price) if you multiply the result of PRICEMAT() by 10 and then add the accrued interest. Multiplication by 10 is necessary because PRICE-MAT() uses a par value of 100.

See Also ACCRINTM(), COUPDAYBS(), COUPDAYSNC(), DAYS360(), PRICEMAT()

> ### Sample Files
> Use the ACCRINT worksheet in the Simple Interest Calculation.xls or Simple Interest Calculation.xlsx sample file. The sample files are found in the Chapter15 folder. For more information about the sample files, see the section titled "Using the Sample Files" on page xxiii.

ACCRINTM()

Syntax ACCRINTM(*Issue,Settlement,Nominal_Interest,Par_Value,Basis*)

Definition The function ACCRINTM() calculates the accrued interest of a debt due in full intra-annually or the accrued interest of a fixed-interest security with one interest payment per year.

Arguments

- ***Issue* (required)** The date of the issue of the security.

- ***Settlement* (required)** The date when the ownership of the security changes.

- ***Nominal_Interest* (required)** The agreed-upon interest rate of the security based on one year.

- ***Par_Value* (optional)** The nominal value of the security. If this argument is not specified, Excel calculates with 1000 monetary units (contrary to the information in Excel Help in Excel 2003 and earlier versions).

- ***Basis* (optional)** Defines the method you want to use for determining the days in the year according to Table 15-2, shown in the section titled "AMORDEGRC()."

All function arguments that concern a date use the date without the time. In other words, fractions are rounded. The *Frequency* and *Basis* arguments also require integers and truncate decimal places.

If invalid dates are used or no numbers are entered where required, the function returns the error #VALUE!. If invalid numbers are entered for nondate arguments, the function returns the #NUMBER! error.

Background This function is a simplified version of the function ACCRINT(). The difference lies in using only one given interest period, which is identical to one entire year (not necessarily a calendar year). Because of the similarities mentioned earlier, all applicable background information about ACCRINT() applies.

Examples The following examples illustrate the function.

Debt Due in Full The accrued interest from the example for the function ACCRINT() in the previous section is calculated with the formula

```
=ACCRINTM(C2,C3,4%,1000,4)
```

where C2 contains the issue date and C3 the date of the change of ownership.

Federal Government Bond The German federal government bond WKN 113517 was issued on October 25, 2000, with a nominal interest rate of 5.5 percent and one interest payment per year, and it is callable on January 4, 2031.

On August 30, 2010, the price was €143.27. How much did the buyer have to pay (without fees) to purchase it?

When solving this problem, note that you cannot use October 25, 2000, as the issue date. Instead, you must use the day of the last interest payment: January 4, 2010:

```
=ACCRINTM(C24,C25,5.5%,100,4)
```

(C24 contains 4/1/2010, and C25 contains 30/8/2010). To the purchasing rate of €143.27 you still need to add €3.61 in accrued interest per bond section.

> **Tip**
> To determine the yield for investing in such a security, you can use the YIELD() function. Unlike YIELDMAT(), which is used in the intra-annual scope, YIELD() works with compound interest.

See Also ACCRINT()

> **Sample Files**
> Use the ACCRINTM worksheet in the Simple Interest Calculation.xls or Simple Interest Calculation.xlsx sample file. The sample files are found in the Chapter15 folder. For more information about the sample files, see the section titled "Using the Sample Files" on page xxiii.

AMORDEGRC()

Syntax   AMORDEGRC(*Cost,Date,First_Period,Residual_Value,Period,Rate,Basis*)

Definition   This function calculates the depreciation amount for assets depending on the desired period based on the French accounting system. The calculated amount is rounded to an integer.

Arguments

- *Cost* **(required)** The purchase cost (net purchase price plus incidental purchase expenses minus reduction of purchase cost) of an asset. If you don't use a number, the error #VALUE! is displayed. If the entered number is negative, the error #NUMBER! is displayed.

- *Date* **(required)** The purchase date of the asset; in other words, the beginning of the depreciation.

- **First_Period (required)** Refers to the date at the end of the first period in the depreciation period. The period gets the number zero.

- **Residual_Value (required)** The anticipated remaining value of the asset after the years of depreciation. If you are using a number that is larger than *Cost*, the error #NUMBER! is returned. The same error value is displayed if a negative number is used.

- **Period (required)** Specifies the time period for which the depreciation amount should be calculated. Only use integers that are greater than or equal to zero.

- **Rate (required)** The (initially linear) depreciation percentage.

- **Basis (optional)** Defines the method you want to use for counting the days. The possible values are shown in Table 15-2.

Table 15-2 **Methods for Counting the Days of the Year**

Basis	Method	Meaning
0	30/360 (NASD method)	Each months has 30 days; each year has 12 months. If the start date is the 31st of a month, this date is converted to the 30th of the same month. If the end date is the 31st of a month and the start date is a date before the 30th of a month, the end date is converted to the 1st of the next month. The end date is always the 30th of the same month.
1	Exact/Exact	Each month has the same amount of days as in the commonly used calendar. The sum of all months is the number of days in the year.
2	Exact/360 days	Each month has the same amount of days as in the commonly used calendar. A year always has 360 days.
3	Exact/365 days	Each month has the same amount of days as in the commonly used calendar. A year always has 365 days.
4	30/360 (European method)	Each months has 30 days; each year has 12 months. Each start and end date that is on the 31st of a month is converted into the 30th of the same month.

Background Depreciation is used to determine the loss of value of an asset and make that loss visible. It should not be confused with depreciation because of abrasion/use, which refers to the cost of purchasing an asset as part of operation expenses from a tax point of view.

The depreciation percentage that is given by the rate is initially interpreted as a linear depreciation rate and thus determines the depreciation duration (5 percent equals 20 years, 10 percent equals 10 years, 20 percent equals 5 years, and so on). Degressive depreciation is created by an additional weighting (multiplication) of the depreciation rate with a factor according to the following rule:

- Factor 1.5 for a rate larger than 25 percent (corresponding to a depreciation duration of three to four years).

- Factor 2 for a rate between 16.66 and 25 percent (corresponding to a depreciation duration of five to six years).

- Factor 2.5 for a rate of less than 16.67 percent (corresponding to a depreciation duration of more than six years).

If you are depreciating to a residual value of zero, this value cannot be reached within the required periods (it becomes smaller and smaller, but only vanishes when the decimal places are also removed by rounding). This is why the residual value in the third period before the end is divided over the two last periods.

If you are depreciating to a residual value that is larger than zero, the depreciation ends in the period in which a book value that is less than or equal to the given residual value is reached. This function returns a depreciation value of zero in the following periods. However, you must use the final book value as the final depreciation value.

Note that the depreciation amount of the first period gets the number zero. It is prorated only for the year, and the days are counted as explained earlier in Table 15-2.

Example   An asset is purchased on June 6, 2010, for a cost of $1,000.00. It is depreciated in the first year with a depreciation of 10 percent, independent of the assumed residual value of $142.00. The result is achieved with the formula

```
=AMORDEGRC(1000,"6/6/2010","12/31/2010",0,0,10%,4)
```

The numbers usually reference the cells where these numbers are located. You can try to calculate this amount by using the formula =DAYS360("6/6/2010","12/31/2010",TRUE) to determine the number of days. The formula should look like this:

```
=ROUND(1000*10%*2.5*DAYS360("6/6/2010","12/31/2010",TRUE)/360,0)
```

The later depreciation amounts can be determined more easily from the respective book values at the end of the previous period multiplied by 10 percent x 2.5.

See Also AMORLINC(), COUPDAYBS(), DAYS360()

Sample Files

Use the AMORDEGRC worksheet in the Depreciation Calculation.xls or Depreciation Calculation.xlsx sample file. The sample files are found in the Chapter15 folder. For more information about the sample files, see the section titled "Using the Sample Files" on page xxiii.

Chapter 15

AMORLINC()

Syntax AMORLINC(*Cost,Date,First_Period,Residual_Value,Period,Rate,Basis*)

Definition This function calculates the depreciation amount in the desired period by using linear depreciation of assets. The calculations are based on the French accounting system, but can be adjusted to tax laws of other countries or regions with a few additional considerations regarding the depreciation calculation.

Arguments

- *Cost* **(required)** The purchase cost (net purchase price plus incidental purchase expenses minus reduction of purchase cost) of an asset. If you don't use a number, the error #VALUE! is displayed. If the entered number is negative, the error #NUMBER! is displayed.

- *Date* **(required)** The purchase date of the asset; that is, the beginning of the depreciation.

- *First_Period* **(required)** Refers to the date at the end of the first period in the depreciation period. The period gets the number zero.

- *Residual_Value* **(required)** The anticipated remaining value of the asset after the years of depreciation. If you are using a number that is larger than *Cost*, the error #NUMBER! is returned. The same error value is displayed if a negative number is used.

- *Period* **(required)** Specifies the time period for which the depreciation amount should be calculated. Only use integers that are greater than or equal to zero.

- *Rate* **(required)** The (initially linear) depreciation percentage, usually determined reciprocally to the planned depreciation duration (10 years yields 10 percent, 5 years yields 20 percent, and so on).

- *Basis* **(optional)** Defines the method to use for counting the days. The possible values were shown earlier in Table 15-2.

Background Depreciation is used to determine the loss of value of an asset and make that loss visible. It should not be confused with depreciation because of abrasion/use, which refers to the cost of purchasing an asset as part of operation expenses from a tax point of view.

The depreciation percentage that is determined by the rate is a linear depreciation rate and thus specifies the depreciation duration.

Note that the depreciation amount of the first period gets the number zero. It is prorated for the year, and the days are counted by using different methods.

If you are depreciating to a residual value of zero and the first period is not an entire year, the end result will contain one more period than initially anticipated. What is left over from the abbreviated first period is depreciated in the final period.

If you are depreciating to a residual value that is larger than zero, the depreciation usually ends before the final (originally assumed) period is reached. The reason for this is that the depreciation percentage is always used against the cost and not (as might be customary in some countries) against the difference between cost and residual value.

If you want to use this function, for instance, according to the German tax law, you can work with *Basis* = 4 in the case of a complete depreciation (*residual value* =0) and a purchase date (argument date) that is the first day of the month when the actual purchase took place. Then select January 1 of the following year as the date for *First_Period*. This ensures that the starting month of the purchase is considered with 1/12 of the cost. Corresponding examples will convince you very quickly that the last day of the previous month with the end of the period on December 31 should not be chosen as the purchase date. (For example, from February 28 until the end of the year there are 302 days and not 300).

Example   On October 5, 2010, you purchase a personal computer for $3,000. Because of the three-year depreciation duration, the depreciation percentage is 33.333 percent. The following formula calculates the depreciation of the first year (period 0):

```
=AMORLINC(3000,DATE(YEAR("5/10/2010"),MONTH("5/10/2010"),1),
    "1/1/2011",0,0,33.333%,4)
```

where instead of the concrete values, the cell references to cells with these values should be displayed. You can also recreate the result of $250.00 with

```
=3000*33.333%*DAYS360(DATE(YEAR("5/10/2010"),
    MONTH("5/10/2010"),1),"1.1.2011",TRUE)/360
```

Instead of using DAYS360(), you can simply use

```
=3000*33.333%*(13-MONTH("5/10/2010"))/12
```

as an alternative.

See Also AMORDEGRC(), COUPDAYBS(), DAYS360()

> **Sample Files**
>
> Use the AMORLINC worksheet in the Depreciation Calculation.xls or Depreciation Calculation.xlsx sample file. The sample files are found in the Chapter15 folder. For more information about the sample files, see the section titled "Using the Sample Files" on page xxiii.

Chapter 15

COUPDAYBS()

Syntax   COUPDAYBS(*Settlement,Maturity,Frequency,Basis*)

Definition   This function determines the number of days that have passed between the last interest payment and the change of ownership of a fixed-interest security with regular coupon dates.

Arguments

- *Settlement* **(required)** The date when the ownership of the security changes.

- *Maturity* **(required)** The date when the repayment of the loan certified by the security takes place.

- *Frequency* **(required)** Because it is quite common to have fixed-interest securities with several interest dates per year, the required argument *Frequency* supplies the dates-per-year number. Allowed values are: 1 = annual; 2 = biannual; 4 = quarterly.

- *Basis* **(optional)** The method you want to use for determining the days in the year according to Table 15-2, shown earlier. If this argument is omitted, Excel calculates with *Basis* = 0.

The arguments have the following requirements:

- Date specifications must not have a time; decimal places are truncated. The arguments *Frequency* and *Basis* are also truncated to integers.

- If date arguments cannot be resolved to a valid date, the function returns the #VALUE! error.

- If *Frequency* cannot be resolved to 1, 2, or 4, or *Basis* cannot be resolved to a number from 0 through 4, the function returns the #NUMBER! error. The same happens when the settlement date is later than the maturity.

> **Important**
>
> Excel Help contains the following note:
>
> "Dates should be entered with the DATE() function or as results of other formulas or functions. Problems might occur if dates are entered as text."

Background   Regular coupon interest for a fixed-interest security (bond) is paid according to the maturity date and the frequency within a year.

The result of this function can be used to calculate the interest that the future owner has to pay for the days passed in the current interest period (which is called *accrued interest*) in addition to the purchase price. Different annual day counters can lead to different results in the intra-annual scope.

Example   This function was used in the detailed calculations of the examples for RATE() and YIELD(). See those sections for examples of the use of this function.

See Also COUPDAYS(), COUPDAYSNC(), COUPNCD(), COUPNUM(), COUPPCD(), DAYS360(), PRICE(), YIELD()

> ## Sample Files
> Use the PRICE and YIELD worksheets in the Price Calculation.xls or Price Calculation.xlsx sample file. The sample files are found in the Chapter15 folder. For more information about the sample files, see the section titled "Using the Sample Files" on page xxiii.

Chapter 15

COUPDAYS()

Syntax   COUPDAYS(*Settlement,Maturity,Frequency,Basis*)

Definition   This function determines the number of days of the interest period into which the change of ownership of a fixed-interest security with regular coupon dates falls.

Arguments

- *Settlement* **(required)** The date when the ownership of the security changes.

- *Maturity* **(required)** The date when the repayment of the loan certified by the security takes place.

- *Frequency* **(required)** Because it is quite common to have fixed-interest securities with several interest dates per year, the required argument *Frequency* supplies the dates-per-year number. Allowed values are: 1 = annual; 2 = biannual; 4 = quarterly.

- *Basis* **(optional)** The method you want to use for determining the days in the year according to Table 15-2, shown earlier. If this argument is omitted, Excel calculates with *Basis* = 0.

The arguments have the following requirements:

- Date specifications must not have a time; decimal places are truncated. The arguments *Frequency* and *Basis* are also truncated to integers.

- If date arguments cannot be resolved to a valid date, the function returns the #VALUE! error.

- If *Frequency* cannot be resolved to 1, 2, or 4, or *Basis* cannot be resolved to a number from 0 through 4, the function returns the #NUMBER! error. The same happens when the settlement date is later than the maturity.

Important

Excel Help contains the following note:

"Dates should be entered with the DATE() function or as results of other formulas or functions. Problems might occur if dates are entered as text."

Background   Regular coupon interest for a fixed-interest security (bond) is paid according to the maturity date and the frequency within a year. Different annual day counters can lead to different results in the intra-annual scope.

Examples   This function was used in the detailed calculations of the examples for RATE() and YIELD(). See those sections for examples of the use of this function.

See Also COUPDAYBS(), COUPDAYSNC(), COUPDAYSNCD(), COUPNUM(), COUPPCD(), DAYS360(), PRICE(), YIELD()

Sample Files

Use the PRICE and YIELD worksheets in the Price Calculation.xls or Price Calculation.xlsx sample file. The sample files are found in the Chapter15 folder. For more information about the sample files, see the section titled "Using the Sample Files" on page xxiii.

COUPDAYSNC()

Syntax   COUPDAYSNC(*Settlement,Maturity,Frequency,Basis*)

Definition   This function determines the number of days between the day on which the change of ownership of a fixed-interest security with regular coupon dates took place and the next coupon date.

Arguments

- **Settlement (required)** The date when the ownership of the security changes.

- **Maturity (required)** The date when the repayment of the loan certified by the security takes place.

- **Frequency (required)** Because it is quite common to have fixed-interest securities with several interest dates per year, the required argument *Frequency* supplies the dates-per-year number. Allowed values are: 1 = annual; 2 = biannual; 4 = quarterly.

- **Basis (optional)** The method you want to use for determining the days in the year according to Table 15-2, shown earlier. If this argument is omitted, Excel calculates with *Basis* = 0.

The arguments have the following requirements:

- Date specifications must not have a time; decimal places are truncated. The arguments *Frequency* and *Basis* are also truncated to integers.

- If date arguments cannot be resolved to a valid date, the function returns the #VALUE! error.

- If *Frequency* cannot be resolved to 1, 2, or 4, or *Basis* cannot be resolved to a number from 0 through 4, the function returns the #NUMBER! error. The same happens when the settlement date is later than the maturity.

> **Important**
>
> Excel Help contains the following note:
>
> "Dates should be entered with the DATE() function or as results of other formulas or functions. Problems might occur if dates are entered as text."

Chapter 15

Background   Regular coupon interest for a fixed-interest security (bond) is paid according to the maturity date and the frequency within a year.

This function's result can be used to calculate the interest that the new owner will still receive in the remaining interest period, or to perform a cash value calculation of payments at the interest date of a fractional period. Different annual day counters can lead to different results in the intra-annual scope.

Examples   This function was used in the detailed calculations of the examples for RATE() and YIELD(). See those sections for examples of the use of this function.

See Also COUPDAYS(), COUPDAYBS(), COUPNCD(), COUPNUM(), COUPPCD(), DAYS360(), PRICE(), YIELD()

> ## Sample Files
> Use the PRICE and YIELD worksheets in the Price Calculation.xls or Price Calculation.xlsx sample file. The sample files are found in the Chapter15 folder. For more information about the sample files, see the section titled "Using the Sample Files" on page xxiii.

COUPNCD()

Syntax   COUPNCD(*Settlement,Maturity,Frequency,Basis*)

Definition   This function determines the date of the first coupon interest payment after a fixed-interest security with regular coupon dates has changed ownership.

Arguments

- *Settlement* **(required)** The date when the ownership of the security changes.

- *Maturity* **(required)** The date when the repayment of the loan certified by the security takes place.

- *Frequency* **(required)** Because it is quite common to have fixed-interest securities with several interest dates per year, the required argument *Frequency* supplies the dates-per-year number. Allowed values are: 1 = annual; 2 = biannual; 4 = quarterly.

- *Basis* **(optional)** The method you want to use for determining the days in the year according to Table 15-2, shown earlier. If this argument is omitted, Excel calculates with *Basis* = 0.

The arguments have the following requirements:

- Date specifications must not have a time; decimal places are truncated. The arguments *Frequency* and *Basis* are also truncated to integers.

- If date arguments cannot be resolved to a valid date, the function returns the #VALUE! error.

- If *Frequency* cannot be resolved to 1, 2, or 4, or *Basis* cannot be resolved to a number from 0 through 4, the function returns the #NUMBER! error. The same happens when the settlement date is later than the maturity.

> **Important**
>
> Excel Help contains the following note:
>
> "Dates should be entered with the DATE() function or as results of other formulas or functions. Problems might occur if dates are entered as text."

Background   Regular coupon interest for a fixed-interest security (bond) is paid according to the maturity date and the frequency within a year. Different annual day counters can lead to different results in the intra-annual scope.

Examples   This function was used in the detailed calculations of the examples for RATE() and YIELD(). See those sections for examples of the use of this function.

See Also COUPDAYBS(), COUPDAYS(), COUPDAYSN(),COUPNUM(), COUPPCD(), DAYS360(), RATE(), YIELD()

> **Sample Files**
>
> Use the PRICE and YIELD worksheets in the Price Calculation.xls or Price Calculation.xlsx sample file. The sample files are found in the Chapter15 folder. For more information about the sample files, see the section titled "Using the Sample Files" on page xxiii.

Chapter 15

COUPNUM()

Syntax   COUPNUM(*Settlement,Maturity,Frequency,Basis*)

Definition   This function determines the number of interest payments (coupon dates) the new owner is facing after buying a fixed-interest security with regular coupon dates.

Arguments

- **Settlement (required)** The date when the ownership of the security changes.

- **Maturity (required)** The date when the repayment of the loan certified by the security takes place.

- **Frequency (required)** Because it is quite common to have fixed-interest securities with several interest dates per year, the required argument *Frequency* supplies the dates-per-year number. Allowed values are: 1 = annual; 2 = biannual; 4 = quarterly.

- **Basis (optional)** The method you want to use for determining the days in the year according to Table 15-2. If this argument is omitted, Excel calculates with *Basis* = 0.

The arguments have the following requirements:

- Date specifications must not have a time; decimal places are truncated. The arguments *Frequency* and *Basis* are also truncated to integers.

- If date arguments cannot be resolved to a valid date, the function returns the #VALUE! error.

- If *Frequency* cannot be resolved to 1, 2, or 4, or *Basis* cannot be resolved to a number from 0 through 4, the function returns the #NUMBER! error. The same happens when the settlement date is later than the maturity.

> **Important**
>
> Excel Help contains the following note:
>
> "Dates should be entered with the DATE() function or as results of other formulas or functions. Problems might occur if dates are entered as text."

Background   Regular coupon interest for a fixed-interest security (bond) is paid according to the maturity date and the frequency within a year.

The result of this function can be used to calculate the cash value of the future payments from the security (price) at the next interest date. For comparison, take a look at the explanations in the detailed calculation example of the PRICE() and YIELD() functions. Different annual day counters can lead to different results in the intra-annual scope.

Example   This function was used in the detailed calculations of the examples for RATE() and YIELD(). See those sections for examples of the use of this function.

See Also COUPDAYBS(), COUPDAYS(), COUPDAYSNC(), COUPNCD(), COUPPCD(), DAYS360(), PRICE(), YIELD()

> ## Sample Files
>
> Use the PRICE and YIELD worksheets in the Price Calculation.xls or Price Calculation.xlsx sample file. The sample files are found in the Chapter15 folder. For more information about the sample files, see the section titled "Using the Sample Files" on page xxiii.

COUPPCD()

Syntax   COUPPCD(*Settlement,Maturity,Frequency,Basis*)

Definition   This function determines the date of the latest interest payment before the change of ownership of a fixed-interest security with regular coupon dates.

Arguments

- *Settlement* **(required)** The date when the ownership of the security changes.

- *Maturity* **(required)** The date when the repayment of the loan certified by the security takes place.

- *Frequency* **(required)** Because it is quite common to have fixed-interest securities with several interest dates per year, the required argument *Frequency* supplies the dates-per-year number. Allowed values are: 1 = annual; 2 = biannual; 4 = quarterly.

- *Basis* **(optional)** The method you want to use for determining the days in the year according to Table 15-2. If it is omitted, Excel calculates with *Basis* = 0.

The arguments have the following requirements:

- Date specifications must not have a time; decimal places are truncated. The arguments *Frequency* and *Basis* are also truncated to integers.

- If date arguments cannot be resolved to a valid date, the function returns the #VALUE! error.

- If *Frequency* cannot be resolved to 1, 2, or 4, or *Basis* cannot be resolved to a number from 0 through 4, the function returns the #NUMBER! error. The same happens when the settlement date is later than the maturity.

> ## Important
>
> Excel Help contains the following note:
>
> "Dates should be entered with the DATE() function or as results of other formulas or functions. Problems might occur if dates are entered as text."

Background   Regular coupon interest for a fixed-interest security (bond) is paid according to the maturity date and the frequency within a year.

The result of this function can be used to manually calculate accrued interest (see the COUPDAYBS() function) or to include the date in a worksheet for better orientation. Different annual day counters can lead to different results in the intra-annual scope.

Example   This function was used in the detailed calculations of the examples for RATE(). See the examples in that section for more information about this function.

See Also COUPDAYBS(), COUPDAYS(), COUPDAYSNC(), COUPNCD(), COUPNUM(), DAYS360(), PRICE(), YIELD()

> ## Sample Files
>
> Use the PRICE worksheet in the Price Calculation.xls or Price Calculation.xlsx sample file. The sample files are found in the Chapter15 folder. For more information about the sample files, see the section titled "Using the Sample Files" on page xxiii.

CUMIPMT()

Syntax   CUMIPMT(*Rate,Nper,Pv,Start_Period,End_Period,Type*)

Definition   This function calculates the accrued interest that is paid between two points in time when a loan is repaid as an annuity loan.

Arguments

- *Rate* **(required)** The nominal interest of the loan.

- *Nper* **(required)** The total number of periods in which the loan is repaid.

- *Pv* **(rquired)** The loan amount.

- *Start_Period* **(required)** The first period of the calculation.

- *End_Period* **(required)** The last period of the calculation.

- *Type* **(required)** With the (by way of exception, required) maturity argument *M*, you can specify whether the payments become interest effective at the start of the periods (*Type* = 1) or at the end of the period (*Type* = 0).

If the values of function arguments (which require integers) are evaluated as fractions, the decimal places are truncated.

The arguments *Rate*, *Nper*, and *Pv* must be positive numbers, otherwise CUMPRINC() returns the error #NUMBER!.

The other arguments must make sense as well: *Start_Period* must be greater than or equal to 1. *End_Period* must be greater than or equal to 1 and not less than *Start_Period*.

Type must return 0 or 1.

Background   The repayment of loans can take place in various ways. One way is for the debtor to pay the same amount each period. This amount is composed of a repayment part (which increases as time passes) and an interest part (which decreases as time passes). The change in this composition is because the loan that needs to be repaid shrinks over time. This version is called *annuity repayment*. The total amount is called *annuity*, even though its payment does not necessarily happen annually.

Although adding up partial repayments is correct (this is how the residual debt is determined), adding up the interest has no finance mathematical relevance. It is a popular method for comparing loans (even financial institutions do it), but it is not a finance mathematical comparison. Adding up interest therefore makes sense only after the interest's evaluation at the time of the loan agreement. If a debtor takes out a loan of $100,000.00, he pays back only that amount. If he pays it back later, he has to pay interest as well.

> **Note**
>
> In loan agreements, an annual interest rate is very frequently formulated as a nominal interest rate (debit interest), but the payment takes place intra-annually. In such cases, you need to determine the intra-annual period interest rate by dividing the annual interest rate by the number of payments per year. The total number of periods results from the periods per year multiplied by the number of years.

Example   In the "Repayment Calculation (Annuity Repayment)" example in the description of the PV() function, the following data was specified: A debtor takes out a loan in the amount of $176,121.76, which he pays back at 5.5 percent with $1,000.00 per month over 30 years.

The repayment plan shows a residual debt of $172,513.25 in the 19th month. $18,000.00 of the loan has been paid back, and you would like to find out how much of it is interest only (in spite of the issues mentioned). The residual debt tells you that $3,608.51 has been paid; therefore, the difference of $14,391.49 must be the amount of interest. You can check this result with the function CUMIPMT(), even though there may be rounding errors.

```
=-CUMIPMT(5.5%/12,30*12,176121.76,1,18,0)
```

(The correct numbers are derived from references to the cells in which the data are located). The result is negative (it has a minus sign), because the payment flow has the opposite direction of the cash value (loan amount).

Rounding errors occur frequently when the integrated functions are used. After all, they cannot take into consideration what actually happens at the bank counter: In the real world, money is calculated with only two decimal places. If you are writing down a repayment plan month by month, you need to use the ROUND() function to show what is actually happening.

See Also CUMPRINC(), FV(), IPMT(), NPER(), PMT(), PV(), RATE()

> **Sample Files**
>
> Use the PV worksheet in the Repayment Calculation.xls or Repayment Calculation.xlsx sample file. The sample files are found in the Chapter15 folder. For more information about the sample files, see the section titled "Using the Sample Files" on page xxiii.

CUMPRINC()

Syntax   CUMPRINC(*Rate,Nper,Pv,Start_Period,End_Period,Type*)

Definition   This function calculates the part of the repayment that is paid between two points in time when a loan is repaid as an annuity loan.

Arguments

- *Rate* **(required)** The nominal interest of the loan.

- *Nper* **(required)** Specifies the total number of periods in which the loan is repaid.

- *Pv* **(required)** Contains the loan amount.

- *Start_Period* **(required)** The first period of the calculation.

- *End_Period* **(required)** The last period.

- *Type* **(required)** With the (by way of exception, required) maturity argument *Type*, you can specify whether the payments become interest effective at the start of the periods (*Type* = 1) or at the end of the periods (*Type* = 0).

If the values of function arguments (which require integers) are evaluated as fractions, the decimal places are truncated.

The arguments *Rate*, *Nper*, and *Pv* must be positive numbers, otherwise CUMPRINC() returns the error #NUMBER!.

The other arguments must make sense as well: *Start_Period* must be greater than or equal to 1. *End_Period* must be greater than or equal to 1 and not less than *Start_Period*.

Type must return 0 or 1.

Background   The repayment of loans can take place in various ways. One way is for the debtor to pay the same amount each period. This amount is composed of a repayment part (which increases as time passes) and an interest part (which decreases as time passes). The change in this composition is because the loan that needs to be repaid shrinks over time. This version is called *annuity repayment*. The total amount is called *annuity*, even though its payment does not necessarily happen annually.

The function calculates the (compounded) part that was used with the annuity payment for loan repayment. This part, therefore, does not represent interest payments. By adding up all past periods, you can determine the residual debt of the original loan.

> **Note**
>
> In loan agreements, an annual interest rate is very frequently formulated as a nominal interest rate, but the payment takes place intra-annually. In such cases, you need to determine the intra-annual period interest rate by dividing the annual interest rate by the number of payments per year. The total number of periods results from the periods per year multiplied by the number of years.

Examples   The following examples illustrate the CUMPRINC() function.

Interest Commitment Over the Entire Duration   In the "Repayment Calculation (Annuity Repayment)" example in the description of the PV() function, shown earlier, the following data was specified: A debtor takes out a loan in the amount of $176,121.76, which he pays back at 5.5 percent with $1,000.00 per month over 30 years. The repayment plan shows a residual debt of $172,513.25 in the 19th month. Therefore, $3,608.51 has been repaid. You can check this result with the function CUMPRINC(), but there might still be rounding errors.

```
=-CUMPRINC(5.5%/12,30*12,176121.76,1,18,0)
```

(The correct numbers are derived from references to the cells in which the data are located). The result is negative (it has a minus sign), because the payment flow has the opposite direction of the cash value (loan amount).

Rounding errors occur frequently when the integrated functions are used. After all, they cannot take into consideration what actually happens at the bank counter: In the real world, money is calculated with only two decimal places. If you are entering data for a repayment plan month by month, you need to use the function ROUND() to show what is actually happening.

Fixed Interest Only at the Beginning of a Loan   Mortgage loans frequently have a fixed interest. However, the time until the interest conditions change is too short for complete repayment. In this case, the debtor can use the residual debt to determine how high his risk would be if interest rates increase, and if necessary he can compare different loan offers. If he does not want to write out a detailed repayment plan, he can determine the residual debt by subtracting the amount repaid within the fixed-interest period from the loan amount. This amount is calculated by CUMPRINC(). The amount is calculated as shown in the previous example.

See Also CUMIPMT(), FV(), IPMT(), NPER(), PMT(), PV(), RATE()

> ## Sample Files
>
> Use the PV worksheet in the Repayment Calculation.xls or Repayment Calculation.xlsx sample file. The sample files are found in the Chapter15 folder. For more information about the sample files, see the section titled "Using the Sample Files" on page xxiii.

DB()

Syntax   DB(*Purchase_Value,Residual_Value,Life,Period,Months*)

Definition   This function calculates the depreciation amounts for an asset by using the geometric-degressive depreciation method, where part of a year (in complete months) is considered in the first depreciation period.

Arguments

- *Purchase_Value* **(required)** The purchase cost (net purchase price plus incidental purchase expenses minus reduction of purchase cost) of an asset. If you don't use a value that can be evaluated as a number, the #VALUE! error is displayed. If the entered number is negative, the #NUMBER! error is displayed.

- *Residual_Value* **(required)** The value of the asset at the end of the depreciation duration. If you don't use a number, the #VALUE! error is displayed. If the entered number is negative, the #NUMBER! error is displayed.

- *Life* **(required)** The number of periods in which the asset is depreciated. You should use an integer greater than zero for this argument.

- *Period* **(required)** The period within the depreciation duration for which the depreciation amount is calculated. This value must be a positive integer that is not greater than the value for *Life*.

- *Months* **(optional)** Specifies the duration of a partial period in the purchase year in complete months. If this argument is omitted, Excel calculates with the complete year (12 months).

Background Depreciation is used to determine the loss of value of an asset and make that loss visible. It should not be confused with depreciation resulting from abrasion/use, which refers to the cost of purchasing an asset as part of operation expenses from a tax point of view.

For the geometric-degressive depreciation percentage, the following formula applies:

$$Depreciation\ rate = 1 - \sqrt[Depreciation\ duration]{Residual\ value / Purchase\ cost}$$

This also explains why a residual value of zero does not make sense—the depreciation would occur entirely in the first year. In such cases, a residual value of $1,000.00 is usually assumed.

In Excel, the calculated depreciation value is rounded to three decimal places and each period is used against the book value. The thus-determined depreciation amount reduces the book value for the next period. If the first period is less than one year long, the depreciation rate for this period is divided by 12 accordingly.

Example An asset with a purchase cost of $1,000.00 must be depreciated in five years to a residual value of $100.00 by using the geometric-degressive method. You can calculate the depreciation amount in each period by using SYD() and subtract it from the book value of the previous period.

Alternatively, you can create a depreciation plan that implements the formulas mentioned earlier in this section for calculating the first depreciation amount as well as the processes for calculating the other amounts.

See Also AMORLINC(), DDB(), SLN(), SYD(), VDB()

Sample Files

Use the DB worksheet in the Depreciation Calculation.xls or Depreciation Calculation.xlsx sample file. The sample files are found in the Chapter15 folder. For more information about the sample files, see the section titled "Using the Sample Files" on page xxiii.

DDB()

Syntax   DDB(*Purchase_Value,Residual_Value,Life,Period, Factor*)

Definition   This function calculates the depreciation amounts by using a multiple-rate depreciation method.

Arguments

- *Purchase_Value* **(required)** The purchase cost (net purchase price plus incidental purchase expenses minus reduction of purchase cost) of an asset. If you don't use a value that can be evaluated as a number, the #VALUE! error is displayed. If the entered number is negative, the #NUMBER! error is displayed.

- *Residual_Value* **(required)** The value of the asset at the end of the depreciation duration. If you don't use a number, the #VALUE! error is displayed. If the entered number is negative, the #NUMBER! error is displayed.

- *Life* **(required)** The number of periods in which the asset is depreciated. You should use an integer greater than zero for this argument.

- *Period* **(required)** The period within the depreciation duration for which the depreciation amount is calculated. This value must be a positive integer that is not greater than the value of *Life*.

- *Factor* **(optional)** The multiplier for the (assumed linear) depreciation rate (reciprocal to the depreciation duration). If this argument is not specified, Excel calculates with the number 2.

Background   Depreciation is used to determine the loss of value of an asset and make that loss visible. It should not be confused with depreciation resulting from abrasion/use, which refers to the cost of purchasing an asset as part of operation expenses from a tax point of view.

The method initially targets linear depreciation. The thus-determined depreciation percentage reciprocal to the depreciation duration is multiplied with an additional factor, however, and is used against the respective book value. This makes it a geometrical depreciation. If the factor used is 2, the process is called the *double-declining balance depreciation method*.

Example   An asset with a purchase cost of $1,000.00 must be depreciated in five years to a remainder of $100.00 by using the arithmetic-degressive method. You can calculate the depreciation amount in each period by using DDB() and subtracting it from the book value of the previous period.

Chapter 15

Alternatively, you can create a depreciation plan that implements the calculation. Creating a depreciation plan following your own pattern is especially recommended if you are using methods that are permitted for taxes, because the integrated functions are generally not usable.

See Also AMORLINC(), DB(), SLN, SYD, VDB()

> **Sample Files**
>
> Use the DDB worksheet in the Depreciation Calculation.xls or Depreciation Calculation.xlsx sample file. The sample files are found in the Chapter15 folder. For more information about the sample files, see the section titled "Using the Sample Files" on page xxiii.

DISC()

Syntax   DISC(*Settlement,Maturity,Price,Repayment,Basis*)

Definition   This function calculates the anticipative interest rate (percent markdown, discount, disagio) of a given cash value or final value and the given duration (simple interest yield).

Arguments

- *Settlement* **(required)** The date when the ownership of the security changes.

- *Maturity* **(required)** The date when the payments from the security must take place.

- *Price* **(required)** Specifies the price at which the ownership changes.

- *Repayment* **(required)** Describes the payment at the day of maturity.

- *Basis* **(optional)** Defines the method you want to use for determining the days in the year according to Table 15-2, shown earlier. If this argument is not used, Excel calculates with *Basis* = 0.

All function arguments that concern a date use the date without the time; that is, fractions are rounded. The *Basis* argument also requires an integer, and decimal places are truncated.

If invalid dates are used or no numbers are entered where required, the function returns the #VALUE! error. If invalid numbers are entered for nondate arguments, the function returns the #NUMBER! error.

Important

Excel Help contains the following note:

"Dates should be entered with the DATE() function or as results of other formulas or functions. Problems might occur if dates are entered as text."

The note regarding the par value in the *Price* and *Repayment* arguments is irrelevant, because DISC() returns a ratio.

Background   The principle of anticipative interest yield is based on the assumption that a seed capital amount (deposit amount/loan) results from the repayment amount minus the interest on this amount. This principle is mainly used in the intra-annual scope and differs from the principal based on a regular savings account or mortgage loan. In this case, interest is calculated at the end of a period based on the seed capital (interest yield in arrears).

Note

The functions are connected as follows (in this example, *Basis* = 4):

$$INTRATE() - INTRATE() \cdot DISC() \cdot \frac{DAYS360()}{360} = PREDISC()$$

But that is exactly the principle of anticipative interest yield. The DISC() function resolves the equation assuming that the other specifications are available.

The DISC() function has the following relation to RECEIVED():

$$(1 + RECEIVED()) \cdot (1 - DISC()) = 1$$

This relationship permits you to calculate the equivalent anticipative annual interest rate from an annual interest rate in arrears. *Equivalence* means that two investors who are investing the same amount of capital (one with anticipative interest yield and one with interest yield in arrears) at the end of a year receive the same payment. The YIELDDISC() function is basically the same as RECEIVED(), only the arguments are named differently.

Examples   The following examples explain the DISC() function:

Bill of Exchange Calculation   On May 10, 2010, a businessman presented his bank with a bill of exchange of $5,000.00 and a (remaining) maturity of two months. The bank has credited $4,958.33 to his account (without adding fees). How high was the discount rate?

From the background information, you can read the equation as follows:

$$Bill\ amount - Bill\ amount \cdot Discount\ rate \cdot \frac{DAYS360()}{360} = Credit$$

and use

```
=DISC("10/5/2010","10/7/2010",4958.33,5%,4)
```

to get to a result of 5 percent.

Usually you would use cell references in this function to refer to the concrete numbers located in cells.

Treasury Bonds   At the time of this writing, Germany offered treasury bonds (security ID 111 704) with the following terms: Duration = 1 year, redemption value (value at end of duration) = €500 (the result from the minimum purchase price), and maturity August 22, 2011. On August 30, 2010, the sale price was €497.75. How high did the German Federal Bank specify the sale interest (this is the name for the anticipative markdown)?

DISC() delivers the correct answer: 0.46 percent.

For data acquisition you should read the preceding formula as:

$$Redemption\ value - Redemption\ value \cdot Sales\ interest \cdot \frac{DAYS360}{360} = Sales\ price$$

You can calculate the annuity of the investment of 0.45 percent specified by the German Federal Bank in two steps: Create the difference between the purchase price and revenue and then build a ratio to the purchase price, or you could use YIELDDISC() or RECEIVED().

See Also INTRATE(), PRICEDISC(), YIELDDISC()

Sample Files

Use the Bill of Exchange and Treasure bonds worksheets in the Simple Interest Calcula-tion.xls or Simple Interest Calculation.xlsx sample file. The sample files are found in the Chapter15 folder. For more information about the sample files, see the section titled "Using the Sample Files" on page xxiii.

DOLLARDE()

Syntax   DOLLARDE(*Number,Factor*)

Definition   This function converts a number's decimal point section, which is interpreted as the numerator of a fraction, into a decimal number, if the denominator is given.

Arguments

- **Number (required)** The number whose decimal places are interpreted as the numerator of a fraction.

- **Factor (required)** The denominator of the fraction for which the decimal section of *Number* is interpreted as the numerator. *Factor* expects an integer; therefore, the decimal places are truncated. If *Factor* is less than zero, DOLLARDE() returns the error #NUMBER!. If it is equal to 0, the error #DIV/0! is displayed.

Background   Until 2001, the stock quotations at the large stock markets in the United States were traditionally given in natural fractions. In other countries, interest was usually established in steps of eighths.

This function helps with the conversion and thus facilitates the quotation comparison.

Example   Figure 15-2 shows the function's effects.

	D6			f_x	=DOLLARDE(D$2,$B6)	
	A	B	C	D	E	F
1						
2		Denominator	1.1	2.2	1.01	2.02
3		2	1.5	3	1.05	2.1
4		4	1.25	2.5	1.025	2.05
5		8	1.125	2.25	1.0125	2.025
6		16	1.625	3.25	1.0625	2.125

Figure 15-2 Conversion from halves, quarters, eighths, and sixteenths.

The results in column C interpret the first number 1.1 as 1½, 1¼, and 1⅛ sequentially. The interpretation as 1¹⁄₁₆ is problematic, because the decimal places can be interpreted only up to the tenth. The result is displayed in column E. In column D, the number 2.2 is interpreted—the number to the left of the period is the integer, and the number to the right of the period represents the quarters, eighths, and so on. Sixteenths cannot be interpreted correctly here either.

Chapter 15

CAUTION!

The numbers this function converts can usually only be entered manually and not as the results of calculations (with the exception of DOLLARFR()). However, you can continue to calculate with the conversion results (unlike with DOLLARFR()).

See Also DOLLARFR()

Sample Files

Use the DOLLARDE worksheet in the Other.xls or Other.xlsx sample file. The sample files are found in the Chapter15 folder. For more information about the sample files, see the section titled "Using the Sample Files" on page xxiii.

DOLLARFR()

Syntax DOLLARFR(*Number,Factor*)

Definition This function converts the decimal places of a decimal number into the numerator of a fraction with a given denominator and displays them in the decimal places.

Arguments

- *Number* **(required)** The decimal number whose decimal places are to be converted

- *Factor* **(required)** The denominator for which the numerator is calculated. If *Factor* is not an integer, the decimal places are truncated. A positive *Factor* is expected. If the argument equals zero, DOLLARFR() returns the error #DIV/0!. If it is negative, the error #NUMBER! is displayed.

Background   Until 2001, the stock quotations in the large stock markets in the United States were traditionally done with natural fractions. In other countries, interest was usually established in steps of eighths.

This function helps with the conversion and thus facilitates the quotation comparison.

Example Figure 15-3 on the next page shows the function's effects.

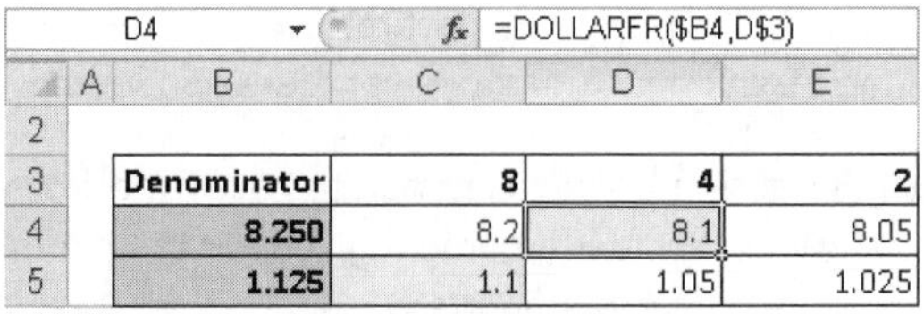

D4 =DOLLARFR($B4,D$3)

	A	B	C	D	E
2					
3		Denominator	8	4	2
4		8.250	8.2	8.1	8.05
5		1.125	1.1	1.05	1.025

Figure 15-3 Conversion to eighths, quarters, and halves.

The results should be read as follows: 8.25 equals 8¼, and 1.125 equals 1⅛.

CAUTION!

The results are only for reading, not for continuing the calculation. If you multiply the result in column D by 10, for example, the first number becomes 81, not 82.5.

See Also DOLLARDE()

Sample Files

Use the DOLLAR worksheet in the Other.xls or Other.xlsx sample file. The sample files are found in the Chapter15 folder. For more information about the sample files, see the section titled "Using the Sample Files" on page xxiii.

DURATION()

Syntax DURATION(*Settlement,Maturity,Nominal_Interest,Yield,Frequency,Basis*)

Definition This function calculates the (average) capital commitment duration of a fixed-interest security. It is called *Macauley Duration*, after its developer.

Arguments

- ***Settlement* (required)** The date when the ownership of the security changes.
- ***Maturity* (required)** The date when the repayment of the loan certified by the security takes place.
- ***Nominal_Interest* (required)** The agreed-upon yearly interest rate as the price for the loaned money.

- *Yield* **(required)** Represents the market interest rate on the settlement day, at which during calculation of the duration all future payments are discounted.

- *Frequency* **(required)** Because it is quite common to have fixed-interest securities with several interest dates per year, this argument gives you their number. Allowed values are 1 = annual; 2 = biannual; 4 = quarterly.

- *Basis* **(optional)** Defines the method you want to use for determining the days in the year according to Table 15-2, shown earlier. If this argument is omitted, Excel calculates with *Basis* = 0.

All function arguments that are dates use the date without the time; that is, fractions are rounded. The *Frequency* and *Basis* arguments also require integers, and decimals are truncated.

If invalid dates are used or no numbers are entered where required, the function returns the #VALUE! error. If invalid numbers are entered for nondate arguments, the function returns the #NUMBER! error.

Important

Excel Help contains the following note:

"Dates should be entered with the DATE() function or as results of other formulas or functions. Problems might occur if dates are entered as text."

The reference to the par value is irrelevant because, due to the creation of the average value, a relative quantity regarding the invested capital is generated.

Background The duration according to Macauley is a weighted arithmetical average value. The cash values of the guaranteed future earnings (interest and repayment) are calculated from the current market interest for the entire duration until maturity by discounting, and are weighted with the time difference until their payment. With slightly more complicated mathematics, it is possible to prove that the thus-calculated *average capital commitment cycle* also determines the date at which a (theoretical) immunization against interest changes takes place. The future value of all payments (calculated with the current market interest) at the date specified by the duration is the average value that is actually reached at that moment, independent of the changing market interest.

The result is then used to compare bonds (fixed-interest securities) with similar conditions (annuity and duration) to each other. A bond with a smaller capital commitment cycle is preferable, because the risk is lower.

Of course, the ratio is no guarantor for the future. Market prices and thus yields are caused by supply and demand, which are caused by many different factors. Therefore, an evaluation done today needs to be corrected in the near future. Again, the duration can be a possible criterion.

Example   On August 30, 2010, the following information for two federal securities was published:

Security	Nominal Interest	Maturity	Price	Yield
Federal loan of 2005	3.25%	July 4, 2015	109.040	1.31%
Federal medium-term bond series 157	2.25%	April 10, 2015	104.500	1.24%

A calculation of the duration returns the following result:

Security	Duration
Federal loan of 2005	4.54 years
Federal medium-term bond series 157	4.40 years

The federal medium-term bond is preferable. However, the difference regarding the duration is very small. There is also another risk advantage for other debtors, and other terms as well as in regard to tax-related aspects (nominal interest must be reduced depending on the rate of taxation).

See Also MDURATION(), PRICE(), YIELD()

> **Sample Files**
> Use the DURATION worksheet in the Price Calculation.xls or Price Calculation.xlsx sample file. The sample files are found in the Chapter15 folder. For more information about the sample files, see the section titled "Using the Sample Files" on page xxiii.

EFFECT()

Syntax   EFFECT(*Nominal_Interest,Periods*)

Definition   This function calculates the equivalent effective annual interest yield (in arrears), also called the *conform interest rate*, from the nominal interest rate (in arrears) that is distributed to different periods of the same length within a year. Even though this is uncommon, a different time unit can also be substituted for the year.

Chapter 15

Arguments

- ***Nominal_Interest* (required)** Returns the annual interest rate which, because of the distribution over the periods, is used for a respective intra-annual interest yield.

- ***Periods* (required)** The number of interest days per year. This number is usually 2, 4, or 12.

Each argument must be evaluated as a number, otherwise, the #VALUE! error is displayed. The *Periods* argument is always turned into an integer by truncating the decimal places. If *Nominal_Interest* is less than or equal to zero, or *Periods* is less than 1, EFFECT() returns the #NUMBER! error.

Background For various financial transactions (such as mortgage loans, building-and-loan savings, interest for certain checking accounts, current accounts, and overdraft credits), an annual interest rate is specified, but it is only used to prepare further modalities. This means that interest is paid in intra-annual periods, not annually. The interest rate used is determined by dividing the nominal interest rate by the number of periods.

To be able to compare different conditions, the interest rate that returns the same result as the intra-annual interest yield for a fixed amount with a one-time interest payment is called the *effective annual interest rate*. The following relationship exists between the two interest rates:

$$1 + Effective\ interest\ rate = \left(1 + \frac{Nominal\ interest\ rate}{Number\ of\ periods}\right)^{Number\ of\ periods}$$

Examples The following examples illustrate how to use this function.

Saving Assume that an investor has an account with monthly interest payments and has deposited $1,000.00 at the beginning of the year. The given annual nominal interest rate is 5 percent. How high is the balance at the end of the year, and what is the effective interest yield?

To answer this question, you can create an account that is credited a monthly interest (make sure to round it correctly to two decimal places after the period). The account balance at the end of the year is $1,051.16.

You get to the same result if you use the FV() function with the corresponding arguments:

=FV(5%/12,12,,-1000)

If you create a ratio between the final account balance and the capital used, you come up with an interest yield of 5.12 percent. This is exactly what =EFFECT(5%,12) calculates as well.

Mortgage Loans A bank advertises a mortgage loan that has a nominal interest (debit interest) of 2.42 percent and promises an (initial) effective annual interest rate of 2.45 percent over five years with a monthly repayment and complete loan disbursement (without disagio).

In this case, you can recreate the effective annual interest rate with EFFECT(), but using this function is not always the way the bank determines its value. The fact that the number is the same down to the two decimal places after the period may be just a coincidence.

See Also NOMINAL(), RATE(), YIELD(),

> ## Sample Files
>
> Use the EFFECT worksheet in the Compound Interest Calculation.xls or Compound Interest Calculation.xlsx sample file. The sample files are found in the Chapter15 folder. For more information about the sample files, see the section titled "Using the Sample Files" on page xxiii.

FV()

Syntax PV(*Rate,Nper,Pmt,Pv,Type*)

Definition The function PV() calculates the future (final) value of a regular payment flow, taking into consideration single payments at the beginning of the time period in question, according to the finance mathematical benefit principle:

Payment of the debtor + payment of the creditor = 0

Arguments

- *Rate* **(required)** The (constant) period interest rate as interest rate in arrears.

- *Nper* **(required)** The number of interest periods. It is assumed that possible regular payments (that is, when the *Pmt* argument is greater than zero) take place at the end or the start of the interest period.

- *Pmt* **(required/optional, see Note)** The amount of the regular payments; this can be interpreted as annuity.

- *Pv* **(required/optional, see Note)** The start value of the process in the time period in question (a positive account balance or the amount of a loan).

- *Type* **(optional)** Specifies whether regular payments take place at the end of the periods ($M = 0$ or not specified) or at the start of the periods ($M = 1$).

Note

If the argument *Pmt* is omitted, *Pv* must be specified. If *Pmt* is present, *Pv* can be omitted. Omitting the arguments has the same effect as specifying them as zero.

Important

The finance mathematical benefit principle means that you need to differentiate between disbursements and deposits in regard to the leading sign (borrowing and repayment, investment and disinvestment). Here Excel differs from the benefit principle used in finance mathematical literature:

Payment of the debtor = payment of the creditor

Background   The five functions PV() = cash value, FV() = future value, PMT() = regular payment, NPER() = interest or payment periods, and RATE() = interest rate, have the following relationship when the benefit principle is implemented:

$$PV \cdot (1 + RATE)^{NPER} + PMT \cdot (1 + M \cdot RATE) \cdot \frac{(1 + RATE)^{NPER} - 1}{RATE} + FV = 0$$

The cash value interest is compounded, and so are the regular payments. Finally, the sum is compared to the future value.

Using one of these functions is equal to the respective basic finance mathematical task: calculation of an unknown variable from the preceding equation, when the other variables are known. The functions thus solve the equation for each of its members. For RATE, an approximation calculation is performed.

Note

Interest rates are usually specified as annual interest rates. These functions work correctly only if the periods match the interest rate. With intra-annual interest yield, the annual interest rate is usually distributed equally over the periods: 12 months at one twelfth of the interest rate, 3 months at a quarter, and half a year at half.

Examples   The headings of the following examples reflect the general linguistic usage of finance mathematical terms.

Compound Interest Calculation   An investor wants to have a small financial cushion for retirement and decides to invest a newly received inheritance of $10,000.00 for 15 years at a fixed interest rate of 4.5 percent. How high is the balance at the end of the duration?

A calculation with

=FV(4.5%,15,,-10000)

returns $19,352.82. The amount of the inheritance has a minus sign, because it is initially handed over.

Annuity Calculation   An investor wants to save $750 at the beginning of each month until he is 60 years old. He can use an account that yields 4.5 percent. He wants to stick to this savings plan for 15 years. How high is the balance at the end? You can determine the future value (in this case, a regular savings rate) with

=FV(4.5%/12,15*12,-750,1)

to get a result of $193,032.17. The 1 represents the anticipative payment of the savings rate. The minus sign represents giving the money to the bank.

The calculation is based on compound interest within one year. Because compound interest cannot be used for a regular savings account, the result is only theoretical.

Repayment Calculation (Annuity Repayment)   A debtor is able to pay back $1,000.00 per month on a loan (repayment plus interest). At an interest rate of 5.5 percent p.a., the interest commitment duration is initially five years. How high is the residual debt at the end of the duration?

FV() can be used here as well (in this case, the repayment calculation is the annuity calculation). You get to a result of $62,689.55 with

=FV(5.5%/12,5*12,-1000,100000)

The amount gets a minus sign because it still has to be repaid.

Unlike for a savings account, a mortgage loan uses a monthly interest of a twelfth of the agreed-upon yearly interest rate (nominal interest).

Chapter 15

> ## Important
>
> Using formulas might be different from keeping detailed notes of an account history with deposits and withdrawals because of rounding errors. This happens because the numbers for a savings account are rounded to two decimal places. If you are recreating such an account with Excel, you should use the function ROUND() for intermediary steps that involve money. Simply limiting the display of the cell value to two decimal places often leads to incorrect results.

See Also PMT(), PPMT(), PV(), RATE()

> ## Sample Files
>
> Use the FV worksheet in the Compound Interest Calculation.xls or Compound Interest Calculation.xlsx, in the Annuity Calculation.xls or Annuity Calculation.xlsx, and in the Repayment Calculation.xls or Repayment Calculation.xlsx sample files. The sample files are found in the Chapter15 folder. For more information about the sample files, see the section titled "Using the Sample Files" on page xxiii.

FVSCHEDULE()

Syntax   FVSCHEDULE(*Capital,Interest*)

Definition   This function calculates the final value for capital with variable period interest rates.

Arguments

- *Capital* (**required**) The capital that will receive interest payments.

- *Interest* (**required**) A list of the interest rates for the periods without gaps, which follows the required order. This argument can be a cell reference or a matrix (values inside of braces, separated by commas). Values that cannot be evaluated as numbers cause the error #VALUE!. Empty cells are handled as if they had the number zero.

Background   This calculation takes into consideration the fact that the interest is added to the capital at the end of the period:

$$Period\ end\ value = (Period\ start\ value) \cdot (1 + Period\ interest\ rate)$$

Of course, this includes compound interest.

However, the result cannot be displayed in clear formulas. A concession must be made to evaluate individual periods more precisely than with a constant interest rate over the entire time.

Example   German Type B federal savings bonds cannot be dealt at the stock exchange. They are securities whose interest is calculated based on annual fixed interest rates. The interest is added to the balance at the end of the interest period and is then paid interest in the remaining periods at the interest rate that is in effect at that time. This is how they differ from type A federal savings bonds, whose interest is paid and not normally reinvested at the same terms.

On August 12, 2008, the German Federal Bank published the data shown in Table 15-3.

Table 15-3   **Conditions for Federal Savings Bonds**

Duration Year	Nominal Interest
2010/2011	0.25%
2011/2012	0.50%
2012/2013	1.00%
2013/2014	1.75%
2014/2015	2.50%
2015/2016	2.75%
2016/2017	2.75%

The yields can be recalculated on a worksheet by using FVSCHEDULE() and RATE(), as shown in Figure 15-4.

	D7		f_x	=FVSCHEDULE($D$4,$C$7:C7)	
A	B	C	C	D	E
2	German Federal Treasury Bills Type B				
4	Investment		$	100.00	
6		Periods	Interest rate	FVSCHEDULE	RATE
7		1 Years	0.25%	$ 100.25	0.25%
8		2 Years	0.50%	$ 100.75	0.37%
9		3 Years	1.00%	$ 101.76	0.58%
10		4 Years	1.75%	$ 103.54	0.87%
11		5 Years	2.50%	$ 106.13	1.20%
12		6 Years	2.75%	$ 109.05	1.45%
13		7 Years	2.75%	$ 112.05	1.64%

Figure 15-4 Yield calculation for federal savings bonds.

The function FVSCHEDULE() determines the status in the individual years by using the interest rates in column C from the beginning to the respective year. RATE() then determines the yield from this value and from the purchase price of $100.00.

This can be interpreted as follows: If the amount was invested at a regular constant interest rate (the same yield), the same result would be reached as with changing interest rates.

See Also PMT(), PPMT(), PV(), RATE()

> ### Sample Files
> Use the FVSCHEDULE worksheet in the Compound Interest Calculation.xls or Compound Interest Calculation.xlsx sample file. The sample files are found in the Chapter15 folder. For more information about the sample files, see the section titled "Using the Sample Files" on page xxiii.

INTRATE()

Syntax   INTRATE(*Settlement,Maturity,Investment,Repayment,Basis*)

Definition   This function calculates the equivalent interest rate in arrears for a security that has received a markdown (discount, disagio) for an intra-annual duration. The only difference between this function and YIELDDISC() is the naming of the arguments.

Arguments

- *Settlement* **(required)** The date when the ownership of the security changes.

- *Maturity* **(required)** The day when the payments from the security must take place.

- *Investment* **(optional)** The purchase price of the security at the day of settlement.

- *Repayment* **(required)** The payment at the day of maturity.

- *Basis* **(optional)** The method you want to use for determining the days in the year according to Table 15-2, shown earlier. If this argument is omitted, Excel calculates with *Basis* = 0.

All function arguments that take a date use the date without time; fractions are rounded. The argument *Basis* also requires an integer, and decimal places are truncated.

Take note of the following:

- If invalid dates are used or no numbers are entered where required, the function returns the error #VALUE!.

- If *Investment* is less than or equal to zero, or *Repayment* is less than or equal to zero, RECEIVED() returns the #NUMBER! error.

- If *Basis* is less than zero or greater than 4, RECEIVED() returns the error #NUMBER!.

- If *Settlement* is greater than or equal to *Maturity*, RECEIVED() returns the error #NUMBER!.

> **Important**
>
> **Excel Help contains the following note:**
>
> **"Dates should be entered with the DATE() function or as results of other formulas or functions. Problems might occur if dates are entered as text."**

Background   In principle, this function belongs to the group of anticipative yield. The principle is based on the assumption that a seed capital amount (deposit amount, loan) results from the repayment amount minus the interest on this amount. This principle is mainly used in the intra-annual scope and differs from the principle based on a savings account or mortgage loan. In this case, interest is calculated at the end of a period based on the seed capital (interest yield in arrears).

To allow you to compare securities with interest payment in arrears, the difference between repayment and price must be put in relation to the price. The result corresponds to the relative increase until maturity (an interest rate in arrears), which, as is done frequently in similar situations, receives the name *Yield*. The calculation is done without compound interest. The interest rate must be extrapolated to one year (with corresponding day counting).

The function DISC() has the following relation to INTRATE():

$$(1 + INTRATE()) \cdot (1 - DISC()) = 1$$

The relationship permits you to calculate the equivalent anticipative annual interest rate from an annual interest rate in arrears. Equivalence means that two investors who are investing the same amount of capital (one with anticipative interest yield and one with interest yield in arrears) at the end of a year receive the same payment.

Example You can use the examples for YIELDDISC() here and use the function RECEIVED() for the calculations.

See Also DISC(), PRICEDISC(), RECEIVED(), TBILLEQ(), YIELDDISC()

> ### Sample Files
>
> Use the Bill of Exchange and Treasury Bonds worksheets in the Simple Interest Calcula-tion.xls or Simple Interest Calculation.xlsx sample file. The sample files are found in the Chapter15 folder. For more information about the sample files, see the section titled "Using the Sample Files" on page xxiii.

IPMT()

Syntax IPMT(*Rate,Per,Nper,Pv,Fv,Type*)

Definition This function determines the part of an annuity that is used for the interest payment of a loan that is repaid according to the principle of annuity repayment.

Arguments

- *Rate* **(required)** The nominal interest of the loan.

- *Per* **(required)** The appropriate number for the desired period.

- *Nper* **(required)** The total number of periods in which the loan is repaid.

- *Pv* **(required)** The loan amount.

- *Fv* **(optional)** Evaluates loans that have not been fully repaid after the total number of periods. Such an effect may happen when mortgages are disbursed with a fixed interest period.

- *Type* **(optional)** Specifies whether the payments become interest effective at the start of the periods ($M = 1$) or at the end of the periods ($M = 0$). If this argument is omitted, Excel uses the value 0.

Background The repayment of loans can take place in various ways. One way is for the debtor to pay the same amount each period. This amount is composed of a repayment part (which increases as time passes) and an interest part (which decreases as time passes).

The change in this composition is a result of the fact that the loan that needs to be repaid shrinks over time. This version is called annuity repayment. The total amount is called annuity, even though its payment does not necessarily happen annually.

The repayment part of the first annuity results from subtracting the interest part from it. This part is the loan sum multiplied by the nominal interest rate specified for the period. The repayment parts of the next periods are (after a few intermediate mathematical steps) determined from:

$$(Repayment\ part\ of\ the\ first\ period) \cdot (1 + Nominal\ interest\ rate)^{Period\ number-1}$$

The interest parts of these periods can be calculated by subtracting the repayment part from the annuity.

> **Note**
>
> In loan agreements, an annual interest rate is very frequently formulated as nominal interest rate, but the payment takes place intra-annually. In such cases, you need to determine the intra-annual period interest rate by dividing the annual interest rate by the number of payments per year. The total number of periods results from the periods per year multiplied by the number of years.

Example   In the "Repayment Calculation" example for the PV() function, the following data was specified: A debtor takes out a loan in the amount of $176,121.76, which he pays back at 5.5 percent with $1,000.00 per month over 30 years. The repayment plan shows an interest part of $791.64 in the 18th month. You can check this result with the function IPMT(), even though there may be rounding errors.

```
=IPMT(5.5%/12,18*12,176121.76)
```

(In practice, this function would use references to the cells in which the data are located.)

The resulting minus sign in front of the number is because the payment is made in the "other direction."

Rounding errors occur frequently when the integrated functions are used. After all, they cannot take into consideration what actually happens at the bank counter: In the real world, money is calculated with only two decimal places. If you are entering data for a repayment plan month by month, you need to use the function ROUND() to show what is actually happening.

See Also CUMPRINC(), FV(), NPER(), PMT(), PPMT(), PV(), RATE()

> ## Sample Files
>
> Use the PV worksheet in the Repayment Calculation.xls or Repayment Calculation.xlsx sample file. The sample files are found in the Chapter15 folder. For more information about the sample files, see the section titled "Using the Sample Files" on page xxiii.

IRR()

Syntax   IRR(*Values,Estimated_Value*)

Definition   This function calculates a value of the dynamic investment calculation: The internal interest rate that turns the cash value of all disbursements and deposits in connection with an investment into zero.

Arguments

- *Values* **(required)** The (actual and/or expected) surpluses from disbursements and deposits, arranged without gaps in a column. Each value represents a period (usually one year) in ascending order and without gaps. Negative surpluses have a minus sign.

- *Estimated_Value* **(optional)** For mathematical reasons, a calculation of the internal interest rate for more than two periods can only be approximate, and therefore this approximation calculation can lead to different and sometimes nonsensical results (such as a negative interest rate). You can influence the calculation with the optional argument *Estimated_Value* as the basis for the approximation calculation. If you don't use this argument, Excel calculates with a base value of 10 percent. In practice, this calculation interest rate is quite common, because it is close to a financially realistic investment.

If the cells of the *Values* argument do not contain numbers or are empty, Excel calculates as if these cells didn't exist. If the functions returns the #NUMBER! error, the approximation calculation was not successful. This might be because of the estimated value used or the data itself (such as only disbursements or only deposits).

Background   The cash value of all disbursements and deposits (also called *net cash value*) is considered the capital value of an investment. It is assumed that the payments take place at the end of a year (the start period gets the number 0, and it usually has only one disbursement). These payments are discounted at a calculation interest rate that in practice lies at 10 percent plus or minus risk premium/deduction. Finance investments are exceptions, because calculations can be made with the regular market yield.

The internal rate of return (internal interest rate) is now the value that turns the capital value into zero:

$$\sum_{n-0}^{Duration} \frac{Deposits\ minus\ Disbursements\ in\ the\ year\ n}{(1 + IRR())^n}$$

Investments where money is lent or borrowed are a special form of investing. When it comes to loans, the rate is called *effective yield*, and for savings investments/bonds it is called *yield*.

Examples   The following examples illustrate how to use the IRR() function.

Investment in Material Assets   The purchase cost for a machine is $80,000.00. The expected annual surpluses (deposits minus disbursements) are estimated as shown in Table 15-4.

Table 15-4   **Estimated Annual Surpluses for the Use of a Machine**

Year	Surplus (in Dollars)
1	15.000
2	19.000
3	25.000
4	27.000
5	17.000
6	7.000

Does this investment make sense, if the interest of the amount used should be at least 10 percent? To answer this question, enter the purchase cost (with a minus sign) in the first row of a table in a worksheet, and below that enter the data from Table 15-4 without gaps. Using IRR() on these values returns an internal interest rate of 10.47 percent, which is slightly above the requested interest rate.

Note that the decimal places are not necessarily important when you are working with real investments whose future surpluses are only estimated.

Financial Investment   Type A federal savings bonds are investments that have future annual payments that are fixed down to the penny. On August 30, 2010, the German Federal Bank issued the information in Table 15-5 and set a yield of 1.44 percent for the last year.

Table 15-5 Terms for Federal Savings Bonds

Duration Year	Nominal Interest
2010/2011	0.25%
2011/2012	0.50%
2012/2013	1.00%
2013/2014	1.75%
2014/2015	2.50%
2015/2016	2.75%

You can recreate this information (with the internal rate of return of 1.44 percent) directly in Excel. The table can look like that shown in Figure 15-5. IRR() returns the desired result.

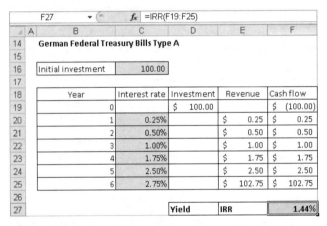

Figure 15-5 Yield calculation with IRR().

See Also MIRR(), NPV(), PV(), RATE(), XIRR(), XNPV()

Sample Files

Use the IRR worksheet in the Investment Calculation.xls or Investment Calculation.xlsx sample file. The sample files are found in the Chapter15 folder. For more information about the sample files, see the section titled "Using the Sample Files" on page xxiii.

ISPMT()

Syntax   ISPMT(*Rate,Per,Nper,Pv*)

Definition   This function calculates the sum of interest that accrues for a certain part of the year with a given annual interest rate and simple yield in arrears. Other time periods are possible, but not common.

For reasons of compatibility, this function was included in Lotus 1-2-3.

Arguments

- **Rate (required)** The annual interest rate in arrears that is to be distributed equally among all the periods in the year

- **Per (required)** Specifies the number of the period (starting with zero) from the end of which the interest is to be calculated until the end of the year

- **Nper (required)** The total amount of periods with the year; determines the factor for the annual interest rate

- **Pv (required)** The present value (cash value) whose interest in arrears is to be calculated

Background   Dividing the annual interest rate into a period interest rate of intra-annual time periods is a process that happens frequently (overdrawing checking accounts, current accounts, or mortgage accounts). However, usually the intra-annual interest rate is used to pay compound interest within the year. This is not taken into consideration by this function.

Example   What the function actually does is best explained with the example of a savings account. If you deposit $100.00 on April 30 to your savings account that has an interest rate of 6 percent, you receive it for 8/12 of the year (assuming that the amount stays in your account until the end of the year). By using

`=ISPMT(6%,4,12,-100)`

you get the result of $4.00.

If you deposit the same amount on May 5, already 135 interest days of the year have passed and you still get interest for 225 days. With

`=ISPMT(6%,135,360,-100)`

you get the amount of $3.75.

See Also ACCRINT(), ACCRINTM(), CUMIPMT(), PPMT()

Chapter 15

> **Sample Files**
>
> Use the ISPMT worksheet in the Simple Interest Calculation.xls or Simple Interest Cal-culation.xlsx sample file. The sample files are found in the Chapter15 folder. For more information about the sample files, see the section titled "Using the Sample Files" on page xxiii.

MDURATION()

Syntax MDURATION(*Settlement,Maturity,Nominal_Interest,Yield,Frequency,Basis*)

Definition This function calculates the figure known as *modified duration* for fixed-interest securities.

Arguments

- *Settlement* **(required)** The date when the ownership of the security changes.

- *Maturity* **(required)** The date when the repayment of the loan certified by the security takes place.

- *Nominal_Interest* **(required)** The agreed-upon annual interest rate as the price for the borrowed money.

- *Yield* **(required)** The market interest rate on the settlement day, at which during cal-culation of the duration all future payments are discounted.

- *Frequency* **(required)** Because it is quite common to have fixed-interest securities with several interest dates per year, the required argument *Frequency* supplies the dates-per-year number. Allowed values are: 1 = annual; 2 = biannual; 4 = quarterly.

- *Basis* **(optional)** The method you want to use for determining the days in the year according to Table 15-2, shown earlier. If this argument is omitted, Excel calculates with *Basis* = 0.

All function arguments that take a date use the date without time; fractions are rounded. The arguments *Frequency* and *Basis* also require integers, and decimal places are truncated.

If invalid dates are used or no numbers are entered where required, the function returns the error #VALUE!. If invalid numbers are entered for nondate arguments, the function returns the #NUMBER! error.

Background   Volatility, or price changes as a reaction to market interest changes, is an important figure for portfolio risk management. Unlike with shares and options, the range of fluctuation for fixed-interest securities decreases towards the end of their duration, because the disbursement amount at the maturity date is fixed.

By using differential calculus, you can determine that the following applies to fixed-interest securities:

$$Relative\ price\ change = -\frac{Duration}{1 + Market\ interest} \cdot (Market\ interest\ change)$$

Duration is the security's Macauley Duration (see DURATION()).

MDURATION() now returns the factor with which the market interest change must be multiplied (unsigned) to calculate the relative price change.

If there are several interest payments per year, the market interest (annual interest rate) is evenly distributed over the interest periods.

Example   A 4.500 percent federal loan initiated in 2003 had a yield of 0.61 percent on August 31, 2010. It will mature on January 4, 2030. Your price on that day was $109.027 (example annual interest rate for the function PRICE()).

If you perform the price calculations of the aforementioned example one more time, but this time with a yield that has been adjusted up by 0.5 percentage points to 1.11 percent (this is the market interest change you expect in the near future), the price changes to 107.800. This means a price loss of 1.13 percent.

You can get approximately the same result by calculating the duration with MDURATION(). With the loan data, MDURATION() results in 2.208. If you multiply this number with the 0.5 percentage points of market interest change, you get a relative price change of 1.1 percent. Because of the mathematical sign, this leads to a price loss of 1.204, which corresponds to an (approximate) future price of $107.824.

Therefore, the figure for modified duration can be supplied together with the price of a loan, so an investor is able to evaluate the structure of a deposit from a risk point of view without extensive recalculation.

See Also DURATION(), PRICE(), PV()

> ## Sample Files
>
> Use the MDURATION worksheet in the Price Calculation.xls or Price Calculation.xlsx sample file. The sample files are found in the Chapter15 folder. For more information about the sample files, see the section titled "Using the Sample Files" on page xxiii.

MIRR()

Syntax   MIRR(*Values,Investment,Reinvestment*)

Definition   This function calculates the internal yield of an investment while evaluating the negative period surpluses with a different interest rate as positive (qualified internal capital yield).

Arguments

- *Values* **(required)** The (actual or expected) surpluses from disbursements and deposits, arranged without gaps in a column. Each value represents the end of a period (usually one year) in ascending order and without gaps. Negative surpluses have a minus sign. At least two values are expected, of which at least one is positive and one negative.

- *Investment* **(required)** The interest rate with which the negative amounts (disbursements) are reduced (discounted) to their cash value.

- *Reinvestment* **(required)** The interest rate with which the positive amounts (deposits) are added to make up the end value.

   If the cells of the *Values* argument do not contain numbers or are empty, Excel calculates as if these cells didn't exist. This is also the case if cell references in the argument refer to such cells.

Background   The method of internal capital yield for evaluating investments is used for dynamic investment calculation. There are advantages and disadvantages when this function is used as described for the functions IRR() and NPV(). One advantage of capital value creation by discounting all future numbers is the open time horizon, which does not require any considerations regarding reinvestment options. A disadvantage is the interest rate for evaluation, which is always fixed.

The method of the qualified internal interest rate limits the time horizon but leaves some room for the evaluation interest rates. All disbursements are evaluated at the *borrowed capital interest rate* by discounting them at their current value, which is the cash value. All deposits are treated as investments. The result is the future value (calculated by adding interest) at the end of the investment.

The qualified internal interest rate is the one that currently leads to the future value of the deposits through disbursements by adding interest to the cash value. It therefore tells you at which interest rate the invested money is returned at the end.

Example   Assume that an investor purchases a medium-term government bond that is paid interest for five years at a rate of 4.25 percent per year. However, for certain reasons, the interest can be reinvested at only 2 percent.

Though the internal capital yield (calculated via IRR()) is 4.25 percent in this case, the mixed interest via MIRR() is only 4.08 per year.

	C17	▾	*fx* =MIRR(C8:C13,D2,D3)				
A	B	C	D	E	F	G
1						
2	Bond rate	(Investment)	4.25%			
3	Reinvestment rate	(Reinvestment)	2.00%			
4						
5	Amount		$ 100.00			
6						
7	Year	MIRR	Investement	Reinvestment		
8	0	$ (100.00)	$ (100.00)	$ -		
9	1	$ 4.25	$ -	$ 4.25		
10	2	$ 4.25	$ -	$ 4.25		
11	3	$ 4.25	$ -	$ 4.25		
12	4	$ 4.25	$ -	$ 4.25		
13	5	$ 104.25	$ -	$ 104.25		
14						
15	IRR	4.25%	Present value of investment	$ (100.00)		
16			Future value of reinvestment	$ 122.12		
17	MIRR	4.08%				
18			Mixed rate	4.08%		

Figure 15-6 Behind MIRR() lies a mixed interest calculation.

Figure 15-6 shows the interpretation: An expenditure of $100.00 has an end result of $122.12 (calculated by adding interest).

See Also IRR(), NPV(), RATE(), XIRR(), XNPV()

Sample Files

Use the MIRR worksheet in the Investment Calculation.xls or Investment Calculation.xlsx sample file. The sample files are found in the Chapter15 folder. For more information about the sample files, see the section titled "Using the Sample Files" on page xxiii.

Chapter 15

NOMINAL()

Syntax   NOMINAL(*Effect_Rate,Periods*)

Definition   This function calculates the nominal interest rate which (finance mathematically) leads to equivalence from a given effective interest rate.

Arguments

- **Effect_Rate (required)**   The given effective annual interest rate, determined from the compound interest of an intra-annual yield.

- **Periods (required)**   The number of interest periods per year. If the *Periods* argument is a number with decimal places, it is truncated to an integer. The result must be greater than zero. Otherwise, NOMINAL() returns the error #NUMBER!. If one of the arguments is not a numeric expression or if *Effect_Rate* is not positive, NOMINAL() also returns the #NUMBER! error.

Background   For various financial transactions (such as mortgage loans, building-and-loan savings, interest for certain checking accounts, current accounts, and overdraft credits), an annual interest rate is specified, but it is used only to prepare further modalities. This means that interest is paid in intra-annual periods, not annually. The interest rate used is determined by dividing the nominal interest rate by the number of periods.

So that you can compare different terms, the interest rate that returns the same result as the intra-annual interest yield with a one-time interest payment is called the *effective annual interest rate*. The following relationship exists between the two interest rates:

$$1 + Effective\ interest\ rate = \left(1 + \frac{Nominal\ interest\ rate}{Number\ of\ periods}\right)^{Number\ of\ periods}$$

The function NOMINAL() solves this equation according to the nominal interest rate.

Examples   The following examples illustrate how to use the NOMINAL() function.

Correlation   The correlation between the nominal and effective interest rates becomes evident in the examples for the EFFECT() function.

ISMA Price and ISMA Yield   In the biannual interest payment example for the PRICE() function, the example includes a recreation of the ISMA price with the integrated Excel function. The yield must be converted with NOMINAL() before the functions can be used.

See Also   EFFECT()

NPER()

Syntax   NPER(*Rate,Pmt,Pv,Fv,Type*)

Definition   The function NPER() calculates the duration of a compound interest rate process, annuity calculation, or repayment calculation. It is based on possible regular payments of the same amount and/or one-time payments at the start or end of the time period, according to the finance mathematical benefit principle

Payment of the creditor + Payment of the debtor = 0

Arguments

- **Rate (required)** The (constant) period interest rate as interest rate in arrears.

- **Pmt (required/optional, see Note)** The amount of the regular payments. This can be interpreted as annuity.

- **Pv (required/optional, see Note)** The start value of one payment direction. For disbursement plans, this is the account balance at the beginning of these considerations; for repayment plans, it is the loan amount.

- **Fv (optional/required, see Note)** The account balance you want to have at the end of the process (for example, a residual balance from disbursement plans or a final repayment in the amount of the residual debt for loans).

- **Type (optional)** Specifies whether regular payments take place at the end of the periods (*Type* = 0 or not specified) or at the start of the periods (*Type* = 1).

> **Note**
>
> At least two of the three arguments *Pmt*, *Pv*, and *Fv* must be specified and must not be zero. Their sign corresponds to the respective "direction of the money flow" (compare to the complex formula in the background section for this function).

> **Important**
>
> The finance mathematical benefit principle means that you need to differentiate between disbursements and deposits in regard to the leading sign (borrowing and repayment, investment and disinvestment). Here Excel differs from the benefit principle used in finance mathematical literature:
>
> *Payment of the creditor = Payment of the debtor*

Background The five functions PV() = cash value, FV() = future value, PMT() = regular payment, NPER() = interest or payment time periods, and RATE() = interest rate, have the following relationship when the benefit principle is implemented:

$$PV \cdot (1 + RATE)^{NPER} + PMT \cdot (1 + M \cdot RATE) \cdot \frac{(1 + RATE)^{NPER} - 1}{RATE} + FV = 0$$

where *M* is the *Type* (timing of payments).

The cash value interest is compounded, and so are the regular payments. At the end, the sum is compared to the future value.

Using one of these functions is equal to the respective basic finance mathematical task: calculation of an unknown variable from the preceding equation, when the other variables are known. The functions solve the equation for each of its members. For RATE, an approximation calculation is performed.

> **Note**
>
> Interest rates are usually specified as annual interest rates. These functions work correctly only if the periods match the interest rate. With intra-annual interest yield, the annual interest rate is usually distributed equally over the periods: 12 months at one twelfth of the interest rate, 3 months at a quarter, and half a year at half.

Examples The headings of the following examples reflect the general usage of finance mathematical terms.

Compound Interest Calculation An investor wants to have a small financial cushion for retirement and decides to invest a newly received inheritance of $10,000.00 at a fixed interest rate of 4.5 percent. He hopes to get a disbursement of at least $25,000.00. How long does he need to leave the money in the bank?

A calculation with

=NPER(4.5%,,-10000,25000)

returns 20.82 years. This means that at the end of the 20th year the target has not been reached, but at the end of the 21st year it has been passed. The concrete account balances can be calculated with the numbers 20 or 21 for the duration argument by using FV(). Alternatively, you can use an account plan.

Annuity calculation A 60-year-old has saved $100,000.00 and would like to be paid an additional monthly annuity of $750.00. Is the saved money enough, if 4.5 percent p.a. is paid on top of the existing balance?

You determine the cash value of the annuity with

```
=NPER(4.5%/12,-750,100000,,1)
```

to get the result of 184.19 months. This means that at the end of the 184th month, the account has been reduced so much that no further withdrawal can be made.

The calculation is based on compound interest within one year. Because compound interest cannot be used for a regular savings account, the result remains only theoretical.

Repayment Calculation (Annuity Repayment)   A debtor is able to pay back $1,000.00 per month on a loan (repayment plus interest). The interest rate for the duration is 5.5 percent. How long does the loan have to be paid back, if the amount of loan is $175,000.00?

NPER() can be used here as well (in this case, the repayment calculation is the annuity calculation). You are using the following to get to a result of 354.24 months:

```
=NPER(5.5%/12,-1000,175000)
```

Therefore, the final payment takes place in the 355th month, and it is smaller than the regular payment.

Note

This example shows that Excel can also handle percentage annuities in the repayment calculation. For those, the repayment amount can be calculated not from the duration (see PMT()) but by displaying the repayment rate that determines the first repayment rate. The sum of the first repayment rate and the interest of the first period is then the regular repayment amount.

Unlike a savings account, a mortgage loan uses a monthly interest of a twelfth of the agreed-upon yearly interest rate (nominal interest).

Important

Using formulas may be different from keeping detailed notes of an account history with deposits and withdrawals because of rounding errors. This happens because the numbers for a savings account are rounded to two decimal places. If you are recreating such an account with Excel, you should use the function ROUND() for intermediary steps that involve money. Simply limiting the display of the cell value to two decimal places often leads to incorrect results.

See Also FV(), IPMT(), PMY(), PPMT(), PV(), RATE()

Sample Files

Use the NPER worksheet in the Compound Interest Calculation.xls or Compound Interest Calculation.xlsx, in the Annuity Calculation.xls or Annuity Calculation.xlsx and in the Repayment Calculation.xls or Repayment Calculation.xlsx sample file. The sample files are found in the Chapter15 folder. For more information about the sample files, see the section titled "Using the Sample Files" on page xxiii.

NPV()

Syntax   NPV(*Rate,Value1,Value2, ...*)

Definition   This function calculates the net cash value of future period surpluses (cash flow) of an investment based on a given calculation interest rate.

Arguments

- *Rate* **(required)** The calculation interest rate supplied by the investor.

- *Value1,Value2,...* **(required)** The (actual and expected) surpluses from disbursements and deposits, arranged without gaps in a column. Each value represents the end of a period (usually one year) in ascending order and without gaps. Negative surpluses have a minus sign.

  If the cells of the *Value* argument do not contain numbers or are empty, Excel calculates as if these cells didn't exist. This is also the case if cell references in the argument refer to such cells.

Background   Dynamic methods of investment calculation are based on the (estimated and predicted) deposits and disbursements and their yield, unlike static methods, which are based on cost and earnings of an investment. Both payment directions are evaluated with a uniform calculation interest rate that results from the experiences of the investor. The sum of all discounted period surpluses is called the *capital value*.

$$Capital\ value = \sum_{n=0}^{Duration} \frac{Deposits\ minus\ Disbursements\ in\ the\ year\ n}{(1 + Rate)^n}$$

An investment is considered financially sound if the capital value is not negative, because then the invested capital plus the yield is returned.

The first value for the *Value* arguments of NPV() represents the end of the first period. The capital value of an investment is determined from NPV() minus the disbursements at the start of the first period.

> **Note**
>
> If the period surpluses are consistent, the function PV() can be used for calculating the net cash value, as an alternative to NPV(). Because PV() permits a future value as an argument, a surplus that deviates from the consistent surpluses and is based on the residual value of the investment can also be taken into consideration.

Example   When reading the following examples, compare them to the explanations about IRR() and the examples in that section.

Investment in Material Assets   The purchase cost for a machine is $80,000.00. The expected annual surpluses (deposits minus disbursements) are estimated as shown in Table 15-6.

Table 15-6 **Estimated Annual Surpluses in the Use of a Machine**

Year	Surplus (in $)
1	15.000
2	19.000
3	25.000
4	27.000
5	17.000
6	7.000

Is the investment economically sound if a calculation interest rate of 10 percent (p.a.) is used?

To answer this question, make sure to note the purchase cost in the first cell, and at another location, note the values from Table 15-6 in a column without gaps. Using NPV() returns an amount of approximately $81,070, which is slightly above the purchase cost. The yield will therefore most likely be paid at a slightly better interest rate than expected.

Note that the decimal places are not necessarily important when you are working with real investments whose future surpluses are only estimated.

Financial Investment   Type A German federal savings bonds with the terms of August 30, 2010, shown in Table 15-7, might seem to have a total yield of about 1.5 percent at first glance.

Table 15-7 **Terms for Federal Savings Bonds**

Duration Year	Nominal Interest
2010/2011	0.25%
2011/2012	0.50%
2012/2013	1.00%
2013/2014	1.75%
2014/2015	2.50%
2015/2016	2.75%

In the sample files for this function, you can find calculations that show that the net cash value for an investment amount of $100.00 is only $99.63. Therefore, an investment at this expected yield does not make sense.

See Also IRR(), MIRR(), PV(), XIRR(), XNPV()

> ### Sample Files
>
> Use the NPV worksheet in the Investment Calculation.xls or Investment Calculation.xlsx sample file. The sample files are found in the Chapter15 folder. For more information about the sample files, see the section titled "Using the Sample Files" on page xxiii.

ODDFPRICE()

Syntax   ODDFPRICE(*Settlement,Maturity,Issue,First_Interest_Date,Rate,Yield,Repayment, Frequency,Basis*)

Definition   Calculates the price of a fixed-interest security while taking into consideration the first interest period, which is shorter or longer than the remaining regular interest periods (quarter, half year, entire year).

Arguments

- *Settlement* **(required)** The date when the loan becomes the property of the purchaser.

- *Maturity* **(required)** The date when the repayment of the certified amount takes place.

- **Issue (required)** The date of the emission of the security.

- **First_Interest_Date (required)** The date of the first interest payment.

- **Rate (required)** The nominal yield (annual interest rate) of the bond.

- **Yield (required)** The market interest rate of bonds of the given duration.

- **Repayment (required)** The percentage of the repayment based on the par value of a security (as if it was 100 monetary units).

- **Frequency (required)** The number of interest payments within a year (annually, biannually, quarterly).

- **Basis (optional)** The method you want to use for determining the days in the year according to Table 15-2, shown earlier. If this argument is omitted, Excel calculates with *Basis* = 0.

Take note of the following:

- Date specifications must not have a time; decimal places are truncated. The arguments *Frequency* and *Basis* are also truncated to integers.

- If date arguments cannot be resolved to a valid date, the ODDFPRICE() function returns the #VALUE! error.

- *Price* and *Yield* require nonnegative numbers. Otherwise ODDFPRICE() returns the #NUMBER! error.

- If *Frequency* cannot be resolved to 1, 2, or 4, or *Basis* cannot be resolved to a number from 0 through 4, ODDFPRICE() returns the error #NUMBER!.

- The same result described in the preceding bullet happens when the correct sort order (*Maturity* is greater than *First_Interest_Date*, which is greater than *Settlement*, which is greater than *Issue*) is not kept.

> **Important**
>
> Excel Help contains the following note:
>
> "Dates should be entered with the DATE() function or as results of other formulas or functions. Problems might occur if dates are entered as text."

Background   To implement the finance mathematical benefit principle

Payment of the creditor = Payment of the debtor

for the start of the transaction, the price of a fixed-interest security (loan) plus potential accrued interest equals the cash value of the debtor's future payments certified in this security. The price is the percentage of the security's par value, as if the par value was 100 monetary units.

The cash value calculation is no problem, if the purchase date (change of ownership) of a security with an annual interest payment is the same as the day of the interest payment. In this case, only the whole year needs to be taken into consideration. A situation in which the change of ownership takes place between interest due dates or in which interest payments take place several times a year is not so easy. In finance mathematics, there are several ways to deal with a year that is broken up into parts. The best known methods are Moosmüller and Braess/Fangmeyer, as well as ISMA.

You can find details about the correlation between the ISMA method and the Excel function calculations in the background information about PRICE() and YIELD().

The formula in Excel Help is reduced to the following, if interest is paid regularly once a year (360 days) and the first interest period is shortened:

$$ODDPRICE = \frac{Repayment}{(1 + Yield)^{N-1+DSC/360}} + \frac{100 \cdot Rate \cdot DFC/360}{(1 + Yield)^{DSC/360}} +$$
$$+ \sum_{k=2}^{N} \frac{100 \cdot Rate}{(1 + Yield)^{k-1+DSC/360}} + 100 \cdot Rate \cdot \frac{A}{360}$$

N is the total number of interest dates, *A* is the time between emission date and settlement date, *DSC* is the time between settlement date and first interest date, and *DFC* is the time between the first interest day and the emission day.)

As you can see, the first period is handled differently, if you compare it to the price formula from the background information for the function PRICE(). It is not part of the summation and cash value creation of the following periods, because the interest payment does not take place with a full coupon.

If *Frequency* is greater than 1 (that is, if it is 2 or 4), *Rate* and *Yield* must be replaced with the regular distributions over the intra-annual periods.

To understand the formula in Excel Help for a first interest period that is longer than the "regular" ones, simply keep in mind that the first period will contain several fictitious interest payments that will become a reality at the end of the period.

Accrued interest in the first period is handled similarly.

As soon as the first interest date is passed, the function is no longer used.

Example   In the sample files for this function, there is an example that shows a calculation for a fictitious bond with a shortened first interest period. It is similar to the calculation in Figure 15-3, shown earlier. The result is the same that the function ODDFPRICE() would deliver.

See Also ODDFYIELD(), ODDLPRICE(), ODDLYIELD(), RATE(), YIELD()

> ## Sample Files
> Use the ODDFPRICE worksheet in the Price Calculation.xls or Price Calculation.xlsx sample file. The sample files are found in the Chapter15 folder. For more information about the sample files, see the section titled "Using the Sample Files" on page xxiii.

ODDFYIELD()

Syntax   ODDFYIELD(*Settlement,Maturity,Issue,First_Interest_Date,Rate,Price,Repayment, Frequency,Basis*)

Definition   This function calculates the yield of a fixed-interest security for the duration from the settlement date to the maturity date. It takes into consideration that the first interest period might be shorter or longer than the other regular interest periods.

Arguments

- *Settlement* **(required)** The date when the bond becomes the property of the purchaser.

- *Maturity* **(required)** The date when the repayment of the certified amount takes place.

- *Issue* **(required)** The date of the emission of the security.

- *First_Interest_Date* **(required)** The date of the first interest payment.

- *Rate* **(required)** The nominal yield (annual interest rate) of the bond.

- *Price* **(required)** The price of the security on the day of settlement as a percentage; it must be interpreted as if the par value of the paper was 100 monetary units.

- *Repayment* **(required)** The percentage of the repayment based on the par value of a security (as if it was 100 monetary units).

- *Frequency* **(required)** The number of interest payments within a year (annually, biannually, quarterly).

- *Basis* **(optional)** The method you want to use for determining the days in the year according to Table 15-2, shown earlier. If this argument is omitted, Excel calculates with *Basis* = 0.

Take note of the following:

- Date specifications must not have a time; decimal places are truncated. The arguments *Frequency* and *Basis* are also truncated to integers.

- If date arguments cannot be resolved to a valid date, the ODDFYIELD() function returns the error #VALUE!.

- *Price* and *Yield* require nonnegative numbers. Otherwise ODDFYIELD() returns the error #NUMBER!.

- If *Frequency* cannot be resolved to 1, 2, or 4, or *Basis* cannot be resolved to a number from 0 through 4, ODDFYIELD() returns the #NUMBER! error.

- The same result as explained in the preceding bullet happens when the correct sort order *Maturity* is greater than *First_Interest_Date*, which is greater than *Settlement*, which is greater than *Issue*) is not kept.

> **Important**
>
> **Excel Help contains the following note:**
>
> **"Dates should be entered with the DATE() function or as results of other formulas or functions. Problems might occur if dates are entered as text."**

Background For information about this function, see the background information for the ODDFPRICE() function.

The ODDFYIELD() function determines the value of the yield in such a way that a desired price (or price payable on the market) is reached, and informs the purchaser about the expected effective yield of the investment.

Example In the sample files for this function, there is an example that shows a calculation for a fictitious bond with a shortened first interest period. It is similar to the calculation shown earlier in Figure 15-7. The calculation follows the pattern of the price calculation (as shown in the example for ODDFPRICE()). The desired yield is then determined with the target value search (an assumed yield changes in such a way that the desired price is calculated). ODDFYIELD() returns the same result.

See Also ODDFPRICE(), ODDLPRICE(), ODDLYIELD(), PRICE(), YIELD()

> **Sample Files**
>
> Use the ODDFYIELD worksheet in the Price Calculation.xls or Price Calculation.xlsx sample file. The sample files are found in the Chapter15 folder. For more information about the sample files, see the section titled "Using the Sample Files" on page xxiii.

ODDLPRICE()

Syntax   ODDLPRICE(*Settlement,Maturity,Last_Interest_Date,Rate,Yield,Repayment, Frequency,Basis*)

Definition   This function calculates the price of a fixed-interest security in a final interest period whose length is different from the regular interest periods in the past. Compound interest is not taken into consideration.

Arguments

- *Settlement* **(required)** The date when the bond becomes the property of the purchaser.

- *Maturity* **(required)** The day when the repayment of the certified amount takes place.

- *Last_Interest_Date* **(required)** The date of the final (regular) interest payment.

- *Rate* **(required)** The nominal yield (annual interest rate) of the bond.

- *Yield* **(required)** The market interest rate of bonds of the given duration.

- *Repayment* **(required)** The percentage of the repayment based on the par value of a security (as if it was 100 monetary units).

- *Frequency* **(required)** The number of interest payments within a year (annually, biannually, quarterly).

- *Basis* **(optional)** The method you want to use for determining the days in the year according to Table 15-2, shown earlier. If this argument is omitted, Excel calculates with *Basis* = 0.

Take note of the following:

- Date specifications must not have a time; decimal places are truncated. The arguments *Frequency* and *Basis* are also truncated to integers.

- If date arguments cannot be resolved to a valid date, the ODDLPRICE() function returns the #NUMBER! error.

- *Rate* and *Yield* require nonnegative numbers. Otherwise ODDLPRICE() returns the #NUMBER! error.

- If *Frequency* cannot be resolved to 1, 2, or 4, or *Basis* cannot be resolved to a number from 0 through 4, ODDLPRICE() returns the error #NUMBER!.

- The same result as explained in the preceding bullet happens when the correct sort order (*Maturity* is greater than *Settlement*, which is greater than *Last_Interest_Date*) is not kept.

> **Important**
>
> Excel Help contains the following note:
>
> **"Dates should be entered with the DATE() function or as results of other formulas or functions. Problems might occur if dates are entered as text."**

Background   To implement the finance mathematical benefit principle

Payment of the creditor = Payment of the debtor

for the start of the transaction, the price of a fixed-interest security (loan) plus potential accrued interest equals the cash value of the debtor's future payments certified in this security. The price is the percentage of the security's par value, as if the par value was 100 monetary units.

The cash value calculation is no problem, if the purchase date (change of ownership) of a security with an annual interest payment is the same as the day of the interest payment. In this case, only the whole year needs to be taken into consideration. A situation in which the change of ownership takes place between interest due dates or in which interest payments take place several times a year is not so easy. In finance mathematics there are several ways to deal with a year that is broken up into parts. The best known methods are Moosmüller and Braess/Fangmeyer as well as ISMA.

You can find details about the correlation between the ISMA method and the Excel function calculations in the background information about PRICE() and YIELD().

In the case being discussed, the principle used by Excel can be formulated as follows as a result of the simple yield (no compound interest) at a given market interest (annual yield):

$$Price + Accrued\ interest = \frac{Par\ value + Interest\ at\ maturity}{1 + Partial\ yield}$$

The accrued interest from the partial interest since the last interest date and the partial yield are calculated from the days until maturity (based on the total number of days in the year).

The function is not used outside the final time period until maturity.

Example   In the sample files for this function there is an example that shows a calculation for a fictitious bond with the required terms. It is similar to the calculation shown earlier in Figure 15-3. The result is the same as what the function ODDLPRICE() would deliver.

See Also ODDFPRICE(), ODDFYIELD(), ODDLYIELD(), PRICE(), PRICEDISC(), YIELD(), YIELDDISC()

Sample Files

Use the ODDLPRICE worksheet in the Simple Interest Calculation.xls or Simple Interest Calculation.xlsx sample file. The sample files are found in the Chapter15 folder. For more information about the sample files, see the section titled "Using the Sample Files" on page xxiii.

ODDLYIELD()

Syntax   ODDLYIELD(*Settlement,Maturity,Last_Interest_Date,Rate,Price,Repayment, Frequency,Basis*)

Definition   This function calculates the yield of a fixed-interest security in a final interest period whose length is different from the regular interest periods in the past. Compound interest is not taken into consideration.

Arguments

- *Settlement* **(required)** The date when the loan becomes the property of the purchaser.

- *Maturity* **(required)** The date when the repayment of the certified amount takes place.

- *Last_Interest_Date* **(required)** The date of the final (regular) interest payment before the purchase date.

- *Rate* **(required)** The nominal yield (annual interest rate) of the bond.

- *Price* **(required)** The price of the security on the day of settlement as a percentage; that is, it must be interpreted as if the par value of the paper was 100 monetary units.

- *Repayment* **(required)** The percentage of the repayment based on the par value of a security (as if it was 100 monetary units).

- *Frequency* **(required)** The number of interest payments within a year (annually, biannually, quarterly).

- *Basis* **(optional)** The method you want to use for determining the days in the year according to Table 15-2, shown earlier. If this argument is omitted, Excel calculates with *Basis* = 0.

Take note of the following:

- Date specifications must not have a time; decimal places are truncated. The arguments *Frequency* and *Basis* are also truncated to integers.

- If date arguments cannot be resolved to a valid date, the ODDLYIELD() function returns the #NUMBER! error.

- *Price* and *Rate* require nonnegative numbers. Otherwise ODDLYIELD() returns the error #NUMBER!.

- If *Frequency* cannot be resolved to 1, 2, or 4, or *Basis* cannot be resolved to a number from 0 through 4, ODDLYIELD() returns the error #NUMBER!.

- The same result as explained in the preceding bullet happens when the correct sort order (*Maturity* is greater than *Settlement*, which is greater than *Last_Interest_Date*) is not kept.

Important

Excel Help contains the following note:

"Dates should be entered with the DATE() function or as results of other formulas or functions. Problems might occur if dates are entered as text."

Background   For more information about this function, see the background information for the ODDLPRICE() function.

The ODDLYIELD() function determines the value of the yield in such a way that a desired price (or price payable on the market) is reached, and informs the purchaser about the expected effective yield of the investment. Because of the principle of simple yield used (no compound interest), the price formula can be resolved to the yield. The formula in Excel Help can be read like this:

$$Yield = \frac{(Repayment + Yield\ at\ maturity) - (Price + Accrued\ interest)}{Price + Accrued\ interest} \cdot \frac{1}{Partial\ period}$$

The partial period based on the year makes the yield an annual interest rate. The interest at maturity results from the interest since the last interest date. The accrued interest is pro-rated based on the time of the last interest payment up until the purchase.

Example   In the sample files for this function there is an example that shows a calculation for a fictitious bond with a changed first interest period. It is similar to the calculation in Figure 15-7, shown earlier. The calculation follows the pattern of the price calculation (as shown in the example for ODDLPRICE()). The desired yield is then determined with the target value search (an assumed yield changes in such a way that the desired price is calculated). ODDLYIELD() returns the same result.

See Also ODDFPRICE(), ODDFYIELD(), ODDLPRICE(), PRICE(), PRICEDISC(), YIELD(), YIELDDISC()

> ## Sample Files
> Use the ODDLYIELD worksheet in the Simple Interest Calculation.xls or Simple Interest Calculation.xlsx sample file. The sample files are found in the Chapter15 folder. For more information about the sample files, see the section titled "Using the Sample Files" on page xxiii.

Chapter 15

PMT()

Syntax PMT(*Rate,Nper,Pv,Fv,Type*)

Definition This function returns the amount of the annuity (regular payment) of a process that is part of an annuity calculation. For a repayment calculation, this is the annuity of a loan that is paid off though annuity repayment.

Important

The finance mathematical benefit principle used in Excel,

Payment of the creditor + Payment of the debtor = 0

means that you need to differentiate between disbursements and deposits in regard to the leading sign (borrowing and repayment, investment and disinvestment).

Here Excel differs from the benefit principle used in finance mathematical literature.

Payment of the debtor = Payment of the creditor

Arguments

- *Rate* **(required)** The period interest rate. This is frequently an annual interest rate.

- *Nper* **(required)** The number of interest dates for the entire duration. It is assumed that these dates coincide with the annuity payment dates.

- *Pv* **(required/optional)** The start value of one payment direction. For disbursement plans, this is the account balance at the beginning of these considerations; for repayment plans, it is the loan amount.

- *Fv* **(required/optional)** The end value of one payment direction. In savings processes, it is the desired savings goal; for disbursement plans, it is a desired account balance at the end of the considerations; and for repayment plans, it is the desired residual debt in the given time.

- *Type* **(optional)** Specifies whether the regular payments take place at the start of the periods (*Type* = 1) or at the end of the periods (*Type* = 0). If this argument is not specified, Excel calculates with *Type* = 0.

One of the two arguments *Pv* or *Fv* must be specified.

Background   The five functions PV() = cash value, FV() = future value, PMT() = regular payment, NPER() = interest or payment periods, and RATE() = interest rate, have the following relationship when the benefit principle used by Excel is implemented:

$$PV \cdot (1 + RATE)^{NPER} + PMT \cdot (1 + M \cdot RATE) \cdot \frac{(1 + RATE)^{NPER} - 1}{RATE} + FV = 0$$

where *M* is the *Type* (timing of payments).

The cash value interest is compounded, and so are the regular payments. Finally, the sum is compared to the future value.

Using one of these functions is equal to the respective basic finance mathematical task: calculation of an unknown variable from the preceding equation, when the other variables are known. The functions thus solve the equation for each of their members. For RATE() an approximation calculation is performed.

> **Note**
>
> Interest rates are usually specified as annual interest rates. The functions used here work correctly only if the periods match the interest rate. With intra-annual interest yield, the annual interest rate is usually distributed equally over the periods: 12 months at one twelfth of the interest rate, three months at a quarter, and half a year at half.

Examples   The headings of the following examples reflect the general usage of finance mathematical terms.

Annuity Calculation   A 60-year-old has saved $100,000.00 and would like to receive an additional monthly annuity. He agrees to 4.5 percent p.a. on the respective current balance for a duration of 15 years. How high is the annuity, if he is planning to use up all the capital? How high is it if he want to still have $10,000.00 in the account after 15 years?

For the first question, you determine the annuity with

```
=PMT(4.5%/12,15*12,-100000)
```

and get a result of $764.99. The second issue can be solved with

```
=PMT(4.5%/12,15*12,-100000,10000)
```

to get the result of $725.99. The minus sign at *Pv* should be interpreted as waiving immediate disbursement. *Fv* and PMT() then "show" the other payment direction.

The calculation is based on compound interest within one year. Because compound interest cannot be used for a regular savings account, the result is a little bit theoretical.

Repayment Calculation (Annuity Repayment) Assume that a debtor has taken out an annuity loan of $100,000. An interest rate of 5.5 percent p.a. with an interest commitment duration of five years was agreed on. The bank informs the debtor that the residual debt after five years is still $80,000.

How high is the (constant) monthly payment (repayment plus interest) for the debtor?

```
=PMT(5.5%/12,5*12,100000,-80000)
```

delivers the result: $748.69 (with a minus sign).

Unlike with a savings account, a mortgage loan uses a monthly interest of a twelfth of the agreed-upon yearly interest rate (nominal interest).

> **Important**
> Using formulas might be different from keeping detailed notes of an account history with deposits and withdrawals, because of rounding errors. This happens because the numbers for a savings account are rounded to two decimal places. If you are recreating such an account with Excel, you should use the function ROUND() for intermediary steps that involve money. Simply limiting the display of the cell value to two decimal places often leads to incorrect results.

See Also FV(), IPMT(), NPER(), PPMT(), PRICE(), PV()

> **Sample Files**
> Use the PMT worksheet in the Annuity Calculation.xls or Annuity Calculation.xlsx and in the Repayment Calculation.xls or Repayment Calculation.xlsx sample files. The sample files are found in the Chapter15 folder. For more information about the sample files, see the section titled "Using the Sample Files" on page xxiii.

PPMT()

Syntax   PPMT(*Rate,Per,Nper,Pv,Fv,Type*)

Definition   This function determines the part of an annuity that is used for the repayment of a loan that is repaid according to the principle of annuity repayment.

Arguments

- **Rate (required)** The nominal interest of the loan.

- **Per (required)** The appropriate number for the desired period.

- **Nper (required)** Specifies the total number of periods in which the loan is repaid.

- **Pv (required)** Contains the loan amount.

- **Fv (optional)** Evaluates loans that have not been fully repaid after the total number of periods. Such an effect might happen when mortgages are disbursed with a fixed interest period.

- **Type (optional)** Specifies whether the payments become interest effective at the start of the periods (*Type* = 1) or at the end of the periods (*Type* = 0). If this argument is omitted, Excel uses the value 0.

Background   The repayment of loans can take place in various ways. One way is for the debtor to pay the same amount each period. This amount is composed of a repayment part (which increases as time passes) and an interest part (which decreases as time passes). The change in this composition is because the loan that needs to be repaid shrinks over time. This version is called *annuity repayment*. The total amount is called *annuity*, even though its payment does not necessarily happen annually.

The repayment part of the first annuity results from subtracting the interest part from it. This part is the loan sum multiplied by the nominal interest rate specified for the period. The repayment parts of the next periods are (after a few intermediate mathematical steps) determined from:

$$(Repayment\ part\ of\ the\ first\ period) \cdot (1 + Nominal\ interest\ rate)^{Period\ number-1}$$

> **Note**
>
> In loan agreements, an annual interest rate is very frequently formulated as a nominal interest rate, but the payment takes place intra-annually. In such cases, you need to determine the intra-annual period interest rate by dividing the annual interest rate by the number of payments per year. The total number of periods results from the periods per year multiplied by the number of years.

Example   In the "Repayment Calculation (Annuity Repayment)" example in the description of the PV() function, the following data was specified: A debtor takes out a loan in the amount of $176,121.76, which he pays back at 5.5 percent with $1,000.00 per month over 30 years. The repayment plan shows an interest part of $791.64 in the 18th month. Therefore, the repayment part for this month is $208.36. You can check this result with the function PPMT(), even though there might be rounding errors.

```
=PPMT(5.5%/12,18,30*12,-176121.76)
```

(The correct numbers are derived from references to the cells in which the data are located).

Rounding errors occur frequently when the integrated functions are used. After all, they cannot take into consideration what actually happens at the bank counter: In the real world, money is calculated with only two decimal places. If you are entering data for a repayment plan month by month, you need to use the function ROUND() to show what is actually happening.

See Also CUMPRINC(), FV(), IPMT(), NPER(), PMT(), PV(), RATE()

> **Sample Files**
>
> Use the PV worksheet in the Repayment Calculation.xls or Repayment Calculation.xlsx sample file. The sample files are found in the Chapter15 folder. For more information about the sample files, see the section titled "Using the Sample Files" on page xxiii.

PRICE()

Syntax   PRICE(*Settlement,Maturity,Rate,Yield,Repayment,Frequency,Basis*)

Definition   This function calculates the price of a fixed-interest security (loan); that is, the purchase price without accrued interest.

Arguments

- *Settlement* **(required)** The date when the ownership of the security changes.

- *Maturity* **(required)** The date when the repayment of the loan certified by the security takes place.

- *Rate* **(required)** The agreed-upon annual interest rate as the price for the borrowed money.

- *Yield* **(required)** The market interest rate on the settlement day, at which during calculation of the duration all future payments are discounted.

- *Repayment* **(required)** The percentage of the par value of a security (as if it was 100 monetary units) at which repayment takes place on the day of maturity.

- *Frequency* **(required)** Because it is quite common to have fixed-interest securities with several interest dates per year, the required argument *Frequency* gives you their number. Allowed values are: 1 = annual; 2 = biannual; 4 = quarterly.

- *Basis* **(optional)** The method you want to use for determining the days in the year according to Table 15-2, shown earlier. If this argument is omitted, Excel calculates with *Basis* = 0.

The arguments of PRICE() have the following requirements:

- Date specifications must not have a time; in other words, decimal places are truncated. The arguments *Frequency* and *Basis* are also truncated to integers.

- If date arguments cannot be resolved to a valid date, the PRICE() function returns the #NUMBER! error.

- *Yield* and *Rate* require nonnegative numbers. *Repayment* requires positive numbers. Otherwise, PRICE() returns the #VALUE! error.

- If *Frequency* cannot be resolved to 1, 2, or 4, and *Basis* cannot be resolved to a number from 0 through 4, PRICE() returns the #NUMBER! error. The same happens when the settlement date is later than the maturity.

Background To implement the finance mathematical benefit principle

Payment of the creditor = Payment of the debtor

for the start of the transaction, the price of a fixed-interest security (loan) plus potential accrued interest equals the cash value of the debtor's future payments certified in this security. The price is the percentage of the security's par value; as if the par value was 100 monetary units.

The cash value calculation is no problem if the purchase date (change of ownership) of a security with an annual interest payment is the same as the day of the interest payment. In this case, only the whole year needs to be taken into consideration. A situation in which the change of ownership takes place between interest due dates or in which interest payments take place several times a year is not so easy. In finance mathematics there are several ways to deal with a year that is divided into parts. The best known methods are *Moosmüller* and *Braess/Fangmeyer* as well as ISMA. ISMA stands for *International Securities Market Association*, an organization that sprang from the Association of International Bond Dealers (AIBD).

The ISMA method returns the same as PRICE() for a one-time interest payment per year and can easily be recreated for biannual and quarterly interest payments by using PRICE().

In Excel terminology and for the functions derived from it, the benefit principle of creating cash values (discounting future payments) for price calculation by Excel works as follows:

$$PRICE = \frac{Repayment}{\left(1 + \frac{Yield}{Frequency}\right)^{COUPNUM - 1 + \frac{COUPDAYSNC}{Days\ of\ the\ interest\ period}}} +$$

$$+ \sum_{K=1}^{COUPNUM} \frac{\frac{RATE}{Frequency} \cdot 100}{\left(1 + \frac{Yield}{Frequency}\right)^{K - 1 + \frac{COUPDAYSNC}{Days\ of\ the\ interest\ period}}} -$$

$$- \frac{RATE}{Frequency} \cdot 100 \cdot \frac{COUPDAYBS}{Days\ of\ the\ interest\ period}$$

COUPNUM is the number of interest payments after the purchase, *COUPDAYSNC* is the number of days until the next interest payment date, and *COUPDAYBS* is the number of days since the last interest payment date.

If *Frequency* = 1, this formula also represents the ISMA method. If *Frequency* equals 2 or 4, Excel calculates with an even distribution of the yield over the periods within the year. The

ISMA method, however, uses a period apportionment following the correlation between nominal and effective interest, which you can find in the function descriptions for EFFECT() or NOMINAL():

$$Period\ yield = \frac{NOMINAL(Annual\ yield, Frequency)}{Frequency}$$

In case of several interest payments per year, you can therefore calculate the price by using the ISMA method with PRICE(). Before you do this, however, you need to convert the "effective" yield into a nominal yield (by using the function NOMINAL()).

CAUTION

The explanations shown here apply only when more than a single interest payment date is left before maturity. Otherwise, Excel does not calculate according to the formula for the price shown here, but uses a fractional yield instead of the fractional duration. PRICE() then returns the same result as PRICEMAT().

Example   The following examples describe how to use the PRICE() function.

Annual Interest Payment   A 4.500 percent federal loan initiated in 2003 had a yield of 0.61 percent on August 31, 2010. It matures on January 4, 2013. How much do you need to pay if you want to purchase securities at a par value of $1,000.00?

Note

This exercise is not a typical situation, because prices are created by supply and demand, and the yield is then calculated from the price. However, the intention is to demonstrate the principle with a security whose behavior you can read daily in the newspapers or on the Internet.

Such price calculations might happen if an issuer issues a security, gives it a "round" nominal interest (1/8 intervals), and wants to launch it with certain yields with price bonuses or discounts.

If you want to determine the ISMA price with the day counter method day exact/day exact without using the function PRICE() (in other words, if you want to learn what exactly PRICE() is converting), you can prepare a worksheet as shown in Figure 15-7.

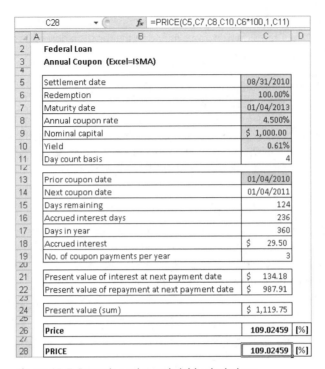

Figure 15-7 Preparing price and yield calculations.

Type in the known data into the first seven cells from C5 through C11. In preparation, enter the day counter mode with 1 (this corresponds to *Basis* = 1 in all of the integrated functions that are used).

Then use `=COUPNCD(C5,C7,1,C11)` to determine the next interest payment date: April 1, 2011. The formula `=COUPDAYSNC(C5,C7,1,C11)` helps you count the days up to this interest date: 126. To calculate the accrued interest, you need the days since the last interest payment date (`=COUPDAYBS(C5,C7,1,C11)` counts 239 here) so that you can use `=C8*C15/C16*C9` to determine an amount of $29.47. The number of remaining interest dates, which you need so that you can discount the future payments, is determined with `=COUPNUM(C5,C7,1,C11)` and returns 3.

Now let's look at discounting. The function PV() helps you here. You can use `=PV(C10,C18-1,- C8*C9,-C8*C9,1)` as a yield calculation to determine the cash value of future interest payments (the result is $134,18) and as a compound interest calculation for discounting the repayment amount with `=PV(C10,C18-1,0,-C6*C9)` to $987.91.

You now need to determine the sum of the two cash values with the ISMA method over the fractional duration of 126 of 365 days with a fractional exponent in the interest formula: `=(C20+C21)/(1+C10)^(C14/C16)` returns $1,119.74.

The price is the percentage (that is, a number based on a par value of 100) that must subtract the value of the accrued interest from the cash value you just calculated: `=(C23-C17)/C9*100`.

The result is the same as with `=PRICE(C5,C7,C8,C10,C6*100,1,C11)`: 109.027.

Note that because of the low yield, there can be deviations from the calculated price on the respective day (rounding errors).

Biannual Interest Payment   There are only a few loans that have more than one interest payment date per year. In the sample files accompanying this book, the loan of the previous example was therefore given a fictitious biannual interest payment so that the calculations could be performed. The Excel price has a different number of decimal places than the ISMA price. If you want to determine the ISMA price, you need to divide the market interest yield evenly over the periods with NOMINAL(*yield,frequency*) and use the function PRICE().

See Also ODDFPRICE(), ODDFYIELD(), ODDLPRICE(), ODDLYIELD(), YIELD()

> **Sample Files**
>
> Use the PRICE worksheet in the Price Calculation.xls or Price Calculation.xlsx sample file. The sample files are found in the Chapter15 folder. For more information about the sample files, see the section titled "Using the Sample Files" on page xxiii.

PRICEDISC()

Syntax   PRICEDISC(*Settlement,Maturity,Disc,Repayment,Basis*)

Definition   This function calculates the disbursement amount of a simply discounted security with anticipative interest yield.

Arguments

- *Settlement* **(required)** The date when the ownership of the security changes.

- *Maturity* **(required)** The day when the payments from the security must take place.

- *Disc* **(required)** The interest rate of the discount (disagio).

- *Repayment* **(required)** The payment at the day of maturity.

- *Basis* **(optional)** The method you want to use for determining the days in the year according to Table 15-2, shown earlier. If this argument is omitted, Excel calculates with *Basis* = 0.

All function arguments that take a date use the date without time; fractions are rounded. The argument *Basis* also requires an integer, and decimal places are truncated.

If invalid dates are used or no numbers are entered where required, the function returns the error #VALUE!. If invalid numbers are entered for nondate arguments, the function returns the #NUMBER! error.

> ## Important
>
> **Excel Help contains the following note:**
>
> **"Dates should be entered with the DATE() function or as results of other formulas or functions. Problems might occur if dates are entered as text."**
>
> **The reference to the par value is wrong.**

Background The principle of anticipative interest yield is based on the assumption that a seed capital amount (deposit amount, loan) results from the repayment amount minus the interest on this amount. This principle is mainly used in the intra-annual scope and differs from the principle based on a savings account or mortgage loan. In this case, interest is calculated at the end of a period based on the seed capital (interest yield in arrears).

> ## Note
>
> **The functions are connected as follows (in this case, *Basis* = 4):**
>
> $$INTRATE() - INTRATE() \cdot DISC() \cdot \frac{DAYS360()}{360} = PREDISC()$$
>
> **But that is exactly the principle of anticipative interest yield.**
>
> **The *Repayment* argument used by the function should be considered with respect to the task of the INTRATE() function.**

Examples   The following examples show how to use PRICEDIS().

Bill of Exchange Calculation   On May 10, 2010, a businessman presented his bank with a bill of exchange in the amount of $5,000 with a (residual) maturity of two months. The bank adds a discount rate of 5 percent p.a. and does not charge fees. How high is the amount that is credited to the account?

From the background information, you can read the equation as follows:

$$Bill\ amount - Bill\ amount \cdot Discount\ rate \cdot \frac{DAYS360()}{360} = Credit$$

and use

```
=PRICEDISC("10/5/2010","10/7/2010",5%,5000,4))
```

to get to a result of $4,958.33. This formula would usually use cell references to refer to concrete numbers.

Treasury Bonds   On August 30, 2010, Germany offered treasury bonds (security ID 111 704) with the following conditions: Duration 1 year; disbursement €500 (results from the minimum purchase price), mature on August 22, 2011; sale interest 0.46 percent (this is the name for the percent anticipative discount). How high is the purchase price?

PRICEDISC() delivers the correct answer here as well: €497.75.

At which interest rate in arrears would a comparable investment (same duration, same usage, same result) have to take place? To answer this question, you just need to create a ratio between the gain and the invested capital and make sure that the duration is 365 of 365 days. The function RECEIVED() is easier to use. It works according to the pattern RECEIVED(*day of purchase,day of maturity,usage,repayment,basis*) and returns 0.46 percent. You can also get the same number for the yield from the German Federal Bank. The function YIELDDISC() works the same as RECEIVED() and returns the same result.

The described process will also work in the future. The number of days you need to use will depend on the specifications of the Federal Bank and the actual purchase date.

Because of the low yield, these results are not very interesting when it comes to more decimal places and the differences to the nominal interest.

See Also DISC(), INTRATE(), RECEIVED(), YIELDDISC()

Chapter 15

> ### Sample Files
>
> Use the Bill of Exchange and Treasury Bonds worksheets in the Simple Interest Calcula-tion.xls or Simple Interest Calculation.xlsx sample file. The sample files are found in the Chapter15 folder. For more information about the sample files, see the section titled "Using the Sample Files" on page xxiii.

PRICEMAT()

Syntax   PRICEMAT(*Settlement,Maturity,Issue,Rate,Yield,Basis*)

Definition   This function returns the price (as a percentage, that is, based on a nominal value) of a security that has a simple interest yield in arrears (no compound interest).

Arguments

- **Settlement (required)** The date when the ownership of the security changes.

- **Maturity (required)** The maturity date of the security.

- **Issue (required)** The date of the emission of the security.

- **Rate (required)** The agreed-upon nominal interest rate of the security based on an entire year.

- **Yield (required)** The current market interest rate or the expected yield of the secu-rity (as an interest rate based on an entire year).

- **Basis (optional)** The method you want to use for determining the days in the year according to Table 15-2, shown earlier. If this argument is omitted, Excel calculates with *Basis* = 0.

The arguments of the function have the following requirements:

- *Settlement*, *Maturity*, and *Issue* require date specifications without a time; that is, decimal places are truncated. Any decimal places of *Basis* are also truncated to make the value an integer.

- If *Account*, *Maturity*, or *Issue* do not have a valid date, PRICEMAT() returns the #VALUE! error. The account date must be earlier than the maturity date.

- If *Rate* or *Yield* is less than zero, PRICEMAT() returns the #NUMBER! error.

- *Basis* must be a number that can be evaluated to a number from 0 through 4, otherwise PRICEMAT() returns the error #NUMBER!.

Important

Excel Help contains the following note:

"Dates should be entered with the DATE() function or as results of other formulas or functions. However, problems might occur if dates are entered as text."

Background   To implement the finance mathematical benefit principle

Payment of creditor = Payment of debtor

for the start of the transaction, the price of a fixed-interest security plus potential accrued interest equals the cash value of the debtor's future payments certified in this security. The price is the percentage of the security's par value, that is, as if the par value was 100 monetary units. In this case, the future payment is the repayment plus the nominal interest. There is no compound interest, because evaluations only take place for the intra-annual timeframe. A divided interest rate according to the duration is used for the discount calculation instead of a divided duration in the exponent (ISMA method).

Example   A debt of $1,000.00, which is due in full with a nominal interest rate of 4 percent p.a. and a repayment by December 1, 2010, was agreed upon on June 1, 2010. On August 9, 2010, there is a change in creditors.

At this date, a real interest rate of 2.5 percent p.a. for the outstanding time until repayment is customary. What price does the person who takes over the debt pay?

You get the price of $100.46, which must be multiplied by 10 because of the par value of $1,000.00, by using

```
=PRICEMAT(C3,C4,C2,4%,4.5%,4)
```

with C3 as the purchase date, C4 as the maturity date, and C2 as the day of issue. Now add the accrued interest of $7.56, which you can calculate manually or by using ACCRINT(). You can find further explanations in the example for the function ACCRINT().

See Also ACCRINT(), COUPDAYS(), YIELDMAT()

Chapter 15

> ### Sample Files
>
> Use the ACCRING worksheet in the Simple Interest Calculation.xls or Simple Interest Calculation.xlsx sample file. The sample files are found in the Chapter15 folder. For more information about the sample files, see the section titled "Using the Sample Files" on page xxiii.

PV()

Syntax   PV(*Rate,Nper,Pmt,Fv,Type*)

Definition   The PV() function calculates the cash value of a regular payment flow, taking into consideration possible single payments at the end of the period in question, according to the finance mathematical benefit principle:

Payment of the debtor + payment of the creditor = 0

Arguments

- **Rate (required)** Specifies the (constant) period interest rate as an annuity interest rate.

- **Nper (required)** Specifies the number of interest periods. It is assumed that possible regular payments (in other words, that the *Pmt* argument is greater than zero) take place at the end or the start of the interest period.

- **Pmt (required/optional, see Note)** Informs you about the amount of the regular payments and can be interpreted as an annuity.

- **Fv (optional/required, see Note)** The account balance you want to have at the end of the process (for example, a residual balance from disbursement plans or a final repayment in the amount of the residual debt for loans).

- **Type (optional)** Specifies whether regular payments take place at the end of the periods (*Type* = 0 or not specified) or at the start of the periods (*Type* = 1).

> ### Note
>
> If the *Pmt* argument is omitted, *Fv* must be specified. If *Pmt* is present, *Fv* can be omitted. Omitting the arguments has the same effect as specifying them as zero.

Important

The preceding finance mathematical benefit principle means that you need to differentiate between disbursements and deposits in regard to the leading sign (borrowing and repayment, investment and disinvestment). Here Excel differs from the benefit principle used in finance mathematical literature:

Payment of the debtor = Payment of the creditor

Background   The five functions PV() = cash value, FV() = future value, PMT() = regular payment, NPER() = interest or payment periods, and RATE() = interest rate, have the following relationship when the benefit principle is implemented:

$$PV \cdot (1 + RATE)^{NPER} + PMT \cdot (1 + M \cdot RATE) \cdot \frac{(1 + RATE)^{NPER} - 1}{RATE} + FV = 0$$

where *M* is the *Type* (timing of payments).

The cash value interest is compounded, and so are the regular payments. Finally, the sum is compared to the future value.

Using one of these functions is equal to the respective basic finance mathematical task: calculation of an unknown variable from the equation when the other variables are known. The functions thus solve the equation for each of its members. For RATE, an approximation calculation is performed.

Note

In practice, the interest rate is almost always specified as an annual interest rate. The functions mentioned here work correctly only if the periods match the interest rate. With intra-annual interest yield, the annual interest rate is usually distributed equally over the periods: 12 months at one-twelfth of the interest rate; 3 months at a quarter, and half a year at half.

Examples   The headings of the following examples reflect the general usage of finance mathematical terms.

Compound Interest Calculation   Assume that an investor wants to have a small financial cushion for retirement and decides to invest a newly received inheritance of $10,000.00

for 15 years at a fixed interest rate of 5 percent. He hopes to get a disbursement of at least $25,000.00. Will the plan succeed?

A calculation with

`=PV(5%,15,,25000)`

returns `-$12,025.43`. This is the amount he would have to invest (thus the inclusion of the minus sign) in order to get the accrued $25,000.00 after 15 years. Therefore, the plan will not succeed.

Annuity Calculation   A 60-year-old person has saved $100,000.00 and would like to get paid an additional monthly annuity of $750.00. Is the saved money enough, if 4.5 percent p.a. is paid on top of the existing balance and payments are planned for 15 years?

You determine the cash value of the annuity with

`=PV(4.5%/12,15*12,750)`

and get `-$98,040.08`. Therefore, there is even a small amount left over after 15 years, because the sum is larger. The minus sign should be interpreted as waiving immediate disbursement.

The calculation is based on compound interest within one year.

Repayment Calculation (Annuity Repayment)   Assume that a debtor is able to pay back $1,000.00 per month on a debt (repayment plus interest). How high could this debt be, if the duration is 30 years at a fixed interest rate of 5.5 percent p.a.?

The cash value formula can be used here as well (in this case, the repayment calculation is the annuity calculation). You are using the following to get to a result of $176,121.76:

`=PV(5.5%/12,30*12,-1000)`

Unlike for a savings account, a mortgage loan actually uses a monthly interest of a twelfth of the agreed-upon yearly interest rate (nominal interest).

Important

Using formulas might be different from keeping detailed notes of an account history with deposits and withdrawals because of rounding errors. This happens because the numbers for a savings account are rounded to two decimal places. If you are re-creating such an account with Excel, you should use the ROUND() function for intermediary steps that involve money. Simply limiting the display of the cell value to two decimal places often leads to incorrect results.

Investment Calculation   The capital value method of the investment calculation determines the cash value of future income surpluses and compares them to the purchase cost. Normally an interest rate of 10 percent is used for the calculation. If the income surpluses are due as regular payments and if the investment asset has a residual value after the disinvestment duration, the capital value can be determined by using the following pattern:

–PV(10%,number of years,annual income surplus,residual value)–purchase cost

The investment makes sense from an economic standpoint, if the calculated amount is positive.

Price Calculation   You can also find ways of using the PV() function in the examples for RATE() and YIELD().

See Also CUMPRINC(), FV(), IPMT(), NPER(), NPV(), PMT(), PPMT(), RATE()

Sample Files

Use the PV worksheet in the Compound Interest Calculation.xls or Compound Interest Calculation.xlsx, Annuity Calculation.xls or Annuity Calculation.xlsx, or Repayment Calculation.xls or Repayment Calculation.xlsx sample file. The sample files are found in the Chapter15 folder. For more information about the sample files, see the section titled "Using the Sample Files" on page xxiii.

Chapter 15

RATE()

Syntax   Rate(*Nper,Pmt,Pv,Fv,Type,Guess*)

Definition   This function determines the applicable interest rate for compound interest tasks and annuity calculation (repayment calculation according to the principle of annuity repayment).

Arguments

- **Nper (required)** The number of interest periods. It is assumed that possible regular payments (that is, the *Pmt* argument is greater than zero) take place at the end (or the start) of the interest periods.

- **Pmt (required/optional, see Note)** The amount of the regular payments, which can be interpreted as annuity.

- **Pv (required/optional, see Note)** The start value of one payment direction. For disbursement plans, this is the account balance at the beginning of these considerations; for repayment plans, it is the loan amount.

- **Fv (required/optional, see Note)** The future value that you want to have at the end of a specific time period.

- **Type (optional)** Specifies whether regular payments take place at the end of the periods (*Type* = 0 or not specified) or at the start of the periods (*Type* = 1).

- **Guess (optional)** Can be used to start the necessary approximation calculation (see the background information for this function). If no value is entered for *Guess*, Excel calculates with a value of 10 percent.

> **Note**
>
> At least two of the three arguments *Pmt*, *Pv*, and *Fv* must be specified and not be zero. Their signs correspond to the respective direction of the money flow (see the formula discussed later in this section).

> **Important**
>
> The finance mathematical benefit principle
>
> *Payment of the creditor + Payment of the debtor = 0*
>
> means that you need to differentiate between disbursements and deposits in regard to the leading sign (borrowing and repayment, investment and disinvestment). Here Excel differs from the benefit principle used in finance mathematical literature:
>
> *Payment of the creditor = Payment of the debtor*

Background The five functions PV() = cash value, FV() = future value, PMT() = regular payment, NPER() = interest or payment time periods, and RATE() = interest rate, have the following relationship when the benefit principle in the preceding Note is implemented:

$$PV \cdot (1 + RATE)^{NPER} + PMT \cdot (1 + M \cdot RATE) \cdot \frac{(1 + RATE)^{NPER} - 1}{RATE} + FV = 0$$

The cash value interest is compounded, and so are the regular payments. Finally, the sum is compared to the future value.

Using one of these functions is equal to the respective basic finance mathematical task: calculation of an unknown variable from the preceding equation, when the other variables are known. The functions thus solve the equation for each of its members. For RATE, an approximation calculation is performed.

Excel starts the calculation as an approximation from the given estimated value and will get to the solution (if it exists) step by step. You can support Excel's search for the solution by varying the estimated value. However, you cannot force a solution of the equation.

> **Note**
>
> Interest rates are usually specified as annual interest rates. The functions discussed here work correctly only if the periods match the interest rate. With intra-annual interest yield, the annual interest rate is usually distributed equally over the periods: 12 months at one twelfth of the interest rate, 3 months at a quarter, and half a year at half.

Examples   Some of the headings of the following examples reflect the general usage of finance mathematical terms.

Compound Interest Calculation   Assume that an investor wants to have a small financial cushion for retirement and decides to invest a newly received inheritance of $10,000.00 for 15 years at a fixed interest rate. He hopes to get a disbursement of at least $25,000.00. At which interest rate will his plan succeed?

A calculation with

=RATE(15,,-10000,25000)

returns a required annual interest rate of 6.3 percent.

Type B German Federal Savings Bonds   With federal savings bonds of type B, paid interest is reinvested according to the agreed-upon terms. In the example for the FVSCHEDULE() function, there is a calculation that uses RATE() to confirm the yield published by the federal bank.

Annuity Calculation   A 60-year-old has saved $100,000.00 and would like to be paid an additional monthly annuity of $750.00. At which interest rate must each current balance be paid interest, if payments are planned at the beginning of each month for 15 years?

You can determine the required monthly interest rate annuity with

=RATE(15*12,-750,100000,,1)

Chapter 15

and get a result of 0.354796 percent (the 1 in the formula represents the beginning of the month). The calculation is based on compound interest within one year. Because compound interest cannot be used for a regular savings account, the result is a little bit theoretical. The specification of the nominal interest (times 12) for a whole year is limited to two decimal places: 4.26 percent p a.. A concrete account must then be kept with a twelfth of this number.

Repayment Calculation (Annuity Repayment)   Assume that an investor is able to pay back $1,000.00 per month on a loan (repayment plus interest). What should the interest rate of the loan be, if $175,000.00 were to be paid back within 30 years?

The repayment calculation is an annuity calculation in this case. Using RATE() with

```
=RATE(30*12,-1000,175000)
```

returns 0.46316 percent. Unlike a savings account, a mortgage loan uses a monthly interest of a twelfth of the agreed-upon yearly interest rate (nominal interest). However, the interest calculated with RATE() still needs to be multiplied by 12 for the year, and the account kept with the resulting nominal interest of 5.56 percent p.a.. To calculate the interest monthly, a twelfth of this interest rate is used. This results in a residual debt after 30 years.

> ## Important
>
> Using formulas might be different from keeping detailed notes of an account history with deposits and withdrawals because of rounding errors. This happens because the numbers for a savings account are rounded to two decimal places. If you are re-creating such an account with Excel, you should use the function ROUND() for intermediary steps that involve money. Simply limiting the display of the cell value to two decimal places often leads to incorrect results.
>
> The example in the sample files for this function leave you room to experiment with the rounding effects, because the account plans are already prepared.

Investment Calculation   If the annual future surpluses are constant in investment evaluations, you can use the function RATE() for determining the internal capital yield instead of the IRR(). The IRR() section contains details about the internal interest rate method.

See Also   FV(), IRR(), NPER(), PMT(), PV()

Sample Files

Use the RATE worksheet in the Compound Interest Calculation.xls or Compound Interest Calculation.xlsx, in the Annuity Calculation.xls or Annuity Calculation.xlsx, and in the Repayment Calculation.xls or Repayment Calculation.xlsx sample files. The sample files are found in the Chapter15 folder. For more information about the sample files, see the section titled "Using the Sample Files" on page xxiii.

RECEIVED()

Syntax   RECEIVED(*Settlement,Maturity,Investment,Redemption,Basis*)

Definition   This function determines the repayment amount of a deposit resulting from a simple anticipative deduction of accrued interest.

Arguments

- **Settlement (required)** The day on which the deposit (investment on the buyer side, borrowing on the seller side) is made

- **Maturity (required)** The date when the repayment of the deposit takes place

- **Investment (required)** The amount of the deposit (the loan)

- **Redemption (required)** Specifies the percentage of the anticipative interest yield

- **Basis (optional)** Defines the method you want to use for determining the days in the year according to Table 15-2, shown earlier

All function arguments that concern a date use the date without the time; that is, fractions are rounded. The *Basis* argument also requires an integer, and decimal places are truncated.

If invalid dates are used or no numbers are entered where required, the function returns the #VALUE! error. If invalid numbers are entered for nondate arguments, the function returns the #NUMBER! error.

Important

Excel Help contains the following note:

"Dates should be entered with the DATE() function or as results of other formulas or functions. However, problems might occur if you enter dates as text."

Background The principle of anticipative interest yield is based on the assumption that a seed capital amount (deposit amount/loan) results from the repayment amount minus the interest on this amount. This principle is mainly used in the intra-annual scope and differs from the principle based on a savings account or mortgage loan. In that case, interest is calculated at the end of a period based on the seed capital (interest yield in arrears).

> **Note**
>
> The functions are connected as follows (noted here in the case of *Basis* = 4):
>
> $$RECEIVED() - RECEIVED() \cdot DISC() \cdot \frac{DAYS360()}{360} = PRICEDISC()$$
>
> But that is exactly the principle of anticipative interest yield. The function RECEIVED() resolves the preceding equation assuming the other specifications are available.

Examples The following examples explain how to use the RECEIVED() function.

Bill of Exchange Calculation On May 10, 2010, a businessman presented his bank with a bill of exchange with a (remaining) maturity of two months. The bank set a discount rate of 5 percent p.a. and credited $4,958.33 to his account. How high was the bill amount?

Of course, this exercise is not a typical situation. Normally you would know the bill amount (the repayment amount, which is called *INTRATE()* in Excel) and would ask for the amount of the disbursement (called *PRICEDISC()*).

From the background information, you can read the equation as follows:

$$Bill\ amount - Bill\ amount \cdot Discount\ rate \cdot \frac{DAYS360()}{360} = Credit$$

and use

```
=RECEIVED("10/5/2010","10/7/2010",4958.33,5%,4)
```

to get to the result of $5,000. Usually this formula would use numbers located in cells and would use cell references.

Treasury Bonds Treasury bonds represent a further example where anticipative interest yield is used. Take a look at the examples for the functions PRICEDISC() and YIELDDISC().

See Also DISC(), INTRATE(), PRICEDISC(), YIELDDISC()

> ## Sample Files
>
> Use the Bill of Exchange worksheet in the Simple Interest Calculation.xls or Simple Interest Calculation.xlsx sample file. The sample files are found in the Chapter15 folder. For more information about the sample files, see the section titled "Using the Sample Files" on page xxiii.

SLN()

Syntax   SLN(*Purchase_Value,Residual_Value,Life*)

Definition   This function calculates the depreciation amounts of capital assets by using the linear depreciation method.

Arguments

- ***Purchase_Value* (required)** The purchase cost (net purchase price plus incidental purchase expenses minus reduction of purchase cost) of an asset. If you do not use a number, the error #VALUE! is displayed. If the entered number is negative, the calculated values cannot be interpreted.

- ***Residual_Value* (required)** The value of the asset at the end of the depreciation duration. If you don't use a number, the error #VALUE! is displayed. If the entered number is negative, the error #NUMBER! is displayed.

- ***Life* (required)** The number of periods in which the asset is depreciated. You should use an integer greater than zero for this argument.

Background   Depreciation is used to determine the loss of value of an asset and make that loss visible. It should not be confused with depreciation because of abrasion/use, which refers to the cost of purchasing an asset as part of operation expenses from a tax point of view.

The depreciation amount, which is the same in each period, is determined from the difference between purchase cost and remainder, divided over the number of periods. This amount reduces the book value in each period.

The linear depreciation method is permitted within some tax laws. However, sometimes a fractional part of the year in the first period must receive special consideration, the function SLN() usually cannot be used. You need to manually adjust the amount of the first depreciation period and write the rest with the help of SLN().

Example An asset with a purchase cost of $1,000.00 should be depreciated in five years to a residual value of $100.00 by using the linear method. You can calculate the depreciation amount in each period by using SLN() and subtract it from the book value of the previous period.

Alternatively, you can create a depreciation plan that implements the formulas for calculating the first depreciation amount as well as the processes for calculating the other amounts.

See Also AMORLINC(), DB(), DDB(), SYD(), VDB()

Sample Files

Use the SLN worksheet in the Depreciation Calculation.xls or Depreciation Calculation.xlsx sample file. The sample files are found in the Chapter15 folder. For more information about the sample files, see the section titled "Using the Sample Files" on page xxiii.

SYD()

Syntax SYD(*Cost,Salvage,Life,Per*)

Definition This function determines the depreciation amounts of an asset according to the arithmetic-degressive method (also called the *digital method*).

Arguments

- *Cost* **(required)** The purchase cost (net purchase price plus incidental purchase expenses minus reduction of purchase cost) of an asset. If you don't use a number, the #VALUE! error is displayed. If the entered number is negative, the calculated values cannot be interpreted.

- *Salvage* **(required)** Returns the value of the asset at the end of the depreciation duration. If you don't use a number, the #VALUE! error is displayed. If the entered number is negative, the #NUMBER! error is displayed.

- *Life* **(required)** The number of periods in which the asset is depreciated. You should use an integer greater than zero for this argument.

- *Per* **(required)** Specifies the period within the depreciation duration for which the depreciation amount should be calculated. You should use an integer greater than zero for this argument.

Background   Depreciation is used to determine the loss of value of an asset and make that loss visible. It should not be confused with depreciation because of abrasion/use, which refers to the cost of purchasing an asset as part of operation expenses from a tax point of view.

Arithmetic-degressive depreciation is based on a constant reduction of the depreciation amount from period to period. The first depreciation amount is determined with the following formula:

$$First\ depreciation = \frac{2 \cdot (Purchase\ cost - Residual\ value)}{Depreciation\ duration - 1}$$

The constant amount that reduces the individual depreciation amounts is calculated by dividing the first depreciation amount by the total number of depreciation periods.

> ## Important
> The arithmetic-degressive depreciation method is not allowed within the tax laws of many countries.

Example   An asset with a purchase cost of $1,000.00 should be depreciated in five years to a residual value of $0 by using the arithmetic-degressive method. You can calculate the depreciation amount in each period by using SYD() and subtract it from the book value of the previous period.

Alternatively, you can create a depreciation plan that implements the formulas mentioned earlier in this section for calculating the first depreciation amount as well as the processes for calculating the other amounts. Creating a depreciation plan following your own pattern is especially recommended if you are using methods that are allowed for taxes, because the integrated functions are not usable in general.

See Also AMORLINC(), DB(), DDB(), SLN(), VDB()

> ## Sample Files
> Use the SYD worksheet in the Depreciation Calculation.xls or Depreciation Calculation.xlsx sample file. The sample files are found in the Chapter15 folder. For more information about the sample files, see the section titled "Using the Sample Files" on page xxiii.

TBILLEQ()

Syntax   TBILLEQ(*Settlement,Maturity,Discount*)

Definition   This function calculates the equivalent annual interest rate in arrears based on 365 days for a given anticipative annual interest rate based on 360 days. The latter is usually formulated as the discount rate of the par value (disagio). It is used for U.S. treasury bills.

Arguments

- **Settlement (required)** The date when the ownership of the security changes

- **Maturity (required)** The date of the repayment of the certified par value

- **Discount (required)** The percent disagio of the par value

There are the following requirements:

- *Settlement* and *Maturity* require a date specification without a time; decimal places are truncated. Invalid date specifications return the #VALUE! error.

- If the start date is not positive, TBILLEQ() returns the #NUMBER! error.

- The same error is generated if the settlement date lies past the maturity date or if the maturity has more than a year of time difference from the settlement.

> **Important**
>
> **Excel Help contains the following note:**
>
> **"Dates should be entered with the DATE() function or as results of other formulas or functions. Problems might occur if dates are entered as text."**

Background   The equivalence between anticipative interest payment and interest payment in arrears is created by the following equation:

$$\left(1 + \frac{Days}{365} \cdot TBILLEQ()\right) \cdot \left(1 - \frac{Days}{360} \cdot Discount\right) = 1$$

Days is the exact day difference between *Maturity* and *Settlement*.

Example   In the sample files for this function, you can find some number experiments that manually recreate this formula and compare the results with those of YIELDDISC() and RECEIVED(). They convert anticipative interest rates to interest rates in arrears.

See Also TBILLPRICE(), TBILLYIELD()

> ### Sample Files
>
> Use the TBILL worksheet in the Simple Interest Calculation.xls or Simple Interest Cal-
> culation.xlsx sample file. The sample files are found in the Chapter15 folder. For more
> information about the sample files, see the section titled "Using the Sample Files" on
> page xxiii.

TBILLPRICE()

Syntax   TBILLPRICE(*Settlement,Maturity,Discount*)

Definition   This function returns the price of a discounted security as a percent, as if the par value was 100 monetary units. It is used for U.S. treasury bills.

Arguments

- *Settlement* **(required)** The date when the ownership of the security changes

- *Maturity* **(required)** The date of the repayment of the certified par value

- *Discount* **(required)** The percent disagio of the par value of the security

There are the following requirements:

- *Settlement* and *Maturity* require a date specification without a time: decimal places are truncated. Invalid date specifications return the #VALUE! error.

- If *Discount* is not positive, TBILLPRICE() returns the #NUMBER! error.

- The same error is generated if the settlement date lies past the maturity date or the maturity has more than a year of time difference from the settlement.

Background   You can calculate the price with a simple percentage calculation: The antici-
pative annual interest rate (disagio) is fractioned into the actual duration. The day counter works with 360 days per year, where each month has as many days as it has in the calendar.

This corresponds to the option *Basis* = 2 for those functions that use an argument, such as the functions in Table 15-2, shown earlier.

$$TBILLPRICE = 100 \cdot \left(1 - \frac{Days}{360} \cdot Discount\right)$$

Example   In the sample files for this function, you can find some number experiments that show the equivalency to the function PRICEDISC(), if the calculation uses the day counter with *Basis* = 2.

See Also TBILLEQ(), TBILLYIELD()

Sample Files

Use the TBILL worksheet in the Simple Interest Calculation.xls or Simple Interest Calculation.xlsx sample file. The sample files are found in the Chapter15 folder. For more information about the sample files, see the section titled "Using the Sample Files" on page xxiii.

TBILLYIELD()

Syntax   TBILLYIELD(*Settlement,Maturity,Price*)

Definition   This function returns the yield of a discounted security as an annual interest rate is arrears. It is used for U.S. treasury bills.

Arguments

- *Settlement* **(required)** The date when the ownership of the security changes

- *Maturity* **(required)** The date of the repayment of the certified par value

- *Price* **(required)** The price of the security on the day of settlement as a percentage; it must be interpreted as if the par value of the security was 100 monetary units

There are the following requirements:

- *Settlement* and *Maturity* require a date specification without a time; decimal places are truncated. Invalid date specifications return the #VALUE! error.

- If *Price* is not positive, TBILLYIELD() returns the #NUMBER! error.

- The same error is generated if the settlement date lies past the maturity date or the maturity has more than a year of time difference from the settlement.

> **Important**
>
> Excel Help contains the following note:
>
> "Dates should be entered with the DATE() function or as results of other formulas or functions. Problems might occur if dates are entered as text."

Background   You can calculate the price with a simple percentage calculation: The gain at the day of maturity, which results from the difference between 100 and the paid purchase price, is put in relation to the purchase price (interest in arrears). Because the paper is held less than one year, the interest has to be extrapolated to an entire year to be able to perform a comparison:

$$TBILLYIELD = \frac{100 - Price}{Price} \cdot \frac{360}{Days}$$

The day counter works with 360 days per year, where each month has as many days as it has in the calendar. This corresponds to the option *Basis* = 2 for those functions that use an argument, such as those in functions Table 15-2, shown earlier.

Example   In the sample files for this function, you can find some number experiments that manually recreate this formula and compare the results with those of YIELDDISC() and RECEIVED(). They convert anticipative interest rates to interest rates in arrears (yields). Both functions return the result TBILLYIELD() if the day counter *Basis* = 2 is used.

See Also TBILLEQ(), TBILLPRICE()

> **Sample Files**
>
> Use the TBILL worksheet in the Simple Interest Calculation.xls or Simple Interest Calculation.xlsx sample file. The sample files are found in the Chapter15 folder. For more information about the sample files, see the section titled "Using the Sample Files" on page xxiii.

VDB()

Syntax   VDB(*Cost,Salvage,Life,Start_Period,End_Period,Factor,No_Switch*)

Definition   This function calculates the depreciation amounts by using the geometrically degressive depreciation method. Optionally, it can be checked to change the depreciation method into linear depreciation (as might be suggested by tax regulations).

Arguments

- *Cost* **(required)** The purchase cost (net purchase price plus incidental purchase expenses minus reduction of purchase cost) of an asset. If you don't use a value that can be evaluated as a number, the error #VALUE! is displayed. If the entered number is negative, the error #NUMBER! is displayed.

- *Salvage* **(required)** The value of the asset at the end of the depreciation duration. If you don't use a number, the error #VALUE! is displayed. If the entered number is negative, the error #NUMBER! is displayed.

- *Life* **(required)** The number of periods in which the asset is depreciated. You should use an integer greater than zero for this argument.

- *Start_Period* **(required)** The period within the depreciation duration at the end of which the calculation of the depreciation amount (possibly summed up over several periods) should begin. The first period has the number zero.

- *End_Period* **(required)** The period within the depreciation duration at the end of which the calculation of the depreciation amount (possibly summed up over several periods) should end.

- *Factor* **(optional)** The multiplier for the (assumed linear) depreciation rate (reciprocal to the depreciation duration). If this argument is not specified, Excel calculates with the number 2.

- *No_Switch* **(optional)** A logical value indicating whether there should be a switch to linear depreciation (because of larger depreciation amounts; see the explanations later in this section). If this argument is FALSE or not specified, the (possibly summed-up) depreciation amount is determined by changing to linear depreciation.

Background Depreciation is used to determine the loss of value of an asset and make that loss visible. It should not be confused with depreciation because of abrasion/use, which refers to the cost of purchasing an asset as part of operation expenses from a tax point of view.

The depreciation percentage used by the function VDB() is determined from the inverse of the depreciation duration multiplied by a factor. If this argument is not specified, Excel calculates with the number 2. The book value at the start of the depreciation period is multiplied by the depreciation percentage. The resulting amount reduces the book value at the end of the period.

The function can also check whether such a depreciation amount is less than the amount that would be created by switching to the linear depreciation (the original residual value), and if that is the case it switches to linear depreciation.

This form of the depreciation method (including the switch to linear depreciation) is permitted within the tax law of some countries. Sometimes there are certain requirements concerning the initial depreciation percentage. These requirements can be regulated by using the factor.

If a fractional part of the year in the first period must receive special consideration, the function VDB() usually cannot be used without additional manual calculations. Recording the depreciation plan by using the percentage calculation and arithmetic links of individual cells is therefore more likely to allow you to achieve the goal.

Example An asset with a purchase cost of $1,000.00 is to be depreciated in 10 years to a residual value of $100.00 by using the geometric-degressive method. You can calculate the depreciation amount in each period by using VDB() and subtract it from the book value of the previous period.

Alternatively, you can create a depreciation plan that implements the formulas for calculating the first depreciation amount as well as the processes for calculating the other amounts.

See Also DB(), DDB(), SLN(), SYD()

Sample Files

Use the VDB worksheet in the Depreciation Calculation.xls or Depreciation Calculation.xlsx sample file. The sample files are found in the Chapter15 folder. For more information about the sample files, see the section titled "Using the Sample Files" on page xxiii.

XIRR()

Syntax XIRR(*Values,Dates,Estimated_Value*)

Definition This function returns the internal interest rate for a series of not-necessarily periodic payments in the intra-annual scope.

Arguments

- ***Values* (required)** The (actual and/or expected) surpluses from disbursements and deposits, arranged without gaps in a column. Each value stands for a date. Negative surpluses have a minus sign.

- ***Dates* (required)** The dates for the surpluses. The order must correspond to the payments in the argument *Values*. The first date specifies the start of the evaluation. All others must be after this date (without necessarily being in a specific order). The error value #NUMBER! indicates that this requirement might not have been met.

- ***Estimated_Value* (optional)** For mathematical reasons a calculation of the internal interest rate for more than two periods can only be approximate, and therefore this approximation calculation can lead to different and sometimes nonsensical results (such as a negative interest rate). You can influence the calculation with the optional argument *Estimated_Value* as the basis for the approximation calculation.

Also note the following:

- Date specifications must not have a time; decimal places are truncated.

- Invalid date specifications return the #VALUE! error.

- XIRR() expects at least one positive and one negative payment. Otherwise the function returns the error #NUMBER!. The first payment itself does not need to be negative.

- If *Values* and *Dates* have a different number of values, XIRR() also returns the error #NUMBER!.

Background Even though the classical investment calculation calculates with annual periods, there are several tasks that need to be taken care of intra-annually. Among those is the evaluation of short-term financial transactions

The calculations are based on the cash value formula for payments, which for fractional annual periods doesn't calculate with a fractional interest rate but rather with a fractional duration. The basis is still an entire year, which is probably because of the fact that a daily interest rate (or even smaller periods) with zeros to the right of the decimal point cannot be imagined well enough during interpretation. The cash value (also called *capital value*) is calculated as follows:

$$Cash\ value = \sum_{k=1}^{Number\ of\ periods} \frac{Payment\ at\ Date_k}{(1 + Annual\ interest)^{(Date_k - Date_1)/365}}$$

The annual interest rate, which makes the cash value zero, is called the *internal interest rate* (yield or effective interest rate).

> ## Note
>
> The value for the calculation cannot be chosen at random. Negative yields suggest that more money has flowed in a direction from which it later does not return. The cause of this problem can be nonapplicable amounts or "false" dates. If an investor invests 100 monetary units and later receives three times 33, there must be a mistake. This is not the case, however, if he invests three times 33 and later receives 100. Number sequences with such effects can be created and nested as desired.
>
> There are only a few special cases in which the equation of the formula shown earlier in this section permits a solution. Therefore, Excel must work with a mathematical approximation. This moves you, step by step, toward a solution (if there is one), assuming that you are working from a good starting position. You can support this iteration by giving it an appropriate estimated value for the internal interest rate, but you cannot force a calculation of a solution.
>
> When you are evaluating financial investments in normal everyday situations, there should be few problems. Evaluating investments in material assets is not recommended in fractional years, because the surpluses are not certain.

Examples   The following examples show how to use the XIRR() function.

Consumer Credit   A dealer advertises a washing machine for $599.00 with a financing option (this is an installment loan or a consumer loan). He asks for a monthly payment of $52.48 for 12 months. How high is the effective interest rate?

To answer this question, enter 13 dates in one-month intervals into a column. Next to the first date, enter the cash price with a plus sign in front, and below this enter the monthly rates with minus signs.

Using XIRR() then returns 9.8 percent.

Chapter 15

Depending on regulations in some countries and regions, it might be that the effective interest rate is calculated by some other special methods.

Insurance Premium in Installments   Insurance companies offer their clients the option of paying their premiums in installments with a surcharge. Normally there is a surcharge of 3 percent for biannual, 5 percent for quarterly, and 8 percent for monthly payments.

At which effective interest rate does the client need to pay back the loan?

One option is to use the cash value formula shown earlier for evaluation.

By now there are also offers that use discounts rather than surcharges. Thus, agreements can be evaluated in the same fashion.

For quarterly payments of a $1,000.00 premium, there is the alternative of four payments of $262.50 each. The insured can initially take the "saved" money of $737.50 to the bank and withdraw $262.50 every three months. XIRR() tells you at which (annual) interest rate the bank would have to pay interest on the balance (interest payments every three months) so that the account will not be overdrawn at the end and the final rate will be available. The result is quite high: 14.2 percent. Therefore, the insured can think about whether he wants to pay the entire premium immediately by using an overdraft credit.

See Also IKV(), IRR(), RATE(), XNPV()

> ## Sample Files
> Use the XIRR worksheet in the Investment Calculation.xls or Investment Calculation.xlsx sample file. The sample files are found in the Chapter15 folder. For more information about the sample files, see the section titled "Using the Sample Files" on page xxiii.

XNPV()

Syntax   XNPV(*Rate,Values,Dates*)

Definition   This function returns the capital value for a series of not-necessarily periodic surpluses (as the difference between deposits and disbursements) in the intra-annual scope.

Arguments

- ***Rate* (required)** The annual interest rate for the calculation. This can be a balance interest rate, an interest rate on a current account, or a market interest rate—whatever best defines the initial situation.

- ***Values* (required)** The (actual and/or expected) surpluses from disbursements and deposits, arranged without gaps in a column. Each value stands for a date. Negative surpluses have a minus sign.

- ***Dates* (required)** The dates for the surpluses. The order must correspond to the payments in the *Values* argument. The first date specifies the start of the evaluation. All others must be after this date (without necessarily being in a specific order). The error value #NUMBER! indicates that this requirement might not have been met.

Also take note of the following:

- Date specifications must not have a time; decimal places are truncated.

- Invalid date specifications return the #VALUE! error.

- XNVP() expects at least one positive and one negative payment. Otherwise the function returns the error #NUMBER!. The first payment itself does not need to be negative.

- If *Values* and *Dates* have a different number of values, XNPV() also returns the error #NUMBER!.

Background   For more information about this function, see the background information for the function XIRR(). The cash value determined with the formula used in the background information is the capital value calculated by XNPV() with a given interest rate.

Example   A dealer offers his customers the option of paying invoices later or receiving a discount for immediate payment. Therefore, paying later represents a form of money lending. Let's assume that there are three invoices with the data from Table 15-8.

Table 15-8 Fictitious Invoice Amounts with Discount Terms

Date	Amount	Discount	Payment Target
1/2/2010	$700.00	0.5%	14 days
4/3/2010	$300.00	1%	4 weeks
7/7/2010	$250.00	2%	2 months

Chapter 15

Does granting this kind of a loan make sense from a finance mathematical point of view, when there are forms of investment that have a yield of 10 percent per year?

The function XNPV() is used for the finance mathematical solution, as shown in Figure 15-8 (but issues regarding customer relations, liquidity, or solvency are not taken into consideration).

	C12		f_x =XNPV(C2,F5:F10,B5:B10)			
	A	B	C	D	E	F
1						
2		Discount rate	10.00%			
3						
4		Day	Amount	Discount	Period (Days)	Cash flow
5		01/02/2010	$ 700.00	0.50%	14	$ (696.50)
6		01/16/2010				$ 700.00
7		04/03/2010	$ 300.00	1.00%	28	$ (297.00)
8		05/01/2010				$ 300.00
9		07/07/2010	$ 250.00	2.00%	60	$ (245.00)
10		09/05/2010				$ 250.00
11						
12		XNPV	$ 2.80			
13						
14		Yield	13.58%			

Figure 15-8 Granting loans with discounts.

Let's assume that the customer does not take advantage of the discount option. Then it is as if the dealer took the money to a fictitious bank upon delivery and then withdrew it when the payment was received. The bank's evaluation according to the cash value principle used here shows a positive capital value. Therefore, the dealer receives more than 10 percent interest per year.

Using XIRR() returns an effective interest of 13.58 percent annually. You also get the same impression by doing a rough calculation in your head, extrapolating the discount rates (which are basically anticipative interest rates): 1 percent for one month is 12 percent for the whole year.

See Also NPV(), PV(), XIRR()

Sample Files

Use the XNPV worksheet in the Investment Calculation.xls or Investment Calculation.xlsx sample file. The sample files are found in the Chapter15 folder. For more information about the sample files, see the section titled "Using the Sample Files" on page xxiii.

YIELD()

Syntax   YIELD(*Settlement,Maturity,Rate,Price,Repayment,Frequency,Basis*)

Definition   This function determines the yield of a fixed-interest security (loan).

Arguments

- **Settlement (required)** The date when the ownership of the security changes.

- **Maturity (required)** The date when the repayment of the loan certified by the security takes place.

- **Rate (required)** The agreed-upon annual interest rate as the price for the borrowed money.

- **Price (required)** The price of the security at the day of settlement (without accrued interest).

- **Repayment (required)** The percentage of the par value of a security (as if it was 100 monetary units) at which repayment takes place on the day of maturity.

- **Frequency (required)** Because it is quite common to have fixed-interest securities with several interest dates per year, the required argument *Frequency* supplies the dates-per-year number. Allowed values are: 1 = annual; 2 = biannual; 4 = quarterly.

- **Basis (optional)** The method you want to use for determining the days in the year according to Table 15-2, shown earlier. If this argument is not used, Excel calculates with *Basis* = 0.

The arguments of YIELD() have the following requirements:

- Date specifications must not have a time; decimal places are truncated. The arguments *Frequency* and *Basis* are also truncated to integers.

- If date arguments cannot be resolved to a valid date, the YIELD() function returns the #VALUE! error.

- *Rate* requires nonnegative numbers. *Repayment* requires positive numbers. Otherwise, YIELD() returns the #NUMBER! error.

- If *Frequency* cannot be resolved to 1, 2, or 4, or *Basis* cannot be resolved to a number from 0 through 4, YIELD() returns the #NUMBER! error. The same happens when the settlement date is later than the maturity.

> **Important**
>
> Excel Help contains the following note:
>
> "Dates should be entered with the DATE() function or as results of other formulas or functions. Problems might occur if dates are entered as text."

Background To implement the finance mathematical benefit principle

Payment of the creditor = Payment of the debtor

for the start of the transaction, the price of a fixed-interest security (loan) plus potential accrued interest equals the cash value of the debtor's future payments certified in this security. The price is the percentage of the security's par value, as if the par value was 100 monetary units.

Because the price is usually determined by market supply and demand, the benefit principle helps you calculate the yield that is used to determine the price with a cash value calculation that corresponds to the market price. This internal interest payment is called *yield*. There is no general resolution formula for this. You need to use a mathematical approximation. With a detailed calculation schema, as shown in the examples later in this section, Excel provides the target value search for solving the equation.

The cash value calculation is no problem, if the purchase date (change of ownership) of a security with an annual interest payment is the same as the day of the interest payment. In this case, only the whole year needs to be taken into consideration. A situation in which the change of ownership takes place between interest due dates, or in which interest payments take place several times a year, is not so easy. In finance mathematics there are several ways to deal with a year that is broken up into parts. The best known methods are Moosmüller and Braess/Fangmeyer, as well as ISMA.

The ISMA method returns the same as YIELD() for a one-time interest payment per year, and YIELD() can easily be recreated for biannual and quarterly interest payments.

In Excel terminology and for the functions derived from it, the benefit principle of creating cash values (discounting future payments) for price calculation by Excel works as shown on the next page.

$$PRICE = \cfrac{Repayment}{\left(1 + \cfrac{Yield}{Frequency}\right)^{COUPNUM-1+\frac{COUPDAYSNC}{Days\ of\ the\ interest\ period}}}$$

$$+ \sum_{K=1}^{COUPNUM} \cfrac{\cfrac{RATE}{Frequency} \cdot 100}{\left(1 + \cfrac{Yield}{Frequency}\right)^{K-1+\frac{COUPDAYSNC}{Days\ of\ the\ interest\ period}}} -$$

$$-\cfrac{RATE}{Frequency} \cdot 100 \cdot \cfrac{COUPDAYBS}{Days\ of\ the\ interest\ period}$$

COUPNUM is the number of interest payments after the purchase, COUPDAYSNC is the number of days until the next interest payment date, and COUPDAYBS is the number of days since the last interest payment date.

If Frequency = 1, this formula also represents the ISMA method. If Frequency equals 2 or 4, Excel calculates with an even distribution of the yield over the periods within the year. The ISMA method, however, uses a period apportionment following the correlation between nominal and effective interest, which you can find in the function descriptions for EFFECT() or NOMINAL():

$$1 + Effective\ interest\ rate = \left(1 + \frac{Nominal\ interest\ rate}{Number\ of\ periods}\right)^{Number\ of\ periods}$$

In case of several interest payments per year, you can therefore calculate the yield by using the ISMA method with YIELD(). Afterwards, you need to convert the "effective" Excel yield by using the function EFFECT().

CAUTION

The explanations here apply only when more than a single interest period is left before maturity. Otherwise, Excel does not calculate according to the formula for the price shown earlier in this section, but uses a fractional yield (simple yield) instead of the fractional duration. YIELD() then returns the same result as YIELDMAT().

Examples   The following examples explain the YIELD() function.

Annual Interest Payment (Coupon)   A 4.500 percent federal loan issued in 2003 had a price of 109.010 on August 31, 2010. It matures on January 4, 2013. Which yield did you find in the corresponding notifications or daily papers?

If you want to determine the ISMA yield with the Exact/Exact day counter method without using the function YIELD() (that is, you want to learn what exactly YIELD() is implementing), you can prepare a worksheet as shown in Figure 15-9.

	B	C
2	**Annual coupon**	
4	**ISMA=Excel**	
6	Settlement date	08/31/2010
7	Settlement price	109.01
8	Redemption	100.00
9	Maturity date	01/04/2013
10	Coupon	4.500%
11	Counting days basis	1
12	Frequency	1
14	Next coupon date	01/04/2011
15	Days remaining	126
16	Accrued interest days	239
17	Days in year	365
18	Accrued interest	2.95
19	No. of coupon payments per year	3
20	Present value of interest at next payment date	13.42
21	Present value of repayment at next payment date	98.78
23	Settlement price	111.96
24	Present value of future payments	111.96
25	Difference	0.0000
27	**Yield p.a.**	**0.6171%**

Figure 15-9 Preparing price and yield calculations.

Enter the known data into the first seven cells from C6 to C10. In preparation, enter the day counter mode by typing 1 (this corresponds to *Basis* = 1 in all of the integrated functions that will be used) and the frequency of the interest payments.

Then use =COUPNCD(C6,C9,C12,C11) to determine the next coupon payment date: April 1, 2011. The formula =COUPDAYSNC(C6,C9,C12,C11) helps you count the days up to this interest date: 126. To calculate the accrued interest, you need the days since the last interest payment date (=COUPDAYBS(C6,C9,C12,C11) counts 239 here) so that you can use =C10*C16/C17*C8 to determine an amount of $2.95. The number of the remaining interest dates, which you need in order to discount the future payments, is determined with =COUPNUM(C6,C9,C12,C11) and returns 3.

Now let's look at discounting. The PV()function helps you here. You can use the formula =PV(C27,C19-1,- C10*C8,-C10*C8,1) as a yield calculation to determine the cash value of future interest payments (the result is 13.42) and as a compound interest calculation for discounting the repayment amount with =PV(C27,C19-1,0,-C8) to get 98.78. For discounting, you first use the assumed yield (4.5 percent) in C27, which can cause different number sequences in both cash values.

You now need to follow the ISMA procedure to determine the sum of the two cash values over the fractional duration of 126 of 365 days with a fractional exponent in the interest formula: =PV(C27,C15/C17,0,-C21-C20) returns 102.92.

Now you compare the sum of the price and the accrued interest (C23) with the sum of the calculated cash values (C24) by creating the difference in C25. On this cell, you run the target value search with a target value of 0 and the modifiable cell C27 (where your yield assumed thus far is located). The result is the same as can be determined with =YIELD(C6,C9,C10,C7,C8,C12,C11): 0.617%.

Biannual Interest Payment (Coupon)   There are only a few loans that have more than one interest payment date per year. In the sample files for this function, the loan of the previous example was therefore given a fictitious biannual interest payment, so the calculations could be performed. The Excel price has a different number of decimal places than the ISMA price. If you want to determine the ISMA yield, you need to evaluate the number calculated with YIELD() (it is twice the correct ISMA biannual yield) with EFFECT(YIELD(),*Frequency*) according to the periods.

See Also DURATION(), MDURATION(), PRICE(), RATE()

> ## Sample Files
>
> Use the YIELD worksheet in the Price Calculation.xls or Price Calculation.xlsx sample file. The sample files are found in the Chapter15 folder. For more information about the sample files, see the section titled "Using the Sample Files" on page xxiii.

YIELDDISC()

Syntax   YIELDDISC(*Settlement,Maturity,Price,Repayment,Basis*)

Definition   This function calculates the annual yield (as an interest rate in arrears) for a security that has received a markdown (discount, disagio) for an intra-annual duration.

The only difference between this function and the RECEIVED() function is the naming of the arguments.

Arguments

- ***Settlement* (required)** The date when the ownership of the security changes.

- ***Maturity* (required)** The day when the payments from the security must take place.

- ***Price* (optional)** The purchase value of the security at the day of settlement.

- ***Repayment* (required)** The payment at the day of maturity.

- ***Basis* (optional)** The method you want to use for determining the days in the year according to Table 15-2, shown earlier. If this argument is omitted, Excel calculates with *Basis* = 0.

All function arguments that take a date use the date without time; 0 fractions are rounded. The argument *Basis* also requires an integer, and decimal places are truncated.

Take note of the following:

- If invalid dates are used or no numbers are entered where required, the function returns the error #VALUE!.

- *Price* and *Repayment* require positive numbers. Otherwise, YIELDDISC() returns the #NUMBER! error.

- If *Frequency* cannot be resolved to 1, 2, or 4, or *Basis* cannot be resolved to a number from 0 through 4, YIELDDISC() returns the #NUMBER! error. The same happens when the settlement date is later than the maturity.

Important

Excel Help contains the following note:

"Dates should be entered with the DATE() function or as results of other formulas or functions. Problems might occur if dates are entered as text."

The notes concerning the par value of 100 are wrong.

Background   In principle, this function belongs to the group of anticipative yield. The principle is based on the assumption that a seed capital amount (deposit amount, loan) results from the repayment amount minus the interest on this amount. This principle is mainly used in the intra-annual scope and differs from the principle based on a savings account or mortgage loan. In this case, interest is calculated at the end of a period based on the seed capital (interest yield in arrears).

So that you can compare securities with interest payment in arrears, the difference between repayment and price must be put into relation to the price. The result corresponds to the relative increase until maturity—an interest rate in arrears—which, as is done frequently in similar situations, receives the name *Yield*. The calculation is done without compound interest. The interest rate must be extrapolated to one year (with corresponding day counting).

Examples   The following examples explain the YIELDDISC() function.

Bill of Exchange Calculation   Bills of exchange have a long tradition in money lending and are a type of supplier loan. Anticipative interest payment is used. If a business owner wants to compare taking up a supplier loan with a bill of exchange against the effective yield of an advance on a current account, he must perform an equivalent conversion of the anticipative interest rate. To do so, he can use YIELDDISC (or RECEIVED()).

On May 10, 2010, a business owner presented his bank with a bill of exchange in the amount of $5,000 with a (residual) maturity of two months. The bank specifies a discount rate of 5 percent p.a. and does not charge fees. He receives a credit of $4,958.33 ($5,000.00 minus 5 percent of the total). How high is the price as interest rate in arrears, with which the bank has him pay the immediate credit?

With

```
=YIELDDISC("10/5/2010","10/7/2010",4958.33,5000,4)
```

you can calculate 5.04 percent as annual interest rate.

Of course, usually the concrete numbers would be located in cells and the formula would use cell references.

Treasury Bonds   On August 30, 2010, Germany offered treasury bonds (security ID 111 704) with the following conditions: Duration 1 year, disbursement €500 (results from the minimum purchase price); maturity on August 22, 2011; sale interest 0.46 percent (this is the name for the percent anticipative discount). What is the effective yield with a purchase price of €497.75?

To answer this question, you just need to create a ratio between the "profit" and the invested capital and make sure that the duration is 360 of 360 days. The formula makes this easier (you can use cell references instead of concrete numbers). The described process will also work in the future. The number of days you need to use then depends on the specifications of the Federal Bank and the actual purchase date:

```
=YIELDDISC("30/8/2010","22/8/2011",497.75,500,4)
```

which return 0.462 percent. You can also get the same number for the yield from the German Federal Bank.

See Also DISC(), INTRATE(), PRICEDISC(), RECEIVED()

> ## Sample Files
> Use the Bill of Exchange and Treasury Bonds worksheets in the Simple Interest Calculation.xls or Simple Interest Calculation.xlsx sample file. The sample files are found in the Chapter15 folder. For more information about the sample files, see the section titled "Using the Sample Files" on page xxiii.

YIELDMAT()

Syntax YIELDMAT(*Settlement,Maturity,Issue,Rate,Price,Basis*)

Definition This function calculates the annual yield of a fixed-interest security in the intra-annual area (without compound interest).

Arguments

- *Settlement* **(required)** The date when the ownership of the security changes.

- *Maturity* **(required)** The maturity date of the security.

- *Issue* **(required)** The date of the emission of the security.

- *Rate* **(required)** The agreed-upon nominal interest rate of the security based on one year.

- *Price* **(required)** The percentage of the par value of a security (as if it was 100 monetary units).

- *Basis* **(optional)** The method you want to use for determining the days in the year according to Table 15-2, shown earlier. If this argument is omitted, Excel calculates with *Basis* = 0.

The arguments of the function have the following requirements:

- *Settlement*, *Maturity*, and *Issue* require a date specification without a time; decimal places are truncated. Any decimal places of *Basis* are also truncated to make the number an integer.

- If *Settlement*, *Maturity*, or *Issue* does not have a valid date, YIELDMAT() returns the #VALUE! error. The settlement date must be earlier than the maturity date.

- If *Rate* or *Price* is less than zero, YIELDMAT() returns the error #NUMBER!.

- If *Basis* cannot be resolved to a number from 0 through 4, YIELDMAT() returns the #NUMBER! error.

> **Important**
>
> **Excel Help contains the following note:**
>
> **"Dates should be entered with the DATE() function or as results of other formulas or functions. Problems might occur if dates are entered as text."**

Background   To implement the finance mathematical benefit principle

Payment of the creditor = Payment of the debtor

for the start of the transaction, the price of a fixed-interest security plus potential accrued interest equals the cash value of the debtor's future payments certified in this security. The price is the percentage of the security's par value, as if the par value was 100 monetary units. In this case, the future payment is the repayment plus the nominal interest. There is no compound interest, because evaluations take place only for the intra-annual timeframe. A divided interest rate according to the duration is used for the discount calculation instead of a divided duration in the exponent (ISMA method).

To calculate the defined yield, the difference between the future payments of the debtor and the current payment of the creditor (purchaser of the security) must be put into a relation to this current payment:

$$\frac{(Repayment + Interest) - (Price + Accrued\ interest)}{Price + Accrued\ interest}$$

The interest is calculated from the annual nominal interest rate in relation to the difference between the maturity date and the emission date. The accrued interest is calculated in the same way, only here the time between the purchase date and the emission date is important. The determined ratio becomes the yield when it is extrapolated to the entire year.

Example   A federal bond issued in the year 2000 has received a coupon of 5.250 percent. The maturity date was specified as January 4, 2011. On August 31, 2010, the price was 101.670. How high was the yield at that time? Using the known data with YIELDMAT() returns 0.32 percent. You also get the same result by using the function YIELD().

See Also PRICEMAT()

Sample Files

Use the YIELDMAT worksheet in the Simple Interest Calculation.xls or Simple Interest Calculation.xlsx sample file. The sample files are found in the Chapter15 folder. For more information about the sample files, see the section titled "Using the Sample Files" on page xxiii.

Mathematical and Trigonometry Functions

T he Microsoft Excel functions for standard mathematical and trigonometry calculations (see Table 16-1) can be divided into the following groups:

- Functions for general mathematical calculations

- Functions for trigonometry calculations

- Functions that cannot be assigned to mathematical or trigonometric calculations

Functions for Mathematical Calculations

This is the largest category of the functions described in this chapter. This category is
divided into the following subcategories:

- **Standard arithmetic operations** Besides addition, subtraction, multiplication,
  and division functions, this chapter also explains the functions for exponentiation,
  root extractions, and logarithmic calculus. The arithmetic operations covered in this
  chapter provide the basis for algebraic calculations.

- **Rounding** The usual mathematical principle is for all values less than five to be
  rounded down and all values greater than or equal to five to be rounded up.
  However, there are several reasons to deviate from this principle. For example, you
  might want to round prices to a multiple of five to get consistent amounts or to
  standardize the values within a range.

- **Arrays** An array consists of numbers in rows and columns, which are also called
  vectors. Arrays are the basis for linear algebraic calculations. Linear algebra calculates equations with multiple variables based on arrays.

Functions for Trigonometry Calculations

Trigonometry is a subarea of geometry that covers triangles. The angles and the length
of sides are important for calculation of right-angled triangle. The longest side of a right
triangle is across from the right angle and is called a *hypotenuse*. The other two (shorter)
sides are the *legs* of the right triangle. The side that is referred to as the *adjacent leg* is
adjacent to the calculated angle, and the *opposite leg* is opposite from the calculated
angle. You can use the angle functions to calculate the legs and hypotenuse of a right
triangle based on the angles. With the arc functions, you can calculate the angles based
on the legs and hypotenuse. The angle functions are explained by using a full circle (360
degrees) that allows for all angle possibilities.

Other Functions

This category includes the ROMAN() function, which converts number values into Roman numerals. (It is not possible to calculate with this function because the result is text.) This function was categorized as a math function by Microsoft even though the authors think it belongs with the text and data functions (see Chapter 8, "Text and Data Functions").

> **Note**
>
> Some mathematical and trigonometry functions are not readily available in the standard installation of Microsoft Office Excel 2003 and earlier versions. To use these functions, you have to activate them in the Add-Ins dialog box (Tools/Add-Ins). You'll find more information in the "Analysis Functions" section in Chapter 2, "Using Functions and PowerPivot."

Table 16-1 Mathematical and Trigonometry Functions

Function	Description
ABS()	Returns the absolute value of a number
ACOS()	Calculates the angle whose cosine is a number
ACOSH()	Returns the inverse hyperbolic cosine of a number
AGGREGATE()	Returns an aggregate in a list or array
ASIN()	Returns the arc sine of a number
ASINH()	Calculates the inverse hyperbolic sine of a number
ATAN()	Returns the arctangent or inverse tangent of a number
ATAN2()	Returns the arctangent or inverse tangent based on an x-coordinate or a y-coordinate
ATANH()	Calculates the inverse hyperbolic tangent of a number
CEILING()	Rounds a number up to the smallest multiple of another value
CEILING.PRECISE()	Rounds a number up regardless of the sign
COMBIN()	Calculates the number of combinations for a given number of items
COS()	Returns the cosine of a number
COSH()	Calculates the hyperbolic cosine of a number
DEGREES()	Converts a radian measure into degrees
EVEN()	Rounds a number to the next even integer
EXP()	Raises a number to a given power
FACT()	Returns the factorial of a number
FACTDOUBLE()	Returns the factorial of a number
FLOOR()	Rounds a number to the multiple of another value

Function	Description
FLOOR.PRECISE()	Rounds a number regardless of the sign
GCD()	Calculates the greatest common divisor
INT()	Rounds a number to the next smaller integer
LCM()	Calculates the least common multiple
LN()	Returns the natural logarithm of a number
LOG()	Calculates the logarithm of a number
LOG10()	Calculates the base-10 logarithm of a number
MDETERM()	Calculates the determinant of an array
MINVERSE()	Returns the inverse array of an array
MMULT()	Calculates the product of two arrays
MOD()	Returns the remainder of a division
MROUND()	Returns a number rounded to a multiple
MULTINOMIAL()	Returns the polynomial coefficient of a number group
ODD()	Rounds a number to the next odd integer
PI()	Returns the pi constant
POWER()	Raises a number to a higher power
PRODUCT()	Multiplies values
QUOTIENT()	Returns the integer part of a division
RADIANS()	Converts degrees into radian measures
RAND()	Returns a random number between 0 and 1 with up to 16 decimal places
RANDBETWEEN()	Returns a random number from a range
ROMAN()	Converts an Arabic number into a Roman numeral
ROUND()	Rounds a number to a certain number of decimal places
ROUNDDOWN()	Rounds a number down
ROUNDUP()	Rounds a number up
SERIESSUM()	Returns the sum of powers (to calculate power series and dichotomous probabilities)
SIGN()	Returns the algebraic sign of a number
SIN()	Calculates the sine of a number
SINH()	Returns the hyperbolic sine of a number
SQRT()	Calculates the square root of a number
SQRTPI()	Calculates the root from a number multiplied by pi
SUBTOTAL()	Calculates a partial result in a list or database
SUM()	Adds the values in the arguments

Function	Description
SUMIF()	Adds the numbers matching a search criterion
SUMIFS()	Adds the numbers matching several search criteria
SUMPRODUCT()	Multiplies the numbers in an array and returns the sum of these products
SUMSQ()	Adds squared arguments
SUMX2MY2()	Adds the differences between the squares of two corresponding arrays
SUMX2PY2()	Adds the sum of the squares of two corresponding arrays
SUMXMY2()	Adds the squares of the differences of two corresponding arrays
TAN()	Calculates the tangent of a number
TANH()	Returns the hyperbolic tangent of a number
TRUNC()	Truncates a number to the specified decimal places

ABS()

Syntax   ABS(*number*)

Definition   This function returns the absolute value of a number. The absolute value of a number is the number without its sign.

Argument

- *number* **(required)** The real number for which you want the absolute value

Background   Consider the following scenario: The integers 3 and –3 are located respectively on the right and left sides of 0 on a number line. However, both integers have the same distance to 0. Thus, both numbers have the same absolute value (see Figure 16-1).

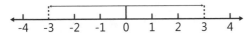

Figure 16-1 Both integers are the same distance from 0.

Absolute values are enclosed in two vertical bars:

$|a| = |-a|$

Example   Absolute values are used in numerous math formulas, for example, in the definition of the artanh. In the following formula, the value *x* is defined as an absolute value:

$$y = \operatorname{artanh} x = \frac{1}{2}\ln\frac{1+x}{1-x} \ with \ |x| < 1$$

More examples for this function are:

- `=ABS(-18)` returns the absolute value 18.

- `=ABS(-3.47)` returns the absolute value 3.47.

- `=ABS(5)` returns the absolute value 5.

See also IMABS(), SIGN(), engineering functions

> **Sample Files**
>
> Use the ROUND worksheet in the Chapter16.xls or Chapter16.xlsx sample file. The sample files are found in the Chapter16 folder. For more information about the sample files, see the section titled "Using the Sample Files" on page xxiii.

ACOS()

Syntax   ACOS(*number*)

Definition   The arccosine is the angle whose cosine is *number*.

Arguments

- ***number* (required)** The cosine of the angle; must be between –1 and 1

Background   Use the ACOS() function to calculate the adjacent angle based on the cosine (see Figure 16-2). The result is a radian measure and has to be converted into degrees with the DEGREES() function. Because each angle occurs two times in a full circle, the value range for an arccosine is restricted:

- If the angle is calculated as a radian measure, the value range spans 0 to π (pi).

- If the angle is calculated in degrees, the value range spans 0 to 180 degrees.

The arccosine is strictly monotonic decreasing. The values of the arccosine in a coordinate plane create the graph shown in Figure 16-2.

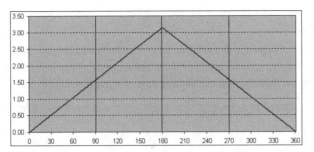

Figure 16-2 The ACOS() function.

Examples   The following examples illustrate the ACOS() function.

Example 1   A 30-foot ladder leans against a house. The distance between the bottom of the ladder and the wall is 7 feet. What is the angle of incline?

First, you calculate the cosine from the adjacent leg (the distance to the wall) and the hypotenuse (length of the ladder).

$$\cos \alpha = \frac{7}{30} = 0.22$$

The angle is calculated from the cosine:

`=DEGREES(ACOS(7/30))`

The angle of incline is 76.51° or 76° and 51 minutes. Because the ACOS() function returns a radian measure, you have to convert the result into degrees.

Example 2   The angle resulting from the cosine 0.707106781 could be 45° as well as 315°. Because the range is limited to 0° to 180°, the result is 45°. The corresponding formula looks like this:

`=DEGREES(ACOS(0.707106781))`

Because the result is a radian measure, you have to convert it by using the DEGREES() function. Here are a few more examples:

- `=ACOS(0)` returns the radian measure `1.570796327` and a 90° angle.

- `=ACOS(-0.5)` returns the radian measure `2.094395102` and a 120° angle.

- `=ACOS(-1)` returns the radian measure `3.141592654` and a 180° angle.

See also COS(), PI()

Chapter 16

> **Sample Files**
>
> Use the SIN_COS worksheet in the Chapter16.xls or Chapter16.xlsx sample file. The sample files are found in the Chapter16 folder. For more information about the sample files, see the section titled "Using the Sample Files" on page xxiii.

ACOSH()

Syntax   ACOSH(*number*)

Definition   This function returns the inverse hyperbolic cosine of a number (see Figure 16-3). The definition range spans $x = +1$ to $+ \infty$.

Argument

- *number* **(required)** A real number equal to or greater than 1.

Background   The inverse hyperbolic functions are also called the *area hyperbolic functions*. They are the inverse functions of the hyperbolic functions. The hyperbolic functions sinh, tanh, and coth are strictly monotonic and have one inverse function. The cosh function, however, has two monotonic intervals symmetrical to the positive segment of the ordinate and two inverse functions:

$y = arcosh\ x$

and

$y = -arcosh\ x$

where:

$$arcosh\ x = \ln\left(x + \sqrt{x^2 - 1}\right)\ \ with\ \ x \in [1, \infty)$$

The graph (see Figure 16-3) starts at point 1.0 and is monotone increasing or decreasing.

> **Note**
>
> Inverse hyperbolic functions have the prefix *ar* in the same way that the inverse trigonometric functions have the prefix *arc*. The notations $sinh^{-1}$, $cosh^{-1}$, or $tanh^{-1}$ are also used.

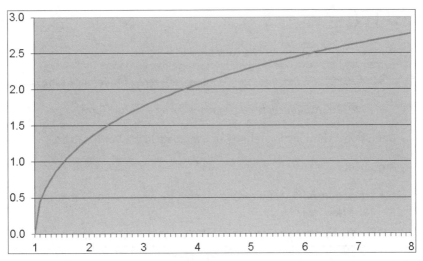

Figure 16-3 The graph of the arcosh shows the monotonic increasing segment in the first quadrant. The monotonic decreasing segment is located inversely under the abscissa.

Example   Two parallel wires with the diameter *d*, length *l*, and distance *a* have the capacitance C.

$$C = \frac{\pi \cdot \varepsilon \cdot l}{arcosh \; \dfrac{a}{d}}$$

$\varepsilon = \varepsilon_0 \, \varepsilon_r$ is the permittivity of the medium.

More examples of this function are:

- =ACOSH(1) returns 0.

- =ACOSH(2) returns 1.3169579.

- =ACOSH(8) returns 2.76865938.

See also ASINH(), ATANH(), COSH(), SINH(), TANH()

Sample Files

Use the Data&Chart and Example worksheets in the ACosH.xls or ACosH.xlsx sample file. The sample files are found in the Chapter16 folder. For more information about the sample files, see the section titled "Using the Sample Files" on page xxiii.

Chapter 16

AGGREGATE()

Syntax This function has two forms:

- AGGREGATE(*function_num, options, ref1, ref2,...*) (reference form)

- AGGREGATE(*function_num, options, array, k*) (array form)

Definition This function returns an aggregate in a list or database.

Arguments

- *function_num* **(required)** A number between 1 and 19 that specifies the function to use (see Table 16-2).

  Table 16-2 **Possible Values for the *function_num* Argument**

function_num	Function
1	AVERAGE()
2	COUNT()
3	COUNTA()
4	MAX()
5	MIN()
6	PRODUCT()
7	STDEV.S()
8	STDEV.P()
9	SUM()
10	VAR.S()
11	VAR.P()
12	MEDIAN()
13	MODE.SNGL()
14	LARGE()
15	SMALL()
16	PERCENTILE.INC()
17	QUARTILE.INC()
18	PERCENTILE.EXC()
19	QUARTILE.EXC()

- *options* **(required)** A numerical value that determines which values to ignore in the evaluation range (see Table 16-3).

Table 16-3 **Possible Values for the *option* Argument**

option	Behavior
0 or omitted	Ignores nested SUBTOTAL() and AGGREGATE() functions
1	Ignores hidden rows and nested SUBTOTAL() and AGGREGATE() functions
2	Ignores error values and nested SUBTOTAL() and AGGREGATE() functions
3	Ignores hidden rows, error values, and nested SUBTOTAL() and AGGREGATE() functions
4	Ignores nothing
5	Ignores hidden rows
6	Ignores error values
7	Ignores hidden rows and error values

- ***ref1* (reference form, required)** The first numeric argument for functions that use multiple numeric arguments for which you want the aggregate value.

- ***ref2* (reference form, optional)** At least two and up to 253 arguments for which you want the aggregate value.

  For functions that take an array, *ref1* is an array, an array formula, or a reference to a range of cells for which you want the aggregate value. *ref2* (*k*) is a second argument that is required for certain functions. The following functions require a *ref2* argument:

  - ○ LARGE(*array,k*)

  - ○ SMALL(*array,k*)

  - ○ PERCENTILE.INC(*array,k*)

  - ○ QUARTILE.INC(*array,quart*)

  - ○ PERCENTILE.EXC(*array,k*)

  - ○ QUARTILE.EXC(*array,quart*)

Chapter 16

> **Note**
>
> If a second *ref* argument is required but not specified, the AGGREGATE() function returns the #VALUE! error. If one or more of the references is a 3-D reference, then AGGREGATE() returns the #VALUE! error.
>
> If the references include additional AGGREGATE() functions, the nested functions could be ignored, so they are not considered multiple. The same applies if the references contain subtotals.

> Remember: The AGGREGATE() function is intended for data columns or vertical ranges, not for rows or horizontal ranges. Hiding a column doesn't affect the result. However, if you hide a row, the result is different.

Background The AGGREGATE() function is very powerful. This function was added to Excel 2010 to remove some restrictions the other functions have. Most functions return an error if the calculated references are incorrect. In such cases in the previous Excel versions, you had to run a complex IFERROR() query. With the AGGREGATE() function you can also control the behavior of hidden cells.

The AGGREGATE() function allows you to calculate formulas for value ranges with subtotals without including the subtotals in the result. See Figure 16-4 for an example of when this function could be useful.

1 2 3		A	B	C
	1		Category	Value
	2		A	21
	3		A	43
	4		A	57
	5		A	#DIV/0!
	6		A Result	#DIV/0!
	7		B	32
	8		B	12
	9		B	50
	10		B	5
	11		B	43
	12		B	59
	13		B Result	201
	14		Total Result	#DIV/0!

Figure 16-4 The SUBTOTAL() function cannot ignore the errors.

In the figure, the SUM() and SUBTOTAL() functions cannot add the values in column C. However, the formula

=AGGREGATE(9,3,C18:C29)

returns a useful result despite the error and the subtotals. You can also ignore hidden cells so that you only add the values in the visible range. With only one click, you can include entire ranges in the result or hide them.

Example This function is used for numerous purposes, such as a series of measurements for which the total is calculated regardless of errors or subtotals.

See also SUBTOTAL()

> **Sample Files**
>
> Use the AGGREGATE.xlsx. The sample files are found in the Chapter16 folder. For more information about the sample files, see the section titled "Using the Sample Files" on page xxiii.

ASIN()

Syntax   ASIN(*number*)

Definition   Use the ASIN() function to calculate the adjacent angle based on the sine (see Figure 16-5).

Argument

- *number* **(required)** The sine of the angle; must be between –1 and 1

Background   This function calculates the angle from a sine value. The result is a radian measure and has to be converted into degrees with the DEGREES() function or by multiplying the result by 180/PI().

Because each angle occurs two times in a full circle, the value range for the arcsine is restricted.

- If the angle is calculated as a radian measure, the value range spans $-\pi/2$ to $\pi/2$.

- If the angle is calculated in degrees, the value range spans –90° to 90°.

The values of the arcsine in a coordinate plane look like this:

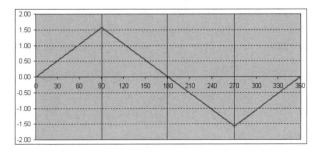

Figure 16-5 The ASIN() function.

Example The ASIN() function is used to calculate the angles of a right triangle based on the opposite leg and the hypotenuse.

$$\theta = arcsin\left(\frac{opposite\ leg}{hypotenuse}\right)$$

More examples for this function are:

- =ASIN(1) returns the radian measure 1.570796327 and a 90° angle.

- =ASIN(0.5) returns the radian measure 0.523598776 and a 150° angle.

- =ASIN(-0.5) returns the radian measure -0.523598776 and a 210° angle.

See also ASINH(), PI(), SIN()

> ## Sample Files
>
> Use the SIN_COS worksheet in the Chapter16.xls or Chapter16.xlsx sample file. The sample files are found in the Chapter16 folder. For more information about the sample files, see the section titled "Using the Sample Files" on page xxiii.

ASINH()

Syntax ASINH(*number*)

Definition This function returns the inverse hyperbolic sine of a number (see Figure 16-6).

Argument

- ***number* (required)** Any real number

Background The inverse hyperbolic functions are the inverse functions of the hyperbolic functions. The formula for the inverse hyperbolic sine (sinh⁻¹) is:

$$y = \operatorname{arsinh} x = \ln\left(x + \sqrt{x^2 + 1}\right)\ with\ \ x \in \Re$$

> ## Note
>
> Inverse hyperbolic functions have the prefix *ar* in the same way that the inverse trigonometric functions have the prefix *arc*.

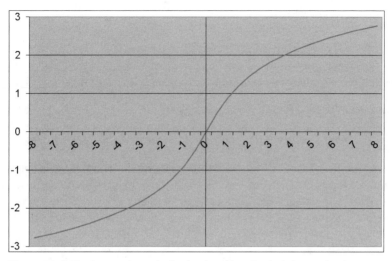

Figure 16-6 The inverse hyperbolic sine is odd and strictly increasing between −∞ and +∞.

More examples of this function are:

- `=ASINH(0)` returns 0.

- `=ASINH(1)` returns 0.88137359.

- `=ASINH(-1)` returns -0.88137359.

- `=ASINH(10)` returns 2.99822295.

- `=ASINH(-10)` returns -2.99822295.

See also ACOSH(), ATANH(), COSH(), SINH(), TANH()

Sample Files

Use the Data&Chart worksheet in the ASinH.xls or ASinH.xlsx sample file. The sample files are found in the Chapter16 folder. For more information about the sample files, see the section titled "Using the Sample Files" on page xxiii.

Chapter 16

ATAN()

Syntax ATAN(*number*)

Definition This function returns the arctangent or inverse tangent of a number.

Argument

- **number (required)** The tangent of the angle you want to calculate

Background Use the ATAN() function to calculate the adjacent angle based on the tangent (see Figure 16-7). In other words, the arctangent is the angle whose tangent is *number*. The result is a radian measure between −π/2 and π/2 and has to be converted into degrees with the DEGREES() function or by multiplying the result with 180/PI().

Because each angle occurs two times in a full circle, the value range for an arctangent is restricted.

- If the angle is calculated as a radian measure, the value range spans −π/2 to π/2.

- If the angle is calculated in degrees, the value range spans −90° to 90°.

The values of the arctangent in a coordinate plane look like those shown in Figure 16-7.

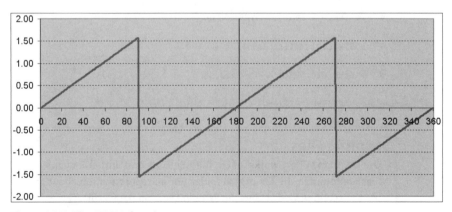

Figure 16-7 The ATAN() function.

Examples The ATAN() function is used to calculate the angles of a right triangle based on the opposite leg and the adjacent leg.

$$\theta = artan\left(\frac{opposite\ leg}{adjacent\ leg}\right)$$

In one example, the angle resulting from tangent 1 could be 45° as well as 225°. Because the range is limited to –90° to 90°, the result is 45°. The corresponding formula looks like this:

```
=DEGREES(ATAN(1))
```

Because the result is a radian measure, you have to convert it by using the DEGREES() function. More examples for this function are:

- `=DEGREES(ATAN(-1))` returns angle α with –45°.

- `=DEGREES(ATAN(0.75355405))` returns angle α with 37°.

- `=DEGREES(ATAN(4.010780934))` returns angle α with 76°.

See also ATAN2(), ATANH(), PI(), TAN()

> ## Sample Files
> Use the SIN_COS worksheet in the Chapter16.xls or Chapter16.xlsx sample file. The sample files are found in the Chapter16 folder. For more information about the sample files, see the section titled "Using the Sample Files" on page xxiii.

ATAN2()

Syntax   ATAN2(*x_num,y_num*)

Definition   This function returns the arctangent based on an x-coordinate or a y-coordinate. The arctangent is the angle between the x-axis and a line through the origin (0, 0) and a point defined by the x-coordinate and y-coordinate.

The angle is returned as a radian measure between –π and π, excluding –π.

Arguments

- ***x_num* (required)** The x-coordinate of the point

- ***y_num* (required)** The y-coordinate of the point

Background   The ATAN2() function is another inverse tangent function (see Figure 16-8). However, the result is not calculated based on a tangent but on an xy-coordinate. The result is a radian measure and has to be converted into degrees with the DEGREES() function or by multiplying the result with 180/PI().

A positive result represents a counterclockwise angle from the x-axis; a negative result represents a clockwise angle.

The result of the formula =ATAN2(*a,b*) equals ATAN(*b/a*), except that *a* can equal zero in ATAN2().

If both *x_num* and *y_num* are zero, the ATAN2() function returns the #DIV/0! error.

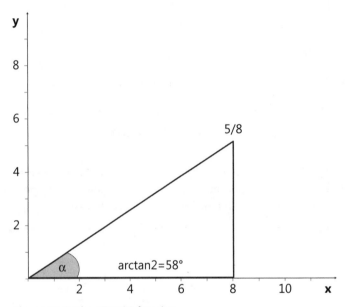

Figure 16-8 The ATAN2() function.

Examples   This function is used to calculate the angle α based on the calculation of x-coordinates and y-coordinates. More examples for this function are:

- =DEGREES(ATAN2(1,2)) returns 85.236° for angle α.

- =DEGREES(ATAN2(-6,-2)) returns –130.601° for angle α.

- =DEGREES(ATAN2(11,2)) returns 10.305° for angle α.

See also ATAN(), ATANH(), PI(), TAN()

Sample Files

Use the ATAN2 worksheet in the Chapter16.xls or Chapter16.xlsx sample file. The sample files are found in the Chapter16 folder. For more information about the sample files, see the section titled "Using the Sample Files" on page xxiii.

ATANH()

Syntax   ATANH(*number*)

Definition   This function returns the inverse hyperbolic tangent of a number (see Figure 16-9). The number must be between –1 and 1.

Argument

- **number (required)**   Any real number between –1 and 1

Background   The inverse hyperbolic functions are the inverse functions of the hyperbolic functions. The formula for the inverse hyperbolic tangent is:

$$y = \operatorname{artanh} x = \frac{1}{2} \ln \frac{1+x}{1-x} \; with \; |x| < 1$$

> **Note**
> Inverse hyperbolic functions have the prefix *ar* in the same way that the inverse trigonometric functions have the prefix *arc*.

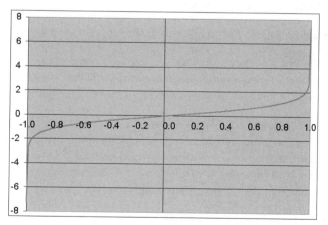

Figure 16-9   The function is odd and is defined only for –1 < *x* < 1.

Examples   Examples of this function are:

- =ATANH(0) returns 0.

- =ATANH(0.5) returns 0.54930614.

- =ATANH(-0.5) returns -0.54930614.

- =ATANH(0.999) returns 3.80020117.

- =ATANH(-0.999) returns -3.80020117.

See also ACOSH(), ASINH(), COSH(), SINH(), TANH()

Sample Files

Use the Data&Chart worksheet in the ATanH.xls or ATanH.xlsx sample file. The sample files are found in the Chapter16 folder. For more information about the sample files, see the section titled "Using the Sample Files" on page xxiii.

CEILING()

Syntax   CEILING(*number,significance*)

Definition   This function rounds a number to the smallest multiple of *significance*.

Arguments

- *number* **(required)** The value you want to round

- *significance* **(required)** The multiple to which you want to round

Background   The CEILING() function allows you to round numbers up to a specified interval limit. This method is especially useful for commercial arithmetic. Of course you could use the other rounding functions in different formulas, but CEILING() is the fastest method.

The sign *number* is taken into consideration when the value is rounded; in other words, for a positive sign the value is rounded up, and for a negative sign the value is rounded down. If *number* is an exact multiple of *significance*, no rounding occurs. If one of the arguments isn't a numeric expression, the CEILING() function returns the #VALUE! error. If *number* and *significance* have different signs, the function returns the #NUM! error.

Example   Assume that you want to calculate the payments in a pay scale table according to the increase in pay rates. All amounts have to be rounded to 50 cents. In other words, you want only amounts with a 0 or a 5 after the decimal point.

The formula

=CEILING(amount,0.5)

returns the correct result.

More examples for this function are:

- =CEILING(2345.47,0.5) returns $2,345.50.

- =CEILING(2345.67,0.5) returns $2,345.50.

See also CEILING.PRECISE(), EVEN(), FLOOR(), FLOOR.PRECISE(), INT(), ODD(), ROUND(), ROUNDDOWN(), ROUNDUP(), TRUNC()

> **Sample Files**
> Use the ROUND worksheet in the Chapter16.xls or Chapter16.xlsx sample file. The sample files are found in the Chapter16 folder. For more information about the sample files, see the section titled "Using the Sample Files" on page xxiii.

CEILING.PRECISE()

Syntax   CEILING.PRECISE(*number,significance*)

Definition   This function rounds a number to the next integer or multiple of *significance*. Regardless of the sign, the value is rounded.

Arguments

- *number* **(required)** The value you want to round.

- *significance* **(optional)** The multiple to which you want to round. The default value for *significance* is 1.

Background   The CEILING.PRECISE() function allows you to round numbers up to a specified interval limit. Of course, you can get this result with other rounding functions, but CEILING.PRECISE is the direct way.

The CEILING.PRECISE() function uses the absolute value of the multiple and returns the upper limit regardless of the sign of *number* and *significance*. The following example shows the difference between CEILING() and CEILING.PRECISE():

CEILING(-3.2,-1) = -4

CEILING.PRECISE(-3.2,-1) = -3

The CEILING.PRECISE() function uses the absolute value to round a number with a negative sign (–3.2) up, and the CEILING() function rounds a number with a negative sign down. The difference between CEILING.PRECISE() and CEILING() is that CEILING.PRECISE() rounds a number with a negative sign up.

Example   A thermometer in a freezer is calibrated to 2 degrees Celsius. You want to round the measured temperature of –17 degrees to a multiple of 2 degrees. The CEILING.PRECISE(–17,–2) function returns –16 degrees.

See also CEILING(), EVEN(), FLOOR(), FLOOR.PRECISE(), INT(), ODD(), ROUND(), ROUNDDOWN(), ROUNDUP(), TRUNC()

> **Sample Files**
> Use the ROUND worksheet in the Chapter16.xls or Chapter16.xlsx sample file. The sample files are found in the Chapter16 folder. For more information about the sample files, see the section titled "Using the Sample Files" on page xxiii.

COMBIN()

Syntax   COMBIN(*number,number_chosen*)

Definition   This function returns the number of combinations for a given number of elements.

Arguments

- *number* **(required)** The number of elements

- *number_chosen* **(required)** The number of elements in each combination

Background   Use the COMBIN() function to determine the total possible number of groups for a given number of elements.

A combination is any set or subset of elements. Combinations are distinct from permutations (see the PERMUT() function in Chapter 12, "Statistical Functions") for which the internal order is significant. This means that ABC equals BCA or CAB.

Because the COMBIN() function uses only values without decimal points, the numeric values are truncated to integers. If one of the arguments isn't a numeric expression, the COMBIN() function returns the #VALUE! error. If there are elements that are less than zero, the

Chapter 16

number of elements in a combination that are less than zero or if there are fewer elements than combinations, the function returns the #NUM! error.

The number of combinations is calculated as follows, where the set of all elements is indicated by *n* and the number of selected elements is *k*:

$$\binom{n}{k} = \frac{P_{k,n}}{k!} = \frac{n!}{k!(n-k)!}$$

where

$$P_{k,n} = \frac{n!}{(n-k)!}$$

Example   You organize a soccer tournament and have to calculate how many soccer games have to take place so that all teams play against each other once. The following teams participate in the tournament: A, B, C, and D.

The possible games are:

1. A + B

2. A + C

3. A + D

4. B + C

5. B + D

6. C + D

The result is 6. The formula looks like this:

=COMBIN(4,2)

See also BINOMDIST(), CRITBINOM(), FACT(), HYPGEOMDIST(), NEGBINOMDIST(), PERMUT()

Sample Files

Use the COMBIN worksheet in the Chapter16.xls or Chapter16.xlsx sample file. The sample files are found in the Chapter16 folder. For more information about the sample files, see the section titled "Using the Sample Files" on page xxiii.

COS()

Syntax COS(*number*)

Definition This function returns the cosine of a number.

Argument

- *number* **(required)** The angle in radians for which you want the cosine

Background In a right triangle, the ratio between the adjacent leg and the hypotenuse depends on the apex angle (see Figure 16-10). The ratio between the adjacent leg of an angle and the hypotenuse is the cosine (cos) of the angle.

$$\cos\alpha = \frac{b}{c}; \cos\beta = \frac{a}{c}$$

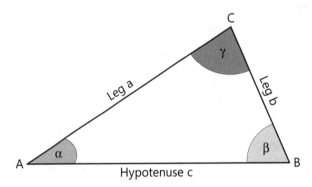

Figure 16-10 Aspect ratios in a right triangle.

If angle α in an unit circle (*c* = 1) increases between 0° and 90°, the cosine decreases between 1 and 0 (see Figure 16-11).

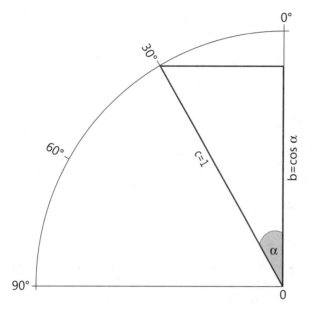

Figure 16-11 Cosine in a unit circle.

In a coordinate system, the angle on the x-axis and the sine of α on the y-axis result in the curve shown in Figure 16-12.

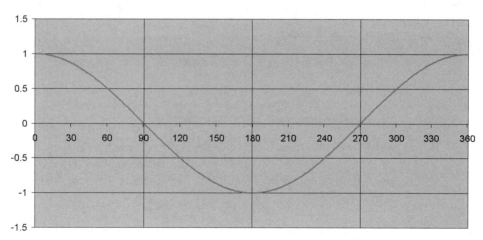

Figure 16-12 The cosine curve.

Example A railroad track has to cross a bridge. Calculate the upward track (*s*) when the slope starts 1,500 m (*l*) before the bridge and the gradient angle α is 1°.

You get the calculation formula with cos α = adjacent leg (*l*) / hypotenuse (*s*) after *s*:

s = *l* / cos α

In Excel the formula is:

=1500/COS(RADIANS(1))

The upward track is 1,500.23 m, which is 23 cm longer than the distance.

See also ACOS(), COSH(), PI()

> **Sample Files**
>
> Use the SIN_COS and trigon worksheets in the Chapter16.xls or Chapter16.xlsx sample file. The sample files are found in the Chapter16 folder. For more information about the sample files, see the section titled "Using the Sample Files" on page xxiii.

COSH()

Syntax COSH(*number*)

Definition This function returns the hyperbolic cosine of a number.

Argument

- *number* **(required)** Any real number.

Background The hyperbolic cosine belongs to the hyperbolic functions, which are (like the circle functions) defined for all real and complex numbers. (However, Excel allows only real arguments, not complex arguments, for hyperbolic functions.) The hyperbolic cosine is defined as follows:

$$\cosh x = \frac{e^x + e^{-x}}{2}$$

A hyperbolic cosine is shown in Figure 16-13.

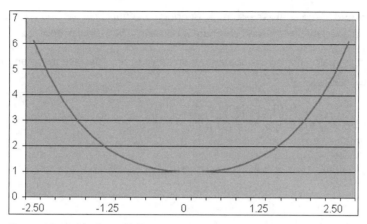

Figure 16-13 The hyperbolic cosine is an even function symmetrical to the y-axis because it has two monotonic intervals.

The hyperbolic cosine is often used for research and development in engineering and natural sciences. The hyperbolic cosine is best known as *catenary*. The catenary describes the form of a freely suspended chain affixed at two points. The equation for the catenary is:

$$y = \alpha \cos \frac{x}{a}$$

α is the distance between the apex and the zero line (lowest point).

See also ACOSH(), ASINH(), ATANH(), SINH(), TANH()

Sample Files

Use the Data&Chart and Example worksheets in the CosH.xls or CosH.xlsx sample file. The sample files are found in the Chapter16 folder. For more information about the sample files, see the section titled "Using the Sample Files" on page xxiii.

Chapter 16

DEGREES()

Syntax   DEGREES(*angle*)

Definition   This function converts radians into degrees.

Argument

- *angle* **(required)** The angle that you want to convert, in radians

Background Angles are measured in degrees (°). A full circle has 360°. A degree is divided in 60 (angular) minutes ('), and a minute is divided in 60 (angular) seconds ('').

For certain math and physics operations, an angle is also specified in radians. A full circle is 2π and the angle π is 180°.

In Excel, this function is important because all angle functions use radians (see Figure 16-14), and the results have to be converted into degrees (see the ACOS() and ASIN() functions).

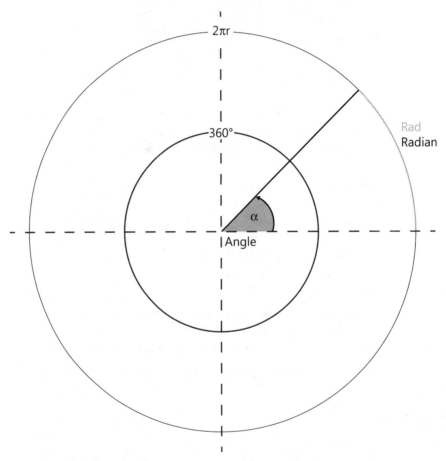

Figure 16-14 Angle and radian.

Examples For circles, the results are returned as radians (see the ATAN() and ATAN2() functions). The DEGREES() function converts the result into degrees:

```
=DEGREES(ACOS(7.5/15))
```

More examples for this function are:

- =DEGREES(1) returns 57.296.

- =DEGREES(0.785) returns 45.

- =DEGREES(1.571) returns 90.

See also RADIANS()

> **Sample Files**
>
> Use the SIN_COS worksheet in the Chapter16.xls or Chapter16.xlsx sample file. The sample files are found in the Chapter16 folder. For more information about the sample files, see the section titled "Using the Sample Files" on page xxiii.

EVEN()

Syntax   EVEN(*number*)

Definition   This function rounds a number up to the nearest even integer.

Argument

- ***number* (required)**   The value to round to the nearest even number. If *number* isn't a numeric expression, the EVEN() function returns the #VALUE! error.

Background   Unlike ROUND(), the EVEN() function always rounds a number up to the nearest even integer. Regardless of the sign of number, a value is rounded up when adjusted based on zero. If *number* is an even integer, no rounding occurs.

All numbers that can be divided by two are even numbers. You can use this function for processing elements that come in pairs.

Examples   Two heirs want to calculate their inheritance. To simplify the calculation, all amounts have to be divisible by 2.

More examples for this function are:

- =EVEN(4.5) returns 6.

- =EVEN(-6.3) returns -8.

- =EVEN(59959) returns 59,960.

Chapter 16

See also CEILING(), CEILING.PRECISE(), FLOOR(), FLOOR.PRECISE(), INT(), ISEVEN(), ISODD(), ODD(), ROUND(), TRUNC()

Sample Files

Use the ROUND worksheet in the Chapter16.xls or Chapter16.xlsx sample file. The sample files are found in the Chapter16 folder. For more information about the sample files, see the section titled "Using the Sample Files" on page xxiii.

EXP()

Syntax   EXP(*number*)

Definition   This function returns the basis *e* raised to the power of a given number.

Argument

- *number* **(required)** The exponent applied to base *e*

Background   Like root extractions and logarithmic calculus, exponentiation belongs to the third level of arithmetic operations. Exponentiation of natural numbers is based on multiplication as multiplication is based on addition. The EXP() function uses the transcendental irrational Euler's number *e* to raise a number to a given power. The constant with the value 2.71828182845904 is the base of the natural logarithm.

Euler's number (named after the Swiss mathematician Leonhard Euler) is an irrational and transcendental number; that is, like pi it cannot be a fraction of two natural numbers. Euler's number plays an important role in differential and integral calculus.

EXP() is the inverse function of LN(), the natural logarithm of *number*. The formula is:

$$x = e^{number} \text{ as product: } x = e_{number} \cdot e_{number-1} \cdot \ldots \cdot e_2 \cdot e_1$$

To calculate powers of other bases, use the exponentiation operator (^). In Excel, the eighth power of 2 (base) is calculated like this:

=2^8 is 256

Note

You will find more information about logarithm systems in the description of LN().

Examples   The exponential function is most often used for probability calculations (stochastic) in physics to calculate radioactive decay, and in biology to calculate the exponential growth of organisms. A detailed description is outside the scope of this book. You will find more information in specialist literature.

More examples for this function are:

- `=EXP(1)` returns `2.71828183` = e.

- `=EXP(2)` returns `7.3890561` = e².

See also IMEXP(), LN(), LOG(), POWER()

> ## Sample Files
>
> Use the EXP worksheet in the Chapter16.xls or Chapter16.xlsx sample file. The sample files are found in the Chapter16 folder. For more information about the sample files, see the section titled "Using the Sample Files" on page xxiii.

FACT()

Syntax   FACT(*number*)

Definition   This function returns the factorial of a number.

Argument

- ***number* (required)** The nonnegative number for which you want the factorial. If *number* isn't an integer, the decimal places are truncated.

Background   The factorial function is used to calculate partial products of natural numbers. The factorial of a number is the result of the product of all natural numbers of 1.

For example, the factorial of the number 4 is calculated as:

$$4! = 1 \cdot 2 \cdot 3 \cdot 4 = 24$$

The formula is:

$$n! = n \cdot (n - 1) \cdot (n - 2) \cdot \ldots \cdot 3 \cdot 2 \cdot 1$$

Note that the factorial of zero is defined: $0! = 1$.

Example   In combinatorics, factorials are important because *n*! is the number of possibilities to arrange *n* discriminable elements.

Assume four runners participate in a marathon. How many different combinations are possible when all runners reach the finish line?

All four runners can make first place. After the first runner passes the finish line, three runners can compete for second place. After the second runner passes the finish line, only two runners are left for third place, and only one runner is left for fourth place. Therefore, 4! = 24 different combinations exist.

The Excel formula is =FACT(4)

See also FACTDOUBLE(), PRODUCT()

Sample Files

Use the FACT worksheet in the Chapter16.xls or Chapter16.xlsx sample file. The sample files are found in the Chapter16 folder. For more information about the sample files, see the section titled "Using the Sample Files" on page xxiii.

FACTDOUBLE()

Syntax FACTDOUBLE(*number*)

Definition This function returns the double factorial of a number.

Argument

- **number (required)** The value for which to return the double factorial. If *number* isn't an integer, the decimal places are truncated.

Background The factorial *n*! of number *n* is defined as follows:

$$n! = n(n-1)(n-2)...(3)(2)(1)$$

The FACTDOUBLE() function for even numbers is defined as follows:

$$n!! = n(n-2)(n-4)...(4)(2)$$

and for odd numbers:

$$n!! = n(n-2)(n-4)...(3)(1)$$

The FACTDOUBLE() function uses numeric values. If *number* isn't a numeric value, the FACT-DOUBLE() function returns the #VALUE! error. If *number* is negative, FACTDOUBLE() returns the #NUM! error value.

More examples:

- =FACTDOUBLE(5) returns 15 (=5 • 3 • 1).

- =FACTDOUBLE(8) returns 384 (=8 • 6 • 4 • 2).

See also FACT(), MULTINOMIAL()

> ## Sample Files
>
> Use the FACT worksheet in the Chapter16.xls or Chapter16.xlsx sample file. The sample files are found in the Chapter16 folder. For more information about the sample files, see the section titled "Using the Sample Files" on page xxiii.

FLOOR()

Syntax   FLOOR(*number,significance*)

Definition   This function rounds a number down to the nearest multiple of *significance*.

Arguments

- *number* **(required)** The numeric value you want to round

- *significance* **(required)** The multiple to which you want to round

Background   The sign of *number* is taken into consideration when a value is rounded; that is, for a number with a positive sign the value is rounded down, and for a number with a negative sign the value is rounded up. If *number* is an exact multiple of *significance*, no rounding occurs.

The FLOOR() function uses numeric values. If one of the arguments isn't a numeric expression, the FLOOR() function returns the #VALUE! error. If *number* and *significance* have different signs, the function returns the #NUM! error.

Example   For a price campaign, assume that you want to round all prices to 25 cents. Figure 16-15 shows a possible solution using the FLOOR() function.

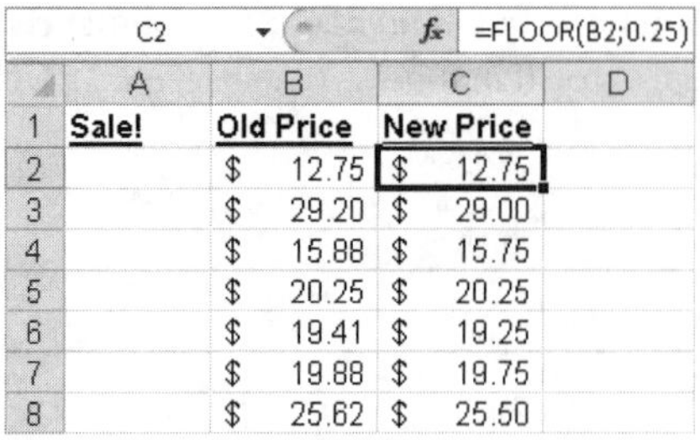

C2 =FLOOR(B2;0.25)

	A	B	C	D
1	Sale!	Old Price	New Price	
2		$ 12.75	$ 12.75	
3		$ 29.20	$ 29.00	
4		$ 15.88	$ 15.75	
5		$ 20.25	$ 20.25	
6		$ 19.41	$ 19.25	
7		$ 19.88	$ 19.75	
8		$ 25.62	$ 25.50	

Figure 16-15 The new prices rounded to 25-cent increments.

See also CEILING(), CEILING.PRECISE(), EVEN(), FLOOR.PRECISE(), INT(), ODD(), ROUND(), ROUNDDOWN(), ROUNDUP(), TRUNC()

Sample Files

Use the FLOOR and ROUND worksheets in the Chapter16.xls or Chapter16.xlsx sample file. The sample files are found in the Chapter16 folder. For more information about the sample files, see the section titled "Using the Sample Files" on page xxiii.

FLOOR.PRECISE()

Syntax FLOOR.PRECISE(*number,significance*)

Definition This function rounds a number down to the next integer or multiple of *significance*. The value is rounded down the same way regardless of the sign. The function returns 0 if *number* or *significance* is zero.

Arguments

- ***number* (required)** The value you want to round.
- ***significance* (optional)** The multiple to which you want to round. The default value for *significance* is 1.

Background The FLOOR.PRECISE() function allows you to round numbers to a specified interval limit. Of course you could use the other rounding functions in different formulas, but FLOOR.PRECISE() is the fastest method.

The FLOOR.PRECISE() function uses the absolute value of the multiple and returns the lower limit regardless of the sign of *number* and *significance*.

The following example shows the difference between FLOOR() and FLOOR.PRECISE():

```
FLOOR(-3.2,-1) = -3
```

```
FLOOR.PRECISE(-3.2,-1) = -4
```

The FLOOR.PRECISE() function rounds the negative number (–3.2) down to the absolute value, whereas the FLOOR() function rounds a number with a negative sign up. The difference between FLOOR.PRECISE() and FLOOR() is that FLOOR.PRECISE() rounds a number with a negative sign down.

Example   A wholesaler can order a minimum of five bicycles from a bicycle manufacturer. As soon as the stock falls below zero, an order has to be placed. The stock can be below zero if no bicycles are in stock and retailers order bicycles. If the stock is –6, then six bicycles are ordered. Therefore, the order is FLOOR.PRECISE(-6,-5) = -10 or ABS(-10) = 10 bicycles. You can combine the two formulas:

```
=ABS(FLOOR.PRECISE(-6,-5))
```

See also CEILING(), CEILING.PRECISE(), EVEN(), FLOOR(), INT(), ODD(), ROUND(), ROUNDDOWN(), ROUNDUP(), TRUNC()

> ## Sample Files
> Use the ROUND worksheet in the Chapter16.xls or Chapter16.xlsx sample file. The sample files are found in the Chapter16 folder. For more information about the sample files, see the section titled "Using the Sample Files" on page xxiii.

Chapter 16

GCD()

Syntax   GCD(*number1,number2,...*)

Definition   This function returns the greatest common divisor of two or more integers.

Arguments

- *number1* **(required) and** *number2* **(optional)** The minimum number of values is 1, and the maximum is 255 (29 in Excel 2003 and earlier versions). At least one value is required, but a second value makes sense so that a common divisor can be found.

Background   The greatest common divisor is the largest integer that divides both *number1* and *number2* without a remainder.

Excel calculates the greatest common divisor based on integers. Decimal places are truncated. If one of the arguments isn't a numeric expression, the GCD() function returns the

#VALUE! error. If one of the arguments is smaller than zero, the function returns the #NUM! error.

The greatest common divisor can be calculated in two ways: with prime factorization or with the Euclidean division algorithm.

Prime Factorization　The greatest common divisor is the product of the common prime factor of all numbers. The numbers are used only once as factors. The greatest common divisor can be calculated by factorizing m and n.

Here is an example:

$m = 36 = 2^2 \cdot 3^2$

$n = 120 = 2^3 \cdot 3 \cdot 5$

The factors found in both numbers are multiplied.

Euclidean Division Algorithm　This method can be used only to calculate the greatest common divisor of two numbers. Divide the larger number by the smaller number. Then divide the divisor by the remainder. Repeat this operation until there is no remainder. The last divisor is the greatest common divisor of the two numbers.

Note

From the greatest common divisor as well as the product of m and n, you can calculate the least common denominator:

$$lcm_{(m,n)} = \frac{m \cdot n}{gcd_{(m,n)}}$$

Example　The floor of a 20-foot by 10-foot room has to be evenly covered with the largest possible tiles. What is the side length of the tiles?

=GCD(20,10) returns 10; the tiles should be 10 feet long.

See also LCM()

Sample Files

Use the GCD_LCM worksheet in the Chapter16.xls or Chapter16.xlsx sample file. The sample files are found in the Chapter16 folder. For more information about the sample files, see the section titled "Using the Sample Files" on page xxiii.

INT()

Syntax   INT(*number*)

Definition   This function rounds a number down to the next smaller integer.

Argument

- **number (required)** The real number to be rounded down to an integer

Background   Real numbers include decimal numbers and extend the rational numbers with irrational numbers. This is necessary for third-level calculus operations—root extraction, logarithmic calculus, and exponentiation—with absolute rational numbers.

Integers are rational numbers and include all positive and negative numbers and 0. The INT() function truncates the decimal places of positive numbers and rounds negative numbers to the nearest smaller number.

Examples   You prepare your tax return and want the amount owed to be an integer rounded down (in your favor).

More examples for this function are:

- `=INT(4,3)` returns 4.

- `=INT(-2.51)` returns –3.

- `=INT(78.8)` returns 78.

See also CEILING(), CEILING.PRECISE(), FLOOR(), FLOOR.PRECISE(), MOD(), MROUND(), ROUND(), TRUNC(),

Sample Files

Use the ROUND worksheet in the Chapter16.xls or Chapter16.xlsx sample file. The sample files are found in the Chapter16 folder. For more information about the sample files, see the section titled "Using the Sample Files" on page xxiii.

Chapter 16

LCM()

Syntax   LCM(*number1,number2;...*)

Definition   This function returns the least common multiple of integers. The least common multiple is the smallest positive integer that is a multiple of all integer arguments (*number1, number2*, and so on). Use LCM() to add fractions with different denominators.

Arguments

- *number1* **(required) and** *number2* **(optional)** The minimum number of values is 1, and the maximum is 255 (29 in Excel 2003 and earlier versions) for which you want the least common multiple. At least one value is required but a second value makes sense so that a least common multiple can be found.

Background   For example, the least common multiple is used to add fractions. The least common multiple is the smallest integer that is a multiple of *number1* (*m*) and *number2* (*n*).

Excel calculates the least common multiple based on integers. Decimal places are truncated. If one of the arguments isn't a numeric expression, the LCM() function returns the #VALUE! error. If one of the arguments is smaller than zero, the function returns the #NUM! error.

Like the greatest common divisor, the least common multiple can be calculated by factorizing *m* and *n*. Examples include:

$m = 36 = 2^2 \cdot 3^2$

$n = 120 = 2^3 \cdot 3 \cdot 5$

All prime factors are multiplied:

$2^3 \cdot 3^2 \cdot 5 = 360$

> **Note**
>
> The greatest common divisor can be calculated from the least common multiple and the product of *m* and *n* (see the GCD() function).
>
> $$gcd(m,n) = \frac{m \cdot n}{lcm(m,n)}$$

Example   Two people run next to each other. The step length of one runner is 1.10 m and the other runner takes 1.43 m steps. Both runners start at the same time. After what distance do the runners tread simultaneously?

=LCM(110,143)

returns 1430; that is, both runners tread simultaneously after 14.30 m.

See also GCD()

> **Sample Files**
>
> Use the GCD_LCM worksheet in the Chapter16.xls or Chapter16.xlsx sample file. The sample files are found in the Chapter16 folder. For more information about the sample files, see the section titled "Using the Sample Files" on page xxiii.

LN()

Syntax   LN(*number*)

Definition   This function returns the natural logarithm of a number. Natural logarithms are based on the constant *e* (2.71828182845904).

Argument

- **number (required)** The positive real number for which you want the natural logarithm

Background   For the equation $b = ax$ where *a* and *b* are known, you can calculate *x* by using logarithmic calculus:

$x = log_a b$

Here is another example:

$2 = log_3 9$

As the logarithm of base *a*, value *x* is indicated with *b*. The logarithm system includes all logarithms with the same base. The base can be any positive number except zero and 1. The logarithm with base 2 is shortened to *lb*.

In natural science, Euler's number e (2.71828182845904) is often used as a base. You can find more information on Euler's number e in the description of EXP(). The abbreviation for logarithms with base e is *ln* (natural logarithm).

Excel provides the LN() function to calculate natural logarithms. LN() is the inverse function of EXP(). The natural logarithm to *log* is:

$$\log_b x = \frac{\ln x}{\ln b}$$

To simplify the calculation, English mathematician Henry Briggs choose base 10. These logarithms are called *Briggs logarithms* or *common logarithms* (see the LOG10() function).

Examples   Similar to the EXP() function, the LN() function is used for growth and decay processes.

More examples for this function are:

- =LN(86) returns 4.4543473, the natural logarithm of 86.

- =LN(2.7182818) returns the natural logarithm for constant $e = 1$.

- =LN(EXP(3)) returns 3, the natural logarithm of the base raised to 3.

See also EXP(), IMLN(), IMLOG10(), IMLOG2(), LOG(), LOG10()

Sample Files

Use the LOG_LN worksheet in the Chapter16.xls or Chapter16.xlsx sample file. The sample files are found in the Chapter16 folder. For more information about the sample files, see the section titled "Using the Sample Files" on page xxiii.

LOG()

Syntax   LOG(*number,base*)

Definition   This function returns the logarithm of a number to the given base.

Arguments

- **number (required)** The positive real number for which you want the logarithm.

- **base (required)** The base of the logarithm. If *base* is omitted, it is assumed to be 10.

Background LOG() is the inverse function of EXP().

Example The exponential function $a = bx$ can use the logarithm as follows:

$x = log_b a$

The logarithm of a product (quotient) is the sum (difference) of the logarithms from the factors (dividend and divisor):

$lg(a\ b) = lg\ a + lg\ b$

$lg(a : b) = lg\ a - lg\ b$

Logarithms return:

- Multiplication and division to addition and subtraction.

- Exponentiation and root extraction to multiplication and division.

Logarithms simplify calculations with multidigit numbers. Unlike the LN() and LOG10() functions, the LOG() function allows you to specify the base. If you don't specify the base, the LOG() function equals LOG10().

See also EXP(), IMLN(), IMLOG10(), IMLOG2(), LN(), LOG10()

> **Sample Files**
>
> Use the LOG_LN and EXP_LOG_LN worksheets in the Chapter16.xls or Chapter16.xlsx sample file. The sample files are found in the Chapter16 folder. For more information about the sample files, see the section titled "Using the Sample Files" on page xxiii.

LOG10()

Syntax LOG10(*number*)

Definition This function returns the common logarithm (base 10) of a number.

Argument

- ***number* (required)** The positive real number for which you want to calculate the base-10 logarithm

Background   The LOG10() function uses the common logarithm with base 10.

Examples   The common logarithm is often used in natural science; for example, to calculate the volume in decibels:

$$L = (\log \frac{P_2}{P_1})\ B = 10(\log \frac{P_2}{P_1})dB$$

You will find more information in specialist literature.

More examples for this function are:

- =LOG10(2) returns 0.301029996.

- =LOG10(6) returns 0.77815125.

- =LOG10(9) returns 0.954242509.

- =LOG10(10) returns 1.

See also   EXP(), IMLN(), IMLOG10(), IMLOG2(), LN(), LOG()

Sample Files

Use the LOG_LN worksheet in the Chapter16.xls or Chapter16.xlsx sample file. The sample files are found in the Chapter16 folder. For more information about the sample files, see the section titled "Using the Sample Files" on page xxiii.

MDETERM()

Syntax   MDETERM(*array*)

Definition   This function returns the determinant of an array.

Argument

- ***array* (required)**   A numeric array with an equal number of rows and columns

Background   The calculation of the determinant is based on a numeric array. An array can be given as the following:

- A cell range (for example, A1:C3)

- An array constant (for example, {1.2.3;4.5.6;7.8.9})

- A name for a cell range or an array constant

If the cells in the array are empty or contain text, the MDETERM() function returns the #VALUE! error. If the array does not have an equal number of rows and columns, the MDETERM() function returns the #VALUE! error.

Determinants are generally used for solving systems of equations. If the determinant is zero, the equation has no (definite) solution.

To calculate the determinant of array A, use the following formulas:

- If A is a 1x1 array:

  $\det(A) = a_{1,1}$

- If A is a 2x2 array:

  $\det(A) = a_{11} \cdot a_{22} - a_{12} \cdot a_{21}$

- If A is an 3x3 array:

  $\det(A) = a_{11} \cdot a_{22} \cdot a_{33} + a_{12} \cdot a_{23} \cdot a_{31} + a_{13} \cdot a_{21} \cdot a_{32} - a_{13} \cdot a_{22} \cdot a_{31} - a_{12} \cdot a_{21} \cdot a_{33} - a_{11} \cdot a_{23} \cdot a_{32}$

Gottfried Leibniz (German philosopher and mathematician, 1646–1716) developed the *Leibniz formula* as a common formula for an $n \cdot n$ array:

$$\det A = \sum_{\sigma \in S_n} (sgn(\sigma)) \prod_{i=1}^{n} a_{i,\sigma(i)}$$

Example See the example for the MINVERSE() function.

See also MINVERSE(), MMULT(), TRANSPOSE()

> ### Sample Files
> Use the ARRAY_FUNCTION and ARRAY_FUNCTION2 worksheets in the Chapter16.xls or Chapter16.xlsx sample file. The sample files are found in the Chapter16 folder. For more information about the sample files, see the section titled "Using the Sample Files" on page xxiii.

MINVERSE()

Syntax MINVERSE(*array*)

Definition This function returns the inverse of an array.

Argument

- ***array*** **(required)** A numeric array with an equal number of rows and columns

Background Inverse arrays are generally used for solving equations involving several variables. For an array to be inverted, it has to be a square array. The array cannot be a singular array—that is, an array whose determinant ≠ 0 (see the description of the MDETERM() function earlier in this chapter).

The inverse of an array is indicated by −1 (array A becomes A–1). The equation Ax=b becomes x=A–1b.

The inverse can be calculated by using the following methods:

- **Gaussian elimination method** The Gaussian elimination method is often used to manually calculate inverses. A detailed description is outside the scope of this book. You will find more information in specialist literature.

- **Cramer's rule** Cramer's rule is interesting for theoretical purposes only because of its complexity. However, for dimensions <=3, you can use Cramer's rule to quickly get a result. You will find more information in specialist literature.

- **The formula**

$$A^{-1} = \frac{1}{\det(A)} \cdot A^{\#}$$

This requires the determinant det(A) and the complementary array A#.

An array can be any of the following:

- A cell range (such as A1:C3)

- An array constant (such as {1.2.3;4.5.6;7.8.9}

- A name for the cell range or the array constant

If the cells in the array are empty or contain text, the MINVERSE() function returns the #VALUE! error. If the array does not have an equal number of rows and columns, the MINVERSE() function returns the #VALUE! error.

Because MINVERSE() returns an array, the formula has to be entered as array formula (with Ctrl+Page Up+Enter).

MINVERSE() is calculated with an accuracy of approximately 16 digits, which may lead to a small numeric error when the rounding is not accurate.

Some square arrays cannot be inverted, in which case MINVERSE() returns the #NUM! error. The determinant for a noninvertable matrix is zero.

Example   Figure 16-16 shows the variables for the following equation:

$Ax = b$

◢	A	B	C	D	E	F	G
2							
3		1	-2	-2			1
4	A =	-2	1	0		b =	2
5		-1	-2	-3			3
6							

Figure 16-16 Variables of the equation.

Solution:

1. Change the formula: $x = A^{-1}b$

2. Check whether the equation can be solved. To do so, use the MDETERM() function to calculate the determinant for array A. If the determinant is not equal to zero, the equation can be solved.

    The formula for the determinant is: =MDETERM(B3:D5).

    Result: The determinant of A is –1.

    Because the determinant of A is not equal to zero, there is a solution for array A.

3. Calculate of the inverse element of A = A^{-1}

    To do this, you specify the following array formula for array A (see Figure 16-17) in the cell range (B9:D11): {=MINVERSE(B3:D5}.

◢	A	B	C	D	E
15					
16		3	2	-2	
17	A^{-1}=	6	5	-4	
18		-5	-4	3	
19					

Figure 16-17 Calculating inverse elements.

4. Check that the inverse array is correct. Do so by multiplying A by A^{-1}. The formula is: {=MMULT(B3:D5;B9:D11)}. The result has to be an unit array (see Figure 16-18).

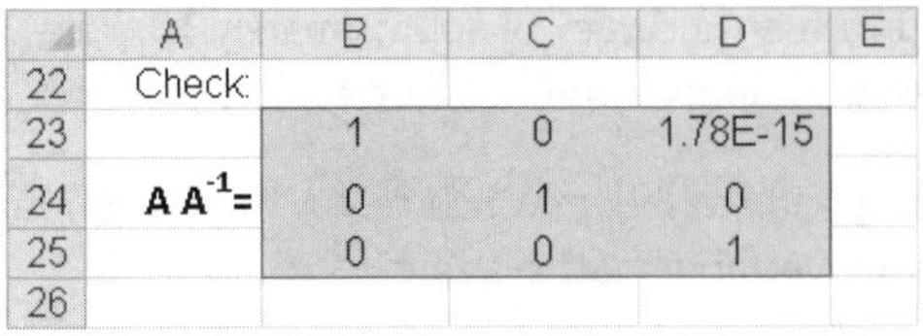

	A	B	C	D	E
22	Check:				
23		1	0	1.78E-15	
24	A A⁻¹=	0	1	0	
25		0	0	1	
26					

Figure 16-18 Verification with an unit array.

5. Finally, A^{-1} is multiplied by b. The formula is {=MMULT(B9:D11;G3:G5)} and the result is x (see Figure 16-19).

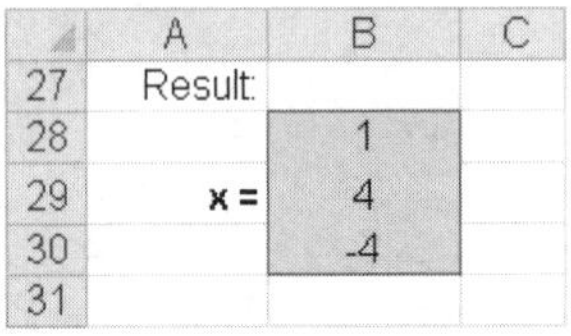

	A	B	C
27	Result:		
28		1	
29	x =	4	
30		-4	
31			

Figure 16-19 The result of the equation

See also INDEX(), MMULT(), TRANSPOSE()

Sample Files

Use the ARRAY_FUNCTION and ARRAY_FUNCTION2 worksheets in the Chapter16.xls or Chapter16.xlsx sample file. The sample files are found in the Chapter16 folder. For more information about the sample files, see the section titled "Using the Sample Files" on page xxiii.

MMULT()

Syntax   MMULT(*array1,array2*)

Definition   This function returns the product of two arrays. The result is an array with the same number of rows as *array1* and the same number of columns as *array2*.

Arguments

- **array1 (required) and array2 (required)** The arrays you want to multiply

Background   The arguments *array1* and *array2* can be any of the following:

- A cell range (such as A1:C3)

- An array constant (such as {1.2.3;4.5.6;7.8.9})

- A name for the cell range or the array constant

To allow the calculation of the product of two arrays, the number of columns in *array1* must be the same as the number of rows in *array2*. Both arrays only can contain numbers.

To calculate the product, the row elements of the first array are multiplied with the column elements of the second array.

$$
\begin{pmatrix} a_{11} & a_{12} & a_{13} \\ a_{21} & a_{22} & a_{23} \end{pmatrix} \cdot \begin{pmatrix} b_{11} & b_{12} \\ b_{21} & b_{22} \\ b_{31} & b_{32} \end{pmatrix}
$$
$$
= \begin{pmatrix} (a_{11} \cdot b_{11} + a_{12} \cdot b_{21} + a_{13} \cdot b_{31}) & (a_{11} \cdot b_{12} + a_{12} \cdot b_{22} + a_{13} \cdot b_{32}) \\ (a_{21} \cdot b_{11} + a_{22} \cdot b_{21} + a_{23} \cdot b_{31}) & (a_{21} \cdot b_{12} + a_{22} \cdot b_{22} + a_{23} \cdot b_{32}) \end{pmatrix}
$$
$$
= \begin{pmatrix} c_{11} & c_{12} \\ c_{21} & c_{22} \end{pmatrix}
$$

Example See the example for the MINVERSE() function.

See also MDETERM(), MINVERSE(), TRANSPOSE()

> **Sample Files**
>
> Use the ARRAY_FUNCTION or ARRAY_FUNCTION2 worksheets in the Chapter16.xls or Chapter16.xlsx sample file. The sample files are found in the Chapter16 folder. For more information about the sample files, see the section titled "Using the Sample Files" on page xxiii.

MOD()

Syntax MOD(*number,divisor*)

Definition This function returns the remainder of a division operation. The result has the same sign as the divisor.

Arguments

- *number* (required) The number for which you want to find the remainder

- *divisor* (required) The number by which you want to divide *number*

Background For certain calculations, you need the remainder of a division operation. This is also called *modulo* (*mod*). For this type of calculation, you can use the MOD() function.

If the divisor is 0, the MOD() function returns the #DIV/0! error.

The MOD() function can be expressed in terms of the INT() function:

=*numerator-divisor* • *INT(numerator/divisor)*

This formula is used for the modulo method in software systems. There are two types of modulo calculations, which return different results for negative arguments:

- **Math method (Excel MOD() function)**

  $Z \bmod D = Z - D \cdot [Z/D]$

  [*Z/D*] is the division in parentheses (for example, –4.3 ≈ –5) and corresponds to the result returned by the =INT(*Z/D*) function. For the math method, the following applies to negative values:

  $(\cdot Z) \bmod D \neq \cdot (Z \bmod D)$

  Here is an example:

  ```
  -7 mod 3 = 2 ≠ -1 = -(7 mod 3)
  ```

  The result has the same sign as the divisor (*D*).

- **Symmetrical method**

  $Z \bmod D = Z - D \cdot (Z \operatorname{div} D)$

  (*Z div D*) is the quotient rounded toward 0 (for example, –4.3 ≈ –4). For the symmetrical method, the following applies to negative values:

  $(\cdot Z) \bmod D = \cdot (Z \bmod D)$

  Here is an example:

  ```
  -7 mod 3 = -1 = -1 = -(7 mod 3)
  ```

  The result has the same sign as the numerator (*Z*).

Example   The MOD() function is often used together with other functions; for example, to add every second line (see Figure 16-20).

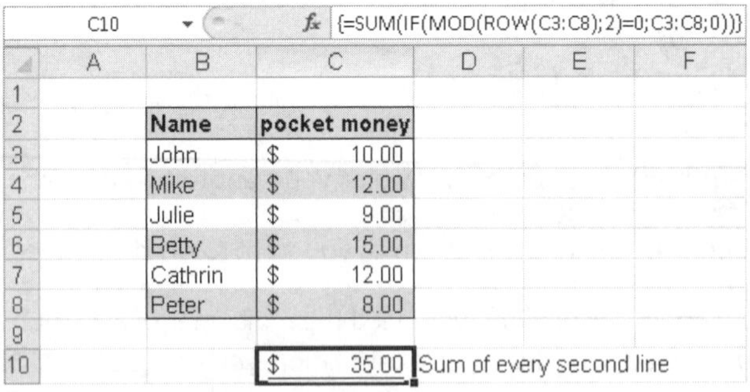

Figure 16-20 Adding every second line.

The formula is {=SUM(IF(MOD(ROW(C3:C8);2)=0;C3:C8;0))}. Because this is an array formula, you have to press Ctrl+Page Up+Enter after you enter the formula.

More examples for this function are:

- =MOD(7,3) returns 1.

- =MOD(-7,3) returns 1 (the value is positive because the divisor is positive).

- =MOD(7,-3) returns -1 (the value is negative because the divisor is negative).

- =MOD(12.56,3.2) returns 2.96.

See also INT(), ROUND(), ROUNDDOWN(), ROUNDUP(), TRUNC()

> ### Sample Files
> Use the MOD worksheet in the Chapter16.xls or Chapter16.xlsx sample file. The sample files are found in the Chapter16 folder. For more information about the sample files, see the section titled "Using the Sample Files" on page xxiii.

MROUND()

Syntax   MROUND(*number,multiple*)

Definition   This function returns a number rounded to a multiple.

Arguments

- ***number* (required)** The value to round

- ***multiple* (required)** The multiple to which you want to round *number*

Background   The MROUND() function allows you to round a number to the multiple of a given value. MROUND() rounds up, away from zero, if the remainder of dividing *number* by multiple is greater than or equal to half the value of *multiple*. If the number is less than or equal to half of the multiple, the number is rounded down.

Examples   All sales prices in a store have to be divisible by 0.05—for example: $10.05, $11.10, $15.25, or $20.00.

- =MROUND(12.31,0.05) returns $12.35.

- =MROUND(0.32,0.05) returns $0.30.

- =MROUND(1.24,0.05) returns $1.25.

See also CEILING(), EVEN(), FLOOR(), ODD(), ROUND(), ROUNDDOWN(), ROUNDUP(), TRUNC()

Sample Files

Use the ROUND worksheet in the Chapter16.xls or Chapter16.xlsx sample file. The sample files are found in the Chapter16 folder. For more information about the sample files, see the section titled "Using the Sample Files" on page xxiii.

MULTINOMIAL()

Syntax MULTINOMIAL(*number1,number2,...*)

Definition This function returns the polynomial coefficient of a set of numbers. The formula for the MULTINOMIAL() function is:

$$MULTINOMIAL(a,b,c) = \frac{(a+b+c)!}{a!\,b!\,c!}$$

Arguments

- *number1* **(required) and** *number2* **(required)** The minimum number of values is 1, and the maximum is 255 (29 in Excel 2003 and earlier versions) for which you want the multinomial

Background The MULTINOMIAL() function calculates the polynomial coefficient for a set of numbers to determine the permutation (the order of identical elements).

With this function, you can also calculate the polynomial distribution.

Example Assume that you want to calculate the number of alternative orders in which five people can sit on a bench with five seats. There are two women (*a*=2), two men (*b*=2), and one child (*c*=1). You use the following formula:

```
=MULTINOMIAL(2,2,1)
```

returns 30. This means that there are 30 different possibilities.

See also FACT(), FACTDOUBLE()

ODD()

Syntax   ODD(*number*)

Definition   This function rounds a number up to the nearest odd integer.

Argument

- *number* **(required)** The value to round

Background   All numbers that cannot be divided by 2 are odd numbers. The ODD() function uses only numeric values. If a number isn't a numeric expression, the ODD() function returns the #VALUE! error.

Regardless of the sign of *number*, the value is rounded up when adjusted based on zero. If *number* is an odd integer, no rounding occurs.

More examples for this function are:

- =ODD(1.9) returns 3.

- =ODD(-2.8) returns -3.

- =ODD(18) returns 19.

See also CEILING(), CEILING.PRECISE(), EVEN(), FLOOR(), FLOOR.PRECISE(), INT(), ISEVEN(), ISODD(), ROUND(), TRUNC()

> **Sample Files**
>
> Use the ROUND worksheet in the Chapter16.xls or Chapter16.xlsx sample file. The sample files are found in the Chapter16 folder. For more information about the sample files, see the section titled "Using the Sample Files" on page xxiii.

PI()

Syntax   PI()

Definition   This function returns the constant pi ($\pi = 3.14159265358979$) accurate to 15 digits.

Arguments   None

Background   Pi (π) defines the ratio of the circumference of a circle to its diameter (d) or radius (r):

$d\,\pi = c$

or

$2r\ \pi = c$

c is the circumference of the circle, and π is an infinite number that can only be approximated. Excel uses 15 decimal places. Rounded to 100 decimal places, π has the following value:

3.141 592 653 589 793 238 462 643 383 279 502 884 197 169 399 375 105 820 974 944 592 307 816 406 286 208 998 628 034 825 342 117 067 0

Examples   Pi is used for calculating circles:

- In geometry:

  ○ Cylinder volume (r = radius, h = height) $V = r^2 \pi h$

  ○ Surface area of a sphere (r = radius) $A_0 = 4\pi r\,2$

- In arithmetic:

  ○ Euler's constant $e^{i\Phi} = \cos(\Phi) + i\,\sin(\Phi)$

- In physics:

  ○ Circular motion $\omega = 2\pi f$ (angular speed = 2π times rotational speed)

See also COS(), SIN(), TAN()

POWER()

Syntax   POWER(*number,power*)

Definition   This function returns a number raised to a power.

Arguments

- ***number* (required)** The base number, which can be any real number

- ***power* (required)** The exponent to which the base number is raised

Background   If a number is raised to a given power, the number is (repeatedly) multiplied with itself.

$$a \cdot a \cdot a \cdot a \cdot ... \cdot a = a^n$$

In this equation, the base number a multiplied with itself to the power n. The following apply:

- a is called the *base* or *cardinal number*.

- n is called the *exponent*.

The result is the power. The logarithm and the root function are inverse functions of POWER().

Instead of the POWER() function, you can use the operator ^ to raise a number; for example, =5^2 instead of =POWER(5,2).

Example   Computers use the dual system for digital processing based on the number 2. The units of digital storage media are the powers to base 2 (power of two). Therefore, 1 kilobyte is 2^{10} bytes = 1024 bytes.

More examples for this function are:

- =POWER(3,2) returns 9.

- =POWER(3.2,3) returns 32.768.

- =POWER(7,1.33) returns 13.3039435426393.

See also SQRT()

Sample Files

Use the POWER worksheet in the Chapter16.xls or Chapter16.xlsx sample file. The sample files are found in the Chapter16 folder. For more information about the sample files, see the section titled "Using the Sample Files" on page xxiii.

PRODUCT()

Syntax   PRODUCT(*number1,number2,...*)

Definition   This function multiplies the arguments and returns the product.

Arguments

- **number1 (required) and number2 (optional)**   The minimum number of values is 1, and the maximum is 255 (30 in Excel 2003 and earlier versions) that you want to multiply. (One number is required, but for a multiplication a second value makes sense.) Instead of using separate numbers, it is also possible to build a product for a range of cells—for example, A1:A5.

Background   The product is the result of multiplication, and the multiplied values are the factors:

$$a_1 \cdot a_2 \cdot a_3 \cdot a_4 \cdot ... \cdot a_n = b$$

In mathematics, analogous to the sum symbol Σ is the symbol Π for product. Π stands for the product of multiple factors.

Example   Multiplication of amounts is very common; for example, in a shopping list (see Figure 16-21).

	E3		f_x	=PRODUCT(C3;D3)	
	A	B	C	D	E
1					
2			Amount	Price Apiece	Total
3		Apples	12	$ 0.12	$ 1.44
4		Mangos	21	$ 1.50	$ 31.50

Figure 16-21 The PRODUCT() function.

See also FACT(), SUM(), SUMPRODUCT()

Sample Files

Use the PRODUCT worksheet in the Chapter16.xls or Chapter16.xlsx sample file. The sample files are found in the Chapter16 folder. For more information about the sample files, see the section titled "Using the Sample Files" on page xxiii.

QUOTIENT()

Syntax   QUOTIENT(*numerator,denominator*)

Definition   This function returns the integer portion of a division operation. If this function is not available and you get the #NAME? error, you need to install and activate the add-in analysis functions.

Arguments

- *numerator* **(required)** The dividend

- *denominator* **(required)** The divisor

Background   The division operation is the inverse of the multiplication operation and can be indicated by a colon, as in *a* : *b* or a fraction line, as in

$$\left.\frac{a \;\; (numerator, divident)}{b \;\; (denominator, divisor)}\right\} quotient$$

The colon and the fraction line are interchangeable signs. However, Excel formulas use the slash (/) as the operator for division.

See Also You will find more information about the use of operators in Excel formulas in Chapter 3, "From Numbers to Formulas."

If one of the arguments isn't a numeric expression, the QUOTIENT() function returns the #VALUE! error. If the divisor is 0, the QUOTIENT() function returns the #DIV/0! error.

Example   Assume that you want to mix a gray paint, so you use one part of black paint and four parts of white paint. The quotient is 1:4. The formula is:

=QUOTIENT(1,4)

The result is 0.25. You need 1 • 0.25 liter of black paint and 4 • 0.25 liter of white paint.

See also MOD()

RADIANS()

Syntax   RADIANS(*angle*)

Definition   This function converts degrees into radian measures.

Argument

- *angle* **(required)** The angle that you want to convert, in degrees

Background   You can calculate the segment of a circle based on the angle as well as on the circumference and arc. This quotient is called a *radian* or *radiant* (see Figure 16-22). Because the angle functions in Excel are based on radians, this function is often used to specify the arguments for angle functions.

The following applies:

Circumference (2πr) / arc (b) = round angle (360°) / angle at center (α)

The measure for the radian is the radiant (rad). The full circumference of a circle is 360° or 2π = 6.28318531 rad. A half-circle is π = 3.14159265 rad.

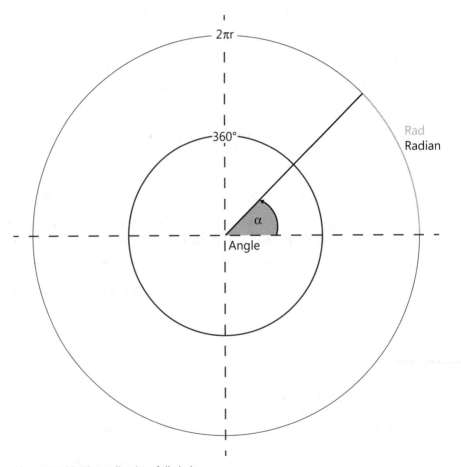

Figure 16-22 The radian in a full circle.

Example   Sea miles are an interesting application. The circumference of the earth is 360° x 60′ = 21,600 arc minutes or sea miles.

More examples for this function are:

- `=RADIANS(1)` returns `0.017453293` rad.

- `=RADIANS(45)` returns `0.785398163` rad.

- `=RADIANS(90)` returns `1.570796327` rad.

See also DEGREES()

> **Sample Files**
> Use the SIN_COS worksheet in the Chapter16.xls or Chapter16.xlsx sample file. The sample files are found in the Chapter16 folder. For more information about the sample files, see the section titled "Using the Sample Files" on page xxiii.

RAND()

Syntax   RAND()

Definition   This function returns a random number between 0 and 1 with up to 16 decimal places.

Arguments   None

Background   The RAND() function returns a random number greater than or equal to 0 and less than 1.

To generate a random real number between *a* and *b*, use:

`=RAND() • (b-a)+a`

A new random number is returned every time the worksheet is calculated.

Example   The RAND() function is often used to fill a table with test data or to simulate processes in engineering and natural sciences. The formula has to be entered in each cell.

Chapter 16

> ### Tip   Use RAND() to generate a random number
>
> If you want to use RAND() to generate a random number but don't want the numbers to change every time the cell is calculated, you can enter =RAND() in the formula bar and then press F9 to change the formula to a random number.
>
> To copy multiple cells containing a formula for random numbers, click the right mouse button in the same range and select Paste Special/Values.

Examples   Some examples of this function are:

- =RAND() • (100-1)+1 returns a random number between 1 and 100.

- =RAND() • (250-150)+150 returns a random number between 150 and 250.

See also RANDBETWEEN()

> ### Sample Files
> Use the RAND worksheet in the Chapter16.xls or Chapter16.xlsx sample file. The sample files are found in the Chapter16 folder. For more information about the sample files, see the section titled "Using the Sample Files" on page xxiii

RANDBETWEEN()

Syntax   RANDBETWEEN(*bottom,top*)

Definition   This function returns a random number from a range. A new random number is returned every time the worksheet is calculated.

Arguments

- ***bottom* (required)** The smallest integer RANDBETWEEN() can return

- ***top* (required)** The largest integer RANDBETWEEN() can return

Background   Random values are necessary in engineering and natural sciences to simulate processes.

To generate a random date, the value has to be a number.

> ## Tip   Use RANDBETWEEN() to generate a random number
>
> If you want to use RANDBETWEEN() to generate a random number but don't want the numbers to change every time the cell is calculated, you can enter =RANDBETWEEN(*bottom,top*) in the formula bar and then press F9 to change the formula to a random number.
>
> To copy multiple cells containing a formula for random numbers, click the right mouse button in the same range and select Paste Special/Values.

Example   See the practical example for the RAND() function.

See also RAND()

> ## Sample Files
>
> Use the RAND worksheet in the Chapter16.xls or Chapter16.xlsx sample file. The sample files are found in the Chapter16 folder. For more information about the sample files, see the section titled "Using the Sample Files" on page xxiii.

ROMAN()

Syntax   ROMAN(*number,form*)

Definition   This function converts an Arabic number into a Roman numeral.

Arguments

- *number* **(required)** The Arabic number you want to convert. You can specify numbers between 0 and 3999. For negative values and numbers greater than 3999, the #VALUE! error is returned.

- *form* **(optional)** A number specifying the type of roman numeral you want. The roman numeral style ranges from Classic to Simplified, becoming more concise as the value of *form* increases (see Figure 16-23). The possible values of *form* are shown in Table 16-4.

Chapter 16

Table 16-4 **Possible Values for the *form* Argument**

Value	Type of Roman Numeral
0	Classic
1	More concise
2	More concise
3	More concise
4	Simplified
TRUE	Classic
FALSE	Simplified

C34		*fx*	=ROMAN($B34;C$3)			
	A	B	C	D	E	F	G
1							
2					**roman**		
3			0	1	2	3	4
4		**arabic**	classic	shorter	shorter	shorter	simplified
34		3,999	MMMCMXCIX	MMMLMVLIV	MMMXMIX	MMMVMIV	MMMIM

Figure 16-23 The different styles for Roman numerals.

Background   Roman numerals consist of basic numerals and auxiliary numerals. The auxiliary numerals were introduced later because numbers written in basic numerals were sometimes too long (see Table 16-5).

Table 16-5 **Roman Numeral Forms**

Basic Numeral		Auxiliary Numeral	
Value	Arabic	Value	Arabic
I	1	V	5
X	10	L	50
C	100	D	500
M	1000		

The following rules for Roman numerals apply:

- The same characters next to each other are added. At most, three of the same characters can be next to each other. (Example: III = 3.)

- Smaller values to the right of greater values are added and to the left of greater values are subtracted. Auxiliary numerals cannot be subtracted. (Example: XI = 11, IX= 9, XLV = 45.)

- The basic numerals I, X, and C can be subtracted only from the nearest larger value. (Examples: CD = 400, CM = 900.)

Roman numerals remained in common use in central Europe until about the 16th century and were continuously adjusted. Arabic numbers became prevalent only at the onset of the letterpress. The Romans didn't use the subtractions just listed. Even today, the number 4 on clock faces labeled with Roman numerals is often written in the original style: IIII.

In addition to the classic Roman numeral style, shorter styles are possible.

Examples   The ROMAN() function converts Arabic numbers into Roman numerals, which are often used for chapters or enumerations:

1 List of references	I List of references
2 Table of Contents	II Table of Contents
3 Introduction	III Introduction

More examples for this function are:

- `=ROMAN(999,0)` returns CMXCIX—classic (type 0).

- `=ROMAN(999,1)` returns LMVLIV—more concise (type 1).

- `=ROMAN(999,2)` returns XMIX—more concise (type 2).

- `=ROMAN(999,3)` returns VMIV—more concise (type 3).

- `=ROMAN(999,4)` returns IM—simplified (type 4).

> **Sample Files**
>
> Use the ROMAN worksheet in the Chapter16.xls or Chapter16.xlsx sample file. The sample files are found in the Chapter16 folder. For more information about the sample files, see the section titled "Using the Sample Files" on page xxiii.

Chapter 16

ROUND()

Syntax   ROUND(*number,num_digits*)

Definition   This function rounds a number to a specified number of decimal places.

Arguments

- ***number* (required)** The number you want to round

- ***num_digits* (required)** The number of decimal places to which you want to round a number

Background   For our number system, rounding is unavoidable. Most number values are rounded at some point. There are many reasons to round numbers: Large numbers are clearer and can be more easily calculated, such as for demographic statistics or pi (π). Also, (almost) all prices are rounded to two decimal places because the smallest unit for money amounts is one cent.

If the number after the number to be rounded is greater than 4, the number is rounded up. If this number is smaller than or equal to 4, the number is rounded down. Examples:

- $3.2549 is rounded to $3.25

- $3.2551 is rounded to $3.26

Negative values are rounded up, away from 0.

- –$3.2549 is rounded to –$3.25

- –$3.2551 is rounded to –$3.26

If *num_digits* is greater than zero, then the number is rounded to the specified number of decimal places. If *num_digits* is zero, then the number is rounded to the nearest integer. If *num_digits* is less than zero, then the number is rounded to the left of the decimal point.

Example   Assume that for a price calculation you want to round the following value to two decimal places: $14.5943.

The formula =ROUND(14.5943,2) returns $14.59.

See also CEILING(), CEILING.PRECISE(), EUROCONVERT(), FLOOR(), FLOOR.PRECISE(), INT(), MOD(), MROUND(), ROUNDDOWN(), ROUNDUP(), TRUNC()

> **Sample Files**
>
> Use the ROUND worksheet in the Chapter16.xls or Chapter16.xlsx sample file. The sample files are found in the Chapter16 folder. For more information about the sample files, see the section titled "Using the Sample Files" on page xxiii.

ROUNDDOWN()

Syntax   ROUNDDOWN(*number,num_digits*)

Definition   This function rounds a number down to the number of digits specified in *num_digits*.

Arguments

- *number* **(required)** The real number to be rounded down

- *num_digits* **(required)** The number of decimal places to which you want to round the number down

Background   Unlike ROUND(), in which numbers less than five round down and greater than or equal to five round up, the ROUNDDOWN() function always rounds a number down. The number is truncated at the position specified in *num_digits*. If *num_digits* is a negative value, the number is rounded down to the specified number of digits before the decimal point.

If *num_digits* is:

- Greater than zero, the number is rounded down to the specified number of decimal places.

- Equal to zero, the number is rounded down to the nearest integer.

- Less than zero, the number is rounded down to the left of the decimal point.

Examples   For a price calculation, assume that you want to round the calculated final amounts of 15.482 and 83.2578 to two decimal places:

- `=ROUNDDOWN(15.482,2)` returns $15.48.

- `=ROUNDDOWN(83.2578,2)` returns $83.25.

A few more examples demonstrate this function further:

- `=ROUNDDOWN(1.9,0)` returns 1.

- `=ROUNDDOWN(-2.846,2)` returns -2.84.

- `=ROUNDDOWN(18,-1)` returns 10.

See also CEILING(), CEILING.PRECISE(), FLOOR(), FLOOR.PRECISE(), INT(), MOD(), MROUND(), ROUND(), ROUNDUP(), TRUNC()

> **Sample Files**
>
> Use the ROUND worksheet in the Chapter16.xls or Chapter16.xlsx sample file. The sample files are found in the Chapter16 folder. For more information about the sample files, see the section titled "Using the Sample Files" on page xxiii.

Chapter 16

ROUNDUP()

Syntax   ROUNDUP(*number,num_digits*)

Definition   This function rounds a number up to any number of decimal places.

Arguments

- *number* **(required)** The real number to be rounded up

- *num_digits* **(required)** The number of decimal places to which you want to round the number

Background   Unlike ROUND(), the ROUNDUP() function always rounds a number up. The *num_digits* argument indicates the number of decimal places to round the number. If the value of *num_digits* is:

- Greater than zero, the number is rounded up to the specified number of decimal places.

- Equal to zero, the number is rounded up to the nearest integer.

- Less than zero, the number is rounded up to the left of the decimal point.

Examples   Assume that you want to wallpaper a room and calculate how many rolls of wallpaper you need for 463 square feet. A roll is 30 feet long and 3 feet wide. The result is three rolls. The corresponding formula looks like this:

```
=ROUNDUP(463/30 • 3,0)
```

First you divide the area you want to wallpaper (463 square feet) by the size of a roll (30 feet x 3 feet). Then you round the result up to an integer because you can only buy entire rolls. You can also include the length of one piece of wallpaper and the estimated waste in the calculation.

More examples for this function are:

- `=ROUNDUP(1.9,0)` returns 2.

- `=ROUNDUP(-2.8,0)` returns -2.

- `=ROUNDUP(18,-1)` returns 10.

See also CEILING(), CEILING.PRECISE(), FLOOR(), FLOOR.PRECISE(), INT(), MOD(), MROUND(), ROUND(), ROUNDDOWN(), TRUNC()

> ## Sample Files
>
> Use the ROUNDUP worksheet in the Chapter16.xls or Chapter16.xlsx sample file. The sample files are found in the Chapter16 folder. For more information about the sample files, see the section titled "Using the Sample Files" on page xxiii.

SERIESSUM()

Syntax   SERIESSUM(*x,n,m,coefficients*)

Definition   SERIESSUM($x,n,m,\{a_1,a_2,a_3,a_4...,a_k\}$) returns the sum of a power series:

$$y = a_1 x^n + a_2 x^{n+m} + a_3 x^{n+2m} + a_4 x^{n+3m} + ... + a_k x^{n+km}$$

The number of values in *coefficients* determines the number of terms in the power series.

Arguments

- *x* **(required)** The value of the independent variable for the power series.

- *n* **(required)** The power of x in the first term.

- *m* **(required)** The increment for n.

- *coefficients* **(required)** An array of coefficients of the power series. The number of values in *coefficients* determines the number of terms in the power series. For example, if there are three values in *coefficients*, then there will be three terms in the power series.

Background   A power series is an infinite series in the form:

$$\sum_{n=0}^{\infty} a_n \left(x - x_0 \right)^n$$

a_n (where $n \in \mathbb{N}_0$) is any series of real or complex numbers. The value x_0 is the expansion point of the power series.

Examples Many functions can be approximated by using the expansion point of the power series. The accuracy of the result depends on the number of terms in the power series: the more terms, the more accurate the result.

Example 1

```
=SERIESSUM(1,0,1,{1,1,0.5,0.16666667,0.04166667,0,00833333,0.00019841})
```

returns `2.71686508`. This function uses:

- $x = 1$

- $n = 0$

- $m = 1$

- $a_1 = 1$

- $a_2 = 1$

- $a_3 = 0.5 = 1/2!$

- $a_4 = 0.16666667 = 1/3!$

- $a_5 = 0.04166667 = 1/4!$

- $a_6 = 0.00833333 = 1/5!$

- $a_7 = 0.00019841 = 1/6!$

These are the first seven terms in the series:

$$1+1+\frac{1}{2}+\frac{1}{6}+\frac{1}{24}+\frac{1}{120}+\frac{1}{720}+\ldots$$

to calculate Euler's number e.

Example 2

This example evaluates the power series shown in Figure 16-24.

	A	B	C	D	E	F	G
	E7	▼	f_x	=SERIESSUM(C3,C4,C5,C6:C9)			
1					**Seriessum**		
2							
3		x	0.785398				
4		n	1		$y = \dfrac{x}{1!} - \dfrac{x^3}{3!} + \dfrac{x^5}{5!} - \dfrac{x^7}{7!} + \cdots$		
5		m	2				
6		a_1	1		This will result in:		
7		a_2	-0.1666667		0.70710635		
8		a_3	0.00833333				
9		a_4	-0.0001984		45.00		
10					0.70710667		
11							
12							
13			0.785398 rad = 45.00°				

Figure 16-24 Evaluating a power series.

Cell E7 contains the result returned by the function based on the specified arguments in the range B3:C9.

Cell E9 contains the formula

=DEGREES(B3)

which converts x in B3 to degrees (45°). Therefore, B3 has to contain a radian measure. Cell D10 contains the formula

=SIN(B3)

which calculates the sine based on 45°. The result matches the value returned by the SERIESSUM() function up to six decimal places.

Sample Files

Use the Seriessum worksheet in the Seriessum.xls or Seriessum.xlsx sample file. The sample files are found in the Chapter16 folder. For more information about the sample files, see the section titled "Using the Sample Files" on page xxiii.

SIGN()

Syntax   SIGN(*number*)

Definition   This function returns the sign of a number. SIGN() returns the following values:

- 1 if the number is positive

- 0 if the number is 0

- –1 if the number is negative

Argument

- *number* **(required)** Any real number

Background   Numbers greater than zero are positive numbers and have the plus sign (+). Numbers less than zero are negative and have a minus sign (–). The plus sign can be omitted. The number 0 is neither positive nor negative.

With the SIGN() function, you can filter values based on their sign.

Example   Assume that you want to filter the subsidiaries that generate negative revenues in a sales list. First, you display the sum of the losses (see Figure 16-25).

	A	B	C	D	E
	E12		*fx* {=SUM(IF(SIGN(B2:B9)=1,B2:B9))}		
1	**Office**	**Profit**	**Sign**		
2	New York	$723,672.00	1		
3	Memphis	-$15,423.00	-1		
4	New Orleans	$12,489.00	1		
5	Toronto	$124,875.00	1		
6	Paris	-$23,534.00	-1		
7	Munich	$62,335.00	1		
8	San Francisco	-$44,347.00	-1		
9	Berlin	$235,612.00	1		
10					
11				Losses	-$83,304.00
12				Profit	$1,158,983.00
13				Balance	$1,075,679.00

Figure 16-25 Revenues with different signs.

You enter the SIGN() function in column C with a reference to the revenue (see Figure 16-26). Now you can filter all revenues with a minus sign.

Figure 16-26 Filtering values with the minus sign.

To display the sum of the losses, you enter the following formula in E11:

`{=SUM(IF(SIGN(B2:B9)=-1,B2:B9))}`

To display the revenues, you enter the following formula:

`{=SUM(IF(SIGN(B2:B9)=1,B2:B9))}`

You have to enter both formulas as array formulas, so you must press Ctrl+Page Up+Enter after you enter the formula.

See also ABS()

Sample Files

Use the SIGN worksheet in the Chapter16.xls or Chapter16.xlsx sample file. The sample files are found in the Chapter16 folder. For more information about the sample files, see the section titled "Using the Sample Files" on page xxiii.

SIN()

Syntax   SIN(*number*)

Definition   This function returns the sine of a number.

Argument

- ***number* (required)** The angle in radians for which you want the sine

Background   In a right triangle, the ratio between the hypotenuse and the opposite leg depends on the apex angle. The ratio between the opposite leg of an angle and the hypotenuse is the *sine* (*sin*) of an angle.

$$\sin \alpha = \frac{a}{c}, \ \sin \beta = \frac{b}{c}$$

The SIN() function requires radians for calculations. If the angle is specified in degrees, you have to multiply the angle by PI()/180 or convert it with the RADIANS() function.

The sine of angle α in an unit circle ($c = 1$) increases up to 90° and has the value 1 in this angle (see Figure 16-27).

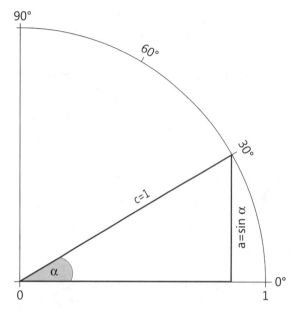

Figure 16-27 Sine in a unit circle.

In a coordinate system, the angle α on the x-axis and the sine of α on the y-axis result in the curve shown in Figure 16-28.

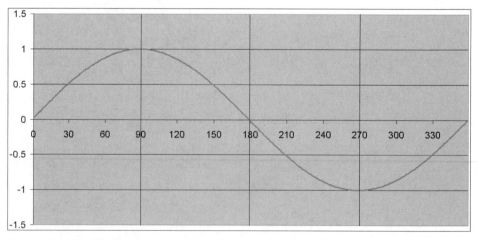

Figure 16-28 Sine curve.

Example Suppose you want to calculate the height of a mountain. The distance between the observation station and the mountaintop is 3.7 miles. The mountaintop appears at an angle of 19.5°. The formula for the sine is:

$$Sin() = \frac{opposite\ leg}{hypotenuse}$$

You enter the existing information in the formula

$$Sin(19.5) = \frac{Height}{3.7miles}$$

Here is the equation to calculate the height:

```
Height = sin(19.5) • 3.7
```

The result is:

```
Height = 1.235 miles ≈ 6,521 feet
```

Enter the following formula in the formula bar:

```
=SIN(RADIANS(19.5)) • 3.7
```

For Excel to be able to calculate the sine for the angle of 19.5°, the angle has to be converted to radians. Then the sine is multiplied by the hypotenuse.

To return the result in feet, you must round the result to three digits and multiply by 5,280.

```
=ROUND((SIN(RADIANS(19.5)) • 3.7),3) • 5280
```

See also ASIN(), PI()

> **Sample Files**
>
> Use the SIN_COS and trigon worksheets in the Chapter16.xls or Chapter16.xlsx sample file. The sample files are found in the Chapter16 folder. For more information about the sample files, see the section titled "Using the Sample Files" on page xxiii.

SINH()

Syntax SINH(*number*)

Definition This function returns the hyperbolic sine of a number.

Argument

- **number (required)** Any real number

Background The hyperbolic sine belongs to the hyperbolic functions which are (like the circle functions) defined for all real and complex numbers. (However, Excel allows only real arguments, not complex arguments, for hyperbolic functions.) The formula for the hyperbolic sine is:

$$\sinh x = \frac{e^x - e^{-x}}{2}$$

A hyperbolic sine is shown in Figure 16-29. The hyperbolic sine is often used for research and development in engineering and natural sciences.

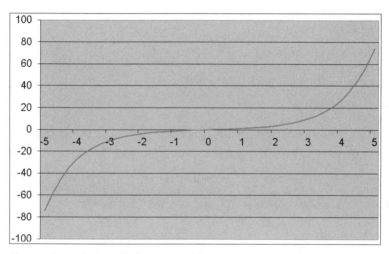

Figure 16-29 The hyperbolic sine is odd and monotonic increasing between -∞ and +∞.

Examples Some examples of this function are:

- =SINH(0) returns 0.

- =SINH(0.5) returns 0.52109531.

- =SINH(-0.5) returns -0.52109531.

Tip Use SINH() to find the probability of an event

One example in Excel Help refers to an empiric cumulative probability distribution. These distribution functions are used for real test series if the behavior of the observed system or its components is not ideal; that is, if the requirements and assumptions for a normal or Poisson distribution are not met.

In this case, a cumulative distribution function, such as a function based on the hyperbolic sine, might be better suited.

See also ACOSH(), ASINH(), ATANH(), COSH(), TANH()

Sample Files

Use the Data&Chart and Distribution worksheets in the SinH.xls or SinH.xlsx sample file. The sample files are found in the Chapter16 folder. For more information about the sample files, see the section titled "Using the Sample Files" on page xxiii.

SQRT()

Syntax SQRT(*number*)

Definition This function returns the square root of a number.

Argument

- *number* **(required)** The number for which you want to calculate the square root

Background The root function is an inverse function to the exponentiation.

$$a^x = b \Leftrightarrow \sqrt[x]{b} = a$$

Base (*b*) is the radicand, and *x* is the order of a root. If the order of a root is 2, it is called a *square root*.

The SQRT() function returns only the square root of a positive number. If *number* is negative, the function returns the #NUM! error.

Example A building lot has the dimensions 19.5 x 10.5 m. You want to know the dimensions of a coextensive square building lot.

The formula

=SQRT(19.5 · 10.5)

as well as the formula

=SQRT(PRODUCT(19.5;10.5))

return 14.309088. To round the result to two decimal places, you use the ROUND() function:

=ROUND((SQRT(PRODUCT(19.5,10.5))),2)

The formula breaks down as follows:

1. You calculate the product of 19.5 and 10.5:

   =PRODUCT(19.5,10.4)

2. You extract the root of the product:

   =SQRT(PRODUCT(19.5;10.5))

3. You round the result to two decimal places:

   =ROUND((SQRT(PRODUCT(19.5,10.5))),2)

The result is 14.31 m.

See also SQRTPI()

> **Sample Files**
>
> Use the SQRT worksheet in the Chapter16.xls or Chapter16.xlsx sample file. The sample files are found in the Chapter16 folder. For more information about the sample files, see the section titled "Using the Sample Files" on page xxiii.

SQRTPI()

Syntax SQRTPI(*number*)

Definition This function returns the root of a number multiplied by pi.

Argument

- *number* **(required)** The number by which pi is multiplied

Background The SQRTPI() function calculates the root of a positive number multiplied by pi. If *number* is less than zero, the function returns the #NUM! error. The following applies:

$$SQRTPI(x) = SQRT(PI() * X) = \sqrt{\pi \cdot x}$$

Examples Some examples for this function are:

- =SQRTPI(12) returns 6.13996025.

- =SQRTPI(5) returns 3.9633273.

See also PI(), SQRT()

SUBTOTAL()

Syntax SUBTOTAL(*function_num,ref1,ref2, ...*)

Definition This function returns a subtotal in a list or database. It is usually easier to create a list with subtotals by using the Data/Subtotal command. After the subtotal list has been created, you can modify it with the SUBTOTAL() function.

Arguments

- ***function_num* (required)** A number between 1 and 11 (including hidden values) or between 101 and 111 (ignoring hidden values) that specifies which function to use when calculating subtotals within a list. The possible values are shown in Table 16-6.

Table 16-6 **Possible Values for the *function_num* Argument**

Code for Unhidden Values	Code for Hidden Values	Function
1	101	AVERAGE()
2	102	COUNT()
3	103	COUNTA()
4	104	MAX()
5	105	MIN()
6	106	PRODUCT()
7	107	STDEV()
8	108	STDEVP()
9	109	SUM()
10	110	VAR()
11	111	VARP()

- ***ref1* (required) and *ref2* (optional)** The range or reference for which you want to calculate the subtotal

Background   Though simple formulas include filtered values, the SUBTOTAL() function can refer to filtered results. If there are other subtotals within the *ref* arguments (*nested subtotals*), these nested subtotals are ignored to avoid double counting.

If any of the references are 3-D references, the SUBTOTAL() function returns the #VALUE! error.

For the *function_num* constants 1 through 11, the SUBTOTAL() function includes the values of rows hidden by the Format/Row/Hide command (Excel 2003) or the Start/Cells/Hide & Unhide command (Excel 2007 or Excel 2010). Use these constants to subtotal hidden and nonhidden numbers in a list.

For the *function_num* constants 101 through 111, the SUBTOTAL() function ignores the values of rows hidden by the Format/Row/Hide command (Excel 2003) or the Start/Cells/ Hide & Unhide command (Excel 2007 or Excel 2010). Use these constants to subtotal only nonhidden numbers in a list.

The SUBTOTAL() function ignores any rows that are not included in the result of a filter, no matter which *function_num* value you use.

The SUBTOTAL() function is designed for columns of data or vertical ranges, not for rows of data or horizontal ranges. For example, when you subtotal a horizontal range using a function constant of 101 or greater, as in =SUBTOTAL(109,B2:G2), hiding a column does not affect the subtotal. However, hiding a row in a subtotal of a vertical range does affect the subtotal.

Example   You can use the SUBTOTAL() function to calculate a sum based on filtered values (see Figure 16-30).

	E1		f_x	=SUBTOTAL(9;C2:C8)	
	A	B	C	D	E
1	**State** ▾	**Company** ▾	**Sales** ▾	**Total Sales**	$ 394,353.00
2	Nebraska	Litware, Inc.	$51,857.00		
3	Michigan	Margie's Travel	$30,090.00		
4	Illinois	Miller Ltd.	$85,164.00		
5	Michigan	Margie's Travel	$84,843.00		
6	New York	Miller Ltd.	$46,536.00		
7	Florida	Coho Winery	$71,731.00		
8	Michigan	Margie's Travel	$24,132.00		

Figure 16-30 The sum of the sales in E1 is calculated for the filtered values.

The formula is: =SUBTOTAL(9,C2:C8).

To view the sales for Michigan, specify a filter in column A (see Figure 16-31).

Figure 16-31 Subtotal of the sales.

See also AGGREGATE(), AVERAGE(), COUNT(), COUNTA(), MAX(), MIN(), PRODUCT(), STDEV(), SUM(), VAR()

Sample Files

Use the SUBTOTAL and SUBTOTAL2 worksheets in the Chapter16.xls or Chapter16.xlsx sample file. The sample files are found in the Chapter16 folder. For more information about the sample files, see the section titled "Using the Sample Files" on page xxiii.

SUM()

Syntax SUM(*number1,number2,...*)

Definition This function adds all numbers specified as arguments.

Arguments

- ***number1* (required) and *number2* (optional)** The minimum number of values is 1, and the maximum is 255 (30 in Excel 2003 and earlier versions) that you want to add (but a second value makes sense for a sum). Instead of separate numbers, it is also possible to build a sum for a range of cells—for example, A1:A5.

Background The result of an addition operation is called the *sum*. The sign for addition is the plus sign (+), but the Σ is also used:

$$x = a + b + c + d + ...$$

or

$$x = \sum (a,b,c,d ...)$$

The arguments for the SUM() function can be numbers, logical values, and numerals when directly entered in the formula. For example:

- The logical value TRUE is converted to 1.

- "12" is treated as 12 even though the value is enclosed in quotation marks.

> **Note**
> Text and logical values in a cell reference are ignored.

If an argument is an array or a reference, only the numbers in that array or reference are counted. Empty cells, logical values, or text in the array or reference are ignored.

Arguments that are error values or text that cannot be converted into numbers cause errors.

Example   There are so many practical uses that Excel provides the Σ symbol in the start bar as well as in the function bar. No Excel user wants to do without this function; for example, to add expenses: =SUM(3.25,5.30,4.70) returns 13.25.

More examples:

- =SUM(1,4,7) returns 12.

- =SUM(A2:B5) adds the values in cell range A2:B5.

- =SUM(A2:B5,12) adds 12 to the sum of cell range A2:B5.

See also AVERAGE(), COUNT(), DCOUNTA(), PRODUCT(), SUMPRODUCT()

> **Sample Files**
> Use the PRODUCT_SUM worksheet in the Chapter16.xls or Chapter16.xlsx sample file. The sample files are found in the Chapter16 folder. For more information about the sample files, see the section titled "Using the Sample Files" on page xxiii.

SUMIF()

Syntax   SUMIF(*range,criteria,sum_range*)

Definition   This function adds all values in a range that match the search criteria.

Arguments

- ***range* (required)** The range in which you want to find the criteria.

- ***criteria* (required)** The criteria in the form of a number, an expression, or text. The criteria determine which cells will be added. For example, the criteria argument can be expressed as 32, ">32", "32", or "apples".

- ***sum_range* (optional)** The actual cells to add.

Background   The SUMIF() function can be used to filter for certain values in a list and add those values. The values in an array are added only if they match the search criterion.

Excel provides additional functions that allow you to analyze data based on a condition. To count text or numbers in an array, use the COUNTIF() function. This function, as well as the AVERAGEIF() and AVERAGEIFS() functions, are explained in Chapter 12.

To return one value or two values based on a condition, such as a sales bonus, use the logical IF() function (see Chapter 9, "Logical Functions").

Example   Assume that you have to add the sales in a list for sales representative Meier (see Figure 16-32).

	B9		*f*_x =SUMIF(A2:A6;A9;B2:B6)	
	A	B	C	
1	**Name**	**Sales**		
2	Meier	$ 350.00		
3	Smith	$ 260.00		
4	Gates	$ 300.00		
5	Meier	$ 360.00		
6	Pedro	$ 240.00		
7				
8	Total sales of:			
9	Meier	$ 710.00		

Figure 16-32 Calculating the sum by using a filter.

Enter the following formula in cell B9:

`=SUMIF(A2:A6,A9,B2:B6)`

1. Specify the array you want to filter (A2:A6).

2. Enter the search criterion (A9).

3. Specify the array containing the values you want to add (B2:B6).

The result is the sum of the sales for the sales representative Meier: $710.

If the *sum_range* argument is omitted, Excel adds the cells that are specified in the *range* argument.

See also AVERAGEIF(), AVERAGEIFS(), COUNTIF(), SUM(), SUMIFS()

> **Sample Files**
> Use the SUMIF worksheet in the Chapter16.xls or Chapter16.xlsx sample file. The sample files are found in the Chapter16 folder. For more information about the sample files, see the section titled "Using the Sample Files" on page xxiii.

SUMIFS()

Syntax   SUMIFS(*sum_range,criteria_range1,criteria1,criteria_range2,criteria2,...*)

Definition   This function adds all numbers in a range matching the search criteria in the criteria ranges.

Arguments

- *sum_range* **(required)** The cell range in which you want to find the criteria.

- *criteria_range1* **(required) and** *criteria_range2* **(optional)** At least one and up to 127 cell ranges in which you want to find the values in *criteria1*, *criteria2*, and so on.

- *criteria1* **(required) and** *criteria2* **(optional)** The criteria in the form of a number, an expression, or text. The criteria determine which cells will be added. For example, the criteria argument can be expressed as 32, ">32", "32", or "apples".

Background   This function was new in Excel 2007 and finally allows the entry of multiple criteria in a SUMIF() calculation. The SUMIFS() function is an extension of the SUMIF() function and can be used to filter for certain values in a list and add those values. The values in an array are added only if they match the search criteria.

Excel provides additional functions that allow you to analyze data based on a condition. To count text or numbers in an array, use the COUNTIF() function. This function, as well as the AVERAGEIF() and AVERAGEIFS() functions, are explained in Chapter 12.

To return one value or two values based on a condition, such as a sales bonus, use the logical IF() function (see Chapter 9).

Example   Assume that you have to add the sales that took place in a certain month in a list for a company and a product. Figure 16-33 shows the solution.

	H5		f_x =SUMIFS(E4:E22;B4:B22;H7;C4:C22;H8;D4:D22;H9)					
	A	B	C	D	E	F	G	H
1								
2								
3		Company	Product	Month	Sales			
4		Alpine Ski House	Desktop P	5	$ 6,214.00			
5		Asian Traiding Corp.	Desktop P	2	$47,570.00		Total Sales	$ 5,723.00
6		Contoso, Ltd	Desktop P	3	$ 5,723.00			
7		Contoso, Ltd	Notebook	4	$ 6,214.00		Company:	Contoso, Ltd
8		Maier & Sons Inc.	Notebook	4	$ 7,321.00		Product	Desktop PC
9		Abrus, Luka	Monitor	2	$ 1,533.00		Month:	3
10		Litware, Inc.	Monitor	1	$ 3,241.00			
11		Contoso, Ltd	iPad	5	$ 2,145.00			
12		Wingtip Toys	Desktop P	6	$12,412.00			
13		Litware, Inc.	Desktop P	7	$ 4,723.00			
14		Contoso, Ltd	Monitor	3	$ 3,240.00			
15		Contoso, Ltd	Desktop P	5	$ 5,132.00			
16		Acevedo, Humberto	Notebook	7	$ 1,533.00			
17		Acevedo, Humberto	Monitor	2	$ 7,321.00			
18		Wingtip Toys	Notebook	3	$ 8,471.00			
19		Graphic Design Institt	Monitor	5	$24,000.00			
20		Coho Vineyard	Desktop P	7	$ 2,547.00			
21		Contoso, Ltd	iPad	1	$ 5,250.00			
22		Coho Vineyard	Monitor	5	$25,400.00			

Figure 16-33 Calculating the sum by using multiple filters.

Cells I7 through I9 contain the filter criteria. Enter the following formula in cell I5:

```
=SUMIFS(E3:E21,B3:B21,I7,C3:C21,I8,D3:D21,I9)
```

1. Specify the array containing the values you want to add (E3:E21). The list is longer than the one shown in Figure 16-33.

   The first array contains the criterion you want to filter (B3:B21).

2. Enter the first search criterion (I7).

3. Enter the second criteria range (C3:C21), the second criterion (I8), and so on.

In month 3, the Contoso, Ltd. company spent $5,723 on the Desktop PC product.

See also AVERAGEIF(), AVERAGEIFS(), COUNTIFS(), SUM(), SUMIF()

> ## Sample Files
>
> Use the SUMIFS and SUMIFS2 worksheets in the Chapter16.xls or Chapter16.xlsx sample file. The sample files are found in the Chapter16 folder. For more information about the sample files, see the section titled "Using the Sample Files" on page xxiii.

Chapter 16

SUMPRODUCT()

Syntax SUMPRODUCT(*array1,array2,array3,...*)

Definition This function multiplies the matching components of the indicated arrays and returns the sum of these products.

Arguments

- ***array1* and *array2* (required) and *array3* (optional)** At least two and up to 255 components of arrays (30 in Excel 2003 and earlier versions) that you want to multiply and add.

Background For a sum product, the values in an array are multiplied and the results are added. The formula is:

$$\begin{matrix} a_1 & b_1 \\ a_2 & b_2 \\ a_3 & b_3 \end{matrix} = \left(a_1 \cdot b_1 + a_2 \cdot b_2 + a_3 \cdot b_3 \right)$$

For example, you can calculate the total price of the products listed in a table.

The array arguments must have the same number of rows and columns. If they do not, the SUMPRODUCT() function returns the #VALUE! error. SUMPRODUCT() treats array entries that are not numeric as if they were zeros.

Example Suppose you want to calculate the total price for the following products:

- 12 apples at $0.39

- 15 pears at $0.42

The result is calculated as follows:

Total price = 12 • 0.39 + 15 • 0.42 = 10.98

In Excel, the initial values are entered in two arrays (see Figure 16-34).

C5		f_x	=SUMPRODUCT(B2:B3;C2:C3)	
	A	B	C	D	E
1		Amount	Price		
2	Apples	12	$ 0.39		
3	Pears	15	$ 0.42		
4					
5		Total Price:	$ 10.98		

Figure 16-34 Arrays containing the amount and price.

Enter the following formula in the formula bar:

=SUMPRODUCT(B2:B3,C2:C3)

See also MMULT(), PRODUCT(), SUM()

> **Sample Files**
>
> Use the SUMPRODUCT worksheet in the Chapter16.xls or Chapter16.xlsx sample file. The sample files are found in the Chapter16 folder. For more information about the sample files, see the section titled "Using the Sample Files" on page xxiii.

SUMSQ()

Syntax SUMSQ(*number1,number2,...*)

Definition This function adds squared arguments.

Arguments

- *number1 (required) and number2 (optional)* Up to 255 arguments (30 in Excel 2003 and earlier versions) to add. You can also use an array with a single row or column or a reference to an array instead of arguments separated by commas.

Background The SUMSQ() function calculates the square numbers of the given arguments and adds those numbers. The formula is:

$$\sum \left(a^2, b^2, c^2, d^2 \dots \right)$$

More examples for this function are:

- =SUMSQ(2,3,4) returns 29 (4+9+16).

- =SUMSQ(5,6) returns 61 (25+36).

- =SUMSQ(12,3) returns 153 (144+9).

> **Sample Files**
>
> Use the PRODUCT_SUM worksheet in the Chapter16.xls or Chapter16.xlsx sample file. The sample files are found in the Chapter16 folder. For more information about the sample files, see the section titled "Using the Sample Files" on page xxiii.

Chapter 16

SUMX2MY2()

Syntax   SUMX2MY2(*array_x,array_y*)

Definition   This function returns the sum of the difference of squares of corresponding values in two arrays (see Figure 16-35).

Arguments

- ***array_x* (required)** The first array or range of values

- ***array_y* (required)** The second array or range of values

Background   The arguments should be numbers or names, arrays, or references containing numbers.

If an array or a reference argument contains text, logical values, or empty cells, those values are ignored. However, cells with the value zero are included. If *array_x* and *array_y* have a different number of values, the SUMX2MY2() function returns the #N/A error.

The equation for the sum of the difference of squares is:

$$\sum \left(x^2 - y^2 \right)$$

The solution for this equation is built for the example (see Figure 16-35) as follows:

1. In two specified ranges:

   ○ Range A: 4, 5

   ○ Range B: 2, 3

   The square number is calculated for each value:

   ○ Range A: 16, 25

   ○ Range B: 4, 9

2. The square numbers of all ranges are added:

   ○ Range A: 41

   ○ Range B: 13

3. The sums are subtracted (see Figure 16-35):

   41 – 13 = 28

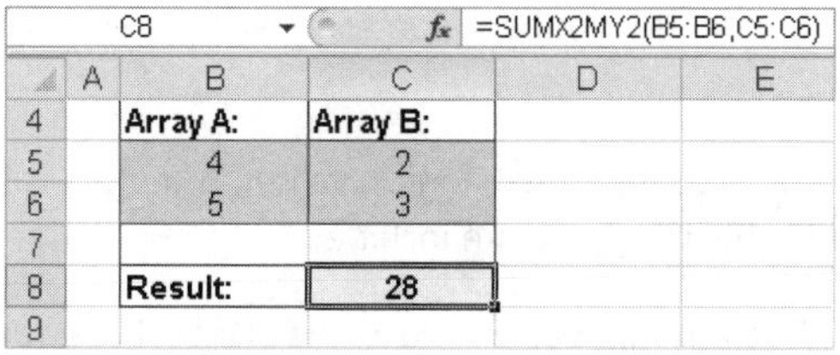

Figure 16-35 The SUMX2MY2() function.

Example   Use this function for statistic tests to evaluate the parallelism, accuracy, or relevance of models. Examples are variance analyses such as:

- The calculation of variances in series of measurements

- The analysis of linear models (significance of the parameters, quality of the model)

For this application, the square sums and the degrees of freedom (*f*-values) for the difference of square sums are calculated. The SUMX2MY2() function provides the foundation for these kinds of calculations. You will find more information in Chapter 12.

See also SUMPRODUCT(), SUMX2PY2(), SUMXMY2()

Sample Files

Use the SUMXY worksheet in the Chapter16.xls or Chapter16.xlsx sample file. The sample files are found in the Chapter16 folder. For more information about the sample files, see the section titled "Using the Sample Files" on page xxiii.

SUMX2PY2()

Syntax   SUMX2PY2(*array_x,array_y*)

Definition   This function returns the sum of the sum of squares of corresponding values in two arrays. The *sum of the sum of squares* is a common term in many statistical calculations (see Figure 16-36).

Arguments

- ***array_x* (required)** The first array or range of values

- ***array_y* (required)** The second array or range of values

Background   The arguments should be numbers, names, arrays, or references containing numbers.

If an array or a reference argument contains text, logical values, or empty cells, those values are ignored. However, cells with the value zero are included.

If *array_x* and *array_y* have a different number of values, the SUMX2PY2() function returns the #N/A error.

The equation for the sum of the difference of squares is:

$$\sum\left(x^2 - y^2\right)$$

The solution of this equation is built for the example (see Figure 16-36) as follows:

1. In two specified ranges:

   ○ Range A: 4, 5

   ○ Range B: 2, 3

   The square number is calculated for each value:

   ○ Range A: 16, 25

   ○ Range B: 4, 9

2. The square numbers of all ranges are added:

   ○ Range A: 41

   ○ Range B: 13

3. The sums are added (see Figure 16-36):

   41 + 13 = 54

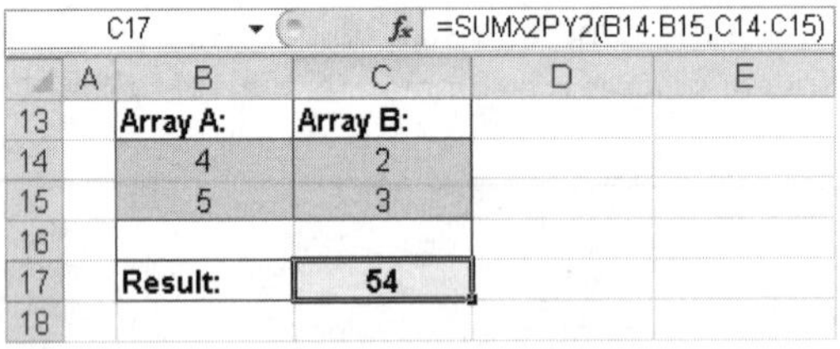

C17		f_x =SUMX2PY2(B14:B15,C14:C15)		

	A	B	C	D	E
13		Array A:	Array B:		
14		4	2		
15		5	3		
16					
17		Result:	54		
18					

Figure 16-36 Square sum of array components.

See also SUMPRODUCT(), SUMX2MY2(), SUMXMY2()

> **Sample Files**
>
> Use the SUMXY worksheet in the Chapter16.xls or Chapter16.xlsx sample file. The sample files are found in the Chapter16 folder. For more information about the sample files, see the section titled "Using the Sample Files" on page xxiii.

SUMXMY2()

Syntax   SUMXMY2(*array_x,array_y*)

Definition   This function returns the sum of squares of differences of corresponding values in two arrays (see Figure 16-37).

Arguments

- *array_x* **(required)** The first array or range of values

- *array_y* **(required)** The second array or range of values

Background   The arguments should be numbers, names, arrays, or references containing numbers.

If an array or a reference argument contains text, logical values, or empty cells, those values are ignored. However, cells with the value zero are included.

If *array_x* and *array_y* have a different number of values, the SUMXMY2() function returns the #N/A error. The equation for the sum of the squared differences is:

$$\sum (x - y)^2$$

The solution of this equation is built for the example (see Figure 16-37) as follows:

1. In two specified ranges:

    - Range A: 4, 5

    - Range B: 2, 3

    The values next to each other are subtracted:

    - First value in the ranges A and B: 4 − 2

    - Second value in the ranges A and B: 5 − 3

2. The square sums are added (see Figure 16-37):

$$2^2 + 2^2 = 4 + 4 = 8$$

	A	B	C	D	E
		C26	f_x =SUMXMY2(B23:B24,C23:C24)		
22		Array A:	Array B:		
23		4	2		
24		5	3		
25					
26		Result:	8		
27					

Figure 16-37 The SUMXMY2() function.

See also SUMPRODUCT(), SUMX2MY2(), SUMX2PY2()

> **Sample Files**
>
> Use the SUMXY worksheet in the Chapter16.xls or Chapter16.xlsx sample file. The sample files are found in the Chapter16 folder. For more information about the sample files, see the section titled "Using the Sample Files" on page xxiii.

TAN()

Syntax   TAN(*number*)

Definition   This function returns the tangent of an angle.

Argument

- *number* **(required)** The angle in radians for which you want the tangent

Background   In a right triangle, the ratio between the opposite leg and the adjacent leg depends on the apex angle. The ratio of the opposite leg of an angle and the adjacent leg is the *tangent (tan)* of an angle.

$$\tan \alpha = \frac{a}{b}; \; \tan \beta = \frac{b}{a};$$

The TAN() function requires radians for calculations. If the angle is specified in degrees, you have to multiply the angle by PI()/180 or convert it with the RADIANS() function.

If angle α in an unit circle ($c = 1$) increases between 0° and 90°, the tangent increases between 0 and ∞ (infinity) (see Figure 16-38).

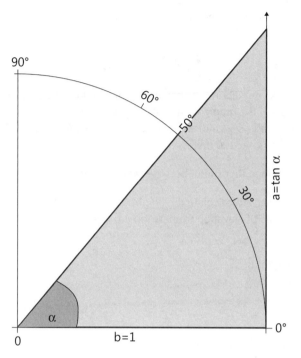

Figure 16-38 The tangent in a unit circle.

In a coordinate system, the angle α on the x-axis and the tangent of α on the y-axis result in the curve shown in Figure 16-39.

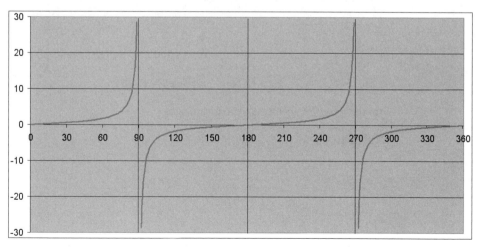

Figure 16-39 the tangent curve.

Chapter 16

The ratio between the tangent and the sine and cosine is:

$$\tan = \frac{\sin}{\cos}$$

The tangent indicates the correlation between the gradient angle and the slope of a straight line. For example, if the gradient angle of a street is 12°, its slope is tan(12°) and approximately 0.21. The traffic sign indicating the slope of the street reads "21%" (an elevation difference of 21 meters per 100 meters).

For a perpendicular, the slope isn't useful because tan(90°) and tan(–90°) are not defined.

Example Suppose you want to calculate the height of a chimney. The chimney is 130 meters away, and the angle of elevation from its top is α=24°50′. How high is the chimney if the eye level is 1.6 meters?

The formula for the tangent is:

$$\tan() = \frac{opposite\ leg}{Adjacent\ leg}$$

You enter the existing information in the formula

$$\tan(24.5) = \frac{chimney\ height\ (h)}{130}$$

The equation to calculate the height is

height = 130 · tan(24.5)

The result is rounded to two decimal places and 1.60 meters (eye level) is added.

h = 59.2444132 ≈ 59.24 m +1.60 m (eye level) = 60.84 m

Enter the following formula in the formula bar:

```
=ROUND(TAN(RADIANS(24.5)) • 130;2)+1.6
```

For Excel to be able to calculate the tangent for the angle of 19.5°, the angle has to be converted to radians. Then the tangent is multiplied by the opposite leg. The result is rounded to two decimal places and 1.60 meters (eye level) is added.

See also ATAN(), ATAN2(), PI()

> ## Sample Files
>
> Use the SIN_COS and trigon worksheets in the Chapter16.xls or Chapter16.xlsx sample file. The sample files are found in the Chapter16 folder. For more information about the sample files, see the section titled "Using the Sample Files" on page xxiii.

TANH()

Syntax   TANH(*number*)

Definition   This function returns the hyperbolic tangent of a number.

Argument

- ***number* (required)** Any real number

Background   The hyperbolic tangent belongs to the hyperbolic functions, which are (like the circle functions) defined for all real and complex numbers. (However, Excel allows only real arguments, not complex arguments, for hyperbolic functions.)

The formula for the hyperbolic tangent is:

$$\tanh x = \frac{e^x - e^{-x}}{e^x + e^{-x}} = \frac{\sinh x}{\cosh x}$$

The last term shows the similarity with the trigonometry functions.

The hyperbolic tangent is often used for research and development in engineering and natural sciences (see Figure 16-40).

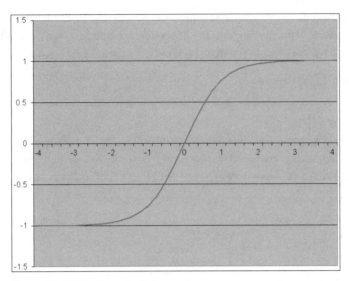

Figure 16-40 The hyperbolic tangent.

You might miss the corresponding cotangent you know from the trigonometry functions: sin, cos, tan, and cot. However, neither the trigonometric cotangent nor the hyperbolic cotangent is implemented as a table function, because cotangent = tangent^{-1}:

- **Cotangent:**

$$\cot x = \frac{1}{\tan x}$$

- **Hyperbolic cotangent:**

$$\coth x = \frac{1}{\tanh x}$$

From this, it follows that the hyperbolic cotangent is:

$$\coth x = \frac{e^x + e^{-x}}{e^x - e^{-x}}$$

Instead of

```
=COTH(A1)
```

(COTH doesn't exist), enter

`=1/TANH(A1)`

Example   The hyperbolic tangent is used to calculate the propagation speed of waves. The formula for the propagation speed υ of waves is:

$$v = \sqrt{\frac{g\lambda}{2\pi}} \tanh \frac{2\pi h}{\lambda}$$

This formula uses the gravity acceleration g [m/s^2], wave length λ [m], and water depth h [m].

If you enter this formula into a table, you can use the following two approximate formulas for shallow and deep water:

- **Shallow water:**

  $$h \ll \lambda \rightarrow v_s = \sqrt{gh}$$

- **Deep water:**

  $$h \gg \lambda \rightarrow v_d = \sqrt{\frac{g\lambda}{2\pi}}$$

More examples of this function are:

- `=TANH(0)` returns 0.

- `=TANH(1)` returns 0.761594156.

- `=TANH(-1)` returns -0.76159416.

- `=TANH(10)` returns 1.

- `=TANH(-10)` returns -1.

See also ACOSH(), ASIN(), ATANH(), COSH(), SINH()

Sample Files

Use the Data&Chart and Water waves worksheets in the TanH.xls or TanH.xlsx sample file. The sample files are found in the Chapter16 folder. For more information about the sample files, see the section titled "Using the Sample Files" on page xxiii.

Chapter 16

TRUNC()

Syntax TRUNC(*number,num_digits*)

Definition This function truncates the decimal places of a number and returns an integer.

Arguments

- *number* **(required)** The number you want to truncate.

- *num_digits* **(optional)** A number indicating the precision of the truncation. The default value for *num_digits* is 0. You can specify positive and negative values for the *num_digits* argument.

Background The TRUNC() function removes the fractional part of a number up to the decimal places specified in *num_digits*. If *num_digits* is omitted, the number is truncated to the integer.

The TRUNC() and ROUND() functions return the same result. The difference between both functions is that specifying the number of digits to truncate is optional for TRUNC(), but for ROUND() it is required.

Example A practical use for this function is the truncation of money amounts, for example, to two decimal places or to even amounts. Here are some more examples:

- =TRUNC(234.4692354,2) returns 234.46.

- =TRUNC(234.4692354,-1) returns 230.

- =TRUNC(9.3) returns 9.

- =TRUNC(-9.3) returns -9.

- =TRUNC(18.628,2) returns 18.62.

See also CEILING(), CEILING.PRECISE(), FLOOR(), FLOOR.PRECISE(), INT(), MOD(), ROUND()

> ### Sample Files
> Use the ROUND worksheet in the Chapter16.xls or Chapter16.xlsx sample file. The sample files are found in the Chapter16 folder. For more information about the sample files, see the section titled "Using the Sample Files" on page xxiii.

Engineering Functions

This chapter explains the engineering functions, which are also called *technical functions*. In the standard Microsoft Excel installation for versions of Excel prior to and including Microsoft Office Excel 2003, these functions led a very secluded existence. Only after the Analysis Functions add-in was enabled were they available in the Function Wizard, in the Technical category, and could be used in formulas (see Chapter 2, "Using Functions and PowerPivot").

In Excel 2010, the analysis functions are located on the Formulas tab in the Function Library group. If you click the More Functions button, five more function categories are displayed. The second category is Engineering, which lists all of the engineering functions in alphabetical order.

How Engineering Functions Are Organized

Engineering functions can be divided into four groups (see Tables 17-1, 17-2, 17-3, and 17-4):

- Conversion functions

- Functions for complex numbers

- Functions for higher mathematics

- Saltus functions

Unlike the alphabetical arrangement in the Excel ribbon list, this chapter looks at the functions according to the preceding grouping.

Conversion Functions

The conversion functions help you convert numbers from one number system into another; for example, from the hexadecimal system common in electronic data processing to the more familiar decimal system.

With CONVERT(), you can convert one physical measurement into another. This is especially helpful when you are dealing with US measurements. For example, who actually knows all the conversion formulas for the various temperature scales from memory? This function shouldn't be too difficult to understand. Usually what is lacking is practice with various number and measurement systems.

Table 17-1 **Conversion Functions**

Function	Description
BIN2DEC()	Converts a binary number into a decimal number
BIN2HEX()	Converts a binary number into a hexadecimal number
BIN2OCT()	Converts a binary number into an octal number
DEC2BIN()	Converts a decimal number into a binary number
DEC2HEX()	Converts a decimal number into a hexadecimal number
DEC2OCT()	Converts an decimal number into an octal number
HEX2BIN()	Converts a hexadecimal number into a binary number
HEX2DEC()	Converts a hexadecimal number into a decimal number
HEX2OCT()	Converts a hexadecimal number into an octal number

Function	Description
OCT2BIN()	Converts an octal number into a binary number
OCT2DEC()	Converts an octal number into a decimal number
OCT2HEX()	Converts an octal number into a hexadecimal number
CONVERT()	Performs conversions between different measurement systems

Functions for Complex Numbers

In principle, Excel permits only real numbers in cells, formulas, and functions. If you want to perform calculations with imaginary or complex numbers, you need to take a detour by using the functions of this group, because Excel is not able to compute the results of complex numbers directly. You can find all the necessary functions in this chapter.

Table 17-2 **Functions for Complex Numbers**

Function	Description
COMPLEX()	Converts real and imaginary coefficients into a complex number
IMABS()	Calculates the absolute value of a complex number
IMAGINARY()	Calculates the imaginary part of a complex number
IMARGUMENT()	Calculates the argument (Φ) of a complex number
IMCONJUGATE()	Calculates the conjugate of a complex number
IMCOS()	Calculates the cosine of a complex number
IMDIV()	Calculates the quotient of two complex numbers
IMEXP()	The exponential function for complex numbers
IMLN()	Calculates the natural logarithm of a complex number
IMLOG10()	Calculates the decadal logarithm of a complex number
IMLOG2()	Calculates the binary logarithm of a complex number
IMPOWER()	Exponentiates a complex number
IMPRODUCT()	Calculates the product of complex numbers
IMREAL()	Returns the real part of a complex number
IMSIN()	Calculates the sine of a complex number
IMSQRT()	Calculates the square root of a complex number
IMSUB()	Calculates the difference between two complex numbers
IMSUM()	Calculates the sum of complex numbers

Functions for Higher Mathematics

The third group contains functions that are typically used in engineering. This is why they are called *engineering functions*. To be able to use these functions, you should have knowledge of higher mathematics, especially of differential equations, error analysis, and probability theory.

Table 17-3 **Functions for Higher Mathematics**

Function	Description
BESSELI()	Calculates a value of the modified Bessel function of the first kind $I_n(x)$
BESSELJ()	Calculates a value of the Bessel function of the first kind $J_n(x)$
BESSELK()	Calculates a value of the modified Bessel function of the second kind $K_n(x)$
BESSELY()	Calculates a value of the Bessel function of the second kind $Y_n(x)$
ERF.PRECISE()/ERF()	Calculates a value of the Gaussian error function
ERFC.PRECISE()/ERFC()	Calculates a value of the complement to the Gaussian error function

Saltus Functions

There are two functions that do not fit into the conventional groupings because they are not continuous. (Mathematicians call them *saltus functions*, so we decided to use this name as a group title.)

> **Note**
>
> The FACTDOUBLE() function was part of the Technical category (now called Engineering) until Excel 2003. In Excel 2007 and Excel 2010, the function is part of the Mathematics and Trigonometry category and is explained in Chapter 16, "Mathematical and Trigonometry Functions."

Table 17-4 **Saltus Functions**

Function	Description
DELTA()	Checks whether two numbers are equal
GESTEP()	Checks whether a number is greater than a given threshold value

Conversion Functions

Conversion functions fall into the following categories: number systems, the binary system, one's complement, and two's complement.

Number Systems

This category contains a series of conversion functions that convert numbers from one number system to another.

The most frequently used and most familiar number system is the *decimal system*, which works with ten distinct symbols and is derived from our ten fingers. In the English language, this connection can still be found: *digit* can mean *finger* as well as *number*.

With the development of data processing, a need arose for a number system that would accommodate the technical factors of the former calculating machines. The general opinion is that the binary system was introduced because calculating machines were binary calculators, and they were able to work with only two states, on and off. (By the way, in 1943, Konrad Zuse built the first programmable binary calculator, the Z3.)

> **Note**
>
> What you just read is only half the truth about the introduction of the binary system into calculation technology: Just as important, or even more so, is the fact that the binary system has much easier calculation rules.
>
> It's hard enough for our abecedarians to learn all the various formulas of our beloved decimal system in math class—3+4, 3+5, 4+7, and so on—and in addition to that, the multiplication tables! To build all that into the mechanical calculation machines was completely impossible back then.
>
> The binary system can basically get by with three calculation rules on which all the others are based:
>
> - 0 + 0 = 0
> - 0 + 1 = 1 or 1 + 0 = 1
> - 1 + 1 = 10

In addition to the familiar decimal system, there are three other systems that are used in calculation technology. Because Excel can use these four number systems, twelve conversion functions are needed: four number systems can each be converted into the three others.

The number systems are:

- Decimal (10)

- Binary (2)

- Octal (8)

- Hexadecimal (16)

The number in parentheses is the base for each number system and thus the number of the digits this number system has. Because the hexadecimal system requires more digits than we have available, the missing digits are represented by the letters A through F. (Not to be confused with the *hexagesimal* system (actually, the *sexagesimal* system) with a base of 60, which is used to measure angles, geographic lengths and widths, and time. It is the foundation for old numbering terms such as *dozen* or *great gross* as well.) Table 17-5 lists the number systems.

Table 17-5 **Number Systems Overview**

System	Base	Digits
Binary system	2	0 and 1
Octal system	8	0 through 7
Decimal system	10	0 through 9
Hexadecimal system	16	0 through 9, A through F

Binary System

Because the binary system allows only two values per number position, binary numbers can quickly become very long and are difficult to read. Therefore, either of the following can be done:

- Three binary digits are combined into one base-8 number system (octal system).

- Four binary digits are combined into one base-16 number system (hexadecimal system).

For example, consider this:

2011 (decimal) = 11111011011 (binary) = 3733 (octal) = 7DB (hexadecimal)

It is obvious that the number system with the largest base (hexadecimal here) is using the fewest digits.

In general, the relationship between the value range *M*, which can be expressed with a number of a certain length in a base-*B* number system, and the number of digits *n* is

$M = B^n$

For example, eight digits ($n = 8$) in the binary system ($B = 2$) can express $M = 2^8 = 256$ numbers as its maximum. The value range is 0 through 255. Because only positive numbers can be represented this way, these numbers are called *unsigned integers*. (This corresponds to the data type *Byte* in Microsoft Visual Basic for Applications [VBA].)

We are familiar with negative numbers with a minus sign in front of them. For a computer with its binary system (based on the two symbols 0 and 1), there is no space for a third symbol, which is the leading sign. Therefore, the leftmost binary number—the most significant bit (MSB)—is reserved to represent negative numbers. Negative numbers have a 1 in this position, and positive numbers have a 0.

One's Complement

For the computer to be able to calculate with these numbers, the direction of the negative numbers must be inverted. For binary numbers, the following applies as well: the larger the absolute value, the smaller the negative number. This is achieved by inverting the individual digits (with the exception of the sign bit). Each 1 becomes a 0, and vice versa. The result is the *one's complement*. This has several disadvantages that will not be explored here, except for the fact that the one's complement has two zero values: +0 and –0, which are mathematically but not technically the same.

Two's Complement

To perfect this number representation, a 1 is added, and a possible overflow is dropped. This results in the *two's complement*. Its value range is –128 to +127. The computer can uniformly apply the calculation rules of the unsigned numbers. The numbers are simply interpreted differently. This basically applies to larger numbers as well, just the number of digits increases. (This is how the data types Integer and Long are represented in VBA.) The binary numbers in Excel also follow this number representation. They can have no more than 10 bits and therefore cover the value range of –512 to +511 (because $2^{10} = 1024$).

Chapter 17

BIN2DEC()

Syntax   BIN2DEC(*Number*)

Definition   This function converts a binary number into a decimal number.

Argument

- ***Number* (required)**   The (at most) 10-digit binary number in two's complement notation (see the earlier discussion) that is to be converted into a decimal number

Background   See the detailed description in the section titled "Number Systems" in the introduction to these functions (page 907).

Examples   The following examples illustrate the BIN2DEC() function.

- =BIN2DEC(1110) returns 14.

- =BIN2DEC(111111111) returns 511.

- =BIN2DEC(1111111111) returns –1.

- =BIN2DEC(1111111110) returns –2.

The worksheet in Figure 17-1 contains many additional examples, including the conversion into the octal and hexadecimal systems.

	A	B	C	D	E
1			Converting Binary Numbers to Other Bases		
2					
3	Numeral System	binary	decimal	octal	hexadecimal
4	Base	2	10	8	16
5		00000001	1	001	01
6		00001001	9	011	09
7		00001010	10	012	0A
8		00010011	19	023	13
9		00010100	20	024	14
10		01100011	99	143	63
11		01100100	100	144	64
12		11000111	199	307	C7
13		11001000	200	310	C8
14		11111111	255	377	FF

Figure 17-1 This Excel worksheet lets you convert binary numbers into numbers of other number systems.

See Also   BIN2HEX(), BIN2OCT(), DEC2BIN(), DEC2HEX(), DEC2OCT(), HEX2BIN(), HEX2DEC(), HEX2OCT(), OCT2BIN(), OCT2DEC(), OCT2HEX()

> ### Sample Files
>
> Use the Binary worksheet in the Numbers.xls or Numbers.xlsx sample file. The sample files are found in the Chapter17 folder. For more information about the sample files, see the section titled "Using the Sample Files" on page xxiii.

BIN2HEX()

Syntax   BIN2HEX(*Number,Places*)

Definition   This function converts a binary number into a hexadecimal number.

Arguments

- ***Number* (required)** The at most 10-digit binary number in two's complement notation (see the section titled "Two's Complement" on page 909) that is to be converted into a hexadecimal number. If *Number* has a negative value, a 10-digit hexadecimal number is returned.

- ***Places* (optional)** Determines how many digits of the hexadecimal number are displayed and is used to display leading zeros in the result. If the argument *Places* is omitted, only the required number of digits is displayed. Possible decimal places after the decimal point are ignored.

Background   See the detailed description in the section titled "Number Systems" in the introduction to these functions (page 907).

CAUTION !

> The result of BIN2HEX() is a string that cannot readily be used for additional calculations. If necessary, you can use text functions for the returned hexadecimal numbers.
>
> You should pay special attention to the fact that formulas that link references to the hexadecimal numbers with arithmetic operators do not generate error messages, as long as those numbers only contain digits from the decimal system (0 to 9). They are interpreted as decimal numbers, and the formula returns a result that is not intended.
>
> The following example shows such a case:
>
> =BIN2HEX(111100100) returns 1E4 as a hexadecimal number. If this value is used via a cell reference in a formula, it could be interpreted as "1.00E+04"; that is, as a completely different number in scientific format. Because no error message is displayed in the table, such an error is hard to find.

Examples The following examples illustrate this function.

- =BIN2HEX(1110) returns the hexadecimal number E.

- =BIN2HEX(1110,4) returns the hexadecimal number 000E.

- =BIN2HEX(111111111) returns 1FF.

- =BIN2HEX(1111111111) returns FFFFFFFFFF(corresponds to $-1_{decimal}$).

- =BIN2HEX(1111111111,4) also returns FFFFFFFFFF (corresponds to $-1_{decimal}$).

You can find additional examples in the »examples for BIN2DEC().

See Also BIN2DEC(), BIN2OCT(), DEC2BIN(), DEC2HEX(), DEC2OCT(), HEX2BIN(), HEX2DEC(), HEX2OCT(), OCT2BIN(), OCT2DEC(), OCT2HEX()

Sample Files

Use the Binary worksheet in the Numbers.xls or Numbers.xlsx sample file. The sample files are found in the Chapter17 folder. For more information about the sample files, see the section titled "Using the Sample Files" on page xxiii.

BIN2OCT()

Syntax BIN2OCT(*Number,Places*)

Definition This function converts a binary number into an octal number.

Arguments

- *Number* **(required)** The (at most) 10-digit binary number in two's complement notation (see the section titled "Two's Complement" on page 909) that is to be converted into an octal number. If *Number* has a negative value, a 10-digit octal number is returned.

- *Places* **(optional)** Determines how many digits of the octal number are displayed, and is used to display leading zeros in the result. If the argument *Places* is omitted, only the required number of digits is displayed. Possible decimal places after the decimal point are ignored.

Background   See the detailed description in the section titled "Number Systems" in the introduction to these functions (page 907).

CAUTION !

> The octal numbers returned by this function are strings that cannot readily be used like common numbers in other formulas. If an octal number is used in a formula with an arithmetic operator, that number is interpreted as a decimal number. For example, if the cells C13 and C14 contain the octal numbers 320 and 377, the formula
>
> =C13+C14
>
> returns the value 697, which is false. It already becomes obvious from the number 697, which is not a valid octal number, because the digit range of the octal system is only 0 through 7, and the digit 9 is not part of it. The octal number 717 would be correct.
>
> The following formula works correctly:
>
> =DEC2OCT(OCT2DEC(C13)+OCT2DEC(C14))

Examples   The following examples illustrate this function.

- =BIN2OCT(1110) returns 16.

- =BIN2OCT(1110,4) returns 0016.

- =BIN2OCT(111111111) returns 777.

- =BIN2OCT(1111111111) returns 7777777777 (corresponds to $-1_{decimal}$).

You can find additional examples in the examples for BIN2DEC().

See Also BIN2DEC(), BIN2HEX(), DEC2BIN(), DEC2HEX(), DEC2OCT(), HEX2BIN(), HEX2DEC(), HEX2OCT(), OCT2BIN(), OCT2DEC(), OCT2HEX()

Sample Files

Use the Binary worksheet in the Numbers.xls or Numbers.xlsx sample file. The sample files are found in the Chapter17 folder. For more information about the sample files, see the section titled "Using the Sample Files" on page xxiii.

Chapter 17

DEC2BIN()

Syntax   DEC2BIN(*Number,Places*)

Definition   This function converts a decimal number into a binary number.

Arguments

- *Number* **(required)** The decimal number that is to be converted into a binary number in two's complement notation (see the section titled "Two's Complement" on page 909). The valid entry values for *Number* are from −512 through +511. If the argument *Number* is not an integer, the decimal places are ignored. If *Number* has a negative value, a 10-digit binary number is returned.

- *Places* **(optional)** Determines how many digits of the binary number are displayed, and is used to display leading zeros in the result. If the argument *Places* is omitted, only the required number of digits is displayed. Possible decimal places after the decimal point are ignored.

Background   See the detailed description in the section titled "Number Systems" in the introduction to these functions (page 907).

CAUTION

Excel functions regard the obtained binary numbers as text. Therefore, these numbers cannot be used for calculations with other formulas without special provisions. Only text functions can be used to process them further.

If formulas with arithmetic operators process references to these binary numbers, Excel does not generate error messages but rather interprets them as decimal numbers, which of course leads to false results.

Examples   The following examples illustrate how to use DEC2BIN().

- =DEC2BIN(14) returns 1110.

- =DEC2BIN(341) returns 101010101.

- =DEC2BIN(6,8) returns 00000110.

- =DEC2BIN(-1) returns 1111111111.

- =DEC2BIN(-1,8) also returns 1111111111.

The worksheet in Figure 17-2 contains many additional examples, including the conversion into the octal and hexadecimal systems.

	A	B	C	D	E
1			Converting Decimal Numbers to Other Bases		
2					
3	Numeral System	decimal	binary	octal	hexadecimal
4	Base	10	2	8	16
5		1	00000001	001	01
6		9	00001001	011	09
7		10	00001010	012	0A
8		19	00010011	023	13
9		20	00010100	024	14
10		99	01100011	143	63
11		100	01100100	144	64
12		199	11000111	307	C7
13		200	11001000	310	C8
14		255	11111111	377	FF

Figure 17-2 This Excel worksheet lets you convert decimal numbers into other number systems.

See Also BIN2DEC(), BIN2HEX(), BIN2OCT(), DEC2HEX(), DEC2OCT(), HEX2BIN(), HEX2DEC(), HEX2OCT(), OCT2BIN(), OCT2DEC(), OCT2HEX()

> ## Sample Files
>
> Use the Decimal worksheet in the Numbers.xls or Numbers.xlsx sample file. The sample files are found in the Chapter17 folder. For more information about the sample files, see the section titled "Using the Sample Files" on page xxiii.

DEC2HEX()

Syntax DEC2HEX(*Number,Places*)

Definition This function converts a decimal number into a hexadecimal number.

Arguments

- *Number* (**required**) The decimal number that is to be converted into a hexadecimal number in two's complement notation (see the section titled "Two's Complement" earlier in this chapter). The valid entry values for *Number* are –549,755,813,888 through +549,755,813,887. If the argument *Number* is not an integer, the decimal places behind the decimal point are ignored. If *Number* has a negative value, a 10-digit hexadecimal number is returned.

- ***Places* (optional)** Determines how many digits of the hexadecimal number are displayed, and is used to display leading zeros in the result. If the argument *Places* is omitted, only the required number of digits is displayed. Possible existing decimal places after the decimal point are ignored.

Background   See the detailed description in the section titled "Number Systems" in the introduction to these functions (page 907).

CAUTION

The result of DEC2HEX() is a string that cannot readily be used for additional calculations. If necessary, you can use text functions for the returned hexadecimal numbers.

You should pay special attention to the fact that formulas that link references to the hexadecimal numbers with arithmetic operators do not generate error messages, as long as those numbers only contain digits from the decimal system (0 through 9). In this case, they are interpreted as decimal numbers, and the formula returns an unintended result.

The following example illustrates such a case:

=DEC2HEX(123456) returns 1E240 as a hexadecimal number. If this value is used through a cell reference in a formula, it can be interpreted as 1E+240, that is, as a completely different number in scientific format.

Examples   The following examples illustrate the function.

- =DEC2HEX(14) returns E.
- =DEC2HEX(31,4) returns 001F.
- =DEC2HEX(341,4) returns 0155.
- =DEC2HEX(-5) returns FFFFFFFFFB.
- =DEC2HEX(-5,4) also returns FFFFFFFFFB.

You can find additional examples in the examples for DEC2BIN() on page 914.

See Also BIN2DEC(), BIN2HEX(), BIN2OCT(), DEC2BIN(), DEC2OCT(), HEX2BIN(), HEX2DEC(), HEX2OCT(), OCT2BIN(), OCT2DEC(), OCT2HEX()

> ## Sample Files
>
> Use the Decimal worksheet in the Numbers.xls or Numbers.xlsx sample file. The sample files are found in the Chapter17 folder. For more information about the sample files, see the section titled "Using the Sample Files" on page xxiii.

DEC2OCT()

Syntax   DEC2OCT(*Number,Places*)

Definition   This function converts a decimal number into an octal number.

Arguments

- *Number* **(required)** The decimal number that is to be converted into an octal number in two's complement notation (see the section titled "Two's Complement" earlier in this chapter). The valid entry values for *Number* are from –536,870,912 through +536,870,911. If the argument *Number* is not an integer, the decimal places are ignored. If *Number* has a negative value, a 10-digit octal number is returned.

- *Places* **(optional)** Determines how many digits of the octal number are displayed, and is used to display leading zeros in the result. If the argument *Places* is omitted, only the required number of digits is displayed. Possible decimal places after the decimal point are ignored.

Background   See the detailed description in the section titled "Number Systems" in the introduction to these functions (page 907).

CAUTION

The octal numbers returned by this function are strings that cannot readily be used like common numbers in other formulas. If an octal number is used in a formula with an arithmetic operator, that number is interpreted as a decimal number. For example, if the cells C13 and C14 contain the octal numbers 320 and 377, the formula

```
=C13+C14
```

returns the value 697, which is false. It already becomes obvious from the number 697, which is not a valid octal number, because the digit range of the octal system is only 0 through 7, and the digit 9 is not part of it. The octal number 717 would be correct.

The following formula works correctly:

```
=DEC2OCT(OCT2DEC(C13)+OCT2DEC(C14))
```

Examples   The following examples illustrate this function.

- =DEC2OCT(14) returns 16.

- =DEC2OCT(31,4) returns 0037.

- =DEC2OCT(341,4) returns 0525.

- =DEC2OCT(-5) returns 7777777773.

- =DEC2OCT(-5,4) also returns 7777777773.

You can find additional examples in the examples for DEC2BIN() on page 914.

See Also BIN2DEC(), BIN2HEX(), BIN2OCT(), DEC2BIN(), DEC2HEX(), HEX2BIN(), HEX2DEC(), HEX2OCT(), OCT2BIN(), OCT2DEC(), OCT2HEX()

Sample Files

Use the Decimal worksheet in the Numbers.xls or Numbers.xlsx sample file. The sample files are found in the Chapter17 folder. For more information about the sample files, see the section titled "Using the Sample Files" on page xxiii.

HEX2BIN()

Syntax   HEX2BIN(*Number,Places*)

Definition   This function converts a hexadecimal number into a binary number.

Arguments

- ***Number* (required)** The (at most) 10-digit hexadecimal number that is to be converted into a binary number in two's complement notation (see the section titled "Two's Complement" on page 909). The valid entry values for *Number* are FFFFFFFE00 ($-512_{decimal}$) through 1FF ($+511_{decimal}$). If *Number* has a negative value, a 10-digit binary number is returned.

- ***Places* (optional)** Determines how many digits of the binary number are displayed, and is used to display leading zeros in the result. If the argument *Places* is omitted, only the required number of digits is displayed. Possible decimal places after the decimal point are ignored.

Background   See the detailed description in the section titled "Number Systems" in the introduction to these functions (page 907).

CAUTION

Excel functions return the obtained binary numbers as text in the default format (left-aligned). Therefore, they cannot be used for calculations with other formulas without special provisions. For further processing, text functions should be used, even though the result looks like a number.

If formulas with arithmetic operators process references to these binary numbers, Excel does not generate error messages but rather interprets them as decimal numbers, which of course leads to false results.

Examples   Here are examples that illustrate this function.

- =HEX2BIN("E") returns 1110.

- =HEX2BIN("E",6) returns 001110.

- =HEX2BIN("155") returns 101010101.

- =HEX2BIN("FFFFFFFFFF") returns 1111111111 (corresponds to $-1_{decimal}$).

- =HEX2BIN("FFFFFFFFFF",6) also returns 1111111111 (corresponds to $-1_{decimal}$).

The worksheet in Figure 17-3 contains many additional examples, including the conversion into the decimal and octal systems.

	A	B	C	D	E
1			Converting Hexadecimal Numbers to Other Bases		
2					
3	Numeral System	hexadecimal	binary	decimal	octal
4	Base	16	2	10	8
5		01	00000001	1	001
6		09	00001001	9	011
7		0A	00001010	10	012
8		13	00010011	19	023
9		14	00010100	20	024
10		63	01100011	99	143
11		64	01100100	100	144
12		C7	11000111	199	307
13		C8	11001000	200	310
14		FF	11111111	255	377

Figure 17-3 This Excel worksheet lets you convert hexadecimal numbers into the other number systems.

Chapter 17

See Also BIN2DEC(), BIN2HEX(), BIN2OCT(), DEC2BIN(), DEC2HEX(), DEC2OCT(), HEX2DEC(), HEX2OCT(), OCT2BIN(), OCT2DEC(), OCT2HEX()

> ## Sample Files
>
> Use the Hexadecimal worksheet in the Numbers.xls or Numbers.xlsx sample file. The sample files are found in the Chapter17 folder. For more information about the sample files, see the section titled "Using the Sample Files" on page xxiii.

HEX2DEC()

Syntax   HEX2DEC(*Number*)

Definition   This function converts a hexadecimal number into a decimal number.

Arguments

- *Number* **(required)** The (at most) 10-digit hexadecimal number in two's complement notation that is to be converted into a decimal number. The valid entry values for *Number* are 8000000000 to 7FFFFFFFFF (that is, from $-549,755,813,888_{decimal}$ through $+549,755,813,887_{decimal}$).

The (optional) *Places* argument is not necessary and not available, because the goal to display leading zeros can easily be reached by formatting the cells.

Background   See the detailed description in the section titled "Number Systems" in the introduction to these functions (page 907).

Examples   The following examples show how to use HEX2DEC().

- =HEX2DEC("E") returns 14.

- =HEX2DEC("155") returns 341.

- =HEX2DEC("FFFFFFFFFF") returns –1.

You can find additional examples in the examples for HEX2BIN() on page 918.

See Also BIN2DEC(), BIN2HEX(), BIN2OCT(), DEC2BIN(), DEC2HEX(), DEC2OCT(), HEX2BIN(), HEX2OCT(), OCT2BIN(), OCT2DEC(), OCT2HEX()

Sample Files

Use the Hexadecimal worksheet in the Numbers.xls or Numbers.xlsx sample file. The sample files are found in the Chapter17 folder. For more information about the sample files, see the section titled "Using the Sample Files" on page xxiii.

HEX2OCT()

Syntax   HEX2OCT(*Number,Places*)

Definition   This function converts a hexadecimal number into an octal number.

Arguments

- *Number* **(required)** The (at most) 10-digit binary number in two's complement notation that is to be converted into an octal number. The valid entry values for *Number* are FFE0000000 (negative) to 1FFFFFFF (positive).

- *Places* **(optional)** Determines how many digits are to be displayed, and is used to display leading zeros in the result. If the argument *Places* is omitted, only the required number of digits is displayed. Possible decimal places after the decimal point are ignored.

Background   See the detailed description in the section titled "Number Systems" in the introduction to these functions (page 907).

CAUTION

The octal numbers returned by this function are strings that cannot readily be used like common numbers in other formulas. If an octal number is used in a formula with arithmetic operators, the number is interpreted as a decimal number. For example, if the cells C13 and C14 contain the octal numbers 320 and 377, the formula

```
=C13+C14
```

returns the value 697, which is false. It already becomes obvious from the number 697, which is not a valid octal number, because the digit range of the octal system is only 0 through 7, and the number 9 is not part of it. The octal number 717 would be correct.

The following formula works correctly:

```
=DEC2OCT(OCT2DEC(C13)+OCT2DEC(C14))
```

Examples   The following examples illustrate this function.

- =HEX20CT("E") returns 16.

- =HEX20CT("E",4) returns 0016.

- =HEX20CT("155") returns 525.

- =HEX20CT("155",4) returns 0525.

- =HEX20CT("FFFFFFFFFF") returns 7777777777 (corresponds to $-1_{decimal}$).

You can find additional examples in the examples for HEX2BIN() on page 918.

See Also BIN2DEC(), BIN2HEX(), BIN2OCT(), DEC2BIN(), DEC2HEX(), DEC2OCT(), HEX2BIN(), HEX2DEC(), OCT2BIN(), OCT2DEC(), OCT2HEX()

Sample Files

Use the Hexadecimal worksheet in the Numbers.xls or Numbers.xlsx sample file. The sample files are found in the Chapter17 folder. For more information about the sample files, see the section titled "Using the Sample Files" on page xxiii.

OCT2BIN()

Syntax   OCT2BIN(*Number,Places*)

Definition   This function converts an octal number into a binary number.

Arguments

- **Number (required)** The (at most) 10-digit octal number in two's complement notation (see the section titled "Two's Complement" earlier in this chapter that is to be converted into a binary number.

- **Places (optional)** Determines how many digits of the binary number are displayed, and is used to display leading zeros in the result. If the argument *Places* is omitted, only the required number of digits is displayed. Possible decimal places after the decimal point are ignored.

Background   See the detailed description in the section titled "Number Systems" in the introduction to these functions (page 907).

CAUTION

Excel functions return the obtained binary numbers as text in the default format (left-aligned). Therefore, they cannot be used for calculations with other formulas without special provisions. For further processing, text functions should be used, even though the result looks like a number.

If formulas with arithmetic operators process references to these binary numbers, Excel does not generate error messages but rather interprets them as decimal numbers, which of course leads to false results.

Examples   The following examples illustrate this function.

● =OCT2BIN(16) returns 1110.

● =OCT2BIN(16,6) returns 001110.

● =OCT2BIN(525) returns 101010101.

● =OCT2BIN(7777777777) returns 1111111111 (corresponds to $-1_{decimal}$).

The worksheet in Figure 17-4 contains many additional examples, including the conversion into the decimal and hexadecimal systems.

	A	B	C	D	E
1		Converting Octal Numbers to Other Bases			
2					
3	Numeral System	octal	binary	decimal	hexadecimal
4	Base	8	2	10	16
5		001	00000001	1	01
6		011	00001001	9	09
7		012	00001010	10	0A
8		023	00010011	19	13
9		024	00010100	20	14
10		143	01100011	99	63
11		144	01100100	100	64
12		307	11000111	199	C7
13		310	11001000	200	C8
14		377	11111111	255	FF

Figure 17-4 This Excel worksheet lets you convert octal numbers into the other number systems.

See Also BIN2DEC(), BIN2HEX(), BIN2OCT(), DEC2BIN(), DEC2HEX(), DEC2OCT(), HEX2BIN(), HEX2DEC(), HEX2OCT(), OCT2DEC(), OCT2HEX()

Chapter 17

OCT2DEC()

Syntax   OCT2DEC(*Number*)

Definition   This function converts an octal number into a decimal number.

Argument

- *Number* **(required)** The (at most) 10-digit octal number in two's complement notation that is to be converted into a decimal number

Background   See the detailed description in the section titled "Number Systems" in the introduction to these functions (page 907).

Examples   The following examples illustrate OCT2DEC().

- =OCT2DEC(16) returns 14.

- =OCT2DEC(525) returns 341.

- =OCT2DEC(7777777777) returns FFFFFFFFFF (corresponds to $-1_{decimal}$).

- =OCT2DEC(7777777777,4)) also returns FFFFFFFFFF (corresponds to $-1_{decimal}$).

You can find additional examples in the examples for OCT2BIN() on page 922.

See Also BIN2DEC(), BIN2HEX(), BIN2OCT(), DEC2BIN(), DEC2HEX(), DEC2OCT(), HEX2BIN(), HEX2DEC(), HEX2OCT(), OCT2BIN(), OCT2HEX()

OCT2HEX()

Syntax   OCT2HEX(*Number,Places*)

Definition   This function converts an octal number into a hexadecimal number.

Arguments

- **Number (required)** The (at most) 10-digit octal number in two's complement nota-tion (see the section titled "Two's Complement" on page 909) that is to be converted into a hexadecimal number. If *Number* has a negative value, a 10-digit hexadecimal number is returned.

- **Places (optional)** Determines how many digits are to be displayed, and is used to display leading zeros in the result. If the argument *Places* is omitted, only the required number of digits is displayed. Possible decimal places after the decimal point are ignored.

Background   See the detailed description in the section titled "Number Systems" in the introduction to these functions (page 907).

CAUTION

The result of OCT2HEX() is a string that cannot be used for additional calculations. If necessary, you can use text functions for the returned hexadecimal numbers. You should pay special attention to the fact that formulas that link references to the hexa-decimal numbers with arithmetic operators do not generate error messages, as long as those numbers only contain digits from the decimal system (0 through 9). In this case, they are interpreted as decimal numbers, and the formula returns an unintended result.

The following example illustrates a special case:

=OCT2HEX(1750) returns 3E8 as a hexadecimal number. If this value is used through a cell reference in a formula, it can be interpreted as 3E+08, that is, as a completely different number in scientific format.

Chapter 17

Examples   The following examples illustrate OCT2HEX():

- =OCT2HEX(16) returns E.

- =OCT2HEX(16,2) returns 0E.

- =OCT2HEX(525) returns 155.

- =OCT2HEX(7777777777) returns FFFFFFFFFF (corresponds to $-1_{decimal}$).

- =OCT2HEX(7777777777,4) also returns FFFFFFFFFF (corresponds to $-1_{decimal}$).

You can find additional examples in the examples for OCT2BIN() on page 922.

See Also BIN2DEC(), BIN2HEX(), BIN2OCT(), DEC2BIN(), DEC2HEX(), DEC2OCT(), HEX2BIN(), HEX2DEC(), HEX2OCT(), OCT2BIN(), OCT2DEC()

Sample Files

Use the Octal worksheet in the Numbers.xls or Numbers.xlsx sample file. The sample files are found in the Chapter17 folder. For more information about the sample files, see the section titled "Using the Sample Files" on page xxiii.

CONVERT()

Syntax   CONVERT(*Number,From_Measurement_Unit,To_Measurement_Unit*)

Definition   This function performs conversions between different measurement systems.

Arguments

- ***Number* (required)** The value to be converted in *From_Measurement_Unit*

- ***From_Measurement_Unit* (required)** The unit of the initial number

- ***To_Measurement_Unit* (required)** The unit into which you want to convert

CONVERT() accepts for *From_Measurement_Unit* and *To_Measurement_Unit* the text values listed in tables in this section as measurement units, which must be put within quotation marks. If these arguments contain cell references, the text in the included cells do not need to be put into quotation marks, because the rules implemented in Excel also mark these text values as text without quotation marks. Pay attention to capitalization! If you don't, you might get the error message #NV.

Some measurement units can also be written differently. In Tables 17-6 through 17-15, the various measurement systems are sorted by category.

> **Note**
> A *slug* is a mass unit within the British Gravitational System (BG) and the English Engineering System (EE).

Table 17-6 (Commercial) Weight Units of the CONVERT() Function

Weight and Mass	Abbreviations for Measurement Units
Gram	g
Slug	sg
Pound (commercial weight)	lbm
u (atomic mass unit)	u
Ounce (commercial weight)	ozm

Table 17-7 Length Units of the CONVERT() Function

Distance	Abbreviations for Measurement Units
Meter	m
Statute mile	mi
Nautical mile	Nmi
Inch	in
Foot	ft
Yard	yd
Angstrom	ang
Pica (1/72 inches)	pica

Table 17-8 Time Units of the CONVERT() Function

Time	Abbreviations for Measurement Units
Year	yr
Day	day
Hour	hr
Minute	mn
Second	sec

Table 17-9 Pressure Units of the CONVERT() Function

Pressure	Abbreviations for Measurement Units
Pascal	Pa, p
Atmosphere (physical)	atm, at
mm of mercury	mmHg

Table 17-10 Force Units of the CONVERT() Function

Force	Abbreviations for Measurement Units
Newton	N
Dyne	dyn, dy
Pound force	lbf

Table 17-11 Energy Units of the CONVERT() Function

Energy	Abbreviations for Measurement Units
Joule	J
Erg	e
Thermodynamic calorie	c
IT calorie	cal
Electron volt	eV, ev
Horsepower-hour	HPh, hh
Watt-hour	Wh, wh
Foot-pound	flb
BTU	BTU, btu

Table 17-12 Performance Units of the CONVERT() Function

Performance	Abbreviations for Measurement Units
Horsepower	HP, h
Watt	W, w

Table 17-13 **Units of the Magnetic Field Intensity of the CONVERT() Function**

Magnetism	Abbreviations for Measurement Units
Tesla	T
Gauss	ga

Table 17-14 **Temperature Units of the CONVERT() Function**

Temperature	Abbreviations for Measurement Units
Degree Celsius (°C)	C, cel
Degree Fahrenheit (°F)	F, fah
Kelvin (K)	K, kel

Table 17-15 **Liquid Measurement Units of the CONVERT() Function**

Liquid Measures	Abbreviations for Measurement Units
Teaspoon	tsp
Tablespoon	tbs
Fluid ounce	oz
Cups	cup
U.S. pint	pt, us_pt
U.K. pint	uk_pt
Quart	qt
Gallon	gal
Liter	l, lt

Table 17-16 lists the increase and decrease factors as well as the unit prefixes. The abbreviated unit prefixes can be used for all metric specifications of *From_Measurement_Unit* and *To_Measurement_Unit*.

Important
You must differentiate between lowercase and capital letters.

Chapter 17

Table 17-16 **Unit Prefixes**

Prefix	Multiplier	Abbreviation
Exa	1E+18 (10^{18})	E
Peta	1E+18 (10^{15})	P
Tera	1E+18 (10^{12})	T
Giga	1E+18 (10^{9})	G
Mega	1E+18 (10^{6})	M
Kilo	1E+18 (10^{3})	k
Hecto	1E+18 (10^{2})	h
Deka	1E+18 (10^{1})	e
Deci	1E–01 (10^{-1})	d
Centi	1E–01 (10^{-2})	c
Milli	1E–01 (10^{-3})	m
Micro	1E–01 (10^{-6})	u
Nano	1E–01 (10^{-9})	n
Pico	1E–01 (10^{-12})	p
Femto	1E–01 (10^{-15})	f
Atto	1E–01 (10^{-18})	a

Background   Traditionally, nonmetric measurements are used in the United States—that is, measurements that are not based on the centimeter-gram-second (CGS) system. In scientific, commercial, and official communication on an international level, only the international units system (SI system) is used, which is becoming more prominent in the United States as well. The conversion between the U.S. and the international units isn't always easy. The CONVERT() function can save you a lot of work here.

CONVERT() can change a metric length specification into yards (and the other way around). However, the units you want to convert must come from the same category. For example, you obviously cannot convert time specifications into length measurements.

> **Important**
>
> Unit names and prefixes are case-sensitive.

Examples   For each possibility of this function, you can find an example in Figure 17-5.

	A	B	C	D	E	F	G	H	I
1					CONVERT()				
2									
3	Weight and Mass					Energy			
4	1	Slug	14,593.90	g		1	Erg	1.00E-07	J
5	1	Pound mass	453.59	g		1	Thermodynamic calorie	4.18	J
6	1	U (atomic mass unit)	1.66E-24	g		1	IT calorie	4.19	J
7	1	Ounce mass	28.35	g		1	electron volt	1.60E-19	J
8						1	Horsepower-hour	2,684,519.54	J
9	Distance					1	Watt-hour	3,600.00	J
10	1	Statute mile	1,609.34	m		1	Foot-pound	1.356	J
11	1	Nautical mile	1,852.00	m		1	BTU	1,055.06	J
12	1	Inch	0.0254	m					
13	1	Foot	0.305	m		Power			
14	1	Yard	0.91	m		1	Horsepower	745.70	W
15	1	Angstrom	1.00E-10	m					
16	1	Pica (1/72 in.)	0.353	mm		Magnetism			
17						1	Gauss	1.00E-04	T
18	Time								
19	1	Year	31,557,600	s		Temperature			
20	1	Day	86,400	s		37	Degree Celsius (°C)	310.15	K
21	1	Hour	3,600	s		98.6	Degree Fahrenheit (°F)	310.15	K
22	1	Minute	60	s					
23						Liquid Measure			
24	Pressure					1	Teaspoon	4.93	ml
25	1	Atmosphere	101,325.00	pa		1	Tablespoon	14.79	ml
26	1	mm of mercury	133.32	pa		1	Fluid ounce	29.57	ml
27						1	Cup	236.59	ml
28	Force					1	U.S. pint	473.18	ml
29	1	Dyne	1.00E-05	N		1	U.K. pint	568.26	ml
30	1	Pound force	4.45	N		1	Quart	946.35	ml
31						1	Gallon	3,785.41	ml

Figure 17-5 The possibilities of the CONVERT() function at a glance.

> **Sample Files**
>
> **Use the Sheet1 worksheet in the Convert.xls or Convert.xlsx sample file. The sample files are found in the Chapter17 folder. For more information about the sample files, see the section titled "Using the Sample Files" on page xxiii**

Functions for Complex Numbers

There are 18 functions total for complex numbers. At this point, this chapter gives you some basic explanations. The individual functions will refer to this passage.

In school, you learned that any number squared is positive:

$$2^2 = 4$$

$$(-2)^2 = 4$$

This also means that it is not possible to take the square root of negative numbers:

$$\sqrt{-4} = ?$$

In the four basic arithmetic calculations, there is an inversion for every operation: addition ↔ subtraction and multiplication ↔ division. Shouldn't this be applicable to exponentiation ↔ extracting a root? Mathematicians could not stop thinking about this problem. They regarded the call for "completeness of mathematics" as a given. This means that at least theoretically it should be possible to solve each and every mathematical problem—and they did find a solution in this case as well. It turned out that the solution was even significant in practice. Many technical calculations are based on it.

To solve these kinds of problems, you must leave the number line of real numbers (our everyday numbers, which go from −∞ through 0 to +∞) and enter the number planes above and below the number line.

The Imaginary Part

Similar to a two-dimensional coordinate system with an x-axis and a y-axis, complex numbers have a Cartesian coordinate system with an *abscissa* (x-axis) and an *ordinate* (y-axis). The number line of real numbers is the abscissa. The ordinate is called the *imaginary unit i* (or sometimes *j*). It has a property that incorporates the mathematical problems mentioned earlier. The y-axis is now called "imaginary" and the x-axis "real." The numbers that can be represented in this coordinate system (*the Argand plane*) are called *complex numbers*.

Therefore, a complex number *z* is displayed like this:

$$z = x + yi$$

This is the *algebraic form*, with *x* as the real part (a line segment on the x-axis) and *y* as the imaginary part (a line segment on the y-axis) of the complex number (see Figure 17-6). The set of all numbers *x* + *yi* represents the *body of complex numbers*, each of which corresponds to an ordered pair (*x;y*). Not only can complex numbers be displayed in arithmetic format, they can also be described with polar coordinates with the value *r* and the angle Φ (the *trigonometric form*):

$$z = r\left(\cos\phi + i\sin\phi\right)$$

The Excel functions IMARGUMENT() on page 939, IMCOS() on page 940, and IMSIN() on page 950 belong to this notation.

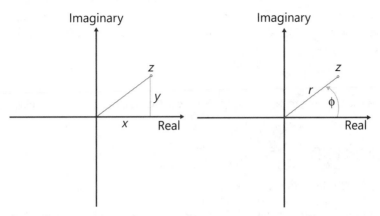

Figure 17-6 Graphical display of a complex number in Cartesian representation and in polar representation.

The complex numbers are the basis for the function theory, in which, among many others, the Bessel functions were developed (see the section titled "Background" for BESSELJ() and others, from pages 958 to page 963).

Important

The special treatment of complex numbers within a spreadsheet program such as Excel is the result of this fact: Complex numbers consist of two numbers, the real part and the imaginary part (or the value and the angle). Table calculations work with cells into which only one value can be entered in each: a text entry, a date/time, an error value, a logical value, a formula, or a number. To avoid this dilemma, in Excel, complex numbers are displayed as text, which concatenates both numbers and can appear in one single cell (similar to other "impossible numbers," such as binary, octal, and hexadecimal numbers).

However, this brings with it the disadvantage that the common calculation operations and the other Excel functions cannot be used for such values, because the Excel functions require "actual" numbers.

From the polar representation in Figure 17-6, you can see that the location of the complex number z is given by the real part x and the imaginary part y. However, the distance from the origin is not yet known. This distance is the length r in the polar representation (shown

Chapter 17

on the right in Figure 17-6). *r* is also called the *modulus* or the *(absolute) value* |z| of the complex number *z*. The absolute value |z| of a complex number is calculated as follows:

$$|z| = \sqrt{x^2 + y^2}$$

This is exactly what the function IMABS() does (see the definition of IMABS() later in this section).

COMPLEX()

Syntax   COMPLEX(*Real_Part,Imaginary_Part,Suffix*)

Definition   COMPLEX() links two real numbers to create a complex number. The first number makes up the real part of the complex number *x*, and the second makes up the imaginary part *y* (*x* + *yi* or *x* + *yj*).

Arguments

- **Real_Part (required)** The real part of the complex number you want to build.

- **Imaginary_Part (required)** The imaginary part of the complex number you want to build.

- **Suffix (optional)** The letter you want to use for the imaginary unit of the complex number. If the *Suffix* argument is not specified, it is assumed to be *i*.

> **Important**
> Complex numbers that are used as arguments in table functions must always be in the algebraic format *a* + *bi*. The imaginary unit can optionally be *i* or *j* and must be lowercase. Within a function's arguments list, the case of the imaginary unit must not change.

Background   The basics of complex numbers are described in the section titled "Functions for Complex Numbers" on page 905.

Examples   The following examples illustrate this function.

- =COMPLEX(3,-4) returns 3-4i.

- =COMPLEX(3,-4,"j") returns 3-4j.

These examples are located among the examples for all of the complex functions in Figure 17-7, on page 936.

See Also IMABS(), IMAGINARY(), IMARGUMENT(), IMEXP(), IMREAL()

Sample Files

Use the Complex worksheet in the Complex.xls or Complex.xlsm sample file. The sample files are found in the Chapter17 folder. For more information about the sample files, see the section titled "Using the Sample Files" on page xxiii.

IMABS()

Syntax   IMABS(*Complex_Number*)

Definition   This function returns the absolute value (modulus) of a complex number. Strings in the format of *x + yi* or *x + yj* are accepted.

Argument

- ***Complex_Number* (required)** The complex number whose absolute value is to be calculated

---

Note

With the COMPLEX() function, you can build a complex number from one number as the real part and a second number as the imaginary part.

Background   The basics of complex numbers are described in the section titled "Functions for Complex Numbers" on page 905.

Example   The following example illustrates the IMABS() function.

`=IMABS("3-4i")` returns 5.

Figure 17-7 shows all of the functions for complex numbers, each illustrated with examples. The cells with a shaded background (C5, C8, and E8) contain values that are required as arguments in the various formulas.

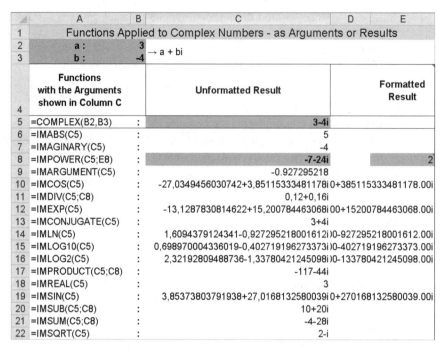

	A	B	C	D	E
1			Functions Applied to Complex Numbers - as Arguments or Results		
2	**a :**	**3**	→ a + bi		
3	**b :**	**-4**			
4	**Functions with the Arguments shown in Column C**		**Unformatted Result**		**Formatted Result**
5	=COMPLEX(B2,B3)	:	**3-4i**		
6	=IMABS(C5)	:	5		
7	=IMAGINARY(C5)	:	-4		
8	=IMPOWER(C5;E8)	:	**-7-24i**		2
9	=IMARGUMENT(C5)	:	-0.927295218		
10	=IMCOS(C5)	:	-27,0349456030742+3,85115333481178i	0+385115333481178.00i	
11	=IMDIV(C5;C8)	:	0,12+0,16i		
12	=IMEXP(C5)	:	-13,1287830814622+15,200784463068i	00+15200784463068.00i	
13	=IMCONJUGATE(C5)	:	3+4i		
14	=IMLN(C5)	:	1,6094379124341-0,927295218001612i	0-927295218001612.00i	
15	=IMLOG10(C5)	:	0,698970004336019-0,402719196273373i	0-402719196273373.00i	
16	=IMLOG2(C5)	:	2,32192809488736-1,33780421245098i	0-133780421245098.00i	
17	=IMPRODUCT(C5;C8)	:	-117-44i		
18	=IMREAL(C5)	:	3		
19	=IMSIN(C5)	:	3,85373803791938+27,0168132580039i	0+270168132580039.00i	
20	=IMSUB(C5;C8)	:	10+20i		
21	=IMSUM(C5;C8)	:	-4-28i		
22	=IMSQRT(C5)	:	2-i		

Figure 17-7 Overview of all available functions for complex numbers in the Engineering Functions (or Technical Functions) category.

INSIDE OUT   Format complex numbers using a VBA function

Note that the function results are often represented by very long numbers, as you can see in column C of the Excel table shown in Figure 17-7. However, the common formatting options cannot be used for complex numbers, for the reasons mentioned previously.

In this table, a formatting function written in VBA was used. This function was, until recently, provided by Microsoft's online support.

However, to be able to perform the examples in this book, you don't need the VBA function and you don't need any knowledge of VBA. The function is already incorporated in the examples. To use this function, you might need to reduce the macro security in Excel. Otherwise you will receive error messages in column E. In Excel 2010, you can do this with the following steps:

1. Click the File tab.

2. Click Options.

3. Select Trust Center.

4. Click the Trust Center Settings button.

5. Click Macro Settings.

6. Select Enable All Macros.

7. Click OK twice to confirm.

In Excel 2003 and earlier versions, you might need to set the macro security to medium (or low). If you haven't done this yet, do the following:

1. Select Tools/Macro/Security.

2. In the Security dialog box, select the Medium option.

3. Click OK to confirm.

The next time you open the Complex.xls workbook, the Security Warning dialog box shown in Figure 17-8 is initially displayed. Clicking the Enable Macros button finally opens the worksheet, activating the VBA module in the background. Now all formulas are completely functional, and you should see the same image as in the example.

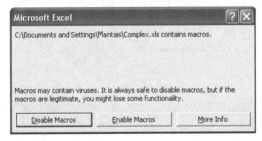

Figure 17-8 When a workbook with macros or VBA code is opened in Excel 2003 (or earlier versions), this dialog box is displayed if the macro security level is medium.

When you no longer need the functions that provide macros and VBA modules, you can increase the macro security back to where it was.

See Also COMPLEX(), IMAGINARY(), IMARGUMENT(), IMEXP(), IMREAL()

Sample Files

Use the Complex worksheet in the Complex.xls or Complex.xlsm sample file. The sample files are found in the Chapter17 folder. For more information about the sample files, see the section titled "Using the Sample Files" on page xxiii.

Chapter 17

IMAGINARY()

Syntax   IMAGINARY(*Complex_Number*)

Definition   This function returns the imaginary part *y* of a complex number that is a string in the format *x + yi* or *x + yj*.

> **Note**
> With the function COMPLEX(), you can build a complex number from one number as the real part and a second as the imaginary part.

Argument

- **Complex_Number (required)** The complex number whose imaginary part is to be determined

Background   The basics of complex numbers are described in the section titled "Functions for Complex Numbers" on page 905.

Example   The following example illustrates this function.

`=IMAGINARY("3–4i")` returns –4.

This example is located among the examples for all of the complex functions, as shown in Figure 17-7 on page 936.

See Also COMPLEX(), IMABS(), IMARGUMENT(), IMEXP(), IMREAL()

> **Sample Files**
> Use the Complex worksheet in the Complex.xls or Complex.xlsm sample file. The sample files are found in the Chapter17 folder. For more information about the sample files, see the section titled "Using the Sample Files" on page xxiii.

IMARGUMENT()

Syntax   IMARGUMENT(*Complex_Number*)

Definition   This function returns the argument (Φ) of a complex number, an angle in radians for displaying a complex number in the trigonometric form (see the right side of Figure 17-6, shown earlier on page 933).

$$x + yi = |x + yi| \cdot (\cos \phi + i \cdot \sin \phi)$$

Argument

- **Complex_Number (required)**   The complex number for which you want to determine the argument Φ

Background   The argument (Φ) of a complex number in the format $x + yi$ is calculated as follows:

$$\phi(x + yi) = \arctan \frac{y}{x}$$

The basics of complex numbers are described in the section titled "Functions for Complex Numbers" on page 906.

Example   The following example shows how to use this function.

`=IMARGUMENT("3-4i")` returns `-0.927295218` (the angle Φ in radians).

This example is located among the examples for all of the complex functions, as shown in Figure 17-7 on page 936.

See Also COMPLEX(), IMABS(), IMAGINARY(), IMREAL()

Sample Files

Use the Complex worksheet in the Complex.xls or Complex.xlsm sample file. The sample files are found in the Chapter17 folder. For more information about the sample files, see the section titled "Using the Sample Files" on page xxiii.

Chapter 17

IMCONJUGATE()

Syntax   IMCONJUGATE(*Complex_Number*)

Definition   This function returns the complex conjugate of a complex number, where the complex number is entered as a string in the format *x + yi* or *x + yj*.

Argument

- **Complex_Number (required)** The complex number whose complex conjugate you want to generate

Background   For the complex conjugate $\bar{z}$ of a complex number $z = x + yi$, the following applies:

$$\bar{z} = x - yi$$

The basics of complex numbers are described in the section titled "Functions for Complex Numbers" on page 905.

Example   The following example explains this function.

`=IMCONJUGATE("3-4i")` returns 3+4i.

This example is located among the examples for all of the complex functions, as shown in Figure 17-7 on page 936.

See Also COMPLEX(), IMAGINARY(), IMREAL()

> ## Sample Files
> Use the Complex worksheet in the Complex.xls or Complex.xlsm sample file. The sample files are found in the Chapter17 folder. For more information about the sample files, see the section titled "Using the Sample Files" on page xxiii.

IMCOS()

Syntax   IMCOS(*Complex_Number*)

Definition   This function returns the cosine of a complex number that is a string in the format *x + yi* or *x + yj*.

Argument

- **Complex_Number (required)** The complex number whose cosine is to be calculated

Background   For the cosine of a complex number, the following applies:

$$\cos(x + yi) = \cos(x) \cdot \cosh(y) - i \cdot \sin(x) \cdot \sinh(y)$$

The basics of complex numbers are described in the section titled "Functions for Complex Numbers" on page 905. Sinh and cosh are the hyperbolic sine and hyperbolic cosine mathematical functions, which you can learn about in Chapter 16.

Example   The following example explains this function.

`=IMCOS("3-4i")` returns `-27.03+3.85i`.

This example (with more decimal places) is located among the examples for all of the complex functions, as shown in Figure 17-7 on page 936.

See Also IMSIN()

Sample Files

Use the Complex worksheet in the Complex.xls or Complex.xlsm sample file. The sample files are found in the Chapter17 folder. For more information about the sample files, see the section titled "Using the Sample Files" on page xxiii.

IMDIV()

Syntax   IMDIV(*Complex_Number1,Complex_Number2*)

Definition   This function returns the quotient of two complex numbers, which are expected as strings in the format *x + yi* or *x + yj*.

Arguments

- **Complex_Number1 (required)** The complex numerator or dividend

- **Complex_Number2 (required)** The complex denominator or divisor

Background For the quotient z of two complex numbers $z1=a+bi$ and $z2=c+di$, the following applies:

$$z = \frac{z_1}{z_2} = \frac{(a+bi)}{(c+di)} = \frac{ac+bd}{c^2+d^2} + i \cdot \frac{bc-ad}{c^2+d^2}$$

The basics of complex numbers are described in the section titled "Functions for Complex Numbers" on page 905.

Example The following example illustrates this function.

`=IMDIV("3-4i","-7-24i")` returns `0.12+0.16i`.

This example is located among the examples for all of the complex functions, as shown in Figure 17-7 on page 936.

See Also IMPRODUCT(), IMSUB(), IMSUM()

> **Sample Files**
>
> Use the Complex worksheet in the Complex.xls or Complex.xlsm sample file. The sample files are found in the Chapter17 folder. For more information about the sample files, see the section titled "Using the Sample Files" on page xxiii.

IMEXP()

Syntax IMEXP(*Complex_Number*)

Definition This function returns the algebraic form of a complex number z, which is the result of the exponential function with a complex exponent:

$$z = e^{(x+yi)}$$

It is therefore the counterpart of the EXP() function, which works with a real number as its argument ($z = e^x$).

The inverse function of IMEXP() is IMLN() (see page 944).

CAUTION

When using the functions IMEXP() and IMLN() for calculating forward and backward, you will notice occasionally that the returned value is not the same as the original one. For example, (1+4i) becomes (–1.77–2.057i) when you use the IMEXP() function. When you take the logarithm of this complex number with the IMLN() function, however, you get (1–2.283i) and not, as expected, the original number of (1+4i).

This (at first glance) strange behavior is a result of the periodicity of the trigonometric functions: With angles of 0° to 360° (or 0 to 2π in radians), the sine runs through values from 0 via 1 back to 0, and then via –1 back to 0. For increasing angles, this sequence is run through repeatedly—periodically with results between –1 and +1.

For the functions IMEXP() and IMLN() to behave reciprocally, the imaginary part y of *Complex_Number* must be in the range of –π to +π for IMEXP(). If y is outside this range, you will receive unexpected (but correct) results when using the inverse function.

Argument

- ***Complex_Number*** (required) The exponent of the exponential function, which must be entered as a string in the format $x + yi$ or $x + yj$

Background For a complex number in exponential notation, the following applies according to Euler's formula:

$$e^{(x+yi)} = e^x \cdot e^{yi} = e^x \cdot \left(\cos y + i \cdot \sin y\right)$$

The basics of complex numbers are described in the section titled "Functions for Complex Numbers" on page 905.

Example The following example describes how to use this function.

`=IMEXP("3-4i")` returns –13.13+15.20i.

This example is located among the examples for all of the complex functions, as shown in Figure 17-7 on page 936.

See Also COMPLEX(), EXP(), IMABS(), IMAGINARY(), IMARGUMENT(), IMREAL()

Chapter 17

> ## Sample Files
>
> Use the Complex worksheet in the Complex.xls or Complex.xlsm sample file. The sample files are found in the Chapter17 folder. For more information about the sample files, see the section titled "Using the Sample Files" on page xxiii.

IMLN()

Syntax   IMLN(*Complex_Number*)

Definition   This function returns the natural logarithm of a complex number entered as a string of the format *x + yi* or *x + yj*. It is the version of the real LN() function from the Mathematical and Trigonometric Functions category that is to be used for complex numbers.

The IMLN() function is the inverse function of IMEXP(). Be sure to see the Caution about IMEXP() on page 943!

Argument

- **Complex_Number (required)**   The complex number whose natural logarithm you want to calculate

Background   The following applies to the natural logarithm of a complex number:

$$\ln\left(x+yi\right)=\ln\sqrt{x^{2}+y^{2}}+i\cdot\arctan\frac{y}{x}$$

where

$$\arctan\frac{y}{x}=\phi(x+yi) \text{ and } \phi \in (-\pi,\pi]$$

(a right half-open interval).

The basics of complex numbers are described in the section titled "Functions for Complex Numbers" on page 905.

Example   The following example illustrates how to use this function.

`=IMLN("3-4i")` returns `1.61-0.93i`.

This example (with more decimal places) is located among the examples for all of the complex functions, as shown in Figure 17-7 on page 936.

See Also   IMEXP(), IMLOG10(), IMLOG2(), IMPOWER(),IMROOT(), LN()

IMLOG10()

Syntax   IMLOG10(*Complex_Number*)

Definition   This function returns the base-10 logarithm of a complex number that is entered as a string in the format *x + yi* or *x + yj*.

The common logarithm of a complex number can be calculated from the natural logarithm as follows:

$$\log_{10}(x + yi) = \log_{10} e \cdot \ln(x + yi)$$

Argument

- **Complex_Number (required)**   The complex number whose common (base 10) logarithm you want to calculate

Background   The basics of complex numbers are described in the section titled "Functions for Complex Numbers" on page 905.

Example   The following example explains this function.

`=IMLOG10("3-4i")` returns `0.70-0.40i`.

This example (with higher accuracy) is located among the examples for all of the complex functions, as shown in Figure 17-7 on page 936.

See Also IMEXP(), IMLN(), IMLOG2(), IMPOWER(), IMROOT(), LOG10()

Chapter 17

IMLOG2()

Syntax   IMLOG2(*Complex_Number*)

Definition   This function returns the base-2 logarithm of a complex number that is entered as a string in the format *x + yi* or *x + yj*.

Argument

- **Complex_Number (required)** The complex number whose base-2 logarithm is to be calculated

Background   The base-2 logarithm of a complex number can be calculated from the natural logarithm as follows:

$$\log_2 (x + yi) = \log_2 e \cdot \ln (x + yi)$$

The basics of complex numbers are described in the section titled "Functions for Complex Numbers" on page 905.

Example   The following example illustrates this function.

`=IMLOG2("3-4i")` returns `2.32-1.34i`.

This example (with higher accuracy) is located among the examples for all of the complex functions, as shown in Figure 17-7 on page 936.

See Also IMEXP(), IMLN(), IMLOG10(), IMPOWER(),IMROOT(), LOG()

> ## Sample Files
> Use the Complex worksheet in the Complex.xls or Complex.xlsm sample file. The sample files are found in the Chapter17 folder. For more information about the sample files, see the section titled "Using the Sample Files" on page xxiii.

IMPOWER()

Syntax   IMPOWER(*Complex_Number, Power*)

Definition   This function exponentiates a complex number, which must be a string of the format *x + yi* or *x + yj*, with a real number.

Arguments

- ***Complex_Number* (required)** The complex number you want to exponentiate.

- ***Power* (required)** The exponent with which you want to exponentiate the complex number. The argument *Power* can be an integer, a rational number (a fraction), or negative.

> ## Note
> With the COMPLEX() function, you can build a complex number from one number as the real part and a second number as the imaginary part.

Background The power of a complex number is calculated as follows, using de Moivre's Formula:

$$(x + yi)^n = r^n \cdot e^{n\phi i} = \left[r \cdot (\cos \phi + i \cdot \sin \phi) \right]^n = r^n \cdot (\cos n\phi + i \cdot \sin n\phi)$$

where

$$r = \sqrt{x^2 + y^2}$$

and

$$\phi(x + yi) = \arctan \frac{y}{x}$$

where

$$\phi \in (-\pi, \pi]$$

(a right half-open interval).

The basics of complex numbers are described in the section titled "Functions for Complex Numbers" on page 905.

Example The following example illustrates how this function is used.

`=IMPOWER("3-4i";2)` returns `-7-24i`.

This example is located among the examples for all of the complex functions, as shown in Figure 17-7 on page 936.

See Also IMEXP(), IMLN(), IMLOG10(), IMLOG2(), IMSQRT()

> **Sample Files**
>
> Use the Complex worksheet in the Complex.xls or Complex.xlsm sample file. The sample files are found in the Chapter17 folder. For more information about the sample files, see the section titled "Using the Sample Files" on page xxiii.

IMPRODUCT()

Syntax IMPRODUCT(*Complex_Number1,Complex_Number2,...*)

Definition This function returns the product of complex numbers, which are expected as strings in the format *x + yi* or *x + yj*.

Arguments

- *Complex_Number1* **(required) and** *Complex_Number2* **(optional)** At least one and up to 255 complex numbers that you want to multiply

Background The product of two complex numbers (*a + bi*) and (*c + di*) is calculated as follows:

$$(a+bi)\cdot(c+di) = (ac-bd)+i\cdot(ad+bc)$$

The basics of complex numbers are described in the section titled "Functions for Complex Numbers" on page 905.

Example The following example illustrates this function.

`=IMPRODUCT("3-4i","-1-24i")` returns –117–44i.

This example is located among the examples for all of the complex functions, as shown in Figure 17-7 on page 936.

See Also IMDIV(), IMSUB(), IMSUM(), PRODUCT()

> ## Sample Files
> Use the Complex worksheet in the Complex.xls or Complex.xlsm sample file. The sample files are found in the Chapter17 folder. For more information about the sample files, see the section titled "Using the Sample Files" on page xxiii.

IMREAL()

Syntax   IMREAL(*Complex_Number*)

Definition   This function returns the real part x of a complex number that is a string in the form of $x + yi$ or $x + yj$.

Argument

- ***Complex_Number* (required)**   The complex number whose real part is to be determined

Background   The basics of complex numbers are described in the section titled "Functions for Complex Numbers" on page 906.

Example   The following example illustrates this function.

`=IMREAL("3-4i")` returns 3.

This example is located among the examples for all of the complex functions, as shown in Figure 17-7 on page 936.

See Also COMPLEX(), IMABS(), IMAGINARY(), IMARGUMENT(), IMEXP()

> ## Sample Files
> Use the Complex worksheet in the Complex.xls or Complex.xlsm sample file. The sample files are found in the Chapter17 folder. For more information about the sample files, see the section titled "Using the Sample Files" on page xxiii.

Chapter 17

IMSIN()

Syntax   IMSIN(*Complex_Number*)

Definition   This function returns the sine of a complex number, which must be a string in the format *x + yi* or *x + yj*.

Argument

- **Complex_Number (required)**   The complex number whose sine should be returned

Background   The sine of a complex number is defined as follows:

$$\sin(x + yi) = \sin(x) \cdot \cosh(y) - i \cdot \cos(x) \cdot \sinh(y)$$

The basics of complex numbers are described in the section titled "Functions for Complex Numbers" on page 905. Sinh and cosh are the mathematical functions *hyperbolic sine* and *hyperbolic cosine*, which you can learn about in Chapter 16.

Example   The following example illustrates this function.

`=IMSIN("3-4i")` returns `3.85+27.02i`.

This example (with more decimal places) is located among the examples for all of the complex functions, as shown in Figure 17-7 on page 936.

See Also IMCOS()

> **Sample Files**
> Use the Complex worksheet in the Complex.xls or Complex.xlsm sample file. The sample files are found in the Chapter17 folder. For more information about the sample files, see the section titled "Using the Sample Files" on page xxiii.

IMSQRT()

Syntax   IMSQRT(*Complex_Number*)

Definition   This function returns the square root of a complex number (*x + yi* or *x + yj*).

Argument

- ***Complex_Number* (required)** The complex number whose square root is to be determined

Background   The square root of a complex number is calculated as follows:

$$\sqrt{x+yi} = \sqrt{r}\cdot\left(\cos\frac{\phi}{2}+i\cdot\sin\frac{\phi}{2}\right)$$

where

$$r = \sqrt{x^2+y^2}$$

and

$$\phi = \arctan\frac{y}{x}$$

where

$$\phi \in (-\pi,\pi]$$

(a right half-open interval).

The basics of complex numbers are described in the section titled "Functions for Complex Numbers" on page 905.

Example   The following example illustrates this function.

`=IMSQRT("3-4i")` returns 2-i.

This example is located among the examples for all of the complex functions, as shown in Figure 17-7 on page 936.

See Also IMEXP(), IMLN(), IMLOG10(), IMLOG2() IMPOWER(), SQRT(), Chapter 16

> ### Sample Files
> Use the Complex worksheet in the Complex.xls or Complex.xlsm sample file. The sample files are found in the Chapter17 folder. For more information about the sample files, see the section titled "Using the Sample Files" on page xxiii.

Chapter 17

IMSUB()

Syntax   IMSUB(*Complex_Number1,Complex_Number2*)

Definition   This function returns the difference between of two complex numbers, which both need to be strings in the format of *x + yi* or *x + yj*.

Arguments

- **Complex_Number1 (required)** The complex number from which *Complex_Number2* is to be subtracted

- **Complex_Number2 (required)** The complex number that is to be subtracted from *Complex_Number1*

Background   The difference between two complex numbers is the difference of the real parts and the difference of the imaginary parts.

$$(a+bi)-(c+di)=(a-c)+i\cdot(b-d)$$

This means that the real parts and the imaginary parts of both complex numbers are subtracted separately.

The basics of complex numbers are described in the section titled "Functions for Complex Numbers" on page 905.

Example   The following example illustrates this function.

`=IMSUB("3-4i";"-7-24i")` returns 10+20i.

This example is located among the examples for all of the complex functions, as shown in Figure 17-7 on page 936.

See Also IMDIV(), IMPRODUCT(), IMSUM()

Sample Files

Use the Complex worksheet in the Complex.xls or Complex.xlsm sample file. The sample files are found in the Chapter17 folder. For more information about the sample files, see the section titled "Using the Sample Files" on page xxiii.

IMSUM()

Syntax   IMSUM(*Complex_Number1,Complex_Number2,...*)

Definition   This function returns the sum of complex numbers, which are expected to be strings of the format $x + yi$ or $x + yj$.

Arguments

- **Complex_Number1 (required) and Complex_Number2 (optional)**   At least one and up to 255 complex numbers to be added

Background   The sum of two complex numbers is calculated by adding the real parts and the imaginary parts separately.

$$(a+bi)+(c+di) = (a+c)+i\cdot(b+d)$$

The basics of complex numbers are described in the section titled "Functions for Complex Numbers" on page 905.

Example   The following example illustrates this function.

`=IMSUM("3-4i","-7-24i")` returns –4–28i.

This example is located among the examples for all of the complex functions, as shown in Figure 17-7 on page 936.

See Also IMDIV(), IMPRODUCT(), IMSUB(), SUM(), Chapter 16

> ## Sample Files
>
> Use the Complex worksheet in the Complex.xls or Complex.xlsm sample file. The sample files are found in the Chapter17 folder. For more information about the sample files, see the section titled "Using the Sample Files" on page xxiii.

Chapter 17

Functions for Higher Mathematics

You've heard people refer to "applying mathematics to everyday life," right? What exactly does that mean?

Even though you have learned a lot in school and during our professional training, you don't always apply what you have learned to your observations in everyday life. This is especially true when it comes to mathematics and sciences. You have witnessed this many times.

However, sometimes it just happens. For example, consider a group of boys who are playing with a rope. Among them is Kevin, a boy who is a little younger and shorter than the others, but who is trying to make up for his deficiencies in years and height by being smarter.

Kevin and another boy are handling the rope, which the other boys are jumping. Kevin is now trying to take the rope away from the other boy. But this does not work. The other boy is too big and strong. As soon as the other boy is distracted, Kevin quickly and forcefully moves his hands up and immediately down again. The jerk moves along the rope and rips the rope out of the other boy's hands.

How does the jerk arrive at the other boy's end? Now let's focus on the rope. Luckily Kevin tries to repeat his success, while on the other end the rope is being held tightly again. Another jerk, and then another, but this time his buddy is watching out. A double-jerk: You can clearly see how this jerking can cause several spikes upward and downward, running down the rope. The form of these spikes seems very familiar. Correct—they are sine curves. We are watching a mechanical model for the distribution of electromagnetic waves in an electrical conductor. If you would like to take another look at the sine curves, you can go back to Chapter 16 and read the description of the SIN() function.

Can Kevin show us more? Now our young protagonists are holding the rope still. There is nothing special happening—or is there more to it? Which shape does a hanging rope have? The answer to this question can also be found in Chapter 16, this time under COSH(). You can also look in the index under "catenary," which is the name of this shape.

Now Kevin has tied one end of the rope to a jungle gym and moves the loose end up and down. Are those sine curves again? No. They get smaller toward the tied end, and the shape is different somehow. What Kevin is illustrating so nicely here is called *damped oscillation*. And how can these curves be described mathematically? "By using Bessel functions!" is the answer. These functions are explained in this section. However, you should first take a look at the diagrams for the BESSELJ() and BESSELY() functions (Figures 17-12 and 17-16) on pages 959 and 963.

Bessel Functions

The *Bessel functions* (or *cylindrical functions*) are the solutions found during the integration of Bessel's differential equation by series expansion. For certain electro-technical problems, they offer an exact (or at least close to exact) calculation, for example, for electric displacement in conductors. They are also used for describing vibrations and the associated damping; for calculating the orbits of planets and orbit abnormalities, for which they were introduced by Friedrich Wilhelm Bessel (an astronomer from Königsberg, Germany, 1784–1846); and for the simulation of pump tests in hydrogeology. They are also important in quantum mechanics, satellite geodesy (ground survey), and communication technology. They are usually generated as solutions for wave equations based on cylindrical boundary conditions.

Error Integrals

In addition to the Bessel functions, there are two separate functions. These functions calculate the probability that a certain value is located within or outside of a Gauss distribution (see the description of NORMSDIST() in Chapter 12, "Statistical Functions").

BESSELI()

Syntax   BESSELI(*x,n*)

Definition   This function returns the modified Bessel function of the first kind, $I_n(z)$, which corresponds to the Bessel function J_n evaluated for purely imaginary arguments.

Arguments

- **x (required)** The value for which the function is to be evaluated; x must be a real number and can have values of ±700. (The value range varies with the order n.)

- **n (required)** The order of the Bessel function, which must be positive and an integer. If n is not an integer, the decimal places are ignored; that is, n is truncated, not rounded.

Background $I_n(x)$, like $K_n(x)$, belongs to the modified Bessel functions that increase or decrease exponentially—unlike the normal Bessel functions $J_n(x)$ and $Y_n(x)$, which oscillate. $I_n(x)$ is the solution of the slightly modified Bessel's differential equation

$$x^2 y'' + xy' - \left(x^2 + n^2\right) \cdot y = 0$$

or

$$x^2 \cdot \frac{d^2}{dx^2} y + x \cdot \frac{d}{dx} y - \left(x^2 + n^2\right) \cdot y = 0$$

This modified Bessel function of the first kind $I_n(x)$ can be described as the loop integral

$$I_n(z) = \frac{1}{2\pi i} \cdot \oint e^{\frac{z}{2}\left(t+\frac{1}{t}\right)} t^{-n-1} dt$$

of the nth order. For a real number v, the function can be calculated with

$$I_v(z) = \left(\tfrac{1}{2}z\right)^v \sum_{k=0}^{\infty} \frac{\left(\frac{1}{4}z^2\right)^k}{k!\,\Gamma(v+k+1)}$$

where $\Gamma(y)$ is the gamma function.

Example   Using Bessel functions requires extensive knowledge of the application area. Therefore, this chapter will not use very specific practical examples. Instead, the example is explained through the mathematical properties and their graphical representation, as shown in Figure 17-9.

	A	B	C	D	E	F	G	H	I	J	K	L	M	N	O	P	Q
1	Modified Bessel Function of the First Kind								$I_n(x)$								
2																	
3	Order	x	0.00	0.25	0.50	0.75	1.00	1.25	1.50	1.75	2.00	2.25	2.50	2.75	3.00	3.25	3.50
4	0		1.00	1.02	1.06	1.15	1.27	1.43	1.65	1.93	2.28	2.73	3.29	4.00	4.88	5.99	7.38
5	1		0.00	0.13	0.26	0.40	0.57	0.76	0.98	1.26	1.59	2.00	2.52	3.16	3.95	4.95	6.21
6	2	$I_n(x)$	0.00	0.01	0.03	0.07	0.14	0.22	0.34	0.49	0.69	0.95	1.28	1.70	2.25	2.94	3.83
7	3		0.00	0.00	0.00	0.01	0.02	0.04	0.08	0.13	0.21	0.32	0.47	0.68	0.96	1.33	1.83
8	4		0.00	0.00	0.00	0.00	0.00	0.01	0.01	0.03	0.05	0.09	0.14	0.21	0.33	0.48	0.70

Figure 17-9 Excerpt from the Excel worksheet Bessel_I.xls for calculating the function values for the orders 0 to 4.

The cell with the text *Order* has the reference A3 in the sample file. C4 through Q8 contain the formulas with the BESSELI() functions. The first argument, the x value, is located in the cells above these formulas in row 3. Column A in the same row contains the second argument, the function order, which is the same for all formulas in a row. For example, the complete formula in C4 would be:

```
=BESSELI(C$3,$A4)
```

From the range C3 through Q8, the diagram in Figure 17-10 can be created, which graphically displays the modified Bessel function of the first kind. The exponential increase is easy to see. Even for small x values, it already generates high amounts.

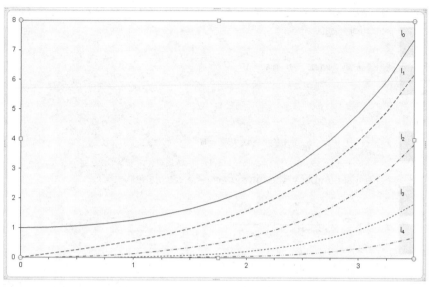

Figure 17-10 Graphical representation of the Bessel function of the first kind, $I_n(x)$, using BESSELI().

See Also BESSELJ(), BESSELK(), BESSELY()

Sample Files

Use the Bessel I and Chart worksheets in the Bessel_I.xls or Bessel_I.xlsx sample file. The sample files are found in the Chapter17 folder. For more information about the sample files, see the section titled "Using the Sample Files" on page xxiii.

BESSELJ()

Syntax   BESSELJ(*x,n*)

Definition   This function returns the Bessel function of the first kind, $J_n(x)$.

Arguments

- **x (required)**   The value for which the function is to be evaluated; *x* must be a real number and can have values between $-1.34 \cdot 10^8$ and $+1.34 \cdot 10^8$. (The value range varies with the order *n*.)

- **n (required)**   The order of the Bessel function; must be positive. If *n* is not an integer, the decimal places are ignored, not rounded.

Chapter 17

Background The Bessel function of the first kind $J_n(x)$ is the solution of Bessel's differential equation

$$x^2 y'' + xy' + \left(x^2 - n^2\right) \cdot y = 0$$

or

$$x^2 \cdot \frac{d^2}{dx^2} y + x \cdot \frac{d}{dx} y + \left(x^2 - n^2\right) \cdot y = 0$$

For a real number ν, the function can be calculated with

$$J_\nu(z) = \sum_{k=0}^{\infty} \frac{(-1)^k z^{n+2k}}{k! \cdot 2^{n+2k} \cdot \Gamma(\nu + k + 1)}$$

where $\Gamma(y)$ is the gamma function.

Example Because of the very special character of the Bessel functions, this book uses only their graphical representation, as with the other Bessel functions.

In the worksheet shown in Figure 17-11, which you can also find in the sample files, the function values for BESSELJ() are calculated with the orders 0 to 4 and displayed in a graph (see Figure 17-12).

	A	B	C	D	E	F	G	H	I	J	K	L	M	N	O
1	Bessel Function of the First Kind							$J_n(x)$							
2															
3	**Order**	**x**	0.00	0.25	0.50	0.75	1.00	1.25	1.50	1.75	2.00	2.25	2.50	2.75	3.00
4	**0**		1.00	0.98	0.94	0.86	0.77	0.65	0.51	0.37	0.22	0.08	-0.05	-0.16	-0.26
5	**1**		0.00	0.12	0.24	0.35	0.44	0.51	0.56	0.58	0.58	0.55	0.50	0.43	0.34
6	**2**		0.00	0.01	0.03	0.07	0.11	0.17	0.23	0.29	0.35	0.40	0.45	0.47	0.49
7	**3**		0.00	0.00	0.00	0.01	0.02	0.04	0.06	0.09	0.13	0.17	0.22	0.26	0.31
8	**4**		0.00	0.00	0.00	0.00	0.00	0.01	0.01	0.02	0.03	0.05	0.07	0.10	0.13

Figure 17-11 Calculation of the BESSELJ() function for the orders $n = 0...4$ (excerpt).

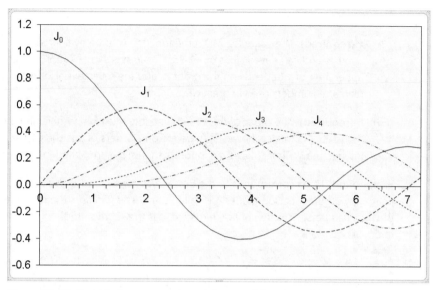

Figure 17-12 Graphical representation of the Bessel function of the first kind, $J_n(x)$, using BESSELJ().

See Also BESSELI(), BESSELK(), BESSELY()

> ## Sample Files
>
> Use the Bessel J and Chart worksheets in the Bessel_J.xls or Bessel_J.xlsx sample file. The sample files are found in the Chapter17 folder. For more information about the sample files, see the section titled "Using the Sample Files" on page xxiii.

BESSELK()

Syntax   BESSELK(*x*,*n*)

Definition   This function returns the modified Bessel function of the second kind, $K_n(x)$.

Arguments

- **x (required)** The value for which the function is to be evaluated; x must be a real number and can have values of $+1 \cdot 10^{-307}$ to more than $+700$. The exact value of the upper limit of x depends on the order n (and the reverse is also true), but it is higher than any numbers used in practice.

- **n (required)** The order of the Bessel function; must be positive and an integer larger than 100. In practice, however, there are only orders of less than 10. If n is not an integer, the decimal places are ignored; that is, n is truncated, not rounded.

Background $K_n(x)$ corresponds to the Bessel functions J_n and Y_n evaluated for purely imaginary arguments. Sometimes it is called the *Basset function*, the *Macdonald function*, or the *modified Bessel function of the third kind*. It is the solution to the modified Bessel's differential equation

$$x^2 y'' + xy' - \left(x^2 + n^2\right) \cdot y = 0$$

or

$$x^2 \cdot \frac{d^2}{dx^2} y + x \cdot \frac{d}{dx} y - \left(x^2 + n^2\right) \cdot y = 0$$

The modified Bessel function of the second kind, $K_n(x)$ of the order n, can be expressed in terms of the modified Bessel function of the first kind, $I_n(x)$:

$$K_n(x) = \lim_{p \to n} \frac{I_{-p}(x) - I_p(x)}{\sin p\pi} \ with \ n = 0,1,2, \ldots$$

Examples Because of the very special character of the Bessel functions, this chapter uses only their graphical representation, as with the other Bessel functions.

In the worksheet shown in Figure 17-13, the function values of the BESSELK() function for the orders $n = 0...4$ can be calculated and graphically displayed, as shown in Figure 17-14.

	A	B	C	D	E	F	G	H	I	J	K	L	M	N	O	P	Q
1	Modified Bessel Function of the Second Kind							$K_n(x)$									
2																	
3	Order	x	0.00	0.10	0.30	0.50	0.70	0.90	1.10	1.30	1.50	1.70	1.90	2.10	2.30	2.50	2.70
4	0			7.02	2.43	1.37	0.92	0.66	0.49	0.37	0.28	0.21	0.17	0.13	0.10	0.08	0.06	0.05
5	1				9.85	3.06	1.66	1.05	0.72	0.51	0.37	0.28	0.21	0.16	0.12	0.09	0.07	0.06
6	2	$K_n(x)$				21.75	7.55	3.66	2.08	1.29	0.85	0.58	0.41	0.30	0.22	0.16	0.12	0.09
7	3						21.97	9.96	5.21	2.99	1.83	1.18	0.78	0.54	0.38	0.27	0.19
8	4							14.66	7.92	4.57	2.78	1.75	1.14	0.77	0.52

Figure 17-13 Calculation of the BESSELK() function for the orders $n = 0...4$.

For the higher orders, the first formulas are omitted, because their function values are too large for a clear graphic.

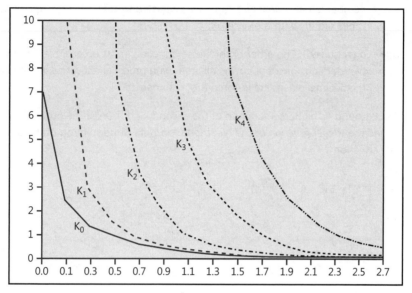

Figure 17-14 Graphical representation of the modified Bessel function of the second kind, $K_n(x)$, using BESSELK().

See Also BESSELI(), BESSELJ(), BESSELY()

Sample Files

Use the Bessel K and Chart worksheets in the Bessel_K.xls or Bessel_K.xlsx sample file. The sample files are found in the Chapter17 folder. For more information about the sample files, see the section titled "Using the Sample Files" on page xxiii.

BESSELY()

Syntax   BESSELY(*x,n*)

Definition   This function returns the Bessel function of the second kind, $Y_n(x)$.

Arguments

- **x (required)** The value for which the function is to be evaluated; x must be a real number larger than 0 and can have values up to $1.34 \cdot 10^8$. (The upper limiting value varies slightly with the order n.)

- **n (required)** The order of the Bessel function; must be positive. The maximum value of n depends on x but covers all areas with practical relevance. If n is not an integer, the decimal places are ignored (not rounded).

Background   The Bessel function of the second kind, $Y_n(x)$ of the order n, which is also called the *Weber function* or the *Neumann function*, is the solution of the Bessel's differential equation

$$x^2 y'' + xy' + \left(x^2 - n^2\right) \cdot y = 0$$

or

$$x^2 \cdot \frac{d^2}{dx^2} y + x \cdot \frac{d}{dx} y + \left(x^2 - n^2\right) \cdot y = 0$$

It can be expressed in terms of the Bessel function of the first kind, $Jn(x)$:

$$Y_n(x) = \lim_{p \to n} \frac{J_p(x)\cos p\pi - J_{-p}(x)}{\sin p\pi} \quad with \ \ n = 0,1,2,\ldots$$

Examples   Because of the very special character of the Bessel functions, this chapter uses only their graphical representation, as with the other Bessel functions.

	A	B	C	D	E	F	G	H	I	J	K	L	M	N	O
1	Bessel Function of the Second Kind						$Y_n(x)$								
2															
3	Order	x	0.25	0.50	0.75	1.00	1.25	1.50	1.75	2.00	2.25	2.50	2.75	3.00	3.25
4	0		-0.93	-0.44	-0.14	0.09	0.26	0.38	0.47	0.51	0.52	0.50	0.45	0.38	0.29
5	1			-1.04	-0.78	-0.58	-0.41	-0.25	-0.11	0.03	0.15	0.25	0.32	0.38
6	2					-0.93	-0.76	-0.62	-0.50	-0.38	-0.27	-0.16	-0.05
7	3							-0.91	-0.76	-0.64	-0.54	-0.45
8	4									-0.92	-0.77

Figure 17-15 Calculation of the BESSELY() function for the orders n = 0…4.

In the worksheet shown in Figure 17-15, the function values of the BESSELY() function for the orders $n = 0...4$ can be calculated and graphically displayed, as shown in Figure 17-16. For the higher orders, the first formulas are omitted, because their function values are too large for a clear graphic.

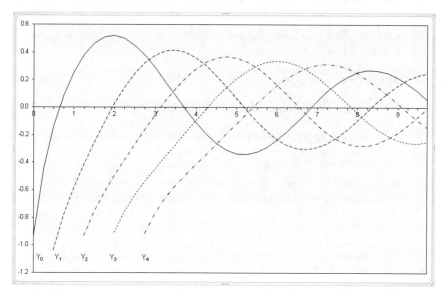

Figure 17-16 Graphical representation of the Bessel function of the second kind $Y_n(x)$.

See Also BESSELI(), BESSELJ(), BESSELK()

> ## Sample Files
>
> Use the Bessel Y and Chart worksheets in the Bessel_Y.xls or Bessel_Y.xlsx sample file. The sample files are found in the Chapter17 folder. For more information about the sample files, see the section titled "Using the Sample Files" on page xxiii.

ERF.PRECISE()/ERF()

Syntax

- ERF.PRECISE(*Limit*)

- ERF(*Lower_Limit,Upper_Limit*)

Definition These functions return the values of the probability integral (also called the *Gauss error integral* or the *error function*). For Excel 2010, the algorithm of the ERF() function has been improved. In addition, a similar function was introduced that does nearly the same thing but has a new name: ERF.PRECISE(), which can accept only one argument. This function calculates the error function in the range of 0 up to *Limit*. If *Limit* is negative, the lower limit is given by *Limit*, and the upper limit is set to 0. If you require backward compatibility, the earlier version of the function can be used without any disadvantages, and the following explanations apply as well.

Arguments

- *Lower_Limit* **(required)** The lower limit for the integration into ERF().

- *Upper_Limit* **(optional)** The upper limit for the integration into ERF(). If this argument is missing, ERF() integrates from zero to *Lower_Limit*.

Background The Gaussian error function erf(z) is returned by integrating the normal distribution of the normalized format of the Gauss function. It has the following format:

$$\mathrm{erf}\left(z\right) = \frac{2}{\sqrt{\pi}} \int_{0}^{z} e^{-t^2}\, dt$$

In the Excel function, the lower limit is also a variable and can be entered as the first argument to allow coverage of special cases. With the integration limits z_1 and z_2, the "generalized error function" erf(z_1,z_2) is defined as follows:

$$\mathrm{erf}\left(z_1, z_2\right) = \frac{2}{\sqrt{\pi}} \int_{z_1}^{z_2} e^{-t^2}\, dt$$

Examples The following examples illustrate this function.

- =ERF(0,0.5) returns 0.520499878.

- =ERF(0.5) also returns 0.520499878.

- =ERF(0.5,1) returns 0.322200915.

Figure 17-17 shows more examples of the function values of ERF() with the arguments *Lower_Limit* = 0 and *Upper_Limit* = 0...3. As a comparison, the function values of the ERFC() function in the same interval are listed next to it.

The diagram (Figure 17-18) graphically displays the connection between ERF() and ERC(): Both functions total a value of 1 at each location.

	A	B	C	D
1	**Error Function *erf()* and Complementary Error Function *erfc()***			
2				
3	**x**	**erf(x)**	**erfc(x)**	**erf(x) + erc(x)**
4	0.00	0	1	1.00
5	0.25	0.27632639	0.72367361	1.00
6	0.50	0.52049988	0.47950012	1.00
7	0.75	0.71115563	0.28884437	1.00
8	1.00	0.84270079	0.15729921	1.00
9	1.25	0.92290013	0.07709987	1.00
10	1.50	0.96610515	0.03389485	1.00
11	1.75	0.98667167	0.01332833	1.00
12	2.00	0.99532227	0.00467773	1.00
13	2.25	0.99853728	0.00146272	1.00
14	2.50	0.99959305	0.00040695	1.00
15	2.75	0.99989938	0.00010062	1.00
16	3.00	0.99997791	0.00002209	1.00

Figure 17-17 In this worksheet, you can see how the results of the ERF() function (column B) and the ERFC() function (column C) added up to return the value 1 (column D).

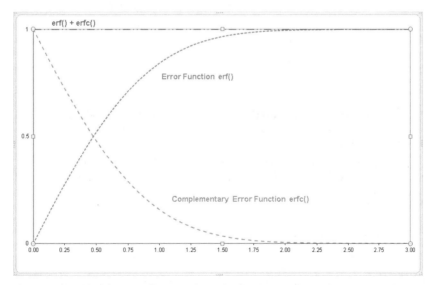

Figure 17-18 This diagram illustrates how the functions ERF() and ERFC() complete each other.

See Also ERFC(), ERFC.PRECISE()

> **Sample Files**
>
> Use the Data and Chart worksheets in the Gauss.xls or Gauss.xlsx sample file. The
> sample files are found in the Chapter17 folder. For more information about the sample
> files, see the section titled "Using the Sample Files" on page xxiii.

ERFC.PRECISE()/ERFC()

Syntax

- ERFC.PRECISE(*Lower_Limit*)

- ERFC(*Lower_Limit*)

Definition   These functions return the complement to the Gaussian error function in the
range of *Lower_Limit* up to infinity. For Excel 2010, the algorithm of the ERFC() function has
been improved. Now it can accept a negative argument. In addition, a similar function was
introduced that does nearly the same thing, but it has a new name: ERFC.PRECISE(). If you
require backward compatibility, the former version of the function can be used without any
disadvantages, and the explanations here apply as well.

Argument

- ***Lower_Limit* (required)**   The lower limit for the integration into ERFC(). This function
  recognizes only one argument.

Background   The complement erfc(z) of the Gaussian error function erf(z) (see the
"Background" section in the description of ERF() on page 964) results from the following
relationship:

$$\text{erfc}(z) = 1 - \text{erf}(z) = \frac{2}{\sqrt{\pi}} \int_z^\infty e^{-t^2} \, dt$$

The upper integration limit is set to infinity (∞). ERFC(z) requires only one variable, z (the
only argument, which consequently is also called *Lower_Limit*).

Example   See the examples section for ERF.PRECISE()/ERF() on page 964 for more examples for this function.

See Also ERF(), ERF.PRECISE()

> **Sample Files**
>
> Use the Data and Chart worksheets in the Gauss.xls or Gauss.xlsx sample file. The sample files are found in the Chapter17 folder. For more information about the sample files, see the section titled "Using the Sample Files" on page xxiii.

Saltus Functions

This section introduces two mathematical functions that work like switches. Unlike most of the Excel functions (such as sine), which deliver a result value from an original value with no surprises, the saltus functions recognize only two result values: 0 and 1. Depending on the amount of the original value, they toggle between 0 and 1. The DELTA() function only recognizes one instance for which it returns 1. Otherwise, it always returns 0. The GESTEP() function, however, continuously toggles between 0 and 1, when the original value reaches or crosses a fixed minimum (a threshold).

The *Dirac delta function* δ(x) is the mathematical ancestor of these Excel functions. Like the two Excel functions, it belongs to the saltus functions. The saltus functions as they are taught in mathematics change their result value at a certain location (or at several locations) without transition by jumping, and are therefore not continuous at this location.

The definition range of the Dirac delta function spans from $x = -\infty$ to $x = +\infty$, and at the location $x = 0$ it becomes infinite (not 1!). It is used, for example, in mechanics and electricity to represent momentary impulses.

DELTA()

Syntax   DELTA(*Number1,Number2*)

Definition   The DELTA() function checks whether two numbers are equal. The function returns 1 if *Number1* and *Number2* are exactly the same; otherwise it returns 0 (zero).

Arguments

- *Number1* **(required) and** *Number2* **(optional)** Any two real numbers. If the argument *Number2* is omitted, it is assumed to be zero.

Background   If the second (optional) argument for this function is omitted or is set to equal 0, you have almost the direct equivalent of the Dirac delta function: The DELTA() function returns for every value of *Number1* the value 0, but when *Number1* is 0, it returns the value 1. Actually, this last value should not be 1 but ∞ (infinity) instead. However, because calculation systems cannot display the value ∞, programmers have set the value 1 as the result value of this function (see also the introduction for the Saltus functions on page 906).

It does the same as the IF() function when that function is written as follows:

IF(Number1=Number2,1,0)

The advantages of the DELTA() function over the IF() function are a simpler syntax, better overview, and faster execution speed.

Examples   You can use this function to filter a group of values. For example, you can use addition with several DELTA() functions to calculate how many equal number pairs you have.

Example 1   =DELTA(A1,C3) returns 1 if the contents of the cells A1 and C3 are equal; otherwise it returns 0.

Example 2   A completely finished and packed assortment must consist of five products, each with a different and sometimes varying number of pieces. In addition, the packaging progress of the assortment must be displayed in a clear format in an Excel table. The accordance between nominal and current value can be done easily with the DELTA() function. In the Excel worksheet in Figure 17-19, you get only the value 5 (the number of the different products in the assortment) in cell D9 when all nominal and current values are identical.

You would have reached a similar result with the function GESTEP(), shown on page 969. The disadvantage of that function, however, would be that an overcompliance could not be distinguished, whereas with the DELTA() function you could account for this situation. For example, if you change the value in cell C4 in the worksheet in Figure 17-19 from 12 to 13, the result of the DELTA() function in cell D4 will also be changed to 0.

◢	A	B	C	D
1	Product Line A			
2		Sales		
3		Given Value	Actual Value	Correlation
4	Product 1	12	12	1
5	Product 2	5	4	0
6	Product 3	20	17	0
7	Product 4	100	100	1
8	Product 5	3	3	1
9				3

Figure 17-19 It is easy to find out if two values match by using the DELTA() function.

Chapter 17

> **Note**
> When looking at this simple example, one might get the idea that using the DELTA()
> function is superfluous, because upon entering the values it is easy to see at first glance
> whether the match has been achieved. However, in everyday professional life it is rare
> that data entry and data evaluation fall on the same location, date, and time. The val-
> ues in cells B4 through C8 could easily have been linked to this table from other Excel
> workbooks (perhaps over a network). The person who enters the data is not necessarily
> the one who has to evaluate it. Therefore, the DELTA() function highlights the decid-
> ing factor for the user of the worksheet. (Beyond that, imagine processing the data for
> 30,000 products.)

See Also EXACT(), GESTEP()

> **Sample Files**
> Use the Sheet1 worksheet in the Delta.xls or Delta.xlsx sample file. The sample files are
> found in the Chapter17 folder. For more information about the sample files, see the
> section titled "Using the Sample Files" on page xxiii.

GESTEP()

Syntax   GESTEP(*Number,Step*)

Definition   GESTEP() returns the value 1 if the argument *Number* is greater than or equal
to the argument *Step*; otherwise it returns 0 (zero).

Arguments

- *Number* **(required)** The value to be checked against *Step*.

- *Step* **(optional)** The threshold value. If no value is specified for *Step*, GESTEP() works
  with zero.

Background   You can use this function to filter a group of values. For example, you can
add several GESTEP() functions to calculate how many values are larger than a threshold
value. (See also the introduction to the Saltus functions on page 905.)

This function does the same as the IF() function, when that function is written as follows:

=IF(Number>=Step,1,0)

The advantages of the GESTEP() function over the IF() function are a simpler syntax, better overview, and faster execution speed.

Examples   The following examples illustrate GESTEP().

Example 1

- =GESTEP(2,5) returns 0.

- =GESTEP(5,5) returns 1.

- =GESTEP(8,5) returns 1.

Example 2   A school class enters into a sporting competition for the long jump (see Figure 17-20). The coach wants to know which jumps reach or surpass a certain minimum. The range E6:G16 contains the formulas that use the GESTEP() function to compare the respective jump length in the range B6:D16 to the given minimum of 3.80 yd in cell E5 (named *minJump*).

	E6		ƒx	=GESTEP(B6,minJump)				
	A	B	C	D	E	F	G	H
2								
3	Long Jump		Attempts		Required			Number of
4					Minimum Jump			Legal Jumps
5	Competitor	No. 1	No. 2	No. 3	3.80			(≥3.80)
6	Brown	3.78	3.95	3.80	0	1	1	2
7	Cook	4.12	4.07	4.28	1	1	1	3
8	Davis	4.09	3.75	3.79	1	0	0	1
9	Johnson	3.52	4.17	4.32	0	1	1	2
10	Kim	2.95	3.09	3.41	0	0	0	0
11	Low	4.89	4.88	4.87	1	1	1	3
12	Miller	3.66	3.54	3.74	0	0	0	0
13	Orman	3.43	3.39	3.41	0	0	0	0
14	Smith	4.52	4.31	4.78	1	1	1	3
15	Turner	3.94	3.82	4.01	1	1	1	3
16	Wilson	3.62	3.71	3.53	0	0	0	0
17					Sum:			17

Figure 17-20 In the range E6:G16, the GESTEP() function shows with a 1 which jumps exceeded the minimum length of 3.80 yd (provided in cell E5).

See Also EXACT(), DELTA()

Sample Files

Use the Longjump worksheet in the GESTEP.xls or GESTEP.xlsx sample file. The sample files are found in the Chapter17 folder. For more information about the sample files, see the section titled "Using the Sample Files" on page xxiii.

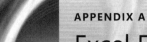

Excel Functions (in Alphabetical Order)

This appendix lists all of the functions in Microsoft Excel alphabetically.

Function	Excel Category	Description
ABS	Math & Trigonometry	Returns the absolute value of a number
ACCRINT	Financial	Returns the accrued interest for a security that pays periodic interest
ACCRINTM	Financial	Returns the accrued interest for a security that pays interest at maturity
ACOS	Math & Trigonometry	Returns the arc cosine or the inverse cosine of a number
ACOSH	Math & Trigonometry	Returns the inverse hyperbolic cosine of a number
ADDRESS	Lookup & Reference	Returns a reference to a table cell as text
AGGREGATE (2010)	Math & Trigonometry	Returns an aggregate in a list or database
AMORDEGRC	Financial	Returns the depreciation amount to apply to a billing cycle based on the French accounting system
AMORLINC	Financial	Calculates the linear depreciation amount for assets
AND	Logical	Returns TRUE if all arguments are true; if the statements of one argument or several arguments are false, the function returns FALSE
AREAS	Lookup & Reference	Returns the number of ranges within a reference
ASC	Text & Data	Converts double-byte characters into single-byte characters
ASIN	Math & Trigonometry	Returns the arc sine of a number
ASINH	Math & Trigonometry	Returns the inverse hyperbolic sine of a number
ATAN	Math & Trigonometry	Returns the arctangent of a number

Function	Excel Category	Description
ATAN2	Math & Trigonometry	Returns the arctangent based on an x-coordinate or y-coordinate
ATANH	Math & Trigonometry	Returns the inverse hyperbolic tangent of a number
AVEDEV	Statistical	Returns the average absolute variance of characteristic values and the average value
AVERAGE	Statistical	Returns the mean average, which is the number value that is calculated by dividing sums
AVERAGEA	Statistical	Calculates the mean value (mean average) of the values in an argument list
AVERAGEIF	Statistical	Returns the mean value (mean average) of all cells in a range that meet a specified criterion
AVERAGEIFS	Statistical	Returns the mean value (mean average) of all cells meeting several criteria
BAHTTEXT	Text & Data	Converts a number into Thai characters and adds the suffix *Baht*
BESSELI	Engineering	Returns the modified Bessel function $I_n(x)$ that corresponds with the Bessel function J_n evaluated for imaginary arguments
BESSELJ	Engineering	Returns the Bessel function $J_n(x)$
BESSELK	Engineering	Returns the modified Bessel function $K_n(x)$ that corresponds with the Bessel functions J_n and Y_n evaluated for imaginary arguments
BESSELY	Engineering	Returns the Bessel function $Y_n(x)$
BETADIST	Statistical (2010 compatibility)	Returns the values of the cumulative beta distribution function
BETA.DIST (2010)	Statistical	See BETADIST
BETAINV	Statistical (2010 compatibility)	Returns the quantile of the given beta distribution
BETA.INV (2010)	Statistical	See BETAINV
BIN2DEC	Engineering	Converts a binary number into a decimal number
BIN2HEX	Engineering	Converts a binary number into a hexadecimal number
BIN2OCT	Engineering	Converts a binary number into an octal number
BINOM.DIST (2010)	Statistical	See BINOMDIST

Function	Excel Category	Description
BINOM.INV (2010)	Statistical	Returns the smallest value for which the cumulative probabilities of the binominal distribution are greater than or equal to a marginal probability
BINOMDIST	Statistical (2010 compatibility)	Returns the probabilities of a binominal distributed random variable
CEILING	Math & Trigonometry	Rounds a number to the smallest multiple of the increments
CEILING.PRECISE (2010)	Math & Trigonometry	See CEILING
CELL	Information	Returns information about the formatting, the position, and the content of the upper-left cell in a reference
CHAR	Text & Data	Returns the code of a character
CHIDIST	Statistical (2010 compatibility)	Returns the values of a distribution function (1 alpha) of a chi-square distributed random variable
CHIINV	Statistical (2010 compatibility)	Returns the quantile of the $\gamma2$ distribution
CHISQ.DIST (2010)	Statistical	Returns the values of the left distribution function (1 alpha) of a chi-square distributed random variable
CHISQ.DIST.RT (2010)	Statistical	Returns the values of the right distribution function (1 alpha) of a chi-square distributed random variable
CHISQ.INV (2010)	Statistical	Returns the quantile of the left $\gamma2$ distribution
CHISQ.INV.RT (2010)	Statistical	Returns the quantile of the right $\gamma2$ distribution
CHISQ.TEST (2010)	Statistical	See CHITEST
CHITEST	Statistical (2010 compatibility)	Returns the test statistics of a γ independence test
CHOOSE	Lookup & Reference	Uses an index to return a value from the value argument list
CLEAN	Text & Data	Deletes all nonprintable characters from the text
CODE	Text & Data	Returns the code of the first character in the text
COLUMN	Lookup & Reference	Returns the column number of a reference

Function	Excel Category	Description
COLUMNS	Lookup & Reference	Returns the number of columns in a matrix or a reference
COMBIN	Math & Trigonometry	Returns the number of combinations without repetition of k elements in an n element set
COMPLEX	Engineering	Converts real and imaginary coefficients into a complex number ($x + yi$ or $x + yj$)
CONCATENATE	Text & Data	Combines several strings into one string
CONFIDENCE	Statistical (2010 compatibility)	Returns a value used to create a confidence interval for the expected value of a random variable
CONFIDENCE.NORM	Statistical	See CONFIDENCE
CONFIDENCE.T (2010)	Statistical	Returns a value used to create a confidence interval for the expected value of a t-distributed random variable
CONVERT	Engineering	Converts a number into a different system of measurement
CORREL	Statistical	Returns the correlation coefficient of a two-dimensional random variable with values in the cell ranges *Matrix1* and *Matrix2*
COS	Math & Trigonometry	Returns the cosine of a number
COSH	Math & Trigonometry	Returns the hyperbolic cosine of a number
COUNT	Statistical	Calculates how many numbers are included in an argument list
COUNTA	Statistical	Calculates how many values are included in an argument list
COUNTBLANK	Statistical	Counts the empty cells in a cell range
COUNTIF	Statistical	Counts the cells of a range whose contents match the search criteria
COUNTIFS	Statistical	Counts the cells of a range whose contents match several criteria
COUPDAYBS	Financial	Returns the number of days from the beginning of the interest date to the settlement date
COUPDAYS	Financial	Returns the number of days of the interest period including the settlement date
COUPDAYSNC	Financial	Returns the number of days between the settlement date and the next interest date (coupon settled day)

Function	Excel Category	Description
COUPNCD	Financial	Returns a number indicating the next interest date after the settlement date
COUPNUM	Financial	Returns the number of interest payments between the settlement date and the due date
COUPPCD	Financial	Returns a number indicating the last interest date before the settlement date
COVAR	Statistical (2010 compatibility)	Returns the covariance, the average of the products of deviations for each data point pair
COVARIANCE.P (2010)	Statistical	See COVAR
COVARIANCE.S (2010)	Statistical	Returns the covariance of a sample, the average of the products of deviations for each data point pair
CRITBINOM	Statistical	Returns the smallest value for which the cumulative probabilities of the binominal distribution are greater than or equal to a marginal probability
CUBEMEMBER	Cube	Returns the dimension element for the given dimension path
CUBEMEMBERPROPERTY	Cube	Returns the requested property (attribute) for a dimension element
CUBEKPIMEMBER	Cube	Returns the requested property for the Key Performance Indicators of a cube
CUBERANKEDMEMBER	Cube	Returns the element in a set defined by the rank
CUBESET	Cube	Returns the defined element set of a cube
CUBESETCOUNT	Cube	Returns the number of elements in a set
CUBEVALUE	Cube	Returns the value for a given address from a data cube
CUMIPMT	Financial	Calculates the cumulated interest payable between two periods
CUMPRINC	Financial	Calculates the accrued loan repayment payable between two periods
DATE	Date & Time	Returns the serial number for a given date
DATEDIF	Date & Time	Calculates the difference between the start and end date in years, months, or days
DATEVALUE	Date & Time	Converts a date formatted as text into a serial number

Function	Excel Category	Description
DAVERAGE	Database	Returns the average values from a list or database column that meets the given conditions
DAY	Date & Time	Returns the day of a date as a serial number
DAYS360	Date & Time	Calculates the number of days between two dates based on a year with 360 days
DB	Financial	Returns the geometric degressive depreciation of an asset for a given period
DCOUNT	Database	Counts the number of cells in a column in a list or database that meets the specified conditions
DCOUNTA	Database	Counts the number of cells in a column in a list or database that meets the specified conditions
DDB	Financial	Returns the depreciation of an asset for a given period using the double-declining-balance depreciation (or the specified multiple-declining method)
DEC2BIN	Engineering	Converts a decimal number into a binary number
DEC2HEX	Engineering	Converts a decimal number into a hexadecimal number
DEC2OCT	Engineering	Converts a decimal number into an octal number
DEGREES	Math & Trigonometry	Converts a radian measure into degrees
DELTA	Engineering	Tests whether two numbers are equal
DEVSQ	Statistical	Returns the sum of the squared variances of data points based on the sample average value
DGET	Database	Extracts the values from a column in a list or database that meets the specified conditions
DISC	Financial	Returns the discount rate for a security (in percent)
DMAX	Database	Returns the highest number from a column in a list or database that meets the specified conditions
DMIN	Database	Returns the lowest number from a column in a list or database that meets the specified conditions

Function	Excel Category	Description
DOLLAR	Text & Data	Converts a number into a text format and assigns a currency format and a currency symbol
DOLLARDE	Financial	Converts a dollar price from a decimal fraction into a decimal number
DOLLARFR	Financial	Converts a dollar price from a decimal number into a decimal fraction
DPRODUCT	Database	Multiplies the values in a column in a list or database that meets the specified conditions
DSTDEV	Database	Calculates the standard variance of the population based on the numbers in a column in a list or database that meets the specified conditions
DSTDEVP	Database	Calculates the standard variance of the full population based on the numbers in a column in a list or database that meets the specified conditions
DSUM	Database	Adds the numbers in a column in a list or database that meets the specified conditions
DURATION	Financial	Returns the Macauley duration for a security
DVAR	Database	Calculates the variance of the population based on a sample using the numbers in a column in a list or database that meets the specified conditions
DVARP	Database	Calculates the variance of the full population based on the numbers in a column in a list or database that meets the specified conditions
EDATE	Date & Time	Returns the serial number of the date that is the indicated number of months before or after the start date
EFFECT	Financial	Returns the effective annual interest rate based on the nominal interest and the number of annual interest payments
EOMONTH	Date & Time	Returns the serial number of the last day of the month that is the indicated number of months before or after the start date
ERF	Engineering	Returns the Gaussian error function
ERF.PRECISE (2010)	Engineering	See ERF

Appendix A

Function	Excel Category	Description
ERFC	Engineering	Returns the complementary Gaussian error function
ERFC.PRECISE (2010)	Engineering	See ERFC
ERROR.TYPE	Information	Returns the number corresponding to one of the error values in Excel or the error value #NV if no error exists
EVEN	Math & Trigonometry	Rounds a number to the next even integer
EXACT	Text & Data	Checks whether two strings are exactly the same
EXP	Math & Trigonometry	Returns e raised to the power of a given number; the constant e equals 2.71828182845904, which is the base of the natural logarithm
EXPON.DIST (2010)	Statistical	See EXPONDIST
EXPONDIST	Statistical (2010 compatibility)	Returns the probabilities of an exponential distributed random variable
F.DIST (2010)	Statistical	Returns the values of a distribution function (1 alpha) of a left f-distributed random variable
F.DIST.RT (2010)	Statistical	Returns the values of a distribution function (1 alpha) of a right f-distributed random variable
F.INV (2010)	Statistical	Returns the quantile of the left f-distribution
F.INV.RT (2010)	Statistical	Returns the quantile of the right f-distribution
F.TEST (2010)	Statistical	See FTEST
FACT	Math & Trigonometry	Returns the factorial of a number equal to 1*2*3*...* *number*
FACTDOUBLE	Math & Trigonometry	Returns the double factorial of a number
FALSE	Logical	Returns the logical value FALSE
FDIST	Statistical (2010 compatibility)	Returns the values of a distribution function (1 alpha) of an f-distributed random variable
FIND	Text & Data	Searches for a string within another string and returns the number of the initial position starting at the first character
FINDB	Text & Data	Searches for a string within another string and returns the number of the initial position starting at the first character based on the bytes of each character

Function	Excel Category	Description
FINV	Statistical (2010 compatibility)	Returns the quantile of the f-distribution
FISHER	Statistical	Returns the Fisher transformation for x
FISHERINV	Statistical	Returns the inversion of the Fisher transformation
FIXED	Text & Data	Formats a number as text with a specified number of decimal places
FLOOR	Math & Trigonometry	Rounds a number
FLOOR.PRECISE (2010)	Math & Trigonometry	See FLOOR
FORECAST	Statistical	Returns the estimated value for a linear trend
FREQUENCY	Statistical	Returns a frequency distribution as a single-column matrix
FTEST	Statistical (2010 compatibility)	Returns the test statistics of a f-test
FV	Financial	Returns the future value (end value) of an investment
FVSCHEDULE	Financial	Returns the accumulated value of the initial capital for several periodic interest rates
GAMMA.DIST (2010)	Statistical	See GAMMADIST
GAMMA.INV (2010)	Statistical	See GAMMAINV
GAMMADIST	Statistical (2010 compatibility)	Returns the probabilities of a gamma-distributed random variable
GAMMAINV	Statistical (2010 compatibility)	Returns the quantile of the gamma distribution
GAMMALN	Statistical	Returns the natural logarithm of the gamma function, $\Gamma(x)$
GAMMALN.PRECISE (2010)	Statistical	See GAMMALN
GCD	Math & Trigonometry	Returns the greatest common divisor
GEOMEAN	Statistical	Returns the geometric mean of a set of positive numbers
GESTEP	Engineering	Checks whether a number is greater than or equal to a given threshold value
GETPIVOTDATA	Database	Returns data from a PivotTable report
GROWTH	Statistical	Returns values from an exponential trend

Function	Excel Category	Description
HARMEAN	Statistical	Returns the harmonic mean of a data set
HEX2BIN	Engineering	Converts a hexadecimal number into a binary number
HEX2DEC	Engineering	Converts a hexadecimal number into a decimal number
HEX2OCT	Engineering	Converts a hexadecimal number into an octal number
HLOOKUP	Lookup & Reference	Searches for values in the first row of a table or matrix and returns a value from a row in the column you specify in the table or matrix
HOUR	Date & Time	Returns the hour of a time specification
HYPERLINK	Lookup & Reference	Creates a connection to open a document saved on a network server or on an intranet or the Internet; can also be used to navigate to another sheet inside the current workbook
HYPGEOM.DIST (2010)	Statistical	Returns the probabilities of a hypergeometric-distributed random variable
HYPGEOMDIST	Statistical (2010 compatibility)	Returns the probabilities of a hypergeometric distributed random variable
IF	Logical	Indicates the logical inquiry to be performed
IFERROR	Logical	Calculates a specified output if an expression contains an error; otherwise returns the result of the expression
IMABS	Engineering	Returns the absolute value of a complex number
IMAGINARY	Engineering	Returns the imaginary part of a complex number in the form of $x + yi$ or $x + yj$
IMARGUMENT	Engineering	Returns the argument (φ) as an angle expressed as a radian measure
IMCONJUGATE	Engineering	Returns the complex conjugate of a complex number ($x + yi$ or $x + yj$)
IMCOS	Engineering	Returns the cosine of a complex number ($x + yi$ or $x + yj$)
IMDIV	Engineering	Returns the quotient of two complex numbers expected as $x + yi$ or $x + yj$
IMEXP	Engineering	Returns the algebraic form of a complex exponential number with an exponent ($x + yi$ or $x + yj$)

Function	Excel Category	Description
IMLN	Engineering	Returns the natural logarithm of a complex number ($x + yi$ or $x + yj$)
IMLOG10	Engineering	Returns the common logarithm of a complex number with a power of 10 ($x + yi$ or $x + yj$)
IMLOG2	Engineering	Returns the base-2 logarithm of a complex number with a power of 2 ($x + yi$ or $x + yj$)
IMPOWER	Engineering	Exponentiates a complex number ($x + yi$ or $x + yj$) with an integer
IMPRODUCT	Engineering	Returns the product of complex numbers expected as $x + yi$ or $x + yj$
IMREAL	Engineering	Returns the real part of a complex number ($x + yi$ or $x + yj$)
IMSIN	Engineering	Returns the sine of a complex number ($x + yi$ or $x + yj$)
IMSQRT	Engineering	Returns the square root of a complex number ($x + yi$ or $x + yj$)
IMSUB	Engineering	Returns the difference of two complex numbers ($x + yi$ or $x + yj$)
IMSUM	Engineering	Returns the sum of complex numbers ($x + yi$ or $x + yj$)
INDEX	Lookup & Reference	Uses an index to select a value from a reference or a matrix
INDIRECT	Lookup & Reference	Returns the reference of a text value; references are immediately evaluated to show the associated values
INFO	Information	Returns information about the current operating system environment
INT	Math & Trigonometry	Rounds a number to the next smaller integer
INTERCEPT	Statistical	Returns the intersection of the regression line
INTRATE	Financial	Returns the amount paid at maturity for a fully invested security
IPMT	Financial	Returns the interest payment of an investment for the given period based on regular invariable payments and an invariable interest rate
IRR	Financial	Returns the internal interest rate of an investment without finance charges or reinvestment gains

Function	Excel Category	Description
ISBLANK	Information	Returns TRUE if the value refers to an empty cell and FALSE if the value refers to a cell that isn't empty
ISERR	Information	Returns TRUE if the value generates an error and FALSE if the value doesn't generate an error, except #N/A
ISERROR	Information	Returns TRUE if the value generates any error and FALSE if the value doesn't generate an error
ISEVEN	Information	Returns TRUE if the number is even and FALSE if the number is odd
ISLOGICAL	Information	Returns TRUE if the value refers to a logical value and FALSE if the value doesn't refer to a logical value
ISNA	Information	Returns TRUE if the value refers to the error value #NA and FALSE if the value doesn't refer to the error value #NA
ISNONTEXT	Information	Returns TRUE if the value isn't text and FALSE if the value is text
ISNUMBER	Information	Returns TRUE if the value is a number (numeric value) and FALSE if the value isn't a number
ISODD	Information	Returns TRUE if the number is odd and FALSE if the number is even
ISPMT	Financial	Calculates the interest for an investment paid within a certain period
ISREF	Information	Returns TRUE if the value is a valid cell reference and FALSE if the value is an invalid cell reference
ISTEXT	Information	Returns TRUE if the value is text and FALSE if the value isn't text; note that this function returns FALSE if the value refers to an empty cell
JIS	Text & Data	Converts Latin single-byte characters or Katakana within a string into Japanese double-byte characters
KURT	Statistical	Returns the kurtosis of a data group
LARGE	Statistical	Returns the highest K-value of a data group
LCM	Math & Trigonometry	Returns the lowest common denominator of the integers specified as arguments

Function	Excel Category	Description
LEFT	Text & Data	Returns the first character(s) of a string based on the specified number of characters
LEN	Text & Data	Returns the number of characters in a string
LINEST	Statistical	Calculates the statistics for a line by using the smallest squares to calculate a straight line appropriate for the data and returns a matrix describing a line
LN	Math & Trigonometry	Returns the natural logarithm of a number
LOG	Math & Trigonometry	Returns the logarithm of a number with the specified power
LOG10	Math & Trigonometry	Returns the base-10 logarithm of a number
LOGEST	Statistical	Calculates the exponential curve in regression analyses and returns a value array describing this curve
LOGINV	Statistical (2010 compatibility)	Returns the quantile of the log-normal distribution of x, where $l_n(x)$ is normally distributed with the parameters *mean* and *standard_dev*
LOGNORM.DIST (2010)	Statistical	See LOGNORMDIST
LOGNORM.INV (2010)	Statistical	See LOGINV
LOGNORMDIST	Statistical	Returns values of the distribution function of a log-normal distributed random variable, where $l_n(x)$ is normally distributed with the parameters *mean* and *standard_dev*
LOOKUP	Lookup & Reference	Searches for values from a vector or matrix
LOWER	Text & Data	Converts text into lowercase
MATCH	Lookup & Reference	Searches for values within a reference or matrix
MAX	Statistical	Returns the highest value in an argument list
MAXA	Statistical	Returns the highest value from an argument list, including numbers, text, and logical values
MDETERM	Math & Trigonometry	Returns the determinant of a matrix

Function	Excel Category	Description
MDURATION	Financial	Returns the modified duration for a security
MEDIAN	Statistical	Returns the median of numbers from an argument list
MID	Text & Data	Returns the number of characters in a string starting at the indicated position based on the specified number of characters
MIN	Statistical	Returns the lowest value within an argument list
MINA	Statistical	Returns the lowest value from an argument list, including numbers, text, and logical values
MINUTE	Date & Time	Converts a serial number (time) into a minute number
MINVERSE	Math & Trigonometry	Returns the inverse of a matrix
MIRR	Financial	Returns the modified internal interest rate for positive and negative cash flows financed to different interest rates
MMULT	Math & Trigonometry	Returns the product of two matrices
MOD	Math & Trigonometry	Returns the remainder of a division operation; the result has the same algebraic sign as the divisor
MODE	Statistical (2010 compatibility)	Returns the most frequent value of a data group
MODE.MULT (2010)	Statistical	Returns a vertical array of the most frequent values in an array or a data range
MODE.SNGL (2010)	Statistical	See MODE
MONTH	Date & Time	Converts a serial number (date) into a month number
MROUND	Math & Trigonometry	Returns a number rounded to a multiple
MULTINOMINAL	Math & Trigonometry	Returns the polynomial coefficient of a number group
N	Information	Returns a value converted into a number
NA	Information	Returns the error value #NA
NEGBINOM.DIST (2010)	Statistical	See NEGBINOMDIST
NEGBINOMDIST	Statistical (2010 compatibility)	Returns the probabilities of a negative binomial distributed random variable

Function	Excel Category	Description
NETWORKDAYS	Date & Time	Returns the number of workdays within a time interval
NETWORKDAY.INTL (2010)	Date & Time	Returns the number of workdays within a time interval considering the weekend definition
NOMINAL	Financial	Returns the annual nominal interest based on the effective interest rate and the number of annual interest periods
NORM.DIST (2010)	Statistical	See NORMDIST
NORM.INV (2010)	Statistical	See NORMINV
NORM.S.DIST (2010)	Statistical	See NORMSDIST
NORM.S.INV (2010)	Statistical	See NORMSINV
NORMDIST	Statistical (2010 compatibility)	Returns the normal distribution for an average value and a standard variance
NORMINV	Statistical (2010 compatibility)	Returns the quantile of the normal distribution
NORMSDIST	Statistical (2010 compatibility)	Returns the values of the distribution function of a standard normally distributed random variable
NORMSINV	Statistical (2010 compatibility)	Returns the quantile of the standard normal distribution
NOT	Logical	Reverts the value of an argument
NOW	Date & Time	Returns the serial number of the current date and time
NPER	Financial	Returns the number of payment periods for an investment based on periodical invariable payments and an invariable interest rate
NPV	Financial	Returns the capital value of an investment based on a discount factor for several periodic payments
OCT2BIN	Engineering	Converts an octal number into a binary number
OCT2DEC	Engineering	Converts an octal number into a decimal number
OCT2HEX	Engineering	Converts an octal number into a hexadecimal number
ODD	Math & Trigonometry	Rounds a number to the next odd integer
ODDFPRICE	Financial	Returns the price per $100 par value of a security with an odd first interest date

Function	Excel Category	Description
ODDFYIELD	Financial	Returns the yield of a security with an odd first interest date
ODDLPRICE	Financial	Returns the price per $100 par value of a security with an odd last interest date
ODDLYIELD	Financial	Returns the yield of a security with an odd last interest date
OFFSET	Lookup & Reference	Returns a reference offset from the specified reference
OR	Logical	Returns TRUE if an argument is true, and FALSE if all arguments are false
PEARSON	Statistical	Returns the Pearson correlation coefficient r
PERCENTILE	Statistical (2010 compatibility)	Returns the alpha quantile of a data group
PERCENTILE.EXC (2010)	Statistical	Returns the k-quantile of a data group where k is between 0 and 1, excluding 0 and 1
PERCENTILE.INC (2010)	Statistical	Returns the k-quantile of a data group where k can be between 0 and 1, including 0 and 1
PERCENTRANK	Statistical (2010 compatibility)	Returns the rank of a value (alpha) as a percentage
PERCENTRANK.EXC (2010)	Statistical	Returns the rank of a value (alpha) as a percentage between 0 and 1
PERCENTRANK.INC (2010)	Statistical	Returns the rank of a value (alpha) as a percentage including 0 and 1
PERMUT	Statistical	Returns the number of possibilities to query k elements from a n element set
PHONETIC	Text & Data	Extracts the phonetic (Furigana) characters from a string
PI	Math & Trigonometry	Returns the value of Pi, 3.14159265358979, accurate to 15 digits
PMT	Financial	Returns the invariable payment of an annuity per period assuming invariable payments and an invariable interest rate
POISSON	Statistical (2010 compatibility)	Returns the probabilities of a Poisson-distributed random variable
POISSON.DIST (2010)	Statistical	See POISSON
POWER	Math & Trigonometry	Returns an exponentiated number

Function	Excel Category	Description
PPMT	Financial	Returns the repayment of principal of an investment for the indicated period
PRICE	Financial	Returns the price per $100 par value of a security that pays periodic interest
PRICEDISC	Financial	Returns the price per $100 par value of a noninterest security
PRICEMAT	Financial	Returns the price per $100 par value of a security that pays interest at maturity
PROB	Statistical	Returns the probability for an interval enclosed in two values
PRODUCT	Math & Trigonometry	Multiplies the arguments and returns the product
PROPER	Text & Data	Converts the first character of all words in a string into uppercase and all other characters into lowercase
PV	Financial	Returns the cash value of an investment
QUARTILE	Statistical (2010 compatibility)	Returns the quartile of a data group
QUARTILE.EXC (2010)	Statistical	Returns the quartile of a data group only based on 0 to 1
QUARTILE.INC (2010)	Statistical	Returns the quartile of a data group including 0 and 1
QUOTIENT	Math & Trigonometry	Returns the integer part of a division operation
RADIANS	Math & Trigonometry	Converts degrees into radian measures
RAND	Math & Trigonometry	Returns a random number between 0 and 1
RANDBETWEEN	Math & Trigonometry	Returns a random integer from an indicated range
RANK	Statistical (2010 compatibility)	Returns the rank of a number within a list of numbers
RANK.AVG (2010)	Statistical	Returns the average rank of a number within a list of numbers
RANK.EQ (2010)	Statistical	See RANK
RATE	Financial	Returns the interest rate of an annuity per period
RECEIVED	Financial	Returns the interest rate of a fully invested security
REPLACE	Text & Data	Replaces part of a string with another string based on the specified number of characters

Function	Excel Category	Description
REPLACEB	Text & Data	Replaces part of a string with another string based on the specified number of bytes
REPT	Text & Data	Repeats text a specified number of times
RIGHT	Text & Data	Returns the last character(s) of a string based on the specified number of characters
ROMAN	Math & Trigonometry	Converts an Arabic number into a roman numeral
ROUND	Math & Trigonometry	Rounds a number to a certain number of decimal places
ROUNDDOWN	Math & Trigonometry	Rounds a number down to *num_digits*
ROUNDUP	Math & Trigonometry	Rounds a number up to *num_digits*
ROW	Lookup & Reference	Returns the row number of a reference
ROWS	Lookup & Reference	Returns the number of rows within a reference or matrix
RSQ	Statistical	Returns the square of the Pearson correlation coefficient according to the data points in *known_y* and *known_x*
RTD	Lookup & Reference	Retrieves real-time data from a program supporting COM automation
SEARCH	Text & Data	Returns the number of a character beginning with the *start_num* at which the wanted character or string was found first
SECOND	Date & Time	Converts a serial number (time) into a second number
SERIESSUM	Math & Trigonometry	Returns the sum of a power series
SIGN	Math & Trigonometry	Returns the algebraic sign of a number
SIN	Math & Trigonometry	Returns the sine of a number
SINH	Math & Trigonometry	Returns the hyperbolic sine of a number
SKEW	Statistical	Returns the skewness of a distribution
SLN	Financial	Returns the linear depreciation of an asset per period

Function	Excel Category	Description
SLOPE	Statistical	Returns the slope of the regression line adjusted to the data points in *known_y* and *known_x*
SMALL	Statistical	Returns the lowest *k*-value of a data group
SQRT	Math & Trigonometry	Returns the square root of a number
SQRTPI	Math & Trigonometry	Returns the root of *number* multiplied by pi
STANDARDIZE	Statistical	Returns the standardized value of a distribution characterized by an average value and a standard variance
STDEV	Statistical (2010 compatibility)	Estimates the standard variance based on a sample
STDEV.P (2010)	Statistical	See STDEVP
STDEV.S (2010)	Statistical	See STDEV
STDEVA	Statistical	Estimates the standard variance based on a sample
STDEVP	Statistical (2010 compatibility)	Calculates the standard variance based on the population
STDEVPA	Statistical	Calculates the standard variance based on a population indicated as arguments, including text and logical values
STEYX	Statistical	Returns the standard error of the predicted y-values for each *x* in a regression
SUBSTITUTE	Text & Data	Replaces old text in a string with new text
SUBTOTAL	Math & Trigonometry	Returns a partial result in a list or database
SUM	Math & Trigonometry	Adds arguments
SUMIF	Math & Trigonometry	Adds numbers matching the search criteria
SUMIFS	Math & Trigonometry	Adds numbers matching several search criteria
SUMPRODUCT	Math & Trigonometry	Multiplies the matching components of the indicated matrices and returns the sum of these products
SUMSQ	Math & Trigonometry	Adds squared arguments
SUMX2MY2	Math & Trigonometry	Adds the differences between the squares of two corresponding matrices

Function	Excel Category	Description
SUMX2PY2	Math & Trigonometry	Adds the sum of the squares of two corresponding matrices
SUMXMY2	Math & Trigonometry	Adds the squares of the differences of two corresponding matrices
SYD	Financial	Returns the arithmetic degressive depreciation of an asset for a specified period
T	Text & Data	Converts arguments into text
T.DIST (2010)	Statistical	Returns the Student's t-distribution of the left end range
T.DIST.2T (2010)	Statistical	Returns the Student's t-distribution of two end ranges
T.DIST.RT (2010)	Statistical	Returns the Student's t-distribution of the right end range
T.INV (2010)	Statistical	See TINV
T.INV.2T (2010)	Statistical	See TINV
T.TEST (2010)	Statistical	See TTEST
TAN	Math & Trigonometry	Returns the tangent of a number
TANH	Math & Trigonometry	Returns the hyperbolic tangent of a number
TBILLEQ	Financial	Converts the interest for a treasury bill into the annual simple interest common for bonds
TBILLPRICE	Financial	Returns the price per $100 par value of a treasury bill
TBILLYIELD	Financial	Returns the yield of a treasury bill
TDIST	Statistical (2010 compatibility)	Returns the values of a distribution function (1 alpha) of a Student's t-distributed random variable
TEXT	Text & Data	Formats a number and converts it into text
TIME	Date & Time	Returns the decimal number of a certain time
TIMEVALUE	Date & Time	Converts a time formatted as text into a serial number (time)
TINV	Statistical (2010 compatibility)	Returns the t-value of the t-distribution as a probability and degrees of freedom
TODAY	Date & Time	Returns the serial number for the current date

Function	Excel Category	Description
TRANSPOSE	Lookup & Reference	Returns the transposed matrix of the indicated matrix
TREND	Statistical	Returns values from a linear trend
TRIM	Text & Data	Deletes the spaces in the text not used as separators between words
TRIMMEAN	Statistical	Returns the average value of a data group without considering the marginal values
TRUE	Logical	Returns the logical value TRUE
TRUNC	Math & Trigonometry	Truncates the decimal places of a number and returns an integer
TTEST	Statistical (2010 compatibility)	Returns the test statistics of a Student's t-test
TYPE	Information	Returns a number indicating the data type of a given value
UPPER	Text & Data	Converts text into uppercase
VALUE	Text & Data	Converts a text argument into a number
VAR	Statistical (2010 compatibility)	Estimates the variance based on a sample
VAR.P (2010)	Statistical	See VARP
VAR.S (2010)	Statistical	See VAR
VARA	Statistical	Estimates the variance based on a sample
VARP	Statistical (2010 compatibility)	Calculates the variance based on the population
VARPA	Statistical	Calculates the variance based on the population, including numbers, text, and logical values
VDB	Financial	Returns the double-declining–balance depreciation of an asset for a given period or a partial period
VLOOKUP	Lookup & Reference	Searches for a value in the left table column and returns a value from the column you specify in the table
WEEKDAY	Date & Time	Converts a serial number into a weekday number, ranging from 1 to 7
WEEKNUM	Date & Time	Returns a number indicating the week with the specified data
WEIBULL	Statistical (2010 compatibility)	Returns the probabilities of a Weibull-distributed random variable
WEIBULL.DIST (2010)	Statistical	See WEIBULL

Function	Excel Category	Description
WORKDAY	Date & Time	Returns the date as a continuous day in the year before or after a certain number of workdays
WORKDAY.INTL (2010)	Date & Time	Returns the date as a continuous day in the year before or after a certain number of workdays, considering the weekend definition for the date
XIRR	Financial	Returns the internal interest rate for a series of nonperiodic payments
XNPV	Financial	Returns the capital value for a series of nonperiodic payments
YEAR	Date & Time	Converts a serial number (date) into a year number
YEARFRAC	Date & Time	Converts the number of whole days between the start and end dates in year fractions
YIELD	Financial	Returns the yield of a security that pays periodic interest
YIELDDISC	Financial	Returns the annual yield of a noninterest security
YIELDMAT	Financial	Returns the annual yield of a security that pays interest at maturity
Z.TEST (2010)	Statistical	Returns the one-tailed probability value for a Gauss test (normal distribution)
ZTEST	Statistical (2010 compatibility)	Returns the one-tailed probability value for a Gauss test (normal distribution)

Excel Functions (by Category)

The Microsoft Excel functions in the following tables are sorted by category.

Date and Time Functions

Function	Description
DATE	Returns the serial number for a date
DATEDIF	Calculates the difference between the start and end dates in years, months, or days
DATEVALUE	Converts a date formatted as text into a serial number
DAY	Converts a serial number into a day of the month
DAYS360	Calculates the number of days between two dates based on a year with 360 days
EDATE	Returns the serial number of the date that is the indicated number of months before or after the start date
EOMONTH	Returns the serial number of the last day of the month that is the indicated number of months before or after the start date
HOUR	Converts a serial number into an hour
MINUTE	Converts a serial number into a minute
MONTH	Converts a serial number into a month
NETWORKDAY.INTL (2010)	Returns the number of workdays within a time interval, considering the weekend definition
NETWORKDAYS	Returns the number of workdays between two dates
NOW	Returns the serial number of the current date and time

Function	Description
SECOND	Converts a serial number into a second
TIME	Returns the serial number for a time
TIMEVALUE	Converts a time formatted as text into a serial number
TODAY	Returns the serial number for the current date
WEEKDAY	Converts a serial number into a week
WEEKNUM	Returns a number indicating the week with the specified data
WORKDAY	Returns the serial number of the date that is the indicated number of workdays before or after the start date
WORKDAY.INTL (2010)	Returns the date as a continuous day in the year before or after a certain number of workdays, considering the weekend definition for the date
YEAR	Converts a serial number into a year
YEARFRAC	Returns the part of the year corresponding to the number of whole days between the start and end dates

Text and Data Functions

Function	Description
ASC	Converts double-byte characters into single-byte characters
BAHTTEXT	Converts a number into Thai characters using the currency format Baht
CHAR	Returns the code of a character
CLEAN	Deletes all nonprintable characters from the text
CODE	Returns the code of the first character in a string
CONCATENATE	Combines several strings into one string
DOLLAR	Converts a number in text using the $ currency format
EXACT	Checks whether two strings are exactly the same
FIND	Searches for a string within another string (case-sensitive)
FINDB	Searches for a string within another string and returns the number of the initial position starting at the first character based on the bytes of each character; this function is used for double-byte characters
FIXED	Formats a number as a string with a specified number of decimal places

Function	Description
LEFT	Returns the first characters in a string
LEFTB	Returns the first characters in a string; this function is used for double-byte characters
LEN	Returns the number of characters in a string
LENB	Returns the number of characters in a string; this function is used for double-byte characters
LOWER	Converts text into lowercase
MID	Returns the number of characters in a string starting at the indicated position
MIDB	Returns the number of characters in a string starting at the indicated position; this function is used for double-byte characters
PHONETIC	Extracts the phonetic (Furigana) characters from a string
PROPER	Converts the first character of all words in the text into uppercase
REPLACE	Replaces characters within a string
REPLACEB	Replaces part of a string with another string; this function is used for double-byte characters
REPT	Repeats text a given number of times
RIGHT	Returns the last characters in a string
RIGHTB	Returns the last characters in a string; this function is used for double-byte characters
SEARCH	Searches for a string within another string (not case-sensitive)
SEARCHB	Searches for a string within another string (not case-sensitive); this function is used for double-byte characters
SUBSTITUTE	Replaces part of a string with a new string
T	Converts an argument into a string
TEXT	Formats a number and converts it into a string
TRIM	Deletes redundant spaces from a string
UPPER	Converts text into uppercase
VALUE	Converts a text argument into a number

Logical Functions

Function	Description
AND	Returns TRUE if all arguments are true
FALSE	Returns the logical value FALSE
IF	Indicates the logical inquiry to be performed
IFERROR	Calculates a specified output if an expression contains an error; otherwise returns the result of the expression
NOT	Reverts the logical value of an argument
OR	Returns TRUE if one of the arguments is true
TRUE	Returns the logical value TRUE

Lookup and Reference Functions

Function	Description
ADDRESS	Returns a reference to a table cell as text
AREAS	Returns the number of ranges within a reference
CHOOSE	Selects a value from a value list
COLUMN	Returns the column number of a reference
COLUMNS	Returns the number of columns associated with a reference
GETPIVOTDATA	Returns data from a PivotTable report
HLOOKUP	Searches in the first row of an array and returns the value in the indicated cell
HYPERLINK	Creates a connection to open a document saved on a network server or on an intranet or the Internet
INDEX	Uses an index to select a value from a reference or an array
INDIRECT	Returns a reference indicated by a text value
LOOKUP	Searches for values within a vector or array (matrix)
MATCH	Searches for values within a reference or array (matrix)
OFFSET	Returns a reference offset from the specified reference
ROW	Returns the row number of a reference
ROWS	Returns the number of rows associated with a reference
RTD	Retrieves real-time data from a program supporting COM automation
TRANSPOSE	Returns the transposed array of the indicated array (matrix)
VLOOKUP	Searches in the first column of an array and returns a cell value from the column you specify per the index

Information Functions

Function	Description
CELL	Returns information about the formatting, the position, and the content of a cell
ERROR.TYPE	Returns a number corresponding to an error type
INFO	Returns information about the current operating system environment
ISBLANK	Returns TRUE if the value refers to an empty cell
ISERR	Returns TRUE if the value is an error value (with the exception of #NV)
ISERROR	Returns TRUE if the value is an error value
ISEVEN	Returns TRUE if the number is even
ISLOGICAL	Returns TRUE if the value is a logical value
ISNA	Returns TRUE if the value is the error value #NV
ISNONTEXT	Returns TRUE if the value isn't text
ISNUMBER	Returns TRUE if the value is a number
ISODD	Returns TRUE if the number is odd
ISREF	Returns TRUE if the value is a reference
ISTEXT	Returns TRUE if the value is text
N	Returns a value converted into a number
NA	Returns the error value #NV
TYPE	Returns a number indicating the data type of a given value

Statistical Functions

Function	Description
AVEDEV	Returns the average absolute variance of data points
AVERAGE	Returns the mean value of arguments
AVERAGEA	Returns the mean value of arguments considering numbers, text, and logical values
AVERAGEIF	Returns the mean value (mean average) of all cells in a range meeting a specified criterion
AVERAGEIFS	Returns the mean value (mean average) of all cells meeting several criteria
BETA.DIST (2010)	See BETADIST

Function	Description
BETA.INV (2010)	See BETAINV
BETADIST	Returns the values of the cumulative beta distribution function
BETAINV	Returns the quantile of the given beta distribution
BINOM.DIST (2010)	See BINOMDIST
BINOM.INV (2010)	Returns the smallest value for which the cumulative probabilities of the binominal distribution are greater than or equal to a marginal probability
BINOMDIST	Returns the probabilities of a binominal-distributed random variable
CHIINV	Returns the quantile of a distribution function (1 alpha) of a chi-square distributed random variable
CHISQ.DIST (2010)	Returns the values of the left distribution function (1 alpha) of a chi-square distributed random variable
CHISQ.DIST.RT (2010)	Returns the values of the right distribution function (1 alpha) of a chi-square distributed random variable
CHISQU.INV (2010)	Returns the quantile of the left $\gamma 2$ distribution
CHISQU.INV.RT (2010)	Returns the quantile of the right $\gamma 2$ distribution
CHISQ.TEST (2010)	See CHITEST
CHIDIST	Returns the values of a distribution function (1 alpha) of a chi-square distributed random variable
CHITEST	Returns the test statistics of a chi-square independence test
CONFIDENCE	Returns a confidence interval for the average value of a population
CONFIDENCE.NORM (2010)	See CONFIDENCE
CONFIDENCE.T (2010)	Returns a value used to create a confidence interval for the expected value of a t-distributed random variable
CORREL	Returns the correlation coefficient of two data sets
COUNT	Calculates how many numbers are included in an argument list
COUNTA	Calculates how many values are included in an argument list
COUNTBLANK	Counts the empty cells in a range
COUNTIF	Counts the cells of a range whose content matches the search criterion
COUNTIFS	Counts the cells of a range whose content matches several criteria
COVAR	Returns the covariance, the average of the products of deviations for each data point pair
COVARIANCE.P (2010)	See COVAR

Function	Description
COVARIANCE.S (2010)	Returns the covariance of a sample, the average of the products of deviations for each data point pair
CRITBINOM	Returns the smallest value for which the cumulative probabilities of the binominal distribution are less than or equal to a marginal probability
DEVSQ	Returns the sum of the squared variances
EXPON.DIST (2010)	See EXPONDIST
EXPONDIST	Returns the exponential distribution
F.DIST (2010)	Returns the values of a distribution function (1 alpha) of a left F-distributed random variable
F.DIST.RT (2010)	Returns the values of a distribution function (1 alpha) of a right F-distributed random variable
F.INV (2010)	Returns the quantile of the left F-distribution
F.INV.RT (2010)	Returns the quantile of the right F-distribution
F.TEST (2010)	See FTEST
FDIST	Returns the F-distribution
FINV	Returns the quantile of the F-distribution
FISHER	Returns the Fisher transformation
FISHERINV	Returns the inversion of the Fisher transformation
FORECAST	Returns a value from a linear trend
FREQUENCY	Returns a frequency distribution as a single-column array (matrix)
FTEST	Returns the result of an f-test
GAMMA.DIST (2010)	See GAMMADIST
GAMMA.INV (2010)	See GAMMAINV
GAMMADIST	Returns the gamma distribution
GAMMAINV	Returns the quantile of the gamma distribution
GAMMALN	Returns the natural logarithm of the gamma function, $\Gamma(x)$
GAMMALN.PRECISE (2010)	See GAMMALN
GEOMEAN	Returns the geometric mean
GROWTH	Returns values from an exponential trend
HARMEAN	Returns the harmonic mean
HYPGEOM.DIST (2010)	Returns the probabilities of a hypergeometric-distributed random variable
HYPGEOMDIST	Returns the hypergeometric distribution

Function	Description
INTERCEPT	Returns the value at which the regression line intercepts the y-axis
KURT	Returns the kurtosis of a data group
LARGE	Returns the highest k-value of a data group
LINEST	Returns the parameters of a linear trend
LOGEST	Returns the parameters of a exponential trend
LOGINV	Returns the quantile of a log-normal distribution
LOGNORM.DIST (2010)	See LOGNORMDIST
LOGNORM.INV (2010)	See LOGINV
LOGNORMDIST	Returns values of the distribution function of a log-normal distributed random variable
MAX	Returns the highest value in an argument list
MAXA	Returns the highest value in an argument list considering numbers, text, and logical values
MEDIAN	Returns the median of numbers
MIN	Returns the lowest value in an argument list
MINA	Returns the lowest value in an argument list considering numbers, text, and logical values
MODE	Returns the most frequent value of a data group
MODE.MULT (2010)	Returns a vertical array of the most frequent values in an array or a data range
MODE.SNGL (2010)	See MODE
NEGBINOM.DIST (2010)	See NEGBINOMDIST
NEGBINOMDIST	Returns the negative binomial distribution
NORM.DIST (2010)	See NORMDIST
NORM.INV (2010)	See NORMINV
NORM.S.DIST (2010)	See NORMSDIST
NORM.S.INV (2010)	See NORMSINV
NORMDIST	Returns the cumulative normal distribution
NORMINV	Returns the quantile of the cumulative normal distribution
NORMSDIST	Returns the standard normal distribution
NORMSINV	Returns the quantile of the standard log-normal distribution
PEARSON	Returns the Pearson correlation coefficient
PERCENTILE	Returns the Alpha quantile of a data set
PERCENTILE.EXC (2010)	Returns the k-quantile of a data group where k is between 0 and 1, excluding 0 and 1

Function	Description
PERCENTILE.INC (2010)	Returns the k-quantile of a data group where k can be between 0 and 1, including 0 and 1
PERCENTRANK	Returns the rank of a value in a data set as a percentage
PERCENTRANK.EXC (2010)	Returns the rank of a value (Alpha) as a percentage between 0 and 1
PERCENTRANK.INC (2010)	Returns the rank of a value (Alpha) as a percentage including 0 through 1
PERMUT	Returns the number of possibilities to query k elements from an n-element set
POISSON	Returns the Poisson distribution
POISSON.DIST (2010)	See POISSON
PROB	Returns the probability for an interval enclosed in two values
QUARTILE	Returns the quartile of a data set
QUARTILE.EXC (2010)	Returns the quartile of a data group only based on 0 to 1
QUARTILE.INC (2010)	Returns the quartile of a data group including 0 through 1
RANK	Returns the rank of a number within a list of numbers
RANK.AVG (2010)	Returns the average rank of a number within a list of numbers
RANK.EQ (2010)	See RANK
RSQ	Returns the square of the Pearson correlation coefficient
SKEW	Returns the skewness of a distribution
SLOPE	Returns the slope of the regression line
SMALL	Returns the lowest k-value of a data group
STANDARDIZE	Returns a normalized value
STDEV	Calculates the standard variance based on a sample
STDEV.P (2010)	See STDEVP
STDEV.S (2010)	See STDEV
STDEVA	Calculates the standard variance based on a sample considering numbers, text, and logical values
STDEVP	Calculates the standard variance based on the population
STDEVPA	Calculates the standard variance based on the population considering numbers, text, and logical values
STEYX	Returns the standard error of the predicted y-values for each x in a regression
T.DIST (2010)	Returns the Student's t-distribution of the left end range
T.DIST.2T (2010)	Returns the Student's t-distribution of two end ranges
T.DIST.RT (2010)	Returns the Student's t-distribution of the right end range

Function	Description
T.INV (2010)	See TINV
T.INV.2T (2010)	See TINV
T.TEST (2010)	See TTEST
TDIST	Returns the Student's t-distribution
TINV	Returns the quantile of a Student's t-distribution
TREND	Returns the values following a linear trend
TRIMMEAN	Returns the average value of a data group without considering the marginal values
TTEST	Returns the probability of a Student's t-test
VAR	Calculates the variance based on a sample
VAR.P (2010)	See VARP
VAR.S (2010)	See VAR
VARA	Calculates the variance based on a sample considering numbers, text, and logical values
VARP	Calculates the variance based on the population
VARPA	Calculates the variance based on the population considering numbers, text, and logical values
WEIBULL	Returns the probabilities of a Weibull distribution random variable
WEIBULL.DIST (2010)	See WEIBULL
Z.TEST (2010)	Returns the one-tailed probability value for a Gauss test (normal distribution)
ZTEST	Returns the one-tailed probability value for a z-test

Database Functions

Function	Description
DAVERAGE	Returns the mean value from the selected database entries
DCOUNT	Counts the cells in a database that contain numbers
DCOUNTA	Counts the cells in a database that are not empty
DGET	Reads a data record from a database that meets the specified search criteria
DMAX	Returns the highest value from the selected database entries
DMIN	Returns the lowest value from the selected database entries
DPRODUCT	Multiplies the values in a field of the database records that meets the specified conditions

Function	Description
DSTDEV	Calculates the standard variance using a sample of database entries
DSTDEVP	Calculates the standard variance using the population from database entries
DSUM	Adds the numbers in the column field in the database records that meet the specified conditions
DVAR	Calculates the variance using a sample of database entries
DVARP	Calculates the variance using the population from database entries

Cube Functions

Function	Description
CUBEKPIMEMBER	Returns the requested property for the Key Performance Indicators of a cube
CUBEMEMBER	Returns the dimension element for the given dimension path
CUBEMEMBERPROPERTY	Returns the requested property (attribute) for a dimension element
CUBERANKEDMEMBER	Returns the element in a set defined by the rank
CUBESET	Returns the defined element set of a cube
CUBESETCOUNT	Returns the number of elements in a set
CUBEVALUE	Returns the value for a given address from a data cube

Financial Functions

Function	Description
ACCRINT	Returns the accrued interest for a security that pays periodic interest
ACCRINTM	Returns the accrued interest for a security that pays interest at maturity
AMORDEGRC	Returns the depreciation amount to apply to a billing cycle using a depreciation coefficient
AMORLINC	Calculates the linear depreciation amount for assets
COUPDAYBS	Returns the number of days from the beginning of the interest date to the settlement date

Function	Description
COUPDAYS	Returns the number of days of the interest period including the settlement date
COUPDAYSNC	Returns the number of days between the settlement date and the next interest date (coupon settled day)
COUPNCD	Returns the next interest date after the settlement date
COUPNUM	Returns the number of interest payments between the settlement date and the due date
COUPPCD	Returns the last interest date before the settlement date
CUMIPMT	Calculates the cumulated interest payable between two periods
CUMPRINC	Calculates the accrued loan repayment payable between two periods
DB	Returns the geometric degressive depreciation of an asset for a given period
DDB	Returns the depreciation of an asset for a given period using the double-declining-balance depreciation (or the specified multiple declining method)
DISC	Returns the discount rate for a security in percent
DOLLARDE	Converts a quotation from a decimal fraction into a decimal number
DOLLARFR	Converts a quotation from a decimal number into a decimal fraction
DURATION	Returns the annual duration for a security that pays periodic interest
EFFECT	Returns the effective annual interest rate
FV	Returns the future value (end value) of an investment
FVSCHEDULE	Returns the accumulated value of the initial capital for several periodic interest rates
INTRATE	Returns the amount paid at maturity for a fully invested security
IPMT	Returns the interest payment for an investment for the indicated period
IRR	Returns the internal interest rate of an investment without finance charges or reinvestment gains
ISPMT	Calculates the interest for an investment paid within a certain period
MDURATION	Returns the modified Macauley duration for a security
MIRR	Returns the internal interest rate for positive and negative cash flows financed to different interest rates

Function	Description
NOMINAL	Returns the annual nominal interest
NPER	Returns the number of payment periods for an investment
NPV	Returns the capital value of an investment based on a discount factor for several periodic payments
ODDFPRICE	Returns the price per $100 par value of a security with an odd first interest date
ODDFYIELD	Returns the yield of a security with an odd first interest date
ODDLPRICE	Returns the price per $100 par value of a security with an odd last interest date
ODDLYIELD	Returns the yield of a security with an odd last interest date
PMT	Returns the periodic payment of an annuity
PPMT	Returns the repayment of principal of an investment for the indicated period
PRICE	Returns the price per $100 par value of a security that pays periodic interest
PRICEDISC	Returns the price per $100 par value of a noninterest security
PRICEMAT	Returns the price per $100 par value of a security that pays interest at maturity
PV	Returns the cash value of an investment
RATE	Returns the interest rate of an annuity per period
RECEIVED	Returns the interest rate of a fully invested security
SLN	Returns the linear depreciation of an asset per period
SYD	Returns the arithmetic degressive depreciation of an asset for a specified period
TBILLEQ	Converts the interest for a treasury bill into the annual simple interest common for bonds
TBILLPRICE	Returns the price per $100 par value of a treasury bill
TBILLYIELD	Returns the yield of a treasury bill
VDB	Returns the degressive depreciation of an asset for a given period or a partial period
XIRR	Returns the internal interest rate for a series of nonperiodic payments
XNPV	Returns the capital value for a series of nonperiodic payments
YIELD	Returns the yield of a security that pays periodic interest
YIELDDISC	Returns the annual yield of a noninterest security, such as a treasury bill
YIELDMAT	Returns the annual yield of a security that pays interest at maturity

Mathematical and Trigonometry Functions

Function	Description
ABS	Returns the absolute value of a number
ACOS	Returns the arccosine or the inverse cosine of a number
ACOSH	Returns the inverse hyperbolic cosine of a number
AGGREGATE (2010)	Returns an aggregate in a list or database
ASIN	Returns the arcsine of a number
ASINH	Returns the inverse hyperbolic sine of a number
ATAN	Returns the arctangent of a number
ATAN2	Returns the arctangent based on an x-coordinate or y-coordinate
ATANH	Returns the inverse hyperbolic tangent of a number
CEILING	Rounds a number to the next integer or the multiple of the increments
CEILING.PRECISE (2010)	See CEILING
COMBIN	Returns the number of combinations for the specified number of objects
COS	Returns the cosine of a number
COSH	Returns the hyperbolic cosine of a number
DEGREES	Converts a radian measure into degrees
EVEN	Rounds a number to the next even integer
EXP	Returns e raised to the power of a given number
FACT	Returns the factorial of a number
FACTDOUBLE	Returns the double factorial of a number
FLOOR	Rounds a number
FLOOR.PRECISE (2010)	See FLOOR
GCD	Returns the greatest common divisor
INT	Rounds a number to the next smaller integer
LCM	Returns the lowest common denominator
LN	Returns the natural logarithm of a number
LOG	Returns the logarithm of a number with the specified power
LOG10	Returns the base-10 logarithm of a number
MDETERM	Returns the determinant of an array (matrix)
MINVERSE	Returns the inverse of an array (matrix)
MMULT	Returns the product of two arrays (matrices)
MOD	Returns the remainder of a division operation

Function	Description
MROUND	Returns a number rounded to a multiple
MULTINOMINAL	Returns the polynomial coefficient of a number group
ODD	Rounds a number to the next odd integer
PI	Returns the value of pi
POWER	Returns an exponentiated number as result
PRODUCT	Multiplies the indicated arguments
QUOTIENT	Returns the integer part of a division operation
RADIANS	Converts degrees into radian measures
RAND	Returns a random number between 0 and 1
RANDBETWEEN	Returns a random integer from an indicated range
ROMAN	Converts an Arabic number into a Roman numeral
ROUND	Rounds a number to a certain number of decimal places
ROUNDDOWN	Rounds a number down to *num_digits*
ROUNDUP	Rounds a number up to *num_digits*
SERIESSUM	Returns the sum of a power series (to calculate power series and dichotomous probabilities)
SIGN	Returns the algebraic sign of a number
SIN	Returns the sine of the indicated angle
SINH	Returns the hyperbolic sine of a number
SQRT	Returns the square root of a number
SQRTPI	Returns the root of a number multiplied by pi
SUBTOTAL	Returns a partial result in a list or database
SUM	Adds the indicated arguments
SUMIF	Adds the cells matching the search criterion
SUMIFS	Adds the cells matching several search criteria
SUMPRODUCT	Multiplies the matching components of the indicated matrices and returns the sum of these products
SUMSQ	Adds squared arguments
SUMX2MY2	Adds the differences between the squares of two corresponding matrices
SUMX2PY2	Adds the sum of the squares of two corresponding matrices
SUMXMY2	Adds the differences between the squares of two corresponding matrices
TAN	Returns the tangent of a number
TANH	Returns the hyperbolic tangent of a number
TRUNC	Truncates a number to an integer

Engineering Functions

Function	Description
BESSELI	Returns the modified Bessel function $I_n(x)$
BESSELJ	Returns the Bessel function $J_n(x)$
BESSELK	Returns the modified Bessel function $K_n(x)$
BESSELY	Returns the Bessel function $Y_n(x)$
BIN2DEC	Converts a binary number into a decimal number
BIN2HEX	Converts a binary number into a hexadecimal number
BIN2OCT	Converts a binary number into an octal number
COMPLEX	Converts real and imaginary coefficients into a complex number
CONVERT	Converts a number into a different system of measurement
DEC2BIN	Converts a decimal number into a binary number
DEC2HEX	Converts a decimal number into a hexadecimal number
DEC2OCT	Converts a decimal number into an octal number
DELTA	Tests whether two numbers are equal
ERF	Returns the error function
ERF.PRECISE (2010)	See ERF
ERFC	Returns the complementary error function
ERFC.PRECISE (2010)	See ERFC
GESTEP	Checks whether a number is greater than a given threshold value
HEX2BIN	Converts a hexadecimal number into a binary number
HEX2DEC	Converts a hexadecimal number into a decimal number
HEX2OCT	Converts a hexadecimal number into an octal number
IMABS	Returns the absolute value of a complex number
IMAGINARY	Returns the imaginary part of a complex number
IMARGUMENT	Returns the argument (theta) as an angle expressed as a radian measure
IMCONJUGATE	Returns the complex conjugate of a complex number
IMCOS	Returns the cosine of a complex number
IMDIV	Returns the quotient of two complex numbers
IMEXP	Returns the exponential value of a complex number
IMLN	Returns the natural logarithm of a complex number
IMLOG10	Returns the base-10 logarithm of a complex number

Function	Description
IMLOG2	Returns the base-2 logarithm of a complex number
IMPOWER	Exponentiates a complex number
IMPRODUCT	Returns the product of two complex numbers
IMREAL	Returns the real part of a complex number
IMSIN	Returns the sine of a complex number
IMSUB	Returns the difference of two complex numbers
IMSUM	Returns the sum of two complex numbers
IMSQRT	Returns the square root of a complex number
OCT2BIN	Converts an octal number into a binary number
OCT2DEC	Converts an octal number into a decimal number
OCT2HEX	Converts an octal number into a hexadecimal number

What's New in Excel 2007 and Excel 2010

This appendix describes the new functions in Microsoft Excel 2007 and Excel 2010 as well as the new internal limits for workbooks, worksheets, cells, formulas, and functions.

New in Excel 2007

The major improvements in Excel 2007 (see Table C-1) include the completely changed user interface and several new worksheet functions:

- The logical functions now include the IFERROR() function that eliminates the need to nest the IF(ISERROR(...);...) functions.

- The statistical functions include three new functions: AVERAGEIF(), AVERAGEIFS(), and COUNTIFS(). AVERAGEIF() and AVERAGEIFS() calculate the average using one or more filter conditions. COUNTIFS() complements COUNTIF() to allow number calculations based on more than one filter condition.

- The math and trigonometry functions include one new function: SUMIFS() complements SUMIF() to allow summations based on more than one filter condition.

- The cube functions category is new. The functions in this category allow formulas to access the data cubes of Microsoft Analysis Services (a database server with special data cubes). The cube functions extend the data access to these databases, which in previous versions was limited to evaluations in PivotTables.

Table C-1 **The New Functions in Excel 2007 (in Alphabetical Order)**

Function	Category	Description
AVERAGEIF	Statistical	Returns the mean value (mean average) of all cells in a range meeting a specified criterion
AVERAGEIFS	Statistical	Returns the mean value (mean average) of all cells meeting several criteria
COUNTIFS	Statistical	Counts the cells of a range whose content matches several criteria

Function	Category	Description
CUBERANKEDMEMBER	Cube	Returns the element in a set specified by the index
CUBEVALUE	Cube	Returns the value for a given address from a data cube
IFERROR	Logical	Calculates a specified output if an expression contains an error or returns the result of the expression
SUMIFS	Math & Trigonometry	Adds numbers matching several search criteria

New Limits

Table C-2 compares several internal limits in Excel 2007 with the limits in Microsoft Office Excel 2003 and earlier versions. You might not know the previous limits, because they are not relevant for normal tasks performed in Excel. The comparison shows the improvements in Excel 2007 in this area.

Table C-2 **Comparison of the Limits in Excel Versions**

Description	Excel 2003 and Earlier	Excel 2007 and Excel 2010
Number of columns in a worksheet	256 (2^8)	$16,384$ (2^{14})
Number of rows in a worksheet	$65,536$ (2^{16})	$1,048,576$ (2^{20})
Maximum number of characters in a cell	$1,024$ (2^{10})	$32,768$ (2^{15})
Maximum length of formulas (characters)	$1,024$ (2^{10})	$8,192$ (2^{13})
Maximum nesting levels in functions	7	64
Maximum number of arguments per function	30	255
Maximum number of array formulas in a worksheet containing references to another identical worksheet	$65,536$ (2^{16})	Unlimited
Maximum number of categories for custom functions	32	255
Maximum number of sort keys	3	64
Maximum number of elements displayed in the AutoFilter picklist	1,000	10,000
Number of rules for conditional formats in a cell	3	Unlimited
Number of different formats in a workbook	4,000	$65,536$ (2^{16})
Number of colors in a workbook	56	$4,294,967,296$ (2^{32})
Maximum usable RAM	1 GB (2^{30})	The max RAM of Windows

> **Important**
>
> The specifications for the new functions and limits apply only if you save your workbook in the file format of Excel 2007 or Excel 2010.

The new file formats save all information (data, formats, and so on) in XML structures. The Microsoft Office Open XML specification has been published and was adopted as an ISO standard. This open standard allows developers to read as well as create the new file format. An exception is the nonstandard binary format that allows you to save and load workbooks quickly.

The XML structures are saved in a compressed file to reduce the file size. Table C-3 lists the new file extensions.

Table C-3 **New File Extensions in Excel 2007 and Excel 2010**

Extension	Description
.xlsx	Excel workbook
.xlsm	Excel workbook with macros
.xltx	Excel workbook template
.xltm	Excel workbook template with macros
.xlam	Excel add-in
.xlsb	Excel binary workbook

New in Excel 2010

Excel 2010 is also available as a 64-bit version. Today, 64-bit processors are a standard even for desktop computers. Compared with 32-bit systems, they can use more virtual and physical memory. The user can work with larger amounts of data and perform more complex calculations. The additional capacity is required by Excel users working with worksheets larger than 2 GB.

Office 2010 includes components that allow you to run the 32-bit version of Excel 2010 on 64-bit Windows by using Windows-32-on-Windows-64 (WOW64), which is an x86 emulator that allow 32-bit Windows-based applications to run on 64-bit systems running the Windows operating system. 32-bit versions of Office 2010 applications running on 64-bit operating systems are supported to ensure the compatibility of controls, add-ins, and Microsoft Visual Basic for Applications (VBA). For more information, see http://technet.microsoft.com/en-us/library/ee681792.aspx.

> **Note**
>
> The 64-bit version of Excel 2010 allows you to save and edit extensive workbooks that you cannot open in Excel 2007.

New Functions

Excel 2010 also includes new worksheet functions:

- Compatibility is a new function category in which you can find the syntax and functionality of all statistical functions that have new function names. These functions aren't listed here because they are mentioned at the beginning of Chapter 12, "Statistical Functions."

- The statistical functions have undergone the most changes. Many functions received new names corresponding to statistics and mathematical terms. The calculation methods of several functions were updated to ensure their accuracy. The renamed, changed, and new statistical functions are listed in Chapter 12.

- The WORKDAY.INTL() and NETWORKDAY.INTL() functions were added to the Date and Time category. These functions complement the WORKDAY() and NETWORK-DAY() functions to allow you to specify weekend days in calculations.

- The ERF.PRECISE() and ERFC.PRECISE() functions were added to the Engineering category (this was called the Construction category in Excel 2007). These functions complement the ERF() and ERFC() functions to provide more accuracy.

- The CEILING.PRECISE() and FLOOR.PRECISE() functions were added to the Mathematical and Trigonometry category. These functions complement the CEILING() and FLOOR() functions to provide more accuracy. Also new is the AGGREGATE() function, which works like the SUBTOTAL() function but is more flexible, because error values and hidden cells are taken into account for calculations.

- The support for calculation clusters is useful for administrators and developers. Excel 2010 allows you to integrate calculation clusters; for example, for compatibility with Windows HPC Server 2008. Excel developers can create cluster-safe functions in XLL add-ins to transfer these function into a calculation cluster for processing.

Support for Calculation Clusters

To support calculation clusters, you must first install the Excel Cluster Connector, an interface between Excel and a cluster connector from a provider. If a supported cluster connector is available, the Excel 2010 user must enable and configure a computer cluster (in the Excel Options dialog box, select Advanced and then Formulas – Configure Computer Cluster).

> **Note**
>
> This feature is available in the Ultimate, Professional Plus, and Enterprise editions of Office 2010.

New Solver

Excel 2010 provides a new version of the Solver add-in. The Solver finds optimal solutions for what-if analyses based on certain data and conditions. The new Solver offers an improved user interface, a new modified Solver based on generic algorithms, new global optimization options, enhanced linear programming, and nonlinear optimization methods as well as new linearity and feasibility reporting. For the 64-bit version of Excel 2010, a 64-bit version of the Solver add-in is available.

PowerPivot

For data analysts, a free add-in is available for Excel 2010. Chapter 2, "Using Functions and PowerPivot," includes an overview of the PowerPivot add-in. With PowerPivot:

- You can use unlimited data lists.

- You can quickly filter and sort lists consisting of millions of rows.

- You can link lists to merge data from different lists.

- You can publish PowerPivot evaluations in Microsoft SharePoint 2010, including all data analysis and update functions.

In PowerPivot lists, you can also save calculation formulas and use a function set called DAX (Data Analysis Expressions).

Index

Symbols

64-bit version, Excel 2010, 1013

1900 date system, for Windows, 42

1904 date system, for Mac, 42, 46

& (ampersand), text operator, 107–108

<> (angle brackets)

> greater than operator, 107, 296, 639

>= greater than or equal to operator, 107, 296, 639

< less than operator, 107, 296, 639

<= less than or equal to operator, 107, 296, 639

<> not equal to operator, 107, 296, 639

<> in search criteria, 638

' (apostrophe), preceding comments in custom functions, 201

* (asterisk)

multiplication operator, 104, 106

wildcard, 637, 639

@ (at sign), in cell references in tables, 117

\ (backslash), indicating fill-aligned text, 349

{} (braces), enclosing array formulas, 119, 120

^ (caret)

exponentiation operator, 104, 106

indicating centered text, 349

: (colon), range operator, 108–110

, (comma)

connection operator, 108, 110

separating function arguments, 143, 144

$ (dollar sign), preceding cell references, 114, 116

" (double quote), indicating right-aligned text, 349

"" (double quotes)

enclosing text or spaces in cells, 107, 108

enclosing text with wildcards, 639

= (equal sign)

assigning results to custom functions, 195

equal to operator, 107, 296, 639

preceding formulas, 103

in search criteria, 639

=? wildcard, 639

=* wildcard, 639

/ (forward slash)

in date values, 41

division operator, 104, 106

- (minus sign)

correcting position of, 55

in date values, 41

negative value operator, 55, 106

subtraction operator, 104, 106

() (parentheses)

cells formatted with, determining, 349

enclosing function arguments, 143

grouping expressions in formulas, 105–106

highlighting of, 106

% (percent operator), 104, 106

+ (plus sign)

addition operator, 104, 106

in keyboard shortcuts, xxii

? (question mark), wildcard, 637, 639

' (single quote), indicating left-aligned text, 349

" " (space)

in database record, 638

in functions, avoiding, 144

highlighting cells containing, 179

including in cells, 108

intersection operator, 108, 110–111

removing from text, 54–55

in search criteria, 638

About the Authors

In this book you will find our combined experience from working with Microsoft Excel on a daily basis in corporate management, software training, statistics, database projects, and programming. Here is who we are:

Sara Unverhau has a degree in international business administration (equivalent to an MBA) with a focus on marketing, corporate management, and languages. She works in marketing and communications. Sara has written many articles and book chapters about topics related to business administration for different publishers.

Jens Bock has a degree in business administration (equivalent to an MBA). Jens specializes in quality control and documentation, which is also the area in which he works. As a consultant for quality control and web applications, he contributed his broad range of experience with Excel.

Dr. Bodo Fienitz has a doctorate in chemistry and since 1991 has been lecturing full-time in adult education. In addition to science (chemistry, physics, and biology), he teaches IT-related topics for theoretical and practical applications. His lectures range from IT basics and operating systems to solutions for the commercial and technical sectors. He first came into contact with data processing in 1971 while studying electrical engineering at the Technische Universität Berlin. For his doctorate in chemistry at the Freie Universität Berlin during the 1980s, he used computer-aided process control, measurement data logging, and measurement data evaluation. Working with the required visualization and subsequent data processing made Dr. Fienitz an Excel expert.

Egbert Jeschke has been working for years as a trainer, application consultant, and application developer. As someone who has committed himself to relational and multidimensional databases, he can appreciate the strengths of Excel and knows how to take advantage of them. Thorough knowledge of SQL, Microsoft Visual Basic for Applications (VBA), and word processing with Microsoft Word make him well-rounded. He is the author and coauthor of several books about Microsoft Office software through Microsoft Press and other publishers.

Dr. Eckehard Pfeifer is a mathematician who works as a freelance consultant, developer, and trainer. He is a Microsoft Certified Application Developer for Microsoft .NET, and his specialty is mainly the Office environment. He writes for various special-interest magazines and loose-leaf editions. He is the coauthor of several books through Microsoft Press (Excel and Microsoft PowerPoint handbooks as well as books on Excel and Microsoft Office 2007 programming).

Helmut Reinke is the guiding spirit of this team and has written numerous publications about Office applications, commercial solutions, project management, and business administration. He is an organization programmer who focuses on success planning and business planning. He has been an Excel guru since the early days of Excel. In addition to benefitting this book with his many years of experience working in sales and commerce, he has contributed his skilled didactical experience as a lecturer and trainer.

How To Download Your eBook

Thank you for purchasing this Microsoft Press® title. Your companion PDF eBook is ready to download from O'Reilly Media, official distributor of Microsoft Press titles.

To download your eBook, go to
http://go.microsoft.com/FWLink/?Linkid=224345
and follow the instructions.

Please note: You will be asked to create a free online account and enter the access code below.

Your access code:

> ## QZDQDHL

Microsoft® Excel® 2010 Formulas and Functions
Inside Out

Your PDF eBook allows you to:

- Search the full text
- Print
- Copy and paste

Best yet, you will be notified about free updates to your eBook.

If you ever lose your eBook file, you can download it again just by logging in to your account.

Need help? Please contact:
mspbooksupport@oreilly.com
or call 800-889-8969.

What do you think of this book?

We want to hear from you!

To participate in a brief online survey, please visit:

microsoft.com/learning/booksurvey

Tell us how well this book meets your needs—what works effectively, and what we can do better. Your feedback will help us continually improve our books and learning resources for you.

Thank you in advance for your input!